Snell's Equity

SNELL'S EQUITY

THIRD CUMULATIVE SUPPLEMENT TO THE THIRTY-FOURTH EDITION

GENERAL EDITOR

JOHN McGHEE KC, MA (Oxon)
of Lincoln's Inn, Barrister

STEVEN ELLIOTT KC, DPhil (Oxon)
of Lincoln's Inn, Barrister

CONTRIBUTORS

MATTHEW CONAGLEN LLB (Hons) (Auck), LLM (Mich), PhD (Cantab)
Professor of Equity and Trusts, University of Sydney; Academic Barrister, New South Wales and Door Tenant at XXIV Old Buildings

PAUL S. DAVIES MA, PhD (Cantab)
of Lincoln's Inn, Barrister; Professor of Commercial Law, University College London

SIMON DOUGLAS DPhil (Oxon)
Associate Professor of Law, Jesus College, Oxford

DAVID FOX PhD (Cantab)
of Lincoln's Inn, Barrister; Professor of Common Law, University of Edinburgh

ANDREW McLEOD BSC (Adv) (Hons), LLB (Hons) (Syd), BCL (Oxon)
of Lincoln's Inn, Barrister

BEN McFARLANE MA (Oxon), BCL
Professor of English Law, University of Oxford; Fellow, St John's College, Oxford

RICHARD NOLAN MA (Cantab)
Professor of Law, University of York; Barrister of the Middle Temple and Door Tenant at Erskine Chambers

JANET O'SULLIVAN MA, PhD (Cantab)
University Senior Lecturer, Faculty of Law, University of Cambridge; Fellow and Director of Studies in Law, Selwyn College, Cambridge

MAGDA RACZYNSKA PhD (UEA)
Associate Professor of Law, University College London

SWEET & MAXWELL

 THOMSON REUTERS

Published and typeset in 2023 by Thomson Reuters,
trading as Sweet & Maxwell
Registered in England & Wales, Company No.1679046.
Registered Office and address for service:
5 Canada Square, Canary Wharf, London E14 5AQ.

For further information on our products and services, visit
www.sweetandmaxwell.co.uk

Printed and bound by CPI Group (UK) Ltd, Croydon, CR0 4YY

A CIP catalogue record for this book is available from the British Library.

ISBN (print): 978-0-414-10995-7

ISBN (e-book): 978-0-414-10998-8

ISBN (print and ebook): 978-0-414-11000-7

TITLE HISTORY

First Edition	(1868) by Edmund Henry Turner Snell
Thirty-Fourth Edition	(2020) by J. A. McGhee and S. Elliott
First Supplement to the Thirty-Fourth Edition	(2021) by J. A. McGhee and S. Elliott
Second Supplement to the Thirty-Fourth Edition	(2022) by J. A. McGhee and S. Elliott
Third Supplement to the Thirty-Fourth Edition	(2023) by J. A. McGhee and S. Elliott

HOW TO USE THIS SUPPLEMENT

This is the Third Cumulative Supplement to the Thirty Fourth Edition of *Snell's Equity* and has been compiled according to the structure of the main volume.

At the beginning of each chapter of this Supplement, a mini table of contents of the sections in the main volume has been included. Where a heading in this table of contents has been marked with a square pointer ■, this indicates that there is relevant information that is new to the Cumulative Supplement to which the reader should refer. Material that has been included from the previous supplements is indicated by the symbol □.

Within each chapter, updating information is referenced to the relevant paragraph in the main volume

This Supplement is up-to-date to 15 September 2022. It has also been possible to include brief references at the proof stage to the decision of the Supreme Court in *Guest v Guest* [2022] UKSC 27 the implications of which will be dealt with fully in the next edition.

TABLE OF CONTENTS

PART IV—EQUITABLE REMEDIES

PART V—TRUSTS

TABLE OF CASES

TABLE OF STATUTES

(References are to paragraph numbers)

TABLE OF STATUTORY INSTRUMENTS

(References are to paragraph numbers)

CHAPTER 2

EQUITABLE PROPERTY

CONTENTS

2. SELECTED EQUITABLE RIGHTS TO PROPERTY

1. Equitable Interests and Mere Equities

(b) Proprietary character of mere equities.

Replace n.28 with:

[28] e.g. *El Ajou v Dollar Land Holdings Plc* [1993] 3 All E.R. 717 (Ch) at 734, per Millett LJ (reversed on other grounds [1994] 2 All E.R. 685 CA); *Shalson v Russo* [2003] EWHC 1637 (Ch); [2005] Ch. 281. See also *Banque Belge pour L'Etranger v Hambrouck* [1921] 1 K.B. 321; *Lonhro Plc v Al Fayed (No.2)* [1992] 1 W.L.R. 1 at 12; *Twinsectra Ltd v Yardley* [1999] Lloyd's Rep. Bank 438 at [98] per Potter LJ (reversed on other grounds: [2002] UKHL 12; [2002] 2 A.C. 164); and *London Allied Holdings Ltd v Lee* [2007] EWHC 2061 (Ch). Similarly, an equity arising from proprietary estoppel may also be enforced against a successor in title and against traceable proceeds, provided that the appropriate remedy would have been to award the claimant a beneficial interest in the original asset: *Re Sangha* [2021] EWHC 1599 (Ch) at [323]. It has been said that an equity to rescind may be defeated when a company goes into voluntary liquidation. The scheme of distribution in s.107 of the Insolvency Act 1986 then governs the distribution of all assets owned beneficially by the company. It may however be enforced against the estate of a bankrupt individual: in *Re Crown Holdings (London) Ltd (In Liquidation)* [2015] EWHC 1876 (Ch). This distinction is open to question.

2-007

CHAPTER 4

PRIORITIES

4. THE BONA FIDE PURCHASER FOR VALUE WITHOUT NOTICE

2. Bona Fides

After "in good faith.", add new n.64a:

[64a] If such a case ever arose, the purchaser's bad faith would need to relate directly to his assertion of **4-021**
the legal estate or interest against the competing equitable interest of the claimant. The estate or interest should not be subordinated to the claimant's right as some general sanction for the purchaser's bad
behaviour in the transaction: *Serious Fraud Office v Litigation Capital Ltd* [2021] EWCA 1272 (Comm)
at [132]-[136] following *Corbett v Halifax Building Society* [2002] EWCA Civ 1849; [2003] 1 W.L.R.
964.

CHAPTER 5

THE MAXIMS OF EQUITY

Replace footnote 2 with:

[2] In *HR Trustees Ltd v Wembley Plc* [2011] EWHC 2974 (Ch), Vos J noted at [53] the "active academic debate as to the desirability of implementing equitable maxims" and quoted extensively from the 32nd edition of this work, which called for "the abolition of the equitable maxims altogether". Contrast, however, H. Smith, "Equity as Meta-Law" (2021) 130 Yale Law Journal 1050 at 1113-1130, arguing that the maxims "relate to the equitable decisionmaking mode as a whole" and exemplify the general operation of equity as meta-law.

5-001

Replace paragraph with:

As a result of the limited utility of maxims, their treatment here is shorter than in some previous editions. Some consideration is still required, however, as equitable maxims continue to feature in judgments[7] and may provide some, limited assistance to courts in two broad types of situation. The first is when there is some uncertainty as to the scope of a particular rule or principle, and a court has to fall back on more basic principles to resolve that uncertainty.[8] The second is when a court is exercising an equitable discretion, and seeks to structure that exercise by referring to broader, underlying principles.[9] This may reflect the fact that maxims were certainly an accepted part of classical rhetoric, and they are still used today by lawyers hoping to invest an argument with ethical appeal.[10]

[7] See, e.g. *Honda Motor Europe Ltd v Powell* [2014] EWCA Civ 437 CA, [41]–[43], where Lewison LJ considered the reach of the maxim that "equity regards as done what ought to be done"; *Lehtimaki v Cooper* [2020] UKSC 33 at [144] where Lady Arden states that "ubi jus ibi remedium is one of the maxims of equity"; *Commissioner of Taxation v Lane* (2020) 385 ALR 92, [87], where the Federal Court

of Australia identifies the "Equality is equity" maxim as underlying a number of doctrines, including the principle of hotchpot.

[8] See, e.g. *Mountney v Treharne* [2003] Ch. 135 CA at [63]–[76] per Jonathan Parker LJ, where the maxim that "equity regards as done what ought to be done" was used in order to justify extending the principle that a purchaser under a specifically enforceable contract acquires an immediate equitable interest so that the making of a property adjustment order in B's favour was also recognised as giving B an immediate equitable interest: see para.5-015. See too *Cruz City 1 Mauritius Holdings v Unitech Ltd* [2014] EWHC 3131 (Comm) at [47], where the maxim that "equity does not act in vain" was taken into account in shaping the principled development (see *JSC VTB Bank v Skurikhin* [2015] EWHC 2131 (Comm) at [35]) of the scope of equitable execution.

[9] See, e.g. *Ming Siu Hung v JF Ming Inc* [2021] UKPC 1, [18] where Lord Briggs refers to the "notion that a person seeking equity must come with clean hands" when noting that "as in the exercise of any discretion on just and equitable principles, the conduct of the party seeking relief may be both relevant and, in particular cases, of real weight in the grant or choice of remedy." *Holiday Inns v Broadhead* (1974) 232 E.G. 951, 1087 (Ch), where the maxim that "equity is equality" was used in order to assist a court in deciding how best to give effect, in practice, to a right of B's arising through proprietary estoppel (or, on another view, under a constructive trust: see, e.g. *Cobbe v Yeoman's Row Management Ltd* [2008] UKHL 55; [2008] 1 W.L.R. 1752 at 24 and 31, per Lord Scott). See too *Ball v Ball* [2020] EWHC 1020 (Ch) at [24], and *MV Productions Ltd v Telegraph Media Group* [2020] EWHC 1357 (Ch) at [62] per HHJ Hodge QC: "[I]t is still one of the maxims of equity that 'equity does not act in vain'; and that broad, underlying principle is relevant when the court is called upon to exercise an equitable, remedial discretion."

[10] See, e.g. E. Corbett & R. Connors, *Classical Rhetoric for the Modern Student*, 4th edn (USA: OUP, 1998) 117: "Because maxims touch upon universal truths about life, they win ready assent from the audience, and because of their air of hoary wisdom they are endowed with a peculiar sanctity".

1.   EQUITY WILL NOT SUFFER A WRONG TO BE WITHOUT A REMEDY

After "abstraction, it is", delete of limited practical use and add:

5-002   rarely applied directly.[11a]

[11a] In *Lehtimaki v Cooper* [2020] UKSC 33, Lady Arden at [144] held that, given that the "facts and circumstances of this case are most unusual", the lack of a previous case in which a court had ordered a fiduciary to cast his vote in a particular way at a company meeting did not prevent a court's making such an order: "ubi jus ibi remedium is one of the maxims of equity and certainly examples can be found where the courts have made directions as to consequential relief in charity cases...". Note that, as explained by Kiefel CJ, Bell and Keane JJ in *Smethurst v Commissioner of Police* [2020] HCA 14, 376 ALR 575 (High Court of Australia), the maxim that equity will not suffer a wrong to be without a remedy "has never meant that the courts of equity would invent a remedy solely because the plaintiff has suffered an injustice for which no remedy was available. A 'wrong' refers to conduct which is recognised as being contrary to law. The maxim means no more than that the court would afford a remedy for the invasion of a subsisting legal or equitable right."

6.   HE WHO COMES INTO EQUITY MUST COME WITH CLEAN HANDS

Replace first paragraph with:

5-010   This maxim is clearly similar to the previous one: it differs as it looks to the past rather than the future. Again, the question is not whether any general moral culpability can be attributed to B,[35] the party seeking relief, but is rather whether relief should be denied because there is a sufficiently close connection between B's alleged misconduct and the relief sought.[36] It is accepted therefore that "the scope of the application of the 'unclean hands' doctrine is limited" and the maxim is applicable only in relation to conduct of B which has "an immediate and necessary relation to the equity sued for", so that B is "seeking to derive advantage from his dishonest conduct in so direct a manner that it is considered unjust to grant him relief".[37] It is also accepted that: "[u]ltimately in each case it is a matter of assessment by the judge, who has to examine all the relevant factors in the case before him to see if the misconduct of the claimant is sufficient to warrant a refusal of the relief sought" and the application of the maxim thus requires "one of those multi-factorial assessments to be conducted by the trial judge, with which an appellate court will be slow to intervene, unless the judge's conclusion was clearly wrong, or based upon some evident failure of analysis".[38]

[35] See e.g. *Loughran v Loughran*, 292 U.S. 216 at 229 (1934) per Brandeis J: "Equity does not demand that its suitors shall have led blameless lives". See too *CF Partners (UK) LLP v Barclays Bank Plc* [2014] EWHC 3049 (Ch) at [1133] per Hildyard J: "The maxim does not, in my view, enforce manners, or require apology; it is reserved for exceptional cases where those seeking to invoke [equity] have put themselves beyond the pale by reason of serious immoral and deliberate misconduct such that the overall result of equitable intervention would not be an exercise but a denial of equity". See too *Gamatronic (UK) Ltd v Hamilton* [2016] EWHC 2225 (QB): Choudhury QC, sitting as a Deputy High Court judge, refused at [227] to regard a party's "brusque and impatient" manner during negotiations as triggering an application of the maxim as it was "well within the rough and tumble of a fraught commercial negotiation".

[36] For example, in *Bott & Co Solicitors v Ryanair DAC* [2022] UKSC 8, [2022] 2 W.L.R. 634 at [98], Lord Burrows recognized that the maxim, "as a well-established equitable doctrine that could be invoked to prevent any abuse" could, in principle, be used to deny a solicitor an equitable lien. In *Michael Wilson & Partners Ltd v Emmott* [2021] NSWCA 315, (2021) 396 A.L.R. 497, Brereton JA used the maxim to explain why a party liable for dishonest assistance in a breach of trust cannot claim contribution from the trustees. Compare, e.g *Murphy v Rayner* [2011] EWHC (Ch) 1 at [351], where it was found that the misconduct of a proprietary estoppel claimant, in lying as to her supposed reliance on the defendant's assurances, had such immediate and necessary relation to the claim as to prevent the claimant having clean hands (although on the facts the maxim did not have to be applied, as the claim was in any case unsuccessful); with, e.g. *Terceira v Terceira* [2011] SC (Bda) 6 Civ; (2010) 13 I.T.E.L.R. 717 at [81]–[82]: the claimant's unreasonable conduct whilst acting as his father's executor did not prevent his invoking a proprietary estoppel, the ingredients of which had arisen before his father's death.

[37] *UBS AG (London Branch) v Kommunale Wasserwerke Leipzig GmbH* [2017] EWCA Civ 1567; [2017] 2 Lloyd's Rep. 621 at [171] (Lord Briggs and Hamblen LJJ); citing the helpful discussion by Aikens LJ in *Royal Bank of Scotland Plc v Highland Financial Partners LP* [2013] EWCA Civ 328 at [158]–[172]; which is also relied on in *Ball v de Marzo* [2019] EWHC 1587 (Ch) at [37]–[39]. See too *Dering v Earl of Winchelsea* (1787) 1 Cox Eq. 318 at 319, 320, per Eyre CB; *Moody v Cox* [1917] 2 Ch. 71 at 87; *Duchess of Argyll v Duke of Argyll* [1967] Ch. 302 at 332; *Grobbelaar v News Group Newspapers* [2002] UKHL 40; [2002] 1 W.L.R. 3024 HL. The formulation given in this paragraph was cited with approval in *Canary Riverside Estate Management Ltd v Coates* [2021] EWHC 1505 (Ch) [83], where it was confirmed by HHJ Hellman at [119] that, as the test is one of "sufficient connection" between the misconduct and the relief sought, "the 'unclean hands' doctrine is not limited to where there is a causal connection between the alleged misconduct and the equitable relief being claimed."

[38] *UBS AG (London Branch) v Kommunale Wasserwerke Leipzig GmbH* [2017] EWCA Civ 1567; [2017] 2 Lloyd's Rep. 621 at [171] (Lord Briggs and Hamblen LJ). See too *Canary Riverside Estate Management Ltd v Coates* [2021] EWHC 1505 (Ch) [114]. In the *UBS* case, the finding at first instance that the clean hands defence was not available was upheld by Lord Briggs and Hamblen LJ ([170]–[177]). Gloster LJ (at [376]) took a different view on this point, however, finding that the inequitable conduct (making of fraudulent misrepresentations) of the party seeking rescission was "so closely connected with the relief sought (namely rescission) that relief should not be granted". Note that the need for an "intense scrutiny of all the facts established at trial" means that it may be inappropriate for a party to attempt to invoke the clean hands principle by way of an application to strike out B's claim: see e.g. *Assertis Ltd v Clarkson* [2021] EWHC 1053 (Ch) (appeal allowed on other grounds: [2022] EWCA Civ 230). For considerations of the principles to be applied to alleged misconduct in relation to freezing orders, see *Fiona Trust & Holding Corp v Privalov* [2015] EWHC 527 (Comm); and *Boreh v Dijibouti* [2015] 3 All E.R. 577. In *Simpkin v Berkeley Group Holdings* [2017] EWHC 1472 (QB); [2017] 4 W.L.R. 116, Garnham J considered (obiter) at [48] that the maxim would have applied on the facts to bar a party from seeking to prevent the disclosure of a confidential and privileged document.

Replace second paragraph with:

This maxim is closely related to the common law maxim ex turpi causa non oritur actio ("no action can arise from a bad cause").[39] When considering that common law maxim in *Patel v Mirza*,[40] the majority of the Supreme Court warned against its mechanical application, emphasising instead the need to consider a "range of factors", looking at the specific policies behind the relevant prohibition and the particular conduct of B, and to consider whether it would be disproportionate to deny relief to B.[41] Although that case did not involve an equitable claim, the majority stated that it would be applicable to determine the effect of illegality on an attempt to establish a beneficial interest under a trust, noting in particular the risk that applying the maxim would be a "disproportionate" response to B's conduct where it would prevent B from enforcing a beneficial interest and leave another party unjustly enriched.[42]

[39] See *Canary Riverside Estate Management Ltd v Coates* [2021] EWHC 1505 (Ch) [118] and *re Smith* [2021] EWHC 1272 (Comm) at [311], citing this paragraph. See too *Assertis Ltd v Clarkson* [2021] EWHC 1053 (Ch) at [87]–[95], where the clean hands and illegality arguments were treated together (appeal allowed on other grounds: [2022] EWCA Civ 230). In *Royal Bank of Scotland Plc v Highland Financial Partners LP* [2012] EWHC 1278 (Comm), Burton J at [176] referred to the equitable maxim as "just a branch, but an important one, being available wherever an equitable remedy is sought, of the principle that abuse of the court process can lead to the court depriving a party of a remedy already obtained (e.g. a freezing order obtained as a result of non-disclosure) or which would otherwise be granted".

[40] *Patel v Mirza* [2016] UKSC 42; [2017] A.C. 467.

[41] See the approach set out by Lord Toulson: [2016] UKSC 42; [2017] A.C. 467 at [95]–[119].

[42] The majority in *Patel v Mirza* [2016] UKSC 42; [2017] A.C. 467 thus rejected the "mechanical" approach to the application of the clean hands maxim in *Tinsley v Milligan* [1994] 1 A.C. 340 HL, but supported the result in that case: see Lord Toulson at [112] and Lord Neuberger at [181]. Lord Neuberger at [151] and [171] also supported the result in *Tribe v Tribe* [1996] Ch. 107 CA as consistent with a general rule (identified at [145]) that a claim is permitted where money has been paid "pursuant to a contract to carry out an illegal activity and the illegal activity is not in the event proceeded with owing to matters beyond the control of either party". ". For discussion of the application of the *Patel v Mirza* approach in this context, see e.g. R Nwabueze, 'Illegality and Trusts: Trusts-creating Primary Transactions and Unlawful Ulterior Purposes' [2019] Conv 29.

Replace third paragraph with:

There is thus, at the least, a close similarity between the operation of equity and of common law in this area,[43] and, in a case where the relevant conduct of B was unlawful, it has been noted that: "it is not obvious why the public policy considerations relied on in *Patel v Mirza* should not equally apply to the equitable maxim".[44] In many cases, it is likely to be possible to explain previous decisions made by applying the equitable maxim as consistent with the multi-factorial approach preferred in *Patel*. Indeed, some instances of its application may serve as useful illustrations of the circumstances where particular policy considerations have been sufficient to deny recovery which would otherwise have been permitted.[45] For example, "Infants have no Privilege to cheat Men",[46] and so if an infant, fraudulently misrepresenting himself to be of age, thereby obtains from his trustees a sum to which he is entitled only on coming of age, neither he nor his assigns can compel the trustees to pay his entitlement when in fact he attains full age.[47]

[43] For example, the question of whether it would be disproportionate to deny B a remedy could be said to have been taken into account already by courts applying the equitable maxim, for example when considering if there are any mitigating factors in B's favour (see, e.g. *Singh v Singh* (1985) 15 Fam. Law 97) and the potential hardship caused to B by denying equitable relief: see, e.g. *CF Partners (UK) LLP v Barclays Bank Plc* [2014] EWHC 3049 (Ch) at [1133].

[44] *Ball v de Marzo* [2019] EWHC 1587 (Ch) at [52], where Morgan J does however also note that the point was not fully argued. See too *re Smith* [2021] EWHC 1272 (Comm) at [312].

[45] Equally, there may be cases where there is a clear reason of policy for allowing B's claim. For example, if public policy renders an instrument void, then B may maintain an action for its delivery up

even if B was a party to the illegality: see *Lord St John v Lady St John* (1805) 11 Ves. 256 at 535; *Lound v Grimwade* (1888) 39 Ch. D. 605. In *Kazakhstan Kagazy Plc v Zhunus* [2017] 1 W.L.R. 1360, the Court of Appeal rejected an attempt to argue that the maxim prevented an alleged fraudster from seeking to issue a contribution notice under the Civil Liability (Contribution) Act 1978 and obtain a freezing injunction in connection with it. As noted by Longmore LJ at [29], the Act itself allows for the possibility of equitable contribution between fraudsters and so "there cannot be any blanket denial of any recovery".

[46] *Evroy v Nicholas* (1733) 2 Eq.Ca.Abr. 488 at 489, per Lord King LC.

[47] See para.8-008.

Replace n.48 with:

[48] For academic consideration of the impact of *Patel v Mirza* in equity, see N. McBride, "The Future of Clean Hands" and P. S. Davies, "Illegality in Equity" in P. S. Davies et al (eds) *Defences in Equity* (Hart, 2018); and P. S. Davies, "Ramifications of Patel v Mirza in the Law of Trusts" in S Green & A Bogg (eds) *Illegality After Patel v Mirza* (Hart, 2018); R Nwabueze, 'Illegality and Trusts: Trusts-creating Primary Transactions and Unlawful Ulterior Purposes' [2019] Conv 29. For a wider consideration of the relationship between the clean hands maxim and the illegality doctrine, see I. Samet, *Equity: Conscience Goes to Market* (OUP, 2018), Ch.4; and also T.L. Anenson, *Judging Equity: The Fusion of Unclean Hands in US Law* (CUP, 2019).

7. DELAY DEFEATS EQUITIES, OR, EQUITY AIDS THE VIGILANT AND NOT THE INDOLENT

Replace paragraph with:

This maxim must also be treated with caution. It can be seen as underpinning, **5-011** in a general sense, the doctrine of laches,[56] which acts as a bar to equitable relief. That doctrine is not based, however, on the mere fact of delay.[57] Something more than mere delay, more even than extremely lengthy delay,[58] is required before B will be denied equitable rights under the doctrine of laches,[59] as the question is whether the lapse of time has given rise to circumstances that now mean it would not be inequitable to deny relief to B. The principal example occurs where, perhaps as a result of having relied on a mistaken belief that B has no relevant right, A would now suffer an irreversible detriment, as a result of B's delay, if B were permitted relief.[60] The doctrine will therefore apply if the delay has resulted in the destruction or loss of evidence by which B's claim might have been resisted,[61] or if B can be said to have released or abandoned any right.[62] There can be no abandonment of a right without full knowledge, legal capacity and free will, so that ignorance or disability or undue influence will be a satisfactory explanation of delay.[63] Laches is also a personal disqualification and will not bind successors in title,[64] although if the circumstances are such as to give rise to a contract between A and B, or a proprietary estoppel based on B's acquiescence, a third party may be bound.[65]

[56] For a discussion of the technical meaning of the term (pronounced "laitches"), see *Partridge v Partridge* [1894] 1 Ch. 351 at 359, 360; J. Brunyate, *Limitation of Actions in Equity* (London: Stevens & Sons, 1932), p.188. In *FMX Food Merchants Import Export Co Ltd v Revenue and Customs Commissioners* [2020] UKSC 1, Lord Briggs at [39], citing this paragraph, confirmed that laches "relates to the pursuit of equitable relief" and so is not available more broadly in relation to other claims.

[57] See e.g. *Re Eustace* [1912] 1 Ch. 561; *Weld v Petre* [1929] 1 Ch. 33 CA; *Rochefoucauld v Boustead* [1897] 1 Ch. 16 CA; *Lazard Bros & Co Ltd v Fairfield Properties Co (Mayfair) Ltd, The Times,* 13 October 1977; *Jones v Stones* [1999] 1 W.L.R. 1739 CA; *Terceira v Terceira* [2011] SC (Bda) 6 Civ; (2010) 13 I.T.E.L.R. 717, where the claimant's unreasonable delay did not lead to laches as it caused no prejudice to the defendants. See also the cogent discussion in *Western Areas Exploration Pty Ltd v Streeter No.3* [2009] W.A.S.C. 213, 431–454. cf. *P & O Nedlloyd BV v Arab Metals Co* [2006] EWCA Civ 1717; [2007] 1 W.L.R. 2288 at 2312 [61] leaving this point open. Note that delay by itself may of course trigger the application of a statutory limitation period.

[58] *Burroughs v Abott* [1922] 1 Ch. 86 (12 years), *Weld v Petrie* [1929] 1 Ch. 33 CA (26 years). In *Cenac v Schafer* [2016] UKPC 25 at [31], it is stated by Sir Kim Lewison that: "in order to resist a claim for specific performance on the ground of delay, it is necessary to show that prejudice has resulted from the delay". See too the discussion at para.17-044 as to the effect of delay in the particular context of applications for specific performance.

[59] As noted by Judge Simon Baker QC in *Mills v Partridge* [2020] EWHC 2171 (Ch) at [117], citing this paragraph. As a result, great caution must be used when considering broad statements such as that of Lord Camden LC in *Smith v Clay* (1767) 3 Bro.C.C. 639n. at 640n: a court of equity "has always refused its aid to stale demands, where a party has slept upon his right and acquiesced for a great length of time. Nothing can call forth this court into activity, but conscience, good faith, and reasonable diligence; where these are wanting, the Court is passive, and does nothing".

[60] This formulation was relied on by Picken J in *Avonwick Holdings Ltd v Azitio Holdings Ltd* [2020] EWHC 1844 (Comm) at [875] (appeal dismissed without discussion of clean hands: [2021] EWCA Civ 1149). See, e.g. *Fisher v Brooker* [2009] UKHL 41; [2009] 1 W.L.R. 1764, 1781 at 64, per Lord Neuberger: "some sort of detrimental reliance is usually an essential ingredient of laches".

[61] *Reimers v Druce* (1857) 23 Beav. 145 CA; *Bourne v Swan & Edgar Ltd* [1903] 1 Ch. 211 at 219, 220. As confirmed in *Fernandes v Fernandes* [2015] EWHC 814 (Ch) at [67], however, the doctrine will not apply simply because of the death of individuals whose value as potential witnesses is "pure speculation".

[62] *Allcard v Skinner* (1887) 36 Ch. D. 145; *Butlin-Sanders v Butlin* (1985) 15 Fam. Law 126. For the relationship between laches and acquiescence, see para.18–041.

[63] See *Rees v De Bernardy* [1896] 2 Ch. 437 at 445; *Allcard v Skinner* (1887) 36 Ch. D. 145 CA; *Beale v Kyte* [1907] 1 Ch. 564. *Labrouche v Frey* [2016] EWHC 268 (Ch) is an example of acquiescence preventing a challenge to fees paid to trustees where the applicants had for a long period had knowledge, and the means of obtaining knowledge, of the fees (see [320]).

[64] *Nwakobi v Nzekwu* [1964] 1 W.L.R. 1019.

[65] See, e.g. *MEPC Ltd v Christian-Edwards* [1978] Ch. 281 CA at 293. For discussion of the circumstances in which a proprietary estoppel claim may bind a third party, see para.12-052.

Replace footnote 70 with:

[70] *Baker v Read* (1854) 18 Beav. 398; *Morse v Royal* (1806) 12 Ves. 355. In *Zarbafi v Zarbafi* [2014] 1 W.L.R. 4122 CA, Briggs LJ noted at [70] that it might reasonably be seen as surprising if laches could be used as a defence "in relation to the assertion of a beneficial interest (rather than, for example, the pursuit of an equitable remedy, or a mere equity)"; in *Fernandes v Fernandes* [2015] EWHC 814 (Ch), laches was considered (but found inapplicable on the facts) in relation to just such an assertion of a beneficial interest.

8.   EQUALITY IS EQUITY: AEQUITAS EST AEQUALITAS

Replace first paragraph with:

5-012   This maxim has been identified as underlying a number of equitable doctrines, each of which has its own distinct requirements.[78a] If applied directly, without reference to those distinct requirements, the maxim again has the potential to mislead. The wisdom of Solomon does not require the baby to be divided in half.[79] Equity is said to "delight in equality",[80] but the application of the maxim in cases where assets are to be distributed between two or more parties does not show the courts adopting a positive preference for equality. Rather, the maxim "provides no more than a fall-back position where no other basis of division is appropriate".[81] So if, for example, a right is held by A, and B provided a proportion of the purchase price, the extent of B's equitable share in the right will be determined by the same reasons for which the existence of that share is acknowledged. So, if B's share arises not as a result of B's reliance on an agreement, but simply as a result of B's financial contribution, B's share will be proportionate to that contribution and there is no need to invoke the maxim.[82] Where assets are held by trustees on a discretionary trust, and a court is compelled to order execution, it would similarly be an error to believe that equal division between the objects of the trust will be the presumptive result. The intention of the settlor is the chief reason justifying the existence of the trust, and, particularly where there is a large class of objects, equal division may well be the last result the settlor would have intended.[83]

[78a] See *Commissioner of Taxation v Lane* (2020) 283 FCR 448, (2020) 385 ALR 92, [87], where the Federal Court of Australia, citing J Pomeroy, *A Treatise on Equity Jurisprudence* (5th edn, 1941) states that the maxim "lay at the foundation of doctrine concerning rights of all who are connected by any common bond of interest or of obligation" and thus is the source of doctrines such as hotchpot and "pro rata distribution, contribution, ownership in common in preference to joint tenancy and survivorship, settlement of insolvent estates, and marshalling".

[79] 1 Kings 3:16–28.

[80] *Petit v Smith* (1695) 1 P.Wms. 7 at 9 per Lord Somers LC; and see *Re Bradberry* [1943] Ch. 35 at 40.

[81] *Waikato Regional Airport Ltd v Attorney General (New Zealand)* [2003] UKPC 50 at 54, per Lord Walker. See too *Jones v Maynard* [1951] Ch. 572, at 575, per Vaisey J: "if you cannot find any other [justice], equality is the proper basis". See too *International Energy Group Ltd v Zurich Insurance Plc UK* [2015] 2 W.L.R. 1471 SC at [61]–[63], where Lord Mance noted the relevance of the maxim to rules of contribution between insurers, but also that the "normal presumption with double insurance that losses should be shared equally" could be departed from "in the present unique circumstances" (of an employer's liability arising from long-term exposure to mesothelioma) so that the rules could instead reflect the "differing lengths of insured exposure".

[82] Note that, in the context of family homes at least, this "presumption of resulting trust" will not apply: *Stack v Dowden* [2007] UKHL 17; [2007] 2 A.C. 432 HL. This can be explained on the basis that, in such cases, it is not the financial contribution alone which justifies the existence of B's share, but rather the fact that the contribution was made pursuant to, and in reliance on, an actual or supposed agreement between A and B.

[83] *McPhail v Doulton* [1971] A.C. 424 HL at 451 per Lord Wilberforce: "to hold that a principle of equal division applies to trusts such as the present is certainly paradoxical. Equal division is surely the last thing the settlor ever intended: equal division among all may, probably would, produce a result beneficial to none. Why suppose that the court would lend itself to a whimsical execution?".

Replace second paragraph with:

5-012

In other cases, however, complications in the facts mean that it will be impossible to work out precisely how the grounds justifying B's acquisition of a right should be used to ascertain the extent of that right.[84] This may be the case, for example, where B's right arises as a result of action taken under a planned joint venture with A, even though the terms of that venture were never conclusively settled by a contract[85]: in such a case, resort may be had to the maxim, although equal division of the assets or profits of the venture is also likely to be accompanied by allowances for the relevant expenditure incurred by A and B as part of the project.[86] Similarly, on the dissolution of a members' club, where the distribution of assets is said to depend on the members' contracts, the terms of those contracts, in the absence of a constitution dealing with the point, may well be unclear, and so equal division, in the absence of a better solution, may be ordered.[87]

[84] In *Re Lehman Brothers International (Europe) (In Administration)* [2010] EWCA Civ 917, Arden LJ noted at [67] that the maxim: "has frequently been applied by the courts to the distribution of assets upon the dissolution of a body or fund". In that case, the maxim was also said to lie behind the application of the pari passu concept in insolvency: [2010] EWCA Civ 917 at [76]. See too *TC01627: Martin Hedley Rogers* [2011] UKFTT 791 (TC) at [117]: "if it is not possible to ascertain from the legal documents or the evidence of what actually transpired precisely how the withdrawals should be allocated across the outstanding policies, we consider that the default position should be that they should be shared equally between them". See too *re Allied Wallet Ltd* [2022] EWHC 1877 (Ch) at [62].

[85] See, e.g. *Holiday Inns v Broadhead* (1974) 232 E.G. 951 at 1087 (Ch).

[86] See, e.g. *Holiday Inns v Broadhead* (1974) 232 E.G. 951 at 1087 (Ch).

[87] See, e.g. *Re Sick and Funeral Society of St John's Sunday School, Golcar* [1973] Ch. 51; *Re Bucks Constabulary Widows' and Orphans' Fund Friendly Society (No.2)* [1979] 1 W.L.R. 936; *Re GKN Bolts & Nuts Ltd (Automotive Division) Birmingham Works Sports and Social Club* [1982] 1 W.L.R. 774. In *Re Horley Town Football Club* [2006] EWHC 2386 (Ch) Lawrence Collins J at [121] explained the result in the *GKN* case as follows: "where, as in that case, there was nothing in the rules or anything else to indicate a different basis, distribution of the assets should be on the basis of equality among the members, irrespective of the length of membership or the amount of subscriptions paid". There may however be a variation between different broad classes of members: see, e.g. *Re Horley Town Football Club* at [118]–[130].

9.   EQUITY LOOKS TO THE INTENT RATHER THAN TO THE FORM

Replace n.90 with:

5-013   [90] "A contract is undoubtedly construed alike both in equity and at law": *Parkin v Thorold* (1852) 16 Beav. 59 at 66–67, per Romilly MR. The contrary view of Harman J in *Smith v Hamilton* [1951] Ch. 174 was rightly described by the editors of *Meagher, Gummow and Lehane's Equity Doctrines and Remedies*, 4th edn (Australia: LexisNexis, 2002) at 3-170 as "nonsense". For further consideration of the importance of form in equity, see e.g. B McFarlane, 'Form and Substance in Equity' in A Robertson & J Goudkamp (eds) *Form and Substance in the Law of Obligations* (Hart, 2019).

10.   EQUITY LOOKS ON AS DONE THAT WHICH OUGHT TO BE DONE

Replace second paragraph with:

5-015   Whilst the principle may well be justifiable,[103] it gains little real support from the maxim. First, where, for example, A is under a duty to grant B a lease, or to assign a right to B by way of security, it seems odd that equity could somehow pretend that the duty had in fact been immediately performed. This leads to the absurdity that, for example, a court, having found that an assignment has not been made, then immediately says that it can, by putting on an equitable hat, regard that assignment as having occurred.[104] Secondly, the notion of what ought to be done is too broad, as the principle bites not on moral obligations of A, but only on duties recognised in equity independently of the maxim.[105] So, for example, it may well be that A ought to keep a gratuitous promise to transfer a right to B, but the mere fact of such a promise is not enough for the principle to apply, as such a promise imposes no duty recognised in equity on A.[106] As a result, rather than supporting the principle, the evident shortcomings in the maxim mean that the principle with which it is associated is exposed to ridicule.[107] An example of the dangers of the maxim is provided by the attempt to use it to justify the imposition of a constructive trust on the proceeds of a bribe received by a fiduciary.[108] It has been recognised that such a trust is justifiable,[109] but the maxim provides no assistance, as it begs the question of why a fiduciary ought to transfer the very right received as a bribe (rather than, e.g. its equivalent value in money) to B.

[103] See, e.g. R. Chambers, "The Importance of Specific Performance" in S. Degeling and J. Edelman (eds), *Equity in Commercial Law* (Sydney: Lawbook Co, 2005), p.431; B. McFarlane & R. Stevens, "The Nature of Equitable Property" (2010) 4 *Journal of Equity* 1.

[104] This clearly involves a fiction, as was noted by Sir Thomas Plumer in *Wall v Bright* (1820) 1 Jac. & W. 494 at 503.

[105] This point was cited with approval by Bell, Keane, Nettle and Edelman JJ in *Commissioner of State Revnue v Rojoda Pty Ltd* [2020] HCA 7, 376 ALR 378 (High Court of Australia) at [47]. Those judges held at [48] that the Western Australian Court of Appeal had misapplied the maxim as it had applied it in a manner which was "unnecessary to give effect to any right or duty recognised by equity". It is possible that the distinction between moral and legal obligations was not given sufficient weight in *Pennington v Waine* [2002] EWCA Civ 227, as the grounds for which A came under a duty to B were not

adequately identified (it may be that B's reliance on A's gratuitous promise was crucial, but the point was not fully analysed by the Court of Appeal).

[106] *Re Anstis* (1886) 31 Ch. D. 596 CA; *Re Plumptre's Marriage Settlement* [1910] 1 Ch. 609.

[107] For an example of such criticism, see e.g. W. Swadling "The Vendor-Purchaser Constructive Trust" in S. Degeling and J. Edelman (eds), *Equity in Commercial Law* (2005), p.463.

[108] *Attorney General for Hong Kong v Reid* [1994] 1 A.C. 324 PC at 336, per Lord Templeman.

[109] *FHR European Ventures LLP v Mankarious* [2014] UKSC 45; [2014] 3 W.L.R. 535.

12. EQUITY ACTS IN PERSONAM

(b) Application of the maxim today: Jurisdiction over property abroad.

Replace footnote 125 with:

[125] See *British South Africa Co v Companhia de Mocambique* [1893] A.C. 602. The same is true under the European Union rules as to jurisdiction: art.22(1) of Regulation (EC) 44/2001, [2001] O.J. L12/1. An amended Regulation (Regulation (EU) 1215/2012, [2012] O.J. L351/1 will take effect from 10 January 2015, but the changes made do not affect the analysis set out here.　　**5-019**

Replace n.135 with:

[135] See, e.g. P. Birks, "In rem or in personam? Webb v Webb" (1994) 8 *Trusts Law International* 99; A. Briggs, *The Conflict of Laws*, 4th edn (Oxford: OUP, 2019), p.59.　　**5-019**

Replace first paragraph with:

A particular danger of the maxim, indeed, is that it may be used as an alternative to analysis. A court may, for example, have to decide on the appropriate law to be applied when B, in a dispute with inter-jurisdictional elements, wishes to appeal to equitable rules and principles. If the maxim is applied, such a "choice of law" question is very easily resolved. The law of the forum should apply, as equity acts in personam and operates on the conscience of A.[137] Such an approach, however, overlooks the fact that many equitable rules and principles operate to confer substantive rights on B,[138] and correlative liabilities or duties on A, and as a result:　　**5-020**

"It is no answer to assert that a claim which invokes the intervention of equity is a claim in personam and part of the law of remedies, and — a highly dubious proposition — as such is governed by the *lex fori*."[139]

Instead, a court must proceed as it would do when considering a common law claim, and must first characterise the specific issue between the parties[140]:

"In the absence of some compelling reason there should be no difference in approach in private international law as between legal and equitable claims."[141]

[137] This approach has won support in Australia: see e.g. *National Commercial Bank v Wimborne* (1978) 5 B.P.R. 11,958; *Attorney General for the United Kingdom v Heinemann Publishers Australia Pty Ltd* (1987) 10 N.S.W.L.R. 86; *Paramasivam v Flynn* [1998] FCA 1711; *Oz-Us Film Productions Pty Ltd v Heath* [2000] NSWSC 967; *Damberg v Damberg* [2001] NSWCA 87; (2001) 52 N.S.W.L.R. 492. But that support is not universal in Australia: see *Murakami v Winyadi* [2010] NSWCA 7.

[138] The *lex fori* approach may however be apt where an equitable rule or principle is genuinely procedural: if, for example, the principle of estoppel by representation (see para.12-035) is regarded as "really a rule of evidence" (*Hopgood v Brown* [1955] 1 W.L.R 213 at 223, per Lord Evershed MR) then the law of the forum should determine if A is, as B claims, precluded from denying the truth of a representation made by A. For a consideration of the conflicts rules applicable where B invokes proprietary estoppel, see B. McFarlane, *The Law of Proprietary Estoppel* (Oxford: OUP, 2nd edn, 2020), paras 10.27–10.40.

[139] *Macmillan Inc v Bishopsgate Investment Trust Plc (No.3)* [1995] 1 W.L.R. 976 at 989 per Millett J. See too *Base Metal Trading Ltd v Shamurin* [2005] 1 W.L.R. 1157 CA, where the Court of Appeal held that an equitable claim based on breach of a director's duties was governed not by English law but by the law of the place of the company's incorporation. Note that the central thesis of T.M. Yeo's powerful monograph, *Choice of Law for Equitable Doctrines* (Oxford: OUP, 2004) is that there is no single or separate choice of law rule for equitable doctrines or remedies.

[140] This is the approach adopted by, for example, L. Collins et al (eds) *Dicey, Morris and Collins: The Conflict of Laws*, 15th edn, (London: Sweet & Maxwell, 2012) Ch.36, s.3.

[141] *OJSC Oil Company Yugraneft (In Liquidation) v Abramovich* [2008] EWHC 2613 at [177], per Christopher Clarke J; relying in part on *Attorney General of England and Wales v R* [2002] N.Z.L.R. 91 at 103, per Tipping J. In the *OJSC Oil* case, for example, Christopher Clarke J therefore rejected the idea that the *lex fori* must govern a claim based on A's dishonest assistance in a breach of fiduciary duty, stating at [223] that: "Dishonest assistance, a form of equitable wrongdoing, is so closely analogous to a claim in tort (as characterised for purely domestic purposes) that it should, I would have thought, be so characterised for private international law purposes".

CHAPTER 6

THE EQUITABLE DOCTRINES

CONTENTS

[15]

1. CONVERSION

1. The Doctrine

(a) Definition

(1) Actual and notional conversion.

Replace n.3 with:

6-002   ³ For an historical survey of the precise scope of the doctrine, see J.S. Anderson, "On the Application of the Doctrine in the Context of Williams & Glyn's Bank Ltd v Boland" (1984) 100 L.Q.R. 86.

2. Cases of Conversion

Change title of paragraph:

(b) Under a contract for the sale of land.³⁰

6-009   ³⁰ See generally P.H. Pettit, "Conversion under a Contract for the Sale of Land" (1960) 24 Conv. (NS) 47.

Replace n.33 with:

³³ *Lawes v Bennett* (1785) 1 Cox Eq. 167.

2. ELECTION

1. The Doctrine of Election

(a) The principle.

Replace n.55 with:

6-015   ⁵⁵ *Cooper v Cooper* (1874-75) L.R. 7 H.L. 53 at 67. See further *Douglas-Menzies v Umphelby* [1908] A.C. 224 at 232; *Brown v Gregson* [1920] A.C. 860 at 870; *Re Gordon's Will Trusts* [1978] Ch. 145 at 154; *Scarfe v Matthews* [2012] EWHC 3071 (Ch); [2012] S.T.C. 2487 at [34].

(c) Other doctrines.

6-020   *Change title of sub-paragraph:*

(3) Election between alternative rights and remedies.

Replace paragraph with:

   Where a person is entitled to the exercise of mutually inconsistent rights or to claim remedies that cannot be enjoyed together, he or she must choose between those rights or remedies. The term "election" is often deployed to describe the choice to be made, but the principles informing the timing and manner of the "election" bear no relation to the equitable doctrine of election.⁶⁶ᵃ

⁶⁶ᵃ *Lissenden v CAV Bosch Ltd* [1940] A.C. 412 at 418. The distinction is sometimes drawn on the basis that "election" between alternative rights or remedies is a doctrine of common law rather than equity: see, e.g., *Agricultural and Rural Finance Pty Ltd v Gardiner* (2008) 238 CLR 570 at [57]–[59]. Whether such a distinction remains accurate or helpful may be questioned, particularly in light of the recognition that the "common law" doctrine applies equally to alternative equitable remedies: para.7-052. See further *United Australia Ltd v Barclays Bank Ltd* [1941] AC 1 at 28-30; *Tang Man Sit v Capacious Investments Ltd* [1996] AC 514 at 521–522.

After the first paragraph, add new paragraph:

For instance, a minor who settles her property on marriage, but whose husband does not bring any property into the settlement, has a right to elect (or choose) to ratify or repudiate the settlement within a reasonable time after attaining full age.[67] This has nothing to do with the equitable doctrine of election.[68] If, however, her husband also settled property, a true case of election would then arise; if she did take back her own property, her interest in the property settled by the husband would be used to compensate the parties disappointed by her repudiation of the settlement.[69]

[67] *Edwards v Carter* [1893] A.C. 360.

[68] *Wilder v Pigott* (1882) 22 Ch. D. 263.

[69] See *Re Vardon's Trusts* (1885) 31 Ch. D. 275.

2.   Conditions to be Satisfied

(e)   Donor's intention.

(2)   Limited interests.

Replace n.102 with:

[102] Administration of Justice Act 1982 s.21. A solicitor's attendance note clearly indicated that the testatrix believed that she was the sole beneficial owner of her house and that the effect of her will would be that the claimant obtained no more than one half of that property. See also *Scarfe v Matthews* [2012] EWHC 3071 (Ch); [2012] S.T.C. 2487 at [42]–[45], [49] (extrinsic evidence admissible both as to identification of the testator's intention as a matter of construction of the will and as to what the testator would have done had he or she realised that the relevant property was not his or hers). **6-032**

3.   PERFORMANCE

5.   Will or Intestacy as Performance of Covenant

(c)   Performance by will.

Replace n.145 with:

[145] See the discussion of the cases in the two previous footnotes by M. Cullity in "Performance and Satisfaction" (1964) 38 Austr. L.J. 147 at 150. **6-057**

4.   SATISFACTION

1.   Nature

Replace n.147 with:

[147] For a critical survey of performance and the satisfaction of debts by legacies, see M. Cullity, "Performance and Satisfaction" (1964) 38 Austr. L.J. 147. **6-059**

4.   Satisfaction of Legacies by Legacies

(b)   Different instruments

Replace paragraph with:

Where the legacies are contained in different instruments, e.g. one in the will and another in a codicil, both legacies are payable unless the legacies are of the same amount and the same motive is expressed for each.[172] The underlying principle, **6-069** judicially described as "a plain rule of law and construction not to be frittered away by a mere balance of probablities",[173] is that the testator intends each and every disposition in his will to take effect, at least where they are not mutually inconsistent.[174] However, where there is the "double coincidence" of the same motive and the same sum it is presumed that the second legacy is no more than a repetition of the first.[175] But if the legacies are of different amounts (even though the same motive may be expressed for each), or if they are of the same amounts but a different motive is expressed for each, or if a motive is expressed for one and not for the other, then they will be cumulative[176] unless it appears from internal evidence[177] or from the circumstances surrounding the execution of the instruments[178] that the second was a mere copy or duplicate of the first.[179]

[172] See, e.g. *Wray v Field* (1826) 2 Russ. 257; affirming (1822) 6 Madd. 300, where at 305 a note classifies over 30 cases of this kind.

[173] *Wilson v O'Leary* (1872) L.R. 7 Ch. 448 at 454, per James LJ.

[174] *Re Resch's WT* [1969] 1 A.C. 514 at 548, where Lord Wilberforce referred to the rules governing this issue as "in reality little more than ordered lists of examples". They are helpfully set out, albeit as "guiding illustrations", in *Theobald on Wills*, 18th edn (London: Sweet & Maxwell, 2018), para.15-033.

[175] *Benyon v Benyon* (1810) 17 Ves. Jr. 34 (legacy of £100 in will, legacy of £100 in codicil, each to beneficiary "for his trouble as executor").

[176] *Hooley v Hatton* (1772) 1 Bro. C.C. 390n; *Roch v Callen* (1848) 6 Hare 531; *Ridges v Morrison* (1784) 1 Bro. C.C. 389.

[177] As, e.g. in *Re Bagnall* [1949] L.J.R. 1.

[178] As, e.g. in *Re Silverston* [1949] Ch. 270.

[179] *Currie v Pye* (1811) 17 Ves. Jr. 462; *Whyte v Whyte* (1873–74) L.R. 17 Eq. 50; *Re Michell* [1929] 1 Ch. 552.

5.   The Presumption Against Double Portions

(b)   Portions

(1)   Nature of portions.

Replace n.196 with:

6-073   [196] *Taylor v Taylor* (1875) L.R. 20 Eq. 155. See *Re George's Will Trusts* [1949] Ch. 154; *Re Livesey* [1953] 1 W.L.R. 1114; and see generally H.I. Elbert, "Advancements: II" (1953) 52 Mich. L.R. 231 at 252.

(f)   Rebutting the presumption

(2)   Extrinsic evidence.

Replace n.240 with:

6-086   [240] *Hall v Hill* (1841) 1 Dr. & War. 94; *Re Shields* [1912] 1 Ch. 591; and see M. Cullity, "Performance and Satisfaction" (1964) 38 Austr. L.J. 147 at 156.

CHAPTER 7

FIDUCIARIES

CONTENTS

1.   FIDUCIARIES AND FIDUCIARY RELATIONSHIPS

2.   Fiduciary Relationships

(b)   Settled categories of fiduciary relationship.

Replace n.10 with:

7-004   [10]   See, e.g. *Keech v Sandford* (1726) 25 E.R. 223; Sel. Cas. Ch. 61; *Dougan v Macpherson* [1902] A.C. 197.

Replace second paragraph with:

Several other categories of relationship are well-settled as fiduciary relationships. In these relationships there is a strong, yet rebuttable, presumption that fiduciary duties are owed.[13] Agents normally owe fiduciary duties to their principals.[14] Solicitors owe fiduciary duties to their clients.[15] Promoters owe fiduciary duties to the company which they are promoting.[16] Partners owe fiduciary duties to each other.[17] Guardians owe fiduciary duties to their wards.[18] A receiver owes fiduciary duties to the person on whose behalf he is acting[19] (e.g. to the mortgagee when appointed under a power contained in the mortgage; not to the mortgagor or subsequent encumbrancers, to whom other, non-fiduciary, duties are owed[20]). Crown servants have been held to owe fiduciary duties to the Crown.[21]

[13]   *Lac Minerals Ltd v International Corona Resources Ltd* (1989) 61 D.L.R. (4th) 14 at 28.

[14]   See, e.g. *De Bussche v Alt* (1878) 8 Ch. D. 286; *Boston Deep Sea Fishing & Ice Co v Ansell* (1888) 39 Ch. D. 339; *Kelly v Cooper* [1993] A.C. 205; *Paper Reclaim Ltd v Aotearoa International Ltd* [2007] NZSC 26 at [33]; [2007] 3 N.Z.L.R. 169; *FHR European Ventures LLP v Cedar Capital Partners LLC* [2014] UKSC 45 at [2]; [2015] A.C. 250. The word "agent" is used in a very broad sense in business, with the consequence that some who are described as agents will not necessarily owe fiduciary duties: *Tonto Home Loans Australia Pty Ltd v Tavares* [2011] NSWCA 389 at [177]. See also *UBS AG v Kommunale Wasserwerke Leipzig GmbH* [2017] EWCA Civ 1567 at [92], [2017] 2 Lloyd's Rep. 621; Watts & Reynolds, *Bowstead & Reynolds on Agency*, 21st edn (2018), para.6-037. Like others, an agent's fiduciary duties must be moulded around the duties which the agent has undertaken in his or her retainer: see para.7-012; *Kelly v Cooper* [1993] A.C. 205, 214–215; *Tigris International NV v China Southern Airlines Co Ltd* [2014] EWCA Civ 1649 at [155].

[15]   See, e.g. *Nocton v Lord Ashburton* [1914] A.C. 932; *Moody v Cox* [1917] 2 Ch. 71; *Boardman v Phipps* [1967] 2 A.C. 46; *Clark Boyce v Mouat* [1994] 1 A.C. 428; *Bristol & West Building Society v Mothew* [1998] Ch. 1.

[16]   See, e.g. *Erlanger v New Sombrero Phosphate Co* (1878) 3 App. Cas. 1218; *Gluckstein v Barnes* [1900] A.C. 240; *Jubilee Cotton Mills Ltd v Lewis* [1924] A.C. 958; *Aequitas v AEFC* [2001] NSWSC 14 at [343]; (2001) 19 A.C.L.C. 1,006. See generally J. Gold, "The Liability of Promoters for Secret Profits in English Law" (1943) 5 U.T.L.J. 21; and see H. Gross, "Who is a Company Promoter" (1970) 86 L.Q.R. 493.

[17]   See, e.g. *Aas v Benham* [1891] 2 Ch. 244; *Thompson's Trustee in Bankruptcy v Heaton* [1974] 1 W.L.R. 605; *Chan v Zacharia* (1984) 154 C.L.R. 178; *Don King Productions Inc v Warren* [2000] Ch. 291; *Kao Lee & Yip v Koo* [2003] W.T.L.R. 1283 (Hong Kong).

[18]   See, e.g. *Hatch v Hatch* (1804) 9 Ves. 292; 32 E.R. 615; *De Manneville v De Manneville* (1804) 10 Ves. 52; 32 E.R. 762; *Clay v Clay* [2001] HCA 9; [2001] W.T.L.R. 393.

[19]   See, e.g. *Nugent v Nugent* [1908] 1 Ch. 546; and see *Re B Johnson & Co (Builders) Ltd* [1955] Ch. 634 at 661–662.

[20]   See, e.g. *Downsview Nominees Ltd v First City Corp Ltd* [1993] A.C. 295 at 312; *Medforth v Blake* [2000] Ch. 86 at 98–102.

[21]   See, e.g. *Reading v Attorney General* [1951] A.C. 507; *Attorney General for Hong Kong v Reid* [1994] 1 A.C. 324; and see *Attorney General v Blake* [2001] 1 A.C. 268 at 280.

Replace third paragraph with:

Company directors have also consistently been held to owe fiduciary duties to the company.[22] This includes de facto directors,[23] and can also include shadow directors,[24] but not directors-elect.[25] The Companies Act 2006 now provides a statutory code of duties for directors in England and Wales, in place of the common law and equitable duties to which directors have hitherto been subject.[26] The result is that directors will no longer be subject to the duties discussed in this chapter, other than insofar as the 2006 Act so provides.[26a] Cases regarding directors which were decided prior to the implementation of the 2006 Act are, however, still relevant in two ways. First, many of them state principles which are of general application to fiduciaries. Secondly, the 2006 Act itself provides that such cases are relevant in interpreting the provisions of that Act.[27] However, caution must be exercised regarding cases decided under the 2006 Act before statements of principle in those cases are treated as statements of principles which apply to fiduciaries generally. The civil consequences of directors acting in breach of the duties contained in the 2006 Act will remain the same as if the corresponding common law or equitable duties had been breached.[28]

[22] See, e.g. *Aberdeen Railway Co v Blaikie Bros* (1854) 1 Macq. 461; 149 R.R. 32; *Imperial Mercantile Credit Association v Coleman* (1873) L.R. 6 H.L. 189; *Parker v McKenna* (1874) L.R. 10 Ch. App. 96; *Regal (Hastings) Ltd v Gulliver* [1967] 2 A.C. 134n.; *Guinness Plc v Saunders* [1990] 2 A.C. 663; *Nanty-glo and Blaina Ironworks Co v Grave* (1878) 12 Ch. D. 738; *Eden v Ridsdales Railway Lamp and Lighting Co Ltd* (1889) 23 Q.B.D. 368.

[23] See, e.g. *Ultraframe (UK) Ltd v Fielding (No.2)* [2003] EWCA Civ 1805 at [39]; *Re Canadian Land Reclaiming & Colonizing Co* (1880) 14 Ch. D. 660 CA at 670 and 673; *Primlake Ltd v Matthews Associates* [2006] EWHC 1227 (Ch) at [284]; *Shepherds Investments Ltd v Walters* [2006] EWHC 836 (Ch) at [78]. On determining when someone is a de facto director, see *Holland v Revenue and Customs Commissioners* [2010] UKSC 51, [2010] 1 W.L.R. 2793; *Wetton v Ahmed* [2011] EWCA Civ 610; *Smithton Ltd v Naggar* [2014] EWCA Civ 939 (also considering shadow directorship).

[24] *Instant Access Properties Ltd (in liq) v Rosser* [2018] EWHC 756 (Ch) at [255]–[275] (emphasising the highly fact-sensitive nature of this question); *Vivendi SA v Richards* [2013] EWHC 3006 (Ch) at [142]–[143]; *Ultraframe (UK) Ltd v Fielding* [2005] EWHC 1638 (Ch) at [1284] and [1289]. See also Companies Act 2006 s.170(5), which was amended in 2015 to make clear that the statute's "general duties apply to a shadow director of a company where and to the extent that they are capable of so applying".

[25] *Lindgren v L & P Estates Ltd* [1968] Ch. 572 at 596 & 604.

[26] Companies Act 2006 s.170(3). For a useful analysis of the duties which applied to company directors before and after 1 October 2007 (when ss.170–181 but not ss.175–177 of the Companies Act 2006 came into force), and before and after 1 October 2008 (when ss.175–177 of the Companies Act 2006 came into force); see *Bhullar v Bhullar* [2017] EWHC 407 (Ch) at [83]–[88].

[26a] For an example of the difference in duties, dealing particularly with the survival of duties after termination of a directorship, see *Burnell v Trans-Tag Ltd* [2021] EWHC 1457 (Ch) at [389]–[413].

[27] Companies Act 2006 s.170(4). See *Burns v Financial Conduct Authority* [2017] EWCA Civ 2140 at [64]–[75]; [2018] 1 W.L.R. 4161.

[28] Companies Act 2006 s.178(1).

Replace n.29 with:

[29] See, e.g. *Peskin v Anderson* [2000] EWCA Civ 326 at [31]–[36], [2001] 1 B.C.L.C. 372; *Kyrris v Oldham* [2003] EWCA Civ 1506 at [142], [2004] 1 B.C.L.C. 305; *Sharp v Blank* [2015] EWHC 3220 (Ch) at [9]–[10]; *Brunninghausen v Glavanics* (1999) 46 N.S.W.L.R. 538; *Coleman v Myers* [1977] 2 N.Z.L.R. 225; *Allen v Hyatt* (1914) 30 T.L.R. 444; *Glandon Pty Ltd v Strata Consolidated Pty Ltd* (1993) 11 A.C.S.R. 543 at 547 (NSWCA).

(c)   Ad hoc fiduciary relationships.

(1) Principles.

Replace second paragraph with:

7-005   There is, however, growing judicial support for the view that:

> "a fiduciary is someone who has undertaken to act for or on behalf of another in a particular matter in circumstances which give rise to a relationship of trust and confidence."[38]

The undertaking can be implied in the circumstances, particularly where someone has taken on a role in respect of which fiduciary duties are appropriate, particularly in the sense that he or she is reasonably expected in that role to act in the interests of the other party, to the exclusion of his or her own several interests.[37] Hence, it has been said that:

> "fiduciary duties are obligations imposed by law as a reaction to particular circumstances of responsibility assumed by one person in respect of the conduct or the affairs of another."[38]

> "The concept encaptures a situation where one person is in a relationship with another which gives rise to a legitimate expectation, which equity will recognise, that the fiduciary will not utilise his or her position in such a way which is adverse to the interests of the principal."[39]

---

[38] *Bristol & West Building Society v Mothew* [1998] Ch. 1 at 18; *Lehtimaki v Cooper* [2020] UKSC 33 at [44], [2021] 1 All E.R. 809; *Arklow Investments Ltd v Maclean* [2000] 1 W.L.R. 594 at 598–600; *Peskin v Anderson* [2000] EWCA Civ 326 at [34], [2001] 1 B.C.L.C. 372; *Hooper v Gorvin* [2001] W.T.L.R. 575 at 590; *Kyrris v Oldham* [2003] EWCA Civ 1506 at [142]; [2001] 1 B.C.L.C. 372; *Maclean v Arklow Investments Ltd* [1998] 3 N.Z.L.R. 680 at 691 and 723; *Button v Phelps* [2006] EWHC 53 (Ch) at [58]–[61]; *Australian Securities and Investments Commission v Citigroup Global Markets Australia Pty Ltd (No.4)* [2007] FCA 963 at [272]; (2007) 160 F.C.R. 35; *South Australia v Peat Marwick Mitchell & Co* (1997) 24 A.C.S.R. 231, 265; *Schipp v Cameron* [1998] NSWSC 997 at [697]; *Galambos v Perez* [2009] SCC 48; [2009] 3 S.C.R. 247; *Grimaldi v Chameleon Mining NL (No.2)* [2012] FCAFC 6 at [177]; (2012) 200 F.C.R. 296; *McWilliam v Norton Finance (UK) Ltd* [2015] EWCA Civ 186 at [40]-[42], [2015] 1 All E.R. (Comm.) 1026; *FHR European Ventures LLP v Cedar Capital Partners LLC* [2014] UKSC 45 at [5]; [2015] A.C. 250; *Farrar v Miller* [2018] EWCA Civ 172 at [75]; *Sheikh Tahnoon v Kent* [2018] EWHC 333 (Comm) at [158]–[159].

[37] *Brandeis (Brokers) Ltd v Black* [2001] 2 All E.R. (Comm.) 980 at [36]–[37]; *Vivendi SA v Richards* [2013] EWHC 3006 (Ch) at [138]–[141].

[38] *F & C Alternative Investments (Holdings) Ltd v Barthelemy (No.2)* [2011] EWHC 1731 (Ch) at [225]; [2012] Ch. 613.

[39] *Arklow Investments Ltd v Maclean* [2000] 1 W.L.R. 594 at 598; *Lehtimaki v Cooper* [2020] UKSC 33 at [47]–[49] and [91], [2021] 1 All E.R. 809; *Farrar v Miller* [2018] EWCA Civ 172 at [75]. See also *Waxman v Waxman* (2004) 7 I.T.E.L.R. 162 at [512] Ont CA; *Brandeis Brokers Ltd v Black* [2001] 2 All E.R. (Comm) 980 at [36]–[37]; *Hughes Aircraft Systems International v Airservices Australia* (1997) 146 A.L.R. 1 (FCA) at 81; *News Ltd v Australian Rugby Football League Ltd* (1996) 64 F.C.R. 410 at 541; *Australian Securities Commission v AS Nominees Ltd* (1995) 62 F.C.R. 504 at 521; (1995) 133 A.L.R. 1 (FCA) at 17; *Glandon Pty Ltd v Strata Consolidated Pty Ltd* (1993) 11 A.C.S.R. 543 at 557 (NSWCA); *Australian Securities and Investments Commission v Citigroup Global Markets Australia Pty Ltd (No.4)* [2007] FCA 963 at [273]; (2007) 160 F.C.R. 35; *Brooker v Friend* [2006] NSWCA 385 at [149]; *John Youngs Insurance Services Ltd v Aviva Insurance Service UK Ltd* [2011] EWHC 1515 (TCC) at [94(3)]; *F & C Alternative Investments (Holdings) Ltd v Barthelemy (No.2)* [2011] EWHC 1731 (Ch) at [223] and [225]; [2012] Ch. 613; *Grimaldi v Chameleon Mining NL (No.2)* [2012] FCAFC 6 at [177]; (2012) 200 F.C.R. 296. This stems from Paul Finn's academic work: see Finn, *"The Fiduciary Principle"* in Equity, Fiduciaries and Trusts (1989) 1 at 54; P. Finn, "Fiduciary Law and the Modern

Commercial World" in E. McKendrick (ed), *Commercial Aspects of Trusts and Fiduciary Obligations* (Oxford: Clarendon Press, 1992) 7 at 8.

Replace n.41 with:

[41] *Vivendi SA v Richards* [2013] EWHC 3006 (Ch) at [139] and [142]; *Tan Yok Koon v Tan Choo Suan* [2017] SGCA 13 at [194] and [199]; [2017] 1 SLR 654..

Replace fourth paragraph with:

Where the fiduciary expectation is appropriate in respect of part only of the arrangement between the parties, it is possible for fiduciary duties to be owed in respect of that part of the arrangement even though it is not fiduciary in general: "a person ... may be in a fiduciary position quoad a part of his activities and not quoad other parts".[42]

[42] *New Zealand Netherlands Society "Oranje" Inc v Kuys* [1973] 1 W.L.R. 1126 at 1130. See also *Lehtimaki v Cooper* [2020] UKSC 33 at [51] and [101], [2021] 1 All E.R. 809; *Breen v Williams* (1996) 186 C.L.R. 71 at 107–108; *Maruha Corp v Amaltal Corp Ltd* [2007] NZSC 40 at [21]–[22]; [2007] 3 N.Z.L.R. 192; *Australian Securities and Investments Commission v Citigroup Global Markets Australia Pty Ltd (No.4)* [2007] FCA 963 at [285]; (2007) 160 F.C.R. 35; *John Youngs Insurance Services Ltd v Aviva Insurance Service UK Ltd* [2011] EWHC 1515 (TCC) at [94(6)], [96].

Replace n.49 with:

[49] See also *John Alexander's Clubs Pty Ltd v White City Tennis Club Ltd* (2010) 241 C.L.R. 1 at [90] and [101]; [2010] HCA 19; *Adventure Golf Systems Australia Pty Ltd v Belgravia Health & Leisure Group Pty Ltd* [2017] VSCA 326 [125]–[126]; (2017) 54 V.R. 625.

(2) Examples.

Replace fourth paragraph with:

Joint venturers have been held to owe fiduciary duties to one another,[63] but not all joint ventures necessarily involve such duties.[64] While it has been suggested that joint ventures may be "inherently fiduciary" because of their similarity to partnership,[65] the term "joint venture" is a business term "which does not have a precise legal meaning".[66] Indeed, it has been said not even to be a term of art in business.[67] It is unwise for such an ill-defined term to be the trigger for a category of fiduciary relationship. Instead, it is preferable for joint ventures not to be treated as a settled category of fiduciary relationship,[68] but an individual joint venture may appropriately be treated as a fiduciary relationship if, "after a meticulous examination of its own facts",[69] the fiduciary expectation[70] is found to be appropriate, bearing in mind the points made above regarding the appropriateness of that expectation between commercial actors[71]:

7-006

> "It is perfectly common for commercial entities to want to enter into cooperative arrangements for a specific purpose, involving a share of profits, but without intending to follow the route of mutual agency and the court should give effect to their intentions."[72]

[63] *United Dominions Corp Ltd v Brian Pty Ltd* (1985) 157 C.L.R. 1 at 7–8, 12–13 and 16; *Fawcett v Whitehouse* (1829) 1 Russ. & M. 132 at 148 (39 E.R. 51 at 57); *Murad v Al-Saraj* [2004] EWHC 1235 (Ch) at [325]–[341]; *Chirnside v Fay* [2006] NZSC 68; [2007] 1 N.Z.L.R. 433; *Schipp v Cameron* [1998] NSWSC 997; *Fraser Edmiston Pty Ltd v AGT (Qld) Pty Ltd* [1988] 2 Qd. R. 1; *Ross River Ltd v Waveley Commercial Ltd* [2013] EWCA Civ 910.

[64] See, e.g. *Global Container Lines Ltd v Bonyad Shipping Co (No.1)* [1998] 1 Lloyd's Rep. 528 at 546–547; *Button v Phelps* [2006] EWHC 53 (Ch) at [59]–[61]; *Ross River Ltd v Cambridge City Football Club Ltd* [2007] EWHC 2115 (Ch) at [197]; *Gibson Motorsport Merchandise Pty Ltd v Forbes* [2006] FCAFC 44 at [2]; (2006) 149 F.C.R. 569; *John Alexander's Clubs Pty Ltd v White City Tennis Club Ltd* [2010] HCA 19 at [44]; (2010) 241 C.L.R. 1; *Farrar v Miller* [2018] EWCA Civ 172 at [75]; *Adventure Golf Systems Australia Pty Ltd v Belgravia Health & Leisure Group Pty Ltd* [2017] VSCA 326 at [134];

(2017) 54 V.R. 625; and see *Explora Group Plc v Hesco Bastion Ltd* [2005] EWCA Civ 646 at [51], citing this paragraph.

[65] *Chirnside v Fay* [2006] NZSC 68 at [14] and [74]; [2007] 1 N.Z.L.R. 433. See also, apparently, *Concrete Pty Ltd v Parramatta Design & Developments Pty Ltd* [2006] HCA 55; (2006) 231 A.L.R. 663 at [156] per Callinan J.

[66] *BBC Worldwide Ltd v Bee Load Ltd* [2007] EWHC 134 (Comm) at [103].

[67] *Ross River Ltd v Waveley Commercial Ltd* [2013] EWCA Civ 910 at [34].

[68] *Paper Reclaim Ltd v Aotearoa Ltd* [2007] NZSC 26 at [31]–[32]; [2007] 3 N.Z.L.R. 169; *Maruha Corp v Amaltal Corp Ltd* [2007] NZSC 40 at [20]–[21]; [2007] 3 N.Z.L.R. 192.

[69] *Cook v Evatt (No.2)* [1992] 1 N.Z.L.R. 676 at 685; *Foster Bryant Surveying Ltd v Bryant* [2007] EWCA Civ 200 at [76], [2007] Bus. L.R. 1565.

[70] See para.7-005 above.

[71] See para.7-005 above.

[72] *BBC Worldwide Ltd v Bee Load Ltd* [2007] EWHC 134 (Comm) at [107].

2. GENERAL NATURE OF FIDUCIARY DUTIES

Replace paragraph with:

7-007   "To say that a man is a fiduciary only begins analysis; it gives direction to further inquiry. To whom is he a fiduciary? What obligations does he owe as a fiduciary? In what respect has he failed to discharge these obligations? And what are the consequences of his deviation from duty?"[74]

[74] *Securities & Exchange Commission v Chenery Corp* 318 U.S. 80 at 85–86; 87 L. Ed. 626 at 632 (1943); quoted with approval in *Re Goldcorp Exchange Ltd (In Receivership)* [1995] 1 A.C. 74 at 98. See also *Boardman v Phipps* [1967] 2 A.C. 46 at 127; *Lehtimaki v Cooper* [2020] UKSC 33 at [35], [2021] 1 All E.R. 809.

1. Loyalty

Replace paragraph with:

7-008   "The distinguishing obligation of a fiduciary is the obligation of loyalty. The principal is entitled to the single-minded loyalty of his fiduciary."[76] This obligation of loyalty has several facets, which are addressed separately below. Millett LJ provided a non-exhaustive list of those facets in his judgment in *Bristol & West Building Society v Mothew*, which is "widely regarded as a masterly survey of the modern law of fiduciary duties"[77]:

> "A fiduciary must act in good faith; he must not make a profit out of his trust; he must not place himself in a position where his duty and his interest may conflict; he may not act for his own benefit or the benefit of a third person without the informed consent of his principal."[78]

The fundamental fiduciary obligation of loyalty comprises two related themes.[79] The first prohibits a fiduciary from acting in a situation where there is a conflict between the fiduciary's duty and his or her interest: "the objective is to preclude the fiduciary from being swayed by considerations of personal interest".[80] The second prohibits a fiduciary from making a profit out of his or her fiduciary position: "the objective is to preclude the fiduciary from actually misusing his position for his personal advantage".[81] It has been suggested that the second of these two themes is merely an instance of the first.[82] In most cases where the profit theme applies, the fundamental conflict theme will also capture the situation and give rise to liability on the part of the fiduciary.[83] The profit theme developed out of the conflict theme,[84] but has reached the point where it applies without the need for any conflict analysis.[85] In other words, the two principles largely overlap but there may be cases where the two do not necessarily both apply.[86]

[76] *Bristol & West Building Society v Mothew* [1998] Ch. 1 at 18; *Boulting v Association of Cinematograph, Television & Allied Technicians* [1963] 2 Q.B. 606 at 636; *KLB v British Columbia* [2003] 2 S.C.R. 403; (2003) 230 D.L.R. (4th) 513 at [48]; *Chirnside v Fay* [2004] 3 N.Z.L.R. 637 at [51]; *Sinclair Investment Holdings SA v Versailles Trade Finance Ltd* [2005] EWCA Civ 722 at [20]; *Ultraframe (UK) Ltd v Fielding* [2005] EWHC 1638 (Ch) at [1285]–[1288]; *Gibson Motorsport Merchandise Pty Ltd v Forbes* [2006] FCAFC 44 at [11]; (2006) 149 F.C.R. 569; *Stevens v Premium Real Estate Ltd* [2009] NZSC 15 at [67]; [2009] 2 N.Z.L.R. 384; *Sinclair Investments (UK) Ltd v Versailles Trade Finance Ltd* [2010] EWHC 1614 (Ch) at [26]; *Rossetti Marketing Ltd v Diamond Sofa Co Ltd* [2012] EWCA Civ 1021 at [20]; *Adventure Golf Systems Australia Pty Ltd v Belgravia Health & Leisure Group Pty Ltd* [2017] VSCA 326 at [124]; (2017) 54 V.R. 625..

[77] *Johnson v EBS Pensioner Trustees Ltd* [2002] EWCA Civ 164 at [37], [2002] Lloyd's Rep. P.N. 309.

[78] *Bristol & West Building Society v Mothew* [1998] Ch. 1 at 18; *Gray v Global Energy Horizons Corp* [2020] EWCA Civ 1668 at [169] (reported in part, but not this part, at [2021] 1 W.L.R. 2264).

[79] *Australian Securities and Investments Commission v Citigroup Global Markets Australia Pty Ltd (No.4)* [2007] FCA 963 at [291]; (2007) 160 F.C.R. 35; *South Australia v Peat Marwick Mitchell & Co* (1997) 24 A.C.S.R. 231, 264; *Sinclair Investments (UK) Ltd v Versailles Trade Finance Ltd* [2010] EWHC 1614 (Ch) at [29]; *Grimaldi v Chameleon Mining NL (No.2)* [2012] FCAFC 6 at [178]; (2012) 200 F.C.R. 296; *Ancient Order of Foresters in Victoria Friendly Society Ltd v Lifeplan Australia Friendly Society Ltd* [2018] HCA 43 at [67]–[69]; (2018) 265 C.L.R. 1.

[80] *Chan v Zacharia* (1984) 154 C.L.R. 178 at 198 (quoted with approval in *Don King Productions Inc v Warren* [2000] Ch. 291 at [40]).

[81] *Chan v Zacharia* (1984) 154 C.L.R. 178 at 199 (quoted with approval in *Don King Productions Inc v Warren* [2000] Ch. 291 at [40]).

[82] See, e.g. *Broughton v Broughton* (1855) 5 De G.M. & G. 160 at 164 (43 E.R. 831 at 833); *Bray v Ford* [1896] A.C. 44 at 51; *Boardman v Phipps* [1967] 2 A.C. 46 at 123; *New Zealand Netherlands Society "Oranje" Inc v Kuys* [1973] 1 W.L.R. 1126 at 1129; *Ratiu v Conway* [2005] EWCA Civ 1302 at [59]; *Huntington Copper & Sulphur Co (Ltd) v Henderson* (1877) 4 S.C. (4th Series) 294 at 299; *FHR European Ventures LLP v Cedar Capital Partners LLC* [2014] UKSC 45 at [5]; [2015] A.C. 250.

[83] See, e.g. *Boston Deep Sea Fishing & Ice Co v Ansell* (1888) 39 Ch. D. 339 at 355, 357.

[84] See generally A. McClean, "The Theoretical Basis of the Trustee's Duty of Loyalty" (1969) 7 Alberta L. Rev. 218.

[85] See, e.g. *Re Lewis* (1910) 103 L.T. 495; *Regal (Hastings) Ltd v Gulliver* [1967] 2 A.C. 134n. at 144–145, 153, 159; *Brown v Inland Revenue Commissioners* [1965] A.C. 244 at 256, 265; *Boardman v Phipps* [1967] 2 A.C. 46 at 100–101, 103, 105, 118; *Queensland Mines Ltd v Hudson* (1978) 18 A.L.R. 1 at 4 (PC).

[86] *Oceanic Life Ltd v HIH Casualty & General Insurance Ltd* [1999] NSWSC 292 at [42].

2. Concurrency of Fiduciary and Non-Fiduciary Duties

Replace paragraph with:

Not all of the duties which a fiduciary owes are properly categorised as fiduci-   **7-009**
ary duties. Only those duties which are an aspect of the fiduciary's duty of loyalty are properly categorised as fiduciary duties, as it is only these duties which are peculiar to fiduciaries.[89] The "essence of a fiduciary relationship is that it creates obligations of a different character from those deriving from the contract",[90] or from tort law, or from non-fiduciary equitable doctrines (e.g. such as those relating to trusts). Thus, a trustee who acts loyally but incompetently is not in breach of his fiduciary duties, although he may be in breach of a duty to exercise due care and skill,[91] or otherwise in breach of trust. Similarly, breach of a contractual duty to ac-

count, in the absence of a trust, is a breach of contract rather than a breach of fiduciary duty.[92] And a solicitor's negligence is not, without more, a breach of fiduciary duty.[93] "Not every breach of duty by a fiduciary is a breach of fiduciary duty."[94]

[89] *Bristol & West Building Society v Mothew* [1998] Ch. 1 at 16; *Attorney General v Blake* [1998] Ch. 439 at 455; *Ocular Sciences Ltd v Aspect Vision Care Ltd* [1997] R.P.C. 289 at 413; *Girardet v Crease & Co* (1987) 11 B.C.L.R. (2d) 361 at 361; *Lac Minerals Ltd v International Corona Resources Ltd* (1989) 61 D.L.R. (4th) 14 at 28; *Permanent Building Society (In Liquidation) v Wheeler* (1994) 14 A.C.S.R. 109 at 157; *Roberts v R.* [2002] 4 S.C.R. 245; (2002) 220 D.L.R. (4th) 1 at [83]. See also *Chirnside v Fay* [2004] 3 N.Z.L.R. 637 at [51].

[90] *Re Goldcorp Exchange Ltd (In Receivership)* [1995] 1 A.C. 74 at 98. See also *Lehtimaki v Cooper* [2020] UKSC 33 at [46], [2021] 1 All E.R. 809; *Ratiu v Conway* [2005] EWCA Civ 1302 at [71]–[72]; *Strother v 3464920 Canada Inc* [2007] SCC 24 at [141]; [2007] 2 S.C.R. 177; *John Youngs Insurance Services Ltd v Aviva Insurance Service UK Ltd* [2011] EWHC 1515 (TCC) at [94(7)].

[91] *Bristol & West Building Society v Mothew* [1998] Ch. 1 at 16, 18. See also *Spread Trustee Co Ltd v Hutcheson* [2011] UKPC 13 at [61]; [2012] 2 A.C. 194.

[92] *Paragon Finance Plc v DB Thakerar & Co* [1999] 1 All E.R. 400 at 415–416; *Coulthard v Disco Mix Club Ltd* [2000] 1 W.L.R. 707 at 728.

[93] *Henderson v Merrett Syndicates Ltd* [1995] 2 A.C. 145 at 205–206; *Nationwide Building Society v Vanderpump & Sykes* [1999] Lloyd's Rep. P.N. 422.

[94] *Hilton v Barker Booth & Eastwood* [2005] UKHL 8; [2005] 1 W.L.R. 567 at [29]; *Bristol & West Building Society v Mothew* [1998] Ch. 1 at 16; *Base Metal Trading Ltd v Shamurin* [2004] EWCA Civ 1316; [2005] 1 All E.R. (Comm) 17 at [19]; *Chirnside v Fay* [2006] NZSC 68 at [15], [72], [73]; [2007] 1 N.Z.L.R. 432; *Strother v 3464920 Canada Inc* [2007] SCC 24 at [34]; [2007] 24 S.C.R. 177; *South Australia v Peat Marwick Mitchell & Co* (1997) 24 A.C.S.R. 231, 266; *John Youngs Insurance Services Ltd v Aviva Insurance Service UK Ltd* [2011] EWHC 1515 (TCC) at [94(2)]; *Novoship (UK) Ltd v Nikitin* [2014] EWCA Civ 908 at [106]; [2015] Q.B. 499.

4. Proscriptive Duties

Replace n.99 with:

7-011   [99] *Attorney General v Blake* [1998] Ch. 439 at 455; *Breen v Williams* (1996) 186 C.L.R. 71 at 95, 113 & 137–138; *Pilmer v Duke Group Ltd (In Liquidation)* [2001] HCA 31 at [74], [127]; (2001) 207 C.L.R. 165; *Youyang Pty Ltd v Minter Ellison Morris Fletcher* [2003] HCA 15 at [41]; (2003) 212 C.L.R. 484; *Aequitas v AEFC* [2001] NSWSC 14; (2001) 19 A.C.L.C. 1,006 at [284]; *Australian Securities and Investments Commission v Citigroup Global Markets Australia Pty Ltd (No.4)* [2007] FCA 963 at [290]; (2007) 160 F.C.R. 35; *Brooker v Friend* [2006] NSWCA 385 at [26]; *Gibson Motorsport Merchandise Pty Ltd v Forbes* [2006] FCAFC 44 at [12]; (2006) 149 F.C.R. 569; *P & V Industries Pty Ltd v Porto* [2006] VSC 131 at [32]–[34], [43]; (2006) 14 V.R. 1; *Commonwealth Oil & Gas Co Ltd v Baxter* [2009] CSIH 75 at [14]; *Eric Preston Pty Ltd v Euroz Securities Ltd* [2010] FCA 97 at [428]–[429]; *Grimaldi v Chameleon Mining NL (No.2)* [2012] FCAFC 6 at [178]; (2012) 200 F.C.R. 296; *Howard v Commissioner of Taxation* [2014] HCA 21 at [31], [56]; (2014) 253 C.L.R. 83; *Moulin Global Eyecare Holdings Ltd v Mei* [2014] 17 H.K.C.F.A.R. 466 at [36]; *Ancient Order of Foresters in Victoria Friendly Society Ltd v Lifeplan Australia Friendly Society Ltd* [2018] HCA 43 at [67]; (2018) 265 C.L.R. 1. cf. *Fassihi v Item Software (UK) Ltd* [2004] EWCA Civ 1244 at [41]; *Sharp v Blank* [2015] EWHC 3220 (Ch) at [23]. See further, Conaglen, *Fiduciary Loyalty: Protecting the Due Performance of Non-Fiduciary Duties* (2010) Ch.7.

5. Scope and Duration of Fiduciary Duties

(a) Scope.

Replace paragraph with:

7-012   The scope of fiduciary duties is "moulded according to the nature of the relationship and the facts of the case".[100] However, application of fiduciary doctrine is not an unprincipled exercise in judicial discretion. Rather, it requires a meticulous examination of the facts of each case in order to determine what non-fiduciary duties are owed, so as to be able to determine the effect that fiduciary principles will have in the case[101]:

> "The fiduciary relationship cannot be superimposed upon the contract in such a way as to alter the operation which the contract was intended to have according to its true construction."[102]

Careful analysis of both fiduciary *and* non-fiduciary duties is crucial.[103] It is nonsensical, for example, to talk of a conflict between duty and interest without careful analysis of what non-fiduciary duties are in fact owed.[104] Those duties will differ with the circumstances of each case. Fiduciary doctrine must be applied in a way that is sensitive to those differences. For this reason, there:

> "is no class of case in which one ought more carefully to bear in mind the facts of the case ... than cases which relate to fiduciary and confidential relations."[105]

[100] *Hospital Products Ltd v United States Surgical Corp* (1984) 156 C.L.R. 41 at 102; *Re Coomber* [1911] 1 Ch. 723 at 729; *New Zealand Netherlands Society "Oranje" Inc v Kuys* [1973] 1 W.L.R. 1126 at 1130; *Lac Minerals Ltd v International Corona Resources Ltd* (1989) 61 D.L.R. (4th) 14 at 28; *Kelly v Cooper* [1993] A.C. 205 at 214; *Henderson v Merrett Syndicates Ltd* [1995] 2 A.C. 145 at 206; *Clay v Clay* [2001] HCA 9 at [46]; *Strother v 3464920 Canada Inc* [2007] SCC 24 at [118], [141]; [2007] 2 S.C.R. 177; *Australian Securities and Investments Commission v Citigroup Global Markets Australia Pty Ltd (No.4)* [2007] FCA 963 at [288]; (2007) 160 F.C.R. 35; *South Australia v Peat Marwick Mitchell & Co* (1997) 24 A.C.S.R. 231 at 266; *Stevens v Premium Real Estate Ltd* [2009] NZSC 15 at 23; [2009] 2 N.Z.L.R. 384; *John Alexander's Clubs Pty Ltd v White City Tennis Club Ltd* [2010] HCA 19 at [91]–[92]; (2010) 241 C.L.R. 1; *Eric Preston Pty Ltd v Euroz Securities Ltd* [2010] FCA 97 at [425]–[426]; *Customer Systems Plc v Ranson* [2012] EWCA Civ 841 at [25]–[29]; *Lehtimaki v Cooper* [2020] UKSC 33 at [79], [2021] 1 All E.R. 809. Thus, e.g. in the case of an agent employed under a contract, the scope of any fiduciary duties of the agent will be determined by reference to the terms of the underlying contract: *John Youngs Insurance Services Ltd v Aviva Insurance Service UK Ltd* [2011] EWHC 1515 (TCC) at [94(1)].

[101] *Howard v Commissioner of Taxation* [2014] HCA 21 at [61]; (2014) 253 C.L.R. 83.

[102] *John Youngs Insurance Services Ltd v Aviva Insurance Service UK Ltd* [2011] EWHC 1515 (TCC) at [94(5)]. See also *Hospital Products Ltd v United States Surgical Corp* (1984) 156 C.L.R. 41 at 97; *John Alexander's Clubs Pty Ltd v White City Tennis Club Ltd* [2010] HCA 19 at [91]; (2010) 241 C.L.R. 1.

[103] See, e.g. *Strother v 3464920 Canada Inc* [2007] SCC 24; [2007] 2 S.C.R. 177; *Australian Securities and Investments Commission v Citigroup Global Markets Australia Pty Ltd (No.4)* [2007] FCA 963. See also Conaglen, *Fiduciary Loyalty: Protecting the Due Performance of Non-Fiduciary Duties* (2010) Ch.7.

[104] cf. *Longstaff v Birtles* [2001] EWCA Civ 1219, [2002] 1 W.L.R. 470 where the court found a conflict between duty and interest while denying the existence of any non-fiduciary duty.

[105] *Re Coomber* [1911] 1 Ch. 723 at 729; *Boardman v Phipps* [1967] 2 A.C. 46 at 125; *Brooker v Friend* [2006] NSWCA 385 at [26]; *Eze v Conway* [2019] EWCA Civ 88 at [39]–[40].

(b) Duration.

Replace paragraph with:

Fiduciary duties are dependent upon the continued existence of an underlying relationship of duty: **7-013**

> "We do not recognise the concept of a fiduciary obligation which continues notwithstanding the determination of the particular relationship which gives rise to it. Equity does not demand a duty of undivided loyalty from a former employee to his former employer."[107]

[107] *Attorney General v Blake* [1998] Ch. 439 at 453; *Bolkiah v KPMG* [1999] 2 A.C. 222 at 235; *CMS Dolphin Ltd v Simonet* [2001] 2 B.C.L.C. 704 at [95]; *Foster Bryant Surveying Ltd v Bryant* [2007] EWCA Civ 200 at [8], [68], [2007] Bus. L.R. 1565; *Walsh v Shanahan* [2013] EWCA Civ 411 at [38]; *Tigris International NV v China Southern Airlines Co Ltd* [2014] EWCA Civ 1649 at [156]–[158].

Replace second paragraph with:

However, to prevent the emasculation of fiduciary duties, a fiduciary may not resign his fiduciary position in order to do that which fiduciary doctrine would otherwise bar him from doing,[110] unless he obtains his principal's fully informed consent, or the principal has made a clear decision no longer to use the fiduciary's services.[111] In this sense fiduciary duties "may endure beyond the termination of the retainer",[112] but this is in order to prevent fiduciary duties from being too easily avoided by the expedient means of resignation,[113] and the breach of fiduciary duty normally takes place before resignation, in the planning and preparation for what comes after resignation.[113a] Furthermore, resignation will not avoid liability under the profit theme of fiduciary loyalty for a fiduciary such as a director:

> "if, after his resignation, he uses for his own benefit property of the company or information which he has acquired while a director."[114]

Nor may a fiduciary arrange a transaction and then resign in order to put the transaction into effect if the transaction could not have been entered into while the fiduciary remained in his fiduciary position.[115] A fiduciary is not, however, barred from resigning and exploiting opportunities within the market in which his principal operates, where he did not resign from his fiduciary position with a view to exploiting such opportunities and where the opportunity was not one which his principal was pursuing at the time of resignation or thereafter.[116]

[110] *Ex p. James* (1803) 8 Ves. 337 at 352 (32 E.R. 385 at 390–391); *Re Boles and British Land Co's Contract* [1902] 1 Ch. 244 at 246–247; *Island Export Finance Ltd v Umunna* [1986] B.C.L.C. 460 at 476; *Edmonds v Donovan* [2005] VSCA 27 [56]–[57] and [60]–[61], (2005) 12 V.R. 513

[111] See, e.g. *In Plus Group Ltd v Pyke* [2002] EWCA Civ 370 at [76] and [90], [2002] 2 B.C.L.C. 201. This line of authority provides only a narrow escape route for fiduciaries: *Recovery Partners GP Ltd v Rukhadze* [2018] EWHC 2918 (Comm) at [402], [2019] Bus. L.R. 1166.

[112] *Longstaff v Birtles* [2001] EWCA Civ 1219 at [1], [2002] 1 W.L.R. 470.

[113] See generally P. Koh "Once a Director, Always a Fiduciary?" [2003] 62 C.L.J. 403; and Conaglen, *Fiduciary Loyalty: Protecting the Due Performance of Non-Fiduciary Duties* (2010) Ch.7.

[113a] *Foster Bryant Surveying Ltd v Bryant* [2007] EWCA Civ 200 at [69], [2007] Bus. L.R. 1565; *Recovery Partners GP Ltd v Rukhadze* [2018] EWHC 2918 (Comm) at [69]–[76], [2019] Bus. L.R. 1166.

[114] *Ultraframe (UK) Ltd v Fielding* [2005] EWHC 1638 (Ch) at [1309].

[115] *Spring v Pride* (1864) 4 De G.J. & S. 395 (46 E.R. 971); *Wright v Morgan* [1926] A.C. 788 at 796; *Industrial Development Consultants Ltd v Cooley* [1972] 1 W.L.R. 443.

[116] *Island Export Finance Ltd v Umunna* [1986] B.C.L.C. 460 at 482, 483. See also *Foster Bryant Surveying Ltd v Bryant* [2007] EWCA Civ 200, [2007] Bus. L.R. 1565.

Replace n.117 with:

[117] Companies Act 2006 s.170(2). This duty "continues" after termination of the directorship: *Burnell v Trans-Tag Ltd* [2021] EWHC 1457 (Ch) at [389]–[413].

6. Authorisation

(a) Principal's consent.

Replace n.127 with:

[127] *Barr, Leary & Co v Hall* (1906) 26 N.Z.L.R. 222 at 225; *York & North-Midland Railway Co v Hudson* (1845) 16 Beav. 485 at 491 (51 E.R. 866 at 868–869); *Coles v Trecothick* (1804) 9 Ves. 234 at 246–247 (32 E.R. 592 at 597).

7-015

Replace third paragraph with:

The materiality of information to be disclosed is determined not by whether it would have been decisive (although, if it would have been decisive, then it clearly was material[131]), but rather by whether it may have affected the principal's consent.[132] Thus, it is no defence to a claim for breach of fiduciary duty for the fiduciary to argue that the principal would have acted in the same way even if the information had been disclosed.[133] Further, consistent with equity's focus on substance rather than form, disclosure is treated in a functional, rather than a formalistic, way, so that the sufficiency of disclosure depends on the sophistication and intelligence of the person to whom disclosure is required to be made.[134]

[131] See, e.g. *Imperial Mercantile Credit Association v Coleman* (1873) L.R. 6 H.L. 189 at 200, 205.

[132] *Johnson v EBS Pensioner Trustees Ltd* [2002] EWCA Civ 164 at [72], [83], [2002] Lloyd's Rep. P.N. 309; *FHR European Ventures LLP v Mankarious* [2011] EWHC 2308 (Ch) at [79].

[133] *Swindle v Harrison* [1997] 4 All E.R. 705 at 733. This fact may affect the remedies available to the principal, as it did in *Swindle v Harrison*.

[134] *McWilliam v Norton Finance (UK) Ltd* [2015] EWCA Civ 186 at [51]-[54], [2015] 1 All E.R. (Comm.) 1026. See also *Farah Constructions Pty Ltd v Say-Dee Pty Ltd* [2007] HCA 22 at [107]–[108]; (2007) 230 C.L.R. 89; *Australian Securities and Investments Commission v Citigroup Global Markets Australia Pty Ltd (No.4)* [2007] FCA 963 at [296]; (2007) 160 F.C.R. 35. Both of these latter cases involved sophisticated principals: cf. the facts in *Maguire v Makaronis* (1997) 188 C.L.R. 449. See also *Medsted Associates Ltd v Canaccord Genuity Wealth (International) Ltd* [2019] EWCA Civ 83; [2019] 1 W.L.R. 4481, which again involved experienced investors.

Replace fourth paragraph with:

The fiduciary must disclose the nature of his interest in the transaction, not merely the existence of the interest.[135] Where the existence of the interest is disclosed, but not the precise nature of that interest, the principal's fully informed consent may not have been obtained, although the fact that the existence of the interest is known to the principal can result in a reduced range of remedies being available to the principal.[136]

[135] *Imperial Mercantile Credit Association v Coleman* (1873) L.R. 6 H.L. 189 at 200 & 205; *Dunne v English* (1874) L.R. 18 Eq. 524 at 533, 534 and 535; *Gray v New Augarita Porcupine Mines Ltd* [1952] 3 D.L.R. 1 at 14; *Movitex Ltd v Bulfield* [1988] B.C.L.C. 104 at 121; *Gwembe Valley Development Co Ltd v Koshy* [2003] EWCA Civ 1048; [2004] 1 B.C.L.C. 131 at [65]; *Wrexham Associated Football Club Ltd v Crucialmove Ltd* [2006] EWCA Civ 237; [2007] B.C.C. 139 at [39].

[136] *Hurstanger Ltd v Wilson* [2007] EWCA Civ 299, [2007] 1 W.L.R. 2351. See also para.7-053. The decision in *Medsted Associates Ltd v Canaccord Genuity Wealth (International) Ltd* [2019] EWCA Civ 83, [2019] 1 W.L.R. 4481 suggests that there is no breach of fiduciary duty where the existence but not nature of the interest is disclosed; this decision is based on a misreading of *Hurstanger*, where the Court of Appeal was clear that there had been a breach of fiduciary duty in that situation (and so an account of profits was available), but held that the remedy of rescission could be refused, in the court's discretion, because the profit was not fully secret (as to which see para.7-053).

Replace n.138 with:

¹³⁸ *FHR European Ventures LLP v Mankarious* [2011] EWHC 2308 (Ch) at [81]–[82]; *McWilliam v Norton Finance (UK) Ltd* [2015] EWCA Civ 186 at [54], [201] 1 All E.R. (Comm.) 1026.

Replace n.140 with:

¹⁴⁰ *De Bussche v Alt* (1878) 8 Ch. D. 286 CA at 312–313; *AB Jnr v MB* [2013] 1 C.I.L.R. 1 at [285].

(b) Consent of person creating fiduciary position.

Replace n.143 with:

7-016 ¹⁴³ *Sargeant v National Westminster Bank Plc* (1991) 61 P. & C.R. 518 CA (Civ Div) at 519, 523.

3. CONFLICTS BETWEEN DUTY AND INTEREST

1. General Principle

Replace footnote 142 with:

7-018 ¹⁴² *Bray v Ford* [1896] A.C. 44 at 51; *Australian Securities and Investments Commission v Citigroup Global Markets Australia Pty Ltd (No.4)* [2007] FCA 963 at [313]; (2007) 160 F.C.R. 35.

Replace n.159 with:

¹⁵⁹ See, e.g. *In Plus Group Ltd v Pyke* [2002] EWCA Civ 370 at [76], [90], [2002] 2 B.C.L.C. 201; *Ultraframe (UK) Ltd v Fielding* [2005] EWHC 1638 (Ch) at [1308]–[1310], [1330]. For more detailed analysis, see Conaglen, *Fiduciary Loyalty: Protecting the Due Performance of Non-Fiduciary Duties* (2010) Ch.7.

Replace n.156 with:

¹⁵⁶ *Bray v Ford* [1896] A.C. 44 at 51; *Australian Securities and Investments Commission v Citigroup Global Markets Australia Pty Ltd (No.4)* [2007] FCA 963 at [313]; (2007) 160 F.C.R. 35.

Replace fourth paragraph with:

It is not necessary to show that there has been a breach of non-fiduciary duty in order for there to have been a breach of fiduciary duty when the fiduciary acted in circumstances involving a conflict between that non-fiduciary duty and his personal interest: "it is quite enough that the thing which he does ... has a tendency to interfere with his duty".¹⁶⁵ Indeed, a fiduciary can be in breach of the fiduciary conflict rule even though his or her conduct has been to the benefit of the fiduciary's principal.¹⁶⁶ The rule is a general rule, based on generalised considerations of risk, rather than one which requires an assessment of whether the fiduciary has actually succumbed to temptation, as that is often too difficult to determine.¹⁶⁷ In this sense, fiduciary doctrine is often described as "prophylactic".¹⁶⁸

¹⁶⁵ *Hamilton v Wright* (1842) 9 Cl. & Fin. 111 at 123 (8 E.R. 357 at 362).

¹⁶⁶ See, e.g. *Ex p. James* (1803) 8 Ves. 337 at 348 (32 E.R. 385 at 389); *Aberdeen Railway Co v Blaikie Bros* (1854) 1 Macq. 461 at 472 (149 R.R. 32 at 39); *Regal (Hastings) Ltd v Gulliver* [1967] 2 A.C. 134 at 153; *Boardman v Phipps* [1967] 2 A.C. 46 at 129.

¹⁶⁷ *Ex p. Lacey* (1802) 6 Ves. 625 at 627 (31 E.R. 1228 at 1229); *Ex p. James* (1803) 8 Ves. 337 at 345 (32 E.R. at 388).

¹⁶⁸ See, e.g. *Harris v Digital Pulse Pty Ltd* [2003] NSWCA 10 at [413]–[414]; (2003) 56 N.S.W.L.R. 298.

Replace n.169 with:

[169] *Ex p. James* (1803) 8 Ves. 337 at 349 (32 E.R. at 389); *Aberdeen Railway Co v Blaikie Bros* (1854) 1 Macq. 461 at 471–472 (149 R.R. 32 at 39); *Parker v McKenna* (1874) L.R. 10 Ch. App. 96 at 124–125; *De Bussche v Alt* (1878) 8 Ch. D. 286 at 316; *Wright v Morgan* [1926] A.C. 788 at 798.

Replace n.172 with:

[172] See, e.g. *Ex p. Lacey* (1802) 6 Ves. 625 at 630 (31 E.R. 1228 at 1230); *Ex p. James* (1803) 8 Ves. 337 at 345 & 348 (32 E.R. 385 at 388 & 389); *Hamilton v Wright* (1842) 9 Cl. & Fin. 111 at 124 (8 E.R. 357 at 362); *Aberdeen Railway Co v Blaikie Bros* (1854) 1 Macq. 461 at 475 (149 R.R. 32 at 41); *De Bussche v Alt* (1878) 8 Ch. D. 286 at 316; *Boston Deep Sea Fishing & Ice Co v Ansell* (1888) 39 Ch. D. 339 at 369.

2. Authorisation

Replace n.179 with:

[179] *Australian Securities and Investments Commission v Citigroup Global Markets Australia Pty Ltd (No.4)* [2007] FCA 963 at [293]; (2007) 160 F.C.R. 35. See also *Downes v Grazebrook* (1817) 3 Mer. 200 at 208 (36 E.R. 77 at 80).

7-019

Replace fourth paragraph with:

It has been said that a fiduciary is liable under the fiduciary conflict rule even if he or she was not aware of the conflicting interest,[187] but this seems unnecessarily harsh.[188] It has been said that a fiduciary is not expected to disclose information of which he or she is unaware.[189] However, a fiduciary should not be able to avoid the effect of the rule where he or she has deliberately refrained from acquiring information about a conflicting interest,[190] or where he or she ought, consistently with his or her professional duty, to have recognised the conflicting interest.[191]

[187] *Lord Selsey v Rhoades* (1824) 2 Sim. & St. 41 at 50 (57 E.R. 260 at 264) (not discussed on appeal: (1827) 1 Bligh N.S. 1 (4 E.R. 774)); *Re Bulmer; Ex p. Greaves* [1937] Ch. 499 at 502–503, 510–511.

[188] It is difficult to see how a fiduciary could be "swayed by interest rather than by duty" (*Bray v Ford* [1896] A.C. 44 at 51) if he or she is completely unaware of the interest. See *In re Piedmont Trust* [2021] JRC 248; [2021] 2 J.L.R. 135 at [59(i)].

[189] *BLB Corp of Australia Establishment v Jacobsen* (1974) 48 A.L.J.R. 372, 378; *Gunasegaram v Blue Visions Management Pty Ltd* [2018] NSWCA 179 at [154]; *Wright v Lemon (No.2)* [2021] WASC 159 at [525].

[190] *BLB Corp of Australia Establishment v Jacobsen* (1974) 48 A.L.J.R. 372 at 378.

[191] *Bulkley v Wilford* (1834) 2 Cl. & Fin. 102 at 177, 181 & 183 (6 E.R. 1094); *Bayly v Wilkins* (1846) 3 Jo. & La T. 630 at 635–636.

3. Application

(b) Self-dealing.

Replace first paragraph with:

"The self-dealing rule is ... that if a trustee sells the trust property to himself, the sale is voidable by any beneficiary ex debito justitiae, however fair the transaction."[200] It is often said that a trustee may not purchase the trust property, but this has never been the true rule.[201] The true rule is that a purchase of trust property by a trustee is voidable at the instance of any beneficiary.[202] However honest and fair the sale may be,[203] and even if it was made at a public auction,[204] or for a price higher than that obtainable on the open market,[205] or on terms which are generous to the trust estate,[206] any beneficiary may have the transaction set aside within a reasonable time after he discovers the circumstances.[207]

7-021

200 *Tito v Waddell (No.2)* [1977] Ch. 106 at 241.

201 *Campbell v Walker* (1800) 5 Ves. 678 at 681 (31 E.R. 801 at 802).

202 *Campbell v Walker* (1800) 5 Ves. 678 at 680 (31 E.R. at 802); *Holder v Holder* [1968] Ch. 353 at 398 (citing an earlier version of this passage).

203 *Ex p. James* (1803) 8 Ves. 337 at 345 & 348–349 (32 E.R. 385 at 388 & 389); *Re Bulmer* [1937] Ch. 499 at 508.

204 *Ex p. James* (1803) 8 Ves. 337 at 349 (32 E.R. at 389); *Newgate Stud Co v Penfold* [2004] EWHC 2993 (Ch) at [222].

205 *Aberdeen Railway Co v Blaikie Bros* (1854) 1 Macq. 461 at 472 (149 R.R. 32 at 39).

206 *Re Thompson's Settlement* [1986] 1 Ch. 99 at 118.

207 *Beningfield v Baxter* (1886) 12 App. Cas. 167; *Randall v Errington* (1805) 10 Ves. 423 (32 E.R. 909); and see *Charter v Trevelyan* (1844) 11 Cl. & Fin. 714 (8 E.R. 712): 37 years' ignorance.

Replace n.213 with:

213 *Ex p. Hughes* (1802) 6 Ves. 617 at 622 (31 E.R. 1223 at 1226); *Attorney General v Earl of Clarendon* (1810) 17 Ves. 491 at 500 (34 E.R. 190 at 194); *Earl of Cardigan v Moore* [2012] EWHC 1024 (Ch) at [41].

Replace sixth paragraph with:

A sale by a trustee to his wife is probably not caught automatically by the rule, especially if the wife has made the purchase on her own initiative, rather than at the instigation of the trustee, and has paid for it out of her own funds.[218] However, the rule may apply where, in circumstances of the case, it is appropriate to treat the wife as acting on behalf of her husband—"there are wives and there are wives".[219] Even where a trustee's sale to his wife is not caught by the self-dealing rule, such a transaction will be viewed cautiously and will be set aside on the slightest suspicion, such as where the transaction is for the benefit of the trustee.[220] In order to be upheld, such a transaction must be shown to have been in the best interests of the fiduciary's principal.[221]

218 See, e.g. *Burrell v Burrell's Trustees*, 1915 S.C. 333 at 337; *Re King's Will Trusts* (1959) 173 E.G. 627. See generally Fleming, "Can a Trustee Sell to His Wife?" (1949) 13 Conv. (N.S.) 248.

219 *Tito v Waddell (No.2)* [1977] Ch. 106 at 240.

220 *Tanti v Carlson* [1948] V.L.R. 401 at 407; *Re McNally (Deceased)* [1967] N.Z.L.R. 521 at 523. See also *Ferraby v Hobson* (1847) 2 Ph. 255 at 261 (41 E.R. 940 at 943), regarding transactions between a trustee and his sister.

221 *Newgate Stud Co v Penfold* [2004] EWHC 2993 (Ch) at [234]–[244].

(c) Fair-dealing.

Replace first paragraph with:

7-022   "The fair-dealing rule is ... that if a trustee purchases the beneficial interest of any of his beneficiaries, the transaction is not voidable ex debito justitiae, but can be set aside by the beneficiary unless the trustee can show that he has taken no advantage of his position and has made full disclosure to the beneficiary, and that the transaction is fair and honest."[233]

The fair-dealing rule and the self-dealing rule apply to different sorts of situations and are therefore treated as distinct rules.[234] The self-dealing rule applies to purchases of trust property by the trustee from himself, whereas the fair-dealing rule applies to purchases by the trustee of his beneficiary's beneficial interest in the trust property. One who alleges that what is in form a purchase by a trustee from himself is in substance a purchase from the beneficiaries must prove this clearly, and has the burden of proving clearly that the beneficiaries:

"had the fullest information upon all material facts; and that, having this information, they agreed to and adopted what was done."[235]

However, the distinction between the fair-dealing and self-dealing rules is best understood as one of convenience rather than one of principle.[236] Both sub-rules are concerned with the conflict between the fiduciary's duty and his interest. In both situations, the transaction can be upheld but only if the fiduciary proves that he obtained consent from his or her principal after making full disclosure of all material facts. The fairness of the transaction in fair-dealing situations is relevant in an evidential capacity rather than substantively: it merely provides objective evidence as to what was disclosed,[237] thereby assisting the court to determine whether fully informed consent was in fact obtained. It is clear, for example, that a fair-dealing transaction can be upheld, despite an unequal exchange of values, provided the principal consented with full information to the transaction in that form[238]:

"The question [is], not, whether the price was fair between the trustees and cestui que trust at the time, but, whether a person, who had a confidential situation previously to the purchase, had at the time of the purchase shaken off that character by the consent of the cestui que trust, freely given, after full information."[239]

Like a self-dealing situation, a fair-dealing transaction is one "of great delicacy, and which the court will watch with utmost diligence"[240] to determine that the beneficiary's consent truly was fully informed.

[233] *Tito v Waddell (No.2)* [1977] Ch. 106 at 241.

[234] *Re Postlethwaite (Deceased)* (1888) 59 L.T. 58 at 59; *Tito v Waddell (No.2)* [1977] Ch. 106 at 241.

[235] *Williams v Scott* [1900] A.C. 499 at 508.

[236] For detailed discussion, see M. Conaglen, "A Re-Appraisal of the Fiduciary Self-Dealing and Fair-Dealing Rules" [2006] C.L.J. 366.

[237] See, e.g. *Luff v Lord* (1864) 34 Beav. 220 at 230 (55 E.R. 619 at 623) (upheld on appeal: (1865) 11 L.T. 695 at 697); *Re Worssam* (1882) 46 L.T. 584 at 591.

[238] See, e.g. *Lord Selsey v Rhoades* (1824) 2 Sim. & St. 41 at 49–50 (57 E.R. 260 at 263–264); *Wright v Lemon (No.2)* [2021] WASC 159 at [291].

[239] *Ex p. James* (1803) 8 Ves. 337 at 353 (32 E.R. 385 at 391); *Downes v Grazebrook* (1817) 3 Mer. 200 at 208–209 (36 E.R. 77 at 80).

[240] *Coles v Trecothick* (1804) 9 Ves. 234 at 244 (32 E.R. 592 at 596).

Replace second paragraph with:

As it is merely an application of the general fiduciary conflict principle, the fair-dealing rule applies to any transaction between fiduciary and principal, even if property does not pass,[245] where the transaction falls within the fiduciary relationship such that there is a conflict between duty and interest. The fair-dealing rule does not apply where the property involved in the transaction was not the subject of the fiduciary relationship,[246] because there is no non-fiduciary duty in conflict with the fiduciary's interest in the transaction.

[245] *Johnson v EBS Pensioner Trustees Ltd* [2002] EWCA Civ 164 at [50], [67], [2002] Lloyd's Rep. P.N. 309; *Swindle v Harrison* [1997] 4 All E.R. 705; *Re Thompson's Settlement* [1986] 1 Ch. 99 at 115.

[246] *Montesquieu v Sandys* (1811) 18 Ves. 302 at 313 (34 E.R. 331 at 336); *Cane v Lord Allen* (1814) 2 Dow. 289 at 294, 297–298 and 299–300 (3 E.R. 869 at 871, 872 and 872–873); *McPherson v Watt* (1877) 3 App. Cas 254 at 270–271; *Wright v Lemon (No.2)* [2021] WASC 159 at [618]–[619].

(d) Fiduciary remuneration.

(5) Court order.

Replace n.287 with:

7-027 [287] *Marshall v Holloway* (1820) 2 Swans. 432 at 453–454 (36 E.R. 681 at 689); *Bainbrigge v Blair* (1845) 8 Beav. 588 at 596–597 (50 E.R. 231 at 234–235); *Re Freeman's Settlement Trusts* (1887) 37 Ch. D. 148 at 152.

(e) Fiduciary expenses.

(1) The right.

Replace n.309 with:

7-031 [309] See, e.g. *Re Beddoe* [1893] 1 Ch. 547 at 558; *Alsop Wilkinson v Neary* [1996] 1 W.L.R. 1220 at 1224. Such payments are not recoverable as expenses paid in management of a trust where the presumption of advancement applies: see *Re Roberts (Deceased)* [1946] Ch. 1.

(3) Beddoe orders.

Replace n.325 with:

7-033 [325] *Alsop Wilkinson v Neary* [1996] 1 W.L.R. 1220 at 1224.

Replace n.330 with:

[330] *Alsop Wilkinson v Neary* [1996] 1 W.L.R. 1220 at 1223–1224; *Re Buckton* [1907] 2 Ch. 406.

4. CONFLICTS BETWEEN DUTY AND DUTY

1. General Principle

Replace n.365 with:

7-036 [365] See, e.g. *Ex p. Bennett* (1805) 10 Ves. 381 (32 E.R. 893); *Transvaal Lands Co v New Belgium (Transvaal) Land & Development Co* [1914] 2 Ch. 488; *Moody v Cox* [1917] 2 Ch. 71; and see *Johnson v EBS Pensioner Trustees Ltd* [2002] EWCA Civ 164 at [43], [2002] Lloyd's Rep. P.N. 309.

2. Application

(a) Potential conflict.

Replace third paragraph with:

7-037 Notwithstanding the potential conflict rule, "a director is at liberty to become a director of a rival company, provided that he or she does not make use of confidential information".[373] The correctness of this proposition has been doubted,[374] but it is important that it be recognised that "[a]t most [it] means that the mere fact of being the director of a company will not preclude the director from engaging in a competing business on his or her own account. But it leaves open any issues of actual conflict, or of conflict reasonably perceived to be within the range of sensible possibilities, arising on the facts of a particular case".[375] A close examination of the director's functions and responsibilities in the company is thus required.[376]

[373] *Bell v Lever Bros Ltd* [1932] A.C. 161, 195; *London & Mashonaland Exploration Co v New Mashonaland Exploration Co* [1891] W.N. 165; *In Plus Group Ltd v Pyke* [2002] EWCA Civ 370 at [72]; [2002] 2 B.C.L.C. 201; *Australian Careers Institute Pty Ltd v Australian Institute of Fitness Pty Ltd* [2016] NSWCA 347 at [134]; (2016) 340 A.L.R. 580.

[374] *In Plus Group Ltd v Pyke* [2002] EWCA Civ 370 at [79]–[88]; [2002] 2 B.C.L.C. 201 per Sedley LJ, although see at [75] per Brooke LJ and at [93] per Jonathan Parker LJ; *Scottish Co-operative Wholesale Society Ltd v Meyer* [1959] A.C. 324 at 368; *Commonwealth Oil & Gas Co Ltd v Baxter* [2009] C.S.I.H. 75 at [4]–[5] and [76]–[77]; S.M. Beck, "The Quickening of Fiduciary Obligation: Canadian Aero Services v O'Malley" (1975) 53 Can. Bar Rev. 771, 789–791; M. Christie, "The Director's Fiduciary Duty not to Compete" (1992) 55 M.L.R. 506. See also *Re Thomson* [1930] 1 Ch. 203.

[375] *Links Golf Tasmania Pty Ltd v Sattler* [2012] FCA 634 at [564], (2012) 213 F.C.R. 1. See also *Australian Careers Institute Pty Ltd v Australian Institute of Fitness Pty Ltd* [2016] NSWCA 347 at [4]; (2016) 340 A.L.R. 580. See also D. Kershaw, "Corporate Law's Fiduciary Personas" (2020) 136 L.Q.R. 454.

[376] *Australian Careers Institute Pty Ltd v Australian Institute of Fitness Pty Ltd* [2016] NSWCA 347 at [136]; (2016) 340 A.L.R. 580.

Replace n.378 with:

[378] *Commonwealth Oil & Gas Co Ltd v Baxter* [2009] CSIH 75 at [4]; *Australian Careers Institute Pty Ltd v Australian Institute of Fitness Pty Ltd* [2016] NSWCA 347; (2016) 340 A.L.R. 580.

(d) Actual conflict.

At the end, add new paragraph:

It is unclear whether the fiduciary commits an actionable breach of duty merely **7-040** by acting in a situation of actual conflict: in *Barrowfen Properties v Patel*, the actual conflict rule was aligned with the inhibition principle, in the sense that a breach of either could give rise to a breach of fiduciary duty, but the judge thought this only possible if the fiduciary went on to commit a conscious breach of duty.[394a] It can be difficult, in any event, to identify what loss might be caused by a breach of the inhibition principle and the actual conflict rule, separate from loss caused by other breaches of non-fiduciary duties.[394b]

[394a] *Barrowfen Properties Ltd v Patel* [2021] EWHC 2055 (Ch) at [299]–[304].

[394b] See the discussion in M. Conaglen, "Remedial Ramifications of Conflicts between a Fiduciary's Duties" (2010) 126 L.Q.R. 72.

5. PROFITS MADE OUT OF FIDUCIARY POSITION

· 1. General Principle

Replace n.400 with:

[400] *Regal (Hastings) Ltd v Gulliver* [1967] 2 A.C. 134. at 154; *Foster Bryant Surveying Ltd v Bryant* **7-041** [2007] EWCA Civ 200 at [88], [101], [2007] Bus. L.R. 1565.

3. Application

(c) Secret profits.

(1) Bribes and secret commissions.

Replace n.448 with:

[448] See, e.g. *FHR European Ventures LLP v Cedar Capital Partners LLC* [2014] UKSC 45 at [37]; **7-047** [2015] A.C. 250; *Shipway v Broadwood* [1899] 1 Q.B. 369 CA at 373; *Tesco Stores Ltd v Pook* [2003] EWHC 823 (Ch) at [41] and [44]; *Daraydan Holdings Ltd v Solland International Ltd* [2004] EWHC 622 (Ch) at [52]; *Aequitas v AEFC* [2001] NSWSC 14; (2001) 19 A.C.L.C. 1,006 at [370]; *Hurstanger Ltd v Wilson* [2007] EWCA Civ 299 at [34], [2007] 1 W.L.R. 2351; *Ross River Ltd v Cambridge City*

Football Club Ltd [2007] EWHC 2115 (Ch) at [203]–[204] and [218]; *Fiona Trust & Holding Corp v Privalov* [2010] EWHC 3199 (Comm) at [1391].

(3) Corporate opportunities.

Replace n.472 with:

7-049   [472] *Industrial Development Consultants Ltd v Cooley* [1972] 1 W.L.R. 443. See also *Recovery Partners GP Ltd v Rukhadze* [2018] EWHC 2918 (Comm), [2019] Bus. L.R. 1166.

Replace n.475 with:

[475] *Bhullar v Bhullar* [2003] EWCA Civ 424 at [27], [2003] 2 B.C.L.C. 241; cf. *CMS Dolphin Ltd v Simonet* [2001] 2 B.C.L.C. 704 at [96].

(d) Duty to disclose misconduct.

Replace first paragraph with:

7-050   A fiduciary's obligation to account to his principal for any profit which he or she receives as a result of the fiduciary position has led some courts to suggest, in a series of obiter comments, that the fiduciary is under a duty to disclose to the principal the fact of the profit having been made:

> "in the case of fiduciaries, such as directors, if they failed to account for secret profits which they have made, then their failure to account must necessarily involve in consequence a failure to reveal a breach of duty which had given rise to that duty to account."[484]

This must be differentiated from the question whether there is a general non-fiduciary duty owed by a fiduciary, such as a director, to disclose conduct which is in breach of non-fiduciary duties.[485]

[484] *Horcal Ltd v Gatland* [1984] B.C.L.C. 549 at 554; *Item Software (UK) Ltd v Fassihi* [2003] EWHC 3116 (Ch) at [54]; *Tesco Stores Ltd v Pook* [2003] EWHC 832 (Ch) at [53]–[65]; *Crown Dilmun v Sutton* [2004] EWHC 52 (Ch) at [181]; *Hanco ATM Systems Ltd v Cashbox ATM Systems Ltd* [2007] EWHC 1599 (Ch); *Bank of Ireland v Jaffery* [2012] EWHC 1377 (Ch) at [301].

[485] As to which see *Sybron Corp v Rochem Ltd* [1984] Ch. 112 at 126–127; *Horcal Ltd v Gatland* [1984] B.C.L.C. 549 at 554; *Balston Ltd v Headline Filters Ltd* [1990] F.S.R. 385 at 408–409; *Item Software (UK) Ltd v Fassihi* [2003] EWHC 3116 (Ch) at [51]–[52]; *British Midland Tool Ltd v Midland International Tooling Ltd* [2003] EWHC 466 (Ch) at [81]–[89].

6.   REMEDIES FOR BREACH OF FIDUCIARY DUTY

1.   General

(a) Disabilities and duties.

Replace n.494 with:

7-051   [494] *Gwembe Valley Development Co Ltd v Koshy (No.3)* [2003] EWCA Civ 1048 at [108]; [2004] 1 B.C.L.C. 131; See also *AB Jnr v MB [2013]* 1 C.I.L.R. 1 at [475].

2.   Rescission

Replace paragraph with:

7-053   A principal may rescind a transaction which was entered into by his or her fiduciary in breach of the fiduciary conflict principle, e.g. the self-dealing rule[505] or the fair-dealing rule.[506] The fact that the fiduciary acted with a conflict, without disclos-

[36]

ing his interest in the transaction and obtaining fully informed consent from his principal, renders the transaction voidable, rather than void.[507] The principal may claim equitable rescission of the transaction, subject to the court's "undoubted discretion to refuse to give effect to the prima facie right to rescind in equity where to do so would be unfair or disproportionate".[508] If the fiduciary asserts that consent was obtained, he bears the onus of proving full disclosure and consent.[509]

[505] See, e.g. *Re Cape Breton Co* (1885) 29 Ch. D. 795 at 803; *Armstrong v Jackson* [1917] 2 K.B. 822 at 823–824; *Re Sherman (Deceased)* [1954] Ch. 653 at 657.

[506] See, e.g. *Hely-Hutchinson v Brayhead Ltd* [1968] 1 Q.B. 549 at 585 and 589–590.

[507] *Campbell v Walker* (1800) 5 Ves. 678, 680 (31 E.R. 801) MR; *Dover v Buck* (1865) 5 Giff. 57, 63 (144 R.R. 344) VC; *Hely-Hutchinson v Brayhead Ltd* [1968] 1 Q.B. 549, 585, 589–90 and 594; *Tito v Waddell (No.2)* [1977] Ch. 106 at 225, 241; *Guinness Plc v Saunders* [1990] 2 A.C. 663 at 697; *Ingram v Inland Revenue Commissioners* [1997] 4 All E.R. 395, 424–25 CA, affirmed on appeal: [2000] 1 A.C. 293, 305 and 310; *Clay v Clay* [2001] HCA 9 at [51]; (2001) 202 C.L.R. 410; *Johnson v EBS Pensioner Trustees Ltd* [2002] EWCA Civ 164 at [77], [2002] Lloyd's Rep. P.N. 309. See generally Conaglen, *Fiduciary Loyalty* (2010) Ch.4. The transaction might be void for other reasons, e.g. breach of the rule requiring two parties to a contract, or if no valid contract was entered into: see, e.g. *Guinness Plc v Saunders* [1990] 2 A.C. 663 at 689.

[508] *UBS AG v Kommunale Wasserwerke Leipzig GmbH* [2017] EWCA Civ 1567 at [162], [2017] 2 Lloyd's Rep. 621. See also *Johnson v EBS Pensioner Trustees Ltd* [2002] EWCA Civ 164 at [57], [77]–[80], [84], [2002] Lloyd's Rep. P.N. 309.

[509] *Rothschild v Brookman* (1831) 2 Dow & Cl. 188 at 197–198 (6 E.R. 699 at 702);*Cavendish Bentinck v Fenn* (1887) 12 App. Cas. 652 at 661, 666; *Maguire v Makaronis* (1997) 188 C.L.R. 449 at 466.

Replace second paragraph with:

Similarly, a principal may also rescind a transaction entered into with a third party where his or her agent has received a bribe or secret commission from the third party in connection with the transaction,[510] provided the third party was aware that the recipient of the bribe was a fiduciary vis-à-vis the principal,[511] or at least under a duty to provide disinterested advice, recommendations or information to the principal,[511a] and had knowledge of the fiduciary's interest in the bribe (the latter point being important where the bribe was not paid directly by the third party to the fiduciary).[512] It is no defence to the person paying the bribe or secret commission to show that he or she believed the fiduciary had informed the principal, if that did not in fact occur.[513] There is no need to show that the bribe or secret commission caused the transaction to be entered into; the fact that the principal has been, to the knowledge of the counterparty, deprived of disinterested advice from his or her agent is sufficient justification for rescission.[514]

[510] *Panama & South Pacific Telegraph Co v India Rubber, Gutta Percha, & Telegraph Works Co* (1875) L.R. 10 Ch. App. 515 at 526; *Grant v Gold Exploration & Development Syndicate Ltd* [1900] 1 Q.B. 233 at 248–249; *Taylor v Walker* [1958] 1 Lloyd's Rep. 490 at 513; *Armagas Ltd v Mundogas SA* [1986] A.C. 717 at 742–743.

[511] *Industries and General Mortgage Co Ltd v Lewis* [1949] 2 All E.R. 573 at 578; *Taylor v Walker* [1958] 1 Lloyd's Rep. 490 at 513; *Ross River Ltd v Cambridge City Football Club Ltd* [2007] EWHC 2115 (Ch) at [205] and [218].

[511a] *Wood v Commercial First Business Ltd* [2021] EWCA Civ 471 at [48]–[49], [53], [66], [92] & [101], denying that a fiduciary relationship is necessary if there is a duty to provide disinterested advice. A person who is obliged to provide advice of that sort will ordinarily have undertaken to provide the advice in circumstances which gives rise to a relationship of trust and confidence, in the sense that he or she is expected to act in the interests of the client to the exclusion of his or her own several interests (i.e., disinterestedly), and so will ordinarily be accurately described as a fiduciary (see para.7-005).

[512] *Logicrose Ltd v Southend United Football Club Ltd* [1988] 1 W.L.R. 1256 (Ch) at 1261.

[513] *Grant v Gold Exploration and Development Syndicate Ltd* [1900] 1 Q.B. 233 at 248–249; *Taylor v Walker* [1958] 1 Lloyd's Rep 490 at 513; *Logicrose Ltd v Southend United Football Club Ltd* [1988] 1 W.L.R. 1256 at 1262; *Ross River Ltd v Cambridge City Football Club Ltd* [2007] EWHC 2115 (Ch) at [205].

[514] *Logicrose Ltd v Southend United Football Club Ltd* [1988] 1 W.L.R. 1256 (Ch) at 1260; *UBS AG v Kommunale Wasserwerke Leipzig GmbH* [2017] EWCA Civ 1567 at [155], [2017] 2 Lloyd's Rep. 621.

Replace n.514 with:

[514] *Logicrose Ltd v Southend United Football Club Ltd* [1988] 1 W.L.R. 1256 (Ch) at 1261–1262; *UBS AG v Kommunale Wasserwerke Leipzig GmbH* [2017] EWCA Civ 1567 at [120], [2017] 2 Lloyd's Rep. 621. Where the third party deals with the principal's agent secretly, and dishonestly assists the agent in breaching its fiduciary duties towards the principal, the third-party's conscience is affected not only where the third party knew the particular form of abuse of the fiduciary relationship which occurred, but also by any other abuse which the agent chose to employ to bring about the impugned transaction: *UBS AG v Kommunale Wasserwerke Leipzig GmbH* [2017] EWCA Civ 1567 at [113], [2017] 2 Lloyd's Rep. 621.

Replace fifth paragraph with:

The principal is entitled to rescind if he neither knew of, nor consented to, the payment made to his fiduciary in breach of fiduciary duty.[517] Where the principal was aware that his fiduciary had been paid a commission by the other party to the transaction but there had been insufficient disclosure for the principal to have given a fully informed consent, the court has, at times, refused to order rescission where it considered that the agreement was fair.[518]

[517] *Ross River Ltd v Cambridge City Football Club Ltd* [2007] EWHC 2115 (Ch) at [203].

[518] *Hurstanger Ltd v Wilson* [2007] EWCA Civ 299 at [43]–[51], [2007] 1 W.L.R. 2351 (the plaintiff was awarded an account). And see *Johnson v EBS Pensioner Trustees Ltd* [2002] EWCA Civ 164, [2002] Lloyd's Rep. P.N. 309. See also *Ross River Ltd v Cambridge City Football Club Ltd* [2007] EWHC 2115 (Ch) at [203]; *Northampton Regional Livestock Centre Co Ltd v Cowling* [2014] EWHC 30 (QB) at [188]–[191]; *Medsted Associates Ltd v Canaccord Genuity Wealth (International) Ltd* [2019] EWCA Civ 83; [2019] 1 W.L.R. 4481; and para.15-016.

Replace n.523 with:

[523] It is the transaction itself which must be undone; the fact that a party has incurred losses to a third party by relying on the validity of the transaction does not mean that restitutio in integrum cannot be achieved: *UBS AG v Kommunale Wasserwerke Leipzig GmbH* [2017] EWCA Civ 1567 at [223]–[225], [2017] 2 Lloyd's Rep. 621.

Replace n.530 with:

[530] See, e.g. *McKenzie v McDonald* [1927] V.L.R. 134; *Mahoney v Purnell* [1996] 3 All E.R. 61; *Robinson v Abbott* (1894) 20 V.L.R. 346; and see generally R.C. Nolan, "Conflicts of Interest, Unjust Enrichment, and Wrongdoing" in W.R. Cornish, R.C. Nolan, J. O'Sullivan & G.J. Virgo (eds), *Restitution: Past, Present and Future* (Oxford: Hart Publishing, 1998) p.87 at paras 114–115.

3. Account of Profits

(a) Availability.

Replace n.534 with:

7-054

[534] *Ancient Order of Foresters in Victoria Friendly Society Ltd v Lifeplan Australia Friendly Society Ltd* [2018] HCA 43 at [70]; (2018) 265 C.L.R. 1.

Replace second paragraph with:

Thus, for example, a director who made a profit on a transaction in which his company was interested but which he entered into personally had to account for the profit to the company.[535] Directors who took shares in a subsidiary of the parent company for which they worked when the parent could not subscribe for all of the subsidiary's shares had to account to the parent company for the profit which they made when the shares were later sold.[536] An agent who bought his principal's ship and sold it on to a third party had to account to his principal for the profit (which was almost 80 per cent of the price at which he bought off his principal) on the transaction.[537] An agent who was detailed to buy sugar on behalf of a partnership had to account for his profit when he bought sugar on the market himself and later sold it to the partnership at full market prices after the market price had increased.[538] And an agent who takes a bribe or secret commission must account for it to his or her principal (the principal may also claim the bribe from the briber, as damages for fraud or as money had and received, if it has not already been recovered from the fiduciary[539]).[540]

[535] *Industrial Development Consultants Ltd v Cooley* [1972] 1 W.L.R. 443 at 454.

[536] *Regal (Hastings) Ltd v Gulliver* [1967] 2 A.C. 134.

[537] *De Bussche v Alt* (1878) 8 Ch. D. 286 at 304 and 317.

[538] *Bentley v Craven* (1853) 18 Beav. 75 (52 E.R. 29).

[539] *Mahesan S/O Thambiah v Malaysia Government Officers' Cooperative Housing Society Ltd* [1979] A.C. 374 at 381 and 383; *Armagas Ltd v Mundogas SA* [1986] A.C. 717 at 743; *Fyffes Group Ltd v Templeman* [2000] 2 Lloyd's Rep. 643 at 660. The payment of a secret commission by a lender to a borrower's broker may also render the relationship between the lender and the borrower unfair for the purposes of s.140A of the Consumer Credit Act 1974: *Wood v Commercial First Business Ltd* [2019] EWHC 2205 (Ch) at [148].

[540] *Boston Deep Sea Fishing & Ice Co v Ansell* (1888) 39 Ch. D. 339; *Lister & Co v Stubbs* (1890) 45 Ch. D. 1 at 12 and 15; *Daraydan Holdings Ltd v Solland International Ltd* [2004] EWHC 622 (Ch) at [51]; *East India Co v Henchman* (1791) 1 Ves. Jun. 287 at 289 (30 E.R. 347 at 348); *Hurstanger Ltd v Wilson* [2007] EWCA Civ 299 at [35], [2007] 1 W.L.R. 2351.

Change title of paragraph:

(b)   Fashioning the account.[542]

[542] Part of an earlier version of this paragraph was cited with approval by Vos J in *Bank of Ireland v Jaffery* [2012] EWHC 1377 (Ch) at [291]. See also M. Conaglen, *"Identifying the Profits for Which a Fiduciary Must Account"* [2020] C.L.J. 38.

7-055

Replace second paragraph with:

The fiduciary must account for all of the profit which he made in breach of fiduciary duty, which means all unauthorized profits falling within the scope of his fiduciary duty.[542a] The obligation to account extends to the actual or net profit,[543] which means that expenses which were properly incurred, and are properly attributable to the gross receipt, will be deducted from the gross profit to determine the amount for which the fiduciary must account.[543a] Net profit can include both revenue and capital profits,[544] and can also include profit which has been earned but not yet realised.[545] Thus, in a simple case, e.g. one involving the purchase and re-sale of trust property by a trustee, the account of profits will take into account all moneys which the trustee received in the impugned transaction, set against all moneys which the fiduciary paid out in respect of the transaction, including allowances for disbursements or expenses properly incurred in respect of the transaction.[546]

[542a] *Gray v Global Energy Horizons Corp* [2020] EWCA Civ 1668 at [126] (reported in part, but not this part, at [2021] 1 W.L.R. 2264).

543 *Bagnall v Carlton* (1877) 6 Ch. D. 371 at 400 and 408 CA; *Emma Silver Mining Co v Grant* (1879) 11 Ch. D. 918 at 940 (MR); *Patel v Brent LBC* [2003] EWHC 3081 (Ch) at [29]. See also *Potton Ltd v Yorkclose Ltd* [1990] F.S.R. 11 at 18 (ChD).

543a *Gray v Global Energy Horizons Corp* [2020] EWCA Civ 1668 at [230] & [233] (reported in part, but not this part, at [2021] 1 W.L.R. 2264).

544 See, e.g. *Murad v Al-Saraj* [2005] EWCA Civ 959; [2005] W.T.L.R. 1573.

545 *Ancient Order of Foresters in Victoria Friendly Society Ltd v Lifeplan Australia Friendly Society Ltd* [2018] HCA 43; (2018) 265 C.L.R. 1.

546 See, e.g. *De Bussche v Alt* (1878) 8 Ch. D. 286 at 307.

Replace third paragraph with:

Like all equitable remedies, the account of profits is discretionary.[550] Thus, in cases which are more complicated than a simple case of the sort described above, the account is fashioned to meet the circumstances of the case. This is done in accordance with settled equitable principles.[551] The profits for which the fiduciary must account must bear some reasonable relationship to the breach of fiduciary duty.[551a] The obligation is to account for profits which have been *made in breach of fiduciary duty*, not simply to account for profits in the abstract[551b]:

> "The courts have long recognised that benefits or the profits derived by a misbehaving fiduciary may be attributable to multiple sources only one of which was the breach of fiduciary duty or trust; personal skill, expertise and exertion, goodwill or the financial contributions of the fiduciary and of third parties may have played their part as well in generating such profits."[551c]

The relevant question is not whether the breach of fiduciary duty caused the profit to be made, but rather whether there is a reasonable connection between the breach of duty and the profit.[551d] The liability is focused more on the fact that making and retaining the profit is itself the breach of fiduciary duty, than on whether the breach caused a profit to be made.

550 *Strother v 3464920 Canada Inc* [2007] SCC 24 at [74]; [2007] 2 S.C.R. 177.

551 *Warman International Ltd v Dwyer* (1995) 182 C.L.R. 544 at 559; *Ultraframe (UK) Ltd v Fielding* [2005] EWHC 1638 (Ch) at [1579]; *Recovery Partners GP Ltd v Ruzhadze* [2022] EWHC 690 (Comm) at [266].

551a *Ultraframe (UK) Ltd v Fielding* [2005] EWHC 1638 (Ch) at [158]; *Gamatronic (UK) Ltd v Hamilton* [2017] B.C.C. 670 at [188]; *Keystone Healthcare Ltd v Parr* [2019] EWCA Civ 1246 at [18]; [2019] 4 W.L.R. 99.

551b *Button v Phelps* [2006] EWHC 53 (Ch) at [66]; *Murad v Al-Saraj* [2005] EWCA Civ 959 at [85], [112] and [115]–[116]; [2005] W.T.L.R. 1573; *Chirnside v Fay* [2006] NZSC 68 at [36]; [2007] 1 N.Z.L.R. 433; *Strother v 3464920 Canada Inc* [2007] SCC 24 at [79] and [89]–[95]; [2007] 2 S.C.R. 177.

551c *Grimaldi v Chameleon Mining NL (No.2)* [2012] FCAFC 6 at [517]; (2012) 200 F.C.R. 296.

551d *Keystone Healthcare Ltd v Parr* [2019] EWCA Civ 1246 at [16]–[18], [2019] 4 W.L.R. 99; *Gray v Global Energy Horizons Corp* [2020] EWCA Civ 1668 at [128] (reported in part, but not this part, at [2021] 1 W.L.R. 2264); *Recovery Partners GP Ltd v Rukhadze* [2022] EWHC 690 (Comm) at [282]–[284]. See also M. Conaglen "Identifying the Profits for Which a Fiduciary Must Account" [2020] C.L.J. 38, esp. at pp. 57–62. Cf the position in Singapore, where "profits sought to be disgorged via an account of profits must be caused by the breaches of fiduciary duty": *UVJ v UVH* [2020] SGCA 49 at [98].

After the third paragraph, add new paragraph:

It is not relevant in that regard for the fiduciary to argue that the principal would have consented to the profit, had he been asked: such considerations can be relevant to the question whether *the principal* has suffered any *loss* as a result of the breach of fiduciary duty, but they are not relevant in determining what *profit* has been made by *the fiduciary* without authorisation and thus in breach of fiduciary duty.[551d] It is that profit for which the fiduciary must account, rather than any profit over and above a hypothetical level to which his principal might potentially have agreed.

[551d] *Regal (Hastings) Ltd v Gulliver* [1967] 2 AC 134n., 144–145; *Murad v Al-Saraj* [2005] EWCA Civ 959 at [67], [136]; [2005] W.T.L.R. 1573; *Keystone Healthcare Ltd v Parr* [2019] EWCA Civ 1246 at [15], [2019] 4 W.L.R. 99; *Gray v New Augarita Porcupine Mines Ltd* [1952] 3 D.L.R. 1 at 15 (PC). See also *United Pan-Europe Communications NV v Deutsche Bank AG* [2000] 2 B.C.L.C. 461 at [47]. cf. *Strother v 3464920 Canada Inc* [2007] SCC 24 at [152]–[158]; [2007] 2 S.C.R. 177.

Replace fourth paragraph with:

Where the profit is made out of a business, rather than a specific asset, given the risks inherent in business activities and the amount of time, effort and skill required to make a business successful, a principal will not necessarily be awarded an account of the entire profits of that business.[554] It remains of first importance, in such cases, "to ascertain precisely what it was that was acquired in consequence of the fiduciary's breach of duty".[555] Thus, where the profit has been generated by carving out the business of the principal, the fiduciary is more likely to be required to account for the entire profit of the new business[555a] but where a company manager set up his own business and deprived the company of a lucrative agency but the new business was also based on contributions other than the business connections of the principal company, the company was awarded an account of the profits of the manager's new business but only for a period of two years.[556] This is based on the understanding that:

> "given the property in question is the goodwill of the company's business, there will in all probability come a time when it can safely be said that any future profits of the new business will be attributable not to the goodwill misappropriated from the claimant company when the new business was set up but rather to the defendants' own efforts in carrying on that business."[557]

[554] See, e.g. *Clegg v Edmondson* (1857) 8 De G.M. & G. 787 at 814–815 (44 E.R. 593 at 604); *Re Jarvis (Deceased)* [1958] 1 W.L.R. 815 at 821; *Warman International Ltd v Dwyer* (1995) 182 C.L.R. 544 at 560–561.

[555] *Warman International Ltd v Dwyer* (1995) 182 C.L.R. 544 at 565. For an example of directions given as to accounts where a licence was obtained in breach of fiduciary duties owed to former partners, see *John Taylors v Masons* [2001] EWCA Civ 2106 at [37]; [2005] W.T.L.R. 1519.

[555a] See, e.g., *Ancient Order of Foresters in Victoria Friendly Society Ltd v Lifeplan Australian Friendly Society Ltd* [2018] HCA 43 at [4], [8], [10], [16, [17]; (2018) 265 C.L.R. 1. And see the analysis in M. Conaglen, *"Identifying the Profits for which a Fiduciary Must Account"* [2020] C.L.J. 38, 53-56.

[556] *Warman International Ltd v Dwyer* (1995) 182 C.L.R. 544.

[557] *Murad v Al-Saraj* [2005] EWCA Civ 959 at [115]; [2005] W.T.L.R. 1573.

At the end of the fourth paragraph, add new paragraph:

The fiduciary bears the onus of convincing the court that an accounting of his or her entire profits is inappropriate in the circumstances.[557a]

[557a] *Warman International Ltd v Dwyer* (1995) 182 C.L.R. 544 at 561–562; *Harris v Digital Pulse Pty Ltd* [2003] NSWCA 10 at [336]; *Ancient Order of Foresters in Victoria Friendly Society Ltd v Lifeplan Australia Friendly Society Ltd* [2018] HCA 43 at [17]; (2018) 265 C.L.R. 1.

Replace the fifth paragraph with:

A fiduciary who has acted in breach of fiduciary duty, and against whom an account of profits is ordered, may be given an allowance for skill and effort employed in obtaining the profit which he has to disgorge,[558] where:

"it would be inequitable now for the beneficiaries to step in and take the profit without paying for the skill and labour which has produced it."[559]

This is most common where the work done by the fiduciary which generated the profit would have had to be done by someone else who would have been remunerated (thus the work may, but need not, be unique[559a]) or where the work done has benefited the property which forms the basis of the account.[559b]The award of such allowances is exceptional and the power to award allowances is exercised sparingly,[559c] out of concern not to encourage fiduciaries to act in breach of fiduciary duty.[560] It will not likely be used where the fiduciary has been involved in surreptitious dealing or has acted dishonestly or in bad faith.[561] However, allowances are not ruled out simply because the fiduciary can be criticised in the circumstances,[562] and there are instances of them being made even where the fiduciary has acted surreptitiously and deceitfully.[563]

[558] See, e.g. *Brown v Litton* (1711) 1 P. Wms. 140 at 142 (24 E.R. 329 at 329); *Lord Provost of Edinburgh v Lord Advocate Ex p. Mclaren* (1879) 4 App.Cas. 823 at 839; *Boardman v Phipps* [1967] 2 A.C. 46 at 104, 112; *O'Sullivan v Management Agency & Music Ltd* [1985] 1 Q.B. 428 at 459, 468 and 472; *Warman International Ltd v Dwyer* (1995) 182 C.L.R. 544 at 568; *Badfinger Music v Evans* [2001] W.T.L.R. 1; *Lindsley v Woodfull* [2004] EWCA Civ 720; [2004] 2 B.C.L.C. 131 at [6], [8]; *Re Macadam* [1946] Ch. 73, 82–83; *Cook v Collingridge* (1823) Jac. 607, 623; *Brown v de Tastet* (1821) Jac. 284 at 294, 298 and 299.

[559] *Phipps v Boardman* [1964] 1 W.L.R. 993 at 1018. See also *Accidia Foundation v Simon C Dickinson Ltd* [2010] EWHC 3058 (Ch) at [94]–[95].

[559a] *Recovery Partners GP Ltd v Rukhadze* [2022] EWHC 690 (Comm) at [456].

[559b] *Recovery Partners GP Ltd v Rukhadze* [2022] EWHC 690 (Comm) at [372].

[559c] *Guinness Plc v Saunders* [1990] 2 A.C. 663 at 693–694 & 700–702; *Gray v Global Energy Horizons Corp* [2020] EWCA Civ 1668 at [209]–[217] & [237] (reported in part, but not this part, at [2021] 1 W.L.R. 2264).

[560] *Guinness Plc v Saunders* [1990] 2 A.C. 663 at 701. cf. the approach in Australia, where allowances are more commonly awarded to fiduciaries: *Mid-City Skin Cancer & Laser Centre v Zahedi-Anarak* [2006] NSWSC 844 at [273], (2006) 67 N.S.W.L.R. 569.

[561] *Phipps v Boardman* [1965] Ch. 992 at 1021; *Crown Dilmun v Sutton* [2004] EWHC 52 (Ch) at [213].

[562] *O'Sullivan v Management Agency & Music Ltd* [1985] Q.B. 428 at 468.

[563] *Murad v Al-Saraj* [2005] EWCA Civ 959 at [88]; [2005] W.T.L.R. 1573. See also *Say-Dee Pty Ltd v Farah Constructions Pty Ltd* [2005] NSWCA 309 at [252], although on appeal it was held that no breach of fiduciary duty had been committed: *Farah Constructions Pty Ltd v Say-Dee Pty Ltd* [2007] HCA 22; (2007) 230 C.L.R. 89.

Delete sixth paragraph.

Replace paragraph with:

A fiduciary does not automatically avoid the obligation to account entirely for a profit made in breach of fiduciary duty by arranging for the profit to be earned through a separate corporate entity.[566] The corporate veil will not protect a profit from being stripped where the company's separate legal personality has been used to conceal the fact that the fiduciary has made the profit,[567] such as where the company is a mere cloak, or alter ego, for the fiduciary.[568] It may also be possible to pierce the corporate veil, if the company's personality has been used to evade the fiduciary's liability, if no other remedy will avail,[569] but not merely because the fiduciary has a substantial interest in a company.[570] Nor can a fiduciary avoid liability to account for unauthorised profits by having those profits diverted or channelled through a partnership of which the fiduciary is a member.[571] But where the profit is earned by a separate corporate entity, it is important to be clear about the basis on which the corporate entity is made to account: it can be made to account if it received the profits as an agent for the fiduciary,[571a] or if it were otherwise involved in the breach of fiduciary duty as an accessory (e.g., having assisted the fiduciary to commit the breach with knowledge).

[566] See, e.g. *Lindsley v Woodfull* [2004] EWCA Civ 165; [2004] 2 B.C.L.C. 131 at [27]–[28]; *Quarter Master UK Ltd v Pyke* [2004] EWHC 1815 (Ch); [2005] 1 B.C.L.C. 245 at [75]; *CMS Dolphin Ltd v Simonet* [2001] 2 B.C.L.C. 704 at [100]–[104].

[567] *Trustor AB v Smallbone (No.2)* [2001] 1 W.L.R. 1177 at [23]; *Sinclair Investment Holdings SA v Versailles Trade Finance Ltd* [2007] EWHC 915 (Ch) at [104] (obiter); [2007] 2 All E.R. (Comm) 993. And see the discussion of *Trustor AB v Smallbone* in *Prest v Petrodel Resources Ltd* [2013] UKSC 34 at [32]–[33], [2013] 2 A.C. 415.

[568] *Gencor ACP Ltd v Dalby* [2000] 2 B.C.L.C. 734 at 744; *Sinclair Investment Holdings SA v Versailles Trade Finance Ltd* [2007] EWHC 915 (Ch) at [104] (obiter); [2007] 2 All E.R. (Comm) 993. See also *Fiona Trust and Holding Corp v Privalov* [2010] EWHC 3199 (Comm) at [1540]; *Grimaldi v Chameleon Mining NL (No.2)* [2012] FCAFC 6 at [243]; (2012) 200 F.C.R. 296. And see the discussion of *Gencor* in *Prest v Petrodel Resources Ltd* [2013] UKSC 34 at [31]–[33], [2013] 2 A.C. 415.

[569] See *Prest v Petrodel Resources Ltd* [2013] UKSC 34, [2013] 2 A.C. 415.

[570] *Ultraframe (UK) Ltd v Fielding* [2005] EWHC 1638 (Ch) at [1576]; *National Grid Electricity Transmission Plc v McKenzie* [2009] EWHC 1817 (Ch) at [117].

[571] *Imperial Mercantile Credit Association v Coleman* (1873) L.R. 6 H.L. 189 at 202 and 207–208; *National Grid Electricity Transmission Plc v McKenzie* [2009] EWHC 1817 (Ch) at [115]–[118].

[571a] *Prest v Petrodel Resources Ltd* [2013] UKSC 34, [2013] 2 A.C. 415 at [31]–[35].

At the end, add new paragraph:

It has been said that the remedy of an account of profits must not be allowed to become a vehicle for the unjust enrichment of the claimant,[571c] but the concept of unjust enrichment has at most a subsidiary role to pay in limiting the liability of a fiduciary to account: it is acknowledged that the liability is a stringent one which is intended to have a deterrent effect, and that the effect of the account can be to confer benefits on the claimant which he or she would not otherwise have been able to reap.[571d]

It may also be inequitable to award an account of profits on the grounds of laches where the claimant stood by for a lengthy period before seeking the remedy despite knowing about the breach, such that it was exposed to none of the risks involved but now seeks all of the rewards.[571e]

[571c] *Warman International Ltd v Dwyer* (1995) 182 C.L.R. 544 at 561; *Murad v Al-Saraj* [2005] EWCA Civ 959 at [64]; [2005] W.T.L.R. 1573.

[571d] *Gray v Global Energy Horizons Corp* [2020] EWCA Civ 1668 at [125]-[127] (reported in part, but not this part, at [2021] 1 W.L.R. 2264).

[571e] *Re Jarvis (Deceased)* [1958] 1 W.L.R. 815; *Edmonds v Donovan* [2005] VSCA 27 at [77]; (2005) 12 V.R. 513. Laches can justify the court refusing to make the fiduciary account for profits; there is some authority that it can also justify a reduction in the amount of profit for which the fiduciary must account (limiting the account to profits made before the principal stood by with sufficient knowledge to make it unconscionable to expect the fiduciary to account: see *Murdoch v Mudgee Dolomite & Lime Pty Ltd* [2022] NSWCA 12 at [204]) but this was not followed in *Recovery Partners GP Ltd v Rukhadze* [2022] EWHC 690 (Comm) at [318].

4. Proprietary Remedies

Replace n.577 with:

7-057 [577] See, e.g. *Eden v Ridsdales Railway Lamp & Lighting Co Ltd* (1889) 23 Q.B.D. 368 CA at 372. A business opportunity is not itself property for this purpose, but the profits generated from that opportunity (if it was pursued in breach of fiduciary duty) can be the subject of an order for transfer: *Gray v Global Energy Horizons Corp* [2020] EWCA Civ 1668 at [459] (reported in part, but not this part, at [2021] 1 W.L.R. 2264).

Replace second paragraph with:

Where a constructive trust of this sort is recognised, the trust arises out of the fiduciary's obligation to transfer the bribe or secret commission to the principal in specie, and so the principal will need to follow or trace the bribe or secret commission in order to identify its current location before claiming a constructive trust over it or its substitute.[579] The Supreme Court has confirmed that the ability to trace in this way is one of the consequences of the principal being able to assert proprietary rights in respect of the bribe or secret commission.[580] The fact that the profit which the fiduciary made was generated through criminal activity, such as might attract a confiscation order against the fiduciary under the Proceeds of Crime Act 2002, does not prevent the principal's claim to a proprietary constructive trust over the profit.[581]

[579] *Ultraframe (UK) Ltd v Fielding* [2005] EWHC 1638 (Ch) at [1519]. cf. *United Pan-Europe Communications NV v Deutsche Bank AG* [2000] 2 B.C.L.C. 461 at [48]. See paras 30-015 to 30-051.

[580] *FHR European Ventures LLP v Cedar Capital Partners LLC* [2014] UKSC 45 at [1]; [2015] A.C. 250.

[581] *Aquila Advisory Ltd v Faichney (Crown Prosecution Service intervening)* [2021] UKSC 49; [2021] 1 W.L.R. 5666.

After "allowance for expenses", add:
properly

5. Equitable Compensation for Loss

(a) Availability.

Replace n.586 with:

7-058 [586] See, e.g. *Swindle v Harrison* [1997] 4 All E.R. 705; *JJ Harrison (Properties) Ltd v Harrison* [2001] 1 B.C.L.C. 158 at 173 (not questioned on appeal: [2001] EWCA Civ 1467 at [21]); *LC Services Ltd v Brown* [2003] EWHC 3024 at [95]; *Warman International Ltd v Dwyer* (1995) 182 C.L.R. 544 at 559; *Breen v Williams* (1996) 186 C.L.R. 71 at 11, 135–136; *Rama v Millar* [1996] 1 N.Z.L.R. 257 (PC); *Aequitas v AEFC* [2001] NSWSC 14; (2001) 19 A.C.L.C. 1,006 at [428] & [442]; *Re MDA Investment Management Ltd* [2003] EWHC 227 (Ch) at [70], [2005] B.C.C. 783; *Cassis v Kalfus (No.2)* [2004] NSWCA 315 at [99]; *Hurstanger Ltd v Wilson* [2007] EWCA Civ 299 at [34]–[35] and [49], [2007] 1 W.L.R. 2351; *Schipp v Cameron* [1998] NSWSC 997 at [741]; *PNC Telecom Plc v Thomas (No.2)* [2007] EWHC 2157 (Ch) at [89]; [2008] 2 B.C.L.C. 95; *Sandhu v Sidhu* [2009] EWHC 983 (Ch) at [122]; *AB Jnr v MB* [2013] 1 C.I.L.R. 1 at [434]–[498]. See also *AIB Group (UK) Plc v Mark Redler & Co Solicitors* [2014] UKSC 58 at [55], [2015] A.C. 1503.

Replace n.595 with:

[595] Although, even there, it must now be approached in the light of *AIB Group (UK) Plc v Mark Redler & Co Solicitors* [2014] UKSC 58, [2015] A.C. 1503.

(b) Causation.

Replace paragraph with:

7-059 Equitable compensation for loss is only available in respect of loss which is shown to have been caused by the breach of fiduciary duty,[598] which requires the court to determine what would have happened but for the breach of fiduciary duty.[599] This can involve consideration of how the principal would have acted if the fiduciary had not acted in breach of fiduciary duty.[600] Compensation cannot, therefore, be recovered where it is clear that the principal would have acted in the same way even if the fiduciary had disclosed all the material facts.[601] In *Swindle v Harrison*, Evans LJ suggested that a fiduciary may be unable to avail himself or herself of this rule where the breach of fiduciary duty involved dishonesty or fraud,[602] but Tuckey LJ has since pointed out that neither Hobhouse LJ nor Mummery LJ appeared to accept Evans LJ's distinction between fraudulent and non-fraudulent breaches of fiduciary duty.[603] In *Gwembe Valley Development Co Ltd v Koshy*, the defendant director was found to have acted dishonestly in not disclosing his interest in a transaction and was nonetheless held not liable to pay equitable compensation on the basis that his breach had not been proven to have caused loss to his company.[604]

[598] *Bentinck v Fenn* (1887) 12 App. Cas. 652 at 661–662 and 669; *Bristol & West Building Society v Daniels & Co* [1997] P.N.L.R. 323 at 328; *Swindle v Harrison* [1997] 4 All E.R. 705; *Wight v Olswang* [2001] W.T.L.R. 291 at 298; *Gwembe Valley Development Co Ltd v Koshy* [2003] EWCA Civ 1048 at [147], [2004] 1 B.C.L.C. 131; *Halton International Inc (Holding) SARL v Guernroy Ltd* [2005] EWHC 1968 (Ch) at [155]; *Blythe v Northwood* [2005] NSWCA 221 at [78]; *Stevens v Premium Real Estate Ltd* [2009] NZSC 15; [2009] 2 N.Z.L.R. 384. This is analogous to the position where there has been a breach of trust: *Target Holdings Ltd v Redferns* [1996] A.C. 421 at 432, 434; *Collins v Brebner* [2000] Lloyd's Rep. P.N. 587 at [64]; *Youyang Pty Ltd v Minter Ellison Morris Fletcher* [2003] HCA 15; (2003) 212 C.L.R. 484.

[599] See, e.g. *Take Ltd v BSM Marketing Ltd* [2006] EWHC 1085 QB at [189], [206]; *Short v Crawley (No.30)* [2007] NSWSC 1322 at [428], [429] and [436]; *Rigg v Sheridan* [2008] NSWCA 79 at [52], [57]; *Nicholls v Michael Wilson and Partners Ltd* [2012] NSWCA 383.

[600] See, e.g. *Satnam Investments Ltd v Dunlop Heywood & Co Ltd* [1999] 3 All E.R. 652 at 668; *Nationwide Building Society v Balmer Radmore* [1999] Lloyd's Rep. P.N. 241 at 278; *Murad v Al-Saraj* [2005] EWCA Civ 959 at [110], [120]; [2005] W.T.L.R. 1573; *Aequitas v AEFC* [2001] NSWSC 14; (2001) 19 A.C.L.C. 1,006 at [443]–[448]; *Edmonds v Donovan* [2005] V.S.C.A. 27 at [78] (2005) 12 V.R. 513. It may also be necessary to consider how third parties would have acted vis-a-vis the principal if there had been no breach of fiduciary duty: see *Nicholls v Michael Wilson and Partners Ltd* [2012] NSWCA 383.

[601] See, e.g. *Swindle v Harrison* [1997] 4 All E.R. 705 at 718, 728 and 735; *Gwembe Valley Development Co Ltd v Koshy* [2003] EWCA Civ 1048; [2004] 1 B.C.L.C. 131 at [147] and [159].

[602] *Swindle v Harrison* [1997] 4 All E.R. 705 at 716–717.

[603] *Collins v Brebner* [2000] Lloyd's Rep. P.N. 587 at [57].

[604] *Gwembe Valley Development Co Ltd v Koshy* [2003] EWCA Civ 1048; [2004] 1 B.C.L.C. 131 at [135], [159].

Replace n.611 with:

[611] *Re MDA Investment Management Ltd* [2004] EWHC 42 (Ch) at [4], [2005] B.C.C. 783.

Replace final paragraph with:

Compensation cannot be recovered for breach of fiduciary duty by a shareholder in a company where the loss is suffered in the form of diminution in value of the shareholding in the company (or in reduced dividends received from the company) as a result of loss suffered by the company if the company had a cause of action for the recovery of that loss; but where the claim is brought in respect of a loss which does not fall within that description, it might succeed, if separate duties were owed to the company and the claimant respectively.[612]

[612] *Marex Financial Ltd v Sevilleja* [2020] UKSC 31, [2021] A.C. 39, as further explained in *Primeo Fund v Bank of Bermuda (Cayman) Ltd* [2021] UKPC 22 (and it is important to bear in mind that the mere fact that duties are owed to a company (as, eg, by directors, but also external fiduciary advisers) does not automatically, nor even normally, mean that those duties are also owed to shareholders in that company: see para.7-004)

(d) Interest.

After "a compound basis.", add:

7-061   The rate of interest must be suited to the economic realities of the times, which can render older decisions less useful as guides, and courts seek a suitable proxy rate for the general characteristics of the claimant that is being awarded equitable compensation.[623a]

[623a] *Watson v Kea Investments Ltd* [2019] EWCA Civ 1759 at [71]-[74]; [2019] 4 W.L.R. 145.

6.   Forfeiture of Fees

Replace second paragraph with:

7-062   If a fiduciary acts dishonestly he will forfeit his right to fees paid or payable by the principal (as distinct from sums paid by a third party, such as a briber).[627] He will also forfeit his right to such fees if he takes a secret profit from a third party which is directly related to performance of the duties in respect of which the fees were payable by the principal,[628] even if the principal has benefited from the fiduciary's performance of those duties.[629] Where the breach lies in a failure to pass on relevant information, rather than the taking of a secret profit, the fiduciary will not forfeit his right to fees unless he acted dishonestly or in bad faith.[629a] And, a fiduciary's fees may not be forfeit if the betrayal of trust has not been in respect of the entire subject-matter of the fiduciary relationship and where forfeiture would be disproportionate and inequitable.[630]

[627] See, e.g. *Andrews v Ramsay* [1903] 2 K.B. 635 at 638; *Hippisley v Knee Brothers* [1905] 1 K.B. 1 at 8; *Ian Scott & Co v Medical Installations Co Ltd* (1981) 258 E.G. 556; *Robinson Scammell & Co v Ansell* [1985] 2 E.G.L.R. 41 at 43–44; *Kelly v Cooper* [1993] A.C. 205 at 216; *Stevens v Premium Real Estate Ltd* [2009] NZSC 15 at [89]; [2009] 2 N.Z.L.R. 384.

[628] *Hippisley v Knee Brothers* [1905] 1 K.B. 1 at 8 & 9; *Price v Metropolitan House Investment & Agency Co (Ltd)* (1907) 23 T.L.R. 630 at 631; *Imageview Management Ltd v Jack* [2009] EWCA Civ 63 at [44] and [46], [2009] Bus. L.R. 1034; *Stupples v Stupples & Co (High Wycombe) Ltd* [2012] EWHC 1226 (Ch) at [21] and [56]; *Avrahami v Biran* [2013] EWHC 1776 (Ch) at [339].

[629] *Rhodes v Macalister* (1923) 29 Com. Cas. 19 at 27; *Imageview Management Ltd v Jack* [2009] EWCA Civ 63 at [47]–[50], [2009] Bus. L.R. 1034; *Rahme v Smith & Williamson Trust Corp Ltd* [2009] EWHC 911 (Ch) at [140]–[141].

[629a] *ACLBDD Holdings Ltd v Staechelin* [2019] EWCA Civ 817 at [81]-[82] and [91] (reported in part, but not this part, at [2019] 3 All E.R. 429).

[630] *Bank of Ireland v Jaffery* [2012] EWHC 1377 (Ch) at [371]–[373].

7.   Limitation Periods

Replace n.634 with:

7-063   [634] *Gwembe Valley Development Co Ltd v Koshy* [2003] EWCA Civ 1048 at [111], [2004] 1 B.C.L.C. 131.

Replace third paragraph with:

The six-year limitation period does not apply where the fiduciary has deliberately concealed from his principal any fact relevant to the principal's cause of action, such as where a fiduciary consciously decided not to disclose his interest in a transaction with his principal and realised that the fact suppressed related to his original wrongdoing.[639] Deliberate concealment can be shown where there is a deliberate breach of duty in circumstances in which it is unlikely to be discovered for some time[640]; this can involve an act or omission, but concealment from the claimant needs to be an intended result of that act or omission,[641] or the wrongdoer must at least have been reckless in that regard.[642]

[639] Limitation Act 1980 s.32(1)(b); *Newgate Stud Co v Penfold* [2004] EWHC 2993 (Ch) at [252]–[256]. See also *Sandhu v Sidhu* [2009] EWHC 983 (Ch) at [158]–[166]; *Canada Square Operations Ltd v Potter* [2021] EWCA Civ 339 at [65]-[77] (it is unnecessary that there be a pre-existing contractual, tortious or fiduciary duty to disclose).

[640] See Limitation Act 1980 s.32(2). Note *Burnden Holdings (UK) Ltd v Fielding* [2018] UKSC 14; [2018] A.C. 857 at [25]–[26].

[641] *Cave v Robinson Jarvis & Rolf* [2002] UKHL 18; [2003] 1 A.C. 384 at [60]; *Brent London Borough Council v Davies* [2018] EWHC 2214 (Ch) at [578].

[642] *Canada Square Operations Ltd v Potter* [2021] EWCA Civ 339 at [85]–[137].

Replace fifth paragraph with:
There has been some controversy as to whether s.21(1)(a) of the Limitation Act 1980, which disapplies the normal six-year limitation period, applies where a fiduciary acted fraudulently or dishonestly,[647] or only applies in respect of claims concerning trust property or property which was held in a fiduciary capacity.[648] The Court of Appeal suggested that some of the decisions which have been based on fraud alone, "may be better explained by reference to the alternative ground of fraudulent concealment".[649] However, in *First Subsea Ltd v Balltec Ltd*,[650] the Court of Appeal held that s.21(1)(a) applies to claims brought against a fiduciary such as a director (who is in a fiduciary position of stewardship regarding the company's property even though not strictly speaking a trustee of that property[651]) for breach of a fiduciary duty which pre-existed the impugned transaction, provided that breach is fraudulent, even if the breach does not involve misappropriation or misapplication of the property which was held in that fiduciary capacity prior to the breach.[652]

[647] See, e.g. *Gwembe Valley Development Co Ltd v Koshy* [2003] EWCA Civ 1048 at [120]–[121], [135]–[136] and [140], [2004] 1 B.C.L.C. 131; *Bank of Credit & Commerce International SA v Saadi* [2005] EWHC 2256 (QB) at [30]–[31].

[648] *Halton International Inc v Guernroy Ltd* [2006] EWCA Civ 801 at [22]. This is also consistent with the majority position in *Williams v Central Bank of Nigeria* [2014] UKSC 10, [2014] A.C. 1189.

[649] *Halton International Inc v Guernroy Ltd* [2006] EWCA Civ 801 at [22] fn.1.

[650] *First Subsea Ltd v Balltec Ltd* [2017] EWCA Civ 186; [2018] Ch. 25.

[651] See also *Burnden Holdings (UK) Ltd v Fielding* [2018] UKSC 14; [2018] A.C. 857 at [11] and [19].

[652] Applied in *Brent London Borough Council v Davies* [2018] EWHC 2214 (Ch) at [549]–[555], which includes discussion of the approach to establishing fraud (applying *Ivey v Genting Casinos (UK) Ltd* [2017] UKSC 67; [2018] A.C. 391 at [74]; *Barlow Clowes International Ltd v Eurotrust International Ltd* [2006] 1 W.L.R. 1476).

Replace sixth paragraph with:
Under s.21(1)(b) of the Limitation Act 1980, the normal six-year limitation period does not apply where the claim is in reality a claim to recover trust property.[653] This includes situations where the fiduciary was not expressly appointed as a trustee but assumed the duties of a trustee by a lawful transaction and that transaction is not impugned,[654] but does not include situations where the "constructive trust" which the principal claims is no more than a formula for

equitable relief.[655] In other words, the "trust" on which the claimant relies must pre-exist the conduct which constitutes the cause of action. Thus, a director of a company who obtains property from the company in breach of fiduciary duty holds that property as a constructive trustee and cannot assert a limitation period against a claim for the return of the property as "his obligations as a trustee in relation to that property predate the transaction by which it was conveyed to him".[656] But claims against a director of a company for an account of profits, and a constructive trust over those profits, would have been time-barred after six years where the claims did not depend on the director having had any pre-existing responsibility for the company's property, but rather on his interest in the transaction which led to the profits[657]; the fact that the profit was made in the context of a pre-existing fiduciary relationship was insufficient to avoid the six-year limitation period under s.21(1)(b)[658] (although the claims were, in the result, not statute-barred because the director had acted fraudulently[659]).

[653] Limitation Act 1980 s.21(1)(b). This can include claims for an account of profits or equitable compensation where the fiduciary has converted property which was held in a fiduciary capacity to his or her own use: *Burnden Holdings (UK) Ltd v Fielding* [2018] UKSC 14; [2018] A.C. 857 at [13].

[654] *Taylor v Davies* [1920] A.C. 636 at 651; *Paragon Finance Plc v DB Thakerar & Co* [1999] 1 All E.R. 400 at 408–409. This approach is confirmed in *Williams v Central Bank of Nigeria* [2014] UKSC 10, [2014] A.C. 1189.

[655] *Paragon Finance Plc v DB Thakerar & Co* [1999] 1 All E.R. 400 at 409–410 and 414–415; *Coulthard v Disco Mix Club Ltd* [2000] 1 W.L.R. 707 at 731. See also *Williams v Central Bank of Nigeria* [2014] UKSC 10, [2014] A.C. 1189. Obviously enough, this is dependent on the appliable statutory provisions; in other jurisdictions, the relevant definitions of "trust" include constructive trustees even where that label is applied only by reason of the transaction impeached: see, e.g. Limitation Act 1969 (NSW) s.11; *Sze Tu v Lowe* (2014) 89 N.S.W.L.R. 317 at [332]–[338].

[656] *J J Harrison (Properties) Ltd v Harrison* [2001] EWCA Civ 1467 at [29], [40]–[41]; *Gwembe Valley Development Co Ltd v Koshy* [2003] EWCA Civ 1048 at [98]–[100], [2004] 1 B.C.L.C. 131; see also *Farrar v Miller* [2018] EWCA Civ 172 at [81]; *Burnden Holdings (UK) Ltd v Fielding* [2018] UKSC 14; [2018] A.C. 857.

[657] *Gwembe Valley Development Co Ltd v Koshy* [2003] EWCA Civ 1048 at [119]; [2004] 1 B.C.L.C. 131. See also *Halton International Inc (Holding) SARL v Guernroy Ltd* [2005] EWHC 1968 (Ch) at [164]; *Halton International Inc v Guernroy Ltd* [2006] EWCA Civ 801 at [10]–[23]; *Slack & Partners Ltd v Slack* [2010] EWCA Civ 204 at [26]–[27] and [39]. This position has been criticized and may be reconsidered in the light of the Supreme Court's decision in *FHR European Ventures LLP v Cedar Capital Partners LLC* [2014] UKSC 45 at [1]; [2015] A.C. 250: see A. Televantos, "Trusts, Limitation Periods and Unauthorised Gains" [2020] Conv. 330.

[658] *Taylor v Davies* [1920] A.C. 636 at 651; *Gwembe Valley Development Co Ltd v Koshy* [2003] EWCA Civ 1048 at [119], [2004] 1 B.C.L.C. 131. See also *Halton International Inc v Guernroy Ltd* [2006] EWCA Civ 801 at [18]; *Sinclair Investments (UK) Ltd v Versailles Trade Finance Ltd (In Administration)* [2010] EWHC 1614 (Ch) at [75].

[659] *Gwembe Valley Development Co Ltd v Koshy* [2003] EWCA Civ 1048 at [120]–[121] and [135]–[136], [2004] 1 B.C.L.C. 131 (applying s.21(1)(a), discussed above).

Replace n.662 with:

[662] *Re Loftus (Deceased)* [2006] EWCA Civ 1124; [2007] 1 W.L.R. 591 at [40]–[41], disapproving apparently contrary observations in *Gwembe Valley Development Co Ltd v Koshy* [2003] EWCA Civ 1048 at [140], [2004] 1 B.C.L.C. 131; see also *Cattley v Pollard* [2006] EWHC 3130 (Ch); [2007] 2 All E.R. 1086 at [151]; *Patel v Shah* [2005] EWCA Civ 157 at [22].

Replace n.666 with:

[666] *Paragon Finance Plc v DB Thakerar & Co* [1999] 1 All E.R. 400 at 415–416; *Coulthard v Disco Mix Club Ltd* [2000] 1 W.L.R. 707 at 728; *Gwembe Valley Development Co Ltd v Koshy* [2003] EWCA Civ 1048 at [86], [2004] 1 B.C.L.C. 131; cf. *Nelson v Rye* [1996] 1 W.L.R. 1378.

7.   RELATIONSHIP WITH OTHER EQUITABLE DOCTRINES OF PROTECTION

2.   Confidential Information

(b)   Duration.

Replace footnote 690 with:

[690] *Bolkiah v KPMG* [1999] 2 A.C. 222 at 235; *Attorney General v Blake* [1998] Ch. 439 at 453; *Walsh*   **7-072**
v Shanahan [2013] EWCA Civ 411 at [38].

CHAPTER 8

FRAUD, UNDUE INFLUENCE AND UNCONSCIONABLE TRANSACTIONS

1. OVERVIEW

1. The Three Doctrines

(b) Fraud is not the underlying basis of the doctrines.

Replace footnote 15 with:

[15] In *Hayward v Zurich Insurance Co Plc* [2015] EWCA Civ 327 at [31], for example, in the context   **8-004**
of rescission for pre-contractual misrepresentation, Briggs LJ stated that: "In my opinion the true
principle is that the equitable remedy of rescission answers the affront to conscience occasioned by holding to a contract a party who has been influenced into making it by being misled or, worse still, defrauded
by his counterparty". The Court of Appeal's decision in that case (denying rescission on the basis that
B, when entering the contract, suspected that A was making fraudulent statements) was reversed on appeal to the Supreme Court ([2017] 2 A.C. 142), but the significance of Briggs LJ's statement for present
purposes lies in the link drawn, at a general level, between the different grounds for rescission.

(c) Unconscionability is not the underlying basis of the doctrines.

Replace first paragraph with:
    At a high level of abstraction, the three doctrines considered in this chapter do   **8-005**
share the basic aim of preventing the unconscionable assertion by A, as against B,
of a right held by A. Each of the three doctrines, however, deals with a quite specific

form of unconscionability and so the requirements and operation of each must be examined separately.[16a] As is the case with the law of equitable estoppel, it would be a mistake to think that the concept of unconscionability, by itself, can provide a workable test as to when any of the doctrines is applicable.[17]

[16a] See Lord Hodge in *Pakistan International Airline Corporation v Times Travel (UK) Ltd* [2021] UKSC 40, [23]: "Unconscionability is not an overarching criterion to be applied across the board without regard to context. Were it so, judges would become arbiters of what is morally and socially acceptable. Equity takes account of the factual and legal context of a case and has identified specific contexts which call for judicial intervention to protect the weaker party." The doctrines of undue influence and of unconscionable bargains are then given as examples of such intervention.

[17] Compare the point made in the context of estoppel: para.12-010. See too Y K Liew, ' "Unconscionability" and the Case Against Lumping: Three Case Studies' (2021) 27 Trusts & Trustees 118.

2. ACTUAL FRAUD

2. The Test for Actual Fraud

Replace paragraph with:

8-007   If, for example, B's entry into a transaction results from a misrepresentation made by A, it has been recognised that an equitable power to rescind the transaction can arise even if A's misrepresentation was wholly innocent.[25] Whilst earlier courts had limited this form of equitable relief to cases of "moral fraud", that notion was stretched so far as to include the action of A who "having obtained a beneficial contract by a statement which he now knows to be false, insists upon keeping the contract".[26] B may nonetheless wish to show that A's statement was fraudulent, as various of the bars to rescission are applied differently, and more leniently to B, if fraud is present.[27] The rules developed in the common law action for deceit may be taken as defining fraud for this purpose: the essence is that A's statement "must be made either with knowledge of its being false, or with a reckless disregard as to whether or not it is true".[28] In such a case, as well as having both a common law and equitable power to rescind the transaction, B will have a claim in the tort of deceit. There is however no independent equitable action for deceit.[29]

[25] *Redgrave v Hurd* (1881) 20 Ch. D. 1 CA.

[26] *Redgrave v Hurd* (1881) 20 Ch. D. 1 CA, per Jessel MR at 13.

[27] See, e.g. paras 15-013 et seq. Note that where a claim for equitable rescission is based on a fraudulent misrepresentation, which would also give rise to a common law claim based on the tort of deceit, then, as a result of s.36(1) of the Limitation Act 1980, the six-year limitation period applied to a claim for deceit will apply by analogy to the claim for rescission: *IGE USA Investments Ltd v Revenue and Customs Commissioners* [2021] EWCA Civ 534, [2021] 3 WLR 313.

[28] *Arkwright v Newbold* (1881) 17 Ch. D. 310 at 320, per Cotton LJ. See too *Standard Chartered Bank v Pakistan National Shipping Corp (No.2)* [1998] 1 Lloyd's Rep. 684 at 704, per Cresswell J; cited with approval in *Niru Battery Manufacturing Co v Milestone Trading Ltd* [2003] EWCA Civ 1443: "The tort of deceit involves a false representation made by the defendant, who knows it to be untrue, or who has no belief in its truth, or who is reckless as to its truth. If the defendant intended that the plaintiff should act in reliance on such representation and the plaintiff in fact does so, the defendant will be liable in deceit for the damage caused". For further detail as to the tort, see M. Jones et al (eds) *Clerk & Lindsell on Torts*, 23rd edn (Sweet & Maxwell, 2020), Ch.17.

[29] *Arkwright v Newbold* (1881) 17 Ch. D. 310 at 320 per Cotton LJ. See too *Banwaitt v Dewji* [2014] EWCA Civ 67 at [84]–[86] where Patten LJ emphasised that an order in equity for repayment by A following rescission by B was not "an award of damages in tort for deceit", but, in ensuring that full restitutio in integrum is made, such an order "should be capable in principle of preventing the defendant from being unjustly enriched at the claimant's expense".

3. UNDUE INFLUENCE

1. Origins and Scope of the Jurisdiction

Replace footnote 40 with:

[40] *Royal Bank of Scotland Plc v Etridge (No.2)* [2002] 2 A.C. 773 HL at [6]. See too *Nature Resorts Ltd v First Citizens Bank Ltd* [2022] UKPC 10, [2022] 1 W.L.R. 2788 at [10]: "Putting to one side illegitimate threats (which are nowadays better viewed as falling within the doctrine of duress: see *Times Travel (UK) Ltd v Pakistan International Airline Corpn* [2021] UKSC 40, [2021] 3 W.L.R. 727, [8]–[9] and [90]) undue influence is concerned with a situation where, by reason of the relationship between them, one party [A] has such influence over the other [B] that [B] does not exercise a free judgment, independent of [A], in relation to the making of a transaction between A and B (or, in a three party situation, between [B] and a third party, C)."

8-009

Replace n.44 with:

[44] See e.g. *Etridge* [2002] 2 A.C. 773 HL at [8] per Lord Nicholls and at [103] per Lord Hobhouse. In *Pakistan International Airline Corporation v Times Travel (UK) Ltd* [2021] UKSC 40, Lord Hodge notes at [2] that "the courts have developed the common law doctrine of duress to include lawful act duress by drawing on the rules of equity in relation to undue influence…morally reprehensible behavior which in equity was judged to render the enforcement of a contract unconscionable in the context of undue influence has been treated by English common law as illegitimate pressure in the context of duress."

8-010

Replace paragraph with:

The exercise of undue influence on a testator is also one of the grounds on which the admittance of a will to probate may be challenged.[49] The probate doctrine must, however, be carefully distinguished from the availability of equitable relief: indeed, it has been suggested that the "only common characteristic with the equitable doctrine is the name".[50] The probate doctrine applies where such pressure has been placed on the testator as to "overpower the volition without convincing the judgment"[51] and it does not permit the party challenging the will to take advantage of any evidential presumption when seeking to prove such pressure.[52] The probate doctrine can be invoked by any party with standing to challenge the will, as it identifies "a species of restraint under which no valid will can be made".[53] The equitable doctrine, by contrast, does not operate so as to render a transaction invalid: a gift or contract entered into by undue influence is valid and so takes effect unless or until B exercises his or her power to rescind the transaction. The equitable doctrine, it is submitted, is based rather on the idea that, as a result of the undue influence, it would be unconscionable, in a broad sense, for A, as against B, to take advantage of the right acquired by A under the impugned transaction.

8-012

[49] See, e.g. *Edwards v Edwards* [2007] EWHC 1119 (Ch), [2007] W.T.L.R. 1387.

[50] P. Ridge, "Equitable Undue Influence and Wills" (2004) 120 L.Q.R. 617 at 621. The distinction between the two doctrines is noted in *re Williams* [2022] EWHC 1334 (Ch) at [70], citing this paragraph. For consideration of which of the two doctrines should be used in relation to will substitutes, see B. Chen and N. Silver (2022) 85 Modern Law Review 295.

[51] *Hall v Hall* (1868) L.R. 1 P. & D. 481 at 481, per Sir J.P. Wilde (later Lord Penzance). In the probate doctrine, "undue influence means coercion": see *Re Good* [2002] EWHC 640 (Ch) per Rimer J; applied in *Ark v Kaur* [2010] EWHC 2314 (Ch) at [18].

[52] See, e.g. *Parfitt v Lawless* (1872) L.R. 2 P. & D. 462; *Craig v Lamoureux* [1920] A.C. 349 PC 356. Note too that if a party unsuccessfully challenges a will on the basis of undue influence when the circumstances were not such as to have led to a reasonable bona fide belief that there were good grounds for such a challenge then that party will generally be liable for costs; indeed, a case based on undue influence is founded on a very serious charge and if the case is particularly weak, costs may be assessed on an indemnity basis: see *Wharton v Bancroft* [2012] EWHC 91 (Ch) at [13] and [18].

[53] *Hall v Hall* (1868) L.R. 1 P. & D. 481 at 481, per Sir J.P. Wilde (later Lord Penzance). For a recent example of a will's being set aside on the grounds of undue influence, see *Schomberg v Taylor* [2013] EWHC 2269 (Ch).

2. The Test for Undue Influence

(a) A unitary doctrine.

Replace paragraph with:

8-014   The leading authority on the doctrine of undue influence is the decision of the House of Lords in *Royal Bank of Scotland Plc v Etridge (No.2)*.[59] It established the important point that, whilst it is common to divide the doctrine into cases of "actual undue influence" on the one hand and "presumed undue influence" on the other, those terms refer only to different methods of proving that the exercise of undue influence caused B to enter into the impugned transaction.[60] It had previously been common to divide cases of undue influence into categories and sub-categories but "the attempt to build up classes or categories may lead to confusion"[61] as evidenced by "the tangle that the case law in this area ha[d] got into"[62] before *Etridge* came to be considered by the House of Lords. Indeed, even after the comprehensive survey undertaken by the Lords in that case, some confusion remains, much of it traceable to the misconception that the "actual" and "presumed" strands identify different concepts, rather than serving as different routes to establishing the single concept of undue influence.[63]

[59] *Etridge* [2002] 2 A.C. 773 HL.

[60] See, e.g. *Etridge* [2002] 2 A.C. 773 HL at [13]–[14] per Lord Nicholls, at [92] per Lord Clyde, at [219] per Lord Scott; *Thompson v Foy* [2009] EWHC 1076 (Ch) at [100]; *Nature Resorts Ltd v First Citizens Bank Ltd* [2022] UKPC 10, [2022] 1 W.L.R. 2788 at [11]: "undue influence is a single concept. It does not have two different forms. The correct analysis of the two categories is that they refer to different ways of *proving* undue influence.".

[61] *Etridge* [2002] 2 A.C. 773 HL at [92] per Lord Clyde. Note too Lord Nicholls' description of the terms "actual" and "presumed" as "a little confusing" ([17]).

[62] *Etridge* [2002] 2 A.C. 773 HL at [218] per Lord Scott.

[63] See the survey and analysis provided by K. Lewison, "Under the Influence" [2011] *Restitution Law Review* 1. For the different argument that the mixed origins of the undue influence authorities mean attempts to reduce it to a core principle are doomed to fail, see R. Honey, "Deconstructing the Equitable Doctrine of Undue Influence: Insights from a Genealogy" (2020) 14 J Eq 58.

(c) Two broad categories of case.

Replace paragraph with:

8-017   The decision of the House of Lords in *Etridge*, as noted above, contains important warnings against placing too much store on categories and sub-categories of undue influence. Lord Nicholls nonetheless noted that: "[e]quity identified broadly two forms of unacceptable conduct".[72] The first "comprises overt acts of improper pressure or coercion such as unlawful threats".[72a] Such a case can be described as involving "actual" undue influence, as B may well be able to point to such coercion to show that he or she acted under an undue weight of influence. The second form "arises out of a relationship between two persons where one has acquired over another a measure of influence, or ascendancy, of which the ascendant person then takes unfair advantage".[73] In such cases, the existence of such a relationship of influence, if coupled with a transaction calling for explanation, may give B the benefit of an evidential presumption of undue influence, and thus assist

B in discharging the onus of proving undue influence. Where B seeks to rely on such a presumption, the case may be seen as involving "presumed" undue influence. When the application of the test for undue influence is considered at paras 8-021 to 8-036, these two categories of case will be examined in turn.[74]

[72] *Etridge* [2002] 2 A.C. 773 HL at [8] per Lord Nicholls.

[72a] *Etridge* [2002] 2 A.C. 773 HL at [8] per Lord Nicholls. In *Pakistan International Airline Corporation v Times Travel (UK) Ltd* [2021] UKSC 40, Lord Burrows at [90] states that in cases of "actual undue influence where the influence was being exerted by a lawful threat" it would be "rational today to treat such cases as examples of duress" rather than of undue influence. Similarly, on the slightly different analysis as to the scope of lawful act duress adopted by other members of the panel, a case such as *Williams v Bayley* (1866) L.R. 1 H.L. 200 is seen as an example of lawful act duress (see Lord Hodge at [7]-[9]). It remains to be seen what effect the confirmation of lawful act duress in the *Times Travel* case will have on the doctrine of actual undue influence. Certainly, in *Nature Resorts Ltd v First Citizens Bank Ltd* [2022] UKPC 10, [2022] 1 W.L.R. 2788 at [10], it was stated that, following *Times Travel*, cases of illegitimate threats are better seen as duress rather than undue influence.

[73] *Etridge* [2002] 2 A.C. 773 HL at [8] per Lord Nicholls. See too *Pakistan International Airline Corporation v Times Travel (UK) Ltd* [2021] UKSC 40 at [90] where Lord Burrows refers to this second form as being "concerned with the standard case of undue influence where the relationship between the parties is such that one party's judgment is not being exercised freely and independently of the other party" referring to such cases as within the "standard area of 'relational' undue influence". Note that in *Libyan Investment Authority v Goldman Sachs International* [2016] EWHC 2530 (Ch), Rose J at [137] stated that in such cases, there is a "protected relationship" and as a result the stronger party has a duty to behave to the vulnerable party with "candour and fairness. If the stronger party then acts in breach of that duty, the transaction can be set aside for undue influence". If such a breach can be proved directly, without the aid of a presumption, the case is one of actual undue influence.

[74] It could be argued that, in principle, there may be situations which lie outside the two categories identified by Lord Nicholls in *Etridge*.

(d)   Is wrongdoing required?

Replace n.77 with:

[77] See e.g. *Etridge* [2002] 2 A.C. 773 HL at [8] per Lord Nicholls. See too *YS GM Marfin II LLC v Lakhani* [2020] EWHC 2629 (Comm) at [95], where Jacobs J, citing *National Commercial Bank (Jamaica) Ltd v Hew* [2003] UKPC 51, refers to "abuse or unfair exploitation of the influence so as to obtain some unfair advantage from the vulnerable party" as a "necessary…element of the undue influence doctrine."   **8-018**

Replace footnote 83 with:

[83] *Hammond v Osborne* [2002] EWCA Civ 885 at [32], per Sir Martin Nourse, citing *Allcard v Skinner* (1887) 36 Ch. D. 145 CA at 171 where Cotton LJ, referring to "presumed" undue influence cases, states: "the court interferes, not on the ground that any wrongful act has in fact been committed by the donee, but on the ground of public policy, and to prevent the relations which existed between the parties and the influence arising therefrom being abused". See too *Jennings v Cairns* [2003] EWCA Civ 1935 at [40], per Arden LJ: "[t]he fact that the conduct of the person exercising influence is unimpeachable is not by itself an answer to a claim in undue influence, though the presumption of undue influence can be rebutted in many ways"; *Pesticcio v Huet* [2004] EWCA Civ 372 at 20, per Mummery LJ: "A transaction may be set aside by the court, even though the actions and conduct of the person who benefits from it could not be criticized as wrongful": Mummery LJ's view was cited with approval in *Nature Resorts Ltd v First Citizens Bank Ltd* [2022] UKPC 10, [2022] 1 W.L.R. 2788 at [15].   **8-018**

Replace n.87 with:

[87] See, e.g. *Hart v Burbidge* [2013] EWHC 1628 (Ch) (upheld on appeal: [2014] EWCA Civ 992) at [142] where Blackburne J stated that: "It would seem quite wrong that [A], however unconscious she may have been of the undue influence that she was exerting on her mother [B], should be entitled to benefit to any degree from the consequences of her conduct"). See too *Royal Bank of Scotland plc v Chandra* [2011] EWCA Civ 192, [26]. As accepted in *YS GM Marfin II LLC v Lakhani* [2020] EWHC 2629 (Comm) at [93], even if a "conscious act of wrongdoing" is required, this "probably does not mean

that the influencing party must subjectively appreciate that he is acting wrongly in a situation where he in fact abuses his influence".

(e)   Undue influence exercised by a third party.

Replace first paragraph with:

8-019   As noted at para.8-011, if B is induced by the undue influence of a third party (X) to make a gift to A, then relief may be available against A, even if A had no knowledge or notice of the undue influence when acquiring the gift.[88] The remedies available to B will however be limited if A, before acquiring any such knowledge or notice, disposed of the gift or otherwise changed his or her position in good faith. If B instead enters a contract with A as a result of X's undue influence, and X was not acting as B's agent,[89] then B will only be entitled to set the contract aside if A, at the time of the entry into the contract, had actual or constructive notice of X's undue influence.[90] Constructive notice can be shown if A is put on inquiry as to the possibility of X's influence and then fails to take reasonable steps to be satisfied that B's consent to the transaction had been properly obtained.[91] If A is a bank or creditor, and B is standing as surety for the debts of another, A will be put on inquiry whenever the relationship between the surety and the debtor is non-commercial[92]: an obvious example consists of a spouse or partner consenting to the charging of his or her property in order to secure a debt owed by that other partner, or by a company.[93]

[88]   See, e.g. *Bridgeman v Green* (1757) Wilmot 58, 97 E.R. 22; *Huguenin v Baseley* (1807) 14 Ves. 273, T 300; 33 E.R. 526, at 536; *Jennings v Cairns* [2003] EWCA Civ 1935.

[89]   See para.37-025. Beyond the surety context, see e.g. *O'Sullivan v Management Agency Ltd* [1985] Q.B. 428 CA, where X was an agent of A, the company with whom B entered into a contract.

[90]   *Barclays Bank Plc v O'Brien* [1994] 1 A.C. 180 at 195–196; and *Etridge* at [34]–[43] and [139]–[150].

[91]   *O'Brien* [1994] 1 A.C. 180 at 196; and *Etridge* at [38].

[92]   *Etridge* [82]–[89] esp. [87].

[93]   *Etridge* [44]–[49] and [109]. See e.g. *Syndicate Bank v Dansingani* [2019] EWHC 3439 (Ch) at [27], finding that A was put on inquiry where a spouse gave a personal guarantee for a loan to a company, even though the spouses had an equal shareholding in the company and were both directors of it. HHJ Dight there cited with approval the analysis in this work.

Replace n.104 with:

[104]   As suggested by J. Cartwright, *Misrepresentation, Mistake and Non-Disclosure*, 5th edn (Sweet & Maxwell, 2019), para.4-77.

(f)   Causation.

Replace paragraph with:

8-020   It is not entirely clear which causal test the courts have settled on for undue influence. In *Bank of Credit and Commerce International SA v Aboody*,[107] the Court of Appeal's joint judgment stated that, at least in ordinary circumstances, it would not be appropriate for a court to grant relief "in a case where the evidence establishes that on the balance of probabilities [B] would have entered the transaction in any event".[108] In *UCB Corporate Services Ltd v Williams*,[109] however, the Court of Appeal rejected the contention that relief depended on B's establishing that, absent the undue influence, B would not have entered into the impugned transaction. It was stated that the approach in *Aboody* was inconsistent with the House of Lords' characterisation of undue influence, in *CIBC Mortgages v Pitt*,[110] as a form of equitable fraud, and with Lord Browne-Wilkinson's statement in that case that "a victim of undue influence is entitled to have the transaction set aside 'as of right'".[111] On the facts of the *UCB* case, B had been the victim of a fraudulent misrepresentation and this justified applying the causal test applied in all cases of actual fraud, which does not permit A to argue that, even in the absence of the fraud, B would have entered the transaction: in cases of fraud, B need only show that the representation was a factor in B's decision to act in a particular way. The actual fraud in the case therefore took it beyond the "ordinary circumstances" referred to in *Aboody*. As noted at para.8-003, however, it would be a mistake to adopt the general position that all cases of undue influence should be seen as examples of actual fraud and so should be governed by that undemanding causal test.[112] Indeed, the quotation from *Pitt* relied on in the *UCB* case refers to "a person who has been induced by undue influence to carry out a transaction",[113] and it can be argued that such inducement has not occurred if B would, in any case, have entered that transaction. It is also worth noting that, where B claims that a benefit was transferred to A as a result of duress, the usual causal test applied is more demanding than showing that the illegitimate pressure was simply a factor in B's decision,[114] and so it is not obvious why a lower standard should be applied in cases of undue influence. Nonetheless, it seems that, at least until further consideration of the matter by the Court of Appeal, the less demanding "a factor" test is now, by convention, the causal test applied in all cases of undue influence.[115]

[107] *Bank of Credit and Commerce International SA v Aboody* [1990] 1 Q.B. 923 CA at 971.

[108] See too *Etridge* [2002] 2 A.C. 773 HL at [223], per Lord Scott, considering the effect of any misrepresentation made to Mrs Etridge: "[the first instance judge] found as a fact that if the nature and contents of the documents had been explained to her, she still would have signed. So, if there had been any misrepresentation as to the nature and content of the documents, it had no relevant causative effect".

[109] *UCB Corporate Services Ltd v Williams* [2002] EWCA Civ 555; [2003] 1 P. & C.R. 12. See too *Syndicate Bank v Dansingani* [2019] EWHC 3439 (Ch) at [96], where HHJ Dight rejected A's argument that B must show that, "had she been fully informed she would not have entered into the transaction", stating instead that: "If [B] did not enter into the transaction of her own free will she did not consent to it and she has a right in principle to set the transaction aside."

[110] *CIBC Mortgages v Pitt* [1994] 1 A.C. 200 HL.

[111] *UCB Corporate Services Ltd v Williams* [2002] EWCA Civ 555; [2003] 1 P. & C.R. 12 at 91, per Jonathan Parker LJ, quoting from *Pitt* at 209.

[112] This observation was approved by Nugee J in *Holyoake v Candy* [2017] EWHC 3397 (Ch) at [407].

[113] *CIBC Mortgages v Pitt* [1994] 1 A.C. 200 HL at 209, per Lord Browne-Wilkinson.

[114] See, e.g. *Huyton SA v Peter Cremer GmbH* [1999] 1 Lloyd's Rep. 620 at 636; *Kolmar Group AG v Traxpo Enterprises Pty Ltd* [2010] EWHC 113 (Comm); [2010] 2 Lloyds Rep. 653 at [92]. The less demanding "a factor" test is applied only in cases of physical duress: *Barton v Armstrong* [1976] A.C. 104 PC. In cases of economic duress, the pressure must be at least a "significant" cause, or a "decisive or clinching" factor (see *KSH Farm Ltd v KSH Plant Ltd* [2021] EWHC 1986 (Ch) [569]–[571]) and it may even be that B must show that B "had no reasonable alternative to giving in to the threat (or pressure)" (Lord Burrows in *Pakistan International Airline Corporation v Times Travel (UK) Ltd* [2021] UKSC 40 at [79]).

[115] In *UCB Group Ltd v Hedworth* [2003] EWCA Civ 1717, in the light of the view taken as to causation in *UCB Corporate Services Ltd v Williams* [2002] EWCA Civ 555, A accepted that undue influence could be found even if B would have entered into the relevant transaction in the absence of such influence. There was no allegation of fraud in that case.

3. Applying the Test for Undue Influence

(a) "Actual" undue influence.

After "transaction requiring explanation.", add new n.115a:

8-021 [115a] As noted above, it remains to be seen what effect the confirmation by the Supreme Court, in *Pakistan International Airline Corporation v Times Travel (UK) Ltd* [2021] UKSC 40, of the category of lawful act duress will have on the doctrine of actual undue influence.

Replace n.129 with:

[129] *Holyoake v Candy* [2017] EWHC 3397 (Ch) at [406]–[407], per Nugee J, who went on to note that "it is not clear to me what, if anything, the plea of actual undue influence adds to the plea of duress". It was held on the facts that, as a threat to litigate does not count as illegitimate pressure for the purposes of duress, it cannot by itself constitute actual undue influence in the absence of any particular relationship between the parties. The practical relevance of actual undue influence may therefore depend on the scope of lawful act duress. In *Pakistan International Airline Corporation v Times Travel (UK) Ltd* [2021] UKSC 40, Lord Hodge (with whom Lord Reed, Lord Lloyd-Jones and Lord Kitchin agreed) identified at [4]–[18] only two sets of cases in which lawful act duress is recognized: exploitation of knowledge of criminal activity (see e.g. *Williams v Bayley* (1866) LR 1 HL 200); and using illegitimate means to manoeuvre [B] into a position of weakness to force him to waive his claim (see e.g. *Borelli v Ting* [2010] UKPC 21). Lord Burrows took a different view of the scope of lawful act duress: ibid [136].

(b) "Presumed" undue influence: Overview.

Replace n.137 with:

8-023 [137] See, e.g. *R. v Attorney General for England and Wales* [2003] UKPC 22 at 24, per Lord Hoffmann. See too *Enal v Singh* [2022] UKPC 13.

(c) "Presumed" undue influence: The special class of established relationships of influence.

Replace footnote 141 with:

8-024 [141] *Etridge* [2002] 2 A.C. 773 HL at [18], per Lord Nicholls; *Nature Resorts Ltd v First Citizens Bank Ltd* [2022] UKPC 10, [2022] 1 W.L.R. 2788 at [12].

Replace n.143 with:

[143] See, e.g. J. Edelman & E. Bant, Unjust Enrichment (2nd edn, Hart, 2016) 232; K. Lewison, "Under the Influence" [2011] *Restitution Law Review* 1, 9; C. Mitchell et al (eds), *Goff & Jones: The Law of Unjust Enrichment*, 9th edn (Sweet & Maxwell, 2016), paras 11–47.

(d) "Presumed" undue influence: Proving a relationship of influence outside the special class.

Replace n.188 with:

8-031 [188] See e.g. Lord Hodge in *Pakistan International Airline Corporation v Times Travel (UK) Ltd* [2021] UKSC 40, [25]–[26] noting that inequality of bargaining power is not sufficient for relief whether on the grounds of undue influence or of an unconscionable bargain, although "such inequality may be a relevant feature in some cases of undue influence" citing Lord Scarman in *National Westminster Bank Plc v Morgan* [1985] A.C. 686 HL, 708. In *Beech v Birmingham CC* [2014] EWCA Civ 830, for example, the Court of Appeal regarded a contention that a relationship of influence arose between an elderly council tenant and an officer of the council as "border[ing] on the unarguable" (at 64, per Etherton C): their dealings were simply as tenant and tenant's agent and the fact that the agent was aware of B's age and frailty clearly did not make the relationship one of influence. See too *Rosesilver Group Corp v Paton* [2015] EWHC 1758 (Ch) at [41] where Mann J stated that: "Undue influence cases cannot be allowed to go forward on the basis of vague statements in evidence, coupled with speculative submissions on the part of counsel, especially in circumstances in which it appears to be a point added as an afterthought". An appeal against Mann J's decision, not challenging the aspect of the case relating to undue influence, was dismissed: [2017] EWCA Civ 158.

(e) "Presumed" undue influence: A transaction calling for explanation.

Replace footnote 201 with:

8-032

[201] *Etridge* [2002] 2 A.C. 773 HL at [24] per Lord Nicholls. As put by Lord Briggs and Lord Burrows in *Nature Resorts Ltd v First Citizens Bank Ltd* [2022] UKPC 10, [2022] 1 W.L.R. 2788 at [12], the requirement is that "the transaction must not be readily explicable on ordinary motives." As shown in that case, the fact that an ordinary commercial transaction with a third party, such as a mortgage entered into by B following advice from A (B's solicitor), turns out to be disadvantageous cannot in itself suffice to make the transaction require an explanation: ibid. at [27]–[28].

Replace third paragraph with:

As is the case with establishing a relationship of influence, the examination of the nature of the transaction is simply part of the central factual inquiry into the presence of undue influence. As a result, the examination is heavily fact-sensitive and cannot be wholly separated from the other factors relevant to the general inquiry,[211] such as those going to the existence of a relationship of influence,[212] nor from those used to rebut a presumption of undue influence should one arise.[213] When considering the transaction, the court must "look at it in its context and see what its general nature was and what it was trying to achieve for the parties".[214] It would therefore be a mistake to think that, because the impugned transaction can be equated with one found to satisfy the test in a previous case, the presumption of undue influence necessarily arises in the present case. With that warning in mind, it can be noted that examples of transactions that have met the test include, but are not limited to, the following: substantial gifts,[215] purchases at an undervalue,[216] sales at an excessive price,[217] leases which damage B's reversion,[218] loans on favourable terms,[219] and transfers which involve an imbalance of benefits.[220] Expert evidence as to the standard terms of a particular transaction may be relevant in determining if, for example, a management agreement entered into between a musician and manager has features which can be seen as unusually oppressive and unreasonable.[221]

[211] See *Libyan Investment Authority v Goldman Sachs International* [2016] EWHC 2530 (Ch) at [350]–[426] for a recent example: Rose J concluded that trades entered into by the authority on the basis of advice from the defendant did not call for an explanation, as the profits made by the defendant were not excessive, and there were commercial reasons why the authority wanted to enter into the trades.

[212] See, e.g. *Glanville v Glanville* [2002] EWHC 1587 (Ch) at [55]–[60].

[213] See, e.g. *de Wind v Wedge* [2008] EWHC 514 (Ch); [2010] W.T.L.R. 794 at [51]–[52].

[214] *Turkey v Awadh* [2005] EWCA Civ 382 at [32], per Buxton LJ. See e.g. *Bhabra v Suri* [2022] EWHC 1652 (Ch) [141], where a father's purported 90-10 division of proceeds between two brothers called for explanation as the evidence showed the father had previously intended to split his assets equally between them; contrast *re Williams* [2022] EWHC 1334 (Ch) at [77], where a minor difference in the gifts made to two daughters did not call for explanation.

[215] For examples following *Etridge* see, e.g. *Re Smith (Deceased)* [2014] EWHC 3926 (Ch) (sale of house and gift of proceeds by mother to daughter where the house was the mother's sole asset of value and the gift thus effectively deprived beneficiaries of the mother's will of any inheritance); *Pesticcio v Huet* [2004] EWCA Civ 372 (brother makes gift of house to his sister); *Jennings v Cairns* [2003] EWCA Civ 1935 (aunt makes outright gift of £35,000 to niece and £170,000 to set up a trust fund); and *Williams v Williams* [2003] EWHC 742 (Ch) (brother makes gift of house to brother and sister-in-law to hold on trust for the three of them). Contrast *Popowski v Popowski* [2004] EWHC 668 (Ch) (mother acquires property subject to secure tenancy at 60 per cent discount, transfers to son on terms that he provides the purchase price and permits her and her husband to live in the property for life).

[216] See e.g. *Enal v Singh* [2022] UKPC 13; *Mahoney v Purnell* [1996] 3 All E.R. 61. Although note that in *Crossfield v Jackson* [2014] EWCA Civ 1548 at [29], a transaction in which B received (effectively) £10,000 in return for allowing A, her brother, to take advantage of B's discount as a council tenant, worth £38,000, in a purchase of the property, did not call for an explanation as B, in rent arrears and lacking access to the funds required to make the purchase, had no other means to access the benefit of the discount.

[217] *Tate v Williamson* (1866) 2 Ch. App. 55.

[218] *Goldsworthy v Brickell* [1987] Ch. 378.

[219] *Nel v Kean* [2003] EWHC 190 (QB).

[220] *Cheese v Thomas* [1994] 1 W.L.R. 129; *Humphreys v Humphreys* [2004] EWHC 2201 (Ch); *Macklin v Dowsett* [2004] EWCA Civ 904.

[221] See *Wadlow v Samuel (aka Seal)* [2006] EWHC 1492 (QB) at [85]–[88]. The facts of the case are instructive in as much as the management agreement was regarded as "not readily explicable by ordinary motives", whereas a later settlement agreement entered into between the same parties did not meet that test, as its terms, in contrast, were not "unreasonable and oppressive": at [93].

(f) "Presumed" undue influence: Rebutting the presumption.

Replace first paragraph with:

8-033   If a court finds that there is a relationship of influence and a transaction calling for explanation, the doctrine of undue influence will apply unless A can show that, in fact, B's entry into that transaction was not procured by undue influence. To do so, A must present evidence to justify a finding that, in relation to the transaction in question, B was in fact sufficiently[229] independent of A and so was able to, and did, consent to the transaction free from any undue influence. The presumption of undue influence arises only if there is no explanation for B's entry into the transaction other than the exertion of undue influence, so, technically, evidence rebutting the presumption does not go to the question of whether there was an understandable reason for which B entered the transaction, but to the different question of whether B's admittedly poor decision-making was the product of undue influence. A must convince the court that B's decision to enter the transaction was made as a result of "full, free and informed thought about it".[230] The presence of such thought is not, of course, a general requirement for the validity of a transaction; but it must be remembered here that, *ex hypothesi*, there is a relationship of influence between A and B and the transaction is one which, in its nature, can only be explained as a result of undue influence. Those concerns can only be met, in effect, by A's showing the procedure through which B formed his or her consent. If the presumption of undue influence is rebutted, then the court has found that B's consent to the transaction was not procured by undue influence and so the doctrine cannot apply.[231]

[229] As noted by Sir William Blackburne in *Hart v Burbidge* [2013] EWHC 1628 (Ch) (approved on appeal: [2014] EWCA Civ 992) at [49], the court's concern is as to whether there has been any "undue" influence: there is thus no need to show that B was free from "everyday" influences.

[230] *Zamet v Hyman* [1961] 1 W.L.R. 1442 at 1444, per Lord Evershed MR; followed in *Re Craig* [1971] Ch. 95 at 105. See too *Nature Resorts Ltd v First Citizens Bank Ltd* [2022] UKPC 10, [2022] 1 W.L.R. 2788 at [13]: "it is for the party seeking to uphold the transaction to rebut the presumption by showing that [B] was not acting under undue influence (ie that [B] exercised free and independent judgment) when entering into the transaction."

[231] See e.g. *Etridge* [2002] 2 A.C. 773 HL at [219] per Lord Scott; *Michael v Cansick* [2004] EWHC 1684 (Ch); [2004] W.T.L.R. 961.

Replace second paragraph with:

The question of whether the presumption of undue influence has been rebutted is a question of fact to be determined on all the evidence.[232] It is not sufficient for A to show simply that B understood what he or she was doing and intended to do it[233]: undue influence consists not of a lack of understanding or an absence of consent but of a lack of sufficient independence in relation to the transaction.[234] Nor is it enough for A to show that his or her behaviour prior to and at the time of B's entry into the transaction was free from any moral blame[235]: as discussed at para.8–018, undue influence may arise even if A's conduct is, in that specific sense, unimpeachable. Nor will it necessarily suffice to show that the initial idea for the transaction was B's.[236] It has been said that:

> "[t]he gift or transaction will be set aside, unless it is proved to have been the spontaneous act of the donor or grantor acting in circumstances which enable him to exercise an independent will and which justify the court in holding that the gift or transaction was the result of a free exercise of his will."[237]

This does not mean, however, that any prior reluctance on B's part to enter the transaction prevents the rebuttal of the presumption: if B changed his or her mind, the question is simply whether that change was the product of thought that was sufficiently independent of A.

[232] As noted in *Nature Resorts Ltd v First Citizens Bank Ltd* [2022] UKPC 10, [2022] 1 W.L.R. 2788 at [23], independent advice from a lawyer is not the only means by which the presumption can be rebutted: B in that case was an experienced businessman undertaking a transaction with an important commercial purpose. Conversely, as noted in *Etridge* at [20] per Lord Nicholls: "In the normal course, advice from a solicitor or other outside adviser can be expected to bring to a complainant a proper understanding of what he or she is about to do. But a person may understand fully the implications of a proposed transaction, for instance a substantial gift, and yet still be acting under the undue influence of another". See also *Papouis v Gibson-West* [2004] EWHC 396 at [5].

[233] This sentence, and the paragraph which follows from the 30th edition of this work, was cited with approval in *Curtis v Pulbrook* [2009] EWHC 782 (Ch) at [143], per Richard Sheldon QC.

[234] This formulation was cited with approval in *Syndicate Bank v Dansingani* [2019] EWHC 3439 (Ch) at [97]. See *Etridge* [2002] 2 A.C. 773 HL at [111], per Lord Hobhouse: "It is their weakness which is being protected not their inability to comprehend".

[235] See, e.g. *Jennings v Cairns* [2003] EWCA Civ 1935 at [40] per Arden LJ: "[t]he fact that the conduct of the person exercising influence is unimpeachable is not by itself an answer to a claim in undue influence, though the presumption of undue influence can be rebutted in many ways". See too *Hammond v Osborne* [2002] EWCA Civ 885 at [32], per Sir Martin Nourse.

[236] See, e.g. *Jennings v Cairns* [2003] EWCA Civ 1935 at [35], per Arden LJ; and *Johnson Vale v Armstrong* [2004] EWHC Ch 1160. See also *Williams v Williams* [2003] EWHC 742 (Ch) (where B suffered from severe mental impairment and wished to be with A).

[237] *Goldsworthy v Brickell* [1987] Ch. 378 at 401, per Nourse L.J. See too *Allcard v Skinner* (1887) 36 Ch. D. 145 CA 171, per Cotton LJ; *Inche Noriah v Shaik Allie Bin Omar* [1929] A.C. 127 PC 133.

4. Remedies

Replace paragraph with:
It has been judicially stated that: **8-037**

> "[t]here is no 'obligation' not to exercise undue influence in order to persuade a party to enter into a contract. The party exercising undue influence incurs no liability. It is merely that the party whose consent was obtained by the exercise of undue influence is entitled to have the contract set aside."[250]

The primary remedy for undue influence is, therefore, rescission and so general rules applying to that form of relief, as set out in Ch.15, are of relevance.[251] For example, the standard equitable defences of laches, acquiescence and confirmation may prevent relief even if undue influence has been established.[252] B's failure to seek relief when remaining under the undue influence should not however be held against B, no matter how long the influence endures.[253] After the influence has ceased B must however commence the proceedings within a reasonable time[254] or the court may draw the inference that he or she has elected to affirm the transaction.[255]

[250] *Agnew v Lansforsakringsbolagens AB* [2001] 1 A.C. 223 HL at 265. Lord Millett's speech was in dissent, but no disagreement was expressed with his observation as to the nature of undue influence.

[251] See too paras 2-006—2-008 for discussion of the effect of a mere equity on a third party. In *Mortgage Express v Lambert* [2016] EWCA Civ 555, Lewison LJ confirmed at [16] that B's right to set aside a transfer of registered land on the grounds of undue influence (or on the grounds of an unconscionable bargain) is a "mere equity" and thus is capable of binding a successor in title to A: s.116(b) of the Land Registration Act 2002. On the facts of that case, however, any such right of B had been overreached as C's mortgage had been granted by two trustees: see [39]. See too *Davies v AIB Group (UK) Plc* [2012] EWHC 2178 (Ch) at [119] where Norris J stated that, had undue influence been found, B would in any case have been estopped from denying liability under the impugned loan contract because of B's acceptance of renewed and especially extended facilities (untainted by any undue influence) under the same loan contract. Note though that if a mortgage procured by undue influence is replaced with a substantially identical mortgage, B has a prima facie power to rescind that substitute mortgage, even if the undue influence did not persist at the time of B's entry into that later mortgage: *Yorkshire Bank Plc v Tinsley* [2004] EWCA Civ 816. See also, N. Gravells "Undue Influence and Substitute Mortgages" [2005] 64 C.L.J. 42.

[252] See, e.g. *Goldsworthy v Brickell* [1987] Ch. 378 at 410; *Elton John v James* [1991] F.S.R. 397. See too *de Sena v Notaro* [2020] EWHC 1031 (Ch) at [233].

[253] *Hatch v Hatch* (1804) 9 Ves. 292 (20 years). An attempt to raise laches was also rejected in *Curtis v Curtis* [2011] EWCA Civ 1602 at [20]–[24].

[254] See *Bullock v Lloyds Bank Ltd* [1955] Ch. 317 (4 years after influence had ceased and discovery of remedy). Compare *Humphreys v Humphreys* [2004] EWHC 2201 (Ch) at [103] (4 years' delay not sufficient to bar claim for undue influence). See also *Allcard v Skinner* (1887) 36 Ch. D. 145 (6 months after influence had ceased and discovery of remedy). But note the exceptional facts of *Allcard v Skinner* where C had had access to legal advice and the inference was drawn that she had made a conscious choice not to seek the return of the property.

[255] For examples of affirmation of transactions induced by undue influence see *Allcard v Skinner* (1887) 36 Ch. D. 145 and *Turner v Collins* (1871) 7 Ch. App. 329. Knowledge of the choice (which will include the legal right to set it aside) will normally be required before B can be held to have affirmed the transaction although if B deliberately declines to investigate circumstances which might give rise to a claim this may give rise to an inference of affirmation: see P Feltham et al (eds) Spencer Bower *Reliance-Based Estoppel* , 5th edn (Bloomsbury, 2017) at 13.26.

Replace second paragraph with:

8-039   It may seem that *Mahoney v Purnell*[268] provides some support for a jurisdiction to order A to pay compensation in an undue influence case: A no longer held the right transferred in the impugned transaction, nor did A retain the proceeds of sale or any other traceable proceeds of that right. May J nonetheless held that "[p]ractical justice in this case requires an award which is akin to damages"[269] and so A was ordered to pay B a sum to prevent B's suffering a loss as a result of A's inability to return the right transferred. The award was said to be based on A's "abuse of trust", however, and it can be readily be explained as a means of redressing A's clear breach of a fiduciary duty owed to B: as a result, it does not provide a general basis for relief premised on B's loss rather than on A's gain.[270]

[268] *Mahoney v Purnell* [1996] 3 All E.R. 61. Note too that in *Jennings v Cairns* [2003] EWCA Civ 1935, where the impugned transaction was a settlement on trusts to pay the school fees of A's children, A was personally ordered to return the value of the money settled, even though the relief sought did not include

setting aside the settlement, and A had received the money, strictly, in her capacity as a trustee. The validity of such a personal order was not however challenged, either at first instance or in the Court of Appeal (see at [45] per Arden LJ) and so the question of law was not considered. The best interpretation may well be that the sums were, in substance, paid for A's benefit, and A had continued access to them, so no hardship was caused by the order that she should repay them.

[269] *Mahoney v Purnell* [1996] 3 All E.R. 61 at 88. In *de Sena v Notaro* [2020] EWHC 1031 (Ch) at [230], HHJ Paul Matthews considered that, if (as was not the case) undue influence had been established, then, as rescission restoring the parties to their previous positions would have been impossible, an enquiry would have been needed as to whether "some other remedy could be awarded, such as equitable compensation".

[270] See too C. Mitchell et al (eds) *Goff and Jones: The Law of Unjust Enrichment*, 9th edn (Sweet & Maxwell, 2016) 11–28. In *Samrai v Kalia* [2022] EWHC 1424 (QB) at [93], there was said to be an arguable issue as to whether equitable compensation is available in response to undue influence, even where there is no breach of fiduciary duty.

4. UNCONSCIONABLE TRANSACTIONS

1. Origins and Scope of the Jurisdiction

Replace footnote 273 with:

[273] See, e.g. *Earl of Aylesford v Morris* (1873) 8 Ch. App. 484. For discussion of the history and development of equity's treatment of unconscionable bargains, see Edelman J in *Australian Securities and Investments Commission v Kobelt* [2019] HCA 18 at [280]–[283]. Differences between the English and Australian law in this area are discussed in Y Liew and D Yu, "The Unconscionable Bargains Doctrine in England and Australia: Cousins or Siblings?" (2021) 45 Melb Univ L Rev 206.

8-041

2. The Test for Unconscionable Transactions

Replace paragraph with:

It is clear that there is no general equitable jurisdiction to relieve B from a transaction simply on the grounds that it is substantively unfair,[281] or simply because its terms are favourable to A as a result of the parties' inequality of bargaining power.[282] In order to obtain relief, therefore, B must show that the requirements of a particular ground of relief, such as undue influence, or the specific unconscionable transaction doctrine, have been met.[283] As regards the latter doctrine, there seem to be three key requirements.[284] First, B is suffering from a particular kind of vulnerability; secondly, the terms of the transaction are oppressive to B; and thirdly, A knowingly took advantage of B's vulnerability.[285] The doctrine can therefore be seen as preventing A's insisting on a right as against B where to do so would "shock the conscience of the court" as it would involve A's benefitting from a knowing exploitation of B's vulnerability.[286] As in relation to proprietary estoppel,[286a] a court is likely to address the three key requirements "in the round", recognizing their overlapping aspects and not addressing them "separately as if they were separate elements of a cause of action in tort".[286b]

8-042

[281] See, e.g. *Boustany v Pigott* (1995) 69 P. & C.R. 298 PC at 303: "it is not sufficient to attract the jurisdiction of equity to prove that a bargain is hard, unreasonable or foolish"; *Export Credit Guarantee Department v Universal Oil Products Co* [1983] 1 W.L.R. 399 HL at 403, per Lord Roskill: "it is not and never has been for the courts to relieve a party from the consequences of what may in the event prove to be an onerous or possibly even a commercially imprudent bargain"; *Union Eagle v Golden Achievement Ltd* [1997] A.C. 514 PC at 519, per Lord Hoffmann: "in many forms of transaction it is of great importance that if something happens for which the contract has made express provision, the parties should know with certainty that the terms of the contract will be enforced. The existence of an undefined discretion to refuse to enforce the contract on the ground that this would be 'unconscionable' is sufficient to create uncertainty". See too *Multiservce Bookbinding v Marden* [1979] Ch. 84 at 110. In

Mountford v Scott [1975] Ch. 258 CA the fact that an option was granted for £1 and thus at an undervalue did not prevent its enforcement.

[282] See e.g. Lord Hodge in *Pakistan International Airline Corporation v Times Travel (UK) Ltd* [2021] UKSC 40, [25] and [26] noting that inequality of bargaining power is not sufficient for relief whether on the grounds of undue influence or of an unconscionable bargain, and that "It is not in dispute that there is in English common law no doctrine of inequality of bargaining power in contract". See too *National Westminster Bank v Morgan* [1985] A.C. 686 HL at 708, per Lord Scarman; rejecting the suggestion of Lord Denning MR in *Lloyds Bank Plc v Bundy* [1975] Q.B. 326 CA at 331.

[283] See *Irvani v Irvani* [2000] 1 Lloyd's Rep. 412 CA at 423 per Buxton LJ: "It is particularly important to keep these distinctions clear, because otherwise there may be a tendency to think that a case that has some elements of undue influence, but is not in law a case of undue influence; and which has some elements of unconscionable bargain, but which is not in law a case of unconscionable bargain; can by the combination of these different and inadequate claims be turned into a case that attracts relief on a vaguer basis of general equity". In *Mortgage Express v Lambert* [2016] EWCA Civ 555, Lewison LJ confirmed at [16], that where B has a power to set aside a transfer of registered land as an unconscionable transaction then (as in the case of undue influence) B has a "mere equity" that is capable of binding a successor in title to A: s.116(b) of the Land Registration Act 2002. On the facts of that case, however, any such right of B had been overreached as C's mortgage had been granted by two trustees: see [39].

[284] Note that the unconscionable transactions doctrine is independent of undue influence as it does not require a pre-existing relationship between the parties and may arise between parties who are completely unknown to each other: see *Irvani v Irvani* [2000] 1 Lloyd's Rep. 412 CA at 424, per Buxton LJ: "Undue influence is concerned with the prior relationship between the contracting parties, and with whether that was the motivation or reason for which the bargain was entered into. Unconscionable bargain is, as its title suggests, concerned with the nature and circumstances of the bargain itself, and can arise without there being any relationship, outside that of the immediate contract, between the parties". See also *Singla v Bashir* [2002] EWHC 883 (Ch) at [25].

[285] *Irvani v Irvani* [2000] 1 Lloyd's Rep. 412 at 424, per Buxton LJ adopting *Chitty on Contracts*, 29th edn (Sweet & Maxwell, 2000), Vol.1 at para.7–078; *Portman Building Society v Dusangh* [2000] 2 All E.R. (Comm) 221 at 228g–h, per Simon Brown LJ; *Mitchell v James* [2001] All E.R. (D) 116 (adopting the same passage in *Chitty*); and *Chagos Islanders v Attorney General* [2003] EWHC 2222 (QB). In *Minder Music Ltd v Sharples* [2015] EWHC 1454 (IPEC) at [34]–[35], the doctrine did not apply as it was not shown that A was aware of the full extent of B's financial difficulties and so it could not be said that A had knowingly taken advantage of that weakness.

[286] This paragraph was cited with approval by Lord Hodge in *Pakistan International Airline Corporation v Times Travel (UK) Ltd* [2021] UKSC 40, [24], noting that, for the doctrine to apply: "Unequal bargaining does not suffice; it is necessary for the claimant to show that unconscientious advantage has been taken of his or her disabling condition or circumstances". As noted by Edelman J in *Australian Securities and Investments Commission v Kobelt* [2019] HCA 18 at [282], these requirements "established a high bar for the vitiation of transactions in twentieth century equity on the ground of unconscionable conduct". As recognised by Rose J in *Libyan Investment Authority v Goldman Sachs International* [2016] EWHC 2530 (Ch) at [161], citing Ward LJ in *Portman Building Society v Dusangh* [2000] 2 All E.R. (Comm) 221, "there must be some impropriety, both in the conduct of the stronger party and in the terms of the transaction itself (though the former may often be inferred from the latter in the absence of an innocent explanation) which in the traditional phrase 'shocks the conscience of the court', and makes it against equity and good conscience of the stronger party to retain the benefit of a transaction he has unfairly obtained". The mere fact, for example, that a party has not had separate legal advice will not suffice to make a transaction unconscionable: see, e.g. *Yedina v Yedin* [2017] EWHC 3319 (Ch).

[286a] See para.12-038.

[286b] See *Stubbings v Jams 2 Pty Ltd* [2022] HCA 6 at [39] (Kiefel CJ, Keane and Gleeson JJ).

3. Application of the Test

(a) Vulnerability.

Replace first paragraph with:

8-043   B must be subject to a special disadvantage: one which affects significantly B's ability to make a judgment as to his or her best interests. Whilst the categories of vulnerability are not closed,[286c] well-established examples are illiteracy or lack of education, age and poverty.[287] The expression "poor and ignorant"[288] is understood today as meaning "member of the lower income group" and "less highly educated".[289] The question of vulnerability must be judged in the light of the transaction in question and of the documentation it involves.[290]

[286c] As noted by Eggers QC (sitting as a Deputy Judge) in *Adare Finance DAC v Yellowstone Capital Management SA* [2020] EWHC 2760 (Comm) at [69], where it is also stated that "mere impecuniosity is not sufficient".

[287] See, e.g. *Portman Building Society v Dusangh* [2000] 2 All E.R. (Comm) 221 at 228: B was "elderly, illiterate and on a very low income"; *Singla v Bashir* [2002] EWHC 883 (Ch) at [7] (where B had limited education, could not read and write and his command of English was poor); and *Chagos Islanders v Attorney General* [2003] EWHC 2222 (Q.B.) at [580]: Bs were "illiterate, ignorant or ill-educated and very poor and in real need of money". Drunkenness or addiction is not a relevant vulnerability, however: see *Irvani v Irvani* [2000] 1 Lloyd's Rep. 412. Compare the position in Australia: see *Blomley v Ryan* (1956) 99 C.L.R. 362 at 405, per Fullagar J. Note that in *Pakistan International Airline Corporation v Times Travel (UK) Ltd* [2021] UKSC 40, Lord Burrows at [77] stated that whilst, in "almost all past English cases on unconscionable bargains, B has been an individual with a mental weakness such as inexperience, confusion because of old age or emotional strain...it is not inconceivable that the relevant weakness could be a very weak bargaining position of a company; and this possibility was recognized 35 years ago by the Court of Appeal in *Alec Lobb (Garages) Ltd v Total Oil Great Britain Ltd* [1985] 1 W.L.R. 173."

[288] See *Fry v Lane* (1888) 40 Ch. D. 312: see para.8-040.

[289] *Cresswell v Potter* (1968) [1978] 1 W.L.R. 255 at 257, 258, per Megarry J; *Backhouse v Backhouse* [1978] 1 W.L.R. 243; *Credit Lyonnais Nederland NV v Burch* [1997] 1 All E.R. 144; and *Steeples v Lea* [1998] 2 F.C.R. 144.

[290] See *Chagos Islanders v Attorney General* [2003] EWHC 2222 (QB) at [545]; *Stubbings v Jams 2 Pty Ltd* [2022] HCA 6 at [40]–[42] (Kiefel CJ, Keane and Gleeson JJ). In *Jones v Morgan* [2001] EWCA Civ 995 at [40] it was held that B (who was described as "naïve, trusting and unbusiness-like") was not acting under a relevant vulnerability because he had the benefit of legal advice: Chadwick LJ stated that "it is for a solicitor to advise the naïve, the trusting or the unbusiness-like in their dealings with the more astute. In such a case the client relies on the solicitor to protect his interests; and, if the solicitor is competent and fulfils his role, the imbalance which would otherwise exist by reason of the client's naiveté, trust and lack of business experience is redressed". In *de Sena v Notaro* [2020] EWHC 1031 (Ch) at [241], HHJ Paul Matthews, using the test for an unconscionable transaction set out at 8-042, found that B was not vulnerable as "she was an experienced business woman who dealt with business transactions day in, day out, as well as being a charity trustee."

(c)   Knowing exploitation of vulnerability.

Replace paragraph with:

The jurisdiction will not be exercised unless the transaction was procured by   **8-045** behaviour that is "characterised by some morally culpability or impropriety"[294] as it involves knowingly taking advantage of B's vulnerability. It is not sufficient that the parties had unequal bargaining power or that the terms of the bargain were more favourable to one party than to another.[295] Although the terms of the transaction may be so oppressive that the court may draw an inference that A behaved unconscionably,[296] a court will not find unconscionable conduct if A was unaware that B was acting under a special vulnerability,[296a] or if, in the course of negotiating the transaction, A behaved properly (i.e. did not use unfair or illegitimate tactics nor sought to take advantage of a mistake).[297]

[294] *Boustany v Pigott* (1995) 69 P. & C.R. 298 PC at 303; relying on *Alec Lobb (Garages) Ltd v Total Oil Great Britain Ltd* [1985] 1 W.L.R. 173 CA at 183, per Dillon J. The High Court of Australia found that this test was met in *Stubbings v Jams 2 Pty Ltd* [2022] HCA 6, a case of high-interest, asset-based

lending where B had no income to meet the loans and no appreciation that he was almost certain to lose the mortgaged property.

[295] *Boustany v Pigott* (1995) 69 P. & C.R. 298 PC at 303. See too *de Sena v Notaro* [2020] EWHC 1031 (Ch) at [241] and *Adare Finance DAC v Yellowstone Capital Management SA* [2020] EWHC 2760 (Comm) at [75].

[296] *Radley v Bruno* [2006] EWHC 2888 (Ch).

[296a] For discussion of the level of knowledge required, see *Gunn v Meiners* [2022] WASC 95 at [143]–[175], holding that wilful ignorance of B's vulnerability will suffice, but mere constructive knowledge will not.

[297] The claim in *Jones v Morgan* [2001] EWCA Civ 995 failed on this basis. The judge found that A was aware that B mistakenly believed that A was obliged to provide further finance and took advantage of it. The Court of Appeal reversed this finding of fact: see [35]–[39].

CHAPTER 9

BREACH OF CONFIDENCE

1.   ORIGINS AND SCOPE OF THE JURISDICTION

1.   Origins

Replace n.1 with:

[1] For recent comprehensive examinations of the detail of the doctrine of breach of confidence, see C.   **9-001**
Phipps et al (eds), *Toulson & Phipps on Confidentiality*, 4th edn (Sweet & Maxwell, 2020); and T. Aplin
et al (eds) *Gurry on Breach of Confidence*, 2nd edn (OUP, 2012). P Stanley, *The Law of Confidentiality:
A Restatement* (Hart, 2008) is shorter but is another useful specialist work.

Replace n.4 with:

[4] As noted in T. Aplin et al (eds) *Gurry on Breach of Confidence*, 2nd edn (2012), 2.87: "*Prince Albert
v Strange* was not the first time the law had protected confidentiality – not by a long way". *Abernethy v
Hutchison* (1825) 1 H. & Tw. 28, 47 E.R. 1313 is suggested as an earlier example of the recognition in
equity of a non-contractual duty of confidence.

2.   Scope

(a)   No need for a contractual relationship or a proprietary right.

Replace paragraph with:

   The decision in *Prince Albert* did not purport to set out an underlying rationale   **9-002**
or foundation for the modern equitable action for breach of confidence. In 1851, for
example, Turner VC said in *Morison v Moat*[6] that: "in some cases it has been
referred to as property, in others as contract, and in others again … as founded upon
trust or confidence". It is clear, however, that A's use of information can be
restrained even if that use would not be a breach of any contractual duty owed by
A to B. In *Saltman Engineering Co Ltd v Campbell Engineering Co Ltd*,[7] for

example, Lord Greene MR explained that a claim for breach of confidence did not require proof that A was in breach of contract, provided that the information has "the necessary quality of confidence about it, namely it must not be something which is public property and public knowledge".[8] Similarly, it is clear that even if it were possible to think of confidential information as "property",[9] such an analysis is neither necessary nor sufficient for the action of breach of confidence.[10] In *Prince Albert v Strange*, Lord Cottenham LC held that it was not necessary for the claimant to establish a property right in the copies or impressions of the etchings since the action "by no means depends solely upon the question of property".[11] An injunction could be given simply "to prevent what this Court considers and treats as a wrong".[12]

[6] *Morison v Moat* (1851) 20 L.J. Ch. 513 at 522.

[7] *Saltman Engineering Co Ltd v Campbell Engineering Co Ltd* (1948) 65 R.P.C. 203.

[8] *Saltman Engineering Co Ltd v Campbell Engineering Co Ltd* (1948) 65 R.P.C. 203 at 215.

[9] A question which has been heavily debated in the cases and the academic literature but which may ultimately involve circular reasoning since it often depends upon what is meant by "property": see Phipps et al (eds), *Toulson & Phipps on Confidentiality*, 4th edn (2020) para.2–033; R. Dean, *The Law of Trade Secrets and Personal Secrets*, 3rd edn (Lawbook Co, 2018) at [2.140]–[2.150]. Compare *Boardman v Phipps* [1967] 2 A.C. 46 HL at 89–90, 102 and 127–128 (Lords Dilhorne, Cohen and Upjohn suggesting that information is not property) with 107 and 115 (Lords Hodson and Guest suggesting that it is). As noted in *Brake v Guy* [2021] 4 W.L.R. 71, [2021] EWHC 671 (Ch) at [218] (affirmed on appeal: [2022] EWCA Civ 235), where a claim to property in the contents of emails as information was discussed, the characterization of a particular resource as property is "context-specific".

[10] "Its rational basis does not lie in proprietary right" but in "an obligation of conscience arising from the circumstances in or through which the information was communicated or obtained": *Moorgate Tobacco Co v Phillip Morris Ltd* (1984) 156 C.L.R. 414 at 438. See too *Cadbury Schweppes v FBI Foods* [1999] S.C.R. 142 at 169; *E I Du Pont de Nemours Powder Co v Masland* 244 U.S. 100 (1917) at 102.

[11] *Prince Albert v Strange* (1849) 1 Mac. & G. 25 at 44; 41 E.R. 1171 at 1178. For a contemporary parallel, see e.g. *Shenzhen Senior Technology Material Co Ltd v Celgard LLC* [2020] EWCA Civ 1293 at [57]–[58], rejecting the claim that confidential information, or trade secrets, are necessarily property.

[12] *Prince Albert v Strange* (1849) 1 Mac. & G. 25 at 46; 41 E.R. 1171 at 1179.

(c) Extension to preventing the misuse of private information.

Replace paragraph with:

9-005   The absence of the requirement of a prior relationship of a confidence also permitted the third crucial step in the development of the modern doctrine: the recognition that it could extend to protecting B from the misuse of private information. There may of course be cases, *Prince Albert v Strange* itself provides an example, where the concern to prevent the misuse of confidential information overlaps with B's interest in privacy. It is now clear, however, there may also be protection for information to which a reasonable expectation of privacy attaches, even if such information might not otherwise be seen as confidential.[19a] In *Campbell v MGN Ltd*,[20] the defendant newspaper published an article about the attendance of Naomi Campbell, the supermodel, at a Narcotics Anonymous meeting. The article was accompanied by an unflattering photo of her leaving the premises. A majority of the House of Lords held that Ms Campbell's right to confidentiality of her personal information had been infringed by the publication of the photograph. Indeed, Lord Nicholls held that a wrong had been committed and that "the essence of the tort is better encapsulated now as misuse of private information".[21]

[19a] In *Brake v Guy* [2021] 4 W.L.R. 71, [2021] EWHC 671 (Ch) (affirmed on appeal: [2022] EWCA Civ 235) it was noted by HHJ Paul Matthews at [224] that "something that is confidential, and protected by the doctrine of breach of confidence, such as trade secrets, may not be *private* as well. It is possible (though perhaps less likely) that something may be private, but not confidential, in the sense that it relates to a person's private life, and yet is known to (say) a section of the public. And it is also possible that something may be both private *and* confidential." See too para.9-007.

[20] *Campbell v MGN Ltd* [2004] 2 A.C. 457 HL.

[21] *Campbell v MGN Ltd* [2004] 2 A.C. 457 HL at [14], not dissenting on this point.

(d) Current scope of the doctrine.

Replace paragraph with:

The fourth crucial development, occurring as a result of the "seminal"[21a] decision in *Campbell v MGN Ltd*, is the separation of a tort of misuse of private information from the equitable doctrine of breach of confidence. Whilst the tort may have developed under the guise of the equitable doctrine, it is now recognised as a "distinct cause of action from breach of confidence" and it was said by Lord Hamblen and Lord Stephens in *ZXC v Bloomberg LP* that it "rests on different legal foundations and protects different interests".[21b] The cumulative impact of these four crucial steps in the development of the modern equitable doctrine of breach of confidence is as follows. First, the doctrine can apply so as to prevent A's misuse of information even where A is under no contractual duty to B, and B has no relevant property right. Secondly, the doctrine can apply even if there is no prior relationship of confidence between A and B. Thirdly, the doctrine has been applied to information in relation to which B has a reasonable expectation of confidentiality, or a reasonable expectation of privacy. As a result, the doctrine has applied where A has revealed, or threatened to reveal, information involving marital secrets,[22] government secrets,[23] or personal information such as B's receipt of therapy for drug addiction,[24] or B's participation in sadomasochistic sex parties.[25] It has also been applied to prevent the publication of a photograph of a child in a public place.[26] Fourth, given that the independence of the tort of misuse of private information has now been recognized, it cannot be assumed that rules or principles developed in cases concerned with private information will necessarily still apply in a case of breach of confidence.

9-006

[21a] The description given in *ZXC v Bloomberg LP* [2022] UKSC 5, [2022] 2 W.L.R. 424 at [45].

[21b] [2022] UKSC 5, [2022] 2 W.L.R. 424 at [45], referring to Lord Nicholls in *Douglas v Hello! Ltd (No 3)* [2008] AC 1 at [255] and *Vidal-Hall v Google Inc* [2016] QB 1003 (CA).

[22] *Duchess of Argyll v Duke of Argyll* [1967] Ch. 302.

[23] *Attorney General v Jonathan Cape Ltd* [1976] Q.B. 752.

[24] *Campbell v MGN Ltd* [2004] 2 A.C. 457 HL.

[25] *Mosley v News Group Newspapers Ltd* [2008] EWHC 1777; [2008] E.M.L.R. 20.

[26] *Murray v Express Newspapers Plc* [2008] EWCA Civ 446; [2009] Ch. 481.

(e) The distinction between confidentiality and privacy.

Replace paragraph with:

In *PJS v News Group Newspapers Ltd*,[27] the Supreme Court reversed the decision of the Court of Appeal to lift an interlocutory injunction restraining A, a newspaper group, from publishing a story about a sexual relationship between B and a party other than B's spouse. It was argued by A that, as the information was in any case available on the internet and on social media, it could no longer be

9-007

regarded as sufficiently confidential to warrant the injunction. In answering that point, Lord Mance[28] noted a distinction between claims based on confidence and those based on privacy. In the former case, a "quantitative test, measuring what has already been disclosed with what is yet to be disclosed...[is] not only appropriate but potentially decisive".[29] Different considerations applied in a privacy claim, however, as "a quantitative approach overlooks the invasiveness and distress involved, even in repetition of private material" and the "hard copy exposure" of information in A's newspapers was "likely to add significantly to the overall intrusiveness and distress involved".[30] Lord Neuberger took a similar approach, stating that "claims based on respect for privacy and family life do not depend on confidentiality (or secrecy) alone" and stated that an injunction may be justified on the grounds of limiting intrusion and distress, even if it can no longer preserve secrecy. He thus affirmed the reasoning in a number of first instance decisions to the effect that intrusion may be relied on to justify an injunction "despite a significant loss of confidentiality".[31] As recognised in *ZXC v Bloomberg LP*, "[i]nformation may be private but not confidential, or confidential but not private. To prove that information is private it is not necessary to show that it is confidential. Often, however, confidentiality and privacy will overlap and confidentiality may well be relevant to whether there is a reasonable expectation of privacy." The courts apply a two stage approach to a claim for misuse of private information, asking at the first stage if B has a "reasonable expectation of privacy in the relevant information" and if so, whether that expectation is "outweighed by the countervailing interest of [A's] right to freedom of expression."[31a] In the *ZXC* case itself, the Supreme Court held that there is a "legitimate starting point"[31b] that where B is under criminal investigation but has not yet been charged, B has a reasonable expectation of privacy in respect of information relating to the investigation.

[27] *PJS v News Group Newspapers Ltd* [2016] A.C. 1081 SC.

[28] With whom Lord Neuberger, Baroness Hale and Lord Reed agreed.

[29] *PJS v News Group Newspapers Ltd* [2016] A.C. 1081 SC at [25]; citing *Sunday Times v United Kingdom (No.2)* (1992) 14 E.H.R.R. 229 at [54]–[55].

[30] *PJS v News Group Newspapers Ltd* [2016] A.C. 1081 SC at [25]. See too at [34]–[37].

[31] *PJS v News Group Newspapers Ltd* [2016] A.C. 1081 SC at [59]–[60], where the first instance decisions are listed. See too Edelman J in *Farm Transparency International Ltd v State of New South Wales* [2022] HCA 23 at [231]: "[i]t may be that personal information should be protected not merely where the information is secret, but also where further disclosure would compromise foundational interests of human dignity and autonomy."

[31a] *ZXC v Bloomberg LP* [2022] UKSC 5, [2022] 2 W.L.R. 424 at [47].

[31b] *ZXC v Bloomberg LP* [2022] UKSC 5, [2022] 2 W.L.R. 424 at [144]–[146].

(f)   Impact of the Human Rights Act 1998.

Replace second paragraph with:

9-008   This does not mean, of course, that all breach of confidence cases necessarily involve a balancing of art.8 and art.10 rights. First, information may be confidential even if it is not private[37]; secondly, confidential information may be misused by means other than communication by A[38]; thirdly, a disclosure of information may be justified in the public interest even if the disclosure does not involve an exercise of A's freedom of expression.[39] Nonetheless, there will be cases where the two rights do conflict, and the approach then to be adopted was set out by Lord Steyn[40]:

"First, neither article has *as such* precedence over the other. Secondly, where the values under the two articles are in conflict, an intense focus on the comparative importance of the specific rights being claimed in the individual case is necessary. Thirdly, the justifications for interfering with or restricting each right must be taken into account. Finally, the proportionality test must be applied to each."

[37] *Douglas v Hello! Ltd* [2008] 1 A.C. 1 at [255], per Lord Nicholls: "a trade secret may be protected as confidential information even though no question of personal privacy is involved". For consideration of when such commercial information may be confidential, see, e.g. *Faccenda Chicken Ltd v Fowler* [1987] Ch. 117 CA; *Lansing Linde Ltd v Kerr* [1991] 1 W.L.R. 251; as applied in, e.g. *Personal Management Solutions Ltd v Brakes Bros Ltd* [2014] EWHC 3495 (QB) at [191]–[196]; and *Marathon Asset Management LLP v Seddon* [2017] EWHC 300 (Comm); [2017] I.C.R. 791 at [115]–[117]. See too *Trailfinders Ltd v Travel Counsellors Ltd* [2020] EWHC 591 (IPEC), where HHJ Hacon at [27] drew on the definition of "trade secret" in Art.2(1) of the Trade Secrets Directive 2016/943, implemented by the Trade Secrets (Enforcement, etc) Regulations 2018, as providing "the best guide to the distinction between information which is confidential and that which is not". An appeal against that decision was dismissed: [2021] EWCA Civ 38. For discussion of the special rules now applying to trade secrets, and their relation to the general rules on breach of confidence, see *Shenzhen Senior Technology Material Co Ltd v Celgard LLC* [2020] EWCA Civ 1293 at [20]–[29].

[38] See para.9-018.

[39] As noted by P. Stanley, *The Law of Confidentiality: A Restatement* (2008) p.88: "it seems strained to analyse the conduct of a person who wishes to report suspicions in confidence to, say, the police or a specific authority under the rubric of 'freedom of expression'".

[40] *In Re S* [2005] 1 A.C. 593 at [17]; summarising the effect of *Campbell v MGN Ltd* [2004] 2 A.C. 457 HL, discussed at para.9-017.

(g) Future of the doctrine.

Replace paragraph with:

The Supreme Court's recognition in *ZXC v Bloomberg LP*[40a] of the distinction between the equitable doctrine of breach of confidence and the tort of misuse of private information is consistent with the view that a single doctrine of breach of confidence is ill-equipped to deal both with misuse of confidential information and misuse of private information, and that, therefore, the two strands should be separated and allowed to develop independently.[41] The treatment in this chapter will focus on breach of confidence, but given the origins of the tort of misuse of private information within that equitable doctrine, privacy issues will be considered where relevant. In *Douglas v Hello (No.3) Ltd*,[42] for example, the Court of Appeal expressed its discomfort at being "required to shoehorn within the cause of action for breach of confidence claims for publication of unauthorised photographs of a private occasion". Certainly, when applying the doctrine, a court will necessarily take account of the particular context of the parties' dispute, and the particular interest of B (confidentiality or privacy) that is at stake. This can be seen from the approach of the Supreme Court in *PJS v News Group Newspapers Ltd*,[43] where, as noted at para.9-007, a clear distinction was made between the protection of confidential information and the prevention of intrusion.

9-009

[40a] *ZXC v Bloomberg LP* [2022] UKSC 5, [2022] 2 W.L.R. 424 at [45].

[41] For arguments to this effect see e.g. T. Aplin, "The Future of Breach of Confidence and the Protection of Privacy" (2007) 7 Oxford University Commonwealth Law Journal 137; C. Phipps et al (eds), *Toulson & Phipps on Confidentiality*, 4th edn (Sweet & Maxwell, 2020), ch.7. In *Sicri v Associated Newspapers Ltd* [2021] 4 W.L.R. 9, [2020] EWHC 3541 (QB), it was stated at [6] that: "Misuse of private information is part of the 'confidentiality genus', but breach of confidence and misuse of private information are separate and distinct wrongs." Note too the view of Edelman J in *Farm Transparency International Ltd v State of New South Wales* [2022] HCA 23 at [225] that breach of confidence is "an overarching doctrine" and in fact encompasses three overlapping categories concerning information that

is private (in the sense of not publicly available): private information that arises in the course of a relationship of confidence; private information that is secret; and private information that is personal in the sense that it concerns the dignity of an individual.

[42] *Douglas v Hello (No.3) Ltd* [2006] Q.B. 125 CA at [53].

[43] *PJS v News Group Newspapers Ltd* [2016] A.C. 26 SC.

After "are actions, including", add:
   now the tort of misuse of private information, as well as

(h)   Nature of the cause of action: is breach of confidence a tort?

Replace n.54 with:

9-010   [54] M. Jones (eds), *Clerk and Lindsell on Tort*, 23rd edn (Sweet & Maxwell, 2020), Ch.26.

Replace second paragraph with:
   The application of the doctrine to misuse of private information certainly invites comparison with torts that can also be said to be founded on the need to protect B's autonomy, such as false imprisonment, battery or defamation. Given the recognition now of a distinct tort of misuse of private information, the question is whether the separate doctrine of breach of confidence should also be analysed as recognizing when A has committed, or is threatening to commit, a wrong against B. It may well be that the doctrine was originally seen as recognising not a duty of A owed to B, but rather A's disability, as against B, to make use of particular information. In that way, it could be seen as identifying a specific sense in which it is unconscionable for A to insist, as against B, on a strict legal right (in this case, a liberty to use information). In the same way that the regulation of fiduciary misconduct may be seen to have shifted from a disability-based to a duty-based approach,[55] however, it seems that, following the analysis of Lord Goff in the *Spycatcher* case,[56] and the application of the doctrine to cases of misuse of private information,[57] it is now possible to identify a duty of confidence, and so to say that A commits a wrong when breaching such a duty.[57a] The question then is whether special rules should apply to equitable wrongs, or whether those wrongs should be treated in the same way as common law wrongs (i.e. torts). In *The Racing Partnership Ltd v SIS Ltd*, Arnold LJ stated that, following *Vidal-Hall v Google*, "breach of confidence and misuse of private information are two separate and distinct causes of action which rest on different legal foundations and protect different interests, and hence a claim for misuse of private information is 'made in tort' even though a claim for breach of confidence is an equitable one."[57b]

[55] See para.7-051. For further discussion see, e.g. C. Mitchell, "Equitable Compensation for Breach of Fiduciary Duty" (2013) 66 C.L.P. 307.

[56] *Attorney General v Guardian Newspapers (No.2)* [1990] 1 A.C. 109 at 281, per Lord Goff. Cited with approval in *Campbell v MGN Ltd* [2004] 2 A.C. 457 HL at [47], per Lord Hoffmann.

[57] In *PJS v News Group Newspapers Ltd* [2016] A.C. 1081 SC, for example, Lord Mance at [32]–[33], [38] and [44] refers to the "tort of invasion of privacy", or to "tortious invasion of privacy". In *TLT v Secretary of State for the Home Department* [2018] EWCA Civ 2217; [2018] 4 W.L.R. 101, for example, a claim for misuse of private information was referred to consistently by Gross LJ as a "tort" claim (e.g. at [15], [18], [26]), although in the context of the case nothing turned on that classification.

[57a] Edelman J in *Farm Transparency International Ltd v State of New South Wales* [2022] HCA 23 at [225] refers to the "equitable wrong of breach of confidence", including within its scope restrictions on private information arising in the course of a relationship of confidence.

[57b] [2021] Ch 233, [2020] EWCA Civ 1300 at [70].

Replace third paragraph with:

The question is of practical relevance when particular rules are said to depend on the classification of B's claim as arising in tort. Care must be taken, however, in considering the particular context in which the question arises. For example, art.5(3) of the Brussels Regulation allows for an exception to the general rule that A should be sued in the place of A's domicile. In "matters relating to tort, delict or quasi-delict", A can instead be sued in "the courts of the place where the harmful event occurred". As has been noted by the Court of Appeal, the term "tort, delict or quasi-delict" must be given an "autonomous" meaning,[58] and so the classification of B's claim as a matter of English law is not decisive. On one view, for example, the term should be given a limited meaning as it is used as a means to justify bringing proceedings outside the courts of A's place of domicile. On another view, the term, by contrast to art.5(1), should refer to any non-contractual claim involving a "harmful event".[59] At one point, the Court of Appeal's starting point, when considering the possible application of art.5(3) to a breach of confidence claim, was that it was clear, as a matter of English law, that a breach of confidence claim "does not arise in tort";[60] however, it is clear that, at least in a case focused on invasion of privacy, or involving an act of unfair competition,[60a] such an approach is now unlikely to be adopted.[61]

[58] *Kitechnology BV v Unicor GmbH Plastmaschinen* [1995] F.S.R. 765 CA at 777–778 per Evans LJ.

[59] In *Kleinwort Benson v Glasgow City Council* [1999] 1 A.C. 153 HL, it was found that art.5(3) does not apply to unjust enrichment claims as, although they are not contractual, they do not depend on there being a "harmful event". In *Douglas v Hello! Ltd (No.3)* [2006] Q.B. 125 at [97] the Court of Appeal suggested, when considering the question of proper law rather than of jurisdiction under the Regulation, that a breach of confidence claim could be categorised as a "restitutionary claim for unjust enrichment". The receipt of a benefit by A at B's expense is not however a requirement of a breach of confidence action, so that analysis can be doubted. Indeed, the suggestion in *Douglas* was based on that of *Dicey & Morris*, and the current edition of that work takes a different view, preferring to regard the claim arising in *Douglas* as involving "issues in tort" and so falling within Pt III of the Private International Law (Miscellaneous Provisions) Act 1995: see L. Collins et al (eds), *Dicey, Morris & Collins: The Conflict of Laws*, 15th edn (Sweet & Maxwell, 2012) at para.34–092.

[60] *Kitechnology BV v Unicor GmbH Plastmaschinen* [1995] F.S.R. 765 at 777, per Evans LJ. See too (in the context of a claim for exemplary damages) *Mosley v News Group Newspapers Ltd* [2008] EWHC 1777; [2008] E.M.L.R. 20 at [190], per Eady J, distinguishing tort from "breach of confidence or any other equitable or restitutionary claim".

[60a] Within the meaning of art.6 of the Rome II Regulation, applying to choice of law: as a result, art.4 then applies even though, as noted by Arnold LJ in *Shenzhen Senior Technology Material Co Ltd v Celgard LLC* [2020] EWCA Civ 1293 at [51], art.4 "is concerned with the law applicable to a non-contractual obligation arising out of a tort/delict, and, as a matter of English law, claims for breach of equitable obligations of confidence are not claims in tort". As noted in *Fetch.ai Ltd v Persons Unknown Category A* [2021] EWHC 2254 (Comm) at [12], this reasoning is based on the application of art.6 to anti-competitive practices and conduct and so it "does not…lead to the conclusion that all breach of confidence cases are capable of coming within art.6."

[61] In *Vidal-Hall v Google Inc* [2016] Q.B. 1003 CA, for example, the question was whether a breach of confidence/misuse of private information claim was a claim "made in tort" where damage had been sustained within the jurisdiction, so that service out of the jurisdiction was permitted by para.3.1(9) of Practice Direction 6B, supplementing Pt 6 of the Civil Procedure Rules. The Court of Appeal drew a distinction between the breach of confidence and misuse of private information claims, finding that the latter had no inherently equitable characteristics and that there was no good reason to regard the claim as not arising in tort, stating at [48] that: "It would seem an odd and adventitious result for the defendant, if the historical accident of the division between equity and the common law resulted in the claimants in the present case being unable to serve their claims out of the jurisdiction". That approach was approved in *Gulati v MGN Ltd* [2016] 2 W.L.R. 1217: see, per Arden LJ at [88]. Note too the distinction between confidence-focused and privacy-focused claims drawn by the Supreme Court in *PJS v News*

Group Newspapers Ltd [2016] A.C. 1081 SC and Lord Mance's references at [32]–[33], [38] and [44] to the "tort of invasion of privacy", or to "tortious invasion of privacy". In *JQL v NTP* [2020] EWHC 1349 (QB), in the context of the publication of confidential and private information, HHJ Lewis at [133] referred to both breach of confidence and misuse of private information as torts.

2. THE TEST AND ITS APPLICATION

9-013   *Change title of paragraph:*

(b)   Reasonable expectation that the information is confidential

Replace paragraph with:

Factors formerly relevant to the question of the "necessary quality of confidence" can now be seen as going to the reasonableness of any expectation of B. For example, it was formerly said that information could not be confidential if it was freely available.[78] However, it has been recognised that such information, such as a photographic image of a child,[79] or an adult,[80] in a public place may be protected by the tort of misuse of private information as:

> "Privacy can be invaded by further publication of information or photographs already disclosed to the public."[81]

[78] *James v James* (1872) 41 L.J. Ch. 353; *Reuters Telegram Co v Byron* (1874) 43 L.J. Ch. 661; *Saltman Engineering Co Ltd v Campbell Engineering Co Ltd* (1948) 65 R.P.C. 203 at 215; [1963] 3 All E.R. 413 at 415, per Lord Greene MR; *Seager v Copydex (No.1)* [1967] 1 W.L.R. 923 CA at 932, per Lord Denning MR; *Coco v A N Clark (Engineers) Ltd* [1969] R.P.C. 41 at 49, per Megarry J; *Woodward v Hutchins* [1977] 1 W.L.R. 760; *O Mustad & Son v Dosen (Note)* [1964] 1 W.L.R. 109. Note that information will not lose the quality of confidence simply because it is known to a small number of people: see, e.g. *AB v Sunday Newspapers (t/a The Sunday World)* [2014] NICA 58 at [26]; and *Warwickshire CC v Matalia* [2015] EWHC B4 (Ch) at [35] (affirmed on appeal: [2017] EWCA Civ 991). See too *Suppipat v Siam Commercial Bank Public Company Ltd* [2022] EWHC 381: a reasonable expectation of confidence arose even though the material had been disclosed in foreign litigation. This is also the case where information is merely used by A, rather than being published by A: *Kerry Ingredients Ltd v Bakkavor Group Ltd* [2016] EWHC 2448 (Ch) at [62] (Newey J). Similarly, information is not rendered non-confidential simply because, with a significant amount of work, that information could be acquired through reverse engineering: ibid. at [67]. In *The Racing Partnership Ltd v SIS Ltd* [2020] EWCA Civ 1300, members of the Court of Appeal took different views as to whether particular racing information, in the very brief period before it became publicly available, could be regarded as confidential: see Arnold LJ at [65]-[77] and contrast with the view of Lewison LJ (with whom Philipps LJ agreed) at [179]-[189]. For discussion see e.g. Saw (2021) 52 Int Rev of IP and Comp Law 752.

[79] *Murray v Express Newspapers Plc* [2008] EWCA Civ 446; [2009] Ch. 481; *Tchenguiz v Imerman* [2010] EWCA Civ 908 at [66]. For discussion of the approach to be taken when considering the art.8 rights of a child, see *Weller v Associated Newspapers Ltd* [2016] 1 W.L.R. 1541 CA. It was stated at [40], for example, that, "although a child's right is not a trump card in the balancing exercise", it may require "very powerful" art.10 reasons to permit publication where this would be harmful to a child. The importance of the interests of children in deciding whether relief by way of interim injunction is available was emphasized in *PJS v News Group Newspapers Ltd* [2016] A.C. 1081 at [37] (Lord Mance) and [74]–[75] (Baroness Hale).

[80] *Campbell v MGN Ltd* [2004] 2 A.C. 457 HL; *Theakston v MGN Ltd* [2002] EWHC 137 (QB).

[81] *Douglas v Hello! Ltd* [2008] 1 A.C. 1 at [255], per Lord Nicholls.

Replace final paragraph with:

In relation to the tort of misuse of private information, the line between information[81a] which is reasonably expected to be private and that which is not can be a very fine one[81b] and it may depend upon the nature of the medium in which the information is held. In *PJS v News Group Newspapers Ltd*,[82] the fact that the information was available on websites and elsewhere outside the jurisdiction did not prevent an interim injunction's being upheld in order to prevent the intrusion and distress (not only to B and B's partner but also to their children)[83] that would result from publication in newspapers and websites in the jurisdiction.[84] Photos of a well-known personality in a brothel, or leaving a Narcotics Anonymous meeting, have been considered to be confidential even though publication of textual information of the same activities was held not to be a breach of confidence.[85] It was also formerly said that B does not have a right to protection of information which is "useless", such as a betting system based on the age of the moon,[86] because "the duty of confidence applies neither to useless information, nor to trivia".[87] It is nonetheless possible that B may have a reasonable expectation of privacy in relation to wholly useless information as to B's private life: if so, misuse of such information may constitute the tort of misuse of private information.[88]

[81a] In *Ukoumunne v University of Birmingham* [2020] EWHC 2927 (IPEC), it was stated at [36] that opinions expressed by a student in very general terms could not constitute "information with a quality of confidence such as to attract protection in law".

[81b] Note that B's intention to publish information at a later date is not fatal to B's claim, whether put on the grounds of breach of confidence or of misuse of private information: see *Duchess of Sussex v Associated Newspapers Ltd* [2022] EWCA Civ 1810.

[82] *PJS v News Group Newspapers Ltd* [2016] A.C. 1081 SC.

[83] As to the relevance of the children's position, see in particular Baroness Hale at [72]–[78].

[84] Lord Mance stated at [35] that it was necessary to give due weight to "the qualitative difference in intrusiveness and distress likely to be involved in what is now proposed by way of unrestricted publication by the English media in hard copy as well as on their own internet sites". It is noteworthy that, in reaching the same conclusion (at [61]–[65]), Lord Neuberger distinguished at [57]–[58] between cases of confidentiality and of privacy: "If PJS's case was simply based on confidentiality (or secrecy), then, while I would not characterise his claim for a permanent injunction as hopeless, it would have substantial difficulties ... However, claims based on respect for privacy and family life do not depend on confidentiality (or secrecy) alone". See too para.9-007. Lord Toulson (dissenting) took a different view on the impact of newspaper publication, stating at [89] that: "If the information is in wide, general circulation from whatever source or combination of sources, I do not see that it should make a significant difference whether the medium of the intended publication is the internet, print journalism, or broadcast journalism. The world of public information is interactive and indivisible".

[85] *Theakston v MGN Ltd* [2002] EWHC 137 (QB); *Campbell v MGN Ltd* [2004] 2 A.C. 457 HL.

[86] *McNichol v Sportsman's Book Stores* (1930) McG. C. C. 116.

[87] *Attorney General v Guardian Newspapers (No.2)* [1990] 1 A.C. 109 HL at 282, per Lord Goff.

[88] *Stephens v Avery* [1988] 1 Ch. 449; *Barrymore v News Group Newspapers Ltd* [1997] F.S.R. 600; *McKennit v Ash* [2008] Q.B. 73 at [21]. cf. *Attorney General v Guardian Newspapers (No.2)* [1990] 1 A.C. 109 at 282.

(c) Knowledge of the confidentiality of the information.

Replace second paragraph with:

It is therefore clear that the doctrine can apply if A has actual knowledge of the circumstances giving rise to B's reasonable expectation of confidentiality or privacy, of if A would have had such knowledge but for A's wilful blindness.[91] If, on the facts actually known to A, a reasonable person would have regarded the information as confidential, then it seems that the doctrine can apply.[92] The more difficult case is where A's actual knowledge or wilful blindness does not extend to facts on which a reasonable person would draw such a conclusion, but a reasonable person in A's position would have discovered such facts. If liability is to be imposed in such a case, it must have an objective element, and so may be harder to reconcile with the underlying concept of unconscionability. There are, nonetheless, a number of state-

9-014

ments of high authority to the effect that A may be liable in such a case,[93] and it has recently been stated that "if the circumstances are such as to bring it to the notice of a reasonable person in the position of [A] that the information, or some of it, may be confidential to another, then the reasonable person's response may be to make enquiries. Whether the reasonable person would make enquiries, and if so what enquiries, is inevitably context- and fact-dependent. If the reasonable person would make enquiries, but the recipient abstains from doing so, then an obligation of confidentiality will arise."[94] It is therefore wrong to think that nothing less than blind-eye knowledge by A will suffice.[95] In some contexts at least, a reasonable person would make enquiries if he or she was aware that some of the information was "likely" to be confidential.[98]

[91] See, e.g. *Attorney General v Guardian Newspapers Ltd (No.2)* [1990] 1 A.C. 109 at 281, per Lord Goff.

[92] See, e.g. *Campbell v MGN Ltd* [2004] 2 A.C. 457 HL; *Vestergaard Frandsen A/S v Bestnet Europe Ltd* [2013] UKSC 31; [2013] 1 W.L.R. 1556 at [23]; *Brake v Guy* [2021] 4 W.L.R. 71, [2021] EWHC 671 (Ch) [229] (HHJ Paul Matthews) (affirmed on appeal: [2022] EWCA Civ 235): "because breach of confidence is an equitable doctrine resting on conscience, the question is not whether the claimant subjectively intended to impose confidentiality on the defendant, but whether a reasonable person in the shoes of the defendant would have appreciated this". Conversely, of course, if a reasonable person in A's position would not have regarded the information as confidential then no liability will arise, even if a more sophisticated legal analysis would have led to the conclusion that the information was confidential: as noted by Lewison LJ in *The Racing Partnership Ltd v SIS Ltd* [2020] EWCA Civ 1300 at [206], it would be wrong to attribute to A an inappropriate "degree of legal knowledge and analytical skills."

[93] See, e.g. *Campbell v MGN Ltd* [2004] 2 A.C. 457 HL at [14], per Lord Nicholls: referring to A's acquiring information which A "knows or ought to know" is reasonably to be regarded as confidential; at [44]–[45] per Lord Hoffmann, referring to A's "actual or constructive" knowledge of the confidentiality.

[94] *Travel Counsellors Ltd v Trailfinders Ltd* [2021] EWCA Civ 38 at [28], where Arnold LJ builds on his analysis in *Primary Group (UK) Ltd v Royal Bank of Scotland* [2014] EWHC 1082 (Ch) at [237]. In the earlier case, even with the application of an objective test, no breach of confidence was made out: see [258]–[260]. However, in the later case, it was found that a reasonable party in A's position would have made enquiries and thereby discovered the confidentiality of the information, and a breach of confidence was established.

[95] That submission was rejected by Arnold LJ in *Travel Counsellors Ltd v Trailfinders Ltd* [2021] EWCA Civ 38 at [29]. It was noted there however that "the position may be different where the issue is not one of primary liability for misuse of confidential information, but accessory liability for misuse by another person. In the latter case, actual knowledge or blind-eye knowledge may be required: *Vestergaard Frandsen A/S v Bestnet Europe Ltd* [2013] UKSC 31; [2013] 1 W.L.R. 1556 at [40]–[43] and *Primary Group (UK) Ltd v Royal Bank of Scotland* [2014] EWHC 1082 (Ch) at [250]." See too 9-010.

[98] *Travel Counsellors Ltd v Trailfinders Ltd* [2021] EWCA Civ 38 at [31]. Note in *Al Fayed v Commissioner of Police for the Metropolis* [2002] EWCA Civ 780 at [16], in the context of receipt of information subject to legal professional privilege and mistakenly disclosed, it was said that A does not have to make enquiries to test any doubts as to whether disclosure was mistaken, and that a duty not to use the information arises only where it is "obvious" that the information was disclosed by mistake. It is possible to see this as simply an application of the general test to the specific context of adversarial litigation. As suggested by P. Stanley, *The Law of Confidentiality: A Restatement* (2008) p.30 an objective test must be applied "sensibly and with regard to its context".

(d) Knowledge of confidentiality where C is a third party.

Replace first paragraph with:

9-015   In a case where A, in breach of a duty of confidence to B, imparts information to C, the law as to when C is also subject to a duty of confidence is less than clear. It has been suggested, correctly it is submitted, that this lack of clarity stems from a failure to distinguish between C's being subject to a primary or a secondary liability.[101] As noted above, the abandonment of the need for a pre-existing relationship of confidence means that C may be primarily liable to B if C has or gains knowledge of the fact that the information obtained by C is confidential. This is the case if, for example, a stranger picks up a diary dropped by B in the street, and there is no reason why the test should differ if C instead receives information as a result of A's breach of confidence. It is therefore submitted that the test to be applied in determining whether C has the necessary knowledge should be the same as discussed at para.9-014.[102]

[101] See *Primary Group (UK) Ltd v Royal Bank of Scotland* [2014] EWHC 1082 (Ch) at [231], per Arnold J; and P. Stanley, *The Law of Confidentiality: A Restatement* (2008) pp.26–30. See too Edelman J in *Farm Transparency International Ltd v State of New South Wales* [2022] HCA 23 at [238], suggesting that different approaches may be required in different categories of breach of confidence (as to which see para.9-009, fn.41).

[102] See *Transport Salaried Staffs Association v Persons Unknown* [2022] EWHC 1497 (QB) at [15], where the test set out in *Travel Counsellors Ltd v Trailfinders Ltd* [2021] EWCA Civ 38 was applied when considering if C, a publisher of a website, could be required to remove a video posted by A where A was in breach of a contractual duty of confidence to B. See too P. Stanley, *The Law of Confidentiality: A Restatement* (2008) p.28: "It would be bizarre indeed if the person who acquired information from a third party who was acting in breach of confidence was in a better position than someone who acquired information directly or without a breach by a third party".

Replace second paragraph with:

The position is, however, different if C has not made, or does not threaten to make, any use of the information. In such a case, if any liability is to be imposed on C, it must be a secondary liability based on C's involvement in A's breach of confidence. This distinction was made by Lord Neuberger in *Vestergaard Frandsen A/S v Bestnet Europe Ltd*[103]:

> "[W]hile a recipient of confidential information may be said to be primarily liable in a case of its misuse, a person who assists her in the [breach] can be liable, in a secondary sense ... as I see it, consistently with the approach of equity in this area, she would normally have to know that the recipient was abusing confidential information. Knowledge in this context would of course not be limited to her actual knowledge, and it would include what is sometimes called 'blind-eye knowledge'. The best analysis of what that involves is to be found in *Royal Brunei Airlines Sdn Bhd v Tan*."[104]

Whilst C's potential secondary liability for assistance in A's breach of a duty of confidence is thus limited to situations where C can be said to have acted dishonestly,[105] there is no need for such dishonesty in a case where B seeks to impose a primary liability on C, by showing that C him or herself misused the confidential information.[106]

[103] *Vestergaard Frandsen A/S v Bestnet Europe Ltd* [2013] UKSC 31; [2013] W.L.R. 1556 at [26].

[104] *Royal Brunei Airlines Sdn Bhd v Tan* [1995] 2 A.C. 378 PC.

[105] Note too that C may also be liable on the basis of a common design if C shares "with the other party, or parties, to the design, each of the features of the design that make it wrongful":*Vestergaard Frandsen A/S v Bestnet Europe Ltd* [2013] UKSC 31; [2013] 1 W.L.R. 1556 at [34], per Lord Neuberger. Where C is A's employer, it seems that C may also be vicariously liable, in a suitable case, for a breach of confidence committed by A in the course of A's employment: see, e.g. *Vestergaard Frandsen A/S v Bestnet Europe Ltd* [2013] UKSC 31; [2013] 1 W.L.R. 1556 at [34], per Lord Neuberger at [27]; *Primary Group (UK) Ltd v Royal Bank of Scotland* [2014] EWHC 1082 (Ch) at [249] per Arnold J. See too *Axon v Ministry of Defence* [2016] EWHC 787 (QB) at [95], where it was found that, had A's employee committed the "tort" of misusing private information, then it would have been a suitable case to find her employer vicariously liable. In *Various Claimants v WM Morrison Supermarkets Plc* [2018] EWCA Civ

2339; [2019] Q.B. 772 it was held that a claim based on an employer's vicarious liability for breach of confidence or misuse of personal information was not expressly or impliedly excluded by the operation of the Data Protection Act 1998 ([148]–[162]). On appeal, the Supreme Court ([2020] UKSC 12) reversed the finding that vicarious liability arose on the facts of the case, but agreed (at [54]-[55]) that the 1998 Act did not exclude liability for misuse of private information and breach of confidence. In *Ali v Luton BC* [2022] EWHC 132 (QB), the defendant local authority was not vicariously liable for a misuse of private information by an employee pursuing a "frolic of her own" (ibid [40]–[43]).

[106] This distinction, unfortunately, was not clearly made by the Court of Appeal in *Thomas v Pearce* [2000] F.S.R. 718 and, as a result, the threshold set for liability in that case was, it is submitted, too high, as the possibility of the defendant's being primarily liable was overlooked. In *Primary Group (UK) Ltd v Royal Bank of Scotland* [2014] EWHC 1082 (Ch) at [234], Arnold J described the decision in *Thomas v Pearce* as "no longer good law on the question of the test to be applied with regard to the imposition of an equitable obligation of confidence in light of the subsequent authorities, and in particular *Campbell v MGN Ltd* [2004] 2 A.C. 457 HL". In *Personal Management Solutions Ltd v Brakes Bros Ltd* [2014] EWHC 3495 (QB), where C1 and C2 had also made use of data obtained by A, reference was made to *Royal Brunei Airlines Sdn Bhd v Tan* [1995] 2 A.C. 378 (PC) and the test applied was said (see [173]–[177]) to turn on whether it would be "unconscionable" for C1 and C2 to make use of that data. That part of the decision is, however, better seen as dealing with a primary liability of C1 and C2: indeed, it was found, following *Primary Group (UK) Ltd v Royal Bank of Scotland Plc* [2014] EWHC 1082 (Ch), that the test was objective, and so the reasoning on this point in *Personal Management Solutions Ltd v Brakes Bros Ltd* can be seen simply as resting on the fact that the equitable jurisdiction to restrain a breach of confidence is ultimately founded on the need to prevent unconscionable conduct: see, e.g. *Vestergaard Frandsen A/S v Bestnet Europe Ltd* [2013] UKSC 31; [2013] 1 W.L.R. 1556 at [25], per Lord Neuberger.

(e) Maintenance of confidentiality is not contrary to the public interest.

Replace first paragraph with:

9-016   Although this requirement has sometimes been described as a "defence of public interest"[107] it is perhaps better regarded as an element of the action for breach of confidence: "the true doctrine is that there is no confidence in an iniquity".[108] The public interest is a malleable term and the authorities do not speak with a single voice on the application of this requirement. The strictest approach would confine the public interest to information which, if suppressed, would be "destructive of the country or its people including matters medically dangerous to the public".[109] It is likely, however, that the public interest will extend to all cases where the maintenance of confidence would suppress the detection, or permit the commission, of crime.[110] As noted at para.9-008, in some cases, but not all, there will be an overlap between the issue of public interest and a consideration of A's right to freedom of expression under art.10 of the European Convention on Human Rights.[110a]

[107] *Beloff v Pressdram Ltd* [1973] 1 All E.R. 241 at 260, per Ungoed Thomas J.

[108] *Gartside v Outram* (1857) 26 L.J. Ch. (NS) 113 at 114, per Sir William Page Wood VC, cited in *Smethurst v Commissioner of the Australian Federal Police* (2020) 376 ALR 575, 647. See too (in the context of the tort of misuse of private information), *Brake v Guy* [2022] EWCA Civ 235 at [70] where it is said that, rather than treating B's iniquity as a defence, B's conduct should be taken into account at an earlier stage in deciding if there was a reasonable expectation of privacy. In *I-Admin (Singapore) Pte Ltd v Hong Ying Ting* [2020] SGA 32 at [61], the Singapore Court of Appeal approaches the question slightly differently, by asking if A's belief that there was a strong public interest in disclosure means that A's conscience is not affected.

[109] *Beloff v Pressdram Ltd* [1973] 1 All E.R. 241 at 260, per Ungoed Thomas J.

[110] *Tournier v National Provincial and Union Bank of England* [1924] 1 K.B. 461 CA at 480–481, 483–484, 486. In *Lachaux v Independent Print Ltd* [2015] EWHC 3677 (QB), it was noted by Sir Michael Tugendhat at [42] that the "public interest in the emergence of the truth" is "commonly held to override what would otherwise be a duty of confidentiality", although it is not of itself a sufficient public interest where the document is subject to legal professional privilege. See too *Glenn v Watson* [2017] 4

W.L.R. 48 at [8]: A cannot be prevented from using confidential information to answer relevant questions at a trial. This does not mean, however, that A is free to reveal the matters before trial: ibid. at [9] and [39]. See too *Re C (a child)* [2015] EWFC 79 at [75], where Sir James Munby emphasised that a desire by a doctor to challenge allegations made by a patient in the press does not necessarily justify disclosure of confidential medical records. In *Heythrop Zoological Gardens v Captive Animals Protection Society* [2016] EWHC 1370 (Ch) at [27]–[29], Birss J regarded the public interest as relevant when considering an application for an interim injunction to prevent publication of photographs of animals at a zoo, as "[o]n the face of it, the material is relevant to a matter of current public debate about the use of animals in entertainment and possible inhumane treatment". The term "public interest" thus extended beyond the boundaries of criminal behaviour. See too *Axon v Ministry of Defence* [2016] EWHC 787 (QB) at [104], where a public interest argument was relevant to disclosure of "gravely serious" misconduct in performing a public function, even if such conduct was not criminal. In *Brake v Guy* [2021] EWHC 670 (Ch) at [82] (affirmed on appeal: [2022] EWCA Civ 235), the "considerable public interest in the law's insolvency systems working as intended" was noted where it was claimed that the information showed an insolvent debtor hiding assets. In *Brevan Howard Asset Management v Reuters Ltd* [2017] EWHC 644 (QB) (affirmed on appeal: [2017] EWCA Civ 950), the court considered an attempt to argue that it was in the public interest to disclose information provided by a hedge fund to potential investors. The argument was rejected and it was noted by Popplewell J at [44], for example, that there was no question of publication being required "to correct a false impression created by [B], to reveal any illegal or immoral dealing, to expose hypocrisy or to expose some improper practice or concealment, nor even to demonstrate incompetence".

[110a] See e.g. *Brake v Guy* [2021] EWHC 670 (Ch) at [30] (affirmed on appeal: [2022] EWCA Civ 235).

(f) Preservation of A's freedom of expression.

Replace paragraph with:

The doctrine of breach of confidence must not be applied in such a way as to interfere unjustifiably with A's right to freedom of expression, protected by art.10 of the European Convention on Human Rights. In *Campbell v MGN Ltd*, for example, Lord Nicholls noted that the first instance judge had gone astray by having "put nothing in the scales under article 10 when striking the balance between articles 8 and 10".[111] As noted at para.9-008, there is a clear procedure to be followed when a court considers the interaction of those two rights; it seems that procedure is relevant not only in cases of the misuse of private information, but also in breach of confidence more generally. The facts of *Campbell* itself provide a useful example.[112] The House of Lords took into account, on the one hand, the fact that the story concerned a public figure who had previously made comments on drug use, and had some status as a role model for the young[113] and, on the other, the fact that publishing the photograph constituted a significant intrusion and added nothing of importance to the textual information.[114] Lord Hope, for example, found that the objective of protecting B's right to respect for her private life was sufficiently important to justify limiting A's freedom of expression and that the means chosen to limit that freedom of expression were rational, fair and not arbitrary, and that they impaired A's right as minimally as was reasonably possible.[115] As a result, the benefits achieved by the publication of the photograph were not proportionate to the harm done by the interference with B's right to privacy, and so the publication could be found to be a breach of confidence without interfering with A's right to freedom of expression.[116] It is important to note that, as stated by Baroness Hale in *Campbell*, that there are "undoubtedly different types of speech, just as there are different types of private information, some of which are more deserving of protection in a democratic society than others".[117] Political speech is "top of the list", and the importance of "intellectual and educational speech" and "artistic speech and expression"[118] has also been emphasised, whereas "celebrity gossip"[119] is less worthy of protection, with pornography still lower in the "hierarchy of speech which

9-017

deserves the protection of the law".[120] On the other side of the scale, it has been recognised that "the weight which should be attached to an obligation of confidence may be enhanced if the obligation is contained in an express contractual agreement", particularly if that agreement was entered into in order to compromise an actual or potential claim.[121] It has been suggested that, in a case where B's right to privacy and A's freedom of expression might otherwise be finely balanced, "[t]hird party rights can be decisive"[122] and so, for example, the privacy and right to family life of a child of B can be important to a finding that disclosure of information relating to B's sexual exploits can be prevented.[123]

[111] *Campbell v MGN Ltd* [2004] 2 A.C. 457 HL at [29].

[112] See too *Commissioner of Police of the Metropolis v Times Newspapers Ltd* [2011] EWHC 2705 (QB) at [73]–[93].

[113] As noted by Lord Hoffmann, for example: "If Ms Campbell had been an ordinary citizen, I think that the publication of information about her attendance at [Narcotics Anonymous] would have been actionable and I do not understand the 'Mirror' to argue otherwise": [2004] 2 A.C. 457 HL at [53].

[114] *Campbell v MGN Ltd* [2004] 2 A.C. 457 HL at [121]–[122], per Lord Hope; at [155]–[156], per Baroness Hale; at [165] per Lord Carswell.

[115] *Campbell v MGN Ltd* [2004] 2 A.C. 457 HL at [119]–[120].

[116] The House of Lords was split on this point, with Lords Nicholls and Hoffmann concluding ([2004] 2 A.C. 457 HL at [28] and [77] respectively) that the proposed interference with the newspaper's freedom of expression was disproportionate, and that, therefore, B was unable to make out all the ingredients of breach of confidence.

[117] *Campbell v MGN Ltd* [2004] UKHL 22 at [148]. See too *BUQ v HRE* [2015] EWHC 1272 (QB) at [47], where Warby J observed that, as A was a blackmailer, his art.10 rights were "limited" and also that his "right to speak publicly of his part in, or of what he knows of, [B's] sexual adventures is one that deserves little weight in striking a fair balance".

[118] *Campbell v MGN Ltd* [2004] UKHL 22 at [148], per Baroness Hale.

[119] In *PJS v News Group Newspapers Ltd* [2016] A.C. 1081, Lord Mance at [24] stated that: "it may be that the mere reporting of sexual encounters of someone like the claimant, however well known to the public, with a view to criticizing them does not even fall within the concept of freedom of expression under Article 10 at all. But, accepting that Article 10 is not only engaged but capable in principle of protecting any form of expression, these cases clearly demonstrate that this type of expression is at the bottom end of the spectrum of importance (compared, for example, with freedom of political speech or a case of conduct bearing on the performance of a public office). For present purposes, any public interest in publishing such criticism must, in the absence of any other, legally recognized, public interest, be effectively disregarded in any balancing exercise and is incapable by itself of outweighing such Article 8 privacy rights as the claimant enjoys".

[120] *Belfast City Council v Miss Behavin' Ltd* [2007] UKHL 19; [2007] 1 W.L.R. 1420 at [38], per Baroness Hale.

[121] *ABC v Telegraph Media Group Ltd* [2018] EWCA Civ 2329 at [24]–[29]; relying on *Mionis v Democratic Press SA* [2017] EWCA Civ 1194, [2018] Q.B. 662.

[122] *BUQ v HRE* [2015] EWHC 1272 (QB) at [49], per Warby J.

[123] *PJS v News Group Newspapers Ltd* [2016] A.C. 1081 SC at [45], [64], and [72]–[78].

(g) Misuse of the information.

Replace first paragraph with:

9-018   A duty of confidence is breached only if A misuses the information in relation to which B has a reasonable expectation of confidence.[123a] Misuse, of course, can be established only where A has made some use of information,[123b] and A may claim, for example, that a particular idea or concept was developed by A independently of any information acquired from B. It is necessary for B to specify the particular information, and the particular way in which it has been misused.[124] An analogy has been drawn with the approach adopted to the question of copying in breach of copyright cases.[125] In a suitable case, B may be able to take advantage of a "strong inference" arising where there are "significant similarities" between the result of A's work and the confidential information, and where A had an opportunity to use that information. A would then need to rebut that inference by proving "independent derivation".[126] It should also be noted that A can misuse information even if A is unaware that A is making use of the information, as when A subconsciously incorporates confidential information into the design of a product.[127]

[123a] Misuse (rather than, e.g., simply enabling access to information by an unauthorized person) is also required for liability in the tort of misuse of private information: see eg *Smith v Talktalk Telcom Group plc* [2022] EWHC 1311 (QB) at [49] and *Underwood v Bounty UK Ltd* [2022] EWHC 888 (QB) at [52]. In *I-Admin (Singapore) Pte Ltd v Hong Ying Ting* [2020] SGA 32, the Singapore Court of Appeal takes a different, wider approach, which allows a breach of confidence to arise from A's accessing or acquiring B's confidential information, unless A can show that A's conscience was not affected, and thus removes the distinct requirement of misuse: ibid [61]. For discussion see B. Wong and D. Tan (2020) 136 LQR 548.

[123b] See e.g. *Warren v DSG Retail Ltd* [2021] EWHC 2168 (QB) at [27]: the misuse requirement was not made out where A had simply suffered a data breach which lead to the disclosure of information on its customers, including B. Note though that retention of information (as when refusing to destroy obviously confidential videos mistakenly disclosed to A) can suffice as misuse: *Chief Constable of Kent Police v Taylor* [2022] EWHC 737 (QB) [54].

[124] *Paymaster (Jamaica) Ltd v Grace Kennedy Remittance Services Ltd* [2017] UKPC 40 at [38]–[41].

[125] *Wade v British Sky Broadcasting Ltd* [2014] EWHC 634 (Ch) at [59], per Birss J. An appeal against Birss J's judgment was dismissed: [2016] EWCA Civ 1214. See too *Vestergaard Frandsen A/S v Bestnet Europe Ltd* [2016] EWCA Civ 541 at [79]–[88].

[126] *Wade v British Sky Broadcasting Ltd* [2014] EWHC 634 (Ch) at [59] per Birss J. An appeal against Birss J's judgment was dismissed: [2016] EWCA Civ 1214.

[127] See *Seager v Copydex Ltd* [1967] 1 W.L.R. 923 CA.

3. REMEDIES

1. Injunctions

Replace first paragraph with:

An injunction may be granted, in a suitable case, to prevent a breach of confidence.[136] The general rules and principles relating to the grant of injunctions are considered in detail in Ch.18. In the specific context of breach of confidence, it should be noted that, if B can show that a threatened act by A would amount to a breach of confidence, the prima facie position is that an injunction will be granted.[137] It remains however a discretionary remedy and there may be "special or exceptional factors"[138] which justify the refusal to grant an injunction.[139] As an injunction to prevent publication will affect the exercise of A's right to freedom of expression, the provisions of s.12 of the Human Rights Act 1998 are also relevant.[140]

9-019

[136] In *Arthur J Gallagher Services UK Ltd v Skriptchenkov* [2016] EWHC 603 (QB), an interim injunction was granted not simply to prevent misuse of confidential information, but also to compel imaging and inspection of a defendant's computer equipment to confirm that the confidential information had been destroyed. See too *Chief Constable of Kent Police v Taylor* [2022] EWHC 737 (QB) [57]–[68], where an order was made that an independent IT expert should (at the expense of the claimant) undertake the permanent deletion of confidential videos mistakenly disclosed to the defendant, and that the defendant should disclose his dealings with the videos. An injunction preventing the disclosure of the content of "private conversations" would be impermissibly vague, but B does not have to identify precisely the

content of the confidential material: *Clearcourse Partnership Acquireco Ltd v Jethwa* [2022] EWHC 1199 (QB) at [53]–[55].

[137] See, e.g. *Ocular Sciences Ltd v Aspect Vision Care Ltd* [1997] R.P.C. 289 at 404, per Laddie J.

[138] *Ocular Sciences Ltd v Aspect Vision Care Ltd* [1997] R.P.C. 289 at 405, per Laddie J.

[139] In the *Ocular Sciences* case, for example, an injunction was refused where the loss caused to B by A's act would be small, the granting of an injunction would be oppressive to A, destroying the company and the livelihoods of its employees, and B's conduct in the litigation had been in many respects vexatious and had included deliberate attempts to mislead the court: [1997] R.P.C. 289 at 407–408.

[140] Those provisions are discussed at para.18-062 and were considered in *PJS v News Group Newspapers Ltd* [2016] A.C. 1081. Section 12 may apply in relation to any remedy or order made in non-criminal proceedings and so may be relevant not only in relation to injunctions but also in relation to, for example, exemplary damages: see para.9-024. In *Attorney General v BBC* [2022] EWHC 826 (QB), it was confirmed that the executive has no general power to impose prior restraints on speech, and that a mere invocation of national security does not suffice to justify an injunction to restrain an alleged breach of confidence. An interim injunction was however granted in that case to prevent the broadcast of a programme, with the real and immediate risk of harm to the intelligence source whose identity the BBC wished to disclose a significant factor.

Replace footnote 150 with:

[150] The term derives from *Terrapin Ltd v Builders' Supply Co (Hayes) Ltd* [1967] R.P.C. 375 at 390: see too *Seager v Copydex Ltd* [1967] 1 W.L.R. 923 CA. For an example of the limits imposed on the duration of confidentiality, see, e.g. *Harrison v Project and Design Co (Redcar) Ltd* [1978] F.S.R. 81. Note the review of the relevant authorities undertaken by Arnold J in *Vestergaard Frandsen A/S v Bestnet Europe Ltd* [2009] EWHC 1456 (Ch); [2010] F.S.R. 2 and the conclusions expressed at [76] (the subsequent appeals did not challenge the judge's analysis of the springboard point). For an application of the "springboard" approach to limit the duration of injunctive relief so as to deny A the improperly obtained "head start" gained by the use of confidential information, see *Kerry Ingredients Ltd v Bakkavor Group Ltd* [2016] EWHC 2448 (Ch) at [110]–[116]. For consideration of the relevant principles, see too *Amob Machinery Ltd v Smith-Hughes* [2022] EWHC 1410 (QB) at [79].

2. Damages and Equitable Compensation

Replace n.156 with:

9-020

[156] See, e.g. *Vestergaard Frandsen A/S v Bestnet Europe Ltd* [2016] EWCA Civ 541, esp. at [87]–[88]; *Argos Pereira Espana SL v Athenian Marine Ltd* [2021] EWHC 554 (Comm) at [5] and [15]. See too *Burrell v Clifford* [2016] EWHC 294 (Ch) at [153]–[163] for discussion of the approach to be taken in assessing appropriate compensation for misuse of private information. In *Marathon Asset Management LLP v Seddon* [2017] EWHC 300 (Comm); [2017] I.C.R. 791, Leggatt J stated at [157] that: "In circumstances where the misuse of confidential information by [A] has neither caused [B] to suffer any financial loss nor resulted in [A] making any financial gain, it is hard to see how [B] could be entitled to any remedy other than an award of nominal damages". In *Douglas v Hello! Ltd (No.8)* [2004] E.M.L.R. 2: Lindsay J found that A was liable to pay just over £1m to B3 (a rival magazine that had paid B1 & B2 for the exclusive right to publish photographs of the wedding) and to pay £14,600 to B1 and B2. The award to B1 was affirmed by the House of Lords ([2008] 1 A.C. 1) and that to B2 and B3 was affirmed by the Court of Appeal (see fn.41), and not contested in the House of Lords. For an illuminating survey of the relevant principles see *Force India Formula One Team Ltd v 1 Malaysia Racing Team* [2012] EWHC 616 (Ch) at [388]–[424]. Arnold J at [392] inclined to the view that the Lord Cairns' Act jurisdiction does not apply to breach of confidence, but that the remedy of equitable compensation is available to provide monetary relief for a party who has suffered financial loss as a result of the defendant's breach of an equitable (i.e. non-contractual) obligation of confidence. Note too *Flogas Britain Ltd v Calor Gas Ltd* [2013] EWHC 3060 (Ch); [2014] F.S.R. 34 at [41], per Proudman J.

Replace second paragraph with:

Whether B seeks damages on the basis of the statutory power, the equitable jurisdiction, or (in an appropriate case) on A's breach of a contractual duty of confidence, the assessment of damages proceeds in the same way[157]: the court calculates the damages based on the sum which would put B in the same position as if the breach of confidence had not occurred.[158] These damages can include consequential losses for distress and disappointment.[159] Although, in line with tort claims, awards for distress and disappointment should be modest,[160] where the distress and exposure of the victim is widespread and significant the damages awarded can be as much as £60,000.[161]

[157] *Johnson v Agnew* [1980] A.C. 367 HL at 400–401, per Lord Wilberforce demonstrates that the assessment under the statute is governed by the same rules applying in the general law.

[158] *Indata Equipment Supplies Ltd v ACL Ltd* [1998] B.C.L.C. 412; C. Phipps et al (eds), *Toulson & Phipps on Confidentiality*, 4th edn (Sweet & Maxwell 2020) 6–164. In *Force India Formula One Team Ltd v 1 Malaysia Racing Team* [2012] EWHC 616 (Ch) at [407] Arnold J cast doubt on the Court of Appeal's willingness in *Indata* to draw an analogy with the tort measure, but it would be a mistake, it is submitted, to view that measure, in this context, as distinct from a "contract measure": whatever the source of A's duty, the central aim of damages is to put B in the position B would have been in had the duty been performed and this means, for example, that relief can be awarded in relation to financial loss, including lost profits, suffered by B as a result of A's breach: see, e.g. *Flogas Britain Ltd v Calor Gas Ltd* [2013] EWHC 3060 (Ch); [2014] F.S.R. 34 at [37]–[41], per Proudman J.

[159] *Campbell v MGN Ltd* [2004] 2 A.C. 457 HL; *Douglas v Hello! Ltd (No.8)* [2004] E.M.L.R. 2; [2006] Q.B. 125 CA. Aggravated damages may also be awarded: see e.g. *JQL v NTP* [2020] EWHC 1349 (QB) [160]-[164]. Consistently with the approach of the Supreme Court in *R. (on the application of Lumba) v Sec of State for the Home Dept* [2012] 1 A.C. 245, damages for breach of confidence or misuse of private information are "not the same as vindicatory damages to vindicate some constitutional right", but can compensate for loss of the right to control the use of private information: see e.g. *Gulati v MGN Ltd* [2016] 2 W.L.R. 1217 at [45]-[49]. Arden LJ also noted there that damages can thus "compensate (if appropriate) for the loss of privacy or autonomy as such arising out of the infringement" (ibid at [168]).

[160] In *Douglas v Hello! Ltd (No.6)* [2006] Q.B. 125, the Court of Appeal upheld an award to each of B1 and B2, of which £3,750 was compensation for the distress caused by the publication of the unauthorised photographs, with a further £7,000 for the cost and inconvenience for having to make a hurried selection of authorised photographs when the magazine to which they had given exclusive rights brought publication forward to compete with A.

[161] *Mosley v News Group Newspapers Ltd* [2008] EWHC 1777; [2008] E.M.L.R. 20. Eady J noted there at [216] that the "scale of the distress and indignity in this case is difficult to comprehend. It is probably unprecedented". See too *Cooper v Turrell* [2011] EWHC 3269 (QB), where A's deliberate dissemination of a falsehood was also a relevant factor in assessing damages and a figure of £40,000 would have been awarded to B if the sole claim had been for breach of confidence. The discussion in this paragraph was referred to by Tugendhat J at [94]. In *Gulati v MGN Ltd* [2016] 2 W.L.R. 1217, the Court of Appeal upheld sizable damages awards for misuse of the private information of victims of phone-hacking, with the highest individual award (based on 31 separate publications) being £260,250.

5. Exemplary Damages

Replace second paragraph with:

It was worth noting that, whilst Eady J refused to characterise breach of   **9-024**
confidence as a "tort",[202] he did not suggest that exemplary damages should be denied merely because of the jurisdictional origin of breach of confidence in the Court of Chancery.[203] As noted above,[204] such questions should instead be determined by the particular nature of the claim made, as well as, of course, the general arguments for and against exemplary damages.[205] It has been observed that any award of exemplary damages for a breach of confidence might constitute a disproportionate interference with A's art.10 right to freedom of expression,[206] although it should not be assumed that art.10 is always engaged where breach of confidence is concerned,[207] and it can also be noted that exemplary damages are in principle available in defamation.[208] Lord Nicholls stated that "the availability of exemplary damages should be co-extensive with its rationale ... the underlying

rationale lies in the sense of outrage which a defendant's conduct sometimes evokes, a sense not always assuaged by a compensatory award of damages, even when the damages are increased to reflect emotional distress".[209] On this view, it is not difficult to think of particular breaches of confidence that might give rise to that sense of outrage.[210]

[202] *Mosley v News Group Newspapers Ltd* [2008] EWHC 1777; [2008] E.M.L.R. 20 at [184] and [190]. Contrast, e.g. *Vidal-Hall v Google Inc* [2016] Q.B. 1003; and *PJS v News Group Newspapers Ltd* [2016] A.C. 1081, where misuse of confidential information has been regarded as, and referred to, as a tort: see fn.37.

[203] Contrast the view taken by Heydon JA in *Harris v Digital Pulse Ltd* [2003] NSWCA 10; (2003) 56 N.S.W.L.R. 298; and criticised by, e.g. A. Burrows, "Remedial Coherence and Punitive Damages in Equity" in S. Degeling & J. Edelman (eds), *Equity in Commercial Law* (Thomson, 2006).

[204] See para 9-010.

[205] For arguments against, see, e.g. Lord Scott in *Kuddus v Chief Constable of Leicestershire* [2002] 2 A.C. 122 at [95]–[111]. For arguments in favour, see, e.g. J. Edelman "In Defence of Exemplary Damages" in C. Rickett (ed), *Justifying Private Law Remedies* (Hart, 2003), 225.

[206] *Mosley v News Group Newspapers Ltd* [2008] EWHC 1777; [2008] E.M.L.R. 20 at [193]. Note too Human Rights Act 1998 s.12(1).

[207] As noted at para.9-018, A's misuse of confidential information need not involve any communication of that information.

[208] See, e.g. *Broome v Cassell & Co Ltd* [1971] 2 Q.B. 354 CA.

[209] *Kuddus v Chief Constable of Leicestershire* [2002] 2 A.C. 122 HL at [65].

[210] See too C. Phipps et al (eds), *Toulson & Phipps on Confidentiality*, 4th edn (Sweet & Maxwell, 2020) 6-187. Note that in *Mosley v News Group Newspapers Ltd* [2008] EWHC 1777; [2008] E.M.L.R. 20, Eady J at [180] rejected a contention, based on Lord Nicholls' "general observations" in *Kuddus*, that "all that is required [for exemplary damages] is conduct characterized as 'outrageous'", and refused to award exemplary damages even whilst noting at [216] that the "scale of the distress and indignity in this case is difficult to comprehend. It is probably unprecedented".

CHAPTER 10

POWERS—GENERAL PRINCIPLES

5. CONTROLLING POWERS

After "first place. The", add:

10-017   first consequence of this difficulty is that the courts are cautious about interfering in the purported exercise of a power: the power holder should be allowed to act unless a good reason can be shown to justify the court's intervention.[41a] The second consequence is that the constraints on the exercise of a power are

[41a] *Lehtimaki v Cooper* [2020] UKSC 33.

1.   Controls on Powers Which Concern the Scope of a Power

(a)   Construction

After the fourth paragraph, add new paragraphs:

10-018   However, that is not to say that they always do. The powers of protectors provide a current example of differing approaches to construction, in three recent cases from three different jurisdictions. Although all cases of construction turn on the exact words at issue, these three cases did address a common issue: where the power of trustees to engage in a particular transaction is subject to the prior consent of one or more protectors, what is the nature and extent of the protectors' power of consent / veto? To put the point more specifically, "does a protector whose consent is required for a trustee to exercise a power have an independent decision-making discretion amounting to a power of veto ('the wider view') or does the protector merely have a discretion to determine that the trustees' decision was rational and valid amounting to a rationality review ('the narrower view')".[54a]

The three cases to consider this question are *PTNZ v AS & Ors*[54b] (England), In the Matter of the *X Trust*[54c] (Bermuda) and In the matter of the *Piedmont Trust and Riviera Trust*[54d] (Jersey). Despite the materially identical language of the powers at issue in the three cases, the courts reached different conclusions. In England and in Jersey, the wider view prevailed, as a matter of objective construction of the relevant words, so the protectors had essentially a power of veto. In Bermuda, the narrower view prevailed, so the protectors could only validly refuse to consent to the trustees' proposed action if it was in essence irrational. The Bermudian court justified its departure from the prima facie meaning of the language conferring the protector's power, and from the court's own prima facie impression of the case, by reference to practicalities: the court thought that a wider (and more natural) construction of the power could lead more easily to deadlock between the trustees and the protector, and that the role of a protector was to act as a watch-dog rather than an independent decision-maker.

With respect to the Bermudian court, the approach of the English and Jersey courts is to be preferred. The role of the protector is to be inferred from the words used to create the office and the powers incidental to it, rather than the converse of limiting words by reference to an a priori conception of the office, particularly as "the term 'protector' is not a term of art and generally 'signifies little more than that a person who is not the (or a) trustee has been granted a power affecting the operation of the trust'."[54e] And as far as practicalities are concerned, first the Bermudian view certainly does not eliminate the possibility of deadlock between trustees and protectors; and secondly, if there is such a deadlock, it is better addressed directly and resolved through the administrative jurisdiction of the court, rather than by means of strained construction.

[54a] Grant, "The Protectors' Power of Consent" (2022) Thought Leaders 4 Private Client 41.

[54b] [2020] EWHC 3114 (Ch).

[54c] [2021] SC (Bda) 72.

[54d] [2021] JRC 24.

[54e] *Poon v Kan* [2014] HKCFA 66 at [67], per Ribeiro PJ, citing Conaglen & Weaver, "Protectors as Fiduciaries: Theory and Practice" (2012) 18 Trusts & Trustees 17.

At the start of the final paragraph, replace "There is, however," with:
  In short, there is

(b) Good Faith

Replace seventh paragraph with:
  Both good faith and bad faith are ascertained prima facie by reference to actual, **10-019**
subjective, states of mind. This has often been emphasised in judicial decisions,
whether they concern trustees,[66] or directors.[67] However, the holder of a fiduciary
power who exercises it in a self-interested way will not be taken to be acting in good
faith.[68] Furthermore, a fiduciary power exercised for reasons of caprice or spite will
not be exercised in good faith.[69]

[66] See, e.g. *Re Smith* [1896] 1 Ch.71 at 76, per Kekewich J (in relation to powers of investment); *Bristol & West Building Society v Mothew* [1998] Ch. 1 at 18; and *Armitage v Nurse* [1998] Ch. 241 at 253–254, per Millett LJ (general principle); *Lehtimaki v Cooper* [2020] UKSC 33 at [100], [187], per Lady Arden. However, the position appears to be different in Australia, where "good faith" is used to encompass matters other than a subjective state of mind: see, e.g. *Re Marsella; Marsella v Wareham (No 2)* [2019] VSC 65 at [36], per McMillan J.

[67] *Re Smith & Fawcett Ltd* [1942] Ch. 304 at 306; *Medforth v Blake* [2000] Ch. 86 at 103, per Scott VC; *Regentcrest Plc (In Liquidation) v Cohen* [2001] 2 B.C.L.C. 80 (ChD) at [120], per Jonathan Parker J. See also *Extrasure Travel Insurances Ltd v Scattergood* [2002] EWHC 3093 (Ch); [2003] 1 B.C.L.C. 598 at [87]–[90], per Jonathan Crow QC.

[68] *Howard Smith Ltd v Ampol Petroleum Ltd* [1974] A.C. 821 at 834, per Lord Wilberforce; citing *Fraser v Whalley* 2 Hem. & M. 10; and *Hogg v Cramphorn Ltd* [1967] Ch. 254.

[69] *Re Smith* at 76; *Bristol & West Building Society v Mothew* [1998] Ch. 1 at 18; *Armitage v Nurse* [1998] Ch. 241 at 253.

After the seventh paragraph, add new paragraph:
  In very unusual circumstances, where a court has approved a course of action as
being in the interests which the fiduciary must further, it would be a breach of the
fiduciary's duty of good faith to do anything other than implement that course of
action.[69a] As Lord Briggs put it in the context of a charitable trust:

> "[O]nce the court's decision about the merits of the transaction is made then, subject to
> any appeal (or perhaps a significant change in circumstances before it is implemented),
> that difficult question has been finally resolved. It ceases to be a question for debate. It is
> binding on all those interested parties joined to the relevant proceedings, and the duty of
> the charity's fiduciaries (whether or not joined as parties) is to use their powers to the end
> that it is implemented, both generally and in accordance with any directions which the
> court may give for that purpose. It would in my view be a plain breach of fiduciary duty
> for a relevant fiduciary of the charity to do otherwise, a fortiori to exercise a fiduciary
> power so as in effect to veto the very transaction which the court has decided should
> proceed in furtherance of the charity's purposes."[69b]

By contrast, good faith action can even include unauthorised action in some cases.[70]

[69a] *Lehtimaki v Cooper* [2020] UKSC 33 at [205]-[235], per Lord Briggs, with whom Lords Wilson and Kitchin agreed.

[69b] *Lehtimaki v Cooper* [2020] UKSC 33 at [208]. See also at [218].

[70] *Armitage v Nurse* [1998] Ch. 241 at 251, 253–254, per Millett LJ.

(c)   Fraud on a Power/Improper Purposes

Replace seventh paragraph with:

10-020   High authority also confirms that the doctrine of abusing a power for an improper purpose is not the same as simply exceeding the power: the proper purposes doctrine and questions of construction are distinct in how they seek to control discretionary power. Lord Wilberforce noted the distinction in *Howard Smith v Ampol Petroleum*:

> "The directors, in deciding to issue shares, forming part of Millers' unissued capital, to Howard Smith, acted under clause 8 of the company's articles of association. This provides, subject to certain qualifications which have not been invoked, that the shares shall be under the control of the directors, who may allot or otherwise dispose of the same to such persons on such terms and conditions and either at a premium or otherwise and at such time as the directors may think fit. Thus, and this is not disputed, the issue was clearly intra vires the directors. But, intra vires though the issue may have been, the directors' power under this article is a fiduciary power: *and it remains the case that an exercise of such a power though formally valid, may be attacked on the ground that it was not exercised for the purpose for which it was granted.*"[85]

Lord Sumption put the matter as follows in *Eclairs Group v JKX Oil & Gas Plc*

> "… the proper purpose rule is not concerned with excess of power by doing an act which is beyond the scope of the instrument creating it as a matter of construction or implication. It is concerned with abuse of power, by doing acts which are within its scope but done for an ulterior purpose."[85a]

[85] *Howard Smith v Ampol Petroleum* [1974] A.C. 821 at 834, emphasis added. See also *Fearon v Desbrisay* (1851) 14 Beav. 635 at 642; 51 E.R. 428 at 431, per Romilly MR; and *Henty v Wrey* (1882) 21 Ch. D. 332 at 355, per Lindley LJ.

[85a] [2015] UKSC 71; [2016] 1 B.C.L.C. 1 at [15].

Ascertaining what amounts to a fraud on a power.

Replace fourth paragraph with:

10-022   The exercise of ascertaining a settlor's expectations may be more or less evidentially difficult. When making its findings, the court may or may not have the assistance of a letter of wishes,[94] or other admissible evidence. Clarke P of the Court of Appeal for Bermuda put it as follows in *Grand View Private Trust Co Ltd v Wong*:

> "[I]t seems to me that, when considering the equitable rule that a power may not be used otherwise than in accordance with the purpose for which it was given (even if the use falls within the scope of the terms of the trust) Equity should not, in a case such as this, close her mind to extrinsic evidence of the settlor's intentions, when setting up the trust and when granting the power, particularly when it is the wishes of the settlor that the trustee is required to take into account when deciding on the exercise of the power. To do so would not offend the rules of construction or implication because the evidence would only be relevant after it had been concluded that the proposed exercise of the power was not outlawed as a matter of construction or implication."[94a]

[94] See *Re Rabiotti's 1989 Settlement* [2000] W.T.L.R. 953 at 967–968, per Deputy Bailiff Birt (Jersey Royal Court, Samedi Division); *Breakspear v Ackland* [2008] EWHC 220 (Ch); [2009] Ch. 32 at [5]–[14], and esp. at [8], per Briggs J, though "[i]t may be that there are some matters in the memorandum [of wishes] which…it would not be proper for the trustees to take into account in the exercise of any, or of a particular, discretionary power": *Hartigan Nominees Pty Ltd v Rydge* (1992) 29 N.S.W.L.R. 405 at 427, per Mahoney JA. See also *Grand View Private Trust Co Ltd v Wong* [2020] CA (Bda) 6 Civ.

[94a] [2020] CA (Bda) 6 Civ at [218]. On 8–10 March 2022, the Privy Council heard an appeal from the judgment of the Bermuda Court of Appeal, but the Privy Council has not yet handed down its own decision.

After the fourth paragraph, add new paragraph:

A court may encounter evidential difficulties in some cases, for example where a trust has more than one settlor, or where a trust has been amended,[95] varied under the Variation of Trusts Act 1958, or created out of another settlement.[96] The terms of a trust (or other organisation) may have evolved over time; and in such a case, the observations of Millett J in *In re Courage Group's Pension Schemes Ryan v Imperial Brewing and Leisure* will be relevant:

> "[I]n the case of an institution of long duration and gradually changing membership like a club or pension scheme, each alteration in the rules must be tested by reference to the situation at the time of the proposed alteration, and not by reference to the original rules at its inception. By changes made gradually over a long period, alterations may be made which would not be acceptable if introduced all at once. Even the main purpose may be changed by degrees…"[96a]

If the court does encounter such problems, then it can supply default implications, if needs be fashioned by reference to "reasonable expectations". This might seem a similar exercise to the control of power in public law by reference to Wednesbury unreasonableness.[97] Nevertheless, the court should be very cautious about any such analogy between private and public law. In the private law context, the court is primarily engaged in a forensic exercise to establish a purpose, or purposes, and should only make implications in so far as it is defeated in that exercise. The court is not, as in public law, applying mandatory rules of law (or at least very strong default presumptions) generated by policy concerns of constitutional legitimacy and propriety.[98] As Lord Sumption put it in *Eclairs Group v JKX Oil & Gas Plc*:

> "Ascertaining the purpose of a power where the instrument is silent depends on an inference from the mischief of the provision conferring it, which is itself deduced from its express terms, from an analysis of their effect, and from the court's understanding of the business context."[98a]

[95] A power to amend trusts is common in pension trusts: see R. Self, *Pension Fund Trustee Handbook*, 9th edn (Haywards Heath: Tottel Publishing, 2005) at para.6.3, and, by way of example, *Imperial Group Pension Trust Ltd v Imperial Tobacco Plc* [1991] 1 W.L.R. 589.

[96] See, generally, A.J. Oakley, *Parker and Mellows: The Modern Law of Trusts*, 9th edn (London: Sweet & Maxwell, 2008) at [18–024]–[18–044]; and Lord Millett, *Encyclopedia of Forms and Precedents*, 5th edn (London: Butterworths, 2001), Vol.40(1) at paras 139 (settled advances); and 4359 and 4405 (powers for trustees to appoint trust funds to distinct settlements).

[96a] [1987] 1 W.L.R. 495, 506, cited with approval by Lord Walker in *Bank of New Zealand v Board of Management of the Bank of New Zealand Officers Provident Association* [2003] UKPC 58 at [19].

[97] *Scott v National Trust* [1998] 2 All E.R. 705 at 718g. The charity involved in this case, the National Trust for Places of Historic Interest or Natural Beauty, is actually a corporation rather than a trust stricto sensu: see the National Trust Act 1907 s.3. That should not affect this point, however.

[98] See *Underhill & Hayton: Law of Trusts and Trustees* (2006), paras 61.12–61.17. Rather ironically, the continuing place of *Wednesbury* unreasonableness in administrative law is moot: see, generally,

H.W.R. Wade & C.F. Forsyth, *Administrative Law*, 9th edn (Oxford: Oxford University Press, 2004) at 371–372.

98a [2015] UKSC 71; [2016] 1 B.C.L.C. 1 at [30].

2. Controls on Power Which Concern Decision-Making

(c) *Consequences of flawed decision-making for the transaction*

Replace footnote 204 with:

10-038   204 See, e.g. *Logicrose v Southend United Football Club Ltd* [1988] 1 W.L.R. 1256 (Ch) at 1261 per Millett J; *Hurstanger Ltd v Wilson* [2007] EWCA Civ 299; [2007] 1 W.L.R. 2351 at [35], [47]–[51] per Tuckey LJ; *Ross River Ltd v Cambridge City Football Club Ltd* [2007] EWHC 2115 (Ch); [2008] 1 All E.R. 1004 at [205], per Briggs J.

Replace footnote 207 with:

10-039   207 See R.P. Meagher, J.D. Heydon, M.J. Leeming, *Meagher, Gummow & Lehane's Equity: Doctrines and Remedies*, 4th edn (Australia: LexisNexis, 2002), paras [24–075]—[24–085]; and note also *Holder v Holder* [1968] Ch. 353 CA (Civ Div); and *Runciman v Walter Runciman Plc* [1992] B.C.L.C. 1084. Note also *Gany Holdings (PTC) SA v Khan* [2018] UKPC 21 at [54]–[58], per Lord Briggs.

CHAPTER 12

ESTOPPEL

1. INTRODUCTION

1. Terminology

After "the parties' actions.", add new n.5a:

[5a] See, e.g. *Mount Wellington Mine Ltd v Renewable Energy Co-operative Ltd* [2021] EWHC 1486 (Ch)   **12-002**
at [45], where HHJ Paul Matthews draws a contrast between estoppel, as a "principle of the common
law of evidence and procedure" and proprietary estoppel as a "principle of substantive obligations/
property law in equity".

2. Estoppel at Common Law

Estoppel by representation.

Replace paragraph with:
  By the nineteenth century the common law had developed a rule that there would   **12-005**
be an estoppel where, by words or conduct, there had been a representation of existing fact[9] (although not of law)[10] which was intended to be acted upon and was in
fact acted upon to his prejudice by the person to whom it was made.[11] The maker
of the representation was then not allowed to allege in proceedings against the
person to whom the representation was made that the facts were other than he or
she had represented them to be. For example, where land[12] or goods[13] were offered for sale and, by standing by and encouraging the sale, the true owner produced
the false impression that the person holding themselves out as the seller was instead

the owner, the sale was binding on the true owner. Similarly, where a company issued certificates indicating that shares were fully paid it was estopped as against a purchaser without notice from asserting the contrary.[14] Estoppel by representation of fact at common law was treated as a rule of evidence and not as a cause of action: this continues to be the case.[15]

[9] See *Jorden v Money* (1854) 5 H.L.C. 185; *Maddison v Alderson* (1883) 8 App. Cas. 467; and *Neville v Wilkinson* (1782) 1 Bro. C.C. 543. The limitation to statements of existing fact was recognised by the House of Lords in *Jorden v Money*: see Jackson "Estoppel as a Sword" (1965) 86 L.Q.R. 84.

[10] *Territorial and Auxiliary Forces Association of the County of London v Nichols* [1949] 1 K.B. 35; *Kai Nam v Ma Kam Chan* [1956] A.C. 358; and *Tomlin v Reid* [1963] E.G.D. 338. But see now *Briggs v Gleeds* [2014] EWHC 1178 (Ch), discussed at para.12-016, fn.67.

[11] See *Pickard v Sears* (1837) 6 Ad. & E. 469 at 472 at 474; *Freeman v Cooke* (1848) 2 Exch. 654 at 663; and *Canadian Pacific Railway v R.* [1931] A.C. 414 at 429. See also *Dean v Bruce* [1952] 1 K.B. 11. The intention of the maker of the representation that it be acted on is judged objectively: see e.g. *Hodgson v Creation Consumer Finance Ltd* [2021] EWHC 2167 (Comm) [84]–[87].

[12] *Price v Neault* (1886) 12 App. Cas. 110; and see *Savage v Foster* (1723) 9 Mod. 35.

[13] *Pickard v Sears* (1837) 6 Ad. & E. 469.

[14] See, e.g. *Burkinshaw v Nicolls* (1878) 3 App. Cas. 1004; *Re Concessions Trust* [1896] 2 Ch. 757; and see *Robinson v Montgomeryshire Brewery Co* [1896] 2 Ch. 841. There is a substantial case law dealing with estoppels arising out of the transfer of shares: see P. Feltham et al (eds), *Spencer Bower's Reliance-Based Estoppel*, 5th edn (Bloomsbury, 2017), paras 10.19-10.21.

[15] See *National Westminster Bank Plc v Somer International (UK) Ltd* [2001] EWCA Civ 970. For the earlier position see *Low v Bouverie* [1891] 3 Ch. 82 at 101; and *Dawson's Bank Ltd v Nippon Menkwa Kabushiki Kaisha* (1935) 51 Ll. L. Rep. 143 at 150. The rule was not always mechanically applied, however. Consider *Simmons v Rose* (1862) 31 Beav. 1 at 7 (where a solicitor was held bound to make good an assertion to court). Compare also *Canada and Dominion Sugar Co Ltd v Canadian National (West Indies) Steam Ships Ltd* [1947] A.C. 46 at 56 where Lord Wright stated that the concept of estoppel by representation of fact should be "more correctly viewed as a substantive rule of law".

3.   Estoppel in Equity

(a)   Relationship with common law estoppel.

Replace n.16 with:

12-006   [16] Although note *Tinkler v Revenue and Customs Commissioners* [2021] 3 W.L.R. 697, [2021] UKSC 39 at [28], where Lord Burrows, referring to several types of estoppel including "estoppel by representation, promissory estoppel proprietary estoppel, estoppel by convention and, most recently, contractual estoppel", states that "Whatever their historical roots, most of these doctrines are nowadays usually regarded as equitable doctrines not least because there is a heavy emphasis in the case law on 'unconscionability' (although, wherever possible, one should seek to clarify what that vague phrase means in relation to the particular facts in play)." For references to promissory estoppel and proprietary estoppel as comprising equitable estoppel, see, e.g. *BP Exploration Co (Libya) Ltd v Hunt (No.2)* [1979] 1 W.L.R. 783 at 810D–E; *Societe Italo-Belge pour le Commerce et L'Industrie SA v Palm and Vegetable Oils (Malaysia) Sdn Bhd; The Post Chaser* [1982] 1 All E.R. 19 at 26; *Scandinavian Trading Tanker Co AB v Flota Petrolera Ecuatoriana; the Scaptrade* [1983] Q.B. 529 at 535; *Motor Oil Hellas (Corinth) Refineries SA v Shipping Corp of India (the "Kanchenjunga")* [1990] Lloyd's Rep. 390 HL, at 398; and *Youell v Bland Welch & Co Ltd (the "Superhulls Cover" Case) (No.2)* [1990] 2 Lloyd's Rep. 431 at 449, and at 454. In *Pacol Lines Ltd v Trade Lines Ltd (the "Henrik Sif")* [1982] 1 Lloyd's Rep. 456 Webster J used the expression "general equitable estoppel" in contradistinction to estoppel by silence or acquiescence and promissory estoppel. But he later doubted the correctness of this terminology: see *Shearson Lehmann Hutton Inc v Maclaine Watson & Co Ltd* [1989] 2 Lloyd's Rep. 570 at 596 and at 604.

(b) No single doctrine of equitable estoppel.

Replace paragraph with:

It would equally be a mistake, it is submitted, to regard the doctrines comprising each of promissory and proprietary estoppel as simply emanations of a broader, unitary principle.[21a] For example, whilst a claim based on proprietary estoppel can arise only where the requirement of detriment has been established,[22] it is very difficult to find any such detriment in a case such as *Central London Property Trust Ltd v High Trees House Ltd*,[23] where the promisee's action in reliance on the promise consists simply of paying a lower sum than that contractually due. Similarly, whilst it is clear that proprietary estoppel can operate as an independent cause of action, the same is not true of the principle applied in the *High Trees* case.

12-008

[21a] See e.g. *Tinkler v Revenue and Customs Commissioners* [2021] 3 W.L.R. 697, [2021] UKSC 39 at [28], where Lord Burrows noted that: "Attempts have been made over the years to try to unify the various estoppels but such unification has proved elusive and the different types of estoppel continue to be seen as having their own particular requirements and effects". Note that here Lord Burrows was referring not only to promissory and proprietary estoppel but also estoppel by representation, estoppel by convention, and contractual estoppel. For discussion of the position in New Zealand, see M Roberts, "Equitable Estoppel in New Zealand: One Overarching Doctrine and its Limitations" [2020] New Zealand Law Review 567.

[22] See para.12-044.

[23] *Central London Property Trust Ltd v High Trees House Ltd* [1947] K.B. 130 at 134.

Replace footnote 24 with:

[24] *Ramsden v Dyson* (1866) L.R. 1 H.L. 129 at 168, per Lord Wensleydale: "If a stranger build on my land, supposing it to be his own, and I, knowing it to be mine, do not interfere, but leave him to go on, equity considers it to be dishonest in me to remain passive and afterwards interfere and take the profit".

12-009

Replace paragraph with:

It may be true that, at a very high level of generality, the various forms of equitable estoppel can be seen as emanations of "a much wider jurisdiction to interfere in cases where the assertion of strict legal rights is found by the court to be unconscionable".[30] In two important decisions,[31] the High Court of Australia flirted with the idea of a unified doctrine based upon unconscionability, but the court later declined the opportunity to rule that there is a single unified doctrine of estoppel.[32] The objection to such a unified doctrine is compelling. A general principle is too abstract and protean to serve as a workable test for intervention. Certainly, an equitable estoppel cannot be founded simply on an unparticularised assertion of unconscionability: as Lord Scott noted in *Cobbe v Yeoman's Row Management Ltd*[33]:

12-010

> "unconscionability of conduct may well lead to a remedy but, in my opinion, proprietary estoppel cannot be the route to it unless the ingredients for a proprietary estoppel are present."

This is not to say that unconscionability, in a broad sense that refers to the general question of whether there are compelling grounds for a court to intervene and make an order against a party, has no role to play in relation to the doctrines comprising equitable estoppel.[34] The point is rather that each of those doctrines addresses a specific form of unconscionable conduct and so references to a unitary notion of unconscionability serve only to obscure the nature and operation of the essential characteristics of each of those doctrines.[35]

[30] *Amalgamated Investment & Property Co Ltd v Texas Commerce International Bank Ltd* [1982] Q.B.

84 at 104, per Robert Goff J. See also *Taylor Fashions Ltd v Liverpool Victoria Trustees Co Ltd* [1982] Q.B. 133n. at 151, 152, and 155; *Grant v Edwards* [1986] Ch. 638 at 656; *W Middlesex Golf Club v Ealing LBC* (1994) 68 P. & C.R. 461 at 482; *John v George* [1996] 1 E.G.L.R. 7; *Lloyds Bank v Carrick* [1996] 4 All E.R. 630 at 640; *Frawley v Neill, The Times,* 5 April 1999; *Jones v Stones* [1999] 1 W.L.R. 1739; *Yaxley v Gotts* [2000] Ch. 162 at 176–177; and *Gillett v Holt* [2001] Ch. 210. For academic support see Lunney, "Towards a Unified Estoppel—The Long and Winding Road" [1992] Conv. 239; and Spence, Protecting Reliance: The Emergent Doctrine of Equitable Estoppel (Hart Publishing, 1999).

[31] See *Waltons Stores (Interstate) Ltd v Maher* (1988) 164 C.L.R. 387; and *Commonwealth of Australia v Verwayen* (1990) 170 C.L.R. 394, esp. at 410–411, 447–453.

[32] *Giumelli v Giumelli* (1999) 196 C.L.R. 101.

[33] *Yeoman's Row Management v Cobbe* [2008] UKHL 55; [2008] 1 W.L.R. 1752 at [16].

[34] See paras 12-020 and 12-045.

[35] In *Preedy v Dunne* [2016] EWCA Civ 805, for example, Vos LJ stated at [59] that: "Estoppels are indeed intended to meet the justice of the case. But they must be based on legal principle, not a vague idea that somehow someone will be able to obtain repayment of monies expended for a worthy purpose". The progress of the litigation in that case also evidences possible overlaps between the distinct forms of estoppel: the case was originally put on the grounds of proprietary estoppel, but the appellant was permitted to argue (ultimately unsuccessfully) for an estoppel by convention as the particulars of claim had contained a "basic allegation of a mutual understanding" (see [44]). For the different uses of the word unconscionability see Finn "Unconscionable Conduct" (1994) 8 J.C.L. 37.

(c) Estoppel by convention.

Replace paragraph with:

12-011 The two chief forms of equitable estoppel are promissory estoppel and proprietary estoppel and this chapter will therefore focus on identifying the different principles applied under each of those labels. As noted at para.12-006, the general doctrine of estoppel by representation is applicable both at common law and in equity and so might also be seen as a form of equitable estoppel. The same seems to be true of a further doctrine that may also prevent a party from denying the truth of a matter where another has acted on the basis of its truth: estoppel by convention. It has been stated that "the circumstances in which an estoppel by convention is likely to arise are likely to be rare and the facts unusual",[36] but the doctrine was indeed applied in that case and may have an important role to play in determining the background against which parties' rights are to be determined: indeed, it was recently applied by the Supreme Court, in relation to non-contractual dealings, in *Tinkler v Revenue and Customs Commissioners*.[37] The Supreme Court there approved of the useful statement of the doctrine[38] made by Lord Steyn, and adopted by the other members of the panel of the House of Lords, in *Republic of India v India Steamship Co Ltd ("The Indian Endurance and The Indian Grace")*[39]:

> "[A]n estoppel by convention may arise where parties to a transaction act on an assumed state of facts or law, the assumption being either shared by them both or made by one and acquiesced in by the other. The effect of an estoppel by convention is to preclude a party from denying the assumed facts or law if it would be unjust to allow him to go back on the assumption.[40] It is not enough that each of the two parties acts on an assumption not communicated to the other. But ... a concluded agreement is not a requirement."

[36] *Blindley Heath Investment Ltd v Bass* [2014] EWHC 1366 (Ch) at [133]. An appeal against that decision was dismissed in *Blindley Heath Investments Ltd v Bass* [2017] Ch. 389, [2015] EWCA Civ 1023. For a further example of the application of the doctrine in a commercial context, see *Bristol Rovers (1883) Ltd v Sainsbury's Supermarkets Ltd* [2016] EWCA Civ 160.

[37] [2021] 3 W.L.R. 697, [2021] UKSC 39. For a further recent example in the contractual context, see *Active Media Services Inc v Burmester Duncker & Joly GmbH* [2021] EWHC 232 (Comm). Note though

Neuberger J's observation in *PW & Co v Milton Gate Investments Ltd* [2004] Ch. 142 at 185: "it would be wrong to extend too readily the circumstances by which estoppel by convention can apply, in light of the concerns expressed by Lord Goff in *Johnson v Gore Wood & Co* [2002] A.C. 1 (HL) 39–40". Certainly, there may be cases where an estoppel by convention cannot arise as the parties are simply acting consistently with a duty imposed by their agreement, rather than acting outside the agreement: see e.g. *Morris Homes Ltd v Cheshire West and Chester Council* [2020] EWCA Civ 1516, [64]–[69]. A claim of estoppel by convention also fell on deaf ears in *Jones v Lydon (No 1)* [2021] EWHC 2321 (Ch).

[38] [2021] 3 W.L.R. 697, [2021] UKSC 39 at [39]. Adopted by Carnwath LJ in *ING Bank NV v Ros Roca SA* [2011] EWCA Civ 353; [2012] 1 W.L.R. 472 at [55]–[60] and described there as "a succinct statement of the modern law, adopted without dissent or qualification by the full House of Lords", the formulation was also accepted by the parties and court in *Robert Sofer v Swissindependent Trustees SA* [2020] EWCA Civ 699 at [53]. For a helpful summary of the "principles applicable to the assertion of an estoppel by convention arising out of non-contractual dealings", see *HMRC v Benchdollar Ltd* [2009] EWHC 1310 (Ch), per Briggs J at [52]; and note too *Mears Ltd v Shoreline Housing Partnership Ltd* [2015] EWHC 1396 (TCC), per Akenhead J at [51].

[39] *Republic of India v India Steamship Co Ltd ("The Indian Endurance and The Indian Grace")* [1998] A.C. 878 at 913–914.

[40] Lord Steyn here cited *K Lokumal & Sons (London) Ltd v Lotte Shipping Co Pty Ltd (The August Leonhardt)* [1985] 2 Lloyd's Rep. 28; *Norwegian American Cruises A/S v Paul Mundy Ltd (The Vistafjord)* [1988] 2 Lloyd's Rep. 343; and G. Treitel, *The Law of Contract*, 9th edn (Sweet & Maxwell, 1995). See now, to the same effect, E. Peel, *Treitel's Law of Contract*, 13th edn (Sweet & Maxwell, 2011), para.3–095.

At the end, add new paragraph:

The Supreme Court also approved the five principles established by Briggs J (as he then was) in *HMRC v Benchdollar*,[40a] and as amended in later decisions such as *Blindley Heath Investments Ltd v Bass*.[40b] Those principles were given in the context of non-contractual dealings but it was suggested in the *Tinkler* case that they are also "a correct statement of the law on estoppel by convention for contractual, as well as non-contractual dealings". The principles are: (i) the common assumption must be expressly shared between A and B, and there must be conduct by the parties, consisting of words or conduct from which the necessary sharing can properly be inferred, that "crosses the line" between them[40c]; (ii) the expression of the common assumption by A must be such that "he may properly be said to have assumed some element of responsibility for it, in the sense of conveying to [B] an understanding that [A] expected [B] to rely upon it"; (iii) "[B] must in fact have relied upon the common assumption, to a sufficient extent, rather than merely upon [B's] own independent view of the matter[40d]; (iv) that reliance must have occurred in connection with some subsequent mutual dealing between the parties; (v) some detriment must thereby have been suffered by [B], or benefit thereby have been conferred upon [A], sufficient to make it unjust or unconscionable for [A] to assert the true legal (or factual) position."[40e]

[40a] [2010] 1 All E.R. 174.

[40b] [2017] Ch. 389, [2015] EWCA Civ 1023. Note that in *Stena Line v Merchant Navy* [2010] EWHC 1805, Briggs J, accepted that modification was needed to his original formulation of this principle in *Benchdollar*, as "[The common assumption] must be expressly, or implicitly by words or conduct from which the necessary sharing can properly be inferred, shared between them"; see too Lord Briggs in *Tinkler v Revenue and Customs Commissioners* [2021] 3 W.L.R. 697, [2021] UKSC 39 at [87].

[40c] See *Tinkler v Revenue and Customs Commissioners* [2021] 3 W.L.R. 697, [2021] UKSC 39 at [49].

[40d] In *Tinkler v Revenue and Customs Commissioners* [2021] 3 W.L.R. 697, [2021] UKSC 39 at [89], Lord Briggs states that B's reliance "may be subordinate to [B's] reliance upon its own view or advice about the reliability of the assumption, but it must have influenced [B's] thinking: see *HMRC v Benchdollar* [2010] 1 All ER 174 at [55]."

40e *HMRC v Benchdollar* [2010] 1 All ER 174 [52] (Briggs J).

Replace paragraph with:

12-012   The doctrine may therefore apply where the party against whom the estoppel by convention is raised made no representation or promise. It nonetheless resembles estoppel by representation in its effect (it determines the facts on which the parties' rights are to be determined, rather than itself providing a cause of action).[41] As a result of the decision of the Court of Appeal in *Amalgamated Investment & Property Co Ltd v Texas Commerce International Bank Ltd*,[42] estoppel by convention is now more often regarded as a variant of equitable estoppel[43] and seen as defining a particular set of circumstances in which it is "unjust",[44] or unconscionable,[45] to allow a party to go back on an underlying assumption that formed the basis of mutual dealings between the parties.[45a] As noted by Lord Burrows in *Tinkler v Revenue and Customs Commissioners*, "unconscionability is unlikely to add anything once the other elements of estoppel by convention have been established and, in particular, where it has been established that [B] has detrimentally relied on the common assumption. However, one can certainly envisage exceptional cases where unconscionability may have a useful additional role to play."[45b] On this view, the role of unconscionability in relation to estoppel by convention is essentially the same as in relation to proprietary estoppel, according to the analysis in para.12-037 below.

[41] See G. Treitel, *Some Landmarks of Twentieth Century Contract Law* (Oxford: OUP, 2002), 38–41, distinguishing between estoppels which relate to facts (such as estoppel by representation or estoppel by convention) and those which instead relate to legal effects (such as promissory estoppel and proprietary estoppel). In *Mears Ltd v Shoreline Housing Partnership Ltd* [2015] EWHC 1396 (TCC), Akenhead J at [71] noted that: "Although there are distinguishing features between the two types of estoppel [by representation and by convention], there must be cases, and this is one, where the two are almost interchangeable on the facts".

[42] *Amalgamated Investment & Property Co Ltd v Texas Commerce International Bank Ltd* [1982] Q.B. 84.

[43] See, e.g. *PW & Co v Milton Gate Investments Ltd* [2004] Ch. 142 at [156], and at [238]; *ING Bank NV v Ros Roca SA* [2011] EWCA Civ 353; [2012] 1 W.L.R. 472 at [73], per Carnwath LJ.

[44] In addition to the statement of Lord Steyn set out at para.12-011, see too *Amalgamated Investment & Property Co Ltd v Texas Commerce International Bank Ltd* [1982] Q.B. 84 at 122, per Lord Denning MR.

[45] *Norwegian American Cruises A/S v Paul Mundy Ltd ("The Vistafjord")* [1988] 2 Lloyds Rep. 343 at 352; *Gloyne v Richardson* [2001] 2 B.C.L.C. 669 CA at 683–684; *PW & Co v Milton Gate Investments Ltd* [2004] Ch. 142 at [156], [165], [209], and [221]. In *Blindley Heath Investments Ltd v Bass* [2017] Ch 389, [2015] EWCA Civ 1023. Hildyard LJ noted at [72] that estoppel by convention was originally developed by the common law courts, but that "especially since the decision of this court in *Amalgamated Investment & Property Co Ltd (in liquidation) v Texas Commerce International Bank Ltd* [1982] 1 Q.B. 84, its principles have largely been explained in equitable terms and expanded as another variant of equitable estoppel" and at [73] referred with approval to this paragraph.

[45a] The mutual dealings need not take the form of a contract or a specific transaction: see *Tinkler v Revenue and Customs Commissioners* [2021] 3 W.L.R. 697, [2021] UKSC 39 [70]–[73]. Note the foregoing sentence of the text was cited with approval in *Trebisol Sud Ouest SAS v Berkley Finance Ltd* [2021] EWHC 2494 (QB) at [92].

[45b] [2021] 3 W.L.R. 697, [2021] UKSC 39 [64] (emphasis in original). Lord Hodge, Lady Arden and Lady Rose agreed with Lord Burrows' judgment and Lord Briggs delivered a brief concurring judgment. In *Tinkler* itself, the need for unconscionability did not prevent the Revenue raising the estoppel by convention, even though it was "primarily at fault" on the facts by "carelessly sending the notice of enquiry to the wrong address and in its consequent misrepresentation to [A]". An example given by Lord Burrows at [64] of a rare case where unconscionability may be relevant is where "fraudulent conduct by the estoppel raiser would rule out the estoppel by convention".

Replace footnote 42 with:

[42] *Amalgamated Investment & Property Co Ltd (in liquidation) v Texas Commerce International Bank Ltd* [1982] 1 Q.B. 84 at 131–132, per Brandon LJ. For this distinction, see too *Astra Asset Management UK Ltd v The Co-operative Bank Plc* [2019] EWHC 897 (Comm) at [132]–[135]. In *Rail for London v Hackney LBC* [2022] EWHC 1075 (Ch), it was said at [55] to be an open question as to whether post-contractual dealings can give rise to an estoppel by convention which places more onerous obligations on a party to the contract. The line between using estoppel by convention to support an independent cause of action, and instead using it to create a cause of action where none had existed, was said to be difficult to draw on the facts of *Geoquip Marine Operations AG v Tower Resources Cameroon SA* [2022] EWHC 531 (Comm) at [146].

At the end, add new paragraph:

In *Tinkler v Revenue and Customs Commissioners*,[47a] the doctrine was applied **12-013** to a mutual assumption arising in a non-contractual context. A, the taxpayer, was prevented from denying that B, the Revenue, had opened a valid enquiry into A's tax return, even though B had sent the statutory notice informing A of the enquiry to the wrong address. B had written as well to A's accountants who, as A's agents, had engaged with B as to the substance of the enquiry and A had first raised the point about the validity of the notice only seven years later. The parties had therefore acted on the assumption that a valid enquiry had been opened, and A (through the accountants as his agents) had positively affirmed B's mistaken assumption by its active engagement in the enquiry, in circumstances where B could reasonably have expected A's accountants to have raised any objection.[47b] A had thus "assumed some element of responsibility" for the common assumption, and B had relied on it by carrying out the enquiry and later issuing a closure notice, suffering detriment by losing the chance to send a second, valid notice of enquiry within the statutory period for doing so.[47c] As a result, B was allowed to enforce A's underlying statutory duty to pay the tax due[47d] and so, as in the *Amalgamated Texas* case, whilst the estoppel by convention did not create an independent cause of action, it did allow B to succeed in a claim which would have failed absent the estoppel.

[47a] [2021] 3 W.L.R. 697, [2021] UKSC 39.

[47b] [2021] 3 W.L.R. 697, [2021] UKSC 39 [59].

[47c] [2021] 3 W.L.R. 697, [2021] UKSC 39 [61]–[63]. At [79]–[83], Lord Burrows rejected the argument that recognizing the estoppel by convention would outflank statutory protection given to the taxpayer, as on the facts there was no undermining of the statutory policy of ensuring a taxpayer had notice of the enquiry, and in any case it was open for the Revenue and a taxpayer to agree a method of giving such notice. Contrast *Zavarco UK plc v Sidhu* [2021] EWHC 1526 (Ch) at [111] where it was stated that an estoppel by convention could not be used to negate a duty imposed on a company by Parliament in the public interest and *Miah v Miah* [2020] EWHC 3374 (Ch) at [71] where it is suggested that an estoppel by convention could not prevent a written declaration of trust determining the parties' beneficial interests as that would be inconsistent with s.53 of the Law of Property Act 1925.

[47d] [2021] 3 W.L.R. 697, [2021] UKSC 39, [76].

Replace paragraph with:

Where a party seeks to rely on an assumption in this way, however, it is not suf- **12-014** ficient to show only that the parties had a common understanding.[48] B must also establish that there was an agreement or convention by which the parties regulated their dealings.[49] It must be established that the shared mistake or assumption "crossed the line".[50] B must show that he or she communicated the mistaken assumption or understanding to A[51] and that A either shared the mistake or acquiesced in it.[52] As explained by Lord Burrows in *Tinkler v Revenue and Customs Commissioners*[52a]: "The person raising the estoppel [B] must know that the person against whom the estoppel is raised [A] shares the common assumption and must be strengthened, or influenced, in its reliance on that common assumption by that knowledge; and [A] must (objectively) intend, or expect, that that will be the effect on [B] of its conduct crossing the line so that one can say that [A] has assumed some element of responsibility for [B's] reliance on the common assumption." The communication may be by words or conduct although there is some doubt as to whether it is necessary to establish a clear and unequivocal assumption of the kind necessary for an estoppel by representation.[53] There is no requirement that A originally induced B's mistaken assumption,[54] indeed, in *Tinkler*, it was B's mistaken conduct which initially gave rise to the assumption that an enquiry had been validly opened.[55] It is not necessary to show that either party subjectively believed the assumed state of facts to be true if they treated them as a true and acted on that assumption.[56] It is, however, necessary to establish that B was induced to act in reliance on the shared convention[57] so that it would be unjust to permit A to depart from it and assert the contrary.[58] B must be able to point to some detriment that would result, as a result of B's reliance on the assumption, if A were free to depart from it, or some benefit that would thereby be conferred on A, "sufficient to make it unjust or unconscionable for [A] to assert the true legal (or factual) position".[59] B's mere entry into a contract cannot, it seem, constitute the necessary reliance in order to support an estoppel by convention relating to the legal effect of that same contract.[60]

[48] See the statement of Lord Steyn in *The Indian Endurance* [1998] A.C. 878 at 913–014, set out at para.12-011. It is possible for the requirements of an estoppel by convention to be met where each party has forgotten a particular matter (see *Blindley Heath Investments Ltd v Bass* [2017] Ch. 389, [2015] EWCA Civ 1023, where Hildyard LJ stated at [79] that: "Whether the true state of affairs has been misappreciated, misremembered or forgotten should make no difference to whether the parties have in the event mutually adopted a common assumption"). In such a case, however, it does not suffice that each party was independently forgetful: it was said at [89] that the "real difficulty" is the evidential one of "showing that something other than forgetfulness played a part in the adoption of the assumption, and that the person sought to be estopped assumed some responsibility for it".

[49] *Amalgamated Investment v Texas Bank* [1982] Q.B. 84 at 122 C–D; *Norwegian American Cruises A/S v Paul Mundy Ltd ("the Vistafjord")* [1988] 2 Lloyd's Rep. 343; *Republic of India v India Steamship Co ("The Indian Endurance") (No.2)* [1998] A.C. 878 at 913E, per Lord Steyn; *Hillingdon LBC v ARC Ltd (No.2)* [2000] R.V.R. 283 at [60] per Arden J; *Commercial First Business Ltd v Munday* [2014] EWCA Civ 1296 at [28] per Patten LJ; *Howe v Motor Insurers' Bureau (No.1)* [2016] 1 W.L.R. 2707 at [102]. For a good example of the difference between a shared understanding and a convention which regulates the parties' dealings, see *Bridgestart Properties Ltd v London Underground Ltd* [2004] EWCA Civ 793; [2005] 1 P. & C.R. 15 (applied in *Khan v Tyne and Wear Passenger Transport Executive (t/a Nexus)* [2015] UKUT 43 (LC)), in which both parties were unaware that a limitation period had expired but continued to negotiate the terms of statutory compensation. It was held, at [23]–[24], that there was no estoppel by convention because there was no convention that A would not take any limitation defence. Similarly, in *Mitchell v Watkinson* [2014] EWCA Civ 1472, it was held at [54]–[55] that as "no-one would have given the slightest thought to the correct legal analysis of what had happened" it could not be said that an estoppel by convention had arisen to the effect that land was occupied under a written tenancy agreement rather than under an implied periodic tenancy.

[50] *The August Leonhardt* [1985] 2 Lloyd's Rep. 28 at 35; *Compania Portorafti Commerciale SA v Ultramar Panama Inc ("The Captain Gregos") (No.2)* [1990] 2 Lloyd's Rep. 395, at 405; *Blindley Heath Investments Ltd v Bass* [2017] Ch. 389, [2015] EWCA Civ 1023 at [93].

[51] See, e.g. *The Indian Endurance* [1998] A.C. 878 at 913, per Lord Steyn: "It is not enough that each of the two parties acts on an assumption not communicated to the other". Note too *K Lokumal & Sons (London) Ltd v Lotte Shipping Co Pty Ltd ("The August Leonhardt")* [1985] 2 Lloyd's Rep. 28 at 35 per Kerr LJ: "All estoppels must involve some statement or conduct by the party alleged to be estopped on which the alleged representee was entitled to rely and did rely. In this sense all estoppels may be regarded as requiring some manifest representation which crosses the line between representor and representee, either by statement or conduct". In *Bridgestart Properties Ltd v London Underground Ltd* [2004] EWCA Civ 793; [2005] 1 P. & C.R. 15, no estoppel by convention arose where the parties had

a shared but unexpressed assumption that no statutory limitation period applied to B's claim: *Bridgestart Properties Ltd v London Underground Ltd* [2004] EWCA Civ 793; [2005] 1 P. & C.R. 15 at 23–24.

[52] Where the estoppel by convention depends on A's acquiescence, it can arise only if A is aware of the specific belief of B in which A is said to acquiesce. As a result, such acquiescence is not present if A and B are at cross purposes as to the meaning of a particular term: see *ABN Amro Bank NV v Royal and Sun Alliance Insurance plc* [2021] EWCA Civ 1789, [2022] 1 W.L.R. 1773 at [87] (note that an estoppel by representation is possible in such a case, as if A has made a representation with the intention that B should rely on it, then A can be prevented from denying the objective meaning of that representation: see [88]). Note however that mere "passive acceptance" by A will not suffice: *Redrow Plc v Pedley* [2002] EWHC 983 (Ch); [2002] P.L.R. 339 at [64], per Morritt VC. This is significant when considering, as in *Redrow*, attempts by trustees of pension schemes to invoke an estoppel by convention against members of the scheme: see too *Briggs v Gleeds* [2014] EWHC 1178 (Ch) at [184], per Newey J.

[52a] [2021] 3 W.L.R. 697, [2021] UKSC 39 [51]. See too *Pearson v Lehman Brothers Finance SA* [2011] EWCA Civ 1544, Lloyd LJ at [106], adopting the formulation given by Briggs J in *HMRC v Benchdollar Ltd* [2009] EWHC 1310 (Ch) at [52].

[53] See the discussion in *Geoquip Marine Operations AG v Tower Resources Cameroon SA* [2022] EWHC 531 (Comm) at [122]–[126], which favours the need for such clarity (as does the view of Morgan J in *Crossco No 4 Unlimited v Jolan Ltd* [2011] EWHC 803 (Ch) at [333]) but notes the different view expressed in *ING Bank NV v Ros Roca SA* [2011] EWCA Civ 353 at [64] and at [69]. Certainly, lack of sufficient clarity as to a claimed shared assumption will prevent an estoppel by convention arising: see, e.g. *Cleveland Bridge UK Ltd v Sarens (UK) Ltd* [2018] EWHC 751 (TCC) (Joanna Smith QC at [126]); *Aras v National Bank of Greece* [2018] EWHC 1389 (Comm) (Picken J at [115]).

[54] See, e.g. see *Government of Swaziland Central Transport Administration v Leila Maritime Co Ltd ("The Leila")* [1985] 2 Lloyd's Rep. 173 at 179, per Mustill LJ; and *John v George* [1996] 1 E.G.L.R. 7 at 11D, per Morritt LJ.

[55] See [2021] 3 W.L.R. 697, [2021] UKSC 39 at [51] where Lord Burrows states that: "it is not a bar to estoppel that HMRC initiated the mistake or that, as in [*HMRC v Benchdollar Ltd* [2010] 1 All E.R. 174], HMRC was careless in relation to that mistake or induced the other party's mistake by misrepresentation." If B argues that an estoppel by convention arises because A failed to correct a mistaken belief of B when A was under a "duty to speak out" then, at least as between parties to legal proceedings, such an argument will succeed only in an "exceptional" case, where there has been some element of "sharp practice or misleading behaviour": see *Costain Ltd v Tarmac Holdings Ltd* [2017] EWHC 319 (Coulson J) at [112]; referring to *Pacol Ltd v Trade Lines Ltd ('The Henrik Sif')* [1982] 1 Lloyd's Rep. 456. In contrast, in *Ted Baker Plc v Axa Insurance UK Plc* [2017] EWCA Civ 4097, Sir Christopher Clarke stated at [88], in the context of an insured-insurer relationship, that a failure to speak could give rise to an estoppel by acquiescence in the absence of dishonesty or intention to mislead, as long as (see [82]) "in the light of the circumstances known to the parties, a reasonable person in the position of [B] would expect the other party (here the insurers) acting honestly and reasonably to take steps to make his position plain".

[56] *Grundt v Great Boulder Proprietary Gold Mines Ltd* (1937) 59 C.L.R. 641 at 676, per Dixon J. Dixon J's analysis on this point was approved by the Privy Council in *Prime Sight Ltd v Lavarello* [2013] UKPC 22; [2014] A.C. 436 at [23] and [46] per Lord Toulson: the general position is that "parties to a transaction may choose to enter into it on the basis that certain facts are to be treated as correct as between themselves for the purposes of the transaction, although both know that they are contrary to the true state of affairs, in which case the necessary convention for an estoppel will be established". See too *ING Bank NV v Ros Roca SA* [2011] EWCA Civ 353; [2012] 1 W.L.R. 472 at [85], where an estoppel by convention arose even though, as Rix LJ noted at [85], one of the parties did not internally share the assumption, but affected and purported to share it externally and objectively. If however a party makes a representation knowing it to be false, and the other party believes it to be true, then it is at least arguable that there is no shared assumption such as to support an estoppel by convention: see *Robert Sofer v Swissindependent Trustees SA* [2020] EWCA Civ 699 at [56].

[57] See the formulation of Lord Denning MR in *Amalgamated Investment v Texas Bank* [1982] Q.B. 84 at 122. Note too the analysis of Brandon LJ at 131: "The transactions took place on the basis of that assumption, and their course was influenced by it in the sense that, if the assumption had not been made, the course of the transactions would without doubt have been different".

[58] See *The Vistafjord* [1998] 2 Lloyd's Rep. 343 at 551; approving *Hamel-Smith v Pycroft & Jetsave Ltd* unreported 5 February 1987; *Credit Suisse v Allerdale BC* [1995] 1 Lloyd's Rep. 315 (approved on

different grounds at [1997] Q.B. 362) where the claim failed because B was not induced to act by the shared convention and it was not unconscionable to permit A to withdraw from it; *Hillingdon LBC v ARC Ltd (No.3)* [2000] 3 E.G.L.R. 97 (where B suffered little prejudice before the representation or shared assumption was withdrawn); *Gloyne v Richardson* [2001] EWCA Civ 716 (shared convention withdrawn); *PW & Co v Milton Gate Investments Ltd* [2004] Ch. 142 (shared convention withdrawn); and *WS Tankship II BV v Kwangju Bank Ltd* [2011] EWHC 3103 (Comm) at [183] (shared convention withdrawn). Contrast *ING Bank NV v Ros Roca SA* [2011] EWCA Civ 353; [2012] 1 W.L.R. 472 in which it was held that it would have been unconscionable to allow ING to go back on the parties' shared assumption: see per Carnwath LJ at [71]–[73]. Note that there is no such requirement of unconscionability if a party relies instead on a contractual estoppel, by claiming that the other party is under a contractual duty not to depart from an assumption: see e.g. *Springwell Navigation Corp v JP Morgan Chase Bank* [2010] EWCA Civ 1221 at [177], per Aikens LJ.

[59] *HMRC v Benchdollar Ltd* [2010] 1 All E.R. 174 at [52], per Briggs J, in a formulation approved by Vos LJ in *Preedy v Dunne* [2016] EWCA Civ 805 at [47]. See *ING Bank NV v Ros Roca SA* [2011] EWCA Civ 353; [2012] 1 W.L.R. 472 at [64], per Carnwath LJ, referring to the requirement of detriment established (in relation to a proprietary estoppel claim) in *Gillett v Holt* [2001] Ch. 210 CA at 232 and the need to conduct a "broad inquiry as to whether repudiation of an assurance is or is not unconscionable in all the circumstances". In *Tinkler v Revenue and Customs Commissioners* [2021] 3 W.L.R. 697, [2021] UKSC 39, it was noted at [63] that A "would stand to gain some £635,000 if estoppel by convention could not be established". In *Costain Ltd v Tarmac Holdings Ltd* [2017] EWHC 319 (TCC), Coulson J at [118] referred to an absence of detriment suffered by B as a result of any common assumption as a reason for rejecting a claimed estoppel. In *General Motors UK v Manchester Ship Canal* [2016] EWHC 2960 (Ch), HHJ Behrens, sitting as a Judge of the High Court, stated that, even if a common assumption had been found, no estoppel by convention would arise, as the detriment suffered by B was very small compared to the loss which would be suffered by A if the estoppel operated to prevent A's seeking relief from forfeiture (the question of estoppel was not considered by the Court of Appeal or Supreme Court in that case: [2018] EWCA Civ 1100; [2019] UKSC 46).

[60] See *Keen v Holland* [1984] 1 W.L.R. 251 at 261–262; *PW & Co v Milton Gate Investments Ltd* [2004] Ch. 142 at [162]–[169].

Replace n.62 with:

12-015 [62] *ING Bank Plc v Ros Roca SA* [2011] EWCA Civ 353; [2012] 1 W.L.R. 472 at [64], per Carnwath LJ; *Reaction Engines Ltd v BNP Paribas Depositary Services (Jersey) Ltd* [2021] EWHC 753 (Ch) [43]. In *The Indian Endurance* [1998] A.C. 878 HL, for example, the relevant assumption was as to the fact that further litigation would be conducted in England.

Replace n.72 with:

12-016 [72] *Cobbe v Yeoman's Row Management Ltd* [2008] UKHL 55; [2008] 1 W.L.R. 1752 at [14].

2. PROMISSORY ESTOPPEL

1. Nature and Origins of the Modern Doctrine

(a) General formulation.

Replace paragraph with:

12-018 A general, judicially approved,[78] formulation of the requirements of promissory estoppel is as follows.[79] Where, by his words or conduct one party to a transaction, (A) freely[80] makes to the other (B) a clear and unequivocal[81] promise or assurance that he or she will not enforce his or her strict legal rights, and that promise or assurance is intended to affect the legal relations between them[82] (whether contractual or otherwise[83]) or was reasonably understood by B to have that effect,[84] and, before it is withdrawn,[85] B acts upon it, altering his or her position[86] so that it would be inequitable to permit the first party to withdraw the promise,[87] the party making the promise or assurance will not be permitted to act inconsistently with it.[88] B must also show that the promise was intended to be binding in the sense that (judged on an objective basis) it was intended to affect the legal relationship between the parties[89] and A either knew or could have reasonably foreseen that B would act on it.[90] Yet B's conduct need not derive its origin solely from A's encouragement or representation. The principal issue is whether A's representation had a sufficiently material influence on B's conduct to make it inequitable for A to depart from it.[91]

[78] *Harvey v Dunbar Assets Plc* [2017] EWCA Civ 60 at [60] (Henderson LJ); *Crossco (No.4) Unlimited v Jolan Ltd* [2011] EWHC 803 (Ch) at [332], where Morgan J approved the formulation, set out as it was then in the 32nd edition of this work. The decision of Morgan J was upheld on appeal ([2011] EWCA Civ 1619; [2012] 2 All E.R. 754), where estoppel was only briefly considered. For a very similar formulation, in the context of contractual rights, see Kitchin LJ in *MWB Business Exchange Centres Ltd v Rock Advertising Ltd* [2016] EWCA Civ 553; [2017] Q.B. 604 at [61]. The Supreme Court allowed an appeal: [2018] UKSC 24; [2018] W.L.R. 1603 but without needing to consider the operation of estoppel in any detail.

[79] See too the formulations of Lord Hodson in *Ajayi v R T Briscoe (Nigeria) Ltd* [1964] 1 W.L.R. 1326 at 1330; of Robert Goff J in *BP Exploration Co (Libya) Ltd v Hunt (No.2)* [1979] 1 W.L.R. 783 at 810; and of Lord Goff in *Motor Oil Hellas (Corinth) Refineries SA v Shipping Corp of India (the "Kanchenjunga")* [1990] 1 Lloyd's Rep. 391 HL at 399. The formulation set out in the text was cited with approval in *Kodric v Bitstamp Holdings NV* [2022] EWHC 210 (Ch) at [129].

[80] *D & C Builders Ltd v Rees* [1966] 2 Q.B. 617 (economic duress may prevent an estoppel's arising).

[81] See, in particular, *Woodhouse AC Israel Cocoa Ltd SA v Nigerian Produce Marketing Co Ltd* [1972] A.C. 741; *Baird Textiles Holdings Ltd v Marks & Spencer Plc* [2001] EWCA Civ 274.

[82] See *High Trees* [1947] K.B. 130 at 134. This was the principal basis on which Denning J distinguished *Jorden v Money* (1854) 5 H.L.C. 185. See also para.12-025.

[83] *Durham Fancy Goods Ltd v Michael Jackson (Fancy Goods) Ltd* [1968] 2 Q.B. 839.

[84] *Baird Textiles Holdings Ltd v Marks & Spencer Plc* [2001] EWCA Civ 274.

[85] *Birmingham and District Land Co v London & NW Railway Co* (1888) 40 Ch. D. 268; and *Ajayi v RT Briscoe (Nigeria) Ltd* [1964] 1 W.L.R. 1326.

[86] See *High Trees* [1947] K.B. 130 at 134; *Commissioner of Inland Revenue v Morris* [1958] N.Z.L.R. 1126 at 1136; *Ajayi v RT Briscoe (Nigeria) Ltd* [1964] 1 W.L.R. 1326 at 1330; *Tool Metal Manufacturing Co Ltd v Tungsten Electric Co Ltd* [1955] 1 W.L.R. 761 at 764, per Lord Simonds and also at 781 per Lord Tucker and at 799 per Lord Cohen.

[87] See *James v Heim Gallery (London) Ltd* (1980) 256 E.G. 819 CA at 823, 825; *Societe Italo-Belge pour le Commerce et L'Industrie SA v Palm and Vegetable Oils (Malaysia) Sdn Bhd ("the Post Chaser")* [1982] 1 All E.R. 19 at 26a; *Motor Oil Hellas (Corinth) Refineries SA v Shipping Corp of India (the "Kanchenjunga")* [1990] 1 Lloyd's Rep. 390 HL at 399; and *Emery v UCB Corporate Services Ltd* [2001] EWCA Civ 675 at [28]. See also para.25-028.

[88] *Hughes v Metropolitan Railway* (1877) 2 App. Cas. 439; *Birmingham & District Land Co v L & NW Ry* (1888) 40 Ch. D. 286; *Central London Property Trust Ltd v High Trees House Ltd* [1947] K.B. 130; *Combe v Combe* [1951] 2 K.B. 215.

[89] *Central London Property Trust Ltd v High Trees House Ltd* [1947] K.B. 130 at 134; and *Baird Textile Holdings Ltd v Marks & Spencer Plc* [2001] EWCA Civ 274. See also para.12-026.

[90] *James v Heim Gallery (London) Ltd* (1980) 256 E.G. 819 at 823.

[91] *Amalgamated Investment & Property Co Ltd v Texas Commerce International Bank Ltd* [1982] Q.B. 84 at 104, 105; and *Lark v Outhwaite* [1991] 1 Lloyd's Rep. 132 at 142.

(c)   The principle in Hughes v Metropolitan Railway Co.

Replace third paragraph with:

It is submitted that the principle to be derived from those two decisions can best **12-020** be explained as follows. It is capable of applying where A claims to have acquired a right (such as, for example, a power to forfeit a lease or to terminate a contract)[98] as a result of particular action or inaction by B. If B's conduct was influenced by a belief, encouraged by A, that, if B so acted or failed to act, A would *not* acquire, or enforce, the right in question, A is then prevented from acquiring, or exercising the benefit of, that right. As noted by Lord Cairns LC in *Hughes*, even if A did not seek to "take advantage of, to lay a trap for, or to lull into false security those with whom he was dealing",[99] it would nonetheless be inequitable for A to benefit from B's conduct, having encouraged B to believe that, if B acted in that way, A would not have that benefit.[100] The principle can thus be seen as falling squarely into an established equitable jurisdiction to prevent the unconscionable insistence on strict legal rights.[101] It is not simply a rule about contractual rights, but can apply whenever A attempts to exercise a right arising as a result of particular action or inaction of B.[102] Nor is it simply a rule about preventing A from enforcing a duty of B, as it can also apply, as in *Hughes* itself, to prevent A's exercise of a power.[103] It may also apply, for example, where A attempts to rely on a limitation period after B, in reliance on a belief encouraged by A that A would not take such a point, failed to commence proceedings within the period prescribed.[104] The principle is, however, incapable of serving as an independent cause of action for B, as it simply prevents A's exercise of a right that A claims to have acquired as a result of B's action or inaction.[105]

[98] See too *Legione v Hateley* (1983) 152 C.L.R. 406, where the High Court of Australia considered the principle in relation to the attempt of A, a vendor of land, to exercise a contractual power to terminate a contract of sale where B had not complied with a notice requiring payment by a particular date.

[99] *Hughes v Metropolitan Railway Co* (1877) 2 App. Cas. 439 at 448.

[100] See D. Gordon, "Creditors' Promises to Forgo Rights" [1963] C.L.J. 222.

[101] See P. Finn, "Equitable Estoppel" in P. Finn (ed), *Essays in Equity* (Lawbook Co Ltd, 1985), p.59. In *Reaction Engines Ltd v BNP Paribas Depositary Services (Jersey) Ltd* [2021] EWHC 753 (Ch), the court in considering *Hughes* referred to the "doctrine of equitable forbearance", although the requirement stated at [17] that A must have made a "clear and unequivocal" promise or representation, albeit one that can be inferred from conduct, is perhaps not easy to square with the result in *Hughes* itself.

[102] See, e.g. *Durham Fancy Goods Ltd v Michael Jackson (Fancy Goods) Ltd* [1968] 2 Q.B. 839: A claimed to have acquired a right, under s.108 of the Companies Act 1948, to sue B personally on a bill of exchange purportedly drawn on a company of which B was a director. That right arose only if B signed a bill on which the company's name was incorrectly recorded. B had so signed a bill, but it was held that A's claim failed as, by having itself incorrectly inscribed the company's name on the bill, A had "implied that acceptance of the bill in that form would be, or would be accepted by them as, a regular acceptance of the bill" (per Donaldson J at 848).

[103] The suggestion that promissory estoppel can apply only to prevent A's exercising a Hohfeldian claim-right (i.e. a right correlating to a duty to B), made by K. Handley, *Estoppel by Conduct and Election* (Sweet & Maxwell, 2006), p.203, should therefore be rejected: see A. Robertson, "Three Models of Promissory Estoppel" (2013) 7 *Journal of Equity* 226 at 234.

[104] See, e.g. *Seechurn v ACE Insurance SA-NV* [2002] EWCA Civ 67 at [51]–[55], although no promissory estoppel arose there as there had been no grounds for any implication that A had encouraged B to believe that it would not take a limitation point. In *Dixon v Santander Asset Finance plc* [2021] EWHC 1044 (Ch) at [142] the court cited the statement in McGee, *Limitation Periods* (8th edn, 2018) 21.025 that establishing an estoppel or waiver in relation to the Limitation Act is likely to be a "formidable task and one which can be accomplished only in the most exceptional cases."

[105] *Combe v Combe* [1951] 2 K.B. 215 CA at 229.

2. The Requirements of Promissory Estoppel

(a) Representation in the nature of a promise.

Replace n.140 with:

[140] Compare, for example, the fact that an unjust enrichment claim based on a failure of consideration **12-024** may be premised on the fact that B conferred a benefit on A on a particular basis, known to and shared by the parties, which has since failed: no promise of A is required: see e.g. *Cobbe v Yeoman's Row Management Ltd* [2008] UKHL 55; [2008] 1 W.L.R. 1752, at [40]–[44]; *Benedetti v Sawiris* [2013] UKSC 50; [2013] 3 W.L.R. 351 at [86] per Lord Reed.

Replace paragraph with:

The promise, or encouragement must be "clear and unequivocal"[141] in the sense that, objectively understood,[142] it makes apparent to B that A's right will not be enforced.[143] If A's conduct is instead capable of a number of different reasonable interpretations, at least one of which is inconsistent with A's right not being enforced, no promissory estoppel may arise.[144] If, for example, B's claim is that he or she was encouraged to believe that a right would be suspended, there must be certainty as to the specific right of A's in question[145] and as to the period of the supposed suspension.[146] A must have encouraged B to believe that A's right would not be enforced: if A's conduct can instead be reasonably understood as involving only advice,[147] a suggestion[148] or even a threat[149] that A may act in a particular way, there are no grounds for a promissory estoppel.

[141] See, e.g. *Woodhouse AC Israel Cocoa Ltd SA v Nigerian Produce Marketing Co Ltd* [1972] A.C. 741 at 756–757, per Lord Hailsham LC; and at 761 per Viscount Dilhorne; *Kim v Chasewood Park Residents Ltd* [2013] EWCA Civ 239 at [23], per Patten LJ: "There is no doubt that in order to found a promissory estoppel (in the same way as any other estoppel based on a representation of fact) the representation or promise must be clear and unambiguous"; *Union of Shop, Distributive and Allied Workers v Tesco Stores Ltd* [2022] EWCA Civ 978 at [53]. In *Joseph v Deloitte NSE LLP* [2020] EWCA Civ 1457 at [33], the Court of Appeal proceeded on the basis that the requirement is met if the promise or representation is "sufficiently clear and unequivocal" or "clear enough" to B, and made reference to the approach in the proprietary estoppel case of *Thorner v Major* [2009] 1 W.L.R. 776 (see para.12-042 below). In *Crown Melbourne Ltd v Cosmopolitan Hotel (Vic) Pty Ltd* [2016] HCA 26, French CJ, Kiefel and Bell JJ at [35] emphasised that the requirement that the promise be precise and unambiguous "does not mean that the words used may not be open to different constructions, but rather that they must be able to be understood in a particular sense by the person to whom the words are addressed. The sense in which they may be understood provides the basis for the assumption or expectation upon which the person to whom they are addressed acts. The words must be capable of misleading a reasonable person in the way that the person relying on the estoppel claims he or she has been misled". Keane J at [147] appeared to apply a more demanding test, stating that: "Where a contractual right or liability is to be altered, coherence in the law requires that a representation which is said to bring about that alteration should be no less certain in its terms than would be required for an effective contractual variation". In contrast, Nettle J at [217] preferred a less demanding test, as has been applied in proprietary estoppel cases, on the basis that the same "more general foundational principle" underlies each form of equitable estoppel.

[142] As the test is objective, an estoppel may arise, preventing the assertion of a right, even if A was, at the time of A's encouragement of B, in fact unaware of A's right: see e.g. the statement of Lord Salmon in *Bremer Handelsgesellschaft mbH v Vanden Avenne-Izegem* [1978] 2 Lloyd's Rep. 10 at 126. See also *Peyman v Lanjani* [1985] Ch. 457, esp. 495B: "waiver or estoppel by conduct, for the operation of which knowledge of the relevant facts is enough, a party does not have to be aware of the legal rights to which those facts give rise"; and *Motor Oil Hellas (Corinth) Refineries SA v Shipping Corp of India (the "Kanchenjunga")* [1990] 1 Lloyd's Rep. 390 at 399: "No question arises of any particular knowledge on the part of the representor".

[143] See, e.g. *Tameside MBC v Barlow Securities Group Services Ltd* [2001] B.L.R. 113 CA at 122: even if A could be said to have represented that it was not necessary for B to have obtained the certificate, required under the contract as part of the final accounting process, this did not entail any representation that A would not enforce any right it might have to rely on the absence of such a certificate if, for

example, making a claim in relation to faulty materials or workmanship. The analysis in this and the following paragraph of the text as to the "clear and unequivocal requirement" were cited with approval by Andrew Burrows QC (sitting as a Judge of the High Court) in *Greenhouse v Paysafe Financial Services Ltd* [2018] EWHC 3296 (Comm) at [17], where it was held at [39] that the requirement for a "clear and unequivocal" promise or representation had not been met.

[144] As pointed out by Lord Salmon in *Woodhouse AC Israel Cocoa Ltd SA v Nigerian Produce Marketing Co Ltd* [1972] A.C. 741 at 771, this does not mean that A's promise or encouragement must be "not only clear and unequivocal but is also incapable of having extracted from it some possible meaning other than its true meaning". Rather, for the estoppel to fail, the competing interpretation must be objectively a reasonable one.

[145] See *Woodhouse AC Israel Cocoa Ltd SA v Nigerian Produce Marketing Co Ltd* [1972] A.C. 741 HL A's statement that "payment can be made in sterling…not only with contracts already entered into but also with future contracts" was not a clear and unequivocal assurance that A would not enforce its contractual right to insist on Nigerian dollars as the currency of account of the contract: it was ambiguous as it might also be interpreted as relating only to the denomination in which payment was to be tendered (see, e.g. at 767–768, per Lord Cross).

[146] In *Woodhouse AC Israel Cocoa Ltd SA v Nigerian Produce Marketing Co Ltd* [1972] A.C. 741 HL: A's statement, set out at fn.144, was also uncertain in as far as it did not specify the duration of the supposed suspension of A's contractual right (see, e.g. at 762, per Lord Pearson).

[147] *Graham v Secretary of State for the Environment* [1993] J.P.L. 353 (assurance "advisory rather than authoritative in tone"); *China-Pacific SA v Food Corp of India ("The Winson")* [1981] Q.B. 403 (reversed on different grounds at [1982] A.C. 939) where the assurance relied on was a statement by solicitors that they had advised their clients that they were liable for a certain sum.

[148] *Marseille Fret SA v D Oltmann Schiffarts GmbH (the "Trado")* [1982] 1 Lloyd's Rep. 157.

[149] *Drexel Burnham Lambert International SA v El Nasr* [1986] 1 Lloyd's Rep. 357.

Replace third paragraph with:

As the effect of a promissory estoppel is to prevent A's enjoying the full benefit of a particular right, and as such an estoppel can arise without any contractual consideration's being provided by B, a court will naturally be cautious in ascertaining whether A did give the required clear and unequivocal encouragement to B.[150] So, whilst it is clear that a promissory estoppel may arise even in the absence of an express statement by A,[151] a court will require clear evidence before finding that A impliedly encouraged B. If, for example, it would not have objectively appeared to B that A was even aware of the right in question, encouragement is likely to be implied from A's course of conduct only if A created the impression that A was willing to "abandon any rights that he might enjoy which were inconsistent with [A's] course of conduct".[152] Further, the general position is that mere silence and inaction by A cannot found a promissory estoppel,[153] as A's failure to act, if capable of communicating anything, will generally be open to differing reasonable interpretations,[154] at least one of which will be inconsistent with A's right not being enforced. There are, however, two exceptions.[154a] First, if A is under a duty to disclose the existence of a particular matter giving rise to a right in A's favour, A's failure to do so may possibly support a promissory estoppel by leading B reasonably to believe that A does not have, or does not intend to enforce, that right.[155] Secondly, if A stands by, knowing that B has a mistaken belief as to B's current legal rights and fails to take a reasonably available opportunity to assert A's inconsistent right, the doctrine of acquiescence may then apply to prevent A's later asserting that right.[156] That doctrine will be discussed separately at para.12-034.

[150] See, e.g. *Collier v P & M J Wright (Holdings) Ltd* [2007] EWCA Civ 1329; [2008] 1 W.L.R. 643 at [45], per Longmore LJ. See too *Chaggar v Chaggar* [2018] EWHC 1203 (QB) at [272], per Morris J. In *MWB Business Exchange Centres Ltd v Rock Advertising Ltd* [2018] UKSC 24; [2018] 2 W.L.R. 1603, Lord Sumption (with whom Baroness Hale, Lord Wilson, and Lord Lloyd-Jones agreed) at [16]

considered that, where the parties have agreed that any variation to their contract must have a particular form (e.g. by agreeing a "No Oral Modification" clause), particular care must be taken to ensure that "the scope of estoppel cannot be so broad as to destroy the whole advantage of certainty for which the parties stipulated...At the very least, (i) there would have to be some words or conduct unequivocally representing that the variation was valid notwithstanding its informality; and (ii) something more would be required for this purpose than the informal promise itself: see *Actionstrength Ltd v International Glass Engineering INGLEN SpA* [2003] 2 A.C. 541 at [9] and [51], per Lord Bingham of Cornhill and Lord Walker of Gestingthorpe." See too *A v B* [2020] EWHC 2790 (Comm) [91] and *Williams v Simm* [2021] EWHC 121 (Ch).

[151] See, e.g. *Paragon Mortgages Ltd v McEwan-Peter* [2011] EWHC 2491 (Comm) at [35]: where the creditor had made it plain that enforcement would occur if the debtor's arrears exceeded three months, this could not be said to be an unequivocal assurance that no enforcement would occur before that point.

[152] *Youell v Bland Welch & Co Ltd (the "Superhulls Cover" Case) (No.2)* [1990] 2 Lloyd's Rep. 431 at 450; applied in *HIH Casualty and General Insurance Ltd v Axa Corporate Solutions* [2002] EWCA Civ 1253 at [25]; and *Glencore Grain Ltd v Flacker Shipping Ltd; The Happy Day* [2002] EWCA Civ 1068. See also *Petromec Inc v Petroleo Brasiliero SA Petrobas* [2004] EWHC 127 (Comm) at [158]: "[T]he deliberate creation or encouragement of an expectation which induces another to act to his detriment may amount to much the same as a representation and may therefore be sufficient to support an estoppel".

[153] Of course, mere silence and inaction must be contrasted with the case in A has not referred explicitly to a particular matter but an implied assurance can still be deduced from A's overall conduct, as in *Vitol SA v Esso Australia Ltd ("The Wise")* [1989] 2 Lloyd's Rep. 451 CA.

[154] See, e.g. *Moorgate Mercantile Co Ltd v Twitchings* [1977] A.C. 890 HL at 903, per Lord Wilberforce: "inaction or silence, by contrast with positive action or statement, is colourless". In *Allied Marine Transport Ltd v Vale do Rio Doce Navegacao SA ("The Leonidas D")* [1985] 1 W.L.R. 925 at 937, the Court of Appeal noted that "it is difficult to imagine how silence and inaction can be anything but equivocal". In *Argo Systems FZE v Liberty Insurance (PTE)* [2011] EWCA Civ 1572, the Court of Appeal reversed a finding at first instance that a party's failure to take a point in litigation established the basis on which a representation founding an estoppel could be implied, Aikens LJ noting, at [46]–[47], that an unequivocal promise is unlikely to be inferred from a party's silence or inaction. See too the analysis of Peter Smith J in *PCE Investors Ltd v Cancer Research UK* [2012] EWHC 884 (Ch) at [80]–[106].

[154a] The formulation in this paragraph was relied on by the court in *Royal Parks Ltd v Bluebird Boats Ltd* [2021] EWHC 2278 (TCC) at [109].

[155] In *Greenwood v Martins Bank* [1933] A.C. 51 a customer failed to comply with his contractual duty to his bank to disclose forgeries of which he was aware, and the customer was estopped from asserting as against the bank that particular cheques were forgeries. That was a case of estoppel by representation. Lord Tomlin at 57 stated that: "Mere silence cannot amount to a representation, but when there is a duty to disclose deliberate silence may become significant and amount to a representation". It is perhaps more difficult, however, to see how such a failure to disclose might be interpreted, in itself, as any assurance or encouragement as to A's future conduct; but an example is provided by *ING Bank NV v Ros Roca SA* [2011] EWCA Civ 353; [2012] 1 W.L.R. 472 where Rix LJ, at [93]–[95], found that an advising bank had a duty to inform its client that its calculations as to the basis on which fees would be charged was incorrect.

[156] See, e.g. *Pacol Ltd v Trade Lines Ltd ("The Henrik Sif")* [1982] 1 Lloyd's Rep. 456; and *The Stolt Loyalty* [1993] 2 Lloyd's Rep. 281; affirmed [1995] 1 Lloyds Rep. 598 CA. It is sometimes said in such cases that A is under a "duty to speak" (see, e.g. *Moorgate Mercantile Co Ltd v Twitchings* [1977] A.C. 890 at 903, per Lord Wilberforce) but this formulation, it is submitted, is inaccurate: the point is rather that, by means of the acquiescence principle, legal consequences may be attached to A's failure to assert a right. In cases within the first exception, in contrast, A is, independently of any estoppel or acquiescence, under a genuine duty to B, such as the contractual duty owed by the customer to the bank in *Greenwood v Martins Bank* [1933] A.C. 51 HL.

(b) B reasonably regarded A's promise or encouragement as intended to affect the parties' rights and as seriously intended by A as capable of being relied upon by B.

Replace footnote 159 with:

12-025 [159] See, e.g. *Baird Textile Holdings Ltd v Marks & Spencer Plc* [2001] EWCA Civ 274 at [92] and at [94], per Mance LJ. In *Trial Lawyers Association of British Columbia v Royal & Sun Alliance Insurance Co of Canada* [2021] SCC 47 at [18]–[23], the majority of the Supreme Court of Canada seem to take a subjective approach to A's intention, holding that the action of an insurer (A), in assisting with the defence of a claim against the insured before knowing of a breach by the insured rendering the policy void, did not give rise to an estoppel as it was not intended by A to affect A's legal relationship with the insured by waiving that breach. On the facts, however, as pointed out by Karakatsanis J at [77] in a concurring judgment, the same result would flow from an objective analysis, as there was no reason for the insured (or the victim claiming against the insured) to believe that A was aware of, and was willing to waive, the insured's breach.

(c) Legal relationship.

Replace footnote 170 with:

12-026 [170] See *Morris v Tarrant* [1971] 2 Q.B. 143 at 160D: "The authorities cited refer to cases in which there was a legal, if not necessarily a contractual, relationship between the parties. I hold that the principle found in these authorities is of no application as between a landowner and a trespasser". Compare Lord Denning MR's view in *Wallis's Cayton Bay Holiday Camp Ltd v Shell-Mex and BP Ltd* [1975] Q.B. 94 at 104 that promissory estoppel could be invoked to prevent a squatter from enforcing his strict rights under the Limitation Act 1939: on the facts of that case, the squatter had simply failed to reply to letters sent by the paper owner, so, even if promissory estoppel is prima facie applicable, it is very hard to find the required promise by A. In *Trial Lawyers Association of British Columbia v Royal & Sun Alliance Insurance Co of Canada* [2021] SCC 47, there was, as noted at [41]–[45], difficulty in finding the required legal relationship where a party bringing a claim against an insured defendant sought to establish an estoppel preventing the insurer from relying on a breach by the insured which rendered the insurance policy void.

Replace second paragraph with:

The better view, it is submitted, is that there is no independent requirement of a legal relationship as such; there is simply the inherent limit that promissory estoppel may only affect a right that A would otherwise have against B.[171] One consequence of this limit is that promissory estoppel cannot, in itself, give rise to a cause of action and it is that restriction that the need for a pre-existing legal relationship is often intended to preserve. So, for example, if B enters into a contract with A on the faith of a representation, not contractually binding, that B will acquire particular rights under that contract, promissory estoppel cannot be used to allow B to enforce that right against A.[172] In *The Henrik Sif*,[173] it was held that where A represents that there is an existing contractual relationship between the parties, such a representation may give rise to a promissory estoppel and so prevent A's later denial that A is under a contractual duty to B. This exception is, however, inconsistent with the clear current position of English law that promissory estoppel cannot be used to found independent rights.[174] As a result, the application of promissory estoppel can be supported[175] only if that restriction, applied as a matter of policy in English law to the broad modern principle, is to be lifted, so that the principle based on ensuring that B suffers no detriment as a result of B's reasonable reliance on A's promise can generate a right even if A's promise does not relate to any property that A owns or is about to acquire.[176]

[171] In an obiter discussion in *Harvey v Dunbar Assets Plc* [2017] EWCA Civ 60 at [62], Henderson LJ noted the view expressed here, and, whilst preferring to express no concluded view on the question, stated that: "it seems clear to me that the weight of existing authority supports the view that promis-

sory estoppel can only arise in the context of an existing legal relationship, as Lord Walker said in *Thorner v Major*". It was therefore doubted that promissory estoppel could apply as a result of a promise (that a guarantee would not be enforced) made to induce B to provide the guarantee to A. In any case, on the facts, it was implausible for B, an experienced business person, to expect that A would under no circumstances enforce the guarantee. Henderson LJ stated at [65] that "It is simply not credible that [B] proceeded to execute the Guarantee on the footing that he was engaging in a solemn farce, and that it would never in any circumstances be enforced against him". In *Umrish Ltd v Gill* [2020] EWHC 1513 (Ch), it was similarly found by Simon Salzedo QC, sitting as a Deputy Judge, that no promissory estoppel could arise from an alleged pre-contractual promise of A not to enforce a guarantee entered into with B, where the reliance would consist of entry into the "very legal relationship which the promise is said to have varied. There is an inherent contradiction between the promise not to enforce certain terms and the act done in supposed reliance upon it, viz. agreement to those very terms." It was also stated at [101] that: "It seems to me, in respectful agreement with Henderson LJ in *Harvey v Dunbar Assets*, that authority in England and Wales is strongly to the effect that promissory estoppel requires the pre-existence of a legal relationship between the promisor and promisee." The nature of the alleged promise meant that, "[e]ven if the law might develop further in terms of broader equitable restraints on conduct, it does not cover a case like this one" (at [102]).

[172] Lord Denning MR was therefore incorrect to find to the contrary in *Evenden v Guildford City Football Club* [1975] Q.B. 917 at 924; a decision overruled in *Secretary of State for Employment v Globe Elastic Thread Co Ltd* [1980] A.C. 506 HL. The reasoning of Lord Denning MR in *Brikom Investments Ltd v Carr* [1979] Q.B. 467 CA at 482–483 can be similarly criticised.

[173] *Pacol Ltd v Trade Lines Ltd ("The Henrik Sif")* [1982] 1 Lloyd's Rep. 456 at 466.

[174] See, e.g. E. Peel, *Treitel's Law of Contract*, 13th edn (2011), para.3–079. In *RPPC v Bank Leumi* [1992] 1 Lloyd's Rep. 515 at 542 it was stated that *The Henrik Sif* depended on its particular facts and in *Parkin v Alba Properties Ltd* [2013] EWHC 2036 (QB) at [77], it was distinguished and so did not support B's claim that: "a cause of action was created, where none had existed before". In *Baird Textiles Holdings Ltd v Marks & Spencer Plc* [2001] EWCA Civ 274, Mance LJ at [89], said that he had "no reason to doubt the outcome" in *The Henrik Sif*, as B was undoubtedly a party to a legal relationship: the only question was whether that relationship was with A, or with X. It is difficult, however, to accept that reasoning, given that the effect of the promissory estoppel was not to prevent A's enforcing a right against B but rather to prevent A's denying that a contract existed between A and B.

[175] It may be possible to defend the decision in *The Henrik Sif* on other grounds, either as an application of the acquiescence principle (see, e.g. para.12-034) or (as suggested by E. Peel, *Treitel's Law of Contract*, 13th edn (2011) at para.9–150) as an example of liability for an actionable non-disclosure.

[176] As appears to be the case in Australia: see *Waltons Stores (Interstate) Ltd v Maher* (1988) 164 C.L.R. 387. Although note that the exact scope of the principle remains a matter of contention, as discussed by A Robertson, "Three Models of Promissory Estoppel" (2013) 7 *Journal of Equity* 226.

(d) Reliance by B.

Replace paragraph with:

It is essential for B to establish that he or she relied on A's promise or encourage-   **12-027**
ment, in the sense that B was thereby induced to alter his or her position.[177] In *High Trees*[178] Denning J stated that a promise would only be binding if it "was in fact so acted upon". More recently, the requirement has been stated in terms of reliance by B of such a kind that it would be unjust or inequitable for B to go back on the promise.[179] Reliance may take the form of inaction rather than action[180] and it seems to be sufficient that A's conduct had a material influence on B.[181] It was suggested by Lord Denning that once B has established that a promise was made which was intended to be acted on, there is a presumption that B relied upon it.[182] Lord Denning's view seems to have focused on the position of A: if A intended B to act on the promise, and such action then occurred, it did not matter whether B in fact relied on the promise, or whether B would suffer a detriment if A were not to honour the promise.[183] Lord Denning's analysis has not, however, been adopted and the better view, as set out convincingly by Neuberger LJ in *Steria Ltd v Hutchison*,[184] is that

the burden of proving reliance remains on B throughout and reliance can never be established through "pure speculation".[185] Of course, the facts of some cases will mean that, unless A can elicit some further evidence to the contrary, inferring such reliance is a simple matter.[186]

[177] In *Tool Metal Manufacturing Co Ltd v Tungsten Electric Co Ltd* [1955] 1 W.L.R. 761 at 764 Viscount Simonds stated that B must be have been led "to alter his position" and this dictum was adopted by Lord Hodson in *Ajayi v RT Briscoe (Nigeria) Ltd* [1964] 1 W.L.R. 1326 at 1330. In *WJ Alan & Co Ltd v El Nasr Export & Import Co* [1972] 2 Q.B. 189 at 213 Lord Denning MR used the formulation that: "[B] must have been led to act differently from what he otherwise would have done". For a case in which B was unable to establish reliance, see *Fontana NV v Mautner* [1980] 1 E.G.L.R. 68 (Ch). In *Crown Melbourne Ltd v Cosmopolitan Hotel (Vic) Pty Ltd* [2016] HCA 26, the majority of the High Court of Australia emphasised that B must show that A can be said to have made a commitment in relation to the expectation on which B actually relies: it does not suffice for B to show that A made a commitment to act in a different way, and that B would have relied in the same way on that commitment (see e.g. French CJ, Kiefel and Bell JJ at [39], Keane J at [158]; although note the different view of Nettle J, drawing on proprietary estoppel cases, at [222]). It may therefore be important to be precise in determining the expectation on which B relied.

[178] *Central London Property Trust Ltd v High Trees House Ltd* [1947] K.B. 130 at 134.

[179] *BP Exploration Co (Libya) Ltd v Hunt (No.2)* [1979] 1 W.L.R. 783 at 810G: "reliance by the representee (whether by action or omission to act) on the representation which renders it inequitable, in all the circumstances, for the representor to enforce his strict rights, or at least to do so until the representee is restored to his former position"; *Motor Oil Hellas (Corinth) Refineries SA v Shipping Corp of India ("the Kanchenjunga")* [1990] 1 Lloyd's Rep. 390 at 399 per Lord Goff: "such reliance by the representee as will render it inequitable for the representor to go back upon his representation"; *Emery v UCB Corporate Services Ltd* [2001] EWCA Civ 675 at [28], per Peter Gibson LJ: "A promissory estoppel, in my judgment, arises where (1) there is a clear and unequivocal promise that strict legal rights will not be insisted upon (2) the promisee has acted in reliance on the promise; and (3) it would be inequitable for the promisor to go back on the promise".

[180] As, for example, where B fails to take steps to protect its position before the expiry of a limitation period: see, e.g. *Seechurn v Ace Insurance SA-NV* [2002] EWCA Civ 67; and note too *Nippon Yusen v Pacifica Navegacion SA (the "Ion")* [1980] 2 Lloyd's Rep. 245 at 250 per Mocatta J: "There was reliance upon the representation by way of omission".

[181] See, e.g. *Steria Ltd v Hutchison* [2006] EWCA Civ 1551; [2007] I.C.R. 445 at [117], per Neuberger LJ: "In order to succeed in a claim based on estoppel, it is probably not necessary for a claimant to satisfy what is known in a somewhat different area of the law as the 'but for' test. In other words in the present case it does not appear to me that Mr Hutchison has to show that, if the representation in question had not been made, he would not have joined the scheme. He merely has to show that the representation was a significant factor which he took into account when deciding whether to join the scheme". In *Lark v Outhwaite* [1991] 1 Lloyd's Rep. 132, Hirst J accepted, at 142, that: "the test is whether the representation influenced the representee, which may include the re-inforcement of a belief already held, or a contribution to lulling the representee into a state of false security". This is certainly consistent with the analysis of Robert Goff J in *Amalgamated Investment & Property Co Ltd v Texas Commerce International Bank Ltd* [1982] Q.B. 84 at 105–107.

[182] See, e.g. *Brikom Investments Ltd v Carr* [1979] Q.B. 467 at 483A: "Once it is shown that a representation was calculated to influence the judgment of a reasonable man, the presumption is that he was so influenced". See also *Greasley v Cooke* [1980] 1 W.L.R. 1306 at 1311H (a proprietary estoppel case).

[183] See, e.g. *Central London Property Trust Ltd v High Trees House Ltd* [1947] K.B. 130 at 134; A.T. Denning, "Recent Developments in the Doctrine of Consideration" (1952) 15 M.L.R. 1 at 5.

[184] *Steria Ltd v Hutchison* [2006] EWCA Civ 1551; [2007] I.C.R. 445 at [128]–[129]. Neuberger LJ's approach was applied in *Univar UK Ltd v Smith* [2020] EWHC 1596 (Ch) at [359]-[360].

[185] See *Steria Ltd v Hutchison* [2006] EWCA Civ 1551; [2007] I.C.R. 445 at [127], per Neuberger LJ; and *Meghraj Bank Ltd v Arsiwalla* CA 10 February 1994, per Peter Gibson LJ: "the court can only decide a question of promissory estoppel on the evidence put before it of what the promisee did in reliance on the promise rather than on speculation as to what the promisee might have done".

[186] See, e.g. *Steria Ltd v Hutchison* [2006] EWCA Civ 1551; [2007] I.C.R. 445 at [130], per Neuberger LJ.

(e)   Inequitable for A to assert A's right.

Replace second paragraph with:

This does not mean, however, that the prospect of detriment is never required.   **12-028**
In cases beyond the scope of either the acceptance of substitute performance
principle, or the principle applied in *Hughes*, it is necessary, it is submitted, for B
to show that he or she would suffer some detriment were A to be wholly free to
revoke A's promise.[192] In the absence of such detriment it will not be possible for
B to show that it would be inequitable for A to assert A's right.[193] This explains why,
for example, Neuberger LJ in *Steria Ltd v Hutchison* stated that, to establish a
promissory estoppel, it will generally be necessary for B to show that "he will suffer some detriment if the defendant is not held to the representation or promise".[194]
Following the seminal analysis of Dixon J in *Grundt v Great Boulder Pty Gold
Mines Ltd*,[195] "the real detriment or harm from which the law seeks to give protection is that which would flow from the change of position if the assumption were
deserted that led to it". This means that the focus is not on harm already suffered
by B, but rather on the detriment that B *would* suffer were A wholly free to enforce
A's right. It also means that the mere absence of a promised benefit does not
constitute detriment.[196] Further, the prospect of detriment must result not merely
from A's enforcement of A's right, but from the course of conduct undertaken by
B in reliance on A's promise that the right would not be enforced.[197] When it comes
to that part of promissory estoppel depending on the broader modern principle,
where detriment is required, there is no reason why the courts should not take
advantage of rules developed to test for detriment in cases of proprietary estoppel.[198]

[192] See, e.g. *Union of Shop, Distributive and Allied Workers v Tesco Stores Ltd* [2022] EWCA Civ 978
at [54]; *Meghraj Bank Ltd v Arsiwalla* CA 10 February 1994, considered at fn.195. In *Fontana NV v
Mautner* [1980] 1 E.G.L.R. 68 (Ch) where B claimed that, as a result of a promise that B could remain
in possession of A's flat, A could be prevented from evicting B, Balcombe LJ rejected the argument of
B's counsel, based on the analysis of Lord Denning MR in *WJ Alan & Co Ltd v El Nasr Export & Import
Co* [1972] 2 Q.B. 189 at 213–214, that there was no need for B to show detriment. That conclusion can
be justified, it is submitted, on the basis that, in *Fontana*, B could not rely on either the acceptance of
substitute performance principle or the *Hughes* principle and so had to rely on the broader modern
principle, where detriment is required.

[193] See, e.g. *Emery v UCB Corporate Services Ltd* [2001] EWCA Civ 675. Peter Gibson LJ, at [28],
stated that there is some controversy as to whether detriment is required, but also noted that "the fact
that the promisee has not altered his position to his detriment is plainly most material in determining
whether it would be inequitable for the promisee to be permitted to act inconsistently with his promise".
In that case, no estoppel arose as B had suffered no detriment by simply making payments that reduced
the debt owed by B to A.

[194] *Steria Ltd v Hutchison* [2006] EWCA Civ 1551; [2007] I.C.R. 445 at [93]. Note there is no presumption of detriment: *Steria Ltd v Hutchison* [2006] EWCA Civ 1551; [2007] I.C.R. 445 at [131].

[195] *Grundt v Great Boulder Pty Gold Mines Ltd* (1938) 59 C.L.R. 641 at 674–675. Approved and applied in *Gillett v Holt* [2001] Ch. 210 CA at 233; and *Steria Ltd v Hutchison* [2006] EWCA Civ 1551;
[2007] I.C.R. 445 at [125].

[196] See *Steria Ltd v Hutchison* [2006] EWCA Civ 1551; [2007] I.C.R. 445 at [125], per Neuberger LJ.
See too *Commercial & General Corporation Pty Ltd v Manassen Holdings Pty Ltd* [2021] SASCFC 40
(Full Court of Supreme Court of South Australia) at [142]–[161].

[197] In *MWB Business Exchange Centres Ltd v Rock Advertising Ltd* [2016] EWCA Civ 553; [2017] Q.B.
604 for example, it was held at [63] that it would not have been inequitable for the creditor to renege
on a promise to defer repayment where it sought to insist on its legal rights only two days later, at a time

when the debtor had made only one repayment (of a sum already due) under the revised schedule. The Supreme Court allowed an appeal in that case [2018] UKSC 24; [2018] W.L.R. 1603 but without needing to consider the operation of estoppel in any detail. See too *Meghraj Bank Ltd v Arsiwalla* CA 10 February 1994: B claimed that A, a secured creditor of B, had promised not to exercise its power to appoint a receiver. Two days after the alleged promise, A did make such an appointment. No promissory estoppel arose as, in the short period before A's revocation of the promise, B had taken no action in reliance on A's promise. So, whilst the appointment of a receiver might well cause harm to B, there was no detriment resulting from any course of conduct adopted by B in reliance on A's promise.

[198] So, for example, the need to consider detriment "in the round" without taking a narrowly financial approach, emphasised in the context of proprietary estoppel in *Gillett v Holt* [2001] Ch. 210 at 225, is also relevant to promissory estoppel. Note that, in *MWB Business Exchange Centres Ltd v Rock Advertising Ltd* [2016] EWCA Civ 553; [2017] Q.B. 604 Kitchin LJ's finding at [65] that the detriment requirement of proprietary estoppel had not been made out was based on the same grounds as the finding (at [63]) that, for the purposes of promissory estoppel, it would not be inequitable for the creditor to assert its rights against the debtor. The Supreme Court allowed an appeal in that case [2018] UKSC 24; [2018] W.L.R. 1603 but without needing to consider the operation of estoppel in any detail.

(f) Illegality.

Replace footnote 226 with:

12-029 [226] *Robertson v Minister of Pensions* [1949] 1 K.B. 227. Where a Minister is required to proceed on a particular basis when exercising a statutory power, then an equitable estoppel cannot preclude the Minister from doing so: see *McHugh v Minister for Immigration, Citizenship, Migrant Services and Multicultural Affairs (No 2)* [2021] FCAFC 152 at [76] (Federal Court of Australia).

Replace second paragraph with:

In *Actionstrength Ltd v International Glass Engineering SpA*,[207] B attempted to rely on estoppel where s.4 of the Statute of Frauds 1677 rendered unenforceable an oral promise to guarantee the liability of a third party. B's claim failed as B was unable to show that any relevant promise or representation had been made by A.[208] On those facts, as Lord Walker noted, an estoppel could arise only if A's oral promise "were to be treated, without more, as somehow carrying in itself a representation that the promise would be treated as enforceable".[209] Such an argument, if accepted, would "wholly frustrate the continued operation of section 4 in relation to contracts of guarantee".[210] Nor could B base any estoppel simply on A's oral guarantee itself, as to do so would be to allow a promissory estoppel to operate as a cause of action. Indeed, even if that limit on promissory estoppel were to be removed, it would seem that the policy behind s.4 would still bar a claim: as Lord Hoffmann noted, where a contract of guarantee is concerned:

"[i]t will always be the case that the creditor will have acted to his prejudice on the faith of the guarantor's promise. To admit an estoppel on these grounds would be to repeal the statute."[211]

[207] *Actionstrength Ltd v International Glass Engineering SpA* [2003] 2 A.C. 541 HL.

[208] See e.g. [2003] 2 A.C. 541 HL, at [9] per Lord Bingham: "There was no representation by [A] that it would honour the agreement despite the absence of writing, or that it was not a contract of guarantee, or that it would confirm the agreement in writing".

[209] *Actionstrength Ltd v International Glass Engineering SpA* [2003] 2 A.C. 541 HL at [52]. See too *Bryce Brougham v Trustees of the Winchester Trust* [2020] NZSC 118, where the Supreme Court of New Zealand adopted the approach in Actionstrength.

[210] *Actionstrength Ltd v International Glass Engineering SpA* [2003] 2 A.C. 541 HL at [52].]. See too *Bryce Brougham v Trustees of the Winchester Trust* [2020] NZSC 118, where the Supreme Court of New Zealand adopted the approach in *Actionstrength*.

[211] *Actionstrength Ltd v International Glass Engineering SpA* [2003] 2 A.C. 541 HL at [26].

Change title of section:

3.   PROPRIETARY ESTOPPEL[232]

[232] See B. McFarlane, *The Law of Proprietary Estoppel* (OUP, 2nd edn, 2020).

12-032

1.   Nature and Origins of the Modern Doctrine

(a)   General formulation.

Replace paragraph with:

In *Thorner v Major*,[235] Lord Walker noted the scholarly consensus that **12-033** proprietary estoppel:

> "is based on three main elements ... a representation or assurance made to the claimant; reliance on it by the claimant; and detriment to the claimant in consequence of his (reasonable) reliance."

In line with this approach, which regards proprietary estoppel as a unitary doctrine, the law will be examined below by reference to the requirements of the general formulation set out above. It is important to note, however, that this general formulation cannot be, nor was intended to serve as, a test that can be applied, without more, to determine the practical operation of proprietary estoppel to a particular set of facts.[236] Rather, it is submitted, a distinction must be made between the three distinct strands that comprise the current law of proprietary estoppel[237]: after all, as noted by Lord Walker,[238] "synthesis and unification, however desirable as objectives, have their dangers".

[235] *Thorner v Major* [2009] UKHL 18; [2009] 1 W.L.R. 776 at [29].

[236] See, e.g. *Macdonald v Frost* [2009] EWHC 2276 (Ch); [2010] 1 P. & C.R.D.G. 14 at [9], per Geraldine Andrews QC, where the three part test is prefaced by the observation that: "there is still no comprehensive and uncontroversial definition of proprietary estoppel".

[237] The approach taken in the following paragraphs to proprietary estoppel was referred to with approval by Morgan J in *Abdulrida v Al-Najar* [2021] EWHC 398 (Ch) [353]–[360]. See too *Nazir v Jagota* [2021] EWHC 2291 (Ch) at [172] and [279] and *Martin v Kogan* [2021] EWHC 24 (Ch) [393]. The distinction between the acquiescence, representation and promise-based strands of proprietary estoppel is made by J. Mee, "Proprietary Estoppel, Promises and Mistaken Belief" in S. Bright (ed.), *Modern Studies in Property Law* (Oxford: Hart Publishing, 2011), Vol.6, pp.175, 181–183; and by B. McFarlane, "Understanding Equitable Estoppel: From Metaphors to Better Laws" (2013) *Current Legal Problems* 1. It is developed in B. McFarlane, *The Law of Proprietary Estoppel* 2nd edn (Oxford: Oxford University Press, 2020). K. Low, "Nonfeasance in Equity" (2012) 128 L.Q.R. 63 at 72–73 and I. Samet, "Proprietary Estoppel and Responsibility for Omissions" (2015) 78 M.L.R. 85, also identify the point that the law of proprietary estoppel may be based on distinct principles which require distinct justifications. In *Hoyl Group Ltd v Cromer Town Council* [2015] EWCA Civ 782, Floyd LJ stated at [72] that: "A proprietary estoppel does not have to fit neatly into the pure acquiescence-based pigeon hole or the assurance one" and also endorsed the broad approach to proprietary estoppel adopted by Oliver J in *Taylors Fashions Ltd v Liverpool Victoria Trustees Co Ltd* [1982] Q.B. 133 at 151–152; but this may simply reflect that, in the *Hoyl Group* case, the relevant conduct of A consisted both of failing to provide information to B and requesting that B complete particular work. In *Mohammed v Gomez* [2019] UKPC 46, the Board doubted at [26] "how far it is possible or useful in the context of proprietary estoppel to draw fine distinctions between different categories", but this may similarly reflect the factual context, as A's failure to object to B's building on A's land was seen by the court below as supporting both the finding of an agreement and a distinct acquiescence-based claim.

[238] *Cobbe v Yeomans Row Management Ltd* [2008] UKHL 55; [2008] 1 W.L.R. 1752 at [48].

(b)   An acquiescence-based principle.

Replace paragraph with:

12-034   In *Fisher v Brooker*, Lord Neuberger stated that: "The classic example of proprietary estoppel, standing by whilst one's neighbour builds on one's land believing it to be his property, can be characterised as acquiescence".[239] The principle is certainly long-established[240]: its operation can be seen, for example, in The *Earl of Oxford's Case*.[241] It applies where B adopts a particular course of conduct in reliance on a mistaken belief as to B's current rights and A, knowing both of B's belief and of the existence of A's own, inconsistent right,[242] fails to assert that right against B.[243] If B would then suffer a detriment if A were free to enforce A's right, the principle applies. It therefore operates in a situation in which it would be unconscionable for A, as against B, to enjoy the benefit of a specific right.[244]

[239] *Fisher v Brooker* [2009] UKHL 41; [2009] 1 W.L.R. 1764 at [62]; referring to *Taylors Fashions Ltd v Liverpool Victoria Trustees Co Ltd* [1982] Q.B. 133 at 151, per Oliver J. It is a curious feature of proprietary estoppel that Oliver J's influential decision is often (as in *Fisher v Brooker*) cited as *Taylor Fashions*, whereas the missing "s" is often added to the citation of *Thorner v Major*. That singular problem has also affected an important Australian decision, *Waltons Stores (Interstate Ltd) v Maher* (1988) 14 C.L.R. 387 (High Court of Australia) from which the "s" of the first word often disappears.

[240] See too *Lester v Woodgate* [2010] EWCA Civ 199 at [27], per Patten LJ: "Many of the earliest cases [of proprietary estoppel] arose out of circumstances in which no express encouragement in the form of words was given by the landowner but where the other party built on or made improvements to the former's land in the mistaken belief that he owned or had rights over it".

[241] The *Earl of Oxford's Case* (1615) Chan. Rep. 1, 21 E.R. 485. See D. Ibbetson, "The Earl of Oxford's Case (1615)" in C. Mitchell and P. Mitchell (eds), *Landmark Cases in Equity* (Oxford: Hart, 2012), pp.1, 26–27.

[242] In *Hoyl Group Ltd v Cromer Town Council* [2015] EWCA Civ 782, it was found at first instance that constructive knowledge of B's belief can suffice, and Floyd LJ stated at [73] that "it is possible by words and conduct to encourage another to believe or assume that he has a right or interest over property when what is encouraged is only consistent with him having some such right. I do not think it was necessary, at this stage at least, for the judge to make a finding of actual knowledge by [A] of [B's] belief". *Rochdale Canal Co v King* (1853) 16 Beav. 630 at 642, 929 supports the view that constructive knowledge will suffice. Certainly, as discussed in the *Hoyl Group* case at [53] and [73], it would therefore be dangerous to read too much into Nourse LJ's dictum in *Brinnand v Ewens* (1987) 19 H.L.R. 415 that: "You cannot encourage a belief of which you do not have any knowledge".

[243] This formulation was adopted by Mr Nicholas Thompsell, sitting as a Deputy Judge of the High Court, in *Nazir v Jagota* [2021] EWHC 2291 (Ch) at [245]. It has been suggested that if B's mistaken work improves the value of A's land, it should, prima facie, also be possible for B to bring an unjust enrichment claim against A by pointing simply to the mistake and the benefit. See e.g. T. Wu, "An Unjust Enrichment Claim for the Mistaken Improver of Land" [2011] Conveyancer and Property Lawyer 8; C. Mitchell et al (eds), *Goff & Jones: The Law of Unjust Enrichment*, 9th edn (Sweet & Maxwell, 2016), para.9–04. There is however no authority for such a claim (either in England or Australia: for the Australian position see S. Degeling and B. Edgeworth, "Improvements to Land Belonging to Another" in L.B. Moses et al (eds), *Property and Security: Selected Essays* (Sydney: Lawbook, 2010) p.277) and it would be surprising if the courts, when confirming the clear requirement that A must have knowingly failed to correct B's error (see, e.g. *Blue Haven Enterprises Ltd v Tully* [2006] UKPC 17; *JS Bloor Ltd v Pavillion Developments Ltd* [2008] EWHC 724 (TCC); [2008] 2 E.G.L.R. 85) had simply overlooked an alternative claim based solely on B's mistake and A's benefit. Indeed, the acquiescence principle has been said to be based on the need to prevent dishonest or fraudulent conduct by A: see, e.g. *Willmott v Barber* (1880) 15 Ch. D. 96 at 105, per Fry J; *Electrolux Ltd v Electrix Ltd* (1954) 71 R.P.C. 23 CA at 33, per Sir Raymond Evershed MR; *Shaw v Applegate* [1977] 1 W.L.R. 970 CA at 978 per Buckley LJ.

[244] This formulation of acquiescence based estoppel was relied on by Judge Simon Baker QC in *Mills v Partridge* [2020] EWHC 2171 (Ch) at [121]. It was suggested in the previous edition (at para.12-016) that the acquiescence principle responds to A's unjust enrichment at B's expense. That suggestion is considered further by K. Low, "Nonfeasance in Equity" (2012) 128 L.Q.R. 63. As noted at fn.239, the principle instead has been said to be based on the need to prevent dishonest or fraudulent conduct

by A: see e.g. *Willmott v Barber* (1880) 15 Ch. D. 96, per Fry J at 105; *Electrolux Ltd v Electrix Ltd* (1954) 71 R.P.C. 23 CA, per Sir Raymond Evershed MR at 33; *Shaw v Applegate* [1977] 1 W.L.R. 970 CA, per Buckley LJ at 978. For discussion of the possible moral bases of the principle, see I. Samet, "Proprietary Estoppel and Responsibility for Omissions" (2015) 78 M.L.R. 85. For the argument that the acquiescence principle can now be seen as part of a broader principle, also applying to promises, see S. Barkehall Thomas, "Proprietary Estoppel by Acquiescence: Does it Survive in Australia?" (2021) 29 Australian Property Law Journal 1.

(c)   A representation-based principle.

Replace n.255 with:

[255] In *Hopgood v Brown* [1955] 1 W.L.R. 213 CA, the estoppel also bound the claimant in the case, a   **12-035**
successor in title to A and this seems to be one respect in which the general rules of estoppel by representation may seem to operate differently in the proprietary context, even if it consists only of extending the scope of the estoppel's preclusive effect, rather than the generation of a cause of action. For full discussion of the rule surrounding the effect of an estoppel by representation on a third party, see e.g. B. McFarlane, *The Law of Proprietary Estoppel*, 2nd edn (2020), 8.47–8.64. Note that a different view is taken in P. Feltham et al (eds) *Spencer Bower's Reliance-Based Estoppel*, 5th edn (Bloomsbury, 2017) where it is argued at 12.3 that an estoppel by representation can give rise to an equitable cause of action where it relates to rights over or in property.

(c)   A promise-based principle.

Replace n.261 with:

[261] For discussion of the principle see B. McFarlane and Sir Philip Sales, "Promises, Detriment, and   **12-036**
Liability: Lessons from Proprietary Estoppel" (2015) 131 L.Q.R. 610. The text in this paragraph was cited with approval in *Christie v Canaccord Genuity Ltd* [2022] EWHC 1130 (QB) at [15].

Replace n.275 with:

[275] *Thorner v Major* [2009] UKHL 18; [2009] 1 W.L.R. 776 at [61] per Lord Walker. A farm, or a testamentary estate, can count as such "identified property" even if its content fluctuates over time: in *Oberman v Collins* [2020] EWHC 3553 (Ch) at [149] it was stated that the doctrine could also apply to an agreement made in relation to a portfolio of properties as "there is an obvious analogy between the promise of a share in a portfolio of assets and the promise of a share in an estate." Note that in *Motivate Publishing FZ LLC v Hello Ltd* [2015] EWHC 1554 (Ch), Birss J held that a proprietary estoppel could arise on the basis of a promise to allow B permission to publish the Middle East edition of *Hello!* magazine, stating at [61] that: "The fact that the licence is a licence of intellectual property rights rather than an interest in land makes no difference". See the discussion by A. Shaw-Mellors, "Proprietary Estoppel and the Enforcement of Promises" [2015] Conv 529. In *Ely v Robson* [2016] EWCA Civ 774, Kitchin LJ stated that the instant case was an "unusual" one for the application of proprietary estoppel, as B was the legal owner of the property and wished to use estoppel to give some effect to an alleged agreement with A that A's beneficial share of the property was smaller than that now claimed by A; nonetheless the court proceeded on the basis that proprietary estoppel was applicable. In contrast, in *Walton Family Estates Ltd v GJD Services Ltd* [2021] EWHC 88 (Comm) at [147], it was held that B's belief that he or she will acquire a licence in relation to A's land cannot form the basis of a proprietary estoppel as a "belief that [B] will acquire a right of a non-proprietary character will not suffice". This, it is submitted, is an unduly narrow test and is inconsistent with decisions such as *Williams v Staite* [1979] Ch 291 (CA) and *Southwell v Blackburn* [2014] EWCA Civ 1347. In *Nazir v Jagota* [2021] EWHC 2291 (Ch) it was held in an obiter discussion of the point at [208] that there would be difficulties in applying proprietary estoppel to a partnership interest, at least in the case of a general trading or professional partnership, as it could lead to an "imbalance in mutual rights and duties".

Replace n.277 with:

[277] In *Christie v Canaccord Genuity Ltd* [2022] EWHC 1130 (QB) at [18]–[19], this paragraph was cited with approval and it was stated by Bruce Carr QC (sitting as a Deputy Judge of the High Court) that the principle is capable of applying where B's promise is as to shares in B's parent company, rather than in relation to property owned or about to be owned by B. However in that case the estoppel claim failed on other grounds. See too, e.g. D. Jackson, "Estoppel as a Sword" (1965) 81 L.Q.R. 223 at 241–243, in a passage quoted with approval by Brennan J in *Waltons Stores (Interstate) Ltd v Maher* (1988) 164

C.L.R. 387 at 426. See too, e.g. N. McBride, "A Fifth Common Law Obligation" (1994) 14 Legal Studies 35; D. Nolan, "Following in their Footsteps: Equitable Estoppel in Australia and the United States" (2000) 11 K.C.L.J. 202; J. Moncrieff & J. Neyers, "(Mis)Understanding Estoppel" [2003] L.M.C.L.Q. 429. See too P. Feltham et al (eds), *Spencer Bower's Reliance-Based Estoppel*, 5th edn (Bloomsbury, 2017) where it is noted at 1.24 that, if the limit on the equitable cause of action is said to be justified by the need to protect the contractual doctrine of consideration, it is hard to see why that concern does not also apply to promises in relation to the acquisition of property. See too B McFarlane, "Equitable Estoppel as a Cause of Action: Neither One Thing Nor One Other" in S Degeling et al (eds) *Contract in Commercial Law* (Lawbook Co, 2017) arguing that the equitable cause of action does not in any case undermine the doctrine of consideration as it does not operate to make a promise immediately binding.

2.   The Requirements of Proprietary Estoppel

(a)   Representation or assurance made to B.

Replace paragraph with:

12-039   The first point to make is that, if B wishes to invoke the acquiescence-based strand of proprietary estoppel, there is no need to prove any express or, it is submitted, implied representation or assurance by A: the relevant conduct of A consists simply of A's failure to disabuse B of a mistaken belief[292]:

> "[I]f all proprietary estoppel cases (including cases of acquiescence or standing-by) are to be analysed in terms of assurance, reliance and detriment, then the landowner's conduct in standing by in silence serves as the element of assurance."[293]

In many acquiescence cases any finding of an implied assurance would be wholly fictional[294] as there is no requirement of any communication between A and B.[295] The hurdles faced by B in an acquiescence case instead come from the need for B to show that he or she acted in a mistaken belief as to his or her *current* rights,[296] and also to show that A failed to assert A's right even though A knew both of B's belief and of the true position.[297]

[292] *Thorner v Major* [2009] UKHL 18; [2009] 1 W.L.R. 776 at [29], per Lord Walker. See too *Optis Cellular Technology LLC v Apple Retail UK Ltd* [2021] EWHC 1739 (Pat) at [340], rejecting A's contention that mere silence or inaction cannot give rise to an estoppel and *A Ward Attachments Ltd v Fabcon Engineering Ltd* [2021] EWHC 2145 (IPEC) at [153], approving the analysis in this paragraph.

[293] *Thorner v Major* [2009] UKHL 18; [2009] 1 W.L.R. 776 at [55], per Lord Walker.

[294] See J. Mee, "Proprietary Estoppel, Promises and Mistaken Belief" in S. Bright (ed), *Modern Studies in Property Law* (Oxford: Hart Publishing, 2011), Vol.6, pp.175, 182.

[295] The principle formulated by Lord Cranworth in *Ramsden v Dyson* (1866) L.R. 1 H.L. 129 at 140–1 (see para.12-034) can apply, for example, even if B was unaware that A was standing-by, and simply acted on a belief independently acquired that particular land belonged to B.

[296] This point was of particular importance in *Ramsden v Dyson* (1866) L.R. 1 H.L. 129: according to Lord Carnworth LC at 142, a crucial factual question was whether B had built in the belief that he *already* had a right to receive a long lease from A, or whether B had done so in the belief that A *would*, in practice, grant B such a lease. See too *Jones v Stones* [1999] 1 W.L.R. 1739 CA at 1746, per Aldous LJ. In *Scottish Newcastle Plc v Lancashire Mortgage Corp Ltd* [2007] EWCA Civ 684 at [44], Mummery LJ stated that: "the court will compel effect to be given to acquiescence by [A] in the known expectation of [B] that [B] has or will have a proprietary right or interest where [B] has acted to his detriment on that basis" but the suggestion that the acquiescence principle can apply where B mispredicts B's future rights is contrary to authority.

[297] See, e.g. *Willmott v Barber* (1880) 15 Ch. D. 96 at 106–107; *Ramsden v Dyson* (1866) L.R. 1 H.L. 129 at 140–141, per Lord Carnworth LC; and at 168 per Lord Wensleydale; *Kammins Ballrooms Co Ltd v Zenith Investments (Torquay) Ltd* [1971] A.C. 850 HL at 884–885, per Lord Diplock. In *Costagliola v English* (1969) 210 E.G. 1425 (Ch) at 1431: B's claim failed as, even if A had been aware that B was modernising B's house, there was nothing to indicate to A that B was doing so in reliance on a mistaken

belief that A had no right of way over B's land. For a recent example where the requirements of an estoppel by acquiescence were met in relation to particular means of asserting intellectual property rights, see *Martin v Kogan* [2021] EWHC 24 (Ch) [390]–[398].

Replace n.298 with:

[298] To adopt the formulation of Lord Scott in *Cobbe v Yeoman's Row Management Ltd* [2008] UKHL 55; [2008] 1 W.L.R. 1752 at [14]. Whilst decisions such as *Territorial and Auxiliary Forces Association of the County of London v Nichols* [1949] 1 K.B. 35; and *Tomlin v Reid* (1963) 185 E.G. 913 CA can be explained on the basis that a representation as to pure law will not found an estoppel, the potential artificiality, in this context, of the distinction between fact and law has been noted (see e.g. *Brikom Investments Ltd v Seaford* [1981] 1 W.L.R. 863 CA at 869, per Ormerod LJ; *Taylors Fashions Ltd v Liverpool Victoria Trustees Co Ltd* [1982] Q.B. 133 at 151 per Oliver J) and it may be that the apparently distinct limit on the scope of estoppel by representation should instead be seen as simply a consequence of the rule that no such estoppel can be based on a statement of A's opinion: see, e.g. *Algar v Middlesex County Council* [1945] 2 All E.R. 243 at 251, per Humphreys J; and *Briggs v Gleeds* [2014] EWHC 1178 (Ch), per Newey J at [35]: see para.12-016, fn.67.

Replace third paragraph with:

The House of Lords' earlier decision in *Cobbe v Yeoman's Row Management Ltd*[305] also provides support for this requirement of a promise. In *Cobbe*, it was found as a matter of "proven facts" at first instance that A, through its agent, "encouraged [B] to believe that, if [B] succeeded in obtaining planning permission in accordance with [A and B's agreement in principle] that agreement would be honoured, even though it was not legally binding".[306] The Court of Appeal upheld the finding of a proprietary estoppel, but the House of Lords allowed A's appeal. As Lord Scott noted, A's behaviour could, in a general sense, be regarded as unconscionable but, whilst:

"unconscionability of conduct may well lead to a remedy ... proprietary estoppel cannot be the route to it unless the ingredients for a proprietary estoppel are present."[307]

[305] *Cobbe v Yeoman's Row Management Ltd* [2008] UKHL 55; [2008] 1 W.L.R. 1752.

[306] *Cobbe* [2005] EWHC 266 (Ch) at [123].

[307] *Cobbe v Yeoman's Row Management Ltd* [2008] UKHL 55; [2008] 1 W.L.R. 1752 at [16].

Replace final paragraph with:

The missing ingredient in *Cobbe*, it is submitted, was a promise by A which B **12-039** could reasonably regard as seriously intended by A as capable of being relied on.[308] No such promise could be found given that, as Lord Neuberger later put it:

"there was total uncertainty as to the nature or terms of any benefit (property interest, contractual right, or money) and, if a property interest, as to the nature of that interest (freehold, leasehold or charge), to be accorded to [B]."[309]

[308] For instructive cases in which the required promise was absent see, e.g. *Cook v Thomas* [2010] EWCA Civ 227; and *Lissimore v Downing* [2003] 2 F.L.R. 308. For further discussion of the principles and factors relevant to the finding of a promise see B. McFarlane, *The Law of Proprietary Estoppel*, 2nd Edn (2020), 2.213–2.249.

[309] *Thorner* [2009] UKHL 18; [2009] 1 W.L.R. 776 at [93]. Such uncertainty also prevented an estoppel's arising in *Pinisetty v Manikonda* [2017] EWHC 838 (QB); see too *Earl of Plymouth v Rees* [2021] EWHC 3180 (Ch) at [32]–[33]. By contrast see, in the commercial context, *Matchmove Ltd v Dowding* [2017] 1 W.L.R. 749, where Etherton VC noted at [35] that there was an oral agreement between the parties which both sides intended to be binding immediately, and which was complete as to all its essential terms. The first instance decision upheld by the Court of Appeal was based on proprietary estoppel and constructive trust, whereas B in the Court of Appeal was content to rely solely on a common intention constructive trust. Compare, in the domestic context, *Southwell v Blackburn* [2014] EWCA Civ 1347, where a successful claim was based on an assurance as to "security of rights of occupation in the house that [A and B] were buying together" and *Arif v Anwar* [2015] EWHC 124 (Fam): a claim

succeeded where the parties' agreement was found at [69] to be one that B should acquire "some sort of interest to be sorted out later".

Replace first paragraph with:

12-040   It is certainly the case that a proprietary estoppel cannot arise where B simply hopes to acquire a right in A's land, and so does not have any belief that he has, or will necessarily acquire, such a right.[310] The submission as to the need for a promise must, nonetheless, be made with some caution, as it is a simple matter to find formulations of the test for proprietary estoppel that refer only to the need for A to have "encouraged" B's belief as to A's future conduct.[311] Indeed, in *Hoyl Group Ltd v Cromer Town Council*, the Court of Appeal adopted "encouragement" as the relevant test, thereby seemingly rejecting counsel's submission that a promise is required where B acts on the basis of a belief as to acquiring rights in the future.[312] On the facts of the case, however, the success of the estoppel claim in *Hoyl Group* is not, it is submitted, inconsistent with the need for a promise[313] and the idea that encouragement alone suffices in a case where B relies on a belief as to acquiring rights in the future is, it is submitted, inconsistent with the result in *Cobbe* and the reasoning of the House of Lords in *Thorner*.[314]

[310] See, e.g. *Cobbe v Yeoman's Row Management Ltd* [2008] UKHL 55; [2008] 1 W.L.R. 1752, per Lord Walker at [64]: "It is not enough to hope, or even to have a confident expectation, that the person who has given assurances will eventually do the right thing". See also *Hoyl Group Ltd v Cromer Town Council* [2015] EWCA Civ 782, per Floyd LJ at [61]: "I accept that it is necessary for [B] to show that they believed that they had or would have a right of way via the garden access". See too *Curran v Collins* [2015] EWCA Civ 404 [69], where Lewison LJ noted that: "it cannot be right that the giving of a reason why someone is not on the title deeds inevitably leads to the inference that it must have been agreed that they would have an interest in the property." If such an excuse is however linked to a "positive representation" that the house would otherwise have been put in joint names (as in *Eves v Eves* [1975] 1 W.L.R. 1338 (CA) and *Grant v Edwards* [1986] Ch 638 (CA)) then it may be possible to infer the required assurance: see Lewison LJ ibid at [69]-[74].

[311] See, e.g. *Taylors Fashions Ltd v Liverpool Victoria Trustees Co Ltd* [1982] Q.B. 133 (Ch) at 145, 151–152; *Re Basham* [1986] 1 W.L.R. 1498 at 1503. Note that cases analysed here as applying the promise-based principle are sometimes said to be part of a doctrine of "estoppel by encouragement" (rather than of "estoppel by standing by"): see, e.g. *Joyce v Epsom and Ewell BC* [2012] EWCA Civ 1398 at [39]; *Hoyl Group Ltd v Cromer Town Council* [2015] EWCA Civ 782 at [65]–[75]; K. Handley, *Estoppel by Conduct and Election* (London: Sweet & Maxwell, 2006), pp.163–165; *Sullivan v Sullivan* [2006] NSWCA 312 at [4].

[312] *Hoyl Group Ltd v Cromer Town Council* [2015] EWCA Civ 782 at [65]–[75] (Floyd LJ). In *Smyth-Tyrrell v Bowden* [2018] EWHC 106 (Ch), having considered *Hoyl*, HHJ Paul Matthews QC at [77] considered that it "seems correct in principle" that a claim can be based on B's reliance on a belief that A will in the future give B a right, even in the absence of a promise by A, if A either knows of B's belief and does nothing to disabuse it or, even if A does not know of B's belief, A "nonetheless positively encourages [B] to act in ways only consistent with [B's] having such a belief (so that, objectively speaking, it should be obvious to [A] what is going on)". See too the view of the same judge in *Gilpin v Legg* [2017] EWHC 3220 (Ch) at [102].

[313] In *Hoyl Group*, it seems first that B was found by the trial judge to have relied on a belief as to its current rights ([2015] EWCA Civ 782 at [63]) and secondly that the facts (like those of *Thorner v Major* [2009] UKHL 18; [2009] 1 W.L.R. 1776) would have supported the finding of an implied promise.

[314] In *Inwards v Baker* [1965] 2 Q.B. 29 CA, the Court of Appeal held expressly that a promise was not required for B to succeed. In that case, however, in contrast to the claimants in *Thorner* and *Cobbe*, B was not seeking to establish a cause of action, but instead wished simply to resist an application for possession made by the trustees of A's will. It may therefore be possible to explain the result in the case by reference to different principles, which do not require a promise to be made, such as waiver (see para.12-021). In *Crabb v Arun DC* [1976] Ch. 179 CA at 188, Lord Denning MR stated explicitly that a cause of action based on proprietary estoppel could arise in cases where A's conduct was "[s]hort of an actual promise", relying on a statement of Cotton LJ in *Birmingham & District Land Co v London & North Western Railway Co (No.2)* (1888) 40 Ch. D. 268 CA at 277. As discussed at para.12-020, however, the

principle applied in the *Birmingham* case cannot operate as a cause of action. It is significant that, in *Cobbe* [2008] UKHL 55; [2008] 1 W.L.R. 1752, Lord Walker (at [79]) described *Crabb* as a "difficult case": it is submitted that the difficulty lies in finding any express or implied promise by A. For support for the contrary view that encouragement short of a promise suffices for a proprietary estoppel claim, even where B's belief relates to A's future conduct, see A Robertson, "The Form and Substance of Equitable Estoppel" in A Robertson & J Goudkamp (eds) *Form and Substance in the Law of Obligations* (Hart, 2019).

Replace paragraph with:

The concept of encouragement has also been used in attempts to formulate a **12-041** single test for proprietary estoppel, capable of capturing the acquiescence and representation-based cases in which no promise is required. Such tests, however, understate the requirements of liability in a case where B has relied on a belief as to A's future conduct: the basic point is that, in an absence of a promise, it is very difficult to justify why A should bear the risk of detriment resulting from B's reliance on such a belief. If, for example, an agreement in principle is expressly stated to be "subject to contract", and A has not expressly or impliedly surrendered A's right to withdraw,[317] no proprietary estoppel can arise: the subject to contract provision means that A has not made the required commitment to B.[318] As demonstrated by the decision of the House of Lords in *Cobbe*,[319] the presence of the term "subject to contact" is not, of course necessary to prevent a claim's arising: the question is simply whether the required promise was made.[320]

[317] The proviso noted by Lord Templeman in *Attorney General of Hong Kong v Humphrey's Estate* [1987] A.C. 114 PC at 124. For consideration of the possibility of a proprietary estoppel claim arising even in a "subject to contract" case see the discussion of Lindsay J in *Gonthier v Orange* [2003] EWCA Civ 873 at [40]–[59]. It has been recognised that a "subject to contract" stipulation can be impliedly withdrawn, so as to allow a contractual claim (*RTS Flexible Systems Ltd v Molkerei Alois Muller GmbH & Co KG* [2010] UKSC 14; [2010] 1 W.L.R. 753) and the same must be true of a proprietary estoppel claim.

[318] See, e.g. *Attorney General of Hong Kong v Humphrey's Estate* [1987] A.C. 114 PC at 124; cited with approval in, e.g. *London & Regional Investments Ltd v TBI Plc* [2002] EWCA Civ 355 at [43]; *Haq v Island Homes Housing Association* [2011] EWCA Civ 805; [2011] 2 P. & C.R. 17 at [60].

[319] *Cobbe* [2008] UKHL 55; [2008] 1 W.L.R. 1752: see, e.g. at [81] per Lord Walker.

[320] See e.g. *Hellfire Entertainment Ltd v Acimar Ltd* [2021] EWHC 1077 (Ch): no proprietary estoppel arose as A and B each "knew and agreed that there would have to be a formal legal agreement signed by both of them before either was bound": ibid, [53]. For an example of the impact of an express "subject to contract" reservation in preventing a proprietary estoppel claim see, e.g. *Generator Developments Ltd v Lidl UK GmbH* [2018] EWCA Civ 396 at [79] (Lewison LJ). It is also clear, for example, that "a statement of *current intentions* as to future conduct is not a *promise* of that conduct": *James v James* [2018] EWHC 43 (Ch) at [24] per HHJ Paul Matthews QC.

Replace first paragraph with:

A proprietary estoppel claim cannot, however, be based on any promise. Whilst **12-042** there is no need for B to have believed that A's promise was intended to be, or was in fact, immediately legally binding,[321] the promise must be one that B reasonably understood as seriously intended by A to be capable of being relied upon by B,[322] and so a clearly casual promise will not suffice. In a formulation acknowledged as "question-begging", it has been suggested that the promise must be "certain enough".[323] The factual context in which A's promise was made will of course be crucial in a determination of whether it was reasonable for B to regard it as seriously intended.[324] A promise will not give rise to a proprietary estoppel claim if it is conditional and the relevant condition has not been fulfilled.[325] Where parties are negotiating towards a contract, a court will rightly require clear evidence that the required promise was made before such a contract was concluded.[326] This does not mean, however, that the underlying requirements of the claim differ in the commercial context: if that were the case, it would be necessary to determine the necessarily unstable line between commercial and other cases.[327]

[321] See, e.g. *Walton v Walton* 14 April 1994 CA; *Sutcliffe v Lloyd* [2007] EWCA Civ 153 at [38], per Wilson LJ; *Herbert v Doyle* [2010] EWCA Civ 1095; *Whittaker v Kinnear* [2011] EWHC 1479 (QB). The contrary position was taken by Lord Scott in *Cobbe* [2008] UKHL 55; [2008] 1 W.L.R. 1752 at [14], but was there based on the very narrow conception of proprietary estoppel as essentially a form of estoppel by representation that was impliedly rejected by the House of Lords' decision in *Thorner v Major* [2009] UKHL 18; [2009] 1 W.L.R. 1776: it would clearly not have been reasonable for David Thorner there to have believed that his uncle had made a legally binding promise.

[322] *Thorner v Major* [2009] UKHL 18; [2009] 1 W.L.R. 1776 at [5], per Lord Hoffmann. In *Creasey v Sole* [2013] EWHC 1410 at [105], it was noted that a claim could not be based on an alleged promise made in the course of a heated argument. See too *Trentelman v The Owners - Strata Plan No 76700* [2021] NSWCA 242, (2021) 106 NSWLR 227 at [147] (Bathurst CJ): the question is not whether the context is domestic or commercial, but rather, "how the representation or promise would be reasonably understood by a person in the position of the persons to whom the representation was made".

[323] *Thorner v Major* [2009] UKHL 18; [2009] 1 W.L.R. 1776 at [56], per Lord Walker: "I would prefer to say (while conscious that it is a thoroughly question-begging formulation) that to establish a proprietary estoppel the relevant assurance must be clear enough. What amounts to sufficient clarity, in a case of this sort, is hugely dependent on context".

[324] In *Layton v Martin* [1986] Fam. 212, a promise of "financial security" was made in a letter to B but that promise did not relate to any specific property and formed part of A's broadly emotive plea for B to return to live with A. *Bradbury v Taylor* [2012] EWCA Civ 1208 provides what may be seen as a borderline example of the requirement's being met: the evidence suggested that A had warned B1 and B2 that A's promise was made as part of a "friendly arrangement", but B2 had already sought assurances from A, and A knew that B1 and B2 were planning to make the significant decision to move from Sheffield to Cornwall in reliance on the arrangement with A. See too *Southwell v Blackburn* [2014] EWCA Civ 1347; and *Arif v Anwar* [2015] EWHC 124 (Fam), discussed at 12-039, fn.309, above. In *Liden v Burton* [2016] EWCA Civ 275, Hamblen LJ emphasised at [24] that: "Context is 'hugely important' as to whether an assurance is sufficiently clear, and the judge was best placed to evaluate that issue, having had the advantage of seeing and hearing the witnesses". In *Ely v Robson* [2016] EWCA Civ 774, for example, in rejecting the argument that any promise by A (B's former cohabiting partner) had been too unclear to form the basis of a proprietary estoppel, Kitchin LJ emphasised at [41] that "[t]his was not a commercial transaction".

[325] See, e.g. *Shaw v Shaw* [2018] EWHC 3196 (Ch) at [231].

[326] See, e.g. *Crossco No.4 Unlimited v Jolan Ltd* [2011] EWCA Civ 1619; [2012] 2 All E.R. 754 at [133] per Arden LJ.

[327] The commercial context is of course significant when applying the tests for proprietary estoppel: see, e.g. *Cobbe v Yeoman's Row Management Ltd* [2008] UKHL 55; [2008] 1 W.L.R. 1752 at [66]–[81], per Lord Walker. Note however that this does not mean a separate legal test is to be applied in commercial cases, as this would involve a court in definitively fixing a definition of such cases, which, it is submitted, would prove impossible: see e.g. *Trentelman v The Owners - Strata Plan No 76700* [2021] NSWCA 242, (2021) 106 NSWLR 227 at [146]). Many cases have both "domestic" and "commercial" elements: see e.g. *Clark v Clark* [2006] EWHC 275 (dispute between two brothers who were also sole and equal shareholders in a company and carried on business from the disputed land); *Jules v Robertson* [2011] EWCA Civ 1322 (promise made to transfer interest in family home to father-in-law, to repay his investment in the promisor's wine bar).

(b) Reliance by B.

Replace second paragraph with:

12-043   The reliance requirement can therefore be seen as raising an issue of causation.[323] It has a strong factual aspect: a judge will have to decide if particular action of B was carried out *on the faith* of a belief that B had or would acquire a right in A's land, rather than merely *in* that belief.[324] Nonetheless, there are instances in which the Court of Appeal has overturned a first instance judge's finding as to reliance, on the basis that the judge did not apply the correct legal test.[335] There is some uncertainty as to the test to be applied when determining if B can establish reliance[336] and it is again useful to distinguish between the three different stands of proprietary estoppel: after all, causal tests may vary according to the particular nature of the legal principle at stake.[337]

[323] See, per Robert Walker LJ in *Campbell v Griffin* [2001] EWCA Civ 990; (2001) 82 P. & C.R. DG23 at [19]: "the judge dealt with the question of reliance (which is really an issue of causation) before he made a finding about detriment".

[324] See in *Taylors Fashions Ltd v Liverpool Victoria Trustees Co Ltd* [1982] Q.B. 133 CA at 156.

[335] See *Wayling v Jones* (1993) 69 P. & C.R. 170 CA; and *Campbell v Griffin* [2001] EWCA Civ 990; (2001) 82 P. & C.R. DG23.

[336] See, e.g. *Steria Ltd v Hutchison* [2006] EWCA Civ 1551; [2007] I.C.R. 445 at [117], per Neuberger LJ. See too JK Ward and S Puttick, "Willpower has no Voltage: Problems with Causation in Equitable Estoppel" (2022) 49 Univ Western Australia Law Rev 230.

[337] As noted by, e.g. Lord Mance in *Durham v BAI (Run Off) Ltd* [2012] UKSC 14; [2012] 1 W.L.R. 867 at [66]. See too Lord Hoffmann, "Causation" (2005) 121 L.Q.R. 592. In *Trentelman v The Owners - Strata Plan No 76700* [2021] NSWCA 242, (2021) 106 NSWLR 227 at [158], reliance was found as B was "sufficiently influenced" by A's promise as to make it unconscionable for A to resile from that promise.

After "liability on A.", add new n.342a:

[342a] Note however that in *Optis Cellular Technology LLC v Apple Retail UK Ltd* [2021] EWHC 1739 (Pat) at [352], it was stated by Meade J that, as a result of *Steria Ltd v Hutchison* [2006] EWCA Civ 1551; [2007] I.C.R. 445, the "significant factor" test should apply. This view, it is submitted, overlooks possible differences between the different strands of proprietary estoppel and is a risk of the "no categorization" approach taken by Meade J at [338]-[339]. **12-043**

Replace fourth paragraph with:

The position in the promise-based strand is less than clear. Certainly, A's promise need not provide the sole reason for B's action: it is very rarely the case that B will act for just one reason and, for example, a claim may still arise even where B cares for A not only as a result of a testamentary promise but also because of the ties of family or friendship.[343] Beyond this, however, it is often merely stated that there must be a "sufficient causal link between the assurance relied upon and the detriment asserted".[344] An argument can be made that the standard "but for" test should apply.[345] Certainly, if A can show that B would have acted in the same way, and so still be facing the same risk of detriment, even in the absence of A's promise, it is difficult to see why A should now bear responsibility for that risk of detriment. In *Wayling v Jones*,[346] a rather odd test was adopted, as the court considered not what B would have done in the absence of A's promise, but rather what B would have done had A informed B that A was not going to honour the promise. Such a test is very favourable to B, and is hard to justify, as the relevant conduct of A on which B's claim is based is the promise, not A's failure to tell B that it will not be honoured.[347] It has also been stated that, whilst A's promise does not have to be the sole inducement for B's conduct, it is sufficient if it is an inducement.[348] Support for a test asking if A's promise was a contributing factor to B's conduct can also be found in *van Dyke v Sidhu*, where four of the judges of the High Court of Australia applied a test which asked if "the promises in question contributed to [B's] conduct"[349] and based their finding of reliance on the fact that A's promises had been found by the primary judge to have "played a part" in B's decision to act.[350] Nonetheless, in almost all of the cases in which B's claim has succeeded,[351] the finding of reliance has been, on the facts, compatible with a test asking if, but for A's promise, B would still have adopted the course of conduct now claimed to give rise to the risk of detriment. For example, in *van Dyke v Sidhu*, the fifth judge, Gageler J adopted, in effect, a "but for" test and found that it too had been met on the facts.[352]

[343] See, e.g. *Campbell v Griffin* [2001] EWCA Civ 990 at [29], per Robert Walker LJ.

[344] See, e.g. *Gillett v Holt* [2001] Ch. 210 CA at 232, per Robert Walker LJ; *Wayling v Jones* (1993) 60 P. & C.R. 170 at 173, per Balcombe LJ.

[345] For a full survey of the different possibilities, and an argument in favour of the standard "but for" test: see B. McFarlane, *The Law of Proprietary Estoppel*, 2nd edn (2020), 3.114–3.212.

[346] *Wayling v Jones* (1993) 69 P. & C.R. 170 CA.

[347] For academic criticism of the *Wayling* test, see, e.g. E. Cooke, "Reliance and Estoppel" (1995) 111 L.Q.R. 389 and *The Modern Law of Estoppel* (Oxford: OUP, 2000) 111; J. Mee, *The Property Rights of Co-Habitees* (Oxford: Hart, 1999) 108; B. McFarlane, *The Law of Proprietary Estoppel*, 2nd edn (2020), 3.114–3.132.

[348] See, e.g. *Campbell v Griffin* [2001] EWCA Civ 990 at [29], per Robert Walker LJ; *Century (UK) Ltd SA v Clibbery* [2004] EWHC 1870 (Ch) at [73], per Blackburne J.

[349] *Van Dyke v Sidhu* [2014] HCA 19 at [66], per French CJ, Kiefel, Bell and Keane JJ.

[350] *Van Dyke v Sidhu* [2014] HCA 19 at [71], per French CJ, Kiefel, Bell and Keane JJ.

[351] *Ottey v Grundy* [2003] EWCA Civ 1176; [2003] W.T.L.R. 1253 may be an exception: see B. McFarlane, *The Law of Proprietary Estoppel*, 2nd edn (2020), 3.125-3.129.

[352] *Van Dyke v Sidhu* [2014] HCA 19 at [93], per Gageler J: the test as stated there asks what B would have done in the absence of the assumption (that B would acquire a right in A's land), but in a promise case, it is more accurate, to ask what B would have done in the absence of A's promise. If B would have had the same belief without A's promise then no claim should arise. Compare *Western Fish Products Ltd v Penwith District Council* [1981] 2 All E.R. 204 CA: no estoppel arose where, independently of any representation by A, B had in any case an "absolute conviction" of the truth of the fact on which it relied.

Replace n.354 with:

[354] *Van Dyke v Sidhu* [2014] HCA 19 at [57]. See too B. McFarlane, *The Law of Proprietary Estoppel*, 2nd edn (2020) 3.233–3.256, also pointing out that Lord Denning had applied principles developed in the context of fraudulent misrepresentations to the quite different context of the promise-based strand of proprietary estoppel.

(c) Detriment.

Replace n.363 with:

12-044 [363] *Gillett v Holt* [2001] Ch. 210 CA at 233. Where B's detriment stems from B's failure to act in a different way, then "it would be unreasonable to expect chapter and verse as to the hypothetical counterfactual": see *Anaghara v Anaghara* [2020] EWHC 3091 (Ch) [34]: B's detriment was established in part by satisfying the judge that, but for A's assurances, B would have used money spent on the property in a different way. Note that in *Cheung Lai Mui v Cheung Wai Shing* [2021] HKCFA 10, the Hong Kong Court of Final Appeal found that detriment relevant to establishing a proprietary estoppel claim cannot be incurred after the death of A/any surviving co-promisor of A: for discussion see S Yee Ching Leung and B Au-Yeung (2021) 5 Trusts and Trustees 1.

Replace n.371 with:

[371] *Lloyd v Dugdale* [2001] EWCA Civ 1754 where the court refused to recognise expenditure incurred by a company owned and controlled by B (although it was prepared to recognise the failure by B to take alternative steps). See too *Brent LBC v Johnson* [2020] EWHC 2526 (Ch) at [242]. Compare *Gillett v Holt* [2001] Ch. 210 (where the court recognised as detriment acts by B's wife as well as acts by B himself).

(d) The role of unconscionability.

Replace n.381 with:

[381] *Cobbe v Yeoman's Row Management Ltd* [2008] UKHL 55; [2008] 1 W.L.R. 1752 at [92] per Lord **12-045**
Walker. For the additional use of this concept of unconscionability in aiding a court to interpret the three
main elements of proprietary estoppel, see B. McFarlane, *The Law of Proprietary Estoppel*, 2nd Edn
(2020), Ch.5.

Replace third paragraph with:

Unconscionability in this broad sense does not refer simply to the specific issue
of A's state of mind; it is rather directed to the general, overarching question of
whether the position of the parties is such that the court is now justified in
intervening. In this way, the concept usefully allows a court to take account of factors that may mean, despite B's apparent satisfaction of the three main elements of
a claimed proprietary estoppel (viz acquiescence, representation, or promise; reliance; and the prospect of detriment), there are nonetheless grounds for denying B's
claim, or, in the acquiescence and promise-based strands, reducing A's liability.[382]

[382] See, e.g. *Guest v Guest*. See too *Optis Cellular Technology LLC v Apple Retail UK Ltd* [2021] EWHC
1739 (Pat) at [332] where Meade J describes unconscionability as a "cross-check which may lead the
Court to revisit its analysis on the three main elements. If an allegation of proprietary estoppel fails when
such cross-check is made, the failure is likely to be expressed in terms of the absence of one or more of
the basic elements." In *Habberfield v Habberfield* [2019] EWCA Civ 890, it was argued by A that B's
earlier refusal to accept an offer to run A's farm in partnership with A meant that it was not unconscionable for A later to fail to keep an assurance that B would take over the running of the farm on A's retirement and then inherit the farm, or at least that any reliance by B after that point should be discounted.
That argument was rejected on the basis that the partnership offer did not fulfil the assurance that B
would be able to run the farm (see [30]) and that A had not made an "unambiguous final offer" that if
rejected would then prevent B from continuing to rely on past assurances by A (at [44]). See too *Gordon
v Havener* [2021] UKPC 26 at [15] where the absence of unconscionability was given by Lord Burrows as one reason why a proprietary estoppel claim cannot be brought by a party in breach of contract
where the relevant promise is "contained in the contract, or is inextricably tied up with the contractual
promise, and that contract has been terminated for breach by the innocent party."

(e) Formality requirements and other possible bars.

Replace n.390 with:

[390] See, e.g. *Chalmers v Pardoe* [1963] 1 W.L.R. 677 PC (distinguished in *Maharaj v Chand* [1986] A.C. **12-046**
898 PC); and in *Brightlingsea Haven Ltd v Morris* [2008] EWHC 1928 (QB); [2009] 2 P. & C.R. 11 at
[60]: for discussion see B. McFarlane, *The Law of Proprietary Estoppel*, 2nd Edn (2020) 6.136–
6.141); *ER Ives (Investments) Ltd v High* (1967) 2 Q.B. 379 at 395 (relief would have been refused if it
had involved an infringement of s.13 of the Land Charges Act 1925); *Mayor and Burgesses of the
London Borough of Bexley v Maison Maurice Ltd* [2006] EWHC 3192 (Ch) at [56] (relief would not
have been granted if it would have involved ordering A to act beyond its legal powers).

Replace second paragraph with:

Section 2 of the Law of Property (Miscellaneous Provisions) Act 1989 provides
that contracts for the sale or other disposition of an interest in land must satisfy
certain formal requirements, although s.2(5) contains an express saving for
constructive trusts.[395] There has been some uncertainty as to the impact of this section on promise-based proprietary estoppel claims. Two principal views are
possible.[396] First, it could be said that s.2 imposes a prima facie bar on such
claims,[397] and therefore they can be made, if at all, only by means of a constructive trust.[398] Secondly, it could be said that no proprietary estoppel claim is caught
by s.2, as the section regulates the requirements of a contract for the sale or other
disposition of an interest in land, and a proprietary estoppel claim, even if promise-

based, is distinct from a contractual claim.[399] The better view, it is submitted, is the latter.[400] In particular, it should be remembered that s.2, on its express wording, does not purport to deny all legal effects to a promise, or to render an agreement void[401]: it clearly applies only to contractual claims. It might be argued that the policy behind the statute is more extensive,[402] but it has been accepted that the statute does not deny all legal effects to informal agreements[403] and also that it has no impact on an acquiescence-based claim[404]: "it would be a strange policy which denied similar relief to a claimant who had acted on a clear promise or representation that he should have an interest in the property".[405] Moreover, there are no examples in the case law of an otherwise valid proprietary estoppel claim failing simply because of the effect of s.2.[406] The only practical impact of the first view is that judges have felt obliged to characterise a successful proprietary estoppel claim as giving rise to a constructive trust even if, on the facts of the case, there is no suggestion that A in fact holds any right on trust for B.[407] The law would therefore be more transparent[408] if it were clearly established that s.2, as was intended by the Law Commission when proposing the reforms that led to the 1989 Act,[409] has no effect on any proprietary estoppel, whether based on A's acquiescence, representation, or promise.

[395] It has also been held that s.2 does not apply to an agreement for a "trivial" disposition of land made as part of an agreement to demarcate a disputed boundary: see, e.g. *Joyce v Rigolli* [2004] EWCA Civ 79. Note that where an express declaration of trust has been made (and conforms with the formality requirements of s.53(1)(b) of the Law of Property Act 1925), it may be overridden by a proprietary estoppel claim "arising in light of representations and promises made after the declaration of trust": see *Bahia v Sidhu* [2022] EWHC 875 (Ch) at [123], relying on *Clarke v Meadus* [2010] EWHC 3117 (Ch).

[396] Further views are possible. For example, it could be argued that s.2 is only of relevance to claims with a "contractual connection" (presumably this would include, at least, claims based on an agreement that, but for the failure to meet the requirements of s.2, would be a valid contract) but not to others, where no contract was contemplated (such as e.g. *Thorner v Major* [2009] UKHL 18; [2009] 1 W.L.R. 776).Whilst a statement of Lord Neuberger in *Thorner* (at [99]) provides some support for that view, it is very hard to see why B should face the prospect of being denied a claim only in the former case where there are in fact more factors that might seem to be in B's favour (e.g. intention to make a legally binding agreement; the provision of consideration; a bargain clear enough to count as a contract) than in the latter case.

[397] See, e.g. *Cobbe v Yeoman's Row Management Ltd* [2008] UKHL 55; [2008] 1 W.L.R. 1752 at [29], per Lord Scott. The view was expressly obiter, and was not followed by Bean J in *Whittaker v Kinnear* [2011] EWHC 1479 (QB) at [28]–[30]. In contrast, in another obiter discussion in *Dudley Muslim Association v Dudley MBC* [2015] EWCA Civ 1123, Lewison LJ at [33] referred with approval to Lord Scott's view.

[398] This seems to have been the assumption adopted by the Court of Appeal in e.g. *Kinane v Mackie-Conteh* [2005] EWCA Civ 45; [2005] W.T.L.R. 345.

[399] This view has been expressed extra-judicially by Lord Neuberger: "The Stuffing of Minerva's Owl? Taxonomy and Taxidermy in Equity" [2009] C.L.J. 537 at 546: "I suggest that section 2 has nothing to do with the matter. In cases such as *Crabb v Arun District Council* and *Thorner v Major*, the estoppel rests on the finding that it would be inequitable for [A] to insist on his strict legal rights. So the fact that, if there was a contract, it would be void is irrelevant: indeed the very reason for mounting the proprietary estoppel claim is that there is no enforceable contract".

[400] The analysis in this paragraph was supported by Morgan J in *Abdulrida v Al-Najar* [2021] EWHC 398 (Ch) [354] and by Snowden J in *Howe v Gossop* [2021] EWHC 637 (Ch) [45]. It was also referred to by Falk J in *Sahota v Prior* [2019] EWHC 1418 (Ch) at [34] as supportive of the conclusion there reached that s.2 did not prevent B's proprietary estoppel claim where A had made assurances as to B's right to remain in occupation of property transferred by B under a sale and leaseback arrangement. It was also favoured by Judge Mark Raeside QC in *Wills v Sowray* [2020] EWHC 939 (Ch) at [259]-[262]. The analysis finds further support in the (obiter) discussion of the point by Kitchin LJ (with whom Floyd and Patten LJJ agreed) in *Farrar v Miller* [2018] EWCA Civ 172 at [57]-[63]. See further B. McFarlane, "Proprietary Estoppel and Failed Contractual Negotiations" [2005] Conv. 501. Versions of

this basic view are also are also supported by M. Dixon, "Confining and Defining Proprietary Estoppel" (2010) 30 L.S. 408; and G. Owen & O. Rees, "Section 2(5) of the Law of Property (Miscellaneous Provisions) Act 1989: A Misconceived Approach" [2011] Conv. 495. See too the very useful discussion of the point by Master Matthews in *Muhammad v ARY Properties Ltd* [2016] EWHC 1698 (Ch) at [32]–[51], respectfully expressing the view at [49] that the exception created by s.2(5) for constructive trusts "appears to be a red herring, because proprietary estoppel is not about enforcing a contract at all". For recent academic discussion of the point see T. Boncey and F. Ng, "'Common Intention' Constructive Trusts Arising from Informal Agreements to Dispose of Land" [2017] Conv. 146 and M. Dixon, "More Moves in Constructive Trusts and Estoppel" [2017] Conv. 89.

[401] In *Cobbe v Yeoman's Row Management Ltd* [2008] UKHL 55; [2008] 1 W.L.R. 1752 at [29], Lord Scott stated, in an expressly obiter view, that "proprietary estoppel cannot be prayed in aid to render enforceable an agreement that statute has declared to be void". This point, it is submitted, is based on an erroneous reading of s.2, as recognising a proprietary estoppel claim does not deny the contractual invalidity of an agreement. The point also seems to be based on Lord Scott's view that proprietary estoppel is, in effect, a form of estoppel by representation (see para.12-035) and so not a cause of action in its own right (compare the discussion at para.12-029 of *Actionstrength Ltd v International Glass Engineering SpA* [2003] 2 A.C. 541 HL).

[402] This is one interpretation of the view of Arden LJ in *Herbert v Doyle* [2010] EWCA Civ 1095 at [10].

[403] See, e.g. *Cobbe v Yeoman's Row Management Ltd* [2008] UKHL 55; [2008] 1 W.L.R. 1752 at [40]–[45]: B's personal claims against A were successful, even though the existence of the parties' agreement was necessarily one of the facts used to establish those claims.

[404] See, e.g. *Yaxley v Gotts* [2000] Ch. 162 CA at 192, per Beldam LJ.

[405] *Yaxley v Gotts* [2000] Ch. 162 CA at 192, per Beldam LJ. See too at 178, per Robert Walker LJ. In *Howe v Gossop* [2021] EWHC 637 (Ch) Snowden J at [64] stated that "Section 2 does not inhibit the grant of equitable relief on the basis of a proprietary estoppel provided that such relief does not amount to enforcing a non-compliant contract."

[406] In *JSC VTB Bank v Skurikhin* [2019] EWHC 1407 (Comm) (affirmed at [2020] EWCA Civ 1337 but without any appeal on this point) the court considered the different question of the impact of s.53(1)(c) of the Law of Property Act 1925 (see para.3-018) on a proprietary estoppel claim, as B sought to base such a claim on an assurance by A of a transfer a beneficial interest to B. It was stated there (by Patricia Robertson QC, sitting as a Deputy High Court judge, at [251]) that permitting such a claim would be inconsistent with the statutory scheme, as it would undermine the purpose of the s.53(1)(c) formality requirement. It is not obvious, however, why s.53(1)(c) should be treated differently in this respect from the other formality rules (not only s.2 of the 1989 Act but also, for example, s.53(1)(a) of the Law of Property Act 1925) that are regularly bypassed by means of a proprietary estoppel claim.

[407] See, e.g. *Yaxley v Gotts* [2000] Ch. 162 CA (no right in fact held on trust by A as A's duty was to grant B a lease, or to pay the value of that lease to B); *Herbert v Doyle* [2010] EWCA Civ 1095 (no right in fact held on trust by A as A's duty was to grant B a lease); *Kinane v Mackie-Conteh* [2005] EWCA Civ 45; [2005] W.T.L.R. 345 (no right held on trust by A as A's duty was to grant B a charge). Note too *McGuane v Welch* [2008] EWCA Civ 785; [2008] 2 P. & C.R. 24 where, on the facts, the terms of the parties agreement precluded a constructive trust (at [35], per Mummery LJ), but a proprietary estoppel was nonetheless found.

[408] Note in particular that in *Stack v Dowden* [2007] 2 A.C. 432 HL at [37], Lord Walker expressed doubts as to the overlap between proprietary estoppel claims and constructive trusts, thus making it more difficult to force such a claim into a constructive trust analysis in order to deal with the perceived s.2 problem.

[409] As noted by Beldam LJ (who had been Chair of the Law Commission at the time of the relevant report) in *Yaxley v Gotts* [2000] Ch. 162 CA at 181–182, although compare Robert Walker LJ's different treatment of the same point, at 176.

3. Relief

(a) Overview.

Replace first paragraph with:

12-047   There is a lack of clarity as to the relevant principles to be applied when determining the court's response to a successful claim of proprietary estoppel.[410] It is suggested here that, in the representation-based strand of proprietary estoppel,[411] where B is relying on the general principles of estoppel by representation, those principles should apply in the usual way, and A will simply be precluded from denying the truth of the representation. The extent of B's potential detriment in the absence of the estoppel will therefore be irrelevant but, crucially, the estoppel, by itself, is not a cause of action and so imposes no independent liability on A.[412] A more difficult question, discussed in the following paragraphs, arises in relation to the acquiescence[413] and promise-based strands,[414] where the success of B's claim does impose a liability on A. It is undeniable that, in such cases, the court has some discretion.[415] It is equally clear, however, that:

> "the court must take a principled approach, and cannot exercise a completely unfettered discretion according to the individual judge's notion of what is fair in any particular case."[416]

[410] The judgment of Lord Briggs in *Guest v Guest* [2022] UKSC 27 (with which Lady Arden and Lady Rose agreed) clarifies the principles to be applied in the promise-based strand, although the dissent of Lord Leggatt (with whom Lord Stephens agreed) provides evidence of the "lively controversy" (see Lewison LJ in *Davies v Davies* [2016] EWCA Civ 463, [2016] 2 P. & C.R. 10 at [39]) which has surrounded the issue.

[411] See para.12-035.

[412] Although, of course, it may be a means of establishing a fact necessary to permit a successful claim by B: see para.12-035.

[413] See para.12-034.

[414] See para.12-036.

[415] See, e.g. *Davies v Davies* [2016] EWCA Civ 463; [2016] 2 P. & C.R. 10 at [39] (Lewison LJ), referring to the court's "broad judgmental discretion". See too *Crabb v Arun DC* [1976] Ch. 179 CA at 189, per Lord Denning MR citing the statement in the 26th edition of this work that "here equity is displayed at its most flexible"; and *Sledmore v Dalby* (1996) 72 P. & C. R. 196 at 204, per Roch LJ citing the equivalent passage in the 29th edition.

[416] *Jennings v Rice* [2003] 1 P. & C.R. 8 CA at [43], per Robert Walker LJ.

(c)   Two competing approaches.

Replace paragraph with:

12-049   Beyond this common ground, however, uncertainty arose as the courts did not choose clearly between two competing approaches.[424] On the first approach, the starting point is that B's expectation will be protected, and a departure from this is permitted only for practical or other reasons, it would not be unconscionable for A to refuse to protect B's expectation: an example occurs where "the magnitude of specific enforcement in full may be so disproportionate to the detriment undertaken by the promisee that something much less than full specific enforcement is needed to clear the conscience of the promisor".[424a] On this view, then, the concept of proportionality[425] has only a negative role to play.[426] On the second approach, there is no presumption in favour of making B's expectation good, and the extent of relief will be determined principally by the need for such relief to do no more than ensuring that B suffers no detriment as a result of B's reasonable reliance on A[427]; although B may be left to suffer some detriment if A can show that such an outcome would not, on the facts, "shock the conscience of the court".[428] The first approach has gained some recent support in Australia[429] and in the Court of Appeal and was, broadly speaking, adopted by the majority of the Supreme Court in *Guest v Guest*,[430a] in relation to promise-based cases and seemingly in relation to proprietary estoppel more generally.[430] The second approach is supported by the reasoning in a number of Court of Appeal[431] and Privy Council[432] cases[433] and informs the approach adopted by the minority in the Supreme Court in *Guest v Guest*.[433a] A logical difficulty with the first approach is that it allows for the possibility that, in two cases where the extent of B's prospective detriment is identical, the value of B's right may increase as a result of the value of B's expectation decreasing.[434] It may well also be the case that the first approach is based on the assumption that proprietary estoppel is an adaptation of estoppel and so A should, generally, be precluded from denying B's expectation.[434a] The difficulty with this view, however, is that, when proprietary estoppel is applied to acquiescence promises, rather than to representations, it escapes the reach of such preclusive logic.[435] The second approach, as it gives a positive role to the need for proportionality, and defines the concept by reference to the extent of B's potential detriment, also improves on the first by providing principles that can be used to determine the extent of B's right even when it is clear that B's expectation should not be protected.[436] It also draws an important link between the grounds on which B's right arises (the need to avoid B's being left to suffer a detriment) and the extent of that right. As noted by Lewison LJ in *Davies v Davies*: "Since the essence of proprietary estoppel is the combination of expectation and detriment, if either is absent the claim must fail. If, therefore, the detriment can be fairly quantified and a claimant receives full compensation for that detriment, that compensation ought, in principle, to remove the foundation of the claim".[437] With one exception,[438] it is also difficult to find decisions where the result reached is inconsistent with the second approach.[439] Nonetheless, the majority of the Supreme Court in *Guest v Guest* rejected the argument that the remedy should focus on ensuring B suffers no detriment, with Lord Briggs stating that:[439a] "The aim remains what it has always been, namely the prevention or undoing of unconscionable conduct. In many cases, once the equity is established, then the fulfilment of the promise is likely to be the starting point, although considerations of practicality, justice between the parties and fairness to third parties may call for a reduced or different award. And justice between the parties may be affected if the proposed remedy is out of all proportion to the reliant detriment, if that can easily be identified without recourse to minute mathematical calculation, and proper regard is had to non-monetary harm." Some recent cases, including *Davies v Davies*,[439b] support as a "useful working hypothesis" the idea of a sliding scale or spectrum, "by which the clearer the expectation, the greater the detriment and the longer the passage of time during which the expectation was reasonably held, the greater the weight to be given to the expectation."[439c] It is not clear however why either the clarity of the expectation (other than as part of a "quasi-bargain"[439d]) nor the mere passage of time should, in themselves, have a bearing on the extent of relief.

[424] See *Davies v Davies* [2016] EWCA Civ 463; [2016] 2 P. & C.R. 10 at [39], where Lewison LJ stated that: "There is a lively controversy about the essential aim of the exercise of this broad judgmental discretion. One line of authority takes the view that the essential aim of the discretion is to give effect to the claimant's expectation unless it would be disproportionate to do so. The other takes the view that

the essential aim of the discretion is to ensure that the claimant's reliance interest is protected, so that she is compensated for such detriment as she has suffered". At one point, it would have been possible to say that English courts favoured the first, more traditional view, and Australian courts the second (see, e.g. the judgments of Mason CJ, Brennan and McHugh JJ and Toohey J in *Commonwealth of Australia v Verwayen* (1990) 170 C.L.R. 394). More recently, it has been possible to say the opposite (compare, e.g. *Sledmore v Dalby* [1996] 72 P. & C.R. 196 CA and *Henry v Henry* [2010] UKPC 3; [2010] 1 All E.R. 988 with, e.g. *Giumelli v Giumelli* (1999) 196 C.L.R. 101, noted by J. Edelman "Remedial Certainty or Remedial Discretion in Estoppel after Giumelli?" (1999) 7 *Journal Contract Law* 179, and the cases noted in fn.411). For further analysis of the Australian case law, see Y. Liew, "The 'Prima Facie Expectation Relief' Approach in the Australian Law of Proprietary Estoppel" (2019) 39 O.J.L.S. 183. In *Low Heng Leon Andy v Low Kian Beng Lawrence* [2018] S.G.C.A. 48, Andrew Phang J argued that the dichotomy between the two approaches is a false one, as both expectation and detriment must be accounted for and the method adopted by the court will depend on how B chooses to plead the case: for discussion and criticism see Y Liew, *"The Remedial Approach to Proprietary Estoppel in Singapore"* [2020] Conv 11.

[424a] Lord Briggs in *Guest v Guest* [2022] UKSC 27 at [6].

[425] The concept of proportionality is itself a source of some uncertainty, as it has not always been clearly defined. In *Jennings v Rice* [2002] EWCA Civ 159; [2003] 1 P. & C.R. 8, for example, Aldous LJ, at 36 emphasised the need for "proportionality between the expectation and the detriment". This may be read to mean that the extent of B's right must be proportionate to both the expectation and detriment (the interpretation given by, e.g. S. Gardner "The Remedial Discretion in Proprietary Estoppel – Again" (2006) 122 L.Q.R. 492, at 498) but, as it is very difficult to see how proportionality to two different measures can be maintained, it seems more likely that, as Aldous LJ was responding to an argument that B's right should be set by B's expectation, the statement means that B's expectation will be protected only if that would be proportionate to the extent of B's detriment (this interpretation is preferred by, e.g. J. Mee, "Expectation and Proprietary Estoppel Remedies" in M. Dixon (ed.) *Modern Studies in Property Law* (Vol.5) pp.389, 404 fn.59).

[426] This view has been favoured in, e.g. *Suggitt v Suggitt* [2012] EWCA Civ 1140; [2012] W.T.L.R. 1607 at [44]–[45], per Arden LJ; *James v James* [2018] EWHC 43 (Ch) at [51]–[52] and [62] and *Brake v Swift* [2020] EWHC 1810 at [151], per HHJ Paul Matthews; and, in Australia, in e.g. *Delaforce v Simpson-Cook* (2010) 78 N.S.W.L.R. 483; and *Harrison v Harrison* [2013] V.S.C.A. 170.

[427] This view can be supported by e.g. *Sledmore v Dalby* (1996) 72 P. & C.R. 196 CA at 208, per Hobhouse LJ (quoting from Mason CJ in *Commonwealth of Australia v Verwayen* (1990) 170 C.L.R. 394, at 413): "A central element of the doctrine is that there must be a proportionality between the remedy and the detriment which is its purpose to avoid"; and *Henry v Henry* [2010] UKPC 3; [2010] 1 All E.R. 988 at [65], per Sir Jonathan Parker: "Proportionality lies at the heart of the doctrine of proprietary estoppel and permeates its every application"; see too *Arif v Anwar* [2015] EWHC 124 (Fam) at [96], where Norris J asked: "what relief is right and conscionable to grant so as to ensure that [B] suffers no detriment".

[428] This seems to follow from Lord Walker's general statement of principle in *Cobbe v Yeoman's Row Management Ltd* [2008] UKHL 55; [2008] 1 W.L.R. 1752 at [92]. As noted at para.12-045, the concept of unconscionability may be invoked in a promise-based case where a significant change of circumstances means that the burden of performance is now much greater than anticipated: in some cases, such a change might not remove A's liability entirely, but rather reduce it, as implied by Mummery LJ in *Uglow v Uglow* [2004] EWCA Civ 987 at [30].

[429] See, e.g. *Giumelli v Giumelli* (1996) 196 C.L.R. 101; *Delaforce v Simpson-Cook* (2010) 78 N.S.W.L.R. 483; and *Harrison v Harrison* [2013] VSCA 170.

[430a] [2022] UKSC 27.

[430] *Suggitt v Suggitt* [2012] EWCA Civ 1140; [2012] W.T.L.R. 1607 at [44]–[45], per Arden LJ.

[431] See *Davies v Davies* [2016] EWCA Civ 463; [2016] 2 P. & C.R. 10 at [39], where Lewison LJ, without having to decide on the facts between the two different approaches set out above, stated that "Logically, there is much to be said for the second approach". See too *Habberfield v Habberfield* [2019] EWCA Civ 890 at [57], where Lewison LJ disagreed with the statement of Arden LJ in *Suggitt v Suggitt* [2012] EWCA Civ 1140 at [44] that there does not need to be a relationship of proportionality between the level of detriment and the relief awarded. In *Moore v Moore* [2018] EWCA Civ 2669, Henderson LJ stated at [89] and [95] that the first instance judge had erred by making an order trying to mirror B's expectation rather than focussing on "the minimum provision that was needed to satisfy

[B's] equity". See too *Dodsworth v Dodsworth* (1973) 228 E.G. 115 CA; *Crabb v Arun District Council* [1976] Ch. 179 at 198, per Scarman LJ (referring to the "minimum equity to do justice"); *Sledmore v Dalby* (1996) 72 P. & C.R. 196 CA at 208, per Hobhouse LJ; *Campbell v Griffin* [2001] EWCA Civ 990; *Jennings v Rice* [2002] EWCA Civ 159; [2003] 1 P. & C.R. 8; *Beale v Harvey* [2003] EWCA Civ 1883; [2004] 2 P. & C.R. 18 at [39], per Peter Gibson LJ; *Powell v Benney* [2007] EWCA Civ 1283.

[432] See *Clarke v Swaby* [2007] UKPC 1 at [18]; *Henry v Henry* [2010] UKPC 3; [2010] 1 All E.R. 988 at [65].

[433] See too, in Australia, *Commonwealth of Australia v Verwayen* (1990) 170 C.L.R. 394 (per Mason CJ, Brennan, McHugh and Toohey JJ); *Sullivan v Sullivan* [2006] NSWCA 312. Note also *Strover v Strover* [2005] EWHC 860 (Ch), treated it seems as an acquiescence case, where B's detriment consisted of losing the chance to propose to his fellow partners a variation in the terms of mirror life insurance policies, and B was awarded 80 per cent of the benefits that would have accrued from that change, to reflect the 20 per cent chance that the other partners might not have consented.

[433a] [2022] UKSC 27.

[434] This point is made by J. Mee, "Expectation and Proprietary Estoppel Remedies" in M. Dixon (ed.), *Modern Studies in Property Law: Volume V* (2009), pp.389, 399–400. For example, in *Jennings v Rice* [2002] EWCA Civ 159; [2003] 1 P. & C.R. 8, it was held that it would be disproportionate for B to receive A's house and furniture, valued at £435,000, and B was instead awarded £200,000. What if the house and furniture had instead been worth £250,000? It might well be said then that it would not be out of all proportion to order that the house and furniture be conveyed to B. If so, the extent of B's right would increase as a result of the decrease in value of A's property. See too Lord Leggatt in *Guest v Guest* [2022] UKSC 27 at [224].

[434a] See too Lord Leggatt in *Guest v Guest* [2022] UKSC 27 at [224].

[435] See para.12-006.

[436] In *Moore v Moore* [2018] EWCA Civ 2669, Henderson LJ at [26] stated an initial view that "although the second approach is logically attractive, I would be wary of according it primacy in a field where cases are so fact sensitive and proportionality has such a prominent role to play". The point may simply be that, as will be seen in para.12-050, the second approach should not be applied in such a way as to mean that simply compensating B for quantifiable reliance loss will always be an appropriate way to satisfy an estoppel equity.

[437] See *Davies v Davies* [2016] EWCA Civ 463; [2016] 2 P. & C.R. 10 at [39], referring to A. Robertson, "The Reliance Basis of Proprietary Estoppel Remedies" [2008] Conv. 295. See too Lord Leggatt in *Guest v Guest* [2022] UKSC 27 at [195].

[438] In *Pascoe v Turner* [1979] 1 W.L.R. 431 CA, A was ordered to transfer A's fee simple to B, where B's reliance on A's promise consisted of expending a relatively small sum on the property. The domestic context was important, and the need to ensure a "clean break" between the parties, so that A could not assert further pressure on B, was highlighted, but it would seem that, even adopting the first approach, the enforcement of B's expectation could be said to be "out of all proportion" to the detriment suffered.

[439] The reasoning in *Suggitt v Suggitt* [2012] EWCA Civ 1140; [2012] W.T.L.R. 1607 (e.g. at [44]–[45]) is certainly consistent only with the first view, but the result in the case may be seen as consistent with the second view once account is taken of the judge's (perhaps, on the facts, exaggerated) finding that B had "positioned his whole life on the basis of the assurances given to him". That finding was certainly important in the Court of Appeal's decision: see, e.g. at [23], [37], and at [38].

[439a] [2022] UKSC 27 at [94].

[439b] [2016] EWCA Civ 463 [41].

[439c] Ibid; see too prevailing *Anaghara v Anaghara* [2020] EWHC 3091 (Ch) at [70]–[72].

[439d] In *Anaghara v Anaghara* [2020] EWHC 3091 (Ch), for example, it was noted at [72] that there was "close to a consensual bargain" between the parties, and B had presumably completed her side of it in the 34 years from the time the expectation was first induced.

(d)   Application of the suggested approach.

Replace first paragraph with:

In a promise-based case, the court will normally start with "the assumption (not   **12-050** presumption) that the simplest way to remedy the unconscionability constituted by the repudiation is to hold the promisor to the promise."[439e] There are certainly cases in which giving effect to B's expectation isalso the only means in practice of removing B's detriment.[440] One sub-set of such cases is where the assurances and reliance "have a consensual character falling not far short of an enforceable contract"[441] and where B has performed B's side of the parties' "quasi-bargain".[442] In such a case, "subject to countervailing considerations, the court is likely to vindicate the claimant's expectations".[443] There is no clear dividing line marking out such cases, but in *Habberfield v Habberfield*, Lewison LJ approved of the following approach, if applied with "an appropriate degree of flexibility"[445]:

> "Looking back from the moment when assurances are repudiated, the nearer the overall outcome comes to the expected reciprocal performance of requested acts in return for the assurance, the stronger will be the case for an award based on or approximating to the expectation interest created by the assurance. That does no more than to recognise party autonomy to decide for themselves what a proportionate reward would be for the contemplated detriment."[446]

[439e] *Guest v Guest* [2022] UKSC 27 at [75].

[440] See, e.g. *Crabb v Arun District Council* [1976] Ch. 179 CA at 199, per Scarman LJ: in the absence of the grant of a right of way by A, B's land would remain inaccessible and "sterilised". Note too cases, such as *Gillett v Holt* [2001] Ch. 210 CA; *Suggitt v Suggitt* [2012] EWCA Civ 1140; [2012] W.T.L.R. 1607; and *Thorner v Major* [2009] UKHL 18; [2009] 1 W.L.R. 776, where B has relied over a long period, or "positioned [his or her] whole life" on the basis of A's promises.

[441] See Robert Walker LJ in *Jennings v Rice* [2002] EWCA Civ 159; [2003] 1 P. & C.R. 8 at [45]; *Habberfield v Habberfield* [2019] EWCA Civ 890 [67]–[68].

[442] See too Lewison LJ in *Davies v Davies* [2016] EWCA Civ 463; [2016] 2 P. & C.R. 10 at [40].

[443] *Habberfield v Habberfield* [2019] EWCA Civ 890 at [62] (Lewison LJ). For an example, see *Rojob v Deb* [2022] EWHC 1572 (Ch) at [134]–[137].

[445] *Habberfield v Habberfield* [2019] EWCA Civ 890 at [69].

[446] *Habberfield v Habberfield* [2019] EWCA Civ 890 at [68].

Replace second paragraph with:

Even in such cases, however, "the court may have to listen to many other reasons from the promisor (or his executors) why something less than full perfromance will negate the unconscionability and therefore satsify the equity."[447] In *Habberfield v Habberfield*, for example, whilst B had completed her side of a non-contractual quid pro quo, the Court of Appeal confirmed that the first instance judge had been correct to "scale down" the remedy awarded as a result of a change in the circumstances of A.[448] In *Guest v Guest*, it was emphasised that a court must also take into account the "acceleration"* of a promised benefit which occurs where, as in that case, a claim is brought before the point in time (eg the death of A where a testamentary promise has been made) when the promise was due to be performed. As noted at 12-048, this is an aspect of the principle that B cannot receive more than was promised by A.[449] The impact of taxation, where relevant, should also be taken into account in framing relief,[450] and in a case, for example, involving a claim for the transfer of valuable assets, the impact of inheritance tax, capital gains tax and income tax will require "careful consideration, with the benefit of expert evidence, or at least submissions from counsel well versed in the relevant areas of tax law".[451]

[447] Lord Briggs in *Guest v Guest* [2022] UKSC 27 at [75]. See too *Habberfield v Habberfield* [2019] EWCA Civ 890 at [71] (Lewison LJ). See too *Moore v Moore* [2018] EWCA Civ 2669 at [30] where Henderson LJ noted that the factors set out by Robert Walker LJ in *Jennings* [2003] 1 P. & C.R. 8 at

[52] (such as the need for a clean break and alternations in A's circumstances) are still relevant when considering a quasi-bargain case, although they are likely to have a less significant influence in such cases. For a reciprocal performance case where alterations in A's circumstances were relevant, see *Habberfield v Habberfield* [2019] EWCA Civ 890 at [41].

448 *Habberfield v Habberfield* [2019] EWCA Civ 890 at [41], [72]. B, a dairy farmer, had expected to acquire a working dairy farm but A had discontinued the dairy unit, and it was not suggested that A had acted culpably in so doing. As a result, the absence of the dairy unit was seen at [41] as "simply a change of circumstance which makes it inappropriate to give full effect to [B's] expectation" as the cost of reinstating the unit was estimated at £400,000. See too *Moore v Moore* [2018] EWCA Civ 2669 at [94], where Henderson LJ pointed out that, even though B had spent his adult life working on A's farm in reliance on promises of inheritance on the death of the survivor of A and A's wife, with proper provision made for A's wife in the meantime, various changes of circumstance (e.g. the worsening health of A and the breakdown of relations in the family) meant that "this was no longer a realistic scenario".

449 [2022] UKSC 27 at [78]-[80].

450 See *Jennings v Rice* [2002] EWCA Civ 159; [2003] 1 P. & C.R. 8 at [52], per Robert Walker LJ; *Habberfield v Habberfield* [2019] EWCA Civ 890 at [20], noting that the first instance judge had ordered A to pay a sum of money to B representing the value of A's farmland, and not to transfer the land itself, as a transfer of the farmland without the farmhouse would be "very tax inefficient" as the farmhouse would not then benefit from agricultural property relief from inheritance tax.

451 *Moore v Moore* [2018] EWCA Civ 2669 at [96] (Henderson LJ). In that case, the first instance judge had made an order for the immediate transfer of assets worth around £5 million from A to B and that order, if implemented, would give rise to "significant CGT and income tax liabilities". Up to date valuations of the relevant assets are also required to allow the tax consequences of a contemplated order to be established. As Henderson LJ noted at [100], if a court does not have such information it may be necessary for a further hearing before the extent of the remedy can be determined.

Replace third paragraph with:

In other cases, where B's reliance is less significant,452 or relatively short-lived,453 there is no need to protect B's expectation and, for example, a monetary award may be justified, even in a case where A made a clear promise to give property to B.454 If A argues that protecting B's expectation would be "out of all proportion" to B's detriment, it should be remembered that, as noted at para.12-044, the assessment of detriment is not a scientific process, not least because detriment includes non-financial consequences,455 and so a court will necessarily have to exercise a judgment.456 In deciding whether to depart from the starting point that A's promise should be enforced, the court must also bear in mind that in *Guest v Guest*, the majority of the Supreme Court chose to "firmly reject the theory that the aim of the remedy for proprietary estoppel is detriment-based".456a The analysis of the majority in *Guest v Guest* does not make clear how a court should take account of B's receipt of any countervailing benefits as a result of his or her acts of reliance457 in assessing the appropriate relief, but previous case-law regards such benefits as potentially relevant and, as the aim of the remedy is to avoid unconscionable conduct by A, that aim is broad enough to permit consideration of such countervailing benefits.458

452 See, e.g. *Powell v Benney* [2007] EWCA Civ 1283 (the reliance on A's promise consisted principally in financial expenditure of £8,830 on fairly minor repairs to those properties). See too *Davies v Davies* [2016] EWCA Civ 463, where Lewison LJ, allowing an appeal and thus reducing the award made to B, emphasised (at [49] and [66]) that it was not a case in which B had made life-changing decisions on the basis of A's promises.

453 See, e.g. *Ottey v Grundy* [2003] EWCA Civ 1176; [2003] W.T.L.R. 1253. A's promise was made in the summer of 1997 and the parties separated in October 1999. B did not give up any specific opportunities as a result of the promise, which was made when A and B were already living together. See too *Davies v Davies* [2016] EWCA Civ 463; [2016] 2 P. & C.R. 10 where Lewison LJ, allowing an appeal and thus reducing the award made to B, emphasised (at [65]) the limited period during which B had relied on A; and *Habberfield v Habberfield* [2018] EWHC 317 (Ch) at [228], where Birss J stated that:

"if the defendant in *Thorner* had died six months after making his promise then the claimant would have been restricted to having his equity satisfied by payment of reasonable remuneration for that period". The decision was upheld on appeal: [2019] EWCA Civ 890.

[454] As noted by Lord Briggs in *Guest v Guest* [2022] UKSC 27 at [10]. In each of *Powell v Benney* [2007] EWCA Civ 1283; and *Ottey v Grundy* [2003] EWCA Civ 1176; [2003] W.T.L.R. 1253, clear promises were made by A. In *Ottey*, the terms of the promise were set out in writing. See too *Sullivan v Sullivan* [2006] NSWCA 312: A's promise was not enforced even though set out clearly in writing: the principal detriment was giving up public housing for which B had had to wait for seven years. The relief, Handley JA dissenting, was that B be allowed to continue in occupation of A's house for a further seven years, presumably on the assumption that B would be able to return to public housing by that point.

[455] The fact that part of B's detriment can be quantified does not mean that B's remedy must be capped at that sum, as there may be other parts of B's detriment that cannot be so quantified: see, e.g. *Habberfield v Habberfield* [2019] EWCA Civ 890 at [47] (Lewison LJ).

[456] See *Davies v Davies* [2016] EWCA Civ 463; [2016] 2 P. & C.R. 10 at [67] where Lewison LJ stated that the court "must do the best we can" in valuing non-financial detriment: "In different situations the court is often called upon to award compensation for non-pecuniary losses, and the difficulty of assessment is no bar to an award". A useful example is provided by *Campbell v Griffin* [2001] EWCA Civ 990; [2001] W.T.L.R. 981. A1 and A2 had come to rely for daily assistance on B, their lodger. They later assured B that he had a home for life. B provided devoted care for A1 and A2 for at least four years, as well as incurring significant out-of-pocket expenses on their behalf. The Court of Appeal reversed the finding of the first instance judge that no proprietary estoppel claim arose. It therefore had to decide on the extent of B's right. Robert Walker LJ rejected B's claim that he was entitled to a life interest in the land, explaining, at [34]–[36], that such a result "would be disproportionate. [B] has a moral (and, as I see it, a legal) claim on the property, but it is not so compelling as to demand total satisfaction, regardless of the effect on other persons with claims on [A1 and A2's] estate". Instead, it was found that B was entitled to a sum of £35,000, to be charged on the property: "the sum payable will not by itself enable [B] to buy a freehold house in Worthing, but it will assist him with rehousing himself".

[456a] [2022] UKSC 27 at [71].

[457] It is not always clear when a benefit will be seen as sufficiently related to B's acts of reliance as to have a countervailing effect: for an examination of the area, see B. McFarlane, *The Law of Proprietary Estoppel*, 2nd Edn (2020) 4.113–4.184. In *Anaghara v Anaghara* [2020] EWHC 3091 (Ch) at [63]–[64], for example, it was found that B's occupation of the matrimonial home during the life of her husband was not a relevant countervailing benefit as it was not "an advantage enjoyed in consequence of the relevant assurances", given that B would have occupied that land in any case.

[458] See e.g. *Sledmore v Dalby* (1996) 72 P. & C.R. 196 CA; *Campbell v Griffin* [2001] EWCA Civ 990; [2001] W.T.L.R. 981; *Powell v Benney* [2007] EWCA Civ 1283; and *Henry v Henry* [2010] UKPC 3; [2010] 1 All E.R. 988 PC (in all four cases, the benefit to B of rent-free use or occupation of A's property was taken into account). Note in particular that in *Henry*, the judgment below was seen as flawed precisely because the judge "did not attempt to weigh the disadvantages suffered by [B] by reason of his reliance on [A's] promises against the countervailing advantages which he enjoyed as a consequence of that reliance".

(e)   Possible forms of relief.

Replace n.459 with:

12-051   [459] For examples of the flexible approach that can be taken to fashioning an appropriate remedy, and of limits to that flexibility, see *Gee v Gee* [2018] EWHC 1393 (Ch) at [140]–[170] and *Morton v Morton* [2022] EWHC 163 (Ch) at [208]–[222].

Replace n.470 with:

12-051   [470] In *Jennings v Rice* [2002] EWCA Civ 159; [2003] 1 P. & C.R. 8, Robert Walker LJ suggested, at [51], that where B's detriment "consists solely of expenditure on improvements to [A's] house" an equitable charge for that expenditure "may be sufficient to satisfy the equity". A fuller analysis was undertaken by Morgan J. in *Abdulrida v Al-Najar* [2021] EWHC 398 (Ch) [356]–[360], where it was stated at [359] that the specific question of whether A's duty to pay B would be secured should be answered by applying the same "principles as to the relevance of expectation and detriment when determining the relief to be granted". On the facts, B would have been unable to recover anything of real value in the absence of security, and B's expectation had been that his detriment (a payment made to A) was made under a valid contract of sale, which would have given B at least a purchaser's lien, so it was held that A's duty to repay B, plus interest, was secured by an equitable charge or lien over the land.

4. Effect on Third Parties.

(b) The acquiescence and promise-based strands: position after a court order in B's favour.

After "fact took free", replace "form" with:
from

12-053

(c) Position before a court order in B's favour.

Replace n.494 with:

[494] As noted, in the context of estoppel licences, by G. Battersby, "Contractual and Estoppel Licences as Proprietary Interests in Land" [1991] 57 Conv. 36. See too *Sangha v Sangha* [2021] EWHC 1599 (Ch) [310] (Deputy Master Bowles): "Arguably, if the proper satisfaction of the equity would not entail the grant of a proprietary interest, but would be satisfied in some other way, then, because a transferee would not, ordinarily be bound by a personal obligation of the transferor, the equity would, or should, only be enforceable against the transferor."

12-054

Replace final paragraph with:

This difficulty may, however, be capable of resolution if the term "equity by estoppel", as used in s.116(a), is interpreted so as to refer only to cases where a court would, at that point, have ordered A to give B a recognised property right[495]; after all, the term "mere equity" in s.116(b) must similarly be limited to cases where B had a power to acquire such a recognised property right, as it cannot apply in every case where some equitable protection would have been available to B against A.[496] If "equity by estoppel" is not interpreted as suggested here, the courts will have the task of finding other ways to protect C in a case where, at the time of C's involvement, A's liability to B would have been satisfied by B's having a purely personal right against A. In *Henry v Henry*, the Privy Council did not rule out the possibility that, even in a case where C is bound by an overriding interest arising through proprietary estoppel, "the particular circumstances surrounding [C's] purchase" may nonetheless "require the court to reassess the extent of [B's] equity in the property".[497] The difficulty with such a view, however, is that a court in effect has to reinvent the wheel by using broader notions of unconscionability to determine when C might be bound. The better solution, it is submitted, is simply to defer to the existing and carefully worked out priority rules, which are structured around the key distinction between personal rights on the one hand and proprietary rights on the other.

[495] This possibility is discussed and advocated by B. McFarlane, *The Law of Proprietary Estoppel* (2nd edn, 2020), paras 8.98–8.117. It is worth noting that in *Re North East Property Buyers Litigation* [2015] A.C. 385 SC, it was found that no equitable proprietary right capable of binding A's mortgagee could be acquired through a proprietary estoppel alleged to arise in the period when A had not yet acquired legal title to the land, but had only rights under a vendor-purchaser constructive trust. For discussion see A. Televantos and L. Maniscalco, "Proprietary Estoppel and Vendor Purchaser Constructive Trusts" [2015] C.L.J. 27.

[496] As noted by e.g. Lord Wilberforce in *National Provincial Bank v Ainsworth* [1965] A.C. 1175 at 1253, "[t]he fact that a contractual right can be specifically performed, or its breach prevented by injunction, does not mean that the right is any the less of a personal character or that a purchaser with notice is bound by it: what is relevant is the nature of the right, not the remedy which exists for its enforcement".

The approach taken in this paragraph was discussed in *Brake v Swift* [2020] EWHC 1810 where the question was whether a proprietary estoppel equity arising as a result of B's reliance on a belief of acquiring a beneficial interest in land amounted to an "interest" in a dwelling-house under the revesting provisions of s.283A of the Insolvency Act 1986. HHJ Paul Matthews stated at [156]-[157] that it was not necessary on the facts to "give any view, much less a concluded view, about the scope of s.116 of the Land Registration Act 2002. It is sufficient for me to say that, in my judgment, the only proprietary estoppel claims which can properly be regarded as 'property' rights under the general law, binding third parties in the appropriate circumstances, are those of claims to already recognized property rights or interests."

[497] *Henry v Henry* [2010] UKPC 3; [2010] 1 All E.R. 988 at [56].

CHAPTER 13

PENALTIES AND FORFEITURE

1. OVERVIEW

(c)   The current rule against penalties as a common law rule.

After "a particular result.", add new n.12a:

[12a] S. Rowan (2021) 84 MLR 1066, 1081-2 argues that the penalties doctrine in England is, along with **13-003** other aspects of contract law, concerned with preventing abuse of rights, but "the right or freedom being abused inheres in the broader right to create mutual rights and duties by agreement, with any abuse occurring and being assessed at the time the contract is made and involving both parties."

Replace n.12 with:

[12] *Andrews v Australia and New Zealand Banking Group Ltd* (2012) 247 C.L.R. 205. Note that M Arden and J Edelman, "Mutual Borrowing and Judicial Dialogue Between the Apex Courts of Australia and the United Kingdom" (2022) 138 L.Q.R. 217, 220 suggest that the difference between England and Australia "might be an illustration of two rational doctrines developing in parallel" with the English view being that "parties cannot agree to a remedy for breach which is of a nature which the law would never have permitted" and the Australian view being that "a security right must be limited to providing security."

(d)   The relationship between the two doctrines.

Replace n.28 with:

[28] Lords Neuberger and Sumption in their joint judgment in *Cavendish* [2015] UKSC 67; [2016] A.C. **13-004** 1172 at [17]–[18]. The Supreme Court's decision in *Vauxhall Motors Ltd v Manchester Ship Canal Co Ltd* [2019] UKSC 46 did not consider in detail the relationship between penalties and forfeiture (although see Lady Arden at [72]–[73]). Note that the issue in that case was seen as one of relief against forfeiture whereas in *Vivienne Westwood Ltd v Conduit Street Development Ltd* [2017] EWHC 350 (Ch) the case was dealt with under the rule against penalties: in each case, B's breach of an agreement for the use of

[133]

A's land led to A's attempting to exercise a contractual power to prevent B continuing to use that land under the existing terms, favourable to B. For academic consideration of the relationship between penalties and forfeiture in light of the Supreme Court's decision in *Vauxhall Motors*, see N Tiverios & B McFarlane, 'Controlling Private Punishment in Three Dimensions: Penalties and Forfeiture in England and Australia' in E Bant et al (eds) *Punishment and Private Law* (Hart, 2021).

2. PENALTIES

2. Scope of the Rule

(a) The limited scope of the rule.

Replace n.69 with:

13-008 [69] See, e.g. Lord Romilly MR in *Parkin v Thorold* (1852) 16 Beav 59, 66; 51 E.R. 698, 701.

(b) The need for a breach of contract.

Replace paragraph with:

13-009 The clear position in English law, confirmed by the Supreme Court's decision in *Cavendish*,[71] is that the penalties doctrine can apply only where a clause attaches a particular consequence to a breach of a contractual duty owed by B to A. The impugned clause can thus be seen as a "secondary provision"[72] imposing a duty on B to A only where a primary obligation owed by B to A has been breached.

[71] *Talal El Makdessi v Cavendish Square Holding BV* [2015] UKSC 67; [2015] 3 W.L.R. 1373: see para.13-003. This approach has also been adopted in Hong Kong: see *Law Ting Pong Secondary School v Chen Wai Wah* [2021] 5 HKC 452.

[72] See, e.g. *Cavendish* [2015] UKSC 67; [2015] 3 W.L.R. 1373 at [73]. In *Banco San Juan Internacional Inc v Petroleos de Venezuela SA* [2021] 2 All ER (Comm) 590, [2020] EWHC 2937 (Comm), Cockerill J noted at [139] that even if the impugned term before him were not a primary obligation, it was in any case outside the scope of the penalty doctrine as it did not arise on a breach of contract by B.

Replace first paragraph with:

13-010 Nonetheless, in *Cavendish*,[82] the Supreme Court confirmed the conventional position in English law that the penalty jurisdiction can apply only to regulate terms which in substance impose consequences on a breach of contract. This perpetuates what Lord Denning called the "absurd paradox"[83] that more protection is given to a contract breaker than to a party who is penalised merely for the non-occurrence of a condition.[84]

[82] *Talal El Makdessi v Cavendish Square Holding BV* [2015] UKSC 67; [2016] A.C. 1172.

[83] *Bridge v Campbell Discount Co Ltd* [1962] A.C. 600 HL at 630.

[84] It may be that the somewhat unclear concept of a "disguised penalty", discussed at para.13-011, can provide some means of dealing with this paradox. For example, in *European Film Bonds AS v Lotus Holdings LLC* [2020] EWHC 1115 (Ch), (upheld on appeal [2021] EWCA Civ 807, but without discussion of the penalty point), the relevant term was contained in a guarantee agreement, so that B, the guarantor, suffered consequences as a result of a breach of contract committed by a different party. It was held that the clause was in any case not penal, so discussion of the point was obiter, but the judge (Andrew Hochhauser QC) noted at [162]-[163] the submission that "the fact that the consequences of the breach are imposed on a different (non-breaching) party cannot be sufficient to turn a provision that is exorbitant or unconscionable into one which is not" as this would allow parties to circumvent the rule against penalties: "the substance of the contractual arrangements must be and are more important than the mere form." See too *Ahuja Investments Ltd v Victorygame Ltd* [2021] EWHC 2382 (Ch) at [132].

(c) The need for the term to impose a secondary obligation.

Replace paragraph with:

The fact that the operation of a term is dependent on a breach of contract by B **13-011** appears to be a necessary but not a sufficient condition of that term falling within the scope of the English rule against penalties. The question is rather whether the term imposes a "secondary" obligation and the approach of Lord Neuberger and Lord Sumption in *Cavendish* shows that a term responding to a breach of contract need not always be a "secondary" obligation.[92] As shown however by the different approach adopted by other members of the Supreme Court when dealing with the terms considered in the *Cavendish* appeal, the meaning of this requirement is not wholly clear.[92a]

[92] *Talal El Makdessi v Cavendish Square Holding BV* [2015] UKSC 67; [2016] A.C. 1172 at [74]–[83]. See too *Adare Finance DAC v Yellowstone Capital Management SA* [2021] 2 B.C.L.C. 140, [2020] EWHC 2760 (Comm) [104], where an acceleration provision, requiring B to pay sums due to A at an earlier date than in the absence of default, was held to be a "conditional primary obligation of the type referred to by Lords Neuberger and Sumption in [Cavendish] at [14]."

[92a] In *Banco San Juan Internacional Inc v Petroleos de Venezuela SA* [2021] 2 All ER (Comm) 590, [2020] EWHC 2937 (Comm) Cockerill J noted at [139] that "there is plainly within [Cavendish] quite a lot of scope for debate about what is meant by a 'secondary obligation'." See too *OCM Maritime Nile LLC v Courage Shipping Co* [2022] EWHC 452 (Comm) at [146] (upheld on appeal: [2022] EWCA Civ 1091). In *Leiman v Noble Resources Ltd* [2020] SGCA 52, the Singapore Court of Appeal, confirming that the penalties doctrine in Singapore, as in England, applies only to terms which "stipulate the way in which a secondary obligation is to be discharged" provided some guidance as to the identification of such terms, stating that the "court should approach the issue as a matter of substance rather than form" and should ask whether the term was "entered into and contemplated as part of the parties' primary obligations under the contract in order to secure some independent commercial purpose or end, or whether it was, in the round, to hold the affected party in terrorem in order thereby to secure his compliance with his primary obligations" ibid [100]–[101]. For discussion see e.g. M. Phua (2021) 137 L.Q.R. 45. See too *Denka Advantech Pte v Seraya Energy Pte* [2020] SGCA 119 [242].

(e) Obligations of B other than a duty to pay money.

Replace n.115 with:

[115] *Cavendish* [2015] UKSC 67; [2016] A.C. 1172 at [16]: "it seems to us that there is no reason why **13-013** an obligation to transfer assets (either for nothing or at an undervalue) should not be capable of constituting a penalty" (Lord Neuberger and Lord Sumption). In *OCM Maritime Nile LLC v Courage Shipping Co* [2022] EWHC 452 (Comm) (upheld on appeal: [2022] EWCA Civ 1091) it was argued that a term that B would lose, on breach, an option to purchase A's boat was penal, but this was rejected at [147] on the basis that the term imposed a condition on A's duty to B rather than imposing a secondary obligation on B.

3. The Test for a Penalty

(a) Summary of the test.

Replace paragraph with:

If a challenged term is identified as falling within the scope of the rule against **13-014** penalties, as it is a secondary obligation arising in response to a breach of contract, then the court will move on to the second stage of the enquiry and consider, in the words of Lords Neuberger and Lord Sumption in *Cavendish*, if the term "imposes a detriment on the contract-breaker out of all proportion to any legitimate interest of the innocent party in the enforcement of the primary obligation."[119] The test was put in slightly different, words by Lord Hodge, who stated that it is "whether the sum or remedy stipulated as a consequence of a breach of contract is exorbitant or unconscionable when regard is had to the innocent party's interest in the performance of the contract."[120] Lord Toulson endorsed that formulation, stating that parties and court should focus on it, bearing in mind both that "it is impossible to lay down abstract rules about what may or may not be 'extravagant or unconscionable', because it depends on the particular facts and circumstances established in the individual case" and that "'exorbitant' and 'unconscionable' are strong words".[121] Lord Toulson also agreed with Lord Mance[122] that: "'unconscionable' in this context means much the same as 'extravagant'".[123]

[119] *Talal El Makdessi v Cavendish Square Holding BV* [2015] UKSC 67; [2016] A.C. 1172 at [32]. Once it is determined that a clause is subject to review as a penalty, a materially identical test of whether the term is out of proportion to the legitimate interests of the innocent party in performance has been applied by the Supreme Court of New Zealand (*127 Hobson Street Ltd v Honey Bees Preschool Ltd* [2020] NZSC 53 at [56]-[57]) and by the High Court of Australia (*Paciocco v Australia and New Zealand Banking Group Ltd* [2016] HCA 28, (2016) 258 C.L.R. 525), as well as by the Hong Kong Court of Appeal (*Law Ting Pong Secondary School v Chen Wai Wah* [2021] 5 HKC 452).

[120] *Cavendish* [2015] UKSC 67; [2016] A.C. 1172 at [255].

[121] *Cavendish* [2015] UKSC 67; [2016] A.C. 1172 at [293].

[122] *Cavendish* [2015] UKSC 67; [2016] A.C. 1172 at [152].

[123] *Cavendish* [2015] UKSC 67; [2016] A.C. 1172 at [293].

(b) The development of the test.

Replace n.132 with:

13-015 [132] *Cavendish* [2015] UKSC 67; [2016] A.C. 1172 at [23] referring in particular to the judgments of Lord Atkinson in *Dunlop Pneumatic* [1915] A.C. 79 HL; and Lord Robertson in *Clydebank* [1905] A.C. 6 HL. Note that a different approach was taken by the Singapore Court of Appeal in *Denka Advantech Pte v Seraya Energy Pte* [2020] SGCA 119, where the court preferred to affirm the conventional understanding of the *Dunlop* test and therefore focus on the question of whether the impugned term is a genuine pre-estimate of loss, rather than focusing on A's legitimate interest in performance: ibid [150]–[158]. For discussion see e.g. R. Halson (2021) 137 LQR 375.

Replace second paragraph with:

13-016 Whilst given only at first instance, the judgment of Colman J in *Lordsvale Finance Plc v Bank of Zambia*[139] proved to be very influential, and was frequently cited with approval by the Court of Appeal.[140] Its focus on a "good commercial reason" is reflected in the language of "legitimate interest" used in *Cavendish*. The court's focus is not solely on the question of whether the clause in question is based on a genuine pre-estimate of the loss A may suffer from B's breach, but rather on the wider question of whether there is a legitimate commercial justification for the clause, so that the dominant purpose of its insertion was not the simple deterrence of B's breach.[141] It should also be noted that the courts themselves, albeit only in exceptional circumstances, may take account of the desirability of deterrence in making a damages award for a breach of contract[142] and so, in those exceptional cases, it must be possible for the parties to agree in advance that B should, for example, give up to A profits acquired by B as a result of a breach of contract.[143]

[139] *Lordsvale Finance Plc v Bank of Zambia* [1996] Q.B. 752.

[140] See e.g. *Cine Bes Filmcilik Ve YapimCilik v United International Pictures* [2003] EWCA Civ 1669 at [15], per Mance LJ; *Murray v Leisureplay Plc* [2005] EWCA Civ 963; [2005] I.R.L.R. 946 at [117], per Buxton LJ; *Euro London Appointments Ltd v Claessens International Ltd* [2006] EWCA Civ 385 at [29]–[30] per Chadwick LJ. For a more recent application of the reasoning of Colman J, see *Banco San Juan Internacional Inc v Petroleos de Venezuela SA* [2021] 2 All ER (Comm) 590, [2020] EWHC 2937 (Comm) [141].

141 See *Cavendish* [2015] UKSC 67; [2016] A.C. 1172 at [28]–[32], [152], [249] and [276].

142 See, e.g. *Attorney General v Blake* [2001] 1 A.C. 268 HL.

143 The validity of such a disgorgement provision was upheld in the New Zealand Court of Appeal in *Attorney General for England & Wales v R.* [2002] 2 N.Z.L.R 91. The issue of its validity was not raised on further appeal to the Privy Council: *R. v Attorney General for England & Wales* [2003] UKPC 22.

(c) The concept of a "legitimate interest in performance".

Replace n.163 with:

163 *Cavendish* [2015] UKSC 67; [2016] A.C. 1172 at [98]. For discussion of the relevance of the wider **13-017** public interest to the concept of a legitimate interest in performance, see see S Rowan, "The 'Legitimate Interest in Performance' in the Law of Penalties" [2019] C.L.J. 148, 170–71. Note too *Harcus Sinclair LLP v Your Lawyers Ltd* [2021] 3 W.L.R. 598, [2021] UKSC 32 at [70] when considering how to determine the "legitimate interests of the promisee", albeit in a different context, the court drew on *Cavendish* in stating that: "one can take into account what the parties (objectively) intended or contemplated, consequent on the contract, at the time the contract was made as well as the contract terms." For criticism of the operation of the test in the context of parking penalties, see D. Campbell and R. Halson [2020] C.L.J. 405, 406-7.

Replace second paragraph with:

It should also be noted that whilst the test, by allowing A to point to considera- **13-018** tions other than the loss directly caused to A by B's breach, does make it difficult for B to show that a term is penal, the mere fact that a clause was thoroughly negoti- ated, and agreed between well-advised commercial parties does not, however, prevent its being penal.[170] The jurisdiction does not respond to inequalities of bargaining power,[171] and so relative equality of such power does not in itself mean that a clause is not penal. It is therefore still possible, even after *Cavendish*, for a term in a commercial contract to be found to be penal.[172]

170 In *Hayfin Opal Luxco v Windermere VII CMBS Plc* [2016] EWHC 782 (Ch), Snowden J (in an obiter consideration of the point at [140]) inclined to the view that a term determining levels of payment to noteholders by imposing high interest rates in the event of default would almost inevitably lead to a duty to pay a sum "many times the amount that would adequately compensate the innocent party for being kept out of its money" and so would be regarded as "exorbitant (if not extortionate)".

171 See, e.g. *Jeancharm Ltd v Barnet Football Club* [2003] EWCA Civ 58 at 20 per Keene LJ: "It is quite clear from the authorities that the concept of a penalty clause is not confined to situations where one party had a dominant bargaining power over the other, although it may, of course, often apply in such a situation". See too *Cavendish* [2015] UKSC 67; [2016] A.C. 1172 at [34] (Lord Neuberger and Lord Sumption); *127 Hobson Street Ltd v Honey Bees Preschool Ltd* [2020] NZSC 53 at [88].

172 See, e.g. *Vivienne Westwood Ltd v Conduit Street Development Ltd* [2017] EWHC 350 (Ch). See too *Hayfin Opal Luxco v Windermere VII CMBS Plc* [2016] EWHC 782 (Ch) at [140]; *First Personnel Services v Halford Ltd* [2016] EWHC 3220 (Ch) at [161]. See too *JT Development Solutions Ltd v Secretary of State for Education* [2021] EWHC 2943 (Ch) at [33].

(d) An obligation which is exorbitant, unconscionable, or out of all proportion.

Replace third paragraph with:

The circumstances in which the parties bargained is likely to affect the court's **13-019** approach. When considering the *Cavendish* appeal, for example, having identified A's interests in securing B's loyalty and in "measuring the price of the business to its value", Lord Neuberger and Lord Sumption did not attempt to place a definite value on such interests, or consider how the parties' contract might have been dif- ferent if the challenged clauses had not been included, remarking that such "were matters for the parties, who were, on both sides, sophisticated, successful and experienced commercial people bargaining on equal terms over a long period with expert legal advice and were the best judges of the degree to which each of them should recognize the proper commercial interests of the other".[176]

[176] *Cavendish* [2015] UKSC 67; [2016] A.C. 1172 at [75]. See too e.g. *European Film Bonds AS v Lotus Holdings LLC* [2020] EWHC 1115 (Ch) at [167]; *Banco San Juan Internacional Inc v Petroleos de Venezuela SA* [2021] 2 All ER (Comm) 590, [2020] EWHC 2937 (Comm) [145]. In *127 Hobson Street Ltd v Honey Bees Preschool Ltd* [2020] NZSC 53 at [80]-[90], the fact that the term had been agreed between two commercial parties, and neither had taken advantage of the other, was relevant to a finding that the remedy it imposed was not out of all proportion to A's legitimate interest in performance. It was noted, for example, that agreeing to the term provided B with a way of making the "watertight commitment" ([16]) A was seeking as a condition of entering the contract.

Replace fifth paragraph with:

An example, post-dating the Supreme Court's decision in *Cavendish*, of a clause being found to be penal is provided by *Vivienne Westwood Ltd v Conduit Street Development Ltd.*[180] The challenged clause there, applying on any non-trivial breach by the tenant, allowed a landlord to terminate an agreement contained in a side letter reducing the rent payable, and would thus require the tenant to pay rent at a substantially higher rate.[181] The clause would take effect in addition to any other remedies available to the landlord for such a breach, and no matter how much time remained of the agreed term. Whilst noting the landlord's legitimate interest in preserving its cash flow and the value of its reversion, Timothy Fancourt QC (sitting as a Deputy Judge of the High Court) concluded that: "[t]he extra financial detriment to [the tenant] does seem exorbitant and unconscionable in comparison with any legitimate interest in full performance that will not otherwise be compensated by interest, costs and damages".[182]

[180] *Vivienne Westwood Ltd v Conduit Street Development Ltd* [2017] EWHC 350 (Ch). See too *Blue-Sky Solutions Ltd v Be Caring Ltd* [2021] EWHC 2619 (QBD), [2022] 2 All ER (Comm) 254 [125] where it was found that particular terms, had they been incorporated into the contract, would have been void as penalties. In *Ahuja Investments Ltd v Victorygame Ltd* [2021] EWHC 2382: it was found that A had a legitimate commercial interest in applying a higher rate of interest to a borrower in default, but, given a 400% increase in the primary interest rate, and the monthly compounding of the new rate, where A had some security for the loan, B was held to have discharged the burden of showing the rate was so "obviously extravagant, exorbitant and oppressive as to constitute a penalty": ibid [144]. Contrast *Permavent Ltd v Makin* [2021] EWHC 467 (Ch) at [77]-[92] where it was found that a payment term, whilst "extremely harsh" was not exorbitant, unconscionable or out of all proportion when taking into account A's interest in maintaining the integrity of intellectual property rights, and the harm A might suffer by B's breaching the contract by challenging those rights.

[181] For the final five years of the lease, the rent due under the side letter was £125,000 per year, whereas under the higher rate it would be £232,500 per year.

[182] *Vivienne Westwood Ltd v Conduit Street Development Ltd* [2017] EWHC 350 (Ch) at [65]. Note the clause on its face also increased the rent due with retrospective effect, but it was held that it was penal even if it had only prospective effect, and also that if it had been penal only because of its retrospective effect, the words in the side letter giving it such effect could validly have been severed: at [71].

(e) Construction and timing.

Replace paragraph with:

13-020 Any label attached by the parties is not conclusive: the court must determine whether the payment stipulated is in truth a penalty.[184] As the matter is judged at the time of the making of the contract,[185] the question of whether the clause imposes a detriment out of all proportion to A's legitimate interest in performance is not answered simply by considering the actual breach or breaches which have occurred.[186] If a challenged clause is penal only because of its inclusion of particular words, it may be possible for the validity of the clause to be upheld if those words are severable.[187]

[184] See, e.g *Triple Point Technology Inc v PTT Public Co Ltd* [2019] EWCA Civ 230 at [71] (the Court of Appeal decision is discussed by E Peel (2019) 135 L.Q.R. 530) and was reversed in part by the Supreme Court ([2021] UKSC 29 although there was no appeal on the penalty point); *Dunlop Pneumatic Tyre Co v New Garage and Motor Co* [1915] A.C. 79 HL at 86, per Lord Dunedin: "Though the parties to a contract who use the words 'penalty' or 'liquidated damages' may prima facie be supposed to mean what they say, yet the expression used is not conclusive. The Court must find out whether the payment stipulated is in truth a penalty or liquidated damages". See e.g. *Alder v Moore* [1961] 2 Q.B. 57 CA; and *Robert Stewart & Sons Ltd v Carapanayoti & Co Ltd* [1962] 1 W.L.R. 34: the use of the term "penalty" to describe a clause was not decisive as the clause in each case was held in fact to be a genuine pre-estimate of damage and so enforceable in full.

[185] As noted by Eder J in *Unaoil Ltd v Leighton Offshore Pte Ltd* [2014] EWHC 2965 (Comm) at [71] "where, as here, the contract is amended in a relevant respect, the relevant date, in my judgment, is the date of such amended contract".

[186] *Jobson v Johnson* [1989] 1 W.L.R. 1026, per Dillon LJ at 1033.

[187] The conditions on which part of a contract rendering it unlawful can be severed are set out in *Marshall v NM Financial Management Ltd* [1995] 1 W.L.R. 1461 at 1466. For an application of those conditions in the penalties context, see *Vivienne Westwood Ltd v Conduit Street Development Ltd* [2017] EWHC 350 (Ch): the analysis there was approved in *Blue-Sky Solutions Ltd v Be Caring Ltd* [2021] EWHC 2619 (QBD), [2022] 2 All ER (Comm) 254 at [117]–[118]. Note that in *Cine Bes Filmcilik Ve YapimClick v United International Pictures* [2003] EWCA Civ 1669 the court refused to sever parts of a clause which provided for a number of different events on breach where the penalty provision was "one component of the whole of the clause the validity of which depended on whether it provided for a genuine pre-estimate of the loss": Thomas LJ at 51.

Change title of paragraph: **13-021**

(f)   Application of the test to breach of primary payment obligations.

Replace second paragraph with:

   A good example is provided by *Lordsvale Finance Plc v Bank of Zambia*.[193] The clause in that case provided for an increase in interest in the event of default on payment under a facility agreement. Such a clause might seem to fall foul of Lord Dunedin's guidance, as B's primary obligation was simply to pay a sum of money but, the clause was not held to be a penalty, as its dominant purpose was to acknowledge that "the borrower in default is not the same credit risk as the prospective borrower with whom the loan agreement was first negotiated".[194] As a result, there was "a good commercial reason for deducing that deterrence of breach is not the dominant contractual purpose of the term".[195]

[193] *Lordsvale Finance Plc v Bank of Zambia* [1996] Q.B. 752: see para.13-016. See too *Banco San Juan Internacional Inc v Petroleos de Venezuela SA* [2021] 2 All ER (Comm) 590, [2020] EWHC 2937 (Comm). See too *Paciocco v Australia and New Zealand Banking Group Ltd* [2016] HCA 28; 258 C.L.R. 525 where a term imposing a duty to pay a set fee of $35 if a customer failed to make monthly credit card repayments on time was held not to be penal.

[194] *Lordsvale Finance Plc v Bank of Zambia* [1996] Q.B. 752 at 763.

[195] *Lordsvale Finance Plc v Bank of Zambia* [1996] Q.B. 752 at 763. Note that in *Cukurova Finance International Ltd v Alfa Telecom Turkey Ltd* [2013] UKPC 20, the Privy Council, when giving B relief against forfeiture, advised that that relief was not conditioned on B's paying interest at the contractually due default rate. This was not based on a finding that the (purely prospective) default interest rate clause was penal, but rather on A's having rejected a sum tendered by B, post-default, of the outstanding principal and interest: see para.13-037. For criticism of the Privy Council's approach as thereby undermining the test for a penalty, see P. Turner (2014) 130 L.Q.R. 188, 192.

4. Remedial Issues

(a) The effect of finding that a term is penal.

Replace first paragraph with:

13-023   The effect of a term's being found to be a penalty is that the clause is void as being contrary to public policy.[211] This follows from the Supreme Court's characterisation, in *Cavendish*, of a penal term as a "species of agreement which the common law considers to be by its nature contrary to the policy of the law."[212] One practical consequence of this view is that a penal clause cannot be enforced pro tanto, that is only up to the level at which it would become out of all proportion to A's legitimate interest in performance. If the clause is penal, A will as a result be entitled only to the remedies, if any,[213] that would have arisen had the clause not been part of the contract.[214]

[211]   The court has the power to sever the penal clause and enforce the remainder of the contract. See *The Angelic Star* [1988] 1 Lloyd's Rep. 122 at 126 per Ralph Gibson LJ: "The rule is, in my judgment, not designed to strike down any more of a lawful contract than is necessary to give effect to the Court's purpose of applying public policy; and, moreover, the rule should be applied so as to interfere as little as possible with the proper enforcement of a lawful contract according to its terms".

[212]   *Talal El Makdessi v Cavendish Square Holding BV* [2015] UKSC 67; [2016] A.C. 1172 at [9] (Lord Neuberger and Lord Sumption).

[213]   See, e.g. *Cavendish* [2015] UKSC 67; [2016] A.C. 1172 at [62]: the loss recoverable by A in a breach of contract claim would be zero, as the loss consisted in a reduction in the value of A's shareholding and was thus reflective of loss to the company itself.

[214]   See e.g. *de Havilland Aircraft of Canada Ltd v Spicejet Ltd* [2021] EWHC 362 (Comm) at [35] (appeal on an unrelated issue: [2021] EWCA Civ 1834): if a clause is penal, the court will not "do a 'reverse Shylock' and deprive the innocent victim of recovery of his loss simply because he claimed what the court has concluded was an excessive pre-estimate of his loss." Note that in *Workers Trust Bank Ltd v Dojap Ltd* [1993] A.C. 573 PC, although the Privy Council stated that a clause allowing for the retention of a deposit of 10 per cent of the purchase price of land would have been enforceable as a reasonable earnest payment, the effect of its finding a clause allowing for the retention of a 25 per cent deposit to be penal was that A had to return all of that deposit, retaining only any sums equating to the loss recoverable in a breach of contract action against B. So, whilst A could have retained a sum equal to 10 per cent of the purchase price had that been agreed, the court did not re-write the terms of the contract so as to allow such a sum to be retained by A.

After "As noted at", replace "para.13-XXX," with:
    para.13-004,

(b)   Effect of an agreed remedy clause on remedies otherwise available.

Replace paragraph with:

13-024   A question also arises if the recoverable loss suffered by A as a result of B's breach exceeds the sum stipulated in an agreed remedy clause. If the contract makes clear that the agreed remedy is intended to be the only remedy available to A on a breach by B then, unless that term is independently challenged,[224] it would seem that A is bound by it.[225] Otherwise, it seems that it should be possible for A to choose not to invoke the agreed remedy clause and instead bring a standard claim for damages for B's breach of contract.[226] On this view, there is no need for A to argue, in order to avoid the limit in the clause, that the clause is penal.[227] It is rather the case that A can simply choose not to invoke the clause.

[224]   It is suggested by *Chitty on Contracts*, 33rd edn (2018) para.26-190 that such a term is probably not caught by the Unfair Contract Terms Act 1977 as it is not a pure exclusion or restriction of liability, given that the same sum is payable whether A's loss is greater or smaller, but that, if in a consumer contract

and not individually negotiated, it would be subject to the Unfair Terms in Consumer Contract Regulations 1999 and the Consumer Rights Act 2015.

[225] See *Eco World - Ballymore Embassy Gardens Co Ltd v Dobler UK Ltd* [2021] EWHC 2207 (TCC) at [111]: "even where a liquidated damages clause is found to be wholly unenforceable as a penalty, it may on a true construction be found to operate as a limitation of liability provision." The effect of the clause will depend on standard principles of contractual interpretation: O'Farrell J there found at [116] that "the objective understanding of the parties in the commercial context of the Contract" was that the clause not only provided an automatic liability for B, but also operated to limit B's liability in a specific way. See too e.g. *Cellulose Acetate Silk Co Ltd v Widnes Foundry (1925) Ltd* [1933] A.C. 20; and *Suisse Altantique Societe d'Armement Maritime SA v NV Rotterdamsche Kolen Centrale* [1967] 1 A.C. 361. As found in *Buckingham Group Contracting Ltd v Peel L&P Investments and Property Ltd* [2022] EWHC 1842 (TCC) [95]–[100], a term intended only to operate in the context of liquidated damages would not then apply to determine general damages.

[226] See *Wall v Rederiaktiebolaget Luggude* [1915] 3 K.B. 66; *Watts, Watts & Co Ltd v Mitsui & Co Ltd* [1917] A.C. 227 at 245, 246; *Cellulose Acetate Silk Co Ltd v Widnes Foundry (1925) Ltd* [1933] A.C. 20 at 26. For academic comment: see e.g. J. Barton (1976) 92 L.Q.R. 20; A. Hudson (1985) 101 L.Q.R. 480; E. Peel, *Treitel's Law of Contract*, 14th edn (Sweet & Maxwell, 2015), para.20-141; J. Carter et al "Contractual Penalties: Resurrecting the Equitable Jurisdiction" (2013) 30 *Journal of Contract Law* 99 at 116–117; N. Tiverios, *Contractual Penalties in Australia and the United Kingdom: History, Theory and Practice* (Federation Press, 2019) pp.195–200.

[227] A term can be penal even if the recoverable loss caused to A by B's particular breach exceeds the sum stipulated in the clause, as the sum may still be "extravagant" in the relevant sense, when judged at the time of the entry into the contract.

3. RELIEF AGAINST FORFEITURE

2. Scope of the Jurisdiction

(b) Protecting a proprietary or possessory right.

Replace first paragraph with:

The jurisdiction is not available in all cases where A's right operates as security: **13-027** it must also be the case that the effect of the forfeiture clause is to deny B a proprietary or possessory right. The jurisdiction is historically associated with protecting mortgagors and leaseholders from the loss of a property right in land. In the past, judges expressed reluctance to extend the jurisdiction beyond those core cases.[244] More recently, however, the jurisdiction has been applied beyond the context of land, and has also been said to apply to possessory rights. It has also been suggested that the jurisdiction should extend still further, although that suggestion is yet to be taken up in English law. This second limit on the scope of the jurisdiction, which confines it to the protection of proprietary or possessory rights (in land or other property) only, was confirmed by the Supreme Court in *Vauxhall Motors Ltd v Manchester Ship Canal Co Ltd.*[245]

[244] See, e.g. *Sport International Bussum BV v Inter-Footwear Ltd* [1984] 1 W.L.R. 776 HL at 788 and 794.

[245] *Vauxhall Motors Ltd v Manchester Ship Canal Co Ltd* [2019] UKSC 46 at [49]–[51]. Lady Arden, in her concurring judgment, was however reluctant to impose such a limit based on the type of right held by the party seeking relief: see [69] and [83]–[87]. For discussion see e.g. M. Cleaver and P. Turner [2020] LMCLQ 191; A. Berriman, (2021) 15 Journal of Equity 306 and F. Lizia (2021) 95 A.L.J. 641.

Replace first paragraph with:

It is clear that the doctrine is not confined to protecting B against the loss of a **13-028** right in real property but can extend to other forms of property, such as intellectual property.[251] In England, however, the jurisdiction has consistently been said to apply only so as to protect B against the forfeiture of proprietary or possessory rights, as opposed to merely contractual rights. This limit was confirmed by the Supreme Court in *Vauxhall Motors Ltd v Manchester Ship Canal Co Ltd*.[252] In 1962, B had been granted by A a licence "in perpetuity", in consideration of an annual payment of £50, to discharge surface water and trade effluent into the canal by means of a complex spillway built and maintained by B on A's land. The contract allowed A to terminate the licence if the annual payment remained in arrears after a warning notice was given. A sought to terminate under that provision in 2014, when the current value of B's right was estimated to be between £300,000 to £440,000 per year. B made an immediate offer to pay the outstanding sum but it was not accepted. It was accepted that B's right was a licence and thus a personal right against A rather than a proprietary right, such as a lease or an easement.[253] The first instance judge was prepared to order relief against forfeiture even if the right was also not strictly a possessory right. The Supreme Court upheld the Court of Appeal's rejection of that suggestion and its confirmation of the requirement that B's right be proprietary or possessory.[254] It was held on the facts that B had established such a possessory right, given the extent of the control it was given over the spillway, as well as over the airspace enclosed by the infrastructure.[255]

[251] See, e.g. *Vauxhall Motors Ltd v Manchester Ship Canal Co Ltd* [2018] EWCA Civ 1100; [2019] Ch. 331 at [45] (Lewison LJ: upheld [2019] UKSC 46), commenting on the effect of *BICC Plc v Burndy Corp* [1985] Ch. 232 CA, where relief was granted in relation to patent rights.

[252] *Vauxhall Motors Ltd v Manchester Ship Canal Co Ltd* [2019] UKSC 46 at [49]–[51], affirming [2019] Ch. 331 CA. In the Court of Appeal Lewison LJ noted at [52]–[53] that, to the extent that Australian law might suggest that the equitable jurisdiction can apply to contractual licences (see Edelman J in *Mineralogy Pty Ltd v Sino Iron Pty Ltd (No.6)* [2015] FCA 825 at [981]; although for a contrasting later view, see now Brereton JA in *Kay v Playup Australia Pty Ltd* [2020] NSWCA 33), this would merely reveal a difference between Australian and English law. For discussion of the Court of Appeal decision see P. Turner [2019] C.L.J. 276–279. Note For discussion of the Supreme Court decision and comparison with the Australian position, see N. Tiverios [2020] C.L.J. 17. For further Australian discussion of the point see, e.g. *Auburn Shopping Village Pty Ltd v Nelmeer Hoteliers Pty Ltd* [2018] NSWCA 114; 19 BPR 38569 at [25] (Bathurst CJ); *Ayers Rock SkyShip Pty Ltd v Voyages Indigenous Tourism Australia Pty Ltd* [2019] NSWSC 828 at [106]–[107] (Drake J).

[253] The structure once built by B became part and parcel of A's land, and the rights granted to B were perpetual and so could not constitute a lease.

[254] *Vauxhall Motors Ltd v Manchester Ship Canal Co Ltd* [2018] EWCA Civ 1100; [2019] Ch. 331 at [55]; [2019] UKSC 46 at [49]–[51]; although note Lady Arden, in her concurring judgment, was in contrast reluctant to impose a limit based on the type of right held by the party seeking relief: [69], [83]–[87].

[255] *Vauxhall Motors Ltd v Manchester Ship Canal Co Ltd* [2018] EWCA Civ 1100; [2019] Ch. 331 at [65]–[71]; [2019] UKSC 46 at [56]–[58].

Replace second paragraph with:

The analysis in *Vauxhall Motors* built on that in *Scandinavian Trading Tanker Co AB v Flota Petrolera Ecuatoriana ("The Scaptrade")*.[256] The House of Lords "robustly"[257] rejected the submission that the withdrawal of a vessel from hire as a result of a time charterer's non-payment of hire was subject to the jurisdiction. In such a case, the time charterer has only a contractual right, and no proprietary right or right to possession. On the same basis, relief against forfeiture is not available in respect of a provision for termination of an exclusive licence granted to the buyer of goods to use the claimant's trade names and trade marks.[258] Further, the transfer of a "bare" possessory right for only a portion of the economic life of the chattel without the option to acquire ownership has also been held to be insufficient to attract the jurisdiction to grant relief.[259]

[256] *Scandinavian Trading Tanker Co AB v Flota Petrolera Ecuatoriana ("The Scaptrade")* [1983] 2 A.C. 694 HL.

[257] The adverb used by Lord Neuberger in *Cukurova Finance International Ltd v Alfa Telecom Turkey Ltd* [2013] UKPC 2 at 89.

[258] *Sport International Bussum BV v Inter-Footwear Ltd* [1984] 1 W.L.R. 776 HL. See too *The Football Association Premier League Ltd v PPLive Sports International Ltd* [2022] EWHC 38 (Comm) [123]–[126] where the jurisdiction was not available on the termination of a licence to broadcast football matches. Contrast *BICC Plc v Burndy Corp* [1985] Ch. 232, where relief was available against forfeiture of patent rights.

[259] *Civil Aviation Trading 71 Ltd v Paramount Airways Private Ltd* [2010] EWHC 185 (Comm) at [57]; explaining *Transag Haulage v Leyland DAF Finance* [1994] 2 B.C.L.C. 88 (hire purchase agreement); *On Demand Information Plc v Michael Gerson (Finance) Ltd* [2002] UKHL 13; [2003] 1 A.C. 368 (equipment lease); and *The Jotunheim* [2005] Lloyd's Rep. 181. Note that in *The Scaptrade* [1983] 2 A.C. 694 HL at 704, Lord Diplock stated that: "the reasoning in my speech has been directed exclusively to time charters that are not by demise. Identical considerations would not be applicable to bareboat charters". In *OCM Maritime Nile LLC v Courage Shipping Co* [2022] EWCA Civ 1091, there was no challenge to the holding at first instance ([2022] EWHC 452 (Comm)) that the jurisdiction can in principle apply to a demise charter with an option to purchase (and indeed a conditional duty to purchase at the end of the charter). Relief was not however granted on the facts.

Replace n.261 with:

[261] *Scandinavian Trading Tanker Co AB v Flota Petrolera Ecuatoriana ("The Scaptrade")* [1983] 2 A.C. 699 HL. The same analysis applies to, e.g. *Sport International Bussum BV v Inter-Footwear Ltd* [1984] 1 W.L.R. 776 HL and *The Football Association Premier League Ltd v PPLive Sports International Ltd* [2022] EWHC 38 (Comm).

(c)   Ousting of the jurisdiction by statute.

Replace paragraph with:

The possibility of relief against forfeiture of a lease formed the principal context **13-030** in which courts of equity developed the jurisdiction. Relief could be granted against forfeiture for non-payment of rent, even after a peaceable re-entry by the landlord without the assistance of the court,[267] for such a proviso was regarded simply as a security for rent,[268] though this jurisdiction would probably not be exercised while the forfeiture was merely threatened and the lessor had neither taken possession nor commenced proceedings for forfeiture.[269] The decision of the House of Lords in *Shiloh Spinners*[270] that there was an equitable jurisdiction to grant relief for breach of covenants other than covenants to pay rent or some other sum of money noted at the same time that, where Parliament had conferred statutory powers of relief,[271] that equitable jurisdiction may have been impliedly excluded. In that vein, in *Billson v Residential Apartments Ltd*,[272] a majority of the Court of Appeal concluded that "the inherent equitable jurisdiction as between landlord and tenant to relieve from forfeiture for wilful breach of covenant (other than a covenant for the payment of rent) has been extinguished by reason of Parliament having legislated comprehensively in that field".[273] The general powers of a lessor to forfeit, including for non-payment of rent, are heavily regulated by statute.[274] The often complex[275] details of these statutory provisions lie outside the scope of this book.[276]

[267] *Howard v Fanshawe* [1895] 2 Ch. 581.

[268] See *Howard v Fanshawe* [1895] 2 Ch. 581 at 588; and *Union Eagle v Golden Achievement Ltd* [1997] A.C. 514 at 519. But cf. *Re Lomax Leisure Ltd* [2000] Ch. 502 (where it was held that the lease itself

was not a form of security and that the relevant provisions of s.10 of the Insolvency Act 1986 did not apply).

269 *Barton Thompson & Co Ltd v Stapling Machines Co* [1966] Ch. 499.

270 *Shiloh Spinners Ltd v Harding* [1973] A.C. 691.

271 LPA 1925 s.146(2), successor to Conveyancing Act 1881 s.14(2) which, as noted by Earl Loreburn LC in *Hyman v Rose* [1912] A.C. 623 HL at 631, provides a "very wide" discretion. The same is true under s.146(2): see, e.g. *Southern Depot Co Ltd v British Railways Board* [1990] 2 E.G.L.R. 39 at 44, per Morritt J.

272 See the decision of the majority of the Court of Appeal in *Billson v Residential Apartments* [1992] 1 A.C. 494: the point was not argued on appeal to the House of Lords.

273 *Billson v Residential Apartments* [1991] 3 W.L.R. 264 CA, at 279 per Lord Browne-Wilkinson. This particular aspect of the case was not in issue when the House of Lords heard a further appeal: [1992] 1 A.C. 494.

274 See, e.g. LPA 1925 s.146; Commonhold and Leasehold Reform Act 2002 ss.167–170. Note too Coronavirus Act 2020 ss.81-83. For a very brief overview of the position, see *Keshwala v Bhalsod* [2021] 1 W.L.R. 4004, [2021] EWCA Civ 492 at [36]–[37]. Note in that case, which concerned forfeiture by way of peaceable re-entry (rather than by an application to court) for non-payment of rent, there was no statutory jurisdiction available to the court, and so it "retains, and exercises, its equitable jurisdiction inherited from the Court of Chancery" (Nugee LJ at [38]).

275 The executive summary to Law Com. No.174, *Landlord and Tenant: Privity of Contract and Estate* (2004) states that the law in this area "is complex, it lacks coherence, and it can lead to injustice". For reform proposals see, e.g. Law Com. No.303 (2006).

276 For a full treatment, see, e.g. S. Bridge et al (eds), *Megarry & Wade: The Law of Real Property*, 9th edn (Sweet & Maxwell, 2019), Ch.17, section 3. For a useful survey of the principles applied under s.146(2) of the LPA 1925, see *Freifeld v West Kensington Court Ltd* [2015] EWCA Civ 806 at [36]–[52]. In *Magnic Ltd v Ul-Hassan* [2015] EWCA Civ 224, when considering the statutory discretion, Patten LJ at [50] drew on *Shiloh Spinners Ltd v Harding* [1973] A.C. 691 HL at 723 when noting that: "The risk of forfeiture is not intended to operate as an additional penalty for breach. It is an ultimate sanction designed to protect the landlord's reversion from continuing breaches of covenant which remain unremedied and to secure performance of the covenants".

3.   The Test for Relief

(a)   General position.

Replace n.279 with:

13-031   279 *Vauxhall Motors Ltd v Manchester Ship Canal Co Ltd* [2018] EWCA Civ 1100; [2019] Ch. 331 at [72]; upheld [2019] UKSC 46. As noted by Morgan J in *re Axminster Carpets Group Retirement Benefits Plan* [2021] EWHC 1652 (Ch) at [259] "there are many examples of relief from forfeiture being granted to a party who has been at fault but where an unrelieved forfeiture would be disproportionate to the fault."

Replace paragraph with:

13-033   In determining whether to grant relief, the court considers the conduct of the applicant for relief[294] (and in particular whether his default was wilful), how grave the breaches were,[295] what disparity there is between the value of the property forfeited and the damage caused by the breach,[296] and the consequences to A of denying forfeiture.[296a] Although this confers an apparently broad discretion, it has been emphasised that a court should exercise caution before preventing A from enforcing a term that is, ex hypothesi, contractually valid: as the jurisdiction ultimately depends on unconscionability, it should be seen as exceptional.[297] Further, "the need for certainty and the desirability of avoiding uncertainty are very relevant considerations".[298] Nonetheless, even in a commercial context, if strict insistence on A's power to forfeit would allow A to abuse a right intended as security for B's performance,[299] where B is in fact ready and willing to perform the substance of that right, and to compensate A for any delay in performance (or where B's failure to remedy the breach will make no practical impact on A's position)[300] then a court will intervene, even in the context of a commercial contract entered into by well-advised parties.[301]

[294] In *Vauxhall Motors Ltd v Manchester Ship Canal Co Ltd* [2018] EWCA Civ 1100; [2019] Ch. 331 (upheld [2019] UKSC 46), it was argued that B's delay in seeking relief was relevant, but that argument was rejected, with Lewison LJ stating at [74] that a defence of laches could arise, but only if it were shown that the delay caused prejudice to A. In *Keshwala v Bhalsod* [2021] 1 W.L.R. 4004, [2021] EWCA Civ 492, Nugee LJ stated at [66] that, whilst there is no statutory time limit applying to a tenant's application for relief from forfeiture of a lease for non-payment of rent in a case of peaceable re-entry, "The longer the tenant leaves it – and a fortiori if he does not have a good explanation for the delay, and fails to keep the landlord informed of his intention – the more likely it is that he will find that the Court will conclude that he has failed to act with reasonable promptitude, and the more likely it will be that intervening events will make it inequitable to grant relief. If the landlord, acting reasonably and not precipitately, has altered his position, it may be unjust to grant relief; as also it may be if the rights of third parties have intervened."

[295] In *Man UK Properties Ltd v Falcon Investments Ltd* [2015] EWHC 1324 (Ch), Warren J at [37] considered that a term allowing A, should B fail to pay its half share of the purchase price of property by 11 months after completion of the purchase, to acquire all of B's shares in the special purpose vehicle set up for the joint purchase of property, was not a forfeiture provision but was rather "a rational and commercial way of dealing with what, in the context of the joint venture, is an important element of the contract between the parties". B's primary duty was to pay the half share within six months of completion, and, as noted at [38], the fact that the clause operated only after a further five months was clearly relevant.

[296] See *Shiloh Spinners Ltd v Harding* [1973] A.C. 691 at 723 and at 724; cited with approval in *Cukurova Finance International Ltd v Alfa Telecom Turkey Ltd* [2013] UKPC 2 at 116. For an example of the factors to be considered in the leasehold context, see e.g. *Patel v K&J Restaurants* [2010] EWCA Civ 1211 at [69]–[104].

[296a] See *OCM Maritime Nile LLC v Courage Shipping Co* [2022] EWCA Civ 1091 at [44]–[52], where the Court of Appeal approved the approach at first instance, which, in denying relief, considered the impact on A (breach of US sanctions rules) if A were required to continue dealing with a party who had been designated as a terrorist under US rules.

[297] See, e.g. *Else (1982) Ltd v Parkland Holding* [1994] 1 B.C.L.C. 130 CA at 145, per Hoffmann LJ; approving the view adopted by the High Court of Australia in *Legione v Hateley* (1983) 152 C.L.R. 406 in the context of a contract for the sale of land, that "the jurisdiction was exceptional and that relief would be granted only in cases in which it was unconscionable of the vendor to rescind the contract".

[298] *Cukurova Finance International Ltd v Alfa Telecom Turkey Ltd* [2013] UKPC 2 at [125]. See too *Union Eagle Ltd v Golden Achievement Ltd* [1997] A.C. 514 PC at 519, per Lord Hoffmann: "in many forms of transaction it is of great importance that if something happens for which the contract has made express provision, the parties should know with certainty that the terms of the contract will be enforced".

[299] Note that, in ascertaining if the forfeiture clause has the purpose of security, a court will look to substance not to form and so, for example, a transfer of a right may be seen as a mortgage even if not expressly labelled as such by the parties: see e.g. *Union Eagle Ltd v Golden Achievement Ltd* [1997] A.C. 514 PC at 521, per Lord Hoffmann: "Equity has always regarded the question of whether a transaction is a mortgage as depending upon substance rather than form". See too *Lavin v Johnson* [2002] EWCA Civ 1138 at [80], per Robert Walker LJ.

[300] See, e.g. *Associated British Ports v CH Bailey Plc* [1990] 2 A.C. 703 HL, discussed at para.13-032.

[301] See, e.g. *Cukurova Finance International Ltd v Alfa Telecom Turkey Ltd* [2013] UKPC 2 at [116]–[126]; *Stern v MacArthur* (1988) 165 C.L.R. 489.

CHAPTER 14

INTRODUCTION

1. LEGAL AND EQUITABLE REMEDIES

After "contracts is a", replace "well known" with:
well-known

14-001

2. DISCRETION

Replace paragraph with:

It is sometimes said that the remedies treated in this part of the book are **14-002** discretionary. The extent of the freedom the court enjoys in deciding whether to grant these remedies, as compared with the freedom it enjoys in relation to other remedies, can be overstated. It consists principally in the need to make what are sometimes fine judgments in order to apply more or less settled principles to the factual circumstances of particular cases. In some cases the description of a remedy as being discretionary only means that its principles are still being worked out.[6] To illustrate, while the decision to rescind a contract is said to be discretionary, the principles according to which that discretion must be exercised have been settled over the years through the articulation of the bars. If rescission has become barred, the court will exercise its discretion to refuse rescission. But it is well established that if restitutio in integrum is possible, and if rescission is not otherwise barred, the claimant is entitled to have the contract rescinded as of right.[7] The same is true of the jurisdiction to compel the performance of a contract, which was said over a century ago to be discretionary but "confined within well-known rules".[8] Of the discretion the court enjoys in deciding whether to grant an injunction, it has been said that "the discretion is not one to be exercised according to the fancy of whoever is to exercise the jurisdiction of equity".[9] And again in relation to the jurisdiction to order that an account of profits be taken, "there is no general, wide-ranging discretion, or justification for the introduction of limits on the account that are not supported by established principles. The fashioning of the remedy is done to fit the nature of the case; but it is done by reference to established equitable principles and to any equitable defences that may be pleaded and proven in a particular case."[9a] Speaking of rectification, the Court of Appeal has emphasised that albeit the origins of the remedy lie in conscience and fair dealing, its principles should be as clear and predictable in their application as possible.[10]

[6] *Vercoe v Rutland Fund Management Limited* [2010] Bus. L.R. D141 at [340].

[7] *Lagunas Nitrate Co v Lagunas Syndicate* [1899] 2 Ch. 393 CA at 456; *Spence v Crawford* [1939] 3 All E.R. 271 HL(Sc) at 280.

[8] *Ryan v Mutual Tontine Westminster Chambers Association* [1893] 1 Ch. 116, at 126.

[9] *Doherty v Allman* (1878) 3 App.Cas. 709, at 728–29.

[9a] *Recovery Partners GP Limited v Rukhadze* [2022] EWHC 690 (Comm) at [261]-[271]. See also *Coomber v Coomber* [1911] 1 Ch. 723; *Warman International Ltd v Dwyer* (1995) 182 C.L.R. 544 at 559; and *Goyal v Florence Care Limited* [2020] EWHC 659 (Ch) at [34]-[44]. Cf. *Walsh v Shanahan* [2013] EWCA Civ 411 at [63], [66] and *Novoship (UK) Ltd v Nikitin* [2015] Q.B. 499 (CA) at [120].

[10] *Daventry District Council v Daventry & District Housing Ltd* [2012] 1 W.L.R. 1333 CA at [194].

3.   MINOR AND DEFUNCT REMEDIES

3.   Ne exeat regno

Replace second paragraph with:

14-006   Following many decades in which few applications were made and none succeeded, there was a revival of interest in the writ in the 1980s,[22] but it has since been said that the writ should not be extended and should only be granted if proportionate and necessary to secure the ends of justice.[23] The court has, however, developed a jurisdiction under s.37(1) of the Senior Courts Act 1981 to restrain defendants and important witnesses from leaving the jurisdiction where necessary to secure compliance with freezing injunctions[24] and search orders,[25] to compel attendance at a means hearing,[25a] and to compel the attendance of the director of a company in liquidation for examination before the Companies Court.[26] Injunctions restraining defendants from leaving the jurisdiction and requiring that their passports be held by the tipstaff or a solicitor are also sometimes granted in family cases,[27] in which context the writ *ne exeat regno* has been said to be *"an anachronism given the availability of the modern form of order"*.[28]

[22] See especially *Al Nahkel for Contracting and Trading Ltd v Lowe* [1986] Q.B. 235.

[23] *Ali v Naseem* (unreported Ch.D., 22 July 2003).

[24] *Bayer A.G. v Winter* [1986] 1 W.L.R. 497 CA; *Lexi Holdings Plc v Luqman* [2008] EWHC 2908 (Ch); *Kuwait Airways Corp v Iraq Airways Co* [2010] EWCA Civ 741. For freezing injunctions see para.18-036 and those following; *JSC Mezhdunarodniy Promyshlenniy Bank v Pugachev* [2015] EWHC 1586 (Ch).

[25] For search orders see, paras 18-044 and those following.

[25a] *Lakatamia Shipping Co Ltd v Su* [2021] EWCA Civ 1187.

[26] *Re Oriental Credit Ltd* [1988] Ch. 204.

[27] The authorities are reviewed in *Re B (a child)* [2015] Fam. 209 CA.

[28] *Bhura v Bhura* [2013] 2 F.L.R. 44 at 51, and see *Young v Young* [2012] Fam. 198.

CHAPTER 15

RESCISSION

3. GROUNDS

1. Misrepresentation

Replace second paragraph with:

Rescission may therefore be available where (a) there was a relevant representa- **15-004**
tion, express or implied; (b) it was made by the other party or with their knowledge;
(c) the representation was false; (d) the rescinding party was aware of the
representation[9a]; and (e) the representation induced the rescinding party to transact.

[9a] *Leeds City Council v Barclays Bank plc* [2021] 2 W.L.R. 1180.

Replace third paragraph with:

The representee always carries the legal burden of proving inducement.[10] In the case of an innocent or negligent misrepresentation, they must prove that they would not have entered into the contract had the representation not been made.[11] In the case of a fraudulent misrepresentation it is enough for the representee to prove that they were materially influenced by it in the sense that it was actively present to their mind when they decided to transact, even if there were also other reasons to have done so.[12] Inducement usually occurs where the rescinding party believes the representation to be true and acts in reliance on it, but exceptionally a fraudulent representation may induce a party to transact even though they do not believe it to be true.[13]

[10] *BV Nederlandse Industrie Van Eiprodukten v Rembrandt Enterprises Inc* [2020] Q.B. 551 CA at [15], [25].

[11] *BV Nederlandse Industrie Van Eiprodukten v Rembrandt Enterprises Inc* [2020] Q.B. 551 CA at [15]; *Assicurazioni Generali SpA v Arab insurance Group* [2003] 1 All E.R. (Comm) 140; *Pan Atlantic Insurance Co Ltd v Pine Top Insurance Co Ltd* [1995] 1 A.C. 501.

[12] *BV Nederlandse Industrie Van Eiprodukten v Rembrandt Enterprises Inc* [2020] Q.B. 551 CA at [32].

[13] *Zurich Insurance Co Plc v Hayward* [2017] A.C. 142.

Replace fourth paragraph with:

A representation is material if it would be likely to induce a person to enter a contract.[14] In cases of fraud it is not necessary that the representation was material provided inducement can be positively proved,[15] although it is open to debate whether there are circumstances in which reliance on an immaterial innocent misrepresentation will support a claim to rescind.[16] But in all cases where the representation was material, provided the rescinding party was aware of it,[16a] there is an evidential presumption of inducement in the sense that inducement is a natural factual inference.[17] The presumption has been said to be "very difficult to rebut" and "particularly strong where the misrepresentation was fraudulent".[18]

[14] *Smith v Chadwick* (1882) 20 Ch. D. 27 CA at 44; on appeal (1884) 9 App. Cas. 187, at 196; *BV Nederlandse Industrie Van Eiprodukten v Rembrandt Enterprises Inc* [2020] Q.B. 551 CA at [32].

[15] *Smith v Kay* (1859) 7 H.L.C. 750; *Pan Atlantic Insurance Co Ltd v Pine Top Insurance Co Ltd* [1995] 1 A.C. 501 at 533.

[16] See the discussion in O'Sullivan, Elliott and Zakrzewski, *The Law of Rescission*, 2nd edn (2014) [4.65]ff. It is clear that reliance on an immaterial innocent misrepresentation will not support rescission of an insurance policy: *Pan Atlantic Insurance Co Ltd v Pine Top Insurance Co Ltd* [1995] 1 A.C. 187.

[16a] *Leeds City Council v Barclays Bank plc* [2021] 2 W.L.R. 1180.

[17] *Mathias v Yetts* (1882) 46 L.T. 497 CA at 502; *Smith v Land and House Property Corp* (1884) 28 Ch. D. 7 CA at 16; *Smith v Chadwick* (1884) 9 App. Cas. 187 at 196; *Barton v County NatWest Ltd* [1999] Lloyd's Rep. Bank 408 CA; *Dadourian v Simms* [2009] 1 Lloyd's Rep. 601 CA at [99]–[101]; *BV Nederlandse Industrie Van Eiprodukten v Rembrandt Enterprises Inc* [2020] Q.B. 551 CA at [32].

[18] *Zurich Insurance Co Plc v Hayward* [2017] A.C. 142 at [34], [37].

2. Non-Disclosure

Replace second paragraph with:

15-005 Exceptionally, non-disclosure is a ground for rescission in relation to contracts of insurance of all types, and also in relation to surety contracts, partnership agreements and family arrangements.[24] Contracts of insurance are said to be contracts uberrimae fide and rescission will lie if either party fails to disclose facts material to the decision to place or accept the risk or the insurer's assessment of the premium.[25] Thus, if a proposing assured fails to disclose that there are rumours circulating about its financial probity, that will entitle the other party to rescind even where it becomes known that those rumours are unfounded.[26] The rescission of insurance policies is something of a special case and, before Judicature, the common law courts and Chancery exercised a coordinate jurisdiction.[27] The court has no discretionary equitable jurisdiction to control the exercise of a right to rescind insurance policies.[28] As to surety contracts, there is no general duty to disclose material facts to the intending surety but the creditor does owe a limited duty to disclose unusual features of the contract between the creditor and the debtor or between the creditor and other creditors of the debtor.[29] As to partnership agreements, a negotiating party owes a duty to disclose all material facts of which he has knowledge and of which the other negotiating parties may not be aware.[30] As to family arrangement cases, it appears that a duty of disclosure applies to settlement agreements between members of the same family intended to be generally and reasonably for the benefit of the family. Such cases are now unusual in England and Wales, but the jurisdiction has been reinvigorated in Asia.[31]

[24] In fiduciary cases governed by the fair dealing rule, non-disclosure is not the ground for rescission, although full disclosure may save the transaction.

[25] As to the duty of proposing assureds, see Marine Insurance Act 1906 s.18(2), stating a test which has been held to apply to all forms of insurance: *Locker and Woolfe Ltd v Western Australian Insurance Co Ltd* [1936] 1 K.B. 408 CA at 415. Exceptions to the disclosure obligation of a proposing assured are enumerated in s.18(3) of the Marine Insurance Act 1906. As to the duty of proposing insurers, see *Banque Keyser Ullmann SA v Skandia (UK) Insurance Co Ltd* [1991] 2 A.C. 249 at 268.

[26] *Brotherton v Asegurada Colseguros SA (No.2)* [2003] 2 All E.R. (Comm) 298 CA.

[27] *Hoare v Bembridge* (1872) 8 Ch. App. 22.

[28] *Brotherton Asegurada Colseguros SA (No.2)* [2003] 2 All E.R. (Comm) 298 CA; *Drake Insurance Plc v Provident Insurance Plc* [2004] Q.B. 601 CA.

[29] *Hamilton v Watson* (1845) 12 Cl. & F. 109 (HL(Sc)) at 119; *Royal Bank of Scotland Plc v Etridge (No.2)* [2002] 2 A.C. 773 at 812, 848; *North Shore Ventures Ltd v Anstead Holdings Inc* [2012] Ch. 31 CA at [14].

[30] *Conlon v Simms* [2008] 1 W.L.R. 484 CA at [127].

[31] *Kuek Siang Wei v Kuek Siew Chew* [2015] 5 S.L.R. 357 CA and *Yang Foo-Oi v Wai Wai Chen* (High Court of the HKSAR, 29 November 2016). In England and Wales, see *Wales v Wadham* [1977] 1 W.L.R. 199; *Crowden v Aldridge* [1993] 1 W.L.R. 433 at 443; and *Bank of Credit and Commerce International SA v Ali* [1999] 1 R.C. 1068 at 1077–78.

4. Fiduciary Misdealing and Bribery

Replace second paragraph with:

Allied to this,[39a] contracts affected by bribery or secret commissions may be **15-007** rescinded,[40] and special presumptions assist claimants in such cases.[41] In some cases the suborned adviser or agent is a fiduciary but it is enough that they were under a duty to provide information, advice or recommendation on an impartial or disinterested basis.[41a] However, if a suborned agent purports to conclude a contract on behalf of their principal (as opposed to the principal contracting at the agent's instance) then they will do so without authority and it appears that the contract is of no effect unless the principal chooses to ratify it,[42] so that there is no need to rescind.

[39a] *Prince Eze v Conway* [2019] EWCA Civ 88 at [38], [43] and [63].

[40] *Panama and South Pacific Telegraph Co v India Rubber, Gutta Percha, and Telegraph Works Co* (1875) L.R. 10 Ch.App. 515; *Logicrose Ltd v Southend United Football Club* [1988] 1 W.L.R. 1256; and see *Hurstanger Ltd v Wilson* [2008] Bus. L.R. 216 CA, where bribery is distinguished from lesser breaches of fiduciary duty by reason of the secrecy it involves. The elements of bribery were authoritatively enumerated in *Industries and General Mortgage Co Ltd v Lewis* [1949] 2 All E.R. 573 at 575.

[41] For example an irrebuttable presumption that the agent was influenced by the bribe: *Hovenden & Sons v Millhof* (1900) 83 L.T. 41 CA at 43.

[41a] *Wood v Commercial First Business Ltd* [2021] 3 W.L.R. 395 CA.

[42] *Heinl v Jyske Bank (Gibraltar) Ltd* [1999] Lloyd's Rep. Bank 511 CA at 521, and see 533; see also O'Sullivan, Elliott and Zakrzewski, *The Law of Rescission*, 2nd edn (2014) [1.85]ff.

5. Undue Influence, Duress and Unconscionability

Replace paragraph with:

15-008   Rescission is available in equity in cases of undue influence and at common law in cases of duress. Undue influence may be shown to have been actually applied, or else the claimant may succeed by proving a relationship of influence, in which case a presumption of undue influence arises which it is for the defendant to rebut.[43] Duress depends on proof (a) of illegitimate pressure arising from a threat coupled with a demand; (b) that the effect of the pressure was to cause coercion in the sense of an absence of practical choice; and (c) that the pressure was a sufficient cause of the victim's entry into the transaction.[44] Pressure may be economic and may even consist in a threat to carry out a lawful act where that threat is not legitimate, demands motivated by commercial self-interest usually being justified.[44a] Unconscionable bargains may also be rescinded,[45] as may contracts concluded by a party suffering from impaired capacity provided only that the other party knew of the impairment.[46]

[43] See Ch.8 above.

[44] *DSND Subsea Ltd v Petroleum Geoservices ASA* [2000] B.L.R. 530 at 545; *Carillion Construction Ltd v Felix (UK) Ltd* [2001] B.L.R. 1. The identification of elements in these cases has been followed in numerous subsequent cases.

[44a] *Times Travel (UK) Ltd v Pakistan International Airlines Corporation* [2021] 3 W.L.R. 727 UKSC.

[45] See Ch.8 above. Trial judges have disagreed about whether the same is true of unconscionable gifts: compare *Langton v Langton* [1995] 2 F.L.R. 890 with *Evans v Lloyd* [2013] W.T.L.R. 1137.

[46] *Hart v O'Connor* [1985] A.C. 1000 PC; *Barclays Bank Plc v Schwartz, The Times,* 2 August 1995 CA.

4.   SELF-HELP RESCISSION AND JUDICIAL RESCISSION

2. Judicial Rescission

Replace second paragraph with:

15-012   Notwithstanding a number of decisions which indicate that rescission always occurs by the act of the innocent party,[55] the foundational authorities presuppose the parallel operation of different mechanisms at law and in equity,[56] and some recent authorities indicate that the judicial mechanism developed in Chancery continues to exist today.[57] Henderson LJ has said that the authorities on the question whether rescission in equity for fraud is a self-help remedy are in such a state of disarray that only the Supreme Court can reconcile them.[57a]

[55] *Reese River Silver Mining Co Ltd v Smith* (1869) L.R. 4 H.L. 64; *Abram Steamship Co Ltd v Westville Shipping Co Ltd* [1923] A.C. 773; *Horsler v Zorro* [1975] 1 Ch. 302 at 310; and more recently *Drake Insurance Plc v Provident Insurance Plc* [2003] Lloyd's Rep. I.R. 78 at [31]–[32]; *Brotherton Aseguradora Colseguros SA* [2003] 2 All E.R. (Comm) 298 CA at [27], [45]–[48]. See however O'Sullivan [2000] C.L.J. 509, arguing that self-help rescission should be abolished.

[56] *Erlanger v The New Sombrero Phosphate Co* (1878) 3 App. Cas. 1218 at 1278; *Spence v Crawford* [1939] 3 All E.R. 271 HL(Sc); *O'Sullivan v Management Agency and Music Ltd* [1985] Q.B. 428 CA at [45]; cf. *Halpern v Halpern* [2008] Q.B. 195 CA.

[57] *Goldsworthy v Bricknell* [1987] Ch. 378 CA at 409–10; *Johnson v EBS Pensioner Trustees Ltd* [2002] Lloyd's Rep. PN 309 CA at [32], [56]–[57], [78]–[79]; *Hurstanger Ltd v Wilson* [2008] Bus L.R. 216 CA at [48]–[51].

[57a] *HMRC v IGE USA Investments Ltd* [2021] 3 W.L.R. 313 CA at [91].

5. EXCLUSION OF RESCISSION

2. Impossibility of Restitutio In Integrum

Replace n.77 with:

[77] *Armstrong v Jackson* [1917] 2 K.B. 822 at 829; *Salt v Stratstone Specialist Ltd (t/a Stratstone Cadillac Newcastle)* [2016] R.L.R. 17 CA at [22].   **15-014**

Replace list with:

- benefits which the rescinding claimant is unable to return because of the defendant's wrongdoing[81];
- benefits the defendant was bound to confer in any event[82];
- assets that were always worthless[83]; and
- insurance premiums in certain cases[84]

[81] *Rees v De Bernardy* [1896] 2 Ch. 437, 446. Similarly, rescission will not be barred by the claimant's inability to restore the defendant to an advantageous position which they obtained through illegitimate means: *Borelli v Ting* [2010] UKPC 21 at 39.

[82] *Hulton v Hulton* [1917] 1 K.B. 813 CA.

[83] *Phosphate Sewage Co v Hartmont* (1875) 5 Ch. D. 394 CA at 454–55; *Halpern v Halpern* [2008] Q.B. 195 CA.

[84] Marine Insurance Act 1906 ss.84(1) and 84(3)(a) (marine insurance); Consumer Insurance (Disclosure and Representations) Act 2012 (consumer insurance); and Insurance Act 2015 (other non-consumer insurance).

4. Disproportionate Effect

Replace paragraph with:

Section 2(2) of the Misrepresentation Act 1967 confers on judges and arbitra-   **15-016**
tors a discretionary power, where rescission is claimed for non-fraudulent misrepresentation, to "declare the contract subsisting and award damages in lieu of rescission".[99] The power was intended to be used where the consequences for the defendant of rescission would be disproportionately hard compared with the consequences for the claimant of the contract remaining on foot, particularly where the misrepresentation relates to a fact of minor importance.[100] The power only exists where rescission would otherwise be available.[101] In effect s.2(2) creates a discretionary bar to rescission in those circumstances, coupled with a power and duty to award damages where the bar is applied. Rescission remains, however, the normal remedy and it should be awarded where possible.[102]

[99] As to the measure of damages, see para.20-060 below.

[100] Law Reform Commission, "Innocent Misrepresentation" (Cmnd. 1782, 1962) paras [11] and [12].

[101] *Salt v Stratstone Specialist Ltd (t/a Stratstone Cadillac Newcastle)* [2016] R.L.R. 17 CA at [17].

[102] *Salt v Stratstone Specialist Ltd (t/a Stratstone Cadillac Newcastle)* [2016] R.L.R. 17 CA at [24].

6. EFFECT OF RESCISSION

3. Consequential Claims and Adjustments

Replace n.120 with:

15-021 [120] *Erlanger v The New Sombrero Phosphate Co* (1878) 3 App. Cas. 1218 at 1278; the party claiming compensation or another adjustment carries the burden of proof: *Salt v Stratstone Specialist Ltd (t/a Stratstone Cadillac Newcastle)* [2016] R.L.R. 17 CA at [30].

After "is otherwise barred.", add new n.128:

[128] Affirmation may impact on causation and the measurement of loss in important ways, as to which see *Motortrak Limited v FCA Australia Pty Ltd* [2018] EWHC 1464 (Comm).

CHAPTER 16

RECTIFICATION

1. NATURE OF RECTIFICATION

1. The Remedy of Rectification

(a) The Role of Rectification.

Replace paragraph with:

Where the terms of a written instrument do not accord with the true agreement **16-001** between the parties,[1] equity has the power to reform, or rectify, that instrument so as to make it accord with the true agreement.[2] What is rectified is not a mistake in the transaction itself, but a mistake in the way in which that transaction has been expressed in writing.[3]

> "Courts of Equity do not rectify contracts; they may and do rectify instruments purporting to have been made in pursuance of the terms of contracts."[4]

[1] Rectification of unilateral transactions is also available; see further para.16-021.

[2] See *M'Cormack v M'Cormack* (1877) 1 L.R.Ir. 119; *Frederick E Rose (London) Ltd v William H. Pim Jnr & Co Ltd* [1953] 2 Q.B. 450. For a more detailed study of this area, see D. Hodge QC, *Rectification: The Modern Law and Practice Governing Claims for Rectification for Mistake* (London: Sweet & Maxwell, 2010).

[3] See *Racal Group Services v Ashmore* [1995] S.T.C. 1151 at 1154; *Allnutt v Wilding* [2007] EWCA Civ 412; [2007] W.T.L.R. 941. This paragraph has recently been cited with approval in e.g. *Saving Stream Security Holding Ltd (In Administration) v Wordley* [2020] EWHC 2849 (Ch) at [11]; *Univar*

UK Ltd v Smith [2020] EWHC 1596 (Ch) at [195] and *Musst Holdings Ltd v Astra Asset Management UK Ltd* [2020] EWHC 337 (Ch) at [33].

[4] *Mackenzie v Coulson* (1869) L.R. 8 Eq. 368 at 375, per James VC. See also *Frederick E Rose (London) Ltd v William H Pim Jnr & Co Ltd* [1953] 2 Q.B. 450 where rectification was refused since, "There was no doubt an erroneous assumption underlying the contract—an assumption for which it might have been set aside on the grounds of misrepresentation or mistake— but that is very different from an erroneous expression of the contract, such as to give rise to rectification".

Replace n.8 with:

[8] This was approved by the Supreme Court of Canada in *Canada (Attorney General) v Fairmont Hotels Inc* [2016] S.C.C. 56 at [13], and in *SPS Technologies Ltd v Moitt* [2020] EWHC 2421 (Ch) at [7].

(b) Discretion.

Replace paragraph with:

16-002   Rectification is a discretionary remedy, "which must be cautiously watched and jealously guarded".[11] But unlike remedies such as specific performance, which are based on the inadequacy of the remedy at law, rectification "gives relief from the inflexibility of the common law, and from the nature of the case involves a contravention of its rules".[12] Rectification may be ordered by consent, but remains at the court's discretion.[13] Rectification will not be decreed if the desired result can conveniently be achieved by other means: by reliance upon common law rights, or by agreement between the parties.

[11] *Whiteside v Whiteside* [1950] Ch. 65 at 71, per Evershed MR; *Racal Group Services v Ashmore* [1995] S.T.C. 1151 at 1154; *Pitt v Holt* [2013] UKSC 26; [2013] 2 A.C. 108. This was cited with approval in *SPS Technologies Ltd v Moitt* [2020] EWHC 2421 (Ch) at [7].

[12] *Thompson v Hickman* [1907] 1 Ch. 550 at 562, per Neville J.

[13] *Burford (Fareham) Ltd v Christian Vision* [2005] EWHC 2533 (Ch).

2.   Documents that will be Rectified

(a)   Contracts and Other Documents Inter Partes.

Replace paragraph with:

16-004   The jurisdiction to rectify is quite general, and may be exercised in respect of a wide range of contracts and documents inter partes.[18a] These include mercantile documents such as a policy of marine insurance,[19] a bill of exchange,[20] a transfer of shares,[21] and a bill of quantities[22]; conveyancing documents such as a convey- ance[23] and a lease[24]; and a consent order, which for this purpose stands on the same footing as an agreement inter partes,[25] even though the mistake on which it is founded is as to the effect of a particular instrument.[26] But the articles of a company will not be rectified[27]; for not only would rectification be inconsistent with the provi- sions of the Companies Acts, but also the articles are (inter alia) a contract between the company and its members,[28] and ex hypothesi the company cannot have had a different intention before incorporation.

[18a] This was approved in *Tyne and Wear Passenger Transport Executive (t/a Nexus) v National Union of Rail at* [2021] EWHC 1388 (Ch) [59], where the court permitted an employer to pursue its claim for rectification of a letter of agreement amending a collective agreement in respect of its employees' terms and conditions.

[19] *Spalding v Crocker* (1897) 2 Com. Cas. 189 at 193.

[20] *Druiff v Lord Parker* (1868) L.R. 5 Eq. 131.

[21] See *Re International Contract Co* (1872) 7 Ch. App. 485 (shares wrongly numbered in transfer).

[22] *Neill v Midland Railway* (1869) 17 W.R. 871.

[23] *Beale v Kyte* [1907] 1 Ch. 564; *Wilson v Wilson* [1969] 1 W.L.R. 1470; *Re Colebrook's Conveyances* [1972] 1 W.L.R. 1397. In *Ralph v Ralph* the Court of Appeal held that, in principle, Land Registry transfer form TR1 could be rectified, although the court left open the question of whether the principles applicable in the context of commercial contracts should apply, especially since there was no negotiation of the contract: [2021] EWCA Civ 1106 at [26]–[32]. Rectification of the Land Register itself does not concern the rectification of a document and raises different considerations: see Land Registration Act 2002 s.65 and Sch.4; see the discussion in *Cherry Tree Investments Ltd v Landmain Ltd* [2012] EWCA Civ 736; [2013] Ch. 305.

[24] *Thomas Bates and Son Ltd v Wyndham's (Lingerie) Ltd* [1981] 1 W.L.R. 505 (rent review clause).

[25] *Huddersfield Banking Co v Henry Lister & Son Ltd* [1895] 2 Ch. 273; and see *Mullins v Howell* (1879) 11 Ch. D. 763 (consent order rectified for unilateral mistake: but the order was made on an interlocutory application, where the rules are not so strict: see *Ainsworth v Wilding* [1896] 1 Ch. 673 at 675, 679).

[26] *Allcard v Walker* [1896] 2 Ch. 369 at 381.

[27] *Scott v Frank F Scott (London) Ltd* [1940] Ch. 794; *Willow International Investments Ltd v Smiths of Smithfield Ltd* [2003] EWHC 568 (Ch); [2003] B.C.C. 769.

[28] Companies Act 2006 s.33. See too *Attorney General of Belize v Belize Telecom Ltd* [2009] UKPC 10; [2009] 1 W.L.R. 1988.

(b) Voluntary Instruments.

Replace paragraph with:

Marriage settlements were early instances of voluntary instruments that could be **16-005** rectified[29]; the same principles now apply to rectification of other unilateral instruments, such as, for example, a trust deed,[30] voluntary dispositions by trustees,[31] disclosure letters,[32] and a notice of severance of a joint tenancy.[33]

[29] See, e.g. *Thin v Thin* (1650) 1 Rep. Ch. 162.

[30] *Lawie v Lawie* [2012] EWHC 2940 (Ch); [2013] W.T.L.R. 85.

[31] *Day v Day* [2013] EWCA Civ 280; [2014] Ch. 114; *Merchant Navy Officers Pension Fund Trustees v Watkins* [2013] EWHC 4741 (Ch). See too *SPS Technologies Ltd v Moitt* [2020] EWHC 2421 (Ch).

[32] *Persimmon Homes Ltd v Hillier* [2019] EWCA Civ 800.

[33] *Lee v Lee* [2018] EWHC 149 (Ch); *Thin v Thin* (1650) 1 Rep. Ch. 162.

(c) Wills.

Replace first paragraph with:

Formerly, short of fraud, there was no power to rectify a will[37]; the furthest the **16-006** court could go was to omit spurious words.[38] Now, however, by statute, if a court is satisfied that a will is so expressed that it fails to carry out the intentions of the testator in consequence of a clerical error[39] or failure to understand his instructions, the court may order that the will be rectified.[40] The action for rectification cannot, without the permission of the court, be commenced later than six months after the grant of probate.[41]

[37] *Harter v Harter* (1872–75) L.R. 3 P. & D. 11; *Collins v Elstone* [1893] P. 1.

[38] *In the Goods of Schott* [1901] P. 190; *Vaughan v Clerk* (1902) 87 L.T. 144.

[39] See *Wordingham v Royal Exchange Trust Co Ltd* [1992] Ch. 412; *Re Segelman (Deceased)* [1996] Ch. 171; *Bell v Georgiou* [2002] W.T.L.R. 1105; *Brown v Bimson* [2010] All E.R. (D) 325 (Jul). Rectification was refused in *Boswell v Lawson* [2011] EWCA Civ 452, because the Court of Appeal held that the will as drafted did in fact represent the testator's intentions. See now the detailed discussion in *Marley v Rawlings* [2014] UKSC 2; [2014] 2 W.L.R. 213, which has been applied in, e.g. *Burnard v Burnard* [2014] EWHC 340 (Ch); *Brooke v Purton* [2014] EWHC 547 (Ch); *Reading v Reading* [2015]

EWHC 946 (Ch); *Bracey v Curley* [2022] EWHC 359 (Ch); [2022] W.T.L.R. 419. The action for rectification cannot, without the permission of the court, be commenced later than six months after the grant of probate*Kelly v Brennan* [2020] EWHC 245 (Ch).

[40] Administration of Justice Act 1982 s.20(1), applying where the testator has died after 1982 (see ss.73(1), 76(11)).

[41] Administration of Justice Act 1982 s.20(2). For the principles to be applied by the court in extending time, see *Re Chittock (Deceased)* [2000] W.T.L.R. 643; *Kelly v Brennan* [2020] EWHC 245 (Ch).

2. SCOPE OF RECTIFICATION

(a) Interpretation.

Replace n.60 with:

16-008 [60] See *Investors Compensation Scheme Ltd v West Bromwich Building Society* [1998] 1 W.L.R. 896 HL at 912 (Lord Hoffmann's third principle). See too *MV Promotions Limited and Micheal Vaughan v Telegraph Media Group Limited and HMRC* [2020] EWHC 1537 (Ch) at [66].

Replace n.54 with:

[54] See *Investors Compensation Scheme Ltd v West Bromwich Building Society* [1998] 1 W.L.R. 896 HL at 912 (Lord Hoffmann's third principle). See too *MV Promotions Limited and Micheal Vaughan v Telegraph Media Group Limited and HMRC* [2020] EWHC 1537 (Ch) at [66].

3. MISTAKE

1. Common Mistake

(a) Prior Agreement.

Replace first paragraph with:

16-014 The prior agreement between the parties on which a claim for rectification is based need not amount to an enforceable contract; it suffices if there is a common intention in regard to the particular provisions of the agreement in question[90] continuing up to the date of the written instrument,[91] together with some outward expression of accord.[92] This requirement of an "outward expression of accord" was once thought to serve only an evidentiary function[93] but is now treated as a legal requirement.[94] However, no outward expression of accord is required proceedings for the rectification of a pension scheme,[94a] in cases where the instrument is not intended to set out an accord between two or more parties (i.e. if the underlying transaction is unilateral); nor where a unilateral transaction requires the consent of another.

[90] *Joscelyne v Nissen* [1970] 2 Q.B. 86; applying *Crane v Hegeman-Harris Co Inc* [1939] 1 All E.R. 662; [1971] 3 All E.R. 245n.; [1971] 1 W.L.R. 1390n. (affirmed [1939] 4 All E.R. 68); and not following dicta in *Lovell and Christmas Ltd v Wall* (1911) 104 L.T. 85; and *Frederick E Rose (London) Ltd v William H. Pim Jnr & Co Ltd* [1953] 2 Q.B. 450. See also *Monaghan CC v Vaughan* [1948] I.R. 306; *Slee v Warke* (1952) 86 C.L.R. 271 at 280, 281.

[91] *Crane v Hegeman Harris Co Inc* [1939] 1 All E.R. 662.

[92] *Joscelyne v Nissen* [1970] Q.B. 86 at 98, criticised by L. Bromley, "Rectification in Equity" (1971) 87 L.Q.R. 532.

[93] *Munt v Beasley* [2006] EWCA Civ 370 at [36], per Mummery LJ.

[94] *FSHC Group Holdings Ltd v Glas Trust Corp Ltd* [2019] EWCA Civ 1361 at [75]–[77]. This does not require that the parties' common intention be declared in express terms, since the shared understanding may be tacit: ibid at [80]–[87]; *Global Display Solutions Ltd v NCR Financial Solutions Group Ltd* [2021] EWHC 1119 (Comm) at [373], [400]–[401]; *Markel Bermuda Ltd v Caesars Entertainment Inc*

[2021] EWHC 1931 (Comm) at [40]; *Ralph v Ralph* [2021] EWCA Civ 1106 at [18], although on the facts no continuing common intention could be found: [33]-[43].

⁹⁴ᵃ *Univar UK Ltd v Smith* [2020] EWHC 1596 (Ch) at [205]-[207]; *Re Colart Pension Scheme* [2020] Pens. L.R. 3 at [7]; *Re Chas A Blatchford & Sons Ltd Group Pension Scheme* [2019] EWHC 2743 (Ch); *Lloyds Bank Plc v Lloyds Banking Group Pensions Trustees Ltd* [2019] EWHC 3775 (Ch); *SPS Technologies Ltd v Moitt* [2020] EWHC 2421 (Ch). See too *FSHC Group Holdings Ltd v Glas Trust Corp Ltd* [2019] EWCA Civ 1361 [78]-[79]. No outward manifestation of an accord is required in cases where the instrument is not intended to set out an accord between two or more parties (i.e. if the underlying transaction is unilateral); nor where a unilateral transaction requires the consent of another: *AMP (UK) Plc v Barker* [2001] Pens. L.R. 77; followed in *Gallaher Ltd v Gallaher Pensions Ltd* [2005] EWHC 42 (Ch); [2005] Pens. L.R. 103.

(b) Continuing Intention.

Replace third paragraph with:

Traditionally, the parties' actual intentions had to be determined; the court could **16-015** only rectify a written instrument if it failed to reflect the actual intentions of the parties.[109] This seems preferable to an objective test of intention; after all, the best evidence of what the parties objectively agreed is to be found in the written document itself. It is difficult to explain why any prior objective agreement should override a later, formal instrument, unless the prior agreement reflects the parties' actual agreement, and continued to do so at the time the instrument was executed.[110] Nevertheless, in *Chartbrook Ltd v Persimmon Homes Ltd*,[111] Lord Hoffmann suggested, obiter, that an objective approach to ascertaining the common intention of the parties is more appropriate, since this is consistent with the approach adopted in interpretation.[112] This view was not contested before the Court of Appeal in *Daventry District Council v Daventry & District Housing Ltd*.[113] Yet the Court in *Daventry* had serious reservations surrounding the test for common mistake,[114] and all three judges differed in their interpretation of what the test required.[115] Significantly, in *Daventry*, the decision of the Court of Appeal in *Britoil Plc v Hunt Overseas Oil Inc*,[116] where the majority demanded a subjective test of intention,[117] was not cited to the court. The law was for some time unsettled in this area, but the very clear judgment of the Court of Appeal in *FSHC Group Holdings Ltd v Glas Trust Corp Ltd* restores the traditional orthodox approach: the parties must have actually made a mistake and had the same actual intention for rectification to be granted, and there must also be an "outward expression of accord".[118] Where rectification is granted in order to give effect to a prior concluded contract rather than a continuing common intention, then the court will give effect to the objective interpretation of the prior agreement where it is clear that both parties actually made a mistake in recording that agreement in the written instrument.[119]

---

[109] See *FSHC Group Holdings Ltd v Glas Trust Corp Ltd* [2019] EWCA Civ 1361 at [51]ff; see too J. Bromley "Recification in Equity" (1971) 87 L.Q.R. 532 and the cases cited therein.

[110] This was referred to with approval in *Simic v New South Wales Land and Housing Corp* [2016] HCA 47 at [48] (Kiefel J). See too *FSHC Group Holdings Ltd v Glas Trust Corp Ltd* [2019] EWCA Civ 1361 at [144].

[111] *Chartbrook Ltd v Persimmon Homes Ltd* [2009] UKHL 38; [2009] 1 A.C. 1101 at [60].

[112] *Chartbrook Ltd v Persimmon Homes Ltd* [2009] UKHL 38; [2009] 1 A.C. 1101 at [60]. See M. Smith "Rectification of Contracts for Common Mistake, Joscelyne v Nissen and Subjective States of Mind" (2007) 123 L.Q.R. 116.

[113] *Daventry District Council v Daventry & District Housing Ltd* [2011] EWCA Civ 1153; [2012] 1 W.L.R. 1333.

[114] See, e.g. Toulson LJ at [173]-[177] and Lord Neuberger MR at [195].

[115] For critical discussion, see P.S. Davies, "Rectifying the course of rectification" (2012) 75 M.L.R. 387.

[116] *Britoil Plc v Hunt Overseas Oil Inc* [1994] C.L.C. 561.

[117] Hobhouse and Glidewell LJJ; Hoffmann LJ dissenting. See *FSHC Group Holdings Ltd v Glas Trust Corp Ltd* [2019] EWCA Civ 1361 at [88]–[97] and [160]–[163].

[118] *FSHC Group Holdings Ltd v Glas Trust Corp Ltd* [2019] EWCA Civ 136 at [176]; noted Davies [2020] C.L.J. 8; Peel (2020) 136 L.Q.R. 205. This decision was described as "seminal" by Sir Geoffrey Vos MR in *Ralph v Ralph* [2021] EWCA Civ 1106 at [14]. The outward expression of accord must exist at the time of the contract: *Musst Holdings Ltd v Astra Asset Management UK Ltd* [2020] EWHC 337 (Ch).

[119] *FSHC Group Holdings Ltd v Glas Trust Corp Ltd* [2019] EWCA Civ 1361 at [140]–[141].

(c) Failure to Represent Agreement.

Replace paragraph with:

16-016   There must be clear and unambiguous evidence that the instrument either does not accurately represent the true agreement of the parties at the time when it was executed,[121] or at least that it is doubtful whether it does.[122] It is not sufficient to show that the parties did not intend what was recorded; they also have to show what they did intend, with some degree of precision.[123]

[121] *Fowler v Fowler* (1859) 4 De G. & J. 250 at 265; *Constantinidi v Ralli* [1935] Ch. 427.

[122] *Walker v Armstrong* (1856) 8 De G.M. & G. 531 (a happy example of judicial scorn appears at [538]); and see *Re Walton's Settlement* [1922] 2 Ch. 509.

[123] *Giles v Royal National Institute for the Blind* [2014] EWHC 1373; *Lee v Lee* [2018] EWHC 149 (Ch). This paragraph was cited with approval in e.g. *Musst Holdings Ltd v Astra Asset Management UK Ltd* [2020] EWHC 337 (Ch) at [33] and *Saving Stream Security Holding Ltd (In Administration) v Wordley* [2020] EWHC 2849 (Ch) at [11], where the court further considered that there is no need to probe into the underlying validity of the agreement when determining the true agreement of the parties (at [23]).

2.   Unilateral Mistake

(b) Rectification in cases where unconscionable advantage taken.

Replace n.150 with:

16-019   [150] See para.12-016. The description of this principle as a species of equitable estoppel was cited by Pennycuick J in *A Roberts & Co Ltd v Leicestershire CC* [1961] Ch. 555; and see more recently *Traditional Structures Ltd v H W Construction Ltd* [2010] EWHC 1530 (TCC); *Caledonian Maritime Assets Limited v HCC International Insurance Company Plc* [2022] EWHC 164 (Ch) at [23].

Replace n.154 with:

[154] Where, however, the defendant does have actual knowledge of the mistake, this will suffice without an additional requirement to establish dishonesty on the part of the defendant: see *Palo Alto Ltd v Alnor Estates Ltd* [2018] UKUT 231 (TCC). See further *Global Display Solutions Ltd v NCR Financial Solutions Group Ltd* [2021] EWHC 1119 (Comm) at [454]–[458].

(d) Unilateral transactions.

Replace paragraph with:

16-021   Where the transaction is unilateral, unilateral mistake suffices for rectification.[165] Thus a deed poll may be rectified on sufficient proof of a mistake[166] in carrying out the intention of the grantor,[167] and so may provisions in deeds of settlement.[168] Nor is there anything to prevent a volunteer claiming rectification,[169] at any rate after the settlor's death.[170] And there is now a statutory jurisdiction to rectify wills.[171] It has recently been suggested that the unilateral mistake required for rectification of a voluntary disposition should be of similar gravity as that required for rescission under *Ogilvie v Littleboy*.[172] However, this elision of the test of mistake for rescission and rectification has perhaps had the unfortunate effect of leading to some judges granting rectification even where there is no mistake as to the terms of the written instrument, and in substance varying or rewriting the trust.[173]

[165] See *Wright v Goff* (1856) 22 Beav. 207 at 214. This paragraph was cited with approval in *Re Webster* [2020] EWHC 2275 (Ch) at [37], [46]-[48], where the judge thought a unilateral tax return submitted by a taxpayer as a consequence of a statutory requirement was not capable of rectification (and would not have granted rectification anyway).

[166] *Bonhote v Henderson* [1895] 1 Ch. 742; [1895] 2 Ch. 202.

[167] *Wright v Goff* (1856) 22 Beav. 207; *Killick v Gray* (1882) 46 L.T. 583; but see *Phillipson v Kerry* (1863) 32 Beav. 628, although this can hardly be read as a decision by Romilly MR denying the jurisdiction to rectify a deed poll that he had exercised in *Wright v Goff*. If the deed is wholly misconceived, it may be cancelled or rescinded.

[168] See, e.g. *Maunsell v Maunsell* (1877) 1 L.R.Ir. 529 (see at 539, 540); *Van der Linde v Van der Linde* [1947] Ch. 306 (deed of covenant); *Lackersteen v Lackersteen* (1860) 30 L.J. Ch. 5. See para.16-005.

[169] *Thompson v Whitmore* (1860) 1 J. & H. 268 at 273; *Weir v Van Tromp* (1900) 16 T.L.R. 531.

[170] *Lister v Hodgson* (1867) L.R. 4 Eq. 30 at 34; *M'Mechan v Warburton* [1896] 1 I.R. 435 at 439.

[171] See para.16-006.

[172] *Day v Day* [2013] EWCA Civ 280; [2013] 3 All E.R. 661 at [39]-[45], per Lewison LJ, relying upon the judgment of Lloyd LJ in the Court of Appeal decision in *Pitt v Holt* [2011] EWCA Civ 197; [2012] Ch. 132; the Supreme Court in *Pitt v Holt* [2013] UKSC 26; [2013] 2 A.C. 108 has also subsequently approved the test in *Ogilvie v Littleboy* (1897) 13 T.L.R. 399 at 400 (affirmed by the House of Lords: *Ogilvie v Allen* (1899) 15 T.L.R. 294). See too the discussion in *Kennedy v Kennedy* [2014] EWHC 4129 (Ch); [2015] B.T.C. 2. For further discussion of this type of "sufficiently serious" mistake, see para.15-006.

[173] Compare, e.g. *Racal Group Services Ltd v Ashmore* [1995] S.T.C. 1151; and *Giles v The Royal National Institute for the Blind* [2014] EWHC 1373 (Ch); with more recent decisions such as *Prowting 1968 Trustee Ltd v Amos-Yeo* [2015] EWHC 2480; [2015] B.T.C. 33; and *RBC Trustees v Stubbs* [2017] EWHC 180 (Ch). cf. *Bullard v Bullard* [2017] EWHC 3. See too *A v D* [2017] EWHC 2222; *Rogge v Rogge* [2019] EWHC 1949 (Ch). See generally P Davies and S Douglas, 'Tax Mistakes Post-Pitt v Holt" (2018) 32 T.L.I. 3.

3. The Standard of Proof

Replace paragraph with:
    The standard of proof remains the civil standard of the balance of probabilities.   **16-022** However, since the alleged intention contradicts the written instrument, "convincing proof"[174] is required to contradict the inherent probability that the written instrument truly represents the parties' intention because it is a document signed by them.[175] Equally, "certainty and ready enforceability would be hindered by constant attempts to cloud the issue by reference to pre-contractual negotiations".[176] It is for these reasons that a person seeking rectification must be able to rely upon "strong irrefragable evidence".[177] The burden of proof is on the party seeking rectification, and this burden is particularly "formidable" if the formal written instrument is detailed and recorded with the benefit of expert legal advice.[178]

[174] *Joscelyne v Nissen* [1970] 2 Q.B. 86; see further *Citifinancial Europe Plc v Davidson* [2014] EWHC 1802 (Ch); and *Vaughan-Jones v Vaughan-Jones* [2015] EWHC 1086 (Ch).

[175] *Thomas Bates and Son v Wyndham's (Lingerie) Ltd* [1981] 1 W.L.R. 505 at 521; *Racal Group Services v Ashmore* [1995] S.T.C. 1151 at 1155. See also *Re H (Minors) (Sexual Abuse: Standard of Proof)* [1996] A.C. 563 at 586–587; *Grupo Torras v Al Sabah* (1999) C.L.C. 1469 (reversed on a different point [2001] C.L.C. 221) (civil fraud). cf. *Heinl v Jyske Bank (Gibraltar) Ltd* [1999] Lloyd's Rep.

Bank 511. Indeed, it would seem that "the test for unilateral mistake in a voluntary transaction should be if anything even more rigorous" than that required in the bilateral case: *Lobler v Revenue and Customs Commissioners* [2015] UKUT 152 (TCC); [2015] B.T.C. 515 at [52] (Proudman J).

[176] *The Olympic Pride* [1980] 2 Lloyds Rep. 67 at 73, per Mustill J.

[177] *Shelburne v Inchiquin* (1784) 1 Bro.C.C. 338 at [341], per Lord Thurlow LC; and see *Townshend v Stangroom* (1801) 6 Ves. 328 at 334; *Lake v Lake* [1989] S.T.C. 865 at 869, per Mervyn Davies J.

[178] See, e.g. *James Hay Pension Trustees Ltd v Hird* [2005] EWHC 1093 (Ch) at [81]. This paragraph was cited and has been approved by Arden LJ in *Scottish Widows Fund and Life Assurance Society v BGC International* [2012] EWCA Civ 607 at [44]; see too *Ashwood Enterprises Ltd v Bank of Ireland* [2014] EWHC 2624 (Ch) at [214]. This paragraph was cited with approval in *Watson v Eyre* [2018] EWHC 500 (Ch) at [81].

4. DEFENCES

1.   Valid Defences

Replace paragraph with:

16-025   Even if the foregoing requirements are satisfied, the court may still refuse to order rectification; for the remedy is equitable and discretionary.[192a] Thus, it will not be granted to the prejudice of a bona fide purchaser for value without notice who takes an interest conferred by the instrument[193]; and laches or acquiescence will bar the claim.[194] Where rectification is sought of a voluntary settlement and one of the trustees objects, the court may in its discretion refuse rectification.[195] Further, it is too late to claim rectification of a contract if it is no longer capable of performance,[196] or if, after being construed by the court, it has been wholly performed under the judgment of the court.[197] Impossibility of restoring the parties to the pre-contract position may also bar rectification, although not if:

> "it would not be difficult to adjust so as to place the parties in a position in which they would receive little or no prejudice from what had been done after the exchange."[198]

[192a] *MV Promotions Limited and Micheal Vaughan v Telegraph Media Group Limited and HMRC* [2020] EWHC 1537 (Ch).

[193] *Bell v Cundall* (1750) Amb. 101; *Garrard v Frankel* (1862) 30 Beav. 445; *Coates v Kenna* (1873) 7 I.R.Eq 113; and see *Smith v Jones* [1954] 1 W.L.R. 1089; *Thames Guaranty Ltd v Campbell* [1985] Q.B. 210 at 240, citing this passage. See too *Mitchells & Butlers Pensions Ltd v Mitchells & Butlers Plc* [2021] EWHC 3017 (Ch); [2022] Pens. L.R. 6 at [210]-[273], approving this passage, with the result that a defendant who became a principal employer under a deed amending an occupational pension scheme could not avail itself of the bona fide purchaser defence since it did not purchase an interest in property.

[194] *Beale v Kyte* [1907] 1 Ch. 564 (holding that time runs from discovery of the mistake); *McCausland v Young* [1949] N.I. 49; cf. *Dormer v Sherman* (1966) 110 S.J. 171 at 172. See also *Milton Keynes Borough Council v Viridor (Community Recycling MK) Ltd* [2017] EWHC 239 (TCC), [100]–[111].

[195] *Re Butlin's Settlement Trusts* [1976] Ch. 251 at 262 (rectification granted).

[196] *Borrowman v Rossell* (1864) 16 C.B.(N.S.) 58; *Retirement Villages Developments Limited v Punch Partnerships (PTL) Limited* [2022] EWHC 65 (Ch) [47].

[197] *Caird v Moss* (1886) 33 Ch. D. 22.

[198] *Beauchamp v Winn* (1873) L.R. 6 H.L. 223 at 232 (Lord Chelmsford).

Replace second paragraph with:
   Performance of the contract will not always amount to a defence, however, at least where the performance was monetary and it is arguable that it (or part of it) is repayable on restitutionary grounds.[199] An order for rectification will also be refused where the parties have already varied their agreement so as to correct the

error, so that the only consequence of the court's order would be to secure a fiscal benefit.[200] In other words, the court will not order rectification of a document as between the parties or as between a grantor or covenantor and an intended beneficiary, if their rights will be unaffected and if the only effect of the order will be to secure a fiscal advantage.[201]

[199] *The Toronto Dominion Bank v Oberoi* [2002] EWHC 3216.

[200] See *Racal Group Services Ltd v Ashmore* [1995] S.T.C. 1151. However, it may be argued that this affords insufficient protection to third parties: see para.16-010.

[201] See *Whiteside v Whiteside* [1950] Ch. 65 CA, where the parties had already entered into a supplementary deed rectifying the error before the matter came to court. See also *Racal Group Services Ltd v Ashmore* [1995] S.T.C. 1151 at 1158, per Peter Gibson LJ; *MV Promotions Limited and Micheal Vaughan v Telegraph Media Group Limited and HMRC* [2020] EWHC 1537 (Ch). However in *Giles v Royal National Institute for the Blind* [2014] EWHC 1373 (Ch) it was no bar to rectification (of a deed of variation of a will) that in executing the deed it was the claimant's objective to relieve the beneficiaries of the indirect burden of inheritance tax.

2. Bad Defences

Replace n.210 with:

[210] See *Racal Group Services Ltd v Ashmore* [1995] S.T.C. 1151 CA at [1157] (Peter Gibson LJ); approving a passage from the judgment of Vinelott J at first instance [1995] S.T.C. 416 at 425. See also *Re Colebrook's Conveyances* [1972] 1 W.L.R. 1397; *Re Slocock's Will Trusts* [1979] 1 All E.R. 358; *Lake v Lake* [1989] S.T.C. 865; *Ware v Ware* [2021] EWHC 694 (Ch).   **16-026**

CHAPTER 17

SPECIFIC PERFORMANCE

1. INTRODUCTION

1. Relation to Remedy at Law

(d) Discretionary nature of relief.

After "a discretionary remedy,", add new n.12a:

[12a] Damages may be awarded in lieu of specific performance, under s.50 of the Senior Courts Act 1981: **17-004** "Where the Court of Appeal or the High Court has jurisdiction to entertain an application for an injunction or specific performance, it may award damages in addition to, or in substitution for, an injunction or specific performance." See e.g. *Rahman v Rahman* [2020] EWHC 2392 (Ch), which holds that such statutory damages in lieu are calculated as at the date when specific performance would have been ordered, not as at the date of breach.

3.   Valid Contractual Obligation Required

Replace n.21 with:

17-006   ²¹ *Gibson v Manchester City Council* [1979] 1 W.L.R. 294; *Gordon v Havener (Antigua and Barbuda)* [2021] UKPC 26.

2.   INADEQUACY OF DAMAGES—THRESHOLD REQUIREMENT FOR AVAILABILITY OF SPECIFIC PERFORMANCE

1.   General Principles and Trends

Replace n.24 with:

17-007   ²⁴ *Co-operative Insurance Society Ltd v Argyll Stores (Holdings) Ltd* [1998] A.C. 1 at 11; [1997] 2 W.L.R. 898. See further para.17-015. For a notable contrast with a Scottish decision on the equivalent issue, see *Sapphire 16 S.A R.L v Marks and Spencer Plc* [2021] CSOH 103.

Replace n.31 with:

³¹ *Cavendish Square Holding BV v Makdessi* [2015] UKSC 67; [2016] A.C. 1172, applied *Westfields Homes Ltd v Keay Homes (Windrush) Ltd* [2020] EWHC 3368 (Ch).

Replace paragraph with:

Damages will generally be considered an adequate remedy even though the claimant regards specific performance as preferable to an award of damages,³² for example because some of his loss is not recoverable in an award of damages or is too remote,³³ or because of his obligation to mitigate his loss. In other words, the court will not, without more, order specific performance merely because its rules on the quantification of damages mean that the claimant's interest in performance is not fully protected.³⁴ However, where the contract itself contains a restriction on the measure of damages available, this may be taken into account by the court when considering whether damages are inadequate so as to justify injunctive relief.³⁵ Damages are generally not considered inadequate even where they are difficult to quantify, though where the calculation of damages would be too speculative this may justify specific performance.³⁶ The defendant's financial situation and potential difficulty in meeting an award of damages are also not generally relevant to whether damages are inadequate.³⁷

³² Presumably true by definition in any case where the claimant is seeking specific performance.

³³ *The Stena Nautica (No. 2)* [1982] 2 Lloyd's Rep. 336 at 342.

³⁴ In *Latin American Investments Ltd v Maroil Trading Inc* [2017] EWHC 1254 (Comm) Teare J held (citing *Peak Hotels and Resorts Ltd v Tarek Investments Ltd* [2015] EWHC 3048 (Ch)) that it was arguable that specific performance might be awarded in circumstances where shareholders were barred from claiming damages because their loss was merely reflective of that of the company. Since such an order would compel payments to be made to the company, it would arguably not fall foul of the reflective loss principle, since it carries no risk of double-recovery and prejudice to creditors. Subsequently in *Broadcasting Investment Group Ltd v Smith* [2021] EWCA Civ 91 Asplin LJ stated that although a superficial reading of the authorities (including *Peak Hotels* and *Latin American Investments*) might lead to the conclusion that claims for specific performance (whether with or without seeking additional or alternative relief in the form of equitable damages) do fall within the reflective loss rule, the matter is complex and "best left to a case in which it is essential to determine the issue".

³⁵ *AB v CD* [2014] EWCA Civ 229, discussed further para.18-035.

³⁶ *Fothergill v Rowland* (1873–1874) L.R. 17 Eq. 132; cf. the position re injunctions *Evans Marshall & Co Ltd v Bertola SA* [1973] 1 W.L.R. 349. See also *Zinc Cobham 1 Ltd (in administration) v Adda Hotels (an unlimited company)* [2018] EWHC 1025 (Ch), and compare *AB v University of XYZ* [2020] EWHC 2978 (QB).

[37] In *Anders Utkilens Rederi A/S v O/Y Lovisa Stevedoring Co A/B and Keller Bryant Transport Co* [1985] 2 All E.R. 669 at 674 Goulding J said: "Commercial life would be subjected to new and unjust hazards if the court were to decree specific performance of contracts normally sounding only in damages simply because of a party's threatened insolvency. Thus I cannot accept the argument based simply on financial instability". The Court of Appeal has declined to order specific performance by analogy with the principle that a claimant will be denied cost of cure damages but will be confined to damages for loss of amenity if it would be "disproportionate" to cure the breach (*Ruxley Electronics and Construction Ltd v Forsyth* [1996] A.C. 344; [1995] 2 All E.R. 268; [1995] 3 W.L.R. 118). In *Newman v Framewood Manor Management Co Ltd* [2012] EWCA Civ 159, the court denied specific performance of a landlord's covenant to provide a jacuzzi, where a sauna had been provided instead. As Arden LJ said, "In my judgment, the judge was correct not to award a specific performance. To incur this cost would be excessive and disproportionate when compared with the loss of amenity".

Replace n.38 with:

[38] *Jan v Torrance* [2002] EWCA Civ 431. See also *Hewavisenti v Wickramsinghe* [2021] EWHC 2045 (Ch) where specific performance was granted to enforce the terms of a settlement agreement between the parties governing the winding up of their joint property venture, in order to achieve finality and because it is "important that the Court ensures that valid settlement agreements are enforced according to their terms".

2. Specific Examples

(a) Land.

After "potential with no intention", insert:
of residing there,   **17-008**

(b) Chattels.

Replace second paragraph with:
The Sale of Goods Act[50] has widened this remedy slightly by giving the court, **17-009** in the case of non-consumer sale of goods contracts, a discretion to order specific performance of a contract to deliver "specific or ascertained goods" without giving the seller the option of retaining the goods and paying damages.[51] In practice, the courts are reluctant to exercise this discretion unless the goods are effectively unique.[52] However, in very exceptional circumstances in which the normal market is not functioning, the courts may be more flexible about specific remedies, even for goods that are not specific or ascertained. In *Sky Petroleum Ltd v VIP Petroleum Ltd*,[53] the plaintiff had a 10-year contract with the defendant under which the plaintiff undertook to obtain all the petrol and diesel required for its filling stations from the defendant. During the oil crisis, the defendant purported to terminate the agreement in breach of contract and, exceptionally, Goulding J was prepared to grant an interlocutory injunction restraining this breach, even though this had the indirect effect of compelling the defendant to supply the petrol and diesel, because the unusual state of the market meant that the plaintiff had little prospect of finding an alternative supply and would otherwise be forced out of business.

[50] As amended by the Consumer Rights Act 2015.

[51] See Sale of Goods Act 1979 s.52(1) (jurisdiction), s.61(1) (meaning of "specific"); and see *Re Wait* [1927] 1 Ch. 606 (on "ascertained"); and *Cohen v Roche* [1927] 1 K.B. 169 (power to order specific performance is discretionary). For the regime for consumer contracts, see now Pt I of the Consumer Rights Act 2015.

[52] *Cohen v Roche* [1927] 1 K.B. 169; *Gregor Fisken Ltd v Carl* [2021] EWCA Civ 792.

[53] *Sky Petroleum Ltd v VIP Petroleum Ltd* [1974] 1 W.L.R. 576; considered in *Land Rover Group Ltd v UPF (UK) Ltd (in Administrative Receivership)* [2002] EWHC 3183 (QB); and *VTB Commodities Trading DAC v JSC Antipinsky Refinery* [2020] EWHC 72 (Comm).

(d) Money.

Replace paragraph with:

17-011   In most cases a monetary remedy of damages or the action for an agreed sum will be an adequate remedy for breach of a contract for the payment of money, but in exceptional cases such a contract may be specifically enforced.[62a] This may occur where the action for an agreed sum would be unavailable or unsuitable, such as where the contract is to pay a third party, so that the damages recoverable by the contracting party would be merely nominal,[63] or where the contract is to make periodical payments, requiring a multiplicity of actions at law to enforce payment.[64] Although the third party cannot himself sue on the contract, he can enforce any order for specific performance which the contracting party obtains.[65] More controversially, in what has been described as "an awkward exception"[66] to the normal requirement that damages should be inadequate, in contracts for the sale of land, the vendor is readily awarded specific performance[67] even though his interest in performance is purely financial and thus damages or the action for an agreed sum would (other than in exceptional cases) be an adequate remedy.[68] This is commonly justified on the basis of mutuality, but this principle is no longer given the weight it traditionally was[69] and, in any event, the purchaser's entitlement to specific performance against the vendor may no longer be absolute.[70]

[62a] Paragraph 17-011 was cited with approval by Picken J in *Avonwick Holdings Ltd v Azitio Holdings Ltd* [2020] EWHC 1844 (Comm). One such exceptional example was referred to by the high court in *Navig8 Chemicals Pool Inc v Aeturnum Energy International Pte Ltd* [2021] EWHC 3132 (Comm) at [68], "It is settled law that the obligations imposed on the indemnifier under a maritime contract of indemnity are amenable to enforcement by a mandatory injunction / order for specific performance: see *Trafigura Maritime Logistics Pte Ltd v Clearlake Shipping Pte Ltd* [2020] EWHC 726 (Comm) (Henshaw J) at [31], *Harmony Innovation Shipping Ltd v Caravel Shipping Inc* [2019] EWHC 1037 (Comm) (Sir Ross Cranston) at [30], *The Bremen Max* [2009] 1 Lloyd's Rep. 81 (Teare J) at [21] and *The Laemthong Glory (No. 2)* [2005] 1 Lloyd's Rep. 632 (Cooke J) at [51]–[52]. Damages are not an adequate remedy in this context."

[63] *Beswick v Beswick* [1968] A.C. 58; [1967] 3 W.L.R. 932.

[64] *Beswick v Beswick* [1968] A.C. 58; [1967] 3 W.L.R. 932.

[65] See *Gurtner v Circuit* [1968] 2 Q.B. 587 at 596, 598, 599, 602, 606.

[66] *Anders Utkilens Rederi A/S v O/Y Lovisa Stevedoring Co A/B and Keller Bryant Transport Co* [1985] 2 All E.R. 669 at 673 per Goulding J.

[67] Lindley LJ in *Hope v Walter* [1900] 1 Ch. 257 described specific performance as allowing the vendor to "thrust" the property "down the throat" of the purchaser, although the remedy was refused on the facts because the vendor had misdescribed the premises as a shop when it was in fact a brothel.

[68] Although the vendor might regard specific performance as more convenient than retaining the property, reselling it and claiming damages, but this would not apply to an action for the agreed sum. The Court of Appeal in *Doherty v Fannigan Holdings Ltd* [2018] EWCA Civ 1615 suggested, without discussion, that the vendor of shares could seek specific performance of the defaulting purchaser's obligation to pay the price.

[69] See *Price v Strange* [1978] Ch. 337; [1977] 3 W.L.R 943 and para.17-024.

[70] See para.17-008.

3. BARS TO SPECIFIC PERFORMANCE

1. The Nature of the Contractual Obligation

(a) Contracts involving personal service.

(1) Employment contracts.

Replace n.80 with:

[80] *Johnson v Shrewsbury and Birmingham Rly Co* (1853) 3 De. G.M. & G. 914, where Knight Bruce LJ said, "We are asked to compel one person to employ against his will another as his confidential servant, for duties with respect to the due performance of which the utmost confidence is required. Let him be one of the best and most competent persons that ever lived, still if the two do not agree, and good people do not always agree, enormous mischief may be done". Lord Wilson in *Geys v Societe Generale* [2012] UKSC 63, [2013] 1 A.C. 523, noted that, "The big question whether nowadays the more impersonal, less hierarchical, relationship of many employers with their employees requires review of the usual unavailability of specific performance has been raised … but is beyond the scope of this appeal."

17-013

(b) Contracts requiring constant supervision.

Replace n.100 with:

[100] *Co-operative Insurance v Argyll Stores* [1998] A.C. 1. The contrary result was reached in Scotland on analogous facts in *Sapphire 16 S.A R.L v Marks and Spencer Plc* [2021] CSOH 103.

17-015

(1) Contracts to carry on an activity.

Replace paragraph with:

Contracts to carry on an activity will often be unsuitable for specific performance for other reasons, because of the difficulty of defining with precision what has to be done[103] or because the inconvenience which would be worked by the decree makes damages a more appropriate remedy.[104] But if a contract as a whole[105] is suitable for specific performance, a decree will not be refused merely because the contract contains a provision which on its own would not be specifically enforced.[106] Further, in a proper case specific performance of an agreement to sign or otherwise execute an instrument will be ordered even if the obligations under that instrument would not themselves be specifically enforced (e.g. because they are obligations to perform personal services[107]) so that breaches of them would sound only in damages.[108]

17-016

[103] *Tito v Waddell (No.2)* [1977] Ch. 106 at 321, 322.

[104] *CH Giles & Co Ltd v Morris* [1972] 1 W.L.R. 307 at 318, 319; approved in *Price v Strange* [1978] Ch. 337 at 359, 360.

[105] For divisible contracts, see para.17-025.

[106] *CH Giles & Co Ltd v Morris* [1972] 1 W.L.R. 307; and see *McCarthy & Stone Ltd v Julian S Hodge & Co Ltd* [1971] 1 W.L.R. 1547.

[107] See para.17-012.

[108] *Wilson v West Hartlepool Railway* (1865) 2 De G.J. & S. 475; *CH Giles & Co Ltd v Morris* [1972] 1 W.L.R. 307.

(2) Contract to build.

Replace n.109 with:

17-017   [109] See *Flint v Brandon* (1803) 8 Ves. 159 at 163.

(e)   Contracts for transient or terminable interests.

Replace n.134 with:

17-020   [134] *Hercy v Birch* (1804) 9 Ves. 357.

(g)   Uncertain obligations.

After "exposed to the", replace "quasicriminal" with:

17-022   quasi-criminal

2.   The Relevance of Other Contractual Obligations

(a)   Mutuality.

Replace n.165 with:

17-024   [165] *Forrer v Nash* (1865) 35 Beav. 167 at 171; and see *Re Bryant and Barningham's Contract* (1890) 44 Ch. D. 218. cf. *Hoggart v Scott* (1830) 1 Russ. & M. 293.

Replace n.174 with:

[174] Buckley LJ in *Price v Strange* [1978] Ch. 337 at 367–368. For an argument that even this formulation affords undue protection to defendants, see A. Burrows, *Remedies for Torts and Breach of Contract*, 4th edn (Oxford: Oxford University Press, 2019), p.427.

3.   Other Reasons for Refusing Specific Performance

(a)   Misrepresentation, non-disclosure and other procedural unfairness.

Replace paragraph with:

17-027   Any misrepresentation, fraudulent or innocent, which justifies the rescission of the contract,[181] affords a defence to proceedings for specific performance against the party misled,[182] even if it affects only a small part of the contract which the party making the misrepresentation offers to waive.[183] The defendant may rely on the claimant's misrepresentation to resist specific performance even if the right to rescind has been lost due to circumstances for which the defendant is not responsible, but not if the reason that the right to rescind was lost was due to the defendant's default.[184] Further, in some cases specific performance may be refused even where there is no right to rescind,[185] e.g. where, although it cannot be proved that the misrepresentation actually induced the contract, it can be inferred that the misrepresentation influenced the defendant.[186] Specific performance will be refused where the contract is tainted with fraud, even if it is not a fraud on the other party to the contract, but on the public.[187] A clause purporting to exclude liability for misrepresentation (including one worded to the effect that the parties acknowledge that no representations have been made or relied upon) is effective at common law, but (if contained in a non-consumer contract) is subject to a test of reasonableness pursuant to s.3 of the Misrepresentation Act 1967. In *Schyde Investments Ltd v Cleaver*,[187a] the Court of Appeal applied this test to cl.7.1.3 of the Standard Conditions of Sale, holding that the vendor had not established that the clause was a reasonable one to have included in the contract at the time when it had been made, and it was thus unenforceable.[187b] Likewise, this sort of condition will fall within the Consumer Rights Act 2015 if the contract is a consumer contract (between a commercial seller and a consumer purchaser), and thus be subject to a test of fairness.

[181] See generally Ch.15. An action for specific performance is sometimes met with a counterclaim by the defendant for rescission on the basis of the claimant's misrepresentation, as in *Andrew v Aitken* (1882) 22 Ch. D. 218; and *Charles Hunt Ltd v Palmer* [1931] 2 Ch. 287; and *Raiffeisen Bank International AG v Asia Coal Energy Ventures Limited, Ashurst LLP* [2020] EWHC 2602 (Comm).

[182] *Walker v Boyle* [1982] 1 W.L.R. 495; *Smelter Corp of Ireland Ltd v O'Driscoll* [1977] I.R. 305.

[183] *Viscount Clermont v Tasburgh* (1819) 1 J. & W. 112.

[184] *Geest Plc v Fyffes* [1999] 1 All E.R. (Comm) 672.

[185] *Lamare v Dixon* (1873) L.R. 6 H.L. 414 at 428; *Re Banister* (1879) 12 Ch. D. 131, at 142, 147, 149.

[186] *Holliday v Lockwood* [1917] 2 Ch. 47 at 56, 57; *Hope v Walter* [1900] 1 Ch. 257.

[187] *Post v Marsh* (1880–81) 16 L.R. Ch. D. 395 (publishers' description of book written by A as being written by B, a well-known author, who in fact wrote none of it).

[187a] [2011] EWCA Civ 929. The purchaser was seeking rescission of the contract for misrepresentation, the vendor resisted on the basis of cl.7.1.3 and counterclaimed for specific performance, which was denied. See also *Cremdean Properties Ltd v Nash* (1977) 241 E.G. 837, and *Shill Properties Ltd v Bunch* [2021] EWHC 2142 (Ch), which considered a non-reliance clause contained in clause 6 of the Standard Conditions of Sale.

[187b] Longmore LJ emphasised that: "the question is not whether the clause is, in general, a reasonable clause. The question is whether it was a reasonable clause in the contract made between this vendor and this purchaser at the time when the contract was made."

Replace n.188 with:

[188] *Mortlock v Buller* (1804) 10 Ves. 292; *Buckley v Irwin* [1960] N.I. 98. This passage was cited with approval by Stocker LJ in *Quadrant Visual Communications v Hutchison Telephone* [1993] B.C.L.C. 442. See also *Arani v Cordic Group* [2021] EWHC 829 (Comm), paras [171]–[172].

(d) Misdescription.

(1) Substantial misdescription.

After "the misdescription is", replace "to prevent the purchaser from really getting the property which he bought," with:
    that the purchaser will not in reality be acquiring the property which he intended **17-035** to purchase,

(2) Slight misdescription.

Replace second paragraph with:
    The principle of granting specific performance with compensation is not one to **17-036** be extended, and will never be applied in an action by the vendor to enforce the contract where he has been guilty of fraud or wilful[234] misrepresentation.[235] Nor will the court apply this principle at the suit of either party if the proper amount of compensation cannot be ascertained.[236] Further, a standard condition is commonly inserted in contracts for the sale of land to the effect that the lots are believed to be correctly described, but that errors shall not annul the sale and that no compensation shall be paid for or in respect of any misdescription.[237] Notwithstanding such a condition, however, the purchaser may treat the contract as repudiated and terminate it if the misdescription is fraudulent or, though not fraudulent, is on a

material and substantial point so that, but for the misdescription, the purchaser would not have entered into the contract.[238]

[234] Quaere whether wilful misdescription here differs from fraud.

[235] See *Price v Macaulay* (1852) 2 De G.M. & G. 339 at 344.

[236] *Lord Brooke v Rounthwaite* (1846) 5 Hare 298 (vendor's action); *Rudd v Lascelles* [1900] 1 Ch. 815 (purchaser's action).

[237] See in particular clause 7.1.3 of the Standard Conditions of Sale.

[238] *Flight v Booth* (1834) 1 Bing. N.C. 370; *Jacobs v Revell* [1900] 2 Ch. 858; *Lee v Rayson* [1917] 1 Ch. 613; *Walker v Boyle* [1982] 1 W.L.R. 495.

(e) Default by the claimant.

Replace n.252 with:

17-038   [252] *Bellamy v Debenham* [1891] 1 Ch. 412; *Pips (Leisure Productions) Ltd v Walton* (1982) 43 P. & C.R. 415; *Pinekerry Ltd v Needs Ltd* (1992) 64 P. & C.R. 245. In *Dreams Ltd v Pavilion Property Trustees Ltd* [2020] EWHC 1169 (Ch), the tenant was in breach of a condition in a surrender agreement to give vacant possession, so the landlord was not required to accept the surrender without vacant possession and the tenant was denied specific performance.

(h) Delay.

Replace paragraph with:

17-044   Even where time is not of the essence of the contract, specific performance may be barred by the claimant's unreasonable delay in seeking the remedy, under the equitable doctrine of laches.[302] The period of delay which will bar a claim to specific performance is to be judged by equitable principles, since an action for specific performance is not sufficiently like an action for damages for breach of contract for the six year limitation period in the Limitation Act to be applicable by analogy.[303] The traditional test for laches was relatively strict: for a claimant to obtain specific performance, he must have shown himself "ready, desirous, prompt, and eager".[304] In practice, however, the courts show some flexibility in assessing the extent, impact of and reasons for the delay, when whether to permit specific performance. So where the claimant has been let into possession under the contract and has obtained the equitable interest, so that all he requires is a mere conveyance of the legal estate, even many years' delay in enforcing his claim will not prejudice him.[305] Moreover, delay in proceeding to trial after the commencement of proceedings will not be fatal unless the defendant is led to believe that only damages are being sought.[306] But even a short delay might preclude specific performance if the subject-matter of the contract is of fluctuating value. Overall, it has been suggested that delay alone is not sufficient to bar specific performance, unless the defendant has been prejudiced by the delay.[307]

[302] *Mills v Haywood* (1877) 6 Ch. D. 196; and see *Walker v Jeffreys* (1842) 1 Hare 341; *Cornwell v Henson* [1900] 2 Ch. 298; *Behzadi v Shaftesbury Hotels* [1992] Ch. 1 at 12.

[303] If a statutory limitation provision (properly interpreted) applies to a claim, then equity will apply it in obedience to the statute; and even where the limitation period does not apply to the claim (because the claim is for an exclusively equitable remedy) the limitation will be applied by analogy if the equitable remedy is "correspondent to the remedy at law": see *P & O Nedlloyd BV v Arab Metals Co* [2006] EWCA Civ 1717 at [34]–[38], per Moore-Bick LJ. However, the remedy of specific performance is not correspondent to any common law remedy; so that no period of limitation applies by analogy at [44]–[52], per Moore-Bick LJ. *P & O Nedlloyd* was applied by Picken J in *Avonwick Holdings Ltd v Azitio Holdings Ltd* [2020] EWHC 72 (Comm) at [1091] – [1096]. Whether a statutory period of limitation

should be applied by analogy to claims for monetary relief in lieu of specific performance remains uncertain.

[304] *Milward v Earl Thanet* (1801) 5 Ves. 720n, per Arden MR; repeated by Cotton LJ in *Mills v Haywood* (1877) 6 Ch. D. 196 at 202.

[305] *Crofton v Ormsby* (1806) 2 Sch. & Lef. 583, at 603; *Shepheard v Walker* (1875) L.R. 20 Eq. 659; *Williams v Greatrex* [1957] 1 W.L.R. 31; *Frawley v Neill, The Times,* 5 April 1999; cf. *Mills v Haywood* (1877) 6 Ch. D. 196. The sentence in the text was cited in *Voyce v Voyce* (1991) 62 P. & C.R. 290 at 293 per Dillon LJ.

[306] *Du Sautoy v Symes* [1967] Ch. 1146. See also *Easton v Brown* [1981] 3 All E.R. 278 (eight years' delay after decree).

[307] Megarry VC in *Lazard Brothers & Co v Fairfield Properties Co (Mayfair) Ltd* (1977) 121 S.J. 793. See also *Taylor v Crotty* [2006] EWCA Civ 1364, where specific performance was ordered despite a delay: the delay was in part caused by the defendant denying the validity of the exercise of the option and where the defendant was "unable to point to any prejudice or equity that has arisen, which would be a ground for denying to the tenant the right to performance of the contract". See further *Avonwick Holdings Ltd v Azitio Holdings Ltd* [2020] EWHC 72 (Comm).

(i)   Great hardship.

Replace fourth paragraph with:

In contrast, the fact that one party has made a poor bargain,[318] or that he is   **17-045** impecunious[319] or financially unable to complete, is not hardship,[320] nor is inadequacy of price a ground for refusing specific performance,[321] unless the purchaser stands in a fiduciary position to the vendor, or enters into the contract as a result of fraud.[322] Nevertheless, occasionally the court may deny specific performance because of commercial hardship. In one case specific performance of an agreement to sell land to a railway company for the purposes of its undertaking was refused after the company had abandoned the project, for the decree would have worked more injustice than justice.[323] More recently, where a flat had purportedly been sold by an agent for the vendor to one party and by the vendor personally to the claimants, thereby generating years of litigation, the Privy Council decided that specific performance of the contract with the claimants would be "wholly unworkable in practice and a recipe for yet further litigation" as well as conflicting with the overriding objective in civil proceedings of dealing with cases justly.[324] Finally, the defendant's financial difficulties might be taken into account when denying specific performance, when coupled with other factors. In one case, the defendant's financial circumstances made compliance with an obligation to build a roundabout pursuant to a development agreement nigh on impossible, whilst difficulties in obtaining planning permission for the development meant that the need for a roundabout was uncertain: in the circumstances the court thought it arguable that the defendant could defend an action for specific performance and declined summary judgment to the claimant.[325]

[318] *Adams v Weare* (1784) 1 Bro.C.C. 567; *Roberts v O'Neill* [1983] I.R. 47 (great increase in value of land after contract).

[319] *RVB Investments Ltd v Bibby* [2013] EWHC 65 (Ch).

[320] *Nicholas v Ingram* [1958] N.Z.L.R. 972. And see *Francis v Cowcliff, The Times,* 30 March 1976 (landlord's financial inability to provide and maintain a lift). See also *Francis v Vista Del Mar Development Ltd (Cayman Islands)* [2019] UKPC 14.

[321] In *Mountford v Scott* [1975] Ch. 258, where an option was granted to the purchaser to purchase the vendor's house for less than its value, the Court of Appeal rejected the vendor's argument that specific performance should not be ordered: "If the owner of a house contracts with his eyes open ... it cannot in my view be right to deny specific performance to the purchaser because the vendor then finds it dif-

ficult to find a house to buy that suits him and his family on the basis of the amount of money in the proceeds of sale".

322 *Coles v Trecothick* (1804) 9 Ves. 234 at 246: *Sullivan v Jacob* (1828) 1 Moll. 472 at 477.

323 *Webb v Direct London & Portsmouth Ry Co* (1852) I De G.M. & G. 521 at 529, 530.

324 *O'Connor v Piccott* [2010] UKPC 4.

325 *North East Lincolnshire BC v Millennium Park (Grimsby) Ltd* [2002] EWCA Civ 1719.

CHAPTER 18

INJUNCTION

CONTENTS

1. INTRODUCTION

3. Jurisdiction

(a) Courts.

Replace n.25 with:

[25] See para.1-038. Moreover, all courts may grant injunctions under the Human Rights Act: *Re G* **18-005**
(Children) [2019] EWCA Civ 1779; [2020] 1 F.L.R. 391.

(c) Parties.

Replace paragraph with:

18-007   Injunctions operate in personam and are generally sought against a party to the proceedings. However, provided the defendant exists, it is not necessary that he be identified: an injunction can be awarded against persons unknown.[35] Similarly, an injunction may be granted against a representative of a group on behalf of all the members of that group.[36] It is also possible for the court to grant an injunction against the whole world.[37]

[35] *Secretary of State for the Environment, Food and Rural Affairs v Meier* [2009] UKSC 11; [2009] 1 W.L.R. 2780. See also *South Cambridgeshire DC v Persons Unknown* [2004] EWCA Civ 1280; [2004] 4 P.L.R. 88; *Bloomsbury Publishing Plc v Newsgroup Newspapers Ltd* [2003] EWHC 1087 (Ch); [2003] 1 W.L.R. 1633; *Vastint Leeds B.V. v Persons Unknown* [2018] EWHC 2456 (Ch) at [19]–[25] (Marcus Smith J); *Boyd v Ineos Upstream Ltd* [2019] EWCA Civ 515; J. Seymour, "Injunctions enjoining non-parties: distinction without difference?" (2007) 66 C.L.J. 605. See too *Olympic Delivery Authority v Persons Unknown* [2012] EWHC 1012 (Ch); *Cameron v Liverpool Victoria Insurance Co Ltd* [2019] UKSC 6; [2019] 1 W.L.R. 1471; *Cuadrilla Bowland Ltd v Persons Unknown* [2020] EWCA Civ 9; [2020] 4 W.L.R. 29; *Canada Goose UK Retail Ltd v Persons Unknown* [2020] EWCA Civ 303; [2020] 1 W.L.R. 2802; *Bromley LBC v Persons Unknown* [2020] EWCA Civ 12; *Birmingham City Council v Afsar* [2020] EWHC 864 (QB); [2020] E.L.R. 341; *City of London Corporation v Persons Unknown* [2021] EWHC 1378 (QB); *Barking and Dagenham LBC v Persons Unknown* [2022] EWCA Civ 13; [2022] 2 W.L.R. 946; *High Speed Two (HS2) Ltd v Persons Unknown* [2022] EWHC 2360 (KB).

[36] *Taff Vale Railway Co v Amalgamated Society of Railway Engineers* [1901] A.C. 426; *Michaels (Furriers) Ltd v Askew* (1983) 127 S.J. 597. However, such an injunction should not be granted if there is an apparent conflict of interest between members of the group: *UK Nirex Ltd v Barton*, *The Times*, 14 October 1986.

[37] Or "*contra mundum*". See, e.g. *Venables v News Group Newspapers Ltd* [2001] Fam. 430; [2001] 2 W.L.R. 1038. See too *OPQ v BJM* [2011] EWHC 1059 (QB); [2011] E.M.L.R. 23; *Re Persons Formerly Known as Winch* [2021] EWHC 1328 (QB); [2021] E.M.L.R. 20 and [2021] EWHC 3284 (QB); [2022] A.C.D. 22.

2. PERPETUAL (OR FINAL) INJUNCTIONS

2. Rights which, if Infringed, may Justify the Grant of a Final Injunction

Replace n.64 with:

18-011   [64] See Ch.30. In *AA v Persons Unknown* [2019] EWHC 3556 (Comm); [2020] 4 W.L.R. 35 Bryan J. held that cryptocurrencies were a form of property and could be subject to proprietary injunctions.

(a) Real property rights.

(1) Trespass.

Replace paragraph with:

18-012   A landowner whose title is not disputed is prima facie entitled to an injunction to restrain a threatened or apprehended[66] trespass on his land even if the trespass will not harm him.[67] An injunction may also be granted against a defendant who disputes the claimant's title, e.g. where he entered and felled a tree and threatened to cut more.[68] But the court refused to enjoin some lepidopterists who committed a mere technical trespass without intending to infringe any rights of property and who desisted on request.[69] Moreover, the court is especially slow to grant an injunction which will exclude even an adult child from his parent's home,[70] but will do so in grave circumstances, such as where the child has assaulted the parent.[71]

[66] On quia timet injunctions generally see para.18-029.

[67] *Patel v WH Smith (Eziot) Ltd* [1987] 1 W.L.R. 853. A hospital is no different from any other landowner when seeking injunctive relief against patients: *University College London Hospitals Foundation Trust v MB* [2020] EWHC 882 (QB). This passage was approved in *High Speed Two (HS2) Ltd v Persons Unknown* [2022] EWHC 2360 (KB) at [74].

[68] *Stanford v Hurlstone* (1873) 9 Ch. App. 116.

[69] *Fielden v Cox* (1906) 22 T.L.R. 411 (Rupert Brooke, who with three other defendants "went to catch a butterfly and caught a writ"; claimant awarded the 1s. damages paid into court and made to pay defendants' costs).

[70] *Waterhouse v Waterhouse* (1905) 94 L.T. 133.

[71] *Stevens v Stevens* (1907) 24 T.L.R. 20; *Egan v Egan* [1975] Ch. 218.

(b) Intellectual property rights.

Replace n.105 with:

[105] *L'Oréal SA v eBay International AG Case C-324/09* [2012] All E.R. (EC) 501; *UPC Telekabel Wien GmbH v Constantin Film Verleih GmbH Case C-314/12* [2014] E.C.D.R. 12. See too, e.g. *Dramatico Entertainment Ltd v British Sky Broadcasting Ltd* [2012] EWHC 268 (Ch); [2012] 3 C.M.L.R. 14; *Twentieth Century Fox Film Corp v Newzbin Ltd* [2010] EWHC 608 (Ch); [2010] E.C.C. 13. For further discussion in the context of "blocking injunctions" see *Cartier International AG v British Telecommunications Plc* [2018] UKSC 28; [2018] 1 W.L.R. 3259; *Nintendo Co Ltd v Sky UK Ltd* [2019] EWHC 2376 (Ch); [2020] 3 All E.R. 83.   **18-016**

(c) Contractual rights.

(3) Personal services.

Replace n.137 with:

[137] Employment Rights Act 1996 s.117. See too *Union of Shop, Distributive and Allied Workers v Tesco Stores Ltd* [2022] EWCA Civ 978.   **18-019**

(g) Statutory Duties.

Replace n.183 with:

[183] Local Government Act 1972 s.222; e.g. *Sharif v Birmingham City Council* [2020] EWCA Civ 1488; [2021] 1 W.L.R. 685. The court's jurisdiction under this section is limited, and does not extend to every order that might be intended to prevent a continuation of a breach of the criminal law: *Worcester CC v Tongue* [2004] EWCA Civ 140.   **18-025**

3.   The Equity to Grant Injunctive Relief

(a) The risk of future interference with the claimant's rights.

(1) The relevance of past interference.

Replace n.191 with:

[191] *Proctor v Bayley* (1889) 42 Ch. D. 390 at 399, 400. This passage was approved in *High Speed Two (HS2) Ltd v Persons Unknown* [2022] EWHC 2360 (KB) at [95].   **18-028**

(2) Claimant's rights not yet interfered with.

Replace n.205 with:

[205] See *Hooper v Rogers* [1975] Ch. 43 at 49 (damages in lieu of quia timet mandatory injunction). See too *Ineos Upstream Ltd v Persons Unknown* [2019] EWCA Civ 515; *High Speed Two (HS2) Ltd v*   **18-029**

Persons Unknown [2022] EWHC 2360 (KB). For critical discussion, see J. Murphy "Rethinking Injunctions in Tort Law" (2007) 27 O.J.L.S. 509.

(d)   The discretion to refuse relief.

(4)   Hardship.

Replace n.284 with:

18-040   ²⁸⁴ *Pride of Derby and Derbyshire Angling Assoc Ltd v British Celanese Ltd* [1953] Ch. 149. *In Priyanka Shipping Ltd v Glory Bulk Carriers Pte Ltd* [2019] EWHC 2804 (Comm); [2019] 1 W.L.R. 6677 at [91] "inconvenience or hardship" was held to be an insufficient reason to refuse injunctive relief; although an injunction may be refused if it would be "unconscionable" or "oppressive", and the may take into account the adequacy of damages: [97].

4.   Damages in Substitution for (or Addition to) Injunction

Replace third paragraph with:

18-044   However, this traditional understanding of the law³²² may no longer be appropriate. In *Coventry v Lawrence*,³²³ the Supreme Court signalled a move away from the *Shelfer* guidelines on the basis that they were "out-dated"³²⁴ and that the broad discretion of the court in this area should not be restricted by a mechanical test.³²⁴ᵃ It may therefore be expected that courts will show a greater willingness to take into account the public interest, and that a broader approach will generally be taken by the courts when deciding whether or not to award damages in lieu of an injunction, even if the defendant still bears a "legal burden" to show why an injunction should not be granted.³²⁵ But even within a wider approach, the factors raised in *Shelfer* are likely to remain relevant as the courts attempt to determine the correct test to apply when considering whether there should be an injunction or damages in lieu.³²⁶

³²² The preceding paragraph was cited with approval by Morgan J in *Loveluck-Edwards v Ideal Developments Ltd* [2012] EWHC 716 (Ch); [2012] 2 P. & C.R. DG2 at [114].

³²³ *Coventry v Lawrence* [2014] UKSC 13; [2014] A.C. 822.

³²⁴ It should be noted that the "working rule" of *Shelfer* [1895] 1 Ch. 287 CA is not necessarily exhaustive, and there may be other situations in which damages may be awarded in lieu of an injunction, e.g. *Jaggard v Sawyer* [1995] 1 W.L.R. 269, 287, per Millett LJ.

³²⁴ᵃ In *Unwired Planet International Ltd v Huawei Technologies (UK) Co Ltd* [2020] UKSC 37 at [162] the Supreme Court approved of Lord Neuberger's approach in Coventry v Lawrence and held that "the court's power to award damages in lieu of an injunction involves a classic exercise of discretion". See too *Alexander Devine Children's Cancer Trust v Housing Solutions Ltd* [2020] UKSC 45; [2020] 1 W.L.R. 4783 at [64].

³²⁵ *Coventry v Lawrence* [2014] UKSC 13; [2014] A.C. 822 at [121] (Lord Neuberger).

³²⁶ See, e.g. *Higson v Guenault* [2014] EWCA Civ 703 [51] (Aikens LJ).); *Priyanka Shipping Ltd v Glory Bulk Carriers Pte Ltd* [2019] EWHC 2804 (Comm); [2019] 1 W.L.R. 6677. For further discussion see, e.g. *Prophet Plc v Huggett* [2014] EWHC 615 (Ch); [2014] I.R.L.R. 618 at [26]–[28] (not considered on appeal: [2014] EWCA Civ 1013; [2014] I.R.L.R. 797); *Comic Enterprise Ltd v Twentieth Century Fox Film Corp* [2014] EWHC 2286 (Ch); [2014] E.T.M.R. 51; *Kerry Ingredients (UK) Ltd v Bakkavor Group Ltd* [2016] EWHC 2448 (Ch) at [74]ff; *Ottercroft Ltd v Scandia Care Ltd* [2016] EWCA Civ 867; *Apexmaster Ltd v URC Thames North Trust* [2018] 2 WLUK 584 [71]–[83]; *Business Mortgage Finance 6 Plc v Greencoat Investments Ltd* [2019] EWHC 2128 (Ch) [96]–[102]; *Beaumont Business Centres Ltd v Florala Properties Ltd* [2020] EWHC 550 (Ch).

3. INTERIM INJUNCTIONS

2. The Jurisdiction to Grant Interim Injunctions

(b) Arbitrations.

Replace paragraph with:

The power of arbitrators to grant interim injunctions may be limited,[342] but the court has the power, unless the parties agree otherwise, to grant interim injunctions in aid of arbitration.[343] Applications must normally be made on notice,[344] but in urgent cases an application for a freezing order or search order may be made ex parte.[345]

18-048

[342] See para.18-006.

[343] Arbitration Act 1996 s.44(1), (2) (this replaces Arbitration Act 1950 s.12(6)).

[344] Arbitration Act 1996 s.44(4). For discussion of this provision and s43(3) when the matter has ceased to be urgent see *VTB Commodities Trading DAC v JSC Antipinsky Refinery v Petraco Oil Co SA* [2020] EWHC 72 (Comm); [2020] 1 W.L.R. 1227.

[345] Arbitration Act 1996 s.44(3); *Cetelem SA v Roust Holdings Ltd* [2005] EWCA Civ 618; [2005] 1 W.L.R. 3555; *Belair LLC v Basel LLC* [2009] EWHC 725 (Comm); *Zim Integrated Shipping Services Ltd v European Container KS* [2013] EWHC 3581 (Comm); [2013] 2 C.L.C. 800; *ETC Export Trading Company SA v Apla Importer* [2020] EWHC 3229 (QB). An injunction will only be granted if "necessary", which is determined using the usual principles applicable to interim relief: *Telenor East Holdings II AS v Altimo Holdings & Investments Ltd* [2010] EWHC 735 (Comm) at [31]. It has been doubted whether the court may grant a freezing order in aid of a foreign arbitration under Civil Jurisdiction and Judgments Act 1982 s.25(3): *ETI Euro Telecom International NV v Republic of Bolivia* [2008] EWCA Civ 880; [2009] 1 W.L.R. 665.

3. Enforcement of Substantive Rights Pending Trial—Prohibitory Injunctions

(b) The principles to be applied.

(1) Serious question.

Replace paragraph with:

At the outset the court must be satisfied that "there is a serious question to be tried". This means something more than the claimant can avoid having the action struck out as frivolous and vexatious in the sense of being one which no reasonable person could treat as bona fide.[357] He does not now have to show a prima facie case, but only an issue for which there is some supporting material and the outcome of which is uncertain.[358] An injunction will be refused to a claimant who has no "real prospect of succeeding in his claim for a permanent injunction at the trial". If the claimant fails to satisfy this requirement, that is an end of the matter.[359] If he does satisfy this requirement, the court must go on to consider the balance of convenience.[360]

18-052

[357] *Mothercare Ltd v Robson Brooks Ltd* [1979] F.S.R. 466; not following *John Walker & Son Ltd v Rothmans International Ltd* [1978] F.S.R. 357 at 361.

[358] *Cayne v Global Natural Resources Plc* [1984] 1 All E.R. 225. A majority of the Court of Appeal recently held that an injunction could be granted to enforce an injunction or undertaking: *Koza Ltd. & Hamdi Akin Ipek v Koza Altin Isletmeleri AS* [2020] EWCA Civ 1018.

[359] *Re Lord Cable* [1977] 1 W.L.R. 7; *Associated British Ports v Transport and General Workers Union* [1989] 1 W.L.R. 939.

360 "… an unfortunate expression. Our business is justice, not convenience": *Francome v Mirror Group Newspapers Ltd* [1984] 1 W.L.R. 892 at 898, per Sir John Donaldson MR. For recent discussion see *Planon Ltd v Gilligan* [2022] EWCA Civ 642; [2022] I.R.L.R. 684.

(2) Balance of convenience.

Replace n.361 with:

18-053 361 *Garden Cottage Foods Ltd v Milk Marketing Board* [1984] A.C. 130. See too *Watson's Dairies Ltd v AG Lambert and Partners* [2020] EWHC 2825 (Ch).

(5) Special factors.

Replace n.374 with:

18-056 374 *Smith v Inner London Education Authority* [1978] 1 All E.R. 411. See too *R. (on the application of the Press Standards Board of Finance Ltd) v Secretary of State for Culture, Media and Sport* [2013] EWHC 3824 (Admin) (no interim injunction to restrain the Secretary of State from placing any charter regarding press regulation before the Privy Council). Indeed, the public interest is important whenever a public authority is involved: *R. (The Governing Body of X) v Office for Standards in Education, Children's Services and Skills* [2020] EWCA Civ 594; [2020] E.M.L.R. 22.

(c) The limits of the Cyanamid guidelines.

(3) No prospect of trial.

Replace n.390 with:

18-060 390 See para.18-061. Cf. *MI Squared Ltd v King* [2022] EWHC 331 (Comm); [2022] 2 B.C.L.C. 279.

(5) Freedom of expression.

Replace n.414 with:

18-062 414 *Cream Holdings Ltd v Banerjee* [2004] UKHL 44 at [22], per Lord Nicholls. See too *CC v AB* [2006] EWHC 3083; [2007] E.M.L.R. 11; *Attorney General v BBC* [2022] EWHC 826 (QB); [2022] 4 W.L.R. 74.

(d) Relief discretionary.

(3) Claimant's undertaking.

Replace second paragraph with:

18-066 Unless the court otherwise orders, an order for an injunction must contain an undertaking by the claimant, to the court, to pay any damages which the respondent(s) (or any other "party" served with or notified of the order) sustain which the court considers the claimant should pay.[446] The grant of the injunction itself does not confer any right to compensation for loss or damage, and it appears that a defendant cannot recover damages in respect of losses suffered by a third party on a cross-undertaking in damages.[447] The undertaking is given to the court, and is not a contract between the claimant and defendant,[448] although analogous principles apply in assessing whether the damages suffered by the defendant are too remote.[449] Because the contractual principles only apply by analogy, and there is in fact no contract, some exceptions from the contractual principles may be appropriate; for example, a claimant may be liable for unforeseeable losses if they arise before the defendant has had any real opportunity to notify the claimant of the likely losses or to apply to the court for a variation.[450]

[446] CPR 25PD para.5.1A gives the court a discretion whether or not to require an undertaking in damages in favour of persons other than the respondent. For consideration of the principles to be applied in assessing the damages payable (which are essentially compensatory), see *Les Laboratoires Servier v Apotex Inc* [2008] EWHC 2347 (Ch); [2009] F.S.R. 3; approved in *AstraZeneca AB v KRKA dd Novo Mesto* [2015] EWCA Civ 484.

[447] *SmithKline Beecham Plc v Apotex Europe Ltd* [2006] EWCA Civ 658; [2007] Ch. 71 at [29]. Moreoever, A cross-undertaking given to the court is not retrospective, and will therefore only affect damages which are suffered by a person after (a) being joined as a party to the proceedings; or (b) being served with (or notified of) the order: see *Smithkline Beecham Plc v Apotex Europe Ltd* [2005] EWHC 1655 (Ch); [2006] 1 W.L.R. 872 at [41] and [49] (not challenged on appeal—see [2006] EWCA Civ 658; [2007] Ch. 71 at [17] and [22]).

[448] It therefore cannot be varied by the parties: *SmithKline Beecham Plc v Apotex Europe Ltd* [2006] EWCA Civ 658; [2007] Ch. 71 at [107].

[449] *Smith v Day* (1882) 2 Ch. D. 421 at 428; *F Hoffman-La Roche & Co AG v Secretary of State for Trade and Industry* [1975] A.C. 295 at 361; *Graham v Campbell* (1878) 7 Ch. D. 490; *Ennismore Fund Management Ltd v Fenris Consulting Ltd* [2022] UKPC 27. For a case where the amount payable was calculated by reference to the change in capital value of the defendant company, see *Johnson Control Systems Ltd v Techni-Track Europa Ltd (in administrative receivership)* [2003] EWCA Civ 1126. See too *SCF Tankers (Formerly Fiona Trust and Holding Corp) v Privalov* [2017] EWCA Civ 1877; *Alta Trading UK Ltd (formerly Arcadia Petroleum Ltd) v Bosworth* [2021] EWHC 1126 (Comm); [2021] 4 W.L.R. 72.

[450] *Hone v Abbey Forwarding Ltd (In Liquidation)* [2014] EWCA Civ 711.

Replace n.451 with:

[451] For the origin of the practice, see *Chappell v Davidson* (1856) 8 De G.M. & G. 1 at 2; *Smith v Day* (1882) 21 Ch. D. 421 at 424; *Attorney General v Albany Hotel Co* [1896] Ch. 696 at 703.

Replace fourth paragraph with:

The claimant should adduce evidence as to his ability to meet the undertaking,[455] and if he gives misleading information as to means on an application without notice, the injunction may be discharged regardless of the merits.[456] The claimant may be required to pay money into court,[457] or, if abroad, to give security for the damages.[458] The court may also require that the claimant's undertaking be fortified by a third party.[459] The court should (i) make an intelligent estimate of the likely amount of loss that a defendant might suffer as a result of the fortification; (ii) the applicant for the fortification should show a sufficient level of risk of loss to require fortification; and (iii) the applicant should show that the contemplated loss would be caused by the grant of the injunction.[460] Fortification will not be ordered where an injunction has been discharged.[461] The undertaking cannot be enforced until it is established at or before trial that the injunction ought not to have been granted[462]; nor can it be enforced if the defendant admits liability and pays money into court which the claimant accepts without going on to claim a perpetual injunction.[463]

[455] *Brigid Foley Ltd v Ellott* [1982] R.P.C. 433e. Although in some cases a lack of funds will not prevent a claimant's obtaining an interim injunction, even where another person will not provide an adequate undertaking: *Allen v Jambo Holdings Ltd* [1980] 1 W.L.R. 1252; *Re DPR Futures Ltd, The Times,* 29 November 1989 CA.

[456] *Luck International Plc v Beswick* [1989] 1 W.L.R. 1268.

[457] *Jones v Pacaya Rubber and Produce Co Ltd* [1911] 1 K.B. 455; *Baxter v Claydon* [1952] W.N. 376.

[458] *Harman Pictures NV v Osborne* [1967] 1 W.L.R. 723 at 739.

[459] For example, *Tarasov v Nassif* unreported 29 June 1994 CA. For general discussion of the principles underpinning fortification of a cross-undertaking in damages see *Energy Venture Partners Ltd v Malabu Oil and Gas Ltd* [2014] EWCA Civ 1295; [2015] 1 W.L.R. 2309; *Alta Trading UK Ltd (formerly Arcadia Petroleum Ltd) v Bosworth* [2021] EWHC 1126 (Comm); [2021] 4 W.L.R. 72.

[460] *Energy Venture Partners Ltd v Malabu Oil and Gas Ltd* [2014] EWCA Civ 1295; [2015] 1 W.L.R. 2309 at [13] (Tomlinson J). It is important that there be a sufficient risk of loss: *JSC Mezhdunarodniy Promyshlenniy Bank v Pugachev* [2015] EWCA Civ 139; [2016] 1 W.L.R. 160; *Brainbox Digital Ltd v Blackboard Media GmbH* [2017] EWHC 2465 (QB); [2018] 1 W.L.R. 1149; *Claimants Listed in Schedule 1 v Spence* [2022] EWCA Civ 500. For consideration of whether an insurance policy can be satisfactory fortification see the discussion in *Candy v Holyoake* [2017] EWCA Civ 92; [2017] 2 All E.R. (Comm) 513 at [79]ff.

[461] *Thai-Lao Lignite (Thailand) Co Ltd v Laos* [2013] EWHC 2466 (Comm); [2013] 2 All E.R. (Comm) 883; *Napp Pharmaceutical Holdings Ltd v Dr Reddy's Laboratories (UK) Ltd* [2019] EWHC 1009 (Pat).

[462] *Ushers Brewery Ltd v PS King & Co (Finance) Ltd* [1972] Ch. 148; approved in *Colledge v Crossley, The Times,* 18 March 1975.

[463] *Wiltshire Bacon Co v Associated Cinema Properties Ltd* [1938] Ch. 268.

5. Preventing the Dissipation of Assets—Freezing Orders

(a) Origins.

Replace n.493 with:

18-070 [493] See SCA 1981 s.37(3) which recognises the court's power to make such orders. In *UL v BK* [2013] EWHC 1735 (Fam); [2014] Fam. 35 at [9]–[14], Mostyn J expressed the view that power to grant a freezing injunction arises from the inherent equitable jurisdiction of the court. For the County Court's jurisdiction, see para.18-015. CPR PD 25 para.1 enables Masters or District Judges to make freezing orders in certain circumstances. Freezing orders can also be granted by the Patents County Court: *Suh v Ryu* [2012] EWPCC 20; [2012] F.S.R 31. The breadth of s.37 was recognized in *Koza Ltd. & Hamdi Akin Ipek v Koza Altin Isletmeleri AS* [2020] EWCA Civ 1018.

(c) Basis.

Replace paragraph with:

18-072 In order to found the jurisdiction to grant a freezing injunction, it has often been said that the claimant must have against the defendant[500] some substantive cause of action justiciable in England,[501] or require relief in relation to "proceedings"[502] which have been or are about to be commenced abroad.[503] As a result of the decision of the House of Lords in *The Siskina,*[504] it used to be thought that the court does not have the power, at common law, to grant a freezing order where there is no pre-existing cause of action against the defendant within the jurisdiction of the court. However, in *Broad Idea International Ltd v Convoy Collateral Ltd*, Lord Leggatt, with whom the majority of the Judicial Committee of the Privy Council agreed, thought that this approach was unnecessarily restrictive and that "[t]he shades of *The Siskina* have haunted this area of the law for far too long and they should now finally be laid to rest".[505] The majority considered that there is no need for a pre-exisiting cause of action,[506] and summarized current practice as follows:[507]

> "a court with equitable and/or statutory jurisdiction to grant injunctions where it is just and convenient to do so has power - and it accords with principle and good practice - to grant a freezing injunction against a party (the respondent) over whom the court has personal jurisdiction provided that:
>
> i)   the applicant has already been granted or has a good arguable case for being granted a judgment or order for the payment of a sum of money that is or will be enforceable through the process of the court;
>
> ii)   the respondent holds assets (or, as discussed below, is liable to take steps other than in the ordinary course of business which will reduce the value of assets) against which such a judgment could be enforced; and
>
> iii)   there is a real risk that, unless the injunction is granted, the respondent will deal

with such assets (or take steps which make them less valuable) other than in the ordinary course of business with the result that the availability or value of the assets is impaired and the judgment is left unsatisfied."

[500] Where there is more than one defendant, the court has power to make a freezing order against a co-defendant against whom no direct cause of action lies, provided that the claim for the freezing order is ancillary and incidental to the claimant's cause of action against at least one of the defendants: see *Yukong Line Ltd v Rendsburg Investments Corp* [2001] 2 Lloyd's Rep. 113 at [121].

[501] *Siskina (Owners of cargo lately laden on board) v Distos Compania Naviera SA* [1979] A.C. 210. In *A v B* [1989] 2 Lloyd's Rep. 423 a conditional injunction was granted in anticipation of a cause of action arising.

[502] Arbitration claims are not "proceedings" for the purposes of Civil Jurisdiction and Judgments Act 1982 s.25(1): *ETI Euro Telecom NV v Republic of Bolivia* [2008] EWCA Civ 880; [2009] 1 W.L.R. 665.

[503] Now that the Civil Jurisdiction and Judgments Act 1982 s.25(1) has been extended: see para.18-047; and *Fourie v Le Roux* [2007] UKHL 1; [2007] 1 W.L.R. 320. See too *Channel Tunnel Group Ltd v Balfour Beatty Construction Ltd* [1993] A.C. 334; [1993] 2 W.L.R. 262. A freezing injunction may be available in respect of some foreign proceedings, by reason of the Civil Jurisdiction and Judgments Act 1982 s.25(1); see, e.g. *United States v Abacha* [2014] EWHC 993 (Comm); [2014] Lloyd's Rep. F.C. 392.

[504] [1979] A.C. 210.

[505] [2021] UKPC 24; [2022] 2 W.L.R. 703 at [120].

[506] The majority therefore considered that *Veracruz Transportation v VC Shipping Co Inc (The Veracruz)* [1992] 1 Lloyd's Rep. 353 was incorrectly decided.

[507] [2021] UKPC 24; [2022] 2 W.L.R. 703 at [101].

At the end, add new paragraph:
Lord Leggatt approved[507a] the view that:

"the heart and core of the *Mareva* injunction is the risk of the defendant removing his assets from the jurisdiction and so stultifying any judgment given by the courts in the action,"[507b]

and such injunctions are most often granted against defendants who are resident abroad. But the jurisdiction is not limited to foreign defendants.[507c] It is exercisable when the defendant is domiciled, resident or present within the jurisdiction, as well as when he is not.[507d] The injunctions may go, not merely to prevent the removal of assets from the jurisdiction, but to restrain the defendant from dissipating them within the jurisdiction.[507e]

[507a] [2021] UKPC 24; [2022] 2 W.L.R. 703 at [11].

[507b] *Barclay-Johnson v Yuill* [1980] 1 W.L.R. 1259 at 1264, per Megarry VC, approved in *Rahman (Prince Abdul) bin Turki al Sudairy v Abu-Taha* [1980] 1 W.L.R. 1268 at 1272.

[507c] *Barclay-Johnson v Yuill* [1980] 1 W.L.R. 1259 (defendant sold flat in London and was believed to be cruising in Mediterranean).

[507d] SCA 1981 s.37(3).

[507e] *Z Ltd v A-Z* [1982] Q.B. 558; not following *A J Bekhor & Co Ltd v Bilton* [1981] Q.B. 923 at 941, 942.

(d) Guidelines.

(1) Disclosure.

Replace paragraph with:

18-074   The claimant must make full and frank disclosure of all matters in his knowledge which are material for the judge to know.[509] This includes the ground of his claim against the defendant and its amount, and also any points which the defendant has made. Full disclosure is particularly important since the injunction is generally first sought ex parte, before the main proceedings have been commenced. The claimant must also make proper inquiries for any relevant additional facts.[510] If there is non-disclosure of material facts, the injunction may be discharged irrespective of the merits of the case[511]; and the defendant may be entitled to damages without waiting for trial.[512] Nevertheless, the court has a discretion to continue the injunction or to make a fresh order; significant factors include the importance of the matters not disclosed, the culpability involved in the non-disclosure, and the severity and duration of the prejudice caused to the defendant.[513] It is important for the court to bear in mind the "overriding objective" of dealing with cases justly[514] and the need for proportionality.[515]

[509] CPR PD 25A para.3.3; *Negocios Del Mar SA v Doric Shipping Corp SA (The Assios)* [1979] 1 Lloyd's Rep. 331. In *UL v BK* [2013] EWHC 1735 (Fam) [2014] Fam. 35 at [50] Mostyn J emphasised this "high duty of candour" and that exceptional urgency would generally be required before granting an injunction ex parte. See too *Kerman v Akhmedova* [2018] EWCA Civ 307; [2018] 4 W.L.R. 52.

[510] *Brink's Mat Ltd v Elcombe* [1988] 1 W.L.R. 1350.

[511] *Lloyd's Bowmaker Ltd v Britannia Arrow Holdings Plc* [1988] 1 W.L.R. 1337; *Swift-Fortune Ltd v Magnifica Marine SA (The Capaz Duckling)* [2007] EWHC 1630 (Comm); [2008] 1 Lloyd's Rep. 54.

[512] *Ali and Fahd Shobokshi Group Ltd v Moneim* [1989] 1 W.L.R. 710 at 722.

[513] *Memory Corp Plc v Sidhu (No.2)* [2000] 1 W.L.R. 1443 at 1455. See also *Brink's Mat Ltd v Elcombe* [1988] 1 W.L.R. 1350; *Behbehani v Salem (Note)* [1989] 1 W.L.R. 723; *Dadourian Group International Inc v Sims* [2007] EWHC 1673 (Ch); *JSC Commercial Bank Privatbank v Kolomoisky* [2019] EWCA Civ 1708; [2020] 2 W.L.R. 993; *Valbonne Estates Ltd v Cityvalue Estates Ltd* [2021] EWCA Civ 973.

[514] CPR r.1.1.

[515] *Memory Corp Plc v Sidhu (No.2)* [2000] 1 W.L.R. 1443 at 1455.

(4) Risk of removal or dissipation.

Replace paragraph with:

18-077   "Dissipation" includes disposition, pledges and charges.[532] However, it does not include handing an asset over to the owner of that asset[533]; nor does it include the right to borrow, the exercise of which is not equivalent to the disposal of an asset.[534] The court will consider whether the dissipation was unjustifiable.[535] It is essential that there be a real risk of the assets being removed or dissipated before the judgment is satisfied[536] : a freezing order will not be granted merely to provide claimants with security, even where this could be done without causing hardship to the defendant.[537]

[532] *CBS UK v Lambert* [1983] Ch. 37; *Z Ltd v A-Z* [1982] 1 Q.B. 558. Both these cases drew upon the language of "otherwise dealing with" in Senior Courts Act 1981 s.37(3). In *Taylor v Van Dutch Marine Holding Ltd* [2017] EWHC 636 (Ch) Mann J held (disapproving *Gangway Ltd v Caledonian Park Investments (Jersey) Ltd* [2001] 2 Lloyd's Rep. 715) that a third-party's enforcing a charge over property which is frozen by the freezing order would not be an act prohibited by the order.

[533] *The Law Society v Shanks* [1988] 1 F.L.R. 504; departing from the speech of Lord Denning in *Z Ltd v A-Z* [1982] 1 Q.B. 558. *Mobil Cerro Negro Ltd v Petroleos de Venezuela SA* [2008] EWHC 532 (Comm); [2008] 2 All E.R. (Comm) 1034 held that the dissipation must be by conduct that is unjustifiable. See too *Fundo Soberano de Angola v dos Santos* [2018] EWHC 2199 (Comm); *Lakatamia Shipping Company Limited v Morimoto* [2019] EWCA Civ 2203; *Organic Grape Spirit Limited v Nueva IQT, S.L.* [2020] EWCA Civ 999.

[534] *JSC BTA Bank v Ablyazov* [2015] UKSC 64; [2015] 1 W.L.R. 4754.

[535] *Candy v Holyoake* [2017] EWCA Civ 92; [2017] 2 All E.R. (Comm) 513; see too *Claremont Group Interiors v Boultbee (Marlybone) Ltd* [2018] EWHC 3886 (TCC); *Nicholas James Care Homes Ltd v Liberty Homes (Kent) Ltd* [2022] EWHC 1203 (TCC); [2022] T.C.L.R. 4.

[536] *Z Ltd v A-Z* [1982] 1 Q.B. 558; *Thane Investments Ltd v Tomlinson* [2003] EWCA Civ 1272; *JSC BTA Bank v Ablyazov* [2015] UKSC 64; [2015] 1 W.L.R. 4754; *Congentra AG v Sixteen Thirteen Marine SA (The Nicholas M)* [2008] EWHC 1615 (Comm); [2009] 1 All E.R. (Comm) 479; *IOT Engineering Projects Ltd v Dangote Fertilizer Ltd* [2014] EWCA Civ 1348; *Lakatamia Shipping Company Limited v Morimoto* [2019] EWCA Civ 2203; *Crowther v Crowther* [2020] EWCA Civ 762; *Les Ambassadeurs Club Limited v Mr Songbo Yu* [2021] EWCA Civ 1310.

[537] *Ninemia Maritime Corp v Trave Schiffahrtsgesellschaft mbH und Co KG* [1983] 1 W.L.R. 1412; *Refco v Eastern Trading Co* [1999] 1 Lloyd's Rep. 159. In *Candy v Holyoake* [2017] EWCA Civ 92; [2017] 2 All E.R. (Comm) 513 the Court of Appeal considered that the same considerations apply to notification injunctions as to freezing injunctions, and considered the correct test in relation to risk of dissipation (at [34]–[48]).

(e)   Form of order.

(5)   Permissible expenses.

Replace n.548 with:

[548] *AJ Bekhor & Co v Bilton* [1981] Q.B. 923; *PCW (Underwriting Agencies) Ltd v Dixon* [1983] 2 All E.R. 158, 697n; *Avant Petroleum Inc v Gatoil Overseas Inc* [1986] 2 Lloyd's Rep. 236. Pre-existing standard of living expenses are permissible, but the court should not speculate about future expenses: *Vneshprombank LLC v Bedzhamov* [2019] EWCA Civ 1992.   **18-085**

(g)   Worldwide freezing orders.

Replace paragraph with:

A freezing order may not be confined to England and Wales but extend   **18-088**
"worldwide" over foreign assets. Such relief is not strictly extraterritorial, since the freezing order only operates in personam on a defendant within the English court's jurisdiction. However, such an order is only granted in exceptional cases, since it has the potential to be considered oppressive and conflict with principles of comity.[566] Worldwide freezing orders may be granted either before judgment[567] or afterwards,[568] and irrespective of the existence or otherwise of assets in England.[569] Although post-judgment worldwide freezing orders are now generally available, there needs to be a sufficient connection with England.[570] It should not be awarded in aid of a foreign judgment where the defendant is resident abroad.[571] The court is permitted to grant relief in support of foreign proceedings,[573] although it will be particularly cautious about granting worldwide freezing orders in support of arbitration.[574] The court will not make a worldwide property freezing order in support of a civil recovery order under Pt 5 of the Proceeds of Crime Act 2002.[575]

[566] e.g. *Masri v Consolidated Contractors International (UK) Ltd (No.2)* [2008] EWCA Civ 303; [2009] 2 W.L.R. 621.

[567] *Republic of Haiti v Duvalier* [1990] Q.B. 202; *Derby & Co v Weldon* [1990] Ch. 48; *Derby & Co v Weldon (Nos 3 & 4)* [1990] Ch. 65.

[568] *Babanaft International Co SA v Bassatne* [1990] Ch. 13.

[569] *Derby & Co v Weldon (Nos 3 & 4)* [1990] Ch. 65. However, the court must be satisfied that there are "grounds for belief" that assets exist somewhere in the world: *Ras al Khaimah v Bestfort* [2017] EWCA Civ 1014.

[570] Either because the English courts have jurisdiction over the defendant, or the assets are located in England: *Masri v Consolidated Contracts International UK Ltd (No.2)* [2008] EWCA Civ 303; [2009] Q.B. 450.

[571] *Banco Nacional de Comercio Exterior SNC v Empresa de Telecomunicationes de Cuba SA* [2007] EWCA Civ 662; [2008] 1 W.L.R. 1936.

[573] CJJA 1982 s.25; see e.g. *Motorola Credit Corp v Uzan* [2003] EWCA Civ 752; [2004] 1 W.L.R. 113; *JSC VTB Bank v Skurikhin* [2014] EWHC 2254 (QB). As regards proceedings commenced before the end of the transition period, it should be noted the relief could be granted in support of proceedings in another Member State: Brussels I Regulation (recast) (1215/2012) art.35. For discussion of the scope of this provision (which mirrors art.31 of the old Brussels I Regulation (44/2001)), see *Masri v Consolidated Contractors International (UK) Ltd* [2008] EWCA Civ 876; [2009] 2 W.L.R. 699, although the European aspects of the case did not need to be considered by the House of Lords: [2009] UKHL 43; [2010] 1 A.C. 90. For an interesting discussion of whether a worldwide freezing order granted in another member state and recognised in England under art.38 of the old Brussels I Regulation is effective immediately or only after a period of time, and whether "measures of enforcement" under art.47(3) includes service of the worldwide freezing order, see *Cyprus Popular Bank Public Co Ltd v Vgenopoulos* [2018] EWCA Civ 1; [2018] Q.B. 886.

[574] *Mobil Cerro Negro Ltd v Petroleos De Venezuela S* [2008] EWHC 532 (Comm); [2008] 2 All E.R. (Comm) 1034.

[575] *Serious Organised Crime Agency v Perry* [2012] UKSC 35; [2013] 1 A.C. 182: by a 7:2 majority, the Supreme Court held that such a civil recovery order in relation to property obtained through criminal conduct could only be made by the High Court in respect of property inside England and Wales. See too *Serious Organised Crime Agency v O'Docherty* [2013] EWCA Civ 518.

Replace n.577 with:

[577] *Dadourian Group International Inc v Simms* [2006] EWCA Civ 399; [2006] 1 W.L.R. 2499 identified eight "guidelines": (1) The principle applying to the grant of permission to enforce a WFO abroad is that the grant of that permission should be just and convenient for the purpose of ensuring the effectiveness of the WFO, and that it is not oppressive to the parties to the English proceedings or to third parties who may be joined in the foreign proceedings. (2) All the relevant circumstances and options need to be considered. In particular consideration should be given to granting relief on terms, e.g. terms as to the extension to third parties of the undertaking to compensate for costs incurred as a result of the WFO and as to the type of proceedings that may be commenced abroad. Consideration should also be given to the proportionality of the steps proposed to be taken abroad, as well as the form of any order. (3) The interests of the applicant should be balanced against the interests of the other parties to the proceedings and any new party likely to be joined to the foreign proceedings. (4) Permission should not normally be given in terms that would enable the applicant to obtain relief in the foreign proceedings which is superior to the relief given by the WFO. (5) The evidence in support of the application for permission should contain all the information (so far as it can reasonably be obtained in the time available) necessary to enable the judge to reach an informed decision, including evidence as to the applicable law and practice in the foreign court, evidence as to the nature of the proposed proceedings to be commenced and evidence as to the assets believed to be located in the jurisdiction of the foreign court and the names of the parties by whom such assets are held. (6) The standard of proof as to the existence of assets that are both within the WFO and within the jurisdiction of the foreign court is a real prospect, i.e. the applicant must show that there is a real prospect that such assets are located within the jurisdiction of the foreign court in question. (7) There must be evidence of a risk of dissipation of the assets in question. (8) Normally the application should be made on notice to the respondent; but in cases of urgency, where it is just to do so, permission may be given without notice to the party against whom relief will be sought in the foreign proceedings—but in such cases the party should have the earliest practicable opportunity of having the matter reconsidered by the court at a hearing of which he is given notice. See too *Lakatamia Shipping Company Limited v Morimoto* [2019] EWCA Civ 2203.

(h) Ancillary orders.

Replace n.580 with:

580 CPR r.25.1(1)(g); *A v C* [1981] Q.B. 956n.; *AJ Bekhor & Co Ltd v Bilton* [1981] Q.B. 923; *Z Ltd v**18-089**
A-Z [1982] Q.B. 558; *JSC Mezhdunarodniy Promyshlenniy Bank v Pugachev* [2015] EWCA Civ 139;
[2015] W.T.L.R. 991. It is important that the court give practical effect to the freezing order to ensure
its efficacy: *JSC BTA Bank v Ablyazov (No.7)* [2011] EWCA Civ 1386; [2012] 1 W.L.R. 1988;
Khrapunov v JSC BTA Bank [2018] EWCA Civ 819. The court has jurisdiction to require a party to sign
a mandate to social media and email providers, authorising them to disclose details of their accounts to
the other party and to a court-appointed independent lawyer: *Lakatamia Shipping Co Ltd v Su* [2020]
EWHC 865 (Comm); [2020] 1 W.L.R. 2852.

7. Anti-suit Injunctions

(b) Foreign proceedings.

Replace paragraph with:

Injunctions to restrain foreign proceedings are to be granted sparingly as they **18-094**
have the appearance of interfering with the process of a foreign court.618 It may be
proper to grant such injunctions where the English court has jurisdiction over the
respondent to the petition619 and an interest to protect, often where proceedings are
continuing in England.620 If the claim is justiciable only abroad it seems unlikely
that an injunction will be granted.621 Where, on the other hand, the parties have
agreed that disputes shall be litigated within a particular jurisdiction, or referred to
arbitration, relief will be granted to enforce that agreement unless strong reasons
can be shown.622 Such cases are thought to cause less offence to foreign courts,623
although in other instances relevant considerations of comity ought to be taken into
account.624

618 *Deutsche Bank v Highland Crusader Offshore Partners LP* [2009] EWCA Civ 725; [2010] 1 W.L.R.
1023 at [50]. See too *Joint Stock Asset Management Co Ingosstrakh-Investments v BNP Paribas SA*
[2012] EWCA Civ 644; [2012] 1 Lloyd's Rep. 649; *SAS Institute Inc v World Programming Ltd* [2020]
EWCA Civ 599.

619 Such jurisdiction may arise because a foreign creditor who proves in an English liquidation or when
bankruptcy is taken to submit to the jurisdiction of the English court: *Rubin v Eurofinance SA* [2012]
UKSC 46; [2013] 1 A.C. 236. On this basis, an anti-suit injunction might be granted to prevent creditors from pursing proceedings in another jurisdiction to gain an unjustifiable priority in liquidation:
Stichting Shell Pensioenfonds v Krys [2014] UKPC 41; [2015] A.C. 616.

620 *Airbus Industrie GIE v Patel* [1999] 1 A.C. 119 at 133. The foreign proceedings should only be
restrained in cases where they are vexatious or oppressive. See the discussion in *Deutsche Bank v
Highland Crusader Offshore Partners LP* [2009] EWCA Civ 725; [2010] 1 W.L.R. 1023. See also *E v
E* [2021] EWHC 743 (Comm); [2021] 4 W.L.R. 66.

621 e.g. *Midland Bank Ltd v Laker Airways Ltd* [1986] Q.B. 689.

622 *Donohue v Armco Inc* [2001] UKHL 64 at [24] (injunction not granted on the facts); *Ust-
Kamenogorsk Hydropower Plant JSC v AES Ust-Kamenogorsk Hydropower Plant LLP* [2013] UKSC
35; [2013] 1 W.L.R. 1889. See too *Welex AG v Rosa Maritime Ltd (The Epsilon Rosa) (No.2)* [2003]
EWCA Civ 938; [2003] 2 Lloyd's Rep. 509 at [48]; *Times Trading Corp v National Bank of Fujairah
(Dubai Branch)* [2020] EWHC 1078 (Comm); [2020] Bus. L.R. 1752 at [38]; *Catlin Syndicate Ltd v
Amec Foster Wheeler USA Corp* [2020] EWHC 2530 (Comm) at [35]–[36].

623 *OT Africa Line Ltd v Magic Sportswear Corp Ltd* [2005] EWCA Civ 710; [2006] 1 All E.R. (Comm)
32. *Ecobank Transnational Inc v Tanoh* [2015] EWCA Civ 1309; [2016] 1 W.L.R. 2231, where the court
also emphasised the need to avoid delay in applying for injunctive relief.

624 *Star Reefers Pool v JFC Group Co Ltd* [2012] EWCA Civ 14; [2012] 2 All E.R. (Comm) 225.

Replace the remaining paragraphs with:

18-094   To avoid parallel proceedings the court has the power to stay proceedings in England,[625] or to restrain either the commencement or continuation of foreign proceedings in a court outside the European Union.[629] Such an order may restrain a person from prosecuting proceedings in a foreign court[630] or from enforcing a judgment obtained abroad.[631] Historically, relief was available where the foreign proceedings were vexatious and oppressive,[632] or where an order had been obtained in breach of contract or by fraud.[633] The principles upon which relief is now granted may be summarised as follows[634]: (i) the court has the power to restrain a defendant over whom it has personal jurisdiction from instituting or continuing proceedings in a foreign court when it is necessary in the interests of justice to do so; (ii) the English court must have a sufficient interest to protect in restraining the foreign proceedings[635]; (iii) injunctive relief may still be available where the proceedings before the foreign court are vexatious or oppressive[636]; (iii) the order is not an order against the foreign tribunal but, rather, an order against the parties; (iv) the prosecution of parallel proceedings in different jurisdictions is undesirable but not necessarily vexatious or oppressive; (v) since the effect of an order is to affect the conduct of litigation abroad, the jurisdiction should be exercised with caution.

[625] *Spiliada Maritime Corp v Cansulex Ltd* [1987] A.C. 460; *Ionian Bank Ltd v Couvreur* [1969] 1 W.L.R. 781; *McHenry v Lewis* (1882) 22 Ch.D. 397; *OT Africa Line Ltd v Magic Sportswear Corp Ltd* [2005] EWCA Civ 710; [2006] 1 All E.R. (Comm) 32. Note that Article 71 of the Brussels I Regulation provides that, for a convention within its scope, the rules of jurisdiction in that convention apply, and the court has no discretion to stay its proceedings in favour of the courts of a non-Contracting State: *Innovia Films Ltd v Frito-Lay North America, Inc* [2012] EWHC 790 (Pat.), [2012] R.P.C. 24; *Conductive Inkjet Technology Ltd v Uni-Pixel Displays Inc* [2013] EWHC 2968 (Ch.); [2014] 1 All E.R. (Comm) 654. For consideration of the applicability of the Regulation, see the discussion immediately below.

[629] *Donohue v Armco Inc* [2001] UKHL 64; *Royal Bank of Scotland Plc v Hicks* [2010] EWHC 2579 (Ch) and [2011] EWHC 287 (Ch).

[630] *Settlement Corp v Hochschild* [1966] Ch. 10.

[631] *Ellerman Lines Ltd v Read* [1928] 2 K.B. 144. For further examples of "anti-enforcement" injunction see, e.g. *Bank St Petersburg v Arkhangelsky* [2014] EWCA Civ 593; [2014] 1 W.L.R. 4360; *Ecobank Transnational Inc v Tanoh* [2015] EWCA Civ 1309; [2016] 1 W.L.R. 2231; *SAS Institute Inc v World Programming Ltd* [2020] EWCA Civ 599.

[632] *McHenry v Lewis* (1882) 22 Ch. D. 397; *Cohen v Rothfield* [1919] 1 K.B. 410; *Orr-Lewis v Orr-Lewis* [1949] P. 347.

[633] *Ellerman Lines Ltd v Read* [1928] 2 K.B. 144.

[634] See, e.g. *Albon (t/a NA Carriage Co) v Naza Motor Trading Sdn Bhd* [2007] EWCA Civ 1124; [2008] 1 All E.R. (Comm) 351; *Glencore International AG v Exeter Shipping Ltd* [2002] EWCA Civ 528; [2002] 2 All E.R. (Comm) 1; *Masri v Consolidated Contractors International Co Sal* [2008] EWCA Civ 625; [2009] Q.B. 503.

[635] For an example of a court issuing an anti-suit injunction in order to protect its jurisdiction under s.5 of Regulation (EU) 1215/2012, [2012] O.J. L351/1 on jurisdiction (known as "Brussels I (recast)"), see *Petter v EMC Europe Ltd* [2015] EWCA Civ 828. On art.4(1) of the Regulation see *Gray v Hurley* [2019] EWCA Civ 2222; [2020] 1 F.L.R. 864 (referred to CJEU).

[636] Foreign proceedings brought in breach of an exclusive jurisdiction or arbitration agreement are usually so considered. See e.g. *Bank St Petersburg v Arkhangelsky* [2014] EWCA Civ 593. However, the threshold of "vexatious and oppressive" is not easy to meet: see *Star Reefers Inc v JFC Group Co Ltd* [2012] EWCA Civ 14; [2012] 2 All E.R. (Comm) 225, in which Rix LJ (at [2]) thought the test was analogous to that employed to determine an abuse of process (*Aktas v Adepta* [2010] EWCA Civ 1170; [2011] 2 W.L.R. 945).

(c) Arbitrations.

Replace paragraph with:

If parties have expressly agreed that their disputes should be resolved under **18-095** arbitration, then the effect of the Arbitration Act 1996 is to identify and limit the court's role. Part of the court's role is to support the arbitral process: by staying court proceedings which fall within the scope of the agreement,[637] and by making interim orders in relation to evidence (e.g. its preservation or inspection), the sale of property, the granting of injunctions and the appointment of a receiver.[638] The court will readily grant injunctions to restrain foreign proceedings brought in breach of an arbitration agreement, especially where the seat of the arbitration is in England.[639] As with breach of jurisdiction agreements, the onus falls on the party seeking to evade the arbitration agreement to show why the injunction should not be granted.

[637] Arbitration Act 1996 s.9. The confidential nature of arbitration proceedings is such, once proceedings have been stayed under s.9, a stranger to the arbitration should not normally be permitted access to documents on the court's file: *Glidepath BV v Thompson* [2005] EWHC 818 (Comm); [2005] 2 All E.R. (Comm) 833; *Emmott v Michael Wilson & Partners Ltd* [2008] EWCA Civ 184; [2008] 2 All E.R. (Comm) 193. Section 9 applies wherever the seat of the arbitration might be: see s.2(1) and s.2(2).

[638] Arbitration Act 1996 s.44; *Hiscox Underwriting Ltd v Dickson Mancester & Co Ltd* [2004] EWHC 479 (Comm); [2004] 1 All E.R. (Comm) 753; *Cetelem SA v Roust Holdings Ltd* [2005] EWCA Civ 618; [2005] 1 W.L.R. 3555. Section 44 applies wherever the seat of the arbitration might be: see s.2(1) and s.2(2).

[639] *Aggeliki Charis Compania Maritima SA v Pagnan SpA, The Angelic Grace* [1995] 1 Lloyd's Rep. 87. This was supported in *Ust-Kamenogorsk Hydropower Plant JSC v AES Ust-Kamenogorsk Hydropower Plant LLP* [2013] UKSC 35; [2013] 1 W.L.R. 1889, in which the Supreme Court also emphasised that s.44 of the Arbitration Act 1996 does not restrict the power of the Court to grant an injunction, under the Senior Courts Act 1981 s.37, to protect a party's contractual right to arbitration in circumstances in which arbitral proceedings are not even pending (provided that the court proceedings in question were not in a jurisdiction within the scope of the Brussels Regulation or Lugano Convention). See also *Western Bulk Shipowning III A/S v Carbofer Maritime Trading ApS* [2012] EWHC 1224 (Comm); [2013] 2 Lloyd's Rep. 163; *Bannai v Erez* [2013] EWHC 3689 (Comm); [2014] B.P.I.R. 4; *Emmott v Michael Wilson & Partners* [2018] EWCA Civ 51; *Grace Ocean Private Ltd v COFCO Global Harvest (Zhangjiagang) Trading Co Ltd* [2020] EWHC 3343 (Comm); [2021] 1 Lloyd's Rep. 194; *Riverrock Securities Limited v International Bank of St Petersburg (Joint Stock Company)* [2020] EWHC 2483 (Comm); [2020] 2 Lloyd's Rep. 591; *AIG Europe SA (formerly AIG Europe Ltd) v John Wood Group Plc* [2022] EWCA Civ 781; *QBE Europe SA/NV v Generali Espana De Seguros Y Reaseguros* QBE Europe SA/NV v Generali España De Seguros Y Reaseguros [2022] EWHC 2062 (Comm). Similar principles apply to a third party to the contract containing the arbitration clause: *Shipowners' Mutual Protection and Indemnity Association (Luxembourg) v Containerships Denizcilik Nakliyat Ve Ticaret A.S. ("Yusuf Cepnioglu")* [2016] EWCA Civ 386; [2016] 3 All E.R. 697; *Qingdao Huiquan Shipping Company v Shanghai Dong He Xin Industry Group Co Ltd* [2018] EWHC 3009 (Comm); [2019] 1 Lloyd's Rep. 520. The Court of Justice of the European Union has confirmed that an anti-suit injunction awarded by an EU-seated arbitral tribunal is not incompatible with the Brussels Regulation: *Gazprom OAO* (C-536/13) [2015] I.L.Pr. 31. For discussion concerning the correct approach to determining the proper law of an arbitration agreement see *Enka Insaat ve Sanayi AS v OOO Insurance Co Chubb* [2020] UKSC 38; [2020] 1 W.L.R. 4117, where it was held (at [180]–[184]) that the principles underpinning anti-suit injunctions in support of arbitration agreements does not depend upon their proper law.

Replace n.640 with:

[640] Arbitration Act 1996 s.32 and s.72. Challenges to an award on the basis of substantive jurisdiction are governed by s.67; *Nori Holding Ltd v Public Joint-Stock Co Bank Otkritie Financial Corp* [2018] EWHC 1343 (Comm); [2018] 2 Lloyd's Rep. 80. See too *Minister of Finance (Inc) v International Petroleum Investment Co* [2019] EWCA Civ 2080; [2020] Bus. L.R. 45.

4. OPERATION OF INJUNCTION

1. Suspension

Replace n.633 with:

18-096   633 *Stollmeyer v Trinidad Lake Petroleum Co Ltd* [1918] A.C. 485; *Vestry of St Mary, Islington v Hornsey UDC* [900] 1 Ch. 695. The court may also stay an injunction pending the outcome of an application for permission to appeal: see, e.g. *Smith & Nephew Plc v ConvaTec Technologies Inc* [2015] EWCA Civ 803. See too *Neurim Pharmaceuticals (1991) Ltd v Generics (UK) Ltd* [2022] EWCA Civ 370.

2. Enforcement

(a)   Committal.

Replace n.665 with:

18-098   665 *Heatons Transport (St. Helens) Ltd v Transport & General Workers' Union* [1973] A.C. 15 at 108, 109. See *Lexi Holdings Plc v Luqman* [2010] EWCA Civ 1116; *JSC BTA Bank v Solodchenko (No.2)* [2011] EWCA Civ 1241; [2012] 1 W.L.R. 350. See too *MBR Acres Ltd v McGivern* [2022] EWHC 2072 (QB). Claimants can recover the costs of a successful application for committal for contempt of court: *Secretary of State for Transport v Cuciurean* [2022] EWCA Civ 661.

CHAPTER 19

RECEIVERS

5.   RECEIVER BY WAY OF EQUITABLE EXECUTION

1.   General

Replace paragraph with:

A judgment creditor normally obtained satisfaction of its judgment by execu- **19-026**
tion at common law, using the writ of fieri facias, attachment of debts and, in the
case of land, the writ of *elegit*.[151] There were cases, however, where the creditor
could not levy execution at law owing to the nature of the property, the principal
case being where the property was merely equitable, such as an interest under a trust
or an equity of redemption.[152] In order to meet this difficulty, the Court of Chancery
evolved a process of enforcement by way of appointing a receiver of the judgment
debtor's interest.[153]

[151] The writ of *elegit* was abolished in 1956 by the Administration of Justice Act 1956 s.34(1), and replaced by the system of charging orders now found in the Charging Orders Act 1979. At the same time, the court was empowered by what is now the Senior Courts Act 1981 s.37(4) to appoint a receiver by way of equitable execution over legal estates and interests in land whether or not a charging order has been obtained.

[152] *Anglo-Italian Bank v Davies* (1878) 9 Ch. D. 275.

[153] *Re Shephard* (1889) 43 Ch. D. 131; *Anglo-Italian Bank v Davies* (1878) 9 Ch. D. 275.

After the first paragraph, add new para.19-026A:

19-026A   By the Judicature Act 1873 the power to appoint a receiver was put on a statutory footing and made available to all divisions of the High Court.[154] The power now contained in the Senior Courts Act 1981 s.37 may be exercised whenever it appears to the court to be "just and convenient" to do so. Notwithstanding the breadth of this language, for a long time the courts considered that the power could only be exercised in circumstances in which the Court of Chancery would have appointed a receiver before the Judicature reforms.[155] In *Parker v London Borough of Camden*, however, Sir John Donaldson MR said he did not accept that the practices of the Court of Chancery "still rule us from their graves".[156] Eventually, in *Masri (No.2)*,[157] the Court of Appeal held that the statutory power is not constrained by reference to pre-1873 practice. Instead, the circumstances in which receivers may be appointed in aid of enforcement may be developed incrementally, applying old principles to new situations. *Masri (No.2)* has been forcefully affirmed by the Privy Council.[158] These decisions substantially enlarge the potential scope and utility of the remedy.

[154] Judicature Act 1873 s.25(8).

[155] *Holmes v Millage* [1893] 1 Q.B. 551 CA; *Edwards & Co v Picard* [1909] 2 K.B. 903; *Harris v Beauchamp Bros* [1894] 1 Q.B. 801 CA; *Morgan v Hart* [1914] 2 K.B. 183 CA; *Maclaine Watson & Co Ltd v International Tin Council* [1988] Ch. 1 aff'd [1989] Ch. 253 CA

[156] *Parker v London Borough of Camden* [1986] Ch. 162 CA 173.

[157] *Masri v Consolidated Contractors International (UK) Ltd (No 2)* [2009] Q.B. 450 CA.

[158] *Tasarruf Mevduati Sigorta Fonu v Merrill Lynch Bank and Trust Co (Cayman) Ltd* [2012] 1 W.L.R. 1721 PC. The Supreme Court of Ireland has followed the same path: *ACC Loan Management Limited DAC v Rickard* [2019] IESC 29.

2.   Land

Replace paragraph with:

19-027   [This sub-section is deleted in the supplement.]

3.   Property not Available for Execution

Replace paragraph with:

19-028   [This sub-section is deleted in the supplement.]

After the third sub-section, add new sub-section:

3A.   Scope and exercise of the jurisdiction

19-029   Until *Masri (No.2)* it was sometimes thought that there was only jurisdiction to appoint a receiver over an asset which would be presently amenable to execution by normal means if only the judgment debtor held the legal interest instead of a mere equitable interest.[159] That is now seen to be an outdated practice rather than a jurisdictional limit. In considering the scope of the jurisdiction, and in exercising that jurisdiction,[160] the demands of justice are the overriding consideration.[161] These include promotion of a policy that English judgments and awards should be complied with and, if necessary, enforced.[162]

The jurisdiction will not be exercised unless there is some hindrance or difficulty in using the normal processes of execution, which may be legal or practical.[163] The classical legal hindrance was the inability of common law execution to reach an equitable interest, but it is no longer necessary that the hindrance should arise out of the nature of the property. Practical difficulties may include steps taken by the judgment debtor to put assets beyond reach in order to frustrate enforcement as well as the holding of assets through multiple chains of companies rendering enforcement complex.[164] The courts are realistic about the difficulties a judgment creditor may face executing overseas against a recalcitrant judgment debtor.[165] It is not necessary to show that execution by other means would be impossible or even very difficult.[166] Receivership may be justified, for example, where it is likely to result in a greater recovery by facilitating the sale of a business a going concern.[167]

A receiver will not be appointed if the court is satisfied that the appointment would be fruitless, for example because there is no property that the receiver can get in.[168] It is enough, however, that there is a reasonable prospect that the appointment will be of practical utility in the enforcement of a judgment or award.[169] **19-030**

The appointment should not be disproportionate and the court may consider less onerous alternatives.[170] In considering whether to make the appointment, the court should have regard to the amount claimed by the judgment creditor, the amount likely to be received by the receiver, and the probable costs of the appointment.[171]

[159] E.g. *Holmes v Millage* [1893] 1 QB 551 CA 555. But cf. *Maclaine Watson & Co v International Tin Council* [1988] Ch. 1 at 19-21.

[160] *Tasarruf Mevduati Sigorta Fonu v Merrill Lynch Bank and Trust Co (Cayman) Ltd* [2012] 1 W.L.R. 1721 PC at [56].

[161] E.g. *JSC VTB Bank v Skurikhin* [2015] EWHC 2131 (Comm) [53].

[162] *Cruz City 1 Mauritius Holdings v Unitech Ltd* [2015] 1 All E.R. (Comm) 336 at [47(a)].

[163] *Cruz City 1 Mauritius Holdings v Unitech Ltd* [2015] 1 All E.R. (Comm) 336 at [47(c)]. CPR 69PD 4.1(3) requires that the written evidence supporting the application give details of "why the judgment cannot be enforced by any other method", as to which see *VB Football Assets v Blackpool Football Club (Properties) Ltd* [2019] B.C.C. 896 at [13]-[14].

[164] *Cruz City 1 Mauritius Holdings v Unitech Ltd* [2015] 1 All E.R. (Comm) 336.

[165] *JSC VTB Bank v Skurikhin* [2021] 1 W.L.R. 434 CA at [76]; *Masri v Consolidated Contractors International Company SAL* [2008] EWHC 2492 (Comm) at [18].

[166] *Masri v Consolidated Contractors International Company SAL* [2008] EWHC 2492 (Comm) at [17].

[167] *VB Football Assets v Blackpool Football Club (Properties) Ltd* [2019] B.C.C. 896 at [15]-[20].

[168] *Manchester & Liverpool District Banking Co Ltd v Parkinson* (1888) 22 Q.B.D. 173; *Morgan v Hart* [1914] 2 K.B. 183; *Maclaine Watson & Co Ltd v International Tin Council* [1988] Ch. 1 (on appeal, see [1989] Ch. 253 at 271); *Bourne v Colodense Ltd* [1985] I.C.R. 291 CA at 302.

[169] *Cruz City 1 Mauritius Holdings v Unitech Ltd* [2015] 1 All E.R. (Comm) 336 at [47(e)].

[170] *JSC VTB Bank v Skurikhin* [2015] EWHC 2131 (Comm) at [56]; *Blight v Brewster* [2012] 1 W.L.R. 2841 at [75]-[76] (where it was more convenient to empower the judgment creditor's solicitor to make the election in question on behalf of the judgment debtor).

[171] CPR 69PD 5.

After the third sub-section, add new sub-section:

3B.   The nature of the relief

19-031   The remedy does not involve "execution" in the ordinary sense of the word, but is a form of equitable relief given in substitution for execution.[172] An application to appoint a receiver is not an action on a judgment to which the Limitation Act 1980 s.24 applies.[173]

The receiver is authorised to receive the assets over which the appointment is made. As such, a third party's payment of an English debt to the receiver will discharge the judgment debtor's claim,[174] and a third party who knows of the receivership will not be discharged if instead they pay the judgment debtor. The receiver will commonly be authorised to take steps to recover the assets, exercising the judgment debtor's rights, including taking legal proceedings against third parties.[175] Amongst other things, a receiver may be authorised to exercise the judgment debtor's rights as a shareholder,[176] under a pension scheme,[177] or as settlor of a revocable trust.[178] The order may give the receiver a power of sale,[179] and a receiver may apply to the court to approve a momentous transaction,[180] such approval conferring on the receiver immunity from claims.[181]

19-032   The receiver's appointment also takes effect as an injunction restraining the judgment debtor from receiving any part of the assets it covers.[182] In consequence, third parties who know of the order will be in contempt of court if they transfer assets to the judgment debtor or otherwise assist in frustrating the receivership.

The court may make such ancillary orders against the judgment debtor as are appropriate in the circumstances to further the purposes of the receivership. For example, the court may require that the judgment debtor not dispose of assets or otherwise deal with them prejudicially to the judgment creditor[183]; or take whatever steps are necessary to transfer assets or powers to the receiver[184]; or provide information about assets[185]; or confirm the receiver's authority and entitlements to third parties.[186]

The appointment of a receiver by way of equitable execution does not have any proprietary effect such as would operate in rem to determine property rights against the world at large.[187] That is, the order itself does not vest any property in the receiver, create an equitable charge, or give the judgment creditor priority over other creditors.

[172] *Re Shepherd* (1889) 43 Ch. D. 131 CA; *Norburn v Norburn* [1894] 1 Q.B. 448.

[173] *Behbehani v Behbehani* [2020] 1 F.C.R 603 CA at [81].

[174] *Masri v Consolidated Contractors International (UK) Ltd (No. 2)* [2009] Q.B. 450 CA at [55]. Whether payment to a receiver of a foreign debt discharges the debt depends on the applicable law of the contract.

[175] *Masri v Consolidated Contractors International (UK) Ltd (No.2)* [2009] Q.B. 450 CA at [22]. The order in that case provided that the receiver could either sue in the name of the judgment debtor or in its own name.

[176] *Cruz City 1 Mauritius Holdings v Unitech Ltd* [2015] 1 All E.R. (Comm) 336 at [48].

[177] *Blight v Brewster* [2012] 1 W.L.R. 2841 at [76] (but no receiver appointed) and more recently *Bacci v Green* [2022] EWHC 486 (Ch); *Brake v Guy* [2022] EWHC 1746 (Ch); and *Lindsay v Michael* [2022] EWHC 1829 (QB).

[178] *Tasarruf Mevduati Sigorta Fonu v Merrill Lynch Bank and Trust Co (Cayman) Ltd* [2012] 1 W.L.R. 1721 PC.

[179] E.g. *JSC BTA Bank v Ablyazov* [2013] EWHC 1361 (Comm).

[180] *VB Football Assets v Blackpool Football Club (Properties) Ltd* [2019] 4 W.L.R. 93.

[181] *Denaxe Ltd v Cooper* [2002] 4 W.L.R. 52.

[182] *Masri v Consolidated Contractors International (UK) Ltd (No.2)* [2009] Q.B. 450 CA at [53]; *Stevens v Hutchinson* [1953] Ch. 299 at 305; *Re Sartoris's Estate* [1892] 1 Ch. 11 CA 12.

[183] *Re Marquis of Anglesey* [1903] 2 Ch. 727; *Lloyd's Bank v Medway Upper Navigation Co* [1905] 2 K.B. 359.

[184] *Tasarruf Mevduati Sigorta Fonu v Merrill Lynch Bank and Trust Co (Cayman) Ltd* [2012] 1 W.L.R. 1721 PC at [61]; *Blight v Brewster* [2012] 1 W.L.R. 2841 at [76].

[185] E.g. *Masri v Consolidated Contractors International (UK) Ltd (No.2)* [2009] Q.B. 450 CA at [23], [28], [183]. The order is helpfully appended to the Court of Appeal's judgment.

[186] E.g. *Masri v Consolidated Contractors International (UK) Ltd (N.2)* [2009] Q.B. 450 CA at [23], [28].

[187] *Masri v Consolidated Contractors International (UK) Ltd (No.2)* [2009] Q.B. 450 CA at [53]-[58], [71]; *JSC VTB Bank v Skurikhin* [2019] EWHC 1407 (Comm) [71]; *Re Potts Ex p Taylor* [1893] 1 QB 648 CA.

After the third sub-section, add new sub-section:

3C.   Assets amenable to equitable execution

It has been said that a receiver by way of equitable execution may be appointed over whatever may be considered in equity as the assets of the judgment debtor,[188] but this seems too narrow. Certainly the classical case is where the judgment debtor has an equitable interest that cannot be reached by legal execution, such as a non-discretionary interest under a trust[189] or an equity of redemption.[190] But the remedy is available more widely: **19-033**

(a)   A receiver may be appointed over assets which the judgment debtor owns absolutely, provided only that there is some hindrance or difficulty in using the normal processes of execution. Assets located outside England are one example.[191] Another is a claim to be indemnified by a third party which is not an attachable debt.[192]

(b)   A receiver may be appointed where there is, for the time being at least, no asset at all, as in the case of future debts,[193] the prospect of assets being distributed by the trustees of a discretionary trust to a nominee for the judgment debtor,[194] or, in an Irish case, future entitlements under a statutory scheme.[195]

(c)   Finally, a receiver may be appointed to exercise a power where this would result in assets vesting in the judgment debtor, such as a settlor's power to revoke a trust.[196] Lord Collins has said that the settlor's rights in such a case are "tantamount to ownership",[197] but this is confusing because the settlor does not have any interest, equitable or otherwise, in any asset until the power is exercised.[198]

[188] *Tasarruf Mevduati Sigorta Fonu v Merrill Lynch Bank and Trust Co (Cayman) Ltd* [2012] 1 W.L.R. 1721 PC at [6].

[189] *Webb v Stanton* (1883) 11 Q.B.D. 518 CA. A pure discretionary beneficiary of a trust has no proprietary interest and receivers cannot be appointed in terms that compel a trustee to exercise the discretion in favour of such a beneficiary. Similarly, de facto control over assets, in the sense that there is a practical likelihood that the holder would act on the judgment debtor' instruction, but no obligation on them to do so, is insufficient. See *JSC VTB Bank v Skurikhin* [2019] EWHC 1407 (Comm) [102]-[109].

[190] *Anglo-Italian Bank v Davies* (1878) 9 Ch. D. 275 CA.

[191] As in *Masri v Consolidated Contractors International (UK) Ltd (No.2)* [2009] Q.B. 450 CA itself.

[192] *Bourne v Colodense Ltd* [1985] I.C.R. 291 CA; *Maclaine Watson & Co Ltd v International Tin Council* [1988] Ch. 1 at 19-21 (Millett J) aff'd [1989] Ch. 253 CA.

[193] *Masri v Consolidated Contractors International (UK) Ltd (No.2)* [2009] Q.B. 450 CA; and see *Soinco SACI v Novokuznetsk Aluminium Plant* [1998] Q.B. 406. In *Holmes v Millage* [1893] 1 Q.B. 551 the Court of Appeal held that equitable execution cannot be used to in relation to future earnings, but they are now regulated by the Attachment of Earnings Act 1971.

[194] JSC *VTB Bank v Skurikhin* [2021] 1 W.L.R. 434 CA at [75].

[195] *ACC Loan Management Limited DAC v Rickard* [2019] IESC 29.

[196] *Quaere* whether a receiver may also be appointed to exercise a beneficiary's power to terminate a trust using the power recognised in *Saunders v Vauthier* (1841) Cr. & Ph. 240.

[197] *Tasarruf Mevduati Sigorta Fonu v Merrill Lynch Bank and Trust Co (Cayman) Ltd* [2012] 1 W.L.R. 1721 PC at [59].

[198] Smith, *"Execution against a power of revocation"* (2013) 129 L.Q.R. 332.

After the third sub-section, add new sub-section:

3D.   Assets outside the jurisdiction

19-034   Because the order does not affect title, but operates in personam, there is no rule preventing the court from making a receivership order by way of equitable execution in relation to foreign assets, provided the court has personal jurisdiction over the judgment debtor and subject matter jurisdiction in relation to the assets.[199] It is not a bar to the appointment of receivers that the English court's order will not or may not be recognised by the foreign court where the assets are located.[200] If the foreign court will not enforce the English court's order, including by recognising the receiver's authority, the order will still regulate the judgment debtor's conduct,[201] and their non-compliance may be sanctioned by contempt proceedings in England. Where assets are located outside England it will usually be appropriate to include in the order modified Babanaft provisos making clear that non-party foreigners are not affected by the order except to the extent it is enforced by a foreign court.[202]

[199] *Masri v Consolidated Contractors International (UK) Ltd (No.2)* [2009] Q.B. 450 CA at [50]-[58]; *Cruz City 1 Mauritius Holdings v Unitech Ltd* [2015] 1 All E.R. (Comm.) 336 at [35].

[200] *Derby & Co Ltd v Weldon (Nos 3 & 4)* [1990] Ch. 65 CA at 86; *Derby & Co Ltd v Weldon (No.6)* [1990] 1 W.L.R. 1139 CA at 1150; *Masri v Consolidated Contractors International (UK) Ltd (No.2)* [2009] Q.B. 450 CA at [69].

[201] In general, the order should not require the judgment debtor to do something which exposes it to a real danger of criminal liability under the law of its home state or the state where the assets are located: *Masri v Consolidated Contractors International Company SAL* [2008] EWHC 2492 (Comm) at [26]; *Cruz City 1 Mauritius Holdings v Unitech Ltd* [2015] 1 All E.R. (Comm) 336 at [39].

[202] *Masri v Consolidated Contractors International (UK) Ltd (No.2)* [2009] Q.B. 450 CA at [61], [71]; *Taurus Petroleum Ltd v State Oil Marketing Co of the Ministry of Oil, Iraq* [2016] 1 Lloyd's Rep. 42 CA at [33]-[37]; *Babanaft International Co SA v Bassatne* [1990] Ch. 13 CA.

CHAPTER 20

PERSONAL MONETARY CLAIMS

2. ACCOUNTING IN EQUITY

2. Accountability for Funds

Replace n.14 with:

[14] *John v Dodwell and Co* [1918] A.C. 563 PC at 569 ("a transmitted fiduciary obligation to ac-   **20-013**
count"); *British America Elevator Co Ltd v Bank of British North America* [1919] A.C. 658 PC at 663–
64; *Arthur v AG of Turks & Caicos Islands* [2012] UKPC 30 at [37]; and see Mitchell and Watterson,
"Remedies for Knowing Receipt" in Mitchell (ed), *Constructive and Resulting Trusts* (2010) and PG
Turner, "Accountability for profits derived from involvement in breach of fiduciary duty" [2018] CLJ
255.

(a) Proceedings for general accounts.

(1)   The right to an account.

Replace first paragraph with:

20-015   "Before a party can be ordered to account, liability to account must be established".[17] This liability arises immediately out of the defendant's receipt of property in an accountable capacity: the "basis of the duty to account is the fiduciary relationship".[18] The claimant bears the onus of proving that the defendant has received property into their control in circumstances sufficient to import an equitable obligation to handle the property for the benefit of another.[19] The liability to account does not depend on the defendant having mishandled the property or otherwise breached their trust.[20] If they wish, however, the claimant may prove specific irregularities at this stage, and if they succeed then the order will direct that the accounts be taken in light of the court's findings.[21] The claimant must also prove that an account has not been provided or is inadequate.[21a]

[17] *Associated Alloys Ltd v CAN 001 452 106 Pty Ltd* (2000) 171 A.L.R. 568 (HCA) at 585.

[18] *Attorney General v Cocke* [1988] Ch. 414 at 420; *Butler v Axco Trustees Ltd* (1997) J.L.R. N-17; *Sinclair Investments (UK) Ltd v Versailles Trade Finance Ltd* [2012] Ch. 453 CA at [45]; *Friends of Burbage School Ltd v Woodhams* [2012] EWHC 1511 (QB) at [10] (citing this passage); *Libertarian Investments Ltd v Hall* [2014] 1 H.K.C. 368 (CFA) at [167]; *Best v Ghose* [2018] IEHC 376 at [43] (citing this passage). It is no objection that the claimant is in turn accountable to a third party: *Barnett v Creggy* [2015] P.N.L.R. 13 at [66] (point not addressed on appeal: [2017] 2 W.L.R. 1054 CA).

[19] *Associated Alloys Ltd v CAN 001 452 106 Pty Ltd* (2000) 171 A.L.R. 568 (HCA) at 585. What must be shown is a fiduciary relationship in the sense of a relationship of custodial responsibility, as opposed to a relationship entailing a duty of undivided loyalty. Accordingly, even bare trustees are accountable. See *Cheong Soh Chin v Eng Chiet Shoong* [2019] 4 S.L.R. 714 at [38]; and *Al-Dowaison v Al-Salam* [2019] EWHC 301 (Ch) [111]–[112] (where the accounting parties were the companies that held the assets not the individuals who dealt with investors and whom the investors trusted).

[20] *Dowse v Gorton* [1891] A.C. 190, 204; *Partington v Reynolds* (1858) 4 Drew. 253 at 255–56, 62 E.R. 98 ("it is sufficient that the Defendant holds the office"); *Hodson v Ball* (1842) 12 L.J. Ch. 80.

[21] For example *Knott v Cottee* (1852) 16 Beav. 77, at 79–80, 51 E.R. 705. The order is reproduced in *Seton's Forms of Judgments and Orders*, 7th edn (1912) Vol.2, 1096–97.

[21a] *Ball v Ball* [2020] EWHC 1020 (Ch) [22].

Replace second paragraph with:

20-015   Since the Judicature reforms the court has enjoyed a discretion whether to order a general accounting even once the requisite relationship is proved. The court will ordinarily order an account where none has been given,[22] especially in cases involving conventional trusts,[22a] but it may refuse relief where the effect of the reversal of the onus of proof would be "to enable the plaintiff to blackmail the defendant",[23] or where an account is unnecessary or disproportionate or premature or unlikely to be fruitful.[24] The court may need to have regard to the information that has already been provided, any difficulties the accounting party may now face, and the motivation for seeking an account.[25] It may be appropriate to order an account only of particular assets or transactions.

[22] *Henchley v Thompson* [2017] W.T.L.R. 1289 at [25], [60]; *Al-Dowaison v Al-Salam* [2019] EWHC 301 (Ch) at [148].

[22a] *Ball v Ball* [2020] EWHC 1020 (Ch) [21], distinguishing commercial cases, where an accounting may only have practical utility if it may lead to a financial claim.

[23] *Campbell v Gillespie* [1900] 1 Ch. 225, at 229.

24 *Libertarian Investments Ltd v Hall* [2014] 1 H.K.C. 368 (CFA) at [172]; *Henchley v Thompson* [2017] W.T.L.R. 1289 (citing a predecessor of this passage).

25 *Al-Dowaison v Al-Salam* [2019] EWHC 301 (Ch) at [150]–[152].

Replace third paragraph with:
A claim to enforce an equitable duty to account (as opposed to a contractual duty)[26] is not subject to any statutory limitation, but the consequences of the passage of time, and any delay in bringing the claim, may be taken into account by the court in exercising its discretion whether to allow the claim.[27] Statutory limitations may affect claims for consequential relief relating to assets or amounts revealed by the account, and the fact that any consequential relief would be time-barred may be a reason to refuse to order an account.[28]

26 *Coultard v Disco Mix Club Ltd* [2000] 1 W.L.R. 707 at 728.

27 *Henchley v Thompson* [2017] W.T.L.R. 1289 at [31]–[33]; *Al-Dowaison v Al-Salam* [2019] EWHC 301 (Ch) at [134]–[144] and [147].

28 *Al-Dowaison v Al-Salam* [2019] EWHC 301 (Ch) at [150]; but compare *Henchley v Thompson* [2017] W.T.L.R. 1289 at [35].

(2) Settled accounts.

Replace paragraph with:
It is a good defence to a claim for an account for the defendant to prove that they **20-016** have been released from their duty to account by a settlement.[29] If the accounts have been settled then the claim will be defeated unless the beneficiary can show that the settlement was obtained by fraud or imposition,[30] or that it contains sufficient errors of sufficient magnitude to warrant setting it aside and taking the accounts from the beginning.[31] If the claimant can only prove errors of a lesser number or magnitude then they will be granted liberty to surcharge and falsify.[32] By this order the master is only directed to rectify specific errors in the settled account, the onus falling on the claimant.

29 *Re Webb* [1894] 1 Ch. 73 CA at 80; *Chng Weng Wah v Goh Bak Heng* [2016] 2 S.L.R. 464 CA. The duty to account is owed to the beneficiaries and cannot be satisfied by a settlement between co-trustees: *Re Fish* [1893] 2 Ch. 413 CA.

30 *Vernon v Vawdry* (1740) 2 Atk. 119, 26 E.R. 474; *Allfrey v Allfrey* (1849) 1 M. & G. 87, at 93, 41 E.R. 1195; *Coleman v Mellersh* (1850) 2 Mac. & G. 309 at 314, 42 E.R. 119; *Re Webb* [1894] 1 Ch. 73 CA at 80.

31 *Williamson v Barbour* (1877) 9 Ch. D. 529.

32 *Dawson v Dawson* (1737) West 171, 25 E.R. 879; 1 Atk 1, 26 E.R. 1; *Pitt v Cholmondeley* (1754) 2 Ves. Sen. 565, 28 E.R. 360; *Gething v Keighley* (1878) 9 Ch. D. 547.

(3) Taking the account.

Replace first paragraph with:
What information and documents an accounting party must provide depends on **20-017** the circumstances and should be considered at the hearing. The essential requirement is the account must say what the assets were, what has been done with them, what the assets now are, and what distributions have taken place.[32a] The account must inform and where necessary explain. Depending on the case, the beneficiaries may therefore be entitled to sufficient material to enable them to understand the movements on the account, the nature of the investments, the monies expended and recovered; the income earned; the expenses paid; and how, and when and on what basis investment decisions were made.[33] In some cases this may require formal trust

accounts but in other cases less formal documents may suffice or a narrative explanation may be required.[34]

[32a] *Ball v Ball* [2020] EWHC 1020 (Ch) [24], [58].

[33] *Best v Ghose* [2018] IEHC 376 at [92]–[97].

[34] *Royal National Lifeboat Institution v Hedley* [2016] EWHC 1948 (Ch) at [11]; *Ball v Ball* [2020] EWHC 1020 (Ch).

(4)   Burden of proof.

Replace n.37 with:

20-018   [37] *Angullia Salleh Angullia v Estate and Trust Agencies* (1927) Ltd [1938] A.C. 624 PC at 637; *Bacon v Clark* (1837) 3 My. & C. 294, 297; 40 E.R. 938; *Jevon v Bush* (1685) 1 Vern. 342, 343; 23 E.R. 508; *Ross River Ltd v Waveley Commercial Ltd* [2014] 1 B.C.L.C. 545 CA at [96]; *Exsus Travel Ltd v Turner* [2015] C.P. Rep. 7 CA at [22] (citing this passage).

(6)   Discharges.

Replace paragraph with:

20-020   Discharge operates in an accounting to extinguish the accountable party's responsibility for their receipts. An accounting party is entitled to a discharge in respect of all payments and transfers necessary to carry out any of the duties and powers they are invested with.[47] What discharges may be claimed depends on the mandate of the particular accounting party. There are three types: first, discharges for proper payments to the beneficiary or at their command;[48] secondly, discharges for proper administrative outlays, collectively known as just allowances[49]; and thirdly, discharges for property lost or stolen through no fault of the accounting party.[50] A trustee who validly exercises a power to sell, exchange or invest trust property will be charged with the proceeds or investment in place of the property used to acquire it.[51]

[47] *Worral v Harford* (1802) 8 Ves. 4 at 8, 32 E.R. 250.

[48] *Nightingale v Lawson* (1784) 1 Cox. 23, 29 E.R. 1045.

[49] *Worral v Harford* (1802) 8 Ves. Jun. 4 at 8, 32 E.R. 250; *Forshaw v Higginson* (1857) 8 De G. M. & G. 827 CA, at 834, 44 E.R. 609; and see s.31 of the Trustee Act 2000.

[50] *Morley v Morley* (1678) 2 Ch. Cas. 2, 22 E.R. 817; *Re Gasquoine* [1894] 1 Ch. 470 CA; *Jobson v Plamer* [1893] 1 Ch. 71; *Job v Job* (1877) 6 Ch. D. 562.

[51] *Re Salmon* (1889) 42 Ch. D. 351 CA at 368.

(7)   Misapplications.

Replace final paragraph with:

20-021   However, in *Target Holdings Ltd v Redferns*,[65] the House of Lords held that, at least in the case of a non-traditional commercial trust, a trustee should not be required to reconstitute a trust from which they have misapplied assets where the same loss (in the sense of abstract harm) would have occurred if the trust had been performed in accordance with its terms. This controversial decision was thought by many to confuse the liability of trustees to pay reparative compensation for losses caused by a breach of trust with their liability to account for the trust property.[66] However, in *AIB Group (UK) Plc v Mark Redler & Co Solicitors*,[67] the Supreme Court declined to reconsider the approach adopted in *Target Holdings Ltd v Redferns*, and indeed extended the approach to traditional trusts. According to the court, the basic model is that the trustee must restore the trust fund to the financial position it would have occupied if the trustee had performed his obligation. Foreseeability of loss is irrelevant, but compensation should not exceed the loss caused by the breach of trust, in the sense that the loss must flow directly from the breach.[68] This decision has not been well received in all quarters[69] and it is clear from subsequent cases that important issues remain to be considered.[69a]

[65] *Target Holdings Ltd v Redferns* [1996] 1 A.C. 421 at 434.

[66] See, e.g. Millett (1998) 114 L.Q.R. 214.

[67] *AIB Group (UK) Plc v Mark Redler & Co Solicitors* [2015] A.C. 1503.

[68] See also *Barnett v Creggy* [2017] 2 W.L.R. 1054 CA, per Sales LJ at [45].

[69] Critics include Millett (2018) 32 Trust LI 44; Gummow (2015) 41 *Australian Bar Review* 5; Watts [2015] L.M.C.L.Q. 118; Lee (2015) 9 *Journal of Equity* 94; Shaw-Mellors [2015] J.B.L. 165; Edelman, Penner and Ho in Degeling and Varuhas (eds), *Equitable Compensation and Disgorgement of Profits* (2017).

[69a] See especially *Main v Giambrone & Law (a firm)* [2018] P.N.L.R. 2 CA; *Interactive Technology Corp Ltd v Ferster* [2018] EWCA Civ 1594; and *Auden McKenzie (Pharma Division) Limited v Patel* [2020] B.C.C. 316 CA.

(8)   Consequential relief.

Replace n.72 with:

[72] *Hancom v Allen* (1774) 2 Dick. 498, 21 E.R. 363; *Target Holdings Ltd v Redferns* [1996] A.C. 421, **20-022** 434; *Hillsdown Plc v Pensions Ombudsman* [1997] 1 All E.R. 862 at 897.

(b)   Accounts on the footing of wilful default.

(1)   Wilful default.

Replace paragraph with:
The term wilful default is used in this branch of the law in a technical sense that **20-024** is synonymous with breach of trust: where custodial fiduciaries "do that which it is their duty not to do, or omit to do that which it is their duty to do then that is wilful neglect and default".[75] It is not necessary that the fiduciary knows that their act constitutes a breach of duty.[76] A failure to meet the applicable standard of care constitutes wilful default as much as intentional wrongdoing.[77] It is sometimes said that wilful default involves passive as opposed to active breach of trust,[78] but this distinction is neither helpful nor correct.[79]

[75] *Re Owens* (1882) 47 L.T. 61 CA; *Shah v Shah* [2020] EWHC 1840 (Ch) [76] (citing this paragraph); and see Stannard [1979] Conv. 345.

[76] *Walker v Symonds* (1818) 3 Swn. 1, 69, 36 E.R. 751; *Re Owens* (1882) 47 L.T. 61 CA, at 63; *AIB Group (UK) Plc v Mark Redler & Co Solicitors* [2015] A.C. 1503 at [54].

[77] *Speight v Gaunt* (1883) 9 App. Cas. 1, 14; *Re Chapman* [1896] 2 Ch. 763 CA at 776, 779–80; *Armitage v Nurse* [1998] Ch. 241 CA at 252.

[78] *Re Wrightson* [1908] 1 Ch. 789 at 799; *Bartlett v Barclays Bank Trust Co Ltd (No.2)* [1980] Ch. 515, 546; *Meehan v Glazier Holdings Pty Ltd* (2002) 54 N.S.W.L.R. 146 at [13]–[14]; *Juul v Northey* [2010] NSWCA 211 at [180].

[79] For example, a trustee who imprudently invests funds on a loss-making but authorised security is chargeable on the basis of wilful default although the misconduct is active: *Re Chapman* [1896] 2 Ch. 763 CA. Similarly a trustee who lets property at less than fair market value: *Noyes v Pollock* (1886) 32 Ch. D. 53 at 61. The distinction between active and passive breaches of trust has been criticised in Australia: *Glazier Holdings Pty Ltd v Australian Men's Health (No.2)* [2001] NSWSC 6 at [56].

(3) Availability.

Replace n.88 with:

20-026   88 *Coope v Carter* (1852) 2 De G.M. & G. 292 at 298, 42 E.R. 884.

(4) Surcharge for wilful default.

Replace paragraph with:

20-027   Where a custodial fiduciary is found to have caused the fund to suffer a loss through their wilful default, their account will be surcharged in the amount of the loss, and the fiduciary will be required to make the loss good.[90] The loss is accounted for on the incoming side of the account as if the fiduciary had received more. This is only a technique used to bring the loss into the *schema* of the account, and it is an error to infer from the fact that the loss is accounted for as if it had been a receipt that the surcharge represents a receipt that never materialised.[90a] It is a double error to infer that the only breaches that can be addressed in this type of proceeding are breaches that result in the custodial fiduciary not receiving an asset that they would have received if they had done their duty.[91] The governing concept is compensation for loss caused by breach of duty, although this has not always been appreciated.[92] It has been held in Singapore that upon an accounting of this type, the court may also order an account of profits.[92a]

90 *AIB Group (UK) Plc v Mark Redler & Co Solicitors* [2015] A.C. 1503 at [54].

90a For example *Sim Poh Ping v Winsta Holding Pte Ltd* [2020] SGCA 35 at [120].

91 For example, a trustee may be charged on the basis of wilful default where they invest the fund negligently, or where they fail to safeguard the fund by monitoring others: *Re Chapman* [1896] 2 Ch. 763 CA; *Re Brier* (1884) 256 Ch. D. 238 CA at 243–44.

92 For example *Meehan v Glazier Holdings Pty Ltd* (2002) 54 N.S.W.L.R. 146 CA at [14], [65]; *Juul v Northey* [2010] NSWCA 211; *Grace v Grace* [2012] NSWSC 976 at [215]–[220].

92a *UVJ v UVH* [2020] SGCA 49, which also contains a valuable general discussion of procedural aspects of accounting on the footing of wilful default.

3. EQUITABLE COMPENSATION

Replace n.93 with:

20-028   93 *Bristol and West Building Society v Mothew* [1998] Ch. 1 CA at 17; *Libertarian Investments Ltd v Hall* [2014] 1 H.K.C. 368 (CFA) at [168] and [170]; *Agricultural Land Management Ltd v Jackson (No.2)* [2014] WASC 102 at [334]–[375]; *Interactive Technology Corp Ltd v Ferster* [2018] EWCA Civ 1594; *Zhang Hong Liv DBS Bank (Hong Kong) Limited* [2019] HKCFA 45; *Sim Poh Ping v Winsta Holding Pte Ltd* [2020] SGCA 35 (a particularly valuable discussion).

1. Reparative Compensation

20-033   **(d) Dishonest assistance.**   Replace n.110 with: See Ch.30 and Elliott and Mitchell (2004) 67 M.L.R. 16.

2. Substitutive Compensation

Replace paragraph with:

20-035   For instance, this concept applies where upon the specific performance of a contract, a vendor is obliged to pay compensation for defects in the asset,[113] and also where upon rescission a party cannot return an asset in specie or cannot return it in the same condition.[114] Classically, where a custodial fiduciary had misapplied assets, on the taking of their account they would be charged with the value of the asset.[115] Their personal liability to pay this amount, conventionally labelled compensation,[116] involved an obligation to perform their duties in respect of the asset substitutively and the compensation was a substitute for the missing asset. However, the effect of *AIB Group (UK) Plc v Mark Redler & Co Solicitors* has been to superimpose an essentially reparative model of liability in this situation to the extent that liability should not exceed the loss that would have occurred if the trustee had done his duty.[117] The extent and limits of this ruling remain unclear. In the most recent appellate decision, *Auden McKenzie (Pharma Division) Limited v Patel*,[117a] the Court of Appeal indicated that liability to restore a payment made by directors of a company in breach of fiduciary duty should not be limited by reference to the (assumed) fact that if the company had not made that payment, it could and would have made a payment of the same amount to the same recipient but in a lawful manner.

[113] See section 6 below.

[114] See section 5 below.

[115] See section 2(a)(7) above. In *Davies v Ford* [2021] EWHC 2550 (Ch) at [106]–[108], the court held that a substitutive form of equitable compensation is appropriate where the breach involved the misappropriation of existing trust property, in which case it is not open to the trustee to argue that the property would have been lost or paid away even if he or she had not been in breach, and on a reparative basis in other cases.

[116] This is sometimes called "restitution" or "restoration", e.g. *Re Paycheck Services 3 Ltd* [2011] Bus L.R. 111 HL at [48], where Lord Hope contrasted this remedy with "damages or equitable compensation", meaning reparative compensation; and *Ahmed v Ingram* [2018] B.P.I.R. 535 CA at [34].

[117] *AIB Group (UK) Plc v Mark Redler & Co Solicitors* [2015] A.C. 1503.

[117a] *Auden McKenzie (Pharma Division) Limited v Patel* [2020] B.C.C. 316 CA.

4. ACCOUNT OF PROFITS

Delete n.118.   20-036

1. Nature of Relief

Replace paragraph with:

Relief given by way of an account of profits is measured by the gain made by   **20-037** the wrongdoer irrespective of whether the claimant has suffered a corresponding loss.[119] On the taking of the account, the object is "to determine as accurately as possible the true measure of the profit or benefit obtained".[120] Typically, the court must determine the sums impermissibly received and deduct any allowable expenses.[121] An account of profits therefore proceeds on a different principle from reparative compensatory damages or equitable compensation. The principle is also different from that which regulates awards of damages on the user basis, where the claimant is compensated for the invasion of their rights by an award reflecting the price at which they might have licensed the relaxation of their right in a hypothetical negotiation.[121] Those damages also deprive the defendant of a gain but it is of a different type to the gain to be disgorged upon an account of profits. The former is, in a sense, objective and the latter, in a sense, subjective. Neither remedy necessarily yields a greater quantum of recovery than the other.[122]

[119] *Attorney General v Blake* [2001] 1 A.C. 268, at 280 (Lord Nicholls); *Murad v Al-Saraj* [2005] W.T.L.R. 1573 CA at [67].

[120] *Warman International Ltd v Dwyer* (1995) 182 C.L.R. 544 at 588; *Re Jarvis* [1958] 1 W.L.R. 815 at 820.

[121] In an intellectual property context, see *Lifestyle Equities CV v Santa Monica Polo Club Limited* [2020] EWHC 688 (Ch) [59] and, in relation to the allowable expenses, *OOO Abbott v Design and Display Ltd* [2017] F.S.R. 43 (IPEC) [57].

[121] As to this distinction and awards on the user basis, see amongst others *Attorney General v Blake* [2001] 1 A.C. 268; *Experience Hendrix LLC v PPX Enterprises Inc* [2003] 1 All E.R. (Comm) 830 CA; *WWF—World Wide Fund for Nature v World Wrestling Federation Entertainment Inc* [2007] Bus L.R. 1252 CA; *Devenish Nutrition Ltd v Sanofi-Aventis SA* [2009] Ch. 390 CA; *Pell Frischmann Engineering Ltd v Bow Valley Iran Ltd* [2011] 1 W.L.R. 2370 PC.

[122] *FHR European Ventures LLP v Cedar Capital Partners LLC* [2015] A.C. 250. The question whether the claimant may elect between personal and proprietary remedies, and the date at which an asset should be valued for the purposes of the personal remedy, were discussed in *Global Energy Horizons Corp v Gray* [2015] EWHC 2232 (Ch) at [128]–[144].

Replace n.123 with:

20-038   [123] *FHR European Ventures LLP v Cedar Capital Partners LLC* [2015] A.C. 250..

2.   Availability

(a)   Breach of fiduciary duty.

Replace paragraph with:

20-040   A fiduciary who gains unauthorised profits within the scope of their duty will generally be obliged to account for those profits to their beneficiary or principal.[125] The same is true of bribes.[126] The liability is strict and inflexible. It is no answer that the principal could not himself have taken up the profitable opportunity or that the fiduciary would have made the profit even if they had acted properly, for example by making full disclosure and obtaining their principal's consent.[127] The applicable principles are considered in Ch.7.

[125] Classical cases include *Keech v Sandford* (1726) Sel. Cas. Ch. 61, 25 E.R. 223; *Regal (Hastings) Ltd v Gulliver* [1942] 1 All E.R. 378; and *Boardman v Phipps* [1967] 2 A.C. 46.

[126] For example *Reading v AG* [1951] A.C. 507.

[127] *Gwembe Valley Development Co Ltd v Koshy* [2004] 1 B.C.L.C. 131 CA; *Murad v Al-Saraj* [2005] W.T.L.R. 1573 CA; *Parr v Keystone Healthcare Ltd* [2019] EWCA Civ 1246; [2019] 4 W.L.R. 99 CA. Contrast the position in Singapore, *UVJ v UVH* [2020] SGCA 49.

(b)   Accessories.

Replace paragraph with:

20-041   Those who assist dishonestly in a breach of trust or of fiduciary duty, and apparently those who knowingly receive trust property,[128] may also be required to account for profits they gain as a result.[129] The remedy is more restricted than that available against a fiduciary. First, an accessory will only be accountable for profits they gain as a sufficiently direct causal result of their misconduct, so that even profits they would not otherwise have gained may be excluded from the account if the misconduct was not their effective cause.[130] Secondly, the court has a discretion to withhold the remedy if, for example, it would be disproportionate.[131] A dishonest assistant is not accountable for profits gained by the primary wrongdoer.[132]

[128] *Ultraframe (UK) Ltd v Fielding* [2005] EWHC 1638 (Ch) at [1577]; and, in Australia, *Grimaldi v Chameleon Mining NL (No.2)* [2012] FCAFC 6 at [253], [555]. See also *Akita Holdings Ltd v Attorney General of the Turks and Caicos Islands* [2017] A.C. 590 (PC –TCI), which, although put on the basis

the company was a knowing recipient, may be better explained on the basis the company was the wrongdoing fiduciary's vehicle and accountable jointly with him.

[129] *Novoship (UK) Ltd v Nikitin* [2015] Q.B. 499 CA confirming a line of first instance authority. The case did not involve a knowing recipient but the Court indicated (at [80]) that the same remedy is in principle available. See generally Elliott and Mitchell "Remedies for Dishonest Assistance" (2004) 67 M.L.R. 17; and Mitchell and Watterson, "Remedies for Knowing Receipt" in Mitchell (ed), *Constructive and Resulting Trusts* (2010); Glister, "Accounts of Profits and Third Parties" in Degeling and Varuhas (eds), *Equitable Compensation and Disgorgement of Profit* (2017).

[130] *Novoship (UK) Ltd v Nikitin* [2015] Q.B. 499 CA at [94]–[115]. See also the High Court of Australia's discussion of related issues in *Ancient Order of Foresters in Victoria Friendly Society Ltd v Lifeplan Australia Friendly Society Ltd* (2018) 360 A.L.R. 1, noted by Ridge (2019) J Eq 69.

[131] *Novoship (UK) Ltd v Nikitin* [2015] Q.B. 499 CA at [119].

[132] *Ultraframe (UK) Ltd v Fielding* [2005] EWHC 1638 (Ch) at [1595]–[1601]; *Novoship (UK) Ltd v Mikhaylyuk* [2012] EWHC 3586 (Comm) [99]; *Electrosteel Castings (UK) Ltd v Metalpol Ltd* [2014] EWHC 2017 (Ch) at [50]–[51]. This proposition has been treated as also applicable where defendants are jointly and severally liable for infringements of intellectual property: *Lifestyle Equities CV v Santa Monica Polo Club Limited* [2020] EWHC 688 (Ch) [35].

(c) Infringement of intellectual property and breach of confidence.

Replace paragraph with:

Courts of equity traditionally awarded accounts of profits gained through the **20-042** infringement of intellectual property or breach of confidence.[133] Relief of this type was seen as a corollary of injunctive relief.[134] As to intellectual property infringements, the remedy has in several cases been put onto a statutory footing.[135] There is unevenness in relation to the question whether an innocent infringer may be made to account. The Patents Act 1977 provides a defence for infringers who were not aware of the patent and had no reasonable grounds for supposing it to exist.[136] By contrast, it has been said, obiter dicta, that there is no similar defence in relation to claims under the Copyrights, Designs and Patents Act 1988.[137] The position is more complicated in relation to passing off and trade mark infringement.[138] A strong line of authority predating the Trade Marks Act 1994 exempted innocent infringers from liability.[139] However it has been held under the 1994 Act that an innocent infringer may be made to account.[140] The principles governing accounts of the profits gained through breaches of confidence are considered in Ch.9.

[133] Damages are available on the user basis for patent infringements and breaches of other intellectual property rights of a proprietary character: *Stoke-on-Trent City Council v W & J Wass Ltd* [1988] 1 W.L.R. 1406 CA at 1410–12; *Experience Hendrix LLC v PPX Enterprises Inc* [2003] 1 All E.R. (Comm) 830 CA at [18] and [26]; *One Step (Support) Ltd v Morris-Garner* [2019] A.C. 649 at [95]. Such damages are usually assessed by reference to a reasonable licence fee: *Henderson v All Around the World Recordings Ltd* [2014] EWHC 2087 (IPEC) at [18]–[19]; *Reformation Publishing Co Ltd v Cruiseco Ltd* [2019] Bus. L.R. 78 at [46].

[134] *Hogg v Kirby* (1803) 8 Ves. Jun 215, 32 E.R. 336; *Cartier v Carlisle* (1862) 31 Beav. 292, 54 E.R. 1151; *Lever v Goodwin* (1887) 36 Ch. D. 1.

[135] The history of these developments is traced in Kremer (2018) 12 J Eq 168.

[136] Patents Act 1977 s.62(1).

[137] *Wienerworld Ltd v Vision Video Ltd* [1998] F.S.R. 832. This had been held to be the case under the Copyrights Act 1956: *Potton Ltd v Yorkclose Ltd* [1990] F.S.R. 11.

[138] See s.14(2) of the Trade Marks Act 1994.

[139] *Edelsten v Edelsten* (1863) 1 De G.J. & S. 185, 26 E.R. 72; *Moet v Couston* (1864) 33 Beav. 578, 55 E.R. 493; *A G Spalding & Bros v A W Gamage Ltd* (1915) 32 R.P.C. 273 HL; *Colbeam Palmer Ltd v Stock Affiliates Pty Ltd* (1968) 122 C.L.R. 25.

[140] *Microsoft Corp v Plato Technology Ltd* [1999] F.S.R. 834; and on appeal (1999) 22 I.P.D. 22108.

(e) Torts.

Replace n.150 with:

20-044 [150] *Forsyth-Grant v Allen* [2008] Env L.R. 41 CA. In *Coventry v Lawrence* [2014] A.C. 822 the Supreme Court left open the possibility of damages assessed by reference to the benefit to the defendant of not suffering an injunction.

5. MONETARY AWARDS RELATING TO RESCISSION

3. Damages in Lieu of Rescission

After "had been rescinded.", add new n.183a:

20-057 [183a] *SK Shipping Europe plc v Capital VLCC 3 Corp* [2020] EWHC 3448 (Comm) at [237], and as to the measurement of damages [247]–[254] (all obiter dicta).

6. MONETARY AWARDS RELATING TO SPECIFIC PERFORMANCE AND INJUNCTIONS

1. Damages Under Lord Cairns' Act

20-058 **(a) Lord Cairns' Act.** *Remove footnote 188 from title.*

(b) Scope of the jurisdiction.

Replace paragraph with:

20-059   The principal object of Lord Cairns' Act was to enable the Court of Chancery, when declining to grant equitable relief and leaving the plaintiff to their remedy at law, to award the plaintiff damages itself instead of sending them to the common law courts to obtain that alternative relief.[189] The merger of jurisdictions brought about by the Judicature Act 1873 had the consequence that any division of the High Court may now award both specific relief and damages in the same proceedings so that the power to award damages in addition to other relief has lost its significance.[189a] The power to award damages in substitution for other relief turned out, however, to have been a substantive innovation with lasting consequences[190] Under this rubric the courts may award damages in two circumstances in which damages were previously not given by any court. First, Lord Cairns' Act created a power to award damages for breach of certain purely equitable rights, such as a covenant running with the land only in equity.[191] Secondly, Lord Cairns' Act created a power to give relief in certain cases where a cause of action has not yet accrued. Damages are recoverable at common law only in respect of causes of action which are complete at the date of the claim form; damages for future or repeated wrongs must be made the subject of fresh proceedings. Damages in substitution for an injunction, however, may encompass prospective loss resulting from continuing infringement[192] and indeed damages may be given in substitution for a quia timet injunction where the wrong has only been threatened.[193] Similarly, damages for breach of contract may be given under Lord Cairns' Act in substitution for specific performance even though the claim form preceded completion so that there was not yet a breach.[194]

[189] *Ferguson v Wilson* (1866) L.R. 2 Ch. App. 77, 88.

[189a] Senior Courts Act 1981 s.49; *Morris-Garner v One Step (Support) Ltd* [2019] A.C. 649 at [43].

[190] Reynolds argues that this was a wrong turn: (2019) 13 J Eq 46.

[191] *Eastwood v Lever* (1863) 4 De G.J. & S. 114, 46 E.R. 859 CA; *Wrotham Park Estate Co v Parkside Homes Ltd* [1974] 1 W.L.R. 798 is a more recent example.

[192] *Bracewell v Appleby* [1975] Ch. 408; *Jaggard v Sawyer* [1995] 1 W.L.R. 269 CA.

[193] *Leeds Industrial Co-operative Society Ltd v Slack* [1924] A.C. 851; *Hooper v Rogers* [1975] Ch. 43 CA

[194] *Hasham v Zenab* [1960] A.C. 316; *Oakacre Ltd v Claire Cleaners (Holdings) Ltd* [1982] Ch. 197.

(c) Availability of the jurisdiction. *Change title of paragraph 20-060 to:* Availability of the jurisdiction. **20-060**

Replace second paragraph with:
   Whether the court has jurisdiction to award damages under Lord Cairns' Act depends on whether, at the date of the claim form, the court *could* (however unwisely) have granted specific relief, not whether it *would* have done so.[197] Jurisdiction will therefore be declined if, at the date of the claim form, it was impossible to grant specific relief.[198] Damages may, however, be awarded if there is jurisdiction to give specific relief but it is refused on some discretionary ground[199] such as laches,[200] acquiescence[201] or mistake,[202] or if a grant of specific relief would for some reason be inappropriate.[203] Burrows argues that the essential question is whether the claimant had an arguable case for specific relief when the proceedings began.[203a]

[197] *City of London Brewery Co v Tennant* (1873) L.R. 9 Ch. App. 212; *Hooper v Rogers* [1975] Ch. 43 at 48; *Pell Frischmann Engineering Ltd v Bow Valley Iran Ltd* [2011] 1 W.L.R. 2370 PC at [48] and [54], Lord Walker said that equitable damages can be given even if the claimant had no prospect of being granted an injunction, but Lord Sumption doubted this in *Morris-Garner v One Step (Support) Ltd* [2019] A.C. 649 at [113].

[198] *Lavery v Pursell* (1888) 39 Ch. D. 508 (lapse of time); *Rogers v Challis* (1859) 27 Beav. 175 (contract to borrow money); *Hipgrave v Case* (1885) 28 Ch. D. 356 (performance impossible because of sale of land by claimant to a third party); *Proctor v Bayley* (1889) 42 Ch. D. 390 (no threat to continue the wrong).

[199] *Wroth v Tyler* [1974] Ch. 30; *Price v Strange* [1978] Ch. 337 at 358–360, 368–370.

[200] *McKenna v Richey* [1950] V.L.R. 360; and see *Eastwood v Lever* (1863) 4 De G.J. & S. 114; *Senior v Pawson* (1866) L.R. 3 Eq. 330; *Sayers v Collyer* (1884) 24 Ch. D. 103, all cases on refusal of injunctions.

[201] *Gafford v Graham* [1999] 41 E.G. 159.

[202] *Dell v Beasley* [1959] N.Z.L.R. 89.

[203] *Tito v Waddell (No.2)* [1977] Ch. 106 at 321–323, 325–328 (damages instead of replanting of trees over a small number of isolated plots). But in an appropriate case the reason which lead the court to refuse specific performance may also lead it to refuse to make an order for damages in substitution thereof: *Gafford v Graham* [1999] 41 E.G. 159 (injunction refused on basis of acquiescence).

[203a] Burrows, *Remedies for Torts, Breach of Contract, and Equitable Wrongs* (4th edn 2019) 315-316.

Replace third paragraph with:
   Where the claimant seeks specific relief, the court may award damages under Lord Cairns' Act even though damages was not included in the prayer.[204] Equally, it has been said that a claimant who is content to receive damages under Lord Cairns' Act is entitled to say so in terms, and does not have to make the pretence of seeking non-monetary relief,[205] but this has been doubted.[205a]

[204] See *Betts v Neilson* (1868) L.R. 3 Ch. App. 429 at 441.

205 *Pell Frischmann Engineering Ltd v Bow Valley Iran Ltd* [2011] 1 W.L.R. 2370 PC at [48]; *Jaggard v Sawyer* [1995] 1 W.L.R. 269 CA at 285.

205a *Morris-Garner v One Step (Support) Ltd* [2019] A.C. 649 at [45] (Lord Reed) and Burrows, *Remedies for Torts, Breach of Contract, and Equitable Wrongs* (4th edn 2019) 315-316.

(d) Damages in substitution for injunctions.

Replace paragraph with:

20-061 The court can properly award damages "once and for all" in respect of future infringements because it awards them in substitution for an injunction and to compensate for those future wrongs which an injunction would have prevented.[206] Since the practical consequence of withholding injunctive relief is to authorise the continuance of an unlawful state of affairs, the doctrine of res judicata operates to prevent the claimant and their successors in title from bringing proceedings thereafter to recover even nominal damages in respect of further wrongs for which the claimant has been fully compensated. For this reason, it has been said that the jurisdiction to award damages in respect of future wrongs (or, rather, the refusal to grant an injunction in respect of such wrongs) should be exercised with caution.[207] On one view, an injunction should not be refused so as to "allow a wrong to continue simply because the wrongdoer is able and willing to pay for the injury he may inflict".[208] However, in *Coventry v Lawrence*[209] the Supreme Court moved away from a mechanical application of the criteria identified in some earlier authorities, at least in cases of nuisance. The decision lies in the unfettered discretion of the court, which is free to take into account, amongst other things, matters of public interest, as well as the effect of a nuisance on third parties.[210] The principles to be applied when considering whether an injunction should be granted are considered in greater detail in Ch.18.

206 *Attorney General v Blake* [2001] 1 A.C. 268 at 281.

207 *Shelfer v City of London Electric Lighting Co* [1895] 1 Ch. 287 at 315–316; also *Cowper v Laidler* [1903] 2 Ch. 337 at 341. For examples of the exercise of such caution, see *Kennaway v Thompson* [1981] Q.B. 88 (limited injunction granted); and *Tetley v Chitty* [1986] 1 All E.R. 663 (damages insufficient remedy).

208 *Shelfer v City of London Electric Lighting Co* [1895] 1 Ch. 287 at 315, 316; applied in *Kelsen v Imperial Tobacco Co (of Great Britain and Ireland) Ltd* [1957] 2 Q.B. 334.

209 *Coventry v Lawrence* [2014] A.C. 822.

210 See especially para.18-044.

(f) Measure of damages.

Replace first paragraph with:

20-063 In *Johnson v Agnew*, Lord Wilberforce said he found in Lord Cairns' Act "no warrant for the court awarding damages differently from common law damages".[211] In *Morris-Garner v One Step (Support) Ltd*, Lord Reed, speaking for a majority of the Supreme Court albeit obiter dicta, indicated that this statement must be read with caution because the measure of damages reflects the special character of the statutory jurisdiction.[212] Damages are said to be given as a monetary substitute for an injunction. They compensate for loss,[213] being the loss the applicant suffers by the refusal of specific relief.[214] However this can be misread. Consistently with earlier cases, what Lord Reed seems to have meant is that damages may be given under the statute as compensation not only for injuries caused by past breaches but also for injuries expected to be caused by future breaches.[214a] Otherwise damages are calculated in the same way in which they would be in a non-statutory case.

[211] *Johnson v Agnew* [1980] A.C. 367 at 400.

[212] *Morris-Garner v One Step (Support) Ltd* [2019] A.C. 649 at [43], [47] and [62]. But compare *Turf Club Auto Emporium Pte Ltd v Yeo Boong Hua* [2018] 2 S.L.R. 655 CA at [286]. The Supreme Court's approach is pointedly criticised by Peel in "Negotiating damages after One Step" (2019) 35 JCL 1.

[213] In *Lunn Poly Ltd v Liverpool & Lancashire Properties Ltd* [2006] 2 E.G.L.R. 29 CA at [22], [24], Neuberger LJ mooted the possibility that within this jurisdiction an account might be given of the profits the defendant had made, is making and will make as a result of the breach, but that is inconsistent with the decision of the Supreme Court in *Morris-Garner v One Step (Support) Ltd* [2019] A.C. 649 at, e.g. [68]–[70], [95(3)]. The Singapore Court of Appeal arrived at the same conclusion in *Turf Club Auto Emporium Pte Ltd v Yeo Boong Hua* [2018] 2 S.L.R. 655 CA at [271].

[214] *Morris-Garner v One Step (Support) Ltd* [2019] A.C. 649 at [44] and [95(3)].

[214a] See *Leeds Industrial Co-operative Society v Slack* [1924] A.C. 851, where Viscount Finlay (at 857 cf. 859) and Lord Dunedin (at 865) both made clear that the damages compensate for the injury caused by the tort (past and future); and *Jaggard v Sawyer* [1995] 1 W.L.R. 269 CA at 276H (Bingham MR) and 286A (Millett LJ), endorsed in *Morris-Garner v One Step (Support) Ltd* [2019] A.C. 649 at [44].

Replace first paragraph with:

In *Johnson v Agnew*, Lord Wilberforce said he found in Lord Cairns' Act "no **20-063** warrant for the court awarding damages differently from common law damages".[211] In *Morris-Garner v One Step (Support) Ltd*, Lord Reed, speaking for a majority of the Supreme Court albeit obiter dicta, indicated that this statement must be read with caution because the measure of damages reflects the special character of the statutory jurisdiction.[212] Damages are said to be given as a monetary substitute for an injunction. They compensate for loss,[213] being the loss the applicant suffers by the refusal of specific relief.[214] However this can be misread. Consistently with earlier cases, what Lord Reed seems to have meant is that damages may be given under the statute as compensation not only for injuries caused by past breaches but also for injuries expected to be caused by future breaches.[214a] Otherwise damages are calculated in the same way in which they would be in a non-statutory case.

[211] *Johnson v Agnew* [1980] A.C. 367 at 400.

[212] *Morris-Garner v One Step (Support) Ltd* [2019] A.C. 649 at [43], [47] and [62]. But compare *Turf Club Auto Emporium Pte Ltd v Yeo Boong Hua* [2018] 2 S.L.R. 655 CA at [286]. The Supreme Court's approach is pointedly criticised by Peel in "Negotiating damages after One Step" (2019) 35 JCL 1.

[213] In *Lunn Poly Ltd v Liverpool & Lancashire Properties Ltd* [2006] 2 E.G.L.R. 29 CA at [22], [24], Neuberger LJ mooted the possibility that within this jurisdiction an account might be given of the profits the defendant had made, is making and will make as a result of the breach, but that is inconsistent with the decision of the Supreme Court in *Morris-Garner v One Step (Support) Ltd* [2019] A.C. 649 at, e.g. [68]–[70], [95(3)]. The Singapore Court of Appeal arrived at the same conclusion in *Turf Club Auto Emporium Pte Ltd v Yeo Boong Hua* [2018] 2 S.L.R. 655 CA at [271].

[214] *Morris-Garner v One Step (Support) Ltd* [2019] A.C. 649 at [44] and [95(3)].

[214a] See *Leeds Industrial Co-operative Society v Slack* [1924] A.C. 851, where Viscount Finlay (at 857 cf. 859) and Lord Dunedin (at 865) both made clear that the damages compensate for the injury caused by the tort (past and future); and *Jaggard v Sawyer* [1995] 1 W.L.R. 269 CA at 276H (Bingham MR) and 286A (Millett LJ), endorsed in *Morris-Garner v One Step (Support) Ltd* [2019] A.C. 649 at [44].

Delete paragraph.

3. Monetary Awards Giving Effect to Specific Performance

(b) Interest.

Replace n.224 with:

20-070   [224] For example cl.7.2 of the Standard Conditions of Sale, 5th edn (The Law Society, 2018 revision).

7. ACCOUNTS BETWEEN CO-OWNERS

1. Background

Replace second paragraph with:

20-073   The Statute of Anne in 1705 gave a joint tenant or tenant in common at law a right to an account against the other co-owners where they had taken more than their fair share of the rents and profits of the land.[250] Courts of equity would direct similar inquiries especially in the case of beneficiaries under trusts. More significantly, in partition actions in which courts of equity had exclusive jurisdiction, the court would inquire into the position between the co-owners so as to adjust accounts between them consequent on making an order for partition or sale.[251] The Statute of Anne was repealed in 1924 and in 1925 legislation abolished partition actions and imposed a trust for sale on all forms of co-ownership.[252] A co-owner who wishes to terminate the joint tenancy may seek an order for sale[253] and as ancillary to the sale the court can direct the same type of accounts as formerly in a partition action.[253a]

[250] Administration of Justice Act 1705 s.27, repealed by Law of Property (Amendment) Act 1924 s.10 and Sch.10. See *Sturton v Richardson* (1844) 13 M. & W. 17, 153 E.R. 7; *Job v Potton* (1875) L.R. 20 Eq. 84.

[251] *Leigh v Dickeson* (1884) 15 Q.B.D. 60 at 67. See E. R. Daniell, *Daniell's Chancery Practice*, 8th edn (Stevens and Sons, 1914) at 1170 and following.

[252] Now a "trust of land".

[253] Under Trusts of Land and Appointment of Trustees Act 1996 s.14.

[253a] The jurisdictional basis of equitable accounting is discussed in *Cheung Lai Mui v Cheung Wai Shing* [2021] 5 H.K.C. 185 HKCFA and in Law (2022) 16 J of Eq 56.

3. Elements of the Account

Replace n.260 with:

20-075   [260] *Brass v Patel* [2007] B.P.I.R. 1049; *Dennis v McDonald* [1982] 2 W.L.R. 275 CA; *Coley v Coley* (1975) 5 Fam. Law. 195 (rent received offset with mortgage payments made). See also *Cheung Lai Mui v Cheung Wai Shing* [2021] 5 H.K.C. 185 HKCFA at [104].

(a) Occupation rent.

Replace paragraph with:

20-076   Whereas the common law took the position that one co-owner would not be liable to pay rent to another absent ouster or some form of agreement,[261] the approach of the Court of Chancery was more flexible.[262] The position adopted in modern cases is that rent may be charged against an occupying co-owner where this is necessary to do broad justice between the parties,[263] taking account of any common intention or arrangement between the parties.[263a] Subject to that, the starting point remains that a co-owner in occupation is not obliged to pay occupation rent merely because they are living in the property and the other co-owner is not.[263b]

Something more has to be shown, for example that the co-owner in occupation has been exploiting the property for their own financial gain, or that they have precluded the other co-owner from exercising a right of occupation that they wished to exercise. The focus is on the behavior of the occupying party and not on the reasonableness of the behavior of the other in not occupying the property. Accordingly, where one co-owner becomes bankrupt, the default rule is that their trustee cannot charge the occupying co-owner rent even though it would not usually be reasonable for the trustee to occupy.[265] In the case of broken cohabiting relationships, the question may depend on whether the claiming party left voluntarily and whether they would be welcome back.[267] Certainly a co-owner cannot, by leaving voluntarily, make the remaining occupier liable for rent.[267a]

[261] See para.20-073 above.

[262] *Dennis v McDonald* [1982] 2 W.L.R. 275; and Cooke [1995] Conv. 391, at 399–403.

[263] *Ali v Khatib* [2022] 4 W.L.R. 50 CA at [68] and [75]; *Murphy v Gooch* [2007] 2 F.L.R. 934 CA at [10]. Compare the more structured approach adopted in *Cheung Lai Mui v Cheung Wai Shing* [2021] 5 H.K.C. 185 HKCFA at [82], discussed in Law (2022) 16 J of Eq 56.

[263a] *Davis v Jackson* [2017] 1 W.L.R. 4005, discussed in *Shilabeer v Lanceley* [2019] EWHC 3380 (QB).

[263b] *Ali v Khatib* [2022] 4 W.L.R. 50 CA at [72].

[265] *Ali v Khatib* [2022] 4 W.L.R. 50 CA at [68] and [74]; preferring the analysis in *Davis v Jackson* [2017] 1 W.L.R. 4005 to that in *French v Barcham* [2009] 1 W.L.R. 1124.

[267] *Re Pavlou* [1993] 1 W.L.R. 1046 at 1050.

[267a] *Re Pavlou* [1993] 1 W.L.R. 1046.

Replace second paragraph with:
In *Stack v Dowden* Baroness Hale and Lord Neuberger indicated that the power to charge an occupation rent is now governed exclusively by ss.12–15 of the Trusts of Land and Appointment of Trustees Act 1996.[268] While the results may often be the same as in Equity, they may differ in some cases because the statute mandates consideration of additional factors such as the welfare of minors and the interests of secured creditors.[269] It is clear that the displacement of equitable accounting in this context is not exhaustive and that the remedy continues to operate where the Trusts of Land and Appointment of Trustees Act does not apply.[270] The extent of the displacement is a matter of some difficulty and there are serious arguments that equitable accounting continues to be the relevant regime, amongst other things, where retrospective adjustments are to be made following a sale.[271]

[268] *Stack v Dowden* [2007] 2 A.C. 432; and see *Murphy v Gooch* [2007] 2 F.L.R. 934 CA.

[269] *Stack v Dowden* [2007] 2 A.C. 432 at [93]–[94]; *Murphy v Gooch* [2007] 2 F.L.R. 934 CA.

[270] *French v Barcham* [2009] 1 W.L.R. 1124 (where the claiming co-owner, the husband's trustee in bankruptcy, did not have a right of occupation); *Davis v Jackson* [2017] 1 W.L.R. 4005; *Ali v Khatib* [2022] 4 W.L.R. 50 CA at [15] (where the circumstances pre-dated the legislation).

[271] See Bright [2009] Conv. 378 at 382–385; Lightman (2008) 22 T.L.I. 11 at 16.

(c)   Improvements and repairs.

After "of the parties.", add:
It may be reasonable to infer that cohabiting couples do not have a common **20-078** intention that either should have to account to the other for sums spent improving their home for their joint benefit.[277a]

[277a] *Lyle v Bedborough* [2021] EWHC 220 (Ch) at [93].

DEFINITION AND CLASSIFICATION OF TRUSTS

3.   TRUSTS COMPARED WITH OTHER RELATIONSHIPS

2.   Fiduciary Relationships

Replace the second paragraph with:

But not all fiduciary relationships can properly be described as trusts. A fiduci-   **21-035**
ary is a trustee only if he has vested in him a fund of property or a power of disposal
over it.[68] Not all trusts involve fiduciary duties. A fiduciary duty must arise from the
voluntary conduct of the person bound by it.[69] Accordingly, a person who becomes
a trustee by operation of law and has not voluntarily undertaken the office may not
owe any fiduciary duties in respect of the trust property. An example is the trust
imposed on a person to strip him of the benefits of his fraudulent conduct.[70] The
trust merely gives effect to the equitable right of the claimant to hold the defendant personally liable to account for his profit, or to recover the property specifically.
While these remedies are commonly enforced against a person who owes fiduciary duties, they are not necessarily an indicator of his status as a fiduciary.[70a] It is

also open to the settlor of an express trust to modify or exclude the operation of the trustee's fiduciary duties under the general law.[71]

[68] See *Paragon Finance v DB Thakerar & Co* [1999] 1 All E.R. 400 at 416.

[69] See generally P.J. Millett (1998) 114 L.Q.R. 214.

[70] *Paragon Finance v DB Thakerar & Co* [1999] 1 All E.R. 400 at 414–415.

[70a] cf. R. Flannigan [2019] Conv. 207.

[71] See above para.7-016.

CHAPTER 22

PRIVATE EXPRESS TRUSTS

1.   VARIETIES OF EXPRESS TRUST

1.   Fixed Trusts

(a)   Nature of the beneficiary's interest.

Replace n.1 with:

22-001   ¹ *Saunders v Vautier* (1841) 4 Beav. 115; affirmed Cr. & Ph. 240. See para.29-030 below.

2.   Discretionary Trusts

(b)   Nature of the beneficiary's interest.

Replace second paragraph with:

22-005   But the beneficiary's interest is nonetheless proprietary in character since it gives him a stronger equitable title to the trust property than any third party with no entitlement to it at all. He would have a sufficient interest to trace and recover any money that the trustee transferred in breach of trust.[22] But his only right would be to compel the third party to reinstate the misapplied money to the trust fund. He could not require the third party to pay the money directly to him since that would give the beneficiary a stronger right against the third party than he had against the trustee himself.[23]

[22] *Gartside v IRC* [1968] A.C. 553 at 617; *Sainsbury v IRC* [1968] A.C. 553 at 617. See generally R.C. Nolan (2006) 122 L.Q.R. 232 at 256–257. The analogy is with the beneficiary of a deceased estate in the course of administration: *Commissioner of Stamp Duties (Queensland) v Livingston* [1965] A.C. 694.

[23] *Target Holdings Ltd v Redferns* [1996] A.C. 421; *Re Diplock* [1948] Ch. 465; *Serious Fraud Office v Litigation Capital Ltd.* [2021] EWHC 127 at [202]–[203], and see below para.30-015.

Replace third paragraph with:

Taken collectively, all the potential beneficiaries of the trust are absolutely entitled to the trust property since the trustee has a duty to distribute it to one or other of them. If all the potential beneficiaries of the trust are sui juris, they can agree to direct the trustee about how he should dispose of the trust assets.[24]

[24] *Re Smith, Public Trustee v Aspinall* [1928] Ch. 915; applying the rule in *Saunders v Vautier* (1841) 4 Beav. 115, affirmed Cr. & Ph. 240; and see below para.29-030. This possibility may however be barred if the trust were subject to a power to add or remove beneficiaries from the class of objects, In that case, the class would not be closed: *Serious Fraud Office v Litigation Capital Ltd.* [2021] EWHC 127 at [202]–[203].

3.   Protective Trusts

(c)   Operative and inoperative events.

Replace first paragraph with:

22-008   A variety of events may determine the primary beneficiary's interest and bring the discretionary trust into existence. These include the bankruptcy of the principal beneficiary, even if this is already existing when the trust first takes effect[38]; the execution by the principal beneficiary of a deed of variation giving up his right to part of the income in certain events[39]; the sequestration of the income[40]; the impounding of part of the income by the trustees to make good sums paid to the principal beneficiary in breach of trust[41]; and the vesting of a right to income in the Custodian of Enemy Property under the Trading with the Enemy Act 1939.[42]

[38] See *Trappes v Meredith* (1871) 7 Ch. App. 248; *Re Public Trustee v Evans* [1920] 2 Ch. 304; *Re Walker, Public Trustee v Walker* [1939] Ch. 974; and see *Re Forder* [1927] 2 Ch. 291, on the effect of an annulment of the bankruptcy.

[39] *Re Dennis's ST* [1942] Ch. 283; see (1942) 58 L.Q.R. 312.

[40] *Re Baring's ST* [1940] Ch. 737.

[41] *Re Balfour's Settlement* [1938] Ch. 928; and, see *Re Richardson's WT* [1958] Ch. 504; *Edmonds v Edmonds* [1965] 1 W.L.R. 58 (orders of divorce court).

[42] *Re Gourju's WT* [1943] Ch. 24. For further detail see the 31st edition of this work at para.20-54.

5. FORMALITIES

1. Declarations of Trusts of Land

(a) Writing.

After "may be fine.", add new n.160a:

[160a] The fineness of the distinction is illustrated in the alternative explanation for s.53(2). On this view, the trust which is enforced when the trustee relies fraudulently on the informality of the transaction is the express trust declared by the settlor. The statute operates as an evidential bar to enforcing it. This view would allow an express trust declared by the settlor for a third party beneficiary to be directly enforceable by the beneficiary himself: A.B. Douglas, [2021] Conv. 128.   **22-036**

(b) Evidence.

Replace n.156 with:

[156] *Forster v Hale* (1798) 3 Ves. 696; *Randall v Morgan* (1806) 12 Ves. 74.   **22-037**

2. Dispositions of interests under Trusts

Replace n.179 with:

[179] *Halley v Law Society* (2003) 6 I.T.E.L.R. 40.   **22-040**

6. CONSTITUTION OF TRUSTS

2. Volunteers

Replace n.183 with:

[183] *Ellison v Ellison* (1802) 6 Ves. 656 at 662.   **22-042**

7. SETTING TRUSTS ASIDE AND UNENFORCEABLE TRUSTS

5. Illegality and Public Policy

(b) Trust created for an unlawful purpose.

Replace n.253 with:

[253] *Bowmakers Ltd v Barnet Instruments Ltd* [1945] K.B. 65;; *Singh v Ali* [1960] A.C. 167 at 176; *Patel v Mirza* [2016] UKSC 42; [2017] A.C. 467 at [110]–[111]; *Grondona v Stoffel & Co* [2020] UKSC 42, [2021] A.C. 540 at [33]–[34].   **22-066**

6. Sham Trusts

(a) Common intention to mislead.

Replace n.266 with:

22-068 [266] *Re The Esteem Settlement* [2003] J.R.C. 092; [2004] 1 W.T.L.R. 1 at [58]; interpreting *Midland Bank Plc v Wyatt* [1995] 1 F.L.R. 696 at 699; and *National Westminster Bank Plc v Jones* [2001] 1 B.C.L.C. 98 at 98; *JSC Mezhdunarodniy Promyshlenniy Bank v Pugachev* [2017] EWHC 2426; (2017) 20 I.T.E.L.R. 905 at [434]. In Jersey the requirement of an intention to mislead is read strictly. A court would not infer an intention to mislead third parties from the alleged trustee's mere indifference to the terms of the trust instrument: *Re Estate of Hanson* [2021] JRC 319 at [102]-[122].

(b) Proof.

Replace n.267 with:

22-069 [267] *Hitch v Stone* [2001] EWCA Civ 63; [2001] S.T.C. 214 at [65]; *JSC Mezhdunarodniy Promyshlenniy Bank v Pugachev* [2017] EWHC 2426; (2017) 20 I.T.E.L.R. 905.

(c) Consequences.

Replace n.276 with:

22-070 [276] *Minwalla v Minwalla* [2004] EWHC 2823 (Fam); [2005] 1 W.L.R. 771; *JSC Mezhdunarodniy Promyshlenniy Bank v Pugachev* [2017] EWHC 2426; (2017) 20 I.T.E.L.R. 905 at [455].

(e) Shams and "illusory" trusts.

Replace second paragraph with:

22-072 An illusory trust is analytically different from a purported trust set out in a sham document. The sham doctrine is concerned with the misleading mismatch between the objective intentions of the parties in the trust instrument and their subjective intentions about the transaction between them.[283] The conclusion that a purported trust is illusory follows from the construction of the trust instrument itself, rather than from a comparison between the terms of trust instrument and the parties' subjective intentions. The court construes the powers and duties of the parties as they are expressed in the trust instrument to work out their true effect. In going about this task, it is concerned with the substance of the transaction rather than its superficial terms. Some indications that the trust may be illusory are that the duties of the trustee stated in the trust instrument are incompatible with the core duties of trusteeship[284]; or that the settlor has reserved such extensive powers to himself as a protector of the trust that the interests of the beneficiaries named under it are unreal.[285]

[283] See para.22-000 above; and *JSC Mezhdunarodniy Promyshlenniy Bank v Pugachev* [2017] EWHC 2426; (2017) 20 I.T.E.L.R. 905 at [436].

[284] *Re the AQ Revocable Trusts* [2010] SC (Bda) 40 Civ; (2010) I.T.E.L.R. 260; *Clayton v Clayton* [2016] NZSC 216; [2016] 1 N.Z.L.R. 551 at [124].

[285] *JSC Mezhdunarodniy Promyshlenniy Bank v Pugachev* [2017] EWHC 2426; (2017) 20 I.T.E.L.R. 905.

CHAPTER 24

TRUSTS ARISING TO ENFORCE AN INFORMALLY EXPRESSED INTENTION

2. TRUSTS GIVING EFFECT TO SPECIFICALLY ENFORCEABLE OBLIGATIONS

1. Vendor's Trusteeship and the Nature of the Purchaser's Interest

Replace n.16 with:

24-003   [16] *Paine v Meller* (1801) 6 Ves. 349 at 352; e.g. Land Charges Act 1972 s.2(4)(iv) (extended definition of "estate contract").

3. TRUSTS TO ENFORCE INCOMPLETE INTER VIVOS GIFTS

1. Circumstances Where an Imperfect Gift may be Complete in Equity

(b) Unconscionability.

Replace paragraph with:

24-007   In *Pennington v Waine*[34] the rule was extended. It was held that, although further acts may remain to be done by the donor to vest the legal interest in the donee, the gift may nonetheless be effective in equity if it would unconscionable for the donor to resile from his intention that the transaction should be complete.[35] In that case the donor executed a share transfer form but did not deliver it to the donee or the company for registration. The donee acted on the assumption that the gift was complete and had been expressly told by the donor's agent that he need take no further action. The gift was held to be complete in equity.[36] But unless the intended donee or a third party relies on the apparent gift, it is unlikely that the transaction would be regarded as complete in equity under the principle in *Pennington v Waine*.[37] The gift is more likely to be complete in equity if it has been publicised to third parties even if doubts remain whether all the steps were taken to vest the legal interest in the donee were in fact taken.[37a]

[34] *Pennington v Waine* [2002] EWCA Civ 227; [2002] 1 W.L.R. 1075.

[35] *Pennington v Waine* [2002] EWCA Civ 227; [2002] 1 W.L.R. 1075 at [64].

[36] An alternative explanation is that the execution of the transfer form in proper form was a complete equitable assignment of the shares, even without delivery: *Pennington v Waine* [2002] EWCA Civ 227; [2002] 1 W.L.R. 1075 at [81]–[83] per Clarke LJ.

[37] *Curtis v Pulbrook* [2011] EWHC 167 (Ch); [2011] B.C.L.C. 638 at [46]. But for an extension which is surely at the outer margins of the principle, see *Khan v Mahmood* [2021] EWHC 597 (Ch).

[37a] *Nosnehpetsj Ltd v Watersheds Capital Partners Ltd* [2020] EWHC 1938 (Ch).

3. Related Ways that an Incomplete Gift may take Effect

(b) Immediate equitable assignment.

Replace n.54 with:

24-011   [54] *Pennington v Waine* [2002] EWCA Civ 227; [2002] 1 W.L.R. 2075 at [71], per Clarke LJ; *Nosnehpetsj Ltd v Watersheds Capital Partners Ltd* [2020] EWHC 1938 (Ch) at [94].

(c) Property vested in donee.

Replace n.60 with:

[60] *Strong v Bird* (1874) L.R. 18 Eq. 315; *Re Stewart* [1908] 2 Ch. 251; *Re Pink, Pink v Pink* [1912] 2 Ch. 528; *Re Nelson, Nelson v Nelson* (1947) 91 S.J. 533. See also *Carter v Hungerford* [1917] 1 Ch. 260. **24-012**

4. TRUSTS GIVING EFFECT TO A DONATIO MORTIS CAUSA

1. Requirements for a donatio mortis causa

(b) Conditional on death.

Replace n.77 with:

[77] See *Edwards v Jones* (1836) 1 My. & Cr. 226; *Tate v Hilbert* (1793) 2 Ves. Jun. 111. **24-019**

(c) Delivery.

Replace n.86 with:

[86] *Miller v Miller* (1735) 3 P. Wms. 356; *Ward v Turner* (1725) 2 Ves. Sen. 431; but see *Tate v Hilbert* (1793) 2 Ves. Jun. 111 at 120. **24-020**

2. Operation of the Condition

(a) The trust to give effect to the condition.

Replace the fourth paragraph with:

If the transfer of the legal interest in the property is not complete, then the gift "leaves the whole title in the donor"[103] until by their death they perfect the gift. The donee's title then becomes complete without any assent by the donor's personal representatives.[104] They hold the property for the donee upon a constructive trust,[105] conferring on them a sufficient title to compel the personal representatives to complete the gift by transfer of the legal interest. The significance of the trust's being constructive is that a *donatio mortis causa* of an interest in land may take effect without the donor leaving any signed writing to record the transfer.[106] **24-021**

[103] *Edwards v Jones* (1836) 1 My. & Cr. 226 at 235, per Lord Cottenham LC.

[104] See *Tate v Hilbert* (1793) 2 Ves. Jun. 111 at 120.

[105] *Snellgrove v Baily* (1744) 3 Atk. 214; *Duffield v Elwes* (1827) 1 Bligh N.S. 497 at 543; *Re Dillon* (1890) 44 Ch. D. 76 at 82.

[106] *Sen v Headley* [1991] Ch. 425 at 440.

5. SECRET TRUSTS

Replace n.113 with:

[113] See *Drakeford v Wilks* (1747) 3 Atk. 539; *McCormick v Grogan* (1869) L.R. 4 H.L. 82 at 88, 89, 97. Lord Jeffreys LC has some claim to paternity: see *Crook v Brooking* (1688) 2 Vern. 50. **24-023**

3.   Basis of Secret Trusts

(a)   Two explanations.

Replace n.134 with:

24-030   134 See *Drakeford v Wilks* (1747) 3 Atk. 539; *McCormick v Grogan* (1869) L.R. 4 H.L. 82 at 88, 89, 97. Lord Jeffreys LC has some claim to paternity: see *Crook v Brooking* (1688) 2 Vern. 50.

7.   Constructive Trusts under the Equity in Pallant v Morgan

Replace n.183 with:

24-038   183 *Pallant v Morgan* [1953] Ch. 43; considered with approval in *Yeoman's Row Management Ltd v Cobbe* [2008] UKHL 55; [2008] 1 W.L.R. 1752 at [24].

1.   The Requirements for the Pallant v Morgan Equity

Replace the first paragraph with:

24-039   A *Pallant v Morgan* equity typically relates to specific property that is not at first owned by either of the parties, A or B.182 A and B form a common intention that A will take steps to acquire the property; and that, if A does so, B will obtain some interest in it. They may contemplate, for example that A will buy the property, subdivide it and convey part of it to B,183 or that it will be acquired by a corporate vehicle, the shares in which will be divided between A and B.184 The common intention need not be recorded in writing,186 but its main term must be agreed between the parties.185 The equity cannot arise where the agreement is expressed to be subject to contract,186 or where A and B realise that their agreement is legally unenforceable because they plan to enter into a binding agreement in the future.187

182 *Yeoman's Row Management Ltd v Cobbe* [2008] UKHL 55; [2008] 1 W.L.R. 1752 at [37].

183 *Pallant v Morgan* [1953] Ch. 43.

184 *Banner Homes Group Plc v Luff Developments Ltd* [2000] Ch. 372.

185 *Generator Developments v Lidl UK Gmbh* [2018] EWCA Civ 396; [2018] 2 P. & C.R. 7 at [78].

186 *Generator Developments v Lidl UK Gmbh* [2018] EWCA Civ 396; [2018] 2 P. & C.R. 7 at [67], [79].

187 *Yeoman's Row Management Ltd v Cobbe* [2008] UKHL 55; [2008] 1 W.L.R. 1752 at [37]; *Herbert v Doyle* [2010] EWCA Civ 1095; [2011] 1 E.G.L.R. 119 at [57]; *Generator Developments Ltd v Lidl UK GmbH* [2018] EWCA Civ 396 at [56].

2.   Basis of the Equity

Replace n.191 with:

24-040   191 *Yeoman's Row Management Ltd v Cobbe* [2008] UKHL 55; [2008] 1 W.L.R. 1752 at [30]; *Generator Developments v Lidl UK Gmbh* [2018] EWCA Civ 396; [2018] 2 P. & C.R. 7 at [72].

Replace n.193 with:

24-040   193 *Generator Developments v Lidl UK Gmbh* [2018] EWCA Civ 396; [2018] 2 P. & C.R. 7 at [36]–[37], [72], [83] where the Court of Appeal considered that agency was the basis on which *Pallant v Morgan* [1953] Ch. 43 was originally decided. As the authorities currently stand, both explanations for the *Pallant v Morgan* equity remain available to be argued: *Dixon v Willan* [2022] EWHC 2160 (Ch).

CHAPTER 25

RESULTING TRUSTS

2.   GRATUITOUS TRANSFER

2.   Purchase of Property in the Name of Another

(c)   Presumption of advancement.

(2)   Between parent and child.

Replace n.41 with:

[41] *Hepworth v Hepworth* (1870) L.R. 11 Eq. 10; *Nelson v Nelson* (1995) 184 C.L.R. 538; *Laskar v*   **25-009**
Laskar [2008] EWCA Civ 347; [2008] 1 W.L.R. 2695 (presumption of some weight between mother
and adult child but rebutted by direct evidence); *Re Watkin (a bankrupt), Wood v Watkin* [2019] EWHC
1311 (Ch).

4. Resulting Trust on Voluntary Transfer of Property

(a) Real property.

(2) After 1925.

Replace n.81 with:

25-017 [81] This preferable explanation has been adopted in *National Crime Agency v Dong* [2017] EWHC 3116 (Ch) and *Ali v Dinc* [2020] EWHC 3055 (Ch), [271]–[278], upheld on appeal [2022] EWCA Civ 34.

4. QUISTCLOSE TRUSTS

Replace n.121 with:

25-033 [121] For an analysis of *Quistclose* Trusts as security interests, see K.C.F. Loy (2012) 128 L.Q.R. 412. The trust typically arises where A loans money to B but it can also arise where A transfers other kinds of property, including land, to B for a limited purpose: *Ali v Dinc* [2020] EWHC 3055 (Ch), upheld on appeal [2022] EWCA Civ 34.

2. Location of Beneficial Interest and Rights of Enforcement

Replace paragraph with:

25-035 B holds the legal interest in the money advanced on trust for A unless and until it is applied in accordance with his directions. B holds it subject to an equitable power to apply it according to the direction. The power may be revocable by A even if the purpose for which A advanced the money could be fulfilled.[133a] The trust arises at the inception when A first advances the money.[134] In the standard case, therefore, it is not necessary to suppose a primary trust under which B holds the property for C or to fulfil the purpose, which then fails and brings into existence a secondary resulting trust for the benefit of A.[135] The beneficial interest in the money remains throughout in A. It provides a proprietary security for his advance until it is applied according to A's direction. In the event of B's insolvency, therefore, the money could be recovered by A by exercising his rights as the beneficiary of a bare trust absolutely entitled to the money. It could not be recovered by C whose rights are limited to those of the object of a mere power. A could by injunction prevent its misapplication, or, if actually misapplied, follow it to a third party receiving it with notice,[136] or trace it into a substituted asset.[137] C may also have a sufficient title to restrain the misapplication of the money or to enforce remedies based on following or tracing since he is the object of an equitable power. But he could not to compel the payment of the money to himself since this would put him in the position of the beneficiary of a trust and diminish A's security. Once the money is properly applied, A's interest is extinguished by overreaching.[138]

[133a] *Ali v Dinc* [2020] EWHC 3055 (Ch), [249]–[253], upheld on appeal [2022] EWCA Civ 34.

[134] *Twinsectra Ltd v Yardley* [2002] UKHL 12; [2002] 2 A.C. 164 at [13], [81], [102]; *Challinor v Juliet Bellis & Co* [2015] EWCA Civ 59 at [63]; [2016] W.T.L.R. 43.

[135] See *Barclays Bank Ltd v Quistclose Investments Ltd* [1970] A.C. 567 at 582.

[136] *Barclays Bank Ltd v Quistclose Investments Ltd* [1970] A.C. 567.

[137] *Twinsectra Ltd v Yardley* [1999] Lloyd's Rep. Bank. 438 CA; reversed on other grounds [2002] UKHL 12; [2002] 2 A.C. 164.

[138] See Ch.4.

CHAPTER 26

TRUSTS ARISING FROM WRONGS

1. GENERAL

Replace n.1 with:

[1] *Muschinski v Dodds* (1985) 160 C.L.R. 583 at 613, per Deane J and para.22-012 above. See para.25-026 where a resulting trust arises from a transaction induced by a fraudulent misrepresentation. **26-001**

3. Duties of Constructive Trustee

After "duties of loyalty.", add new n.15a:

[15a] *Westdeutsche Landesbank Girozentrale v Islington London L.B.C.* [1996] A.C. 669, 705-06; *Ali v Dinc* [2020] EWHC 3055 (Ch), [221]. **26-005**

CHAPTER 27

APPOINTMENT, RETIREMENT AND REMOVAL OF TRUSTEES

CONTENTS

1. CAPACITY TO BE A TRUSTEE

At the start of the paragraph, replace "Two" with:
Three

27-001

1. Corporations

(b) Trust corporations.

Replace n.11 with:

27-003 [11] TA 1925 s.68(1)(18); LPA 1925 s.205(1)(xxviii); SLA 1925 s.117(1)(xxx); LP(Am)A 1926 s.3 (extending the definitions in the former Acts). Certain individuals such as trustees in bankruptcy and trustees under deeds of arrangement are also comprised in the term "trust corporation".

After para.27-004, add new sub-section:

3. Non-Residents

27-004A There is no general rule that prevents a settlor from appointing a person resident abroad as trustee of a trust established in England. Where the appointment is made by a person with the power to appoint a new trustee, or by the court, then it is only in exceptional circumstances that a person resident abroad can be appointed trustee.[21a] Exceptional circumstances include those where the beneficiaries are resident abroad, where it is likely to be for their benefit to have trustees appointed in the same jurisdiction.[21b]

[21a] *Re Whitehead's Will Trusts* [1971] 1 W.L.R. 833.

[21b] *Richard v Mackay* [2008] W.T.L.R. 1667

2. NUMBER OF TRUSTEES

Following para.27-004A add new sub-section at the beginning:

A1. General rule

27-004B Although settlors commonly stipulate that at least two trustees are required in order to exercise the trust powers, in the absence of an express provision the general rule is that there is no minimum number of trustees. Trusts with sole trustees are not normally considered to be desirable given the risk of fraudulent behaviour. Furthermore, sole trustees, except in the case of a trust corporation, cannot give valid receipt for the sale proceeds from land.[21c] There is no general rule that limits the number of trustees, and a trust deed may require any number of trustees to act. However, in light of the normal rule that trustees must act unanimously[21d] there are obvious risks to the appointment of too many trustees.

[21c] See LPA 1925 s.27(2); SLA 1925 ss.18(1), 94; TA 1925 ss.14, 37. cf. SCA 1981 s.114 as to personal representatives (para.31-021).]

[21d] *Luke v South Kensington Hotel Co* (1879) 11 Ch 121.

1. Land

Replace paragraph with:

27-005 Where a settlement of land or a trust of land is created, the number of trustees must not exceed four; and if more than four trustees are named, the first four named who are able and willing to act will alone be the trustees.[22] This rule does not apply in the following cases[23]:

  (i) where land, or the proceeds of sale of land, is held in trust for charitable, ecclesiastical or public purposes;

(ii)   a term of years limited by a settlement on trusts for raising money, e.g. portions; or

(iii)   a term of years created under the statutory remedies for enforcing
rentcharges.[25]

[22] TA 1925 s.34(1). cf. SCA 1981 s.114, replacing JA 1925 s.160; considered in *In b Holland* (1936)
105 L.J.P. 113 as to the number of personal representatives. Before 1926 there was no such restriction;
for the relevant transitional provisions, see TA 1925 s.34(2).). For difficulties where there is a conveyance to the partners of a firm and there are more than four such partners, see: *Vanquish Properties (UK)
Ltd v Brook Street (UK) Ltd* [2016] EWHC 1508.

[23] TA 1925 s.34(3).

[25] The Rentcharges Act 1977 prohibits the creation of new rentcharges.

2.   Exceptions

Replace paragraph with:
[This sub-section is deleted in the supplement.]   **27-006**

3.   APPOINTMENT OF TRUSTEES

After the first sub-section, add new sub-section:

1A.   Trustee's Consent

A person cannot be compelled to act as a trustee, and an intended trustee must   **27-007A**
accept the office of trusteeship.[28a] Acceptance may be express, as where a trustee
signs the declaration of trust[28b] or inferred from their conduct, such as their taking
steps in the administration of the trust.[28c] where an intended trustee has not accepted the office it is not correct to view the appointment as provisionally valid until
the trustee disclaims. Rather, for the appointment to have any legal effect the person
must first consent to their appointment as trustee.[28d] Moreover, where an individual
is pressured into accepting their appointment, or where they are unaware of the
nature and extent of the fiscal liability that they assume on acceptance of the trusteeship, they may apply to have their acceptance rescinded on the ground of equitable
mistake.[28e]

Acceptance of the office of trustee is a separate issue from the vesting of trust
property. A person may accept their appointment as trustee even though no trust
property is vested in him[28f]; conversely, trust property may be conveyed to a person
who subsequently refuses to consent to their appointment as a trustee. In the latter
case, where there is a conveyance to several trustees, and one of their number does
not consent to act as a trustee, the fund will vest in the consenting trustees, who shall
be free to exercise the rights and powers of trusteeship without the concurrence of
the non-consenting individual.[28g] Where there is a conveyance to a sole person who
does not consent to act as trustee (or to several persons who each refuse to act as
trustee), the non-consenting party is not subject to the liabilities, duties and powers of trusteeship.[28h] Their sole duty is to reconvey the fund to the settlor, who will
receive it subject to the originally declared trusts. Where the trust is established by
will, and the intended trustees refuse to act as such, the fund remains vested in the
personal representatives who may either appoint new trustees or administer the
trusts themselves.[28i]

[28a] *Re Sharman's Will Trusts* [1942] Ch. 311 at 314; and see generally on disclaimer *Re Stratton's
Disclaimer* [1958] Ch. 42 (beneficial gift by will).

[28b] *Ong v Ping* [2015] EWHC 1742, [98].

[28c] *James v Frearson* (1840) 1 Y & Coll Ch 370; *In re Stevens* [1897] 1 Ch. 432.

[28d] *Mackay v Wesley* [2020] EWHC 3400.

[28e] *Mackay v Wesley* [2020] EWHC 3400.

[28f] *Ong v Ping* [2015] EWHC 1742 at [98] (this point was not the subject of the appeal in [2017] EWCA Civ 2069).

[28g] *Nicholson v Wordsworth* (1818) 2 Swan 365.

[28h] *Mallott v Wilson* [1903] 2 Ch 494.

[28i] *Re Cockburn's Will Trusts* [1957] Ch 438.

2.   Initial Trustees

Replace paragraph with:

27-008   Normally the first trustees are appointed by the will or settlement. Unless and until new trustees are appointed, the property remains vested in the first trustees (or such of them as do not retire and are not removed[31]), and when one dies, the trust property devolves upon the survivors. On the death of a sole or sole surviving trustee, the trust property, whether real or personal, vests in his personal representatives, still subject to the trust.[32] Until new trustees are appointed, the personal representatives, though they are not bound to accept the position and duties of trustees,[33] are capable of exercising or performing any power or trust which the deceased trustee could have exercised or performed, unless the trust instrument (if any) contains a contrary direction.[34]

[31] See paras 27–033 to 27–036.

[32] AEA 1925 ss.1 and 3 replacing CA 1881 s.30.

[33] *Re Benett* [1906] 1 Ch. 216.

[34] TA 1925 s.18(2) replacing CA 1911 s.8(1). See P.W. Smith (1977) 41 Conv. (NS) 423 for the position where personal representatives die without appointing new trustees.

3.   Subsequent Trustees

Replace paragraph with:

27-009   [This sub-section is deleted in the supplement.]

4.   Appointment of New Trustees

(b)   The Trustee Act 1925.

(1)   The power.

Replace list item "(viii)" with:

27-012   (viii)   He is removed under a power in the trust instrument.[50]

[50] TA 1925 s.36(2). *Re Gleeds Retirement Benefit Scheme* [2015] Ch. 212 (no requirement for a deed, as writing is sufficient).

At the end, add new paragraph:

Outside of these categories the power under s.36 has no application. For instance, where a trustee is appointed under a statute which provides that they shall act for a fixed term, the expiry of that term is not one of the circumstances in which the s.36 power arises.[50a]

[50a] *Rettendon Parish Council v Hart* [2020] EWHC 2221 at [69]–[70].

(2) The appointment.

Replace paragraph with:

The appointment must be made in writing,[51] though it may not be made by the **27-013** will of the last surviving trustee.[52] It may be made by the following persons[53]:

(i) By the person or persons nominated by the trust instrument for the purpose of appointing new trustees. This means the person or persons nominated generally[54] and not merely in certain specified events.[55] If several persons are nominated, the power cannot be exercised by the survivor or survivors[56] unless a contrary intention is shown,[57] or the property is vested in them[58] or they are trustees and hold the power as such[59] or the power was given to a class (e.g. "my sons") of whom at least two still exist.[60] If there is no person able and willing to act under this head (as where the persons nominated cannot be found,[61] or they disagree[62]), the appointment may be made under the next head; namely:

(ii) By the surviving or continuing trustees or trustee. This includes a refusing or retiring trustee, if willing to make the appointment, [63] but not a trustee removed against his will.[64] If there is no such trustee, the appointment may be made—

(iii) By the personal representative of the last surviving or continuing trustee, including the personal representatives of a sole trustee,[65] unless he is appointed by will and predeceases the testator[66];

(iv) If (and probably only if[67]) there is no person able to act, or it is doubtful whether he can act,[68] the court may appoint.[69]

When the appointment is made by the personal representatives, the concurrence of any executor who has renounced or who has not proved is not required[70]; but the appointment may be made by a sole or last surviving executor intending to renounce, or all the executors where they all intend to renounce, without thereby accepting the office of executor.[71] Yet although the appointment may be made before probate, the new trustee's title to act will not be complete before the grant of probate (or letters of administration with will annexed if all renounce).[72] No appointment of a new trustee to take the place of a mentally defective trustee who is also entitled in possession to some beneficial interest in the trust property can be made by the continuing trustee or trustees unless leave has been given by the Court of Protection.[73]

[51] TA 1925 s.36(1).

[52] *Re Parker's Trusts* [1894] 1 Ch. 707.

[53] TA 1925 s.36(1).

[54] *Re Walker & Hughes' Contract* (1883) 24 Ch. D. 698.

[55] *Re Wheeler & De Rochow's Contract* [1896] 1 Ch. 315; *Re Sichel's Settlements* [1916] 1 Ch. 358.

[56] See *Bersel Manufacturing Co Ltd v Berry* [1968] 2 All E.R. 552 at 554, 557.

[57] *Re Harding* [1923] 1 Ch. 182.

[58] See *Re Bacon* [1907] 1 Ch. 475.

[59] TA 1925 s.18(1); and see *Re Smith, Eastwick v Smith* [1904] 1 Ch. 139.

[60] *Jefferys v Marshall* (1870) 19 W.R. 94; but see *Sykes v Sheard* (1863) 2 De G.J. & S. 6.

[61] *Cradock v Witham* [1895] W.N. 75.

[62] *Re Sheppard's ST* [1888] W.N. 234.

63 TA 1925 s.36(8); *Rettendon Parish Council v Hart* [2020] EWHC 2221 (trustee appointed for a fixed term does not 'retire' on expiry of term, and therefore cannot exercise the power).

64 *Re Stoneham's Settlement Trusts* [1953] Ch. 59.

65 *Re Shafto's Trusts* (1885) 29 Ch. D. 247.

66 *Nicholson v Field* [1893] 2 Ch. 511.

67 *Re Gibbon's Trusts* (1882) 30 W.R. 287 (undesirable); *Re Hodson's Settlement* (1851) 9 Hare 118; *Re Higginbottom* [1892] 3 Ch. 132 (probably no jurisdiction).

68 *Re May's Will Trust* [1941] Ch. 109 (absence in enemy territory).

69 TA 1925 s.41; para.27-018.

70 TA 1925 s.36(4).

71 TA 1925 s.36(5).

72 *Re Crowhurst Park* [1974] 1 W.L.R. 583.

73 TA 1925 s.36(9), as amended by Mental Capacity Act 2005 s.68(1), Sch.6 para.3(2)(b)(ii).

(3)   The person appointed.

Replace paragraph with:

27-014   It is expressly provided that the person making the appointment may appoint himself.[74] He should not, however, appoint anyone whom the court would not appoint,[75] although the appointment is not necessarily invalid if he does,[76] nor, if he is a trustee, is such an appointment itself a breach of trust.[77] But if the appointor is a minor, the appointment will be closely scrutinised, and may be set aside.[78]

74 TA 1925 s.36(1), altering on this point TA 1893 s.10; see *Re Sampson* [1906] 1 Ch. 435. Compare the position under express powers (para.27-011) and contrast the power of appointing additional trustees (para.27-016).

75 See para.27-019.

76 *Forster v Abraham* (1874) L.R. 17 Eq. 351 (tenant for life); *Re Earl of Stamford* [1896] 1 Ch. 288 (solicitor to tenant for life); *Re Coode* (1913) 108 L.T. 94 (husband of tenant for life); and see *Re Cotter* [1915] 1 Ch. 307.

77 *Briggs v Parsloe* [1937] 3 All E.R. 831.

78 *Re Parsons* [1940] Ch. 973; quaere what this case decided: see (1941) 57 L.Q.R. 25.

(4)   Number of trustees.

Replace n.88 with:

27-015   88 See *Adam and Co International Trustees Ltd v Theodore Goddard* [2000] W.T.L.R. 349 and *Gelber v Sunderland Foundation* [2018] EWHC 2344.

(c)   Trusts of Land and Appointment of Trustees Act 1996.

Replace paragraph with:

27-017   Section 19 of the Trusts of Land and Appointment of Trustees Act 1996 entitles the beneficiaries to give directions to the trustees either or both to retire and appoint new trustees in certain circumstances. The power is exercisable only where no person is nominated for the purpose of appointing trustees by the trust deed and where the beneficiaries are of full age and capacity and (taken together) are absolutely entitled to the property subject to the trust.[94] Section 19 does not permit such a beneficiary to appoint a trustee directly; such appointment should be made by the existing trustee at the direction of the beneficiary.[94a] Section 20 provides that where a trustee is incapable of performing his functions as trustee, and there is no-one able and willing to appoint a replacement under s.36(1) of the Trustee Act 1925 the beneficiaries may (if they are of full age and capacity and, taken together, are absolutely entitled to the property subject to the trust) appoint a replacement trustee. Sections 19 and 20 can be excluded by express provision in the trust deed in the case of trusts created since 1 January 1997. They can also be excluded in the case of trusts created by disposition before that date by deed made by the settlor or surviving settlors.[95]

[94] TLATA 1996 s.19(1).

[94a] *Malik v Kettle* [2020] EWHC 2568 (Ch).

[95] TLATA 1996 s.21(5), (6).

(d)   The court.

(1)   Trustee Act 1925.

Replace paragraph with:
   Under the Trustee Act 1925[96] the court has a wide power of appointing a new   **27-018** trustee or new trustees either in substitution for or in addition to any existing trustee or trustees, or although there is no existing trustee.[97] The appointment can be made whenever it is expedient to appoint a new trustee and it is found "inexpedient, difficult or impracticable so to do without the assistance of the court", e.g. when a trustee is imprisoned, or is mentally defective, or is bankrupt, or is a corporation which is in liquidation or has been dissolved. The section authorises the displacement of a trustee against his will.[98] The court also has very extensive powers of making vesting orders with regard to trust land, and orders vesting the right to transfer trust stock or sue for trust things in action.[99] Applications for the appointment of a new trustee and for such vesting orders may be made by any beneficiary or trustee.[100]

[96] TA 1925 s.41, replacing TA 1893 s.25. In *Re C Trust* [2019] 22 ITELR 155, the Supreme Court of Bermuda held that the inherent jurisdiction to supervise the administration of a trust extended to the making of an order confirming a trustee's appointment in cases where there some doubt over the validity of the trustee's appointment under a defective deed.

[97] In *Potier v Treasury Solicitor (Bona Vacantia)* [2021] EWHC 1524 (Ch) at [38] it was noted that the discretion under TA 1925 s. 41(1) is a very broad one that will be exercised in a way that is essentially pragmatic; a court is not limited to reinstating the terms of the trust and can, in an appropriate case (such as a bare trust), vest title in the beneficiary. In *Bridge Trustees Ltd v Noel Penny* [2008] EWHC 2054 (Ch); 2008 P.L.R. 345 it was held that this power can only be used to appoint a trustee properly so called, and this does not include an independent trustee under a pension scheme, albeit that the court might appoint him under its inherent power (in that case for the purpose of distributing surplus assets).

[98] *Re Henderson (Charles)* [1940] Ch. 764. cf. *Titterton v Oates* [2001] W.T.L.R. 319 (Australia), where it was held that similar Australian legislation did not authorise the court to remove a trustee against his will.

[99] TA 1925 ss.44–56, replacing TA 1893 ss.26–41.

[100] TA 1925 s.58.

Delete sub-paragraph "Judicial Trustees Act 1896.".   **27-020**

Delete sub-paragraph "Public Trustee Act 1906.".   **27-021**

4.   VESTING OF TRUST PROPERTY

1.   Vesting Declarations

Replace paragraph with:
   The mere appointment of a person as trustee does not by itself vest the trust   **27-022**

property in him; the office of trustee is one thing, the trust property another. On every appointment of a trustee it is accordingly necessary to provide for the vesting of the trust property in the new trustee, either alone (if he is the sole trustee) or jointly with his co-trustees. By virtue of the Trustee Act 1925 s.40,[124] this can often be done without any express conveyance or assignment. The section applies to all trusts, whenever created, unless negatived by the trust instrument, if any[125]; but it does not apply to property held by personal representatives in the course of administration.[126] If the appointment is made by deed, a mere vesting declaration in it suffices to vest the property in those who have become the trustees[127]; and where the deed is made after 1925, then, subject to any express provision to the contrary, it operates as if it contained such a declaration even if none is actually inserted.[128]

[124] Replacing TA 1893 s.12.

[125] TA 1925 s.69(2).

[126] *Re King's Will Trusts* [1964] Ch. 542; sed quaere; see para.21-055. In *Re AMT Coffee Ltd* [2018] EWHC 1562 at [12] the court held than an order appointing a new personal representative under the Administration of Justice Act 1985, s.50 has a similar vesting effect to TA 1925, s.40.

[127] TA 1925 s.40(1), (3).

[128] TA 1925 s.40(1). In *Procter v Procter* [2022] EWHC 1202 at [30] the Court held that a recital in a trust deed that vesting would occur "forthwith" did not amount to a contrary intention that vesting would occur by the same deed.

2.   Exceptions

Replace paragraph with:

27-023   There are three classes of property to which the section does not apply. They are as follows[129]:

  (i)   land held by the trustees by way of mortgage for securing money subject to the trust, except land conveyed on trust for securing debentures or debenture stock;

  (ii)   land held under a lease which contains a covenant not to assign without consent, unless before the execution of the deed the requisite consent has been obtained, or unless by virtue of any statute or rule of law the vesting declaration, express or implied, would not operate as a breach of covenant or give rise to a forfeiture; and

  (iii) any share, stock, annuity, or property which is only transferable in books kept by a company or other body, or in manner directed by or under Act of Parliament.

These forms of property must be vested in the trustee by the appropriate form of conveyance or transfer. The reason for the first exception is to avoid bringing the trusts on to the title; for otherwise on redemption the mortgagor would have to investigate the title to the mortgage, including, e.g. appointments of new trustees, in order to see that he is paying the right persons. The second exception is to avoid accidental breaches of the terms of the lease; and the third exception is made necessary by the normal mode of transferring such property.[129a]

[129] TA 1925 s.40(4).

[129a] *Re AMT Coffee Ltd* [2018] EWHC 1562.

5.   THE PUBLIC TRUSTEE

After para.27-024 add new paragraph:

The title of this section should be changed to: Statutory Trustees

There are three trustees that are creations of statute that require special men-   27-024A
tion, namely the judicial trustee, custodian trustees, and the Public Trustee. Whereas
judicial trustees and custodian trustees are types of trusteeship that can be held by
any appropriate person, the Public Trustee is a corporation sole.[131] The use of statutory trustees, although less common in recent times, is often desirable in cases
where it has proved difficult to find appropriate persons to act as normal trustees,
or where there has been breakdown in relationship between the trustees and
beneficiaries.

[131] Public Trustee Act 1906 s.1.

1.   Appointment and Powers

Replace para.27-025 with:
[This sub-section is deleted in the supplement.]   **27-025**

2.   Limits to Powers

Replace para.27-026 with:
[This sub-section is deleted in the supplement.]   **27-026**

3.   As Custodian Trustee

Replace para.27-027 with:
[This sub-section is deleted in the supplement, including footnote 137 from title.]

After the third sub-section, add new sub-section:

3A.   The Judicial Trustee

(a)   General   Judicial Trustees Act 1896[132] created the role of the 'judicial   27-027A
trustee'. A judicial trustee has the same powers of a normal trustee, but is appointed by and acts under the control of the court. The object of the Act:

> "was to provide a middle course in cases where the administration of the estate by the
> ordinary trustees had broken down and it was not desired to put the estate to the expense
> of a full administration"

by the court.[133] Until recently the Act offered the only way of replacing a personal
representative once a grant had been made and he had begun the administration.[134]
The jurisdiction is commonly resorted to where, for reasons not necessarily involving fault on the part of the representative (e.g. illness or conflicting interest), it is
expedient to replace him.

(b)   Appointment   On an application by the settlor or a trustee or a beneficiary,   27-027B
the court may appoint any fit and proper person nominated in the application,[135] or
an official of the court (usually the Official Solicitor), to be a judicial trustee to act
alone or jointly[136] with any other person and, if sufficient cause is shown, in place
of all or any existing trustees. The Act allows the court to appoint a judicial trustee

to be a Settled Land Act trustee,[137] or to administer the estate of a testator or intestate instead of the executor or administrator,[138] though not to administer part of the estate, since an executorship is indivisible.[139] In all cases the appointment of a judicial trustee is absolutely discretionary.[140]

27-027C **(c) Powers of the judicial trustee** A judicial trustee differs from an ordinary trustee in a number of respects. He is an officer of the court, and as such is subject to its control and supervision; he can at any time obtain the court's directions as to the way in which he is to act, without the necessity of a formal application; he is entitled to such remuneration as the court allows him; every year he must prepare accounts for examination by the court,[141] although a corporate trustee[142] need only submit such accounts to such persons as the court directs[143]; and he cannot appoint a successor under the statutory power[144] for this would usurp the function of the court.[145] In other respects he is in the position of any other trustee, and so, for example, he can compromise claims.[146]

[132] Judicial Trustees Act 1896 s.1; and see Judicial Trustee Rules 1983 (SI 1983/370), replacing with amendments Judicial Trustee Rules 1972 (SI 1972/1096).

[133] *Re Ridsdel* [1947] Ch. 597 at 605, per Jenkins J.

[134] See now Administration of Justice Act 1985 s.50 (power of court to appoint substitute for, or remove, personal representative), para.34-015.

[135] See *Douglas v Bolam* [1900] 2 Ch. 749.

[136] It is not, however, desirable for a judicial trustee and a private trustee to hold office jointly: *Re Martin* [1900] W.N. 129.

[137] *Re Marshall's Will Trusts* [1945] Ch. 217.

[138] *Re Ratcliff* [1898] 2 Ch. 352.

[139] *Re Wells* [1968] 1 W.L.R. 44.

[140] *Re Ratcliff* [1898] 2 Ch. 352.

[141] Judicial Trustee Rules 1983 rr.9, 10, 12. A yearly audit was formerly required: Judicial Trustees Act 1896 s.1(6), partially repealed by Administration of Justice Act 1982 s.75(1) and Sch.9 Pt I.

[142] Judicial Trustee Rules 1983 r.2(1).

[143] Judicial Trustee Rules 1983 r.13.

[144] TA 1925 s.36, above.

[145] *Re Johnston* (1911) 105 L.T. 701.

[146] *Re Ridsdel* [1947] Ch. 597; for the power of compromise, see para.28-026.

4. As Ordinary Trustee

Replace para.27-028 with:

27-028 [This sub-section is deleted in the supplement.]

After the fourth sub-section, add new sub-section:

4A. Custodian Trustees

27-028A **(a) General** The role of custodian trustee was created by the Public Trustee Act 1906.[147] A custodian trustee is appointed along with other trustees known as the 'management trustees'. Whereas the management trustees are responsible for the active management and administration of the trust, the custodian trustee has custody of the trust fund and trust documents.[148] The various bodies who may act as a custodian trustee are prescribed by the rules made under the Public Trustee Act,[149] and include the Public Trustee, the Treasury Solicitor, particular corporations, health authorities, local authorities and other public bodies. A custodian trustee may be appointed by a settlor, anyone with the power to appoint a trustee, or the court.[150]

(b) Powers of the custodian trustee When appointed, the trust property must 27-028B
be transferred to the custodian trustee as if he were sole trustee,[151] and all the securities and documents of title relating to the trust property are to be in his sole custody. Further, all sums payable to or out of the income of the trust property are to be paid to or by him, except that he may allow the dividends and other income to be paid to the other trustees (called the "managing trustees"), or as they may direct. The management of the trust property and the exercise of any power or discretion exercisable by the trustees under the trust remain vested in the managing trustees.[152] Where there is a power to appoint new trustees, this is exercisable by the managing trustees, although the custodian trustee has the power to apply to the court for the appointment of a new trustee.[153] The court has power to determine a custodian trusteeship if it is expedient,[154] e.g. when it is desirable for the trustee to become an ordinary trustee.[155]

[147] Public Trustee Act 1906 s.4(1). See generally S. G. Maurice (1960) 24 Conv. (N.S.) 196.

[148] Public Trustee Act 1906 s.4(2).

[149] Public Trustee Rules 1912 r.30 (as amended).

[150] Public Trustee Act 1906 s.4(1).

[151] Public Trustee Act 1906 s.4(2)(a)-(c).

[152] Public Trustee Act 1906 s.4(2)(b).

[153] Public Trustee Act 1906 s.4(2)(f).

[154] Public Trustee Act 1906 s.4.

[155] *Re Squires Settlement* (1945) 115 L.J.Ch. 90.

5. As Personal Representative

Replace para.27-029 with:
[This sub-section is deleted in the supplement.]   **27-029**

After the fifth sub-section, add new sub-section:

5A. The Public Trustee

(a) General The office of the Public Trustee was established by the Public 27-029A
Trustee Act 1906. The purpose of the Public Trustee was to act in cases where it was otherwise difficult to find a person willing to act as trustee. The chief advantages derived from appointing him to act as a trustee are as follows. First, being a corporation sole, the office has perpetual existence, despite the death or retirement of the individual from time to time holding it; secondly, the Lord Chancellor's Department is responsible for any loss to the trust estate caused by his breaches of trust[156]; and thirdly, he has a wide experience in trust matters, and yet his fees are moderate. He may, if he thinks fit, act as a custodian trustee, as an ordinary trustee, or as a judicial trustee, and may act alone or jointly with another person or other persons[157]; and he may hold land.[158]

(b) Limits to Powers The Public Trustee may decline to accept any trust, and 27-029B
the current practice is that he only accepts trusts as a matter of last resort. However, the Public Trustee must not decline solely on the ground of the smallness of the trust

property.[159] Further, he cannot accept any trust exclusively for religious or charitable purposes,[160] nor any except an English trust[160a], nor any trust under a deed of arrangement for the benefit of creditors; nor can he undertake the administration of any estate known or believed by him to be insolvent. He also, as ordinary trustee, cannot carry on a business without the leave of the Treasury, unless he is satisfied that it can be carried on without risk of loss, and he carries it on:

    (i)   for not more than 18 months; and

    (ii)   with a view to sale, disposition, or winding up.

27-029C **(c) As Custodian Trustee** The Public Trustee may be appointed to act as custodian trustee may be made by the court, or by the settlor, or by the person who has power to appoint new trustees. When so appointed, the Public Trustee has the same powers and duties of a normal custodian trustee.[160b]

27-029D **(d) As Ordinary Trustee** The Public Trustee may be appointed to be an ordinary trustee, either as an original or a new trustee or as an additional trustee, in the same cases and in the same manner and by the same persons or court as if he were a private trustee; and even if the trustees originally appointed were two or more, the Public Trustee may be appointed sole trustee.[160c] The Public Trustee may be appointed as sole trustee and exercise all the powers of the trustees under the trust despite a direction in the trust instrument that on appointment of new trustees the number shall not be reduced below three[160d] and despite a direction that no discretion vested in the trustees may be exercised at any time when there are less than two trustees.[160e] But if the trust instrument prohibits his appointment he may not be appointed a new or additional trustee unless the court otherwise orders.[160f] Further, if it is proposed to appoint him as a new or additional trustee, notice must be given to the beneficiaries; and on the application of any beneficiary, the court may prohibit the appointment if it considers it expedient to do so having regard to the interests of all the beneficiaries.[160g]

27-029E **(e) As Personal Representative** The Public Trustee is also given power to obtain probate of a will or letters of administration.[160h] Further, with the leave of the court an executor who has obtained probate, or an administrator who has obtained letters of administration, may transfer to the Public Trustee the whole future administration of the estate, and in that way escape all liability in respect of the further administration.[160i]

[156] Under s.7 of the Public Trustee Act 1906 the liability was that of the Consolidated Fund. Section 7 was repealed by Public Trustee (Liability and Fees) Act 2002, with result that the liability is now that of the Lord Chancellor's Department: see 390 HL Official Report (6th series) col.261.

[157] Public Trustee Act 1906 s.2.

[158] *Re Leslie's Hassop Estates* [1911] 1 Ch. 611.

[159] Public Trustee Act 1906 s.2(3).

[160] See *Re Hampton* (1919) 88 L.J.Ch. 103. See para.23-064 for the Official Custodian for Charities.

[160a] *Re Hewitts Settlement* [1915] 1 Ch. 228.

[160b] See above.

[160c] Public Trustee Act 1906 s.5(1).

[160d] *Re Moxon* [1916] 2 Ch. 595.

[160e] *Re Duxbury's Settlement Trusts* [1995] 1 W.L.R. 425.

[160f] Public Trustee Act 1906 s.5(3).

160g Public Trustee Act 1906 s.5(4); see *Re Firth (No.1)* [1912] 1 Ch. 806.

160h Public Trustee Act 1906 s.6(1); Public Trustee Rules 1912 r.6.

160i Public Trustee Act 1906 s.6(2).

6.   DETERMINATION OF TRUSTEESHIP

1.   Disclaimer

Replace para.27-030 with:
[This sub-section is deleted in the supplement.]   **27-030**

Delete para.27-031 "Limits to disclaimer.".   **27-031**

Delete para.27-032 "Effect on property.".   **27-032**

2.   Retirement

(b)   Vesting of property.

Replace n.169 with:

169 In Procter v Procter [2022] EWHC 1202 at [48] the court confirmed that (1) where there is a retire-   **27-034**
ment and no appointment of a new trustee, vesting in the continuing trustees occurs under TA 1925
s.40(2); where there is a retirement and simultaneous appointment of a new trustee, vesting in the
continuing and new trustees occurs under TA 1925 s.40(1).

4.   Removal

Replace paragraph with:

   The statutory power to remove a trustee under s.41 of the Trustee Act 1925 is not   **27-036**
applicable in cases where the claim is brought by someone other than the trustee
or beneficiary of the trust. [170a] Furthermore, the statutory power cannot be used for
the simple removal of a trustee, where there is not a corresponding appointment of
new trustee.[170b]. Where the statutory power does not apply, the court has an inherent jurisdiction to remove a trustee (including a trustee of a foreign trust[171]) and to
appoint a new one in his place. As the interests of the trust are of paramount
importance to the court, this jurisdiction will be exercised whenever the welfare of
the beneficiaries requires it,[172] even if the trustees have been guilty of no
misconduct.[173] The welfare of the beneficiaries is also the court's guide in exercising its statutory powers of removal, e.g. on bankruptcy.[174] A bankrupt trustee ought
to be removed from his trusteeship whenever the nature of the trust is such that he
has to receive and deal with trust funds so that he can misappropriate them; but if
there is no danger to the trust property, bankruptcy by itself will not necessarily
induce the court to remove him.[175]

170a s.58(1) TA 1925; *Davidson v Seelig* [2016] EWHC 549 (application by protector refused).

170b *London Capital & Finance Plc (in Admin) v Global Security Trustees Ltd* [2019] EWHC 3339 (Ch).

171 *Chellaram v Chellaram* [1985] Ch. 409.

172 *Re Wrightson* [1908] 1 Ch. 789; *Miller v Cameron* (1936) 54 C.L.R. 572 (Aus H.C.); *Titterton v
Oates* [2001] W.T.L.R. 319 (Australia); *London Capital & Finance Plc (in Admin) v Global Security
Trustees Ltd* [2019] EWHC 3339 (Ch) (threshold for the exercise of the inherent jurisdiction is not higher
than that of the statutory power).

173 *Letterstedt v Broers* (1884) 9 App. Cas. 371.

174 TA 1925 s.41.

175 *Re Barker's Trusts* (1875) 1 Ch. D. 43; *Re Adam's Trust* (1879) 12 Ch. D. 634.

CHAPTER 28

SPECIFIC POWERS: THE ADMINISTRATIVE POWERS OF TRUSTEES

CONTENTS

1. Sale

2. Mode of Sale

After "and minerals separately.", replace "An express power to sell settled land" with:

28-008   Where land is settled under the Settled Land Act 1925, an express power to sell

3. The Price

Replace n.54 with:

28-009   [54] *Marley v Mutual Security Merchant Bank and Trust Co Ltd* [1991] 3 All E.R. 198. In *Kingsley v Kingsley* [2020] 1 WLR 1909, where the court made an order that one beneficiary sell their interest to another (under TLATA 1996, s. 14(2)), it was held that the price could be determined by the court, and there is no absolute requirement that the value of the property be "tested" on the open market. See also *Bagum v Hafiz* [2016] Ch 241.

4. Conditions of Sale

Replace paragraph with:

28-010   Trustees must be careful not to sell under unnecessarily depreciatory conditions,[41] for if the purchase price is thereby rendered inadequate, the beneficiaries can interfere to stop the sale at any time before completion.[41a] After completion, the beneficiaries can hold the trustees personally liable for the loss, but the title of the purchaser will be indefeasible unless he acted in collusion with the trustees.[42]

[41]   See *Dunn v Flood* (1885) 28 Ch. D. 586.

[41a]   Trustee Act 1925, s.13(1).

[42]   TA 1925 s.13(2), replacing TA 1893 s.14.

2. Partition

2. Chattels

Replace n.53 with:

28-013   [53] LPA 1925 s.188. See *Butler v Butler* [2016] EWHC 1793 (Ch).

4. Delegation

1. Employment of Agents

(c)   Part IV of the Trustee Act 2000.

Replace n.82 with:

28-019   [82] TA 2000 s.23.

3. Temporary Delegation

(a)   The power.

Replace n.90 with:

28-021   [90] Mental Capacity Act 2005, s.9(1).

(c) Effect.

Replace n.98 with:

[98] Powers of Attorney Act 1971 s.5(2).   **28-023**

5.   COMPROMISE AND VALUATION

1.   Compromise of Claims

Replace the first paragraph with:

The Trustee Act 1925[109] gives wide powers of compromise and valuation to a   **28-026**
personal representative, to two or more trustees acting together, to a judicial
trustee,[110] or (subject to the restrictions imposed in regard to receipts by a sole
trustee not being a trust corporation) to a sole acting trustee where by the instrument (if any) creating the trust or by statute[111] a sole trustee is authorised to execute
the trusts and powers imposed in him. These persons may, if and as they or he think
or thinks fit:

(i)   accept any property before the time at which it is made transferable or pay-
        able; or
(ii)   sever and apportion any blended trust funds or property; or
(iii)   pay or allow any debt or claim on any evidence that he or they think suf-
        ficient; or
(iv)   accept any composition or security for any debt or for any property
        claimed; or
(v)   allow any time of payment of any debt; or
(vi)   compromise, compound, abandon, submit to arbitration or otherwise set-
        tle any debt or claim.

The powers apply primarily in the context of external disputes between the trustee,
acting on behalf of the trust, and a third party; internal disputes, such as a dispute
between beneficiaries as to the construction of the trust deed, fall outside the scope
of the power.[111a] Although powers are to be given a wide construction,[112] in exercising them the statutory duty of care applies to the trustee.[112a] In compromising a
claim to property in the hands of a beneficiary the trustees may accept a surrender
of his interest in satisfaction of the claim, if satisfied that such a course is expedient for the trust as a whole.[113] A composition of this kind does not amount to a variation or rearrangement of the trusts of the settlement.[114]

[109]   TA 1925 s.15, replacing TA 1893 s.21.

[110]   *Re Ridsdel* [1947] Ch. 597.

[111]   For example, a trustee of a deed of arrangement: see *Re Shenton* [1935] Ch. 651.

[111a] *Re Earl of Strafford* [1980] Ch. 28, 32.

[112]   *Re Earl of Strafford* [1980] Ch. 28 at 47, 51.

[112a] Trustee Act 2000, s.1(1), Sch.1, para.4.

[113]   *Re Earl of Strafford* [1980] Ch. 28.

[114]   *Re Earl of Strafford* [1980] Ch. 28 at 47, 48, 51. See para.29-044.

6. PROTECTION AGAINST CLAIMS

1. Payment into Court

Replace paragraph with:

28-030   In case of difficulty, trustees or personal representatives may obtain a discharge by paying into court any trust money or securities in their hands or under their control[123]; and the receipt or certificate of the proper officer is a sufficient discharge.[124] If they are unanimous, they may make the payment into court merely on filing an affidavit or witness statement[125]; but if only a majority wish to make payment in, they can do so by obtaining an order of the court.[126] Trustees should make a payment in only when there is no other way of obtaining a discharge, as where they cannot obtain a valid receipt[127]; thus a doubt as to which of several persons are entitled to the trust fund should be resolved by instituting proceedings in which those persons are named as defendants.[128] Similarly, doubt as to whether a beneficiary is still living should be resolved by an application for a *Re Benjamin*[128a] order, or an order under the Presumption of Death Act 2013. An application to pay trust monies into court is apt where a beneficiary can be located but is refusing to accept payment or give good receipt to the trustee. Life assurance companies have a somewhat similar power of paying policy moneys into court in cases of difficulty.[129]

[123] TA 1925 ss.63(1), 68(17), replacing TA 1893 ss.42, 50, which replaced earlier legislation. TA 1925 s.63(1) was slightly amended by the Administration of Justice Act 1965 s.36(4), Sch.3.

[124] TA 1925 s.63(2).

[125] CPR Pt 37, PD 9.1; Court Funds Rules 1987 r.14(1)(ii)(b). A personal representative may make a written request for payment in: above r.15(1)(ii)(b).

[126] TA 1925 s.63(3). See s.63(4) for ancillary powers.

[127] See, e.g. *Re Parker's Will* (1888) 39 Ch. D. 303.

[128] See *Re Birkett* (1878) 9 Ch. D. 576; *Re Giles* (1886) 55 L.J.Ch. 695.

[128a] [1902] 1 Ch 723.

[129] Life Assurance Companies (Payment into Court) Act 1896.

2. Advertisement for Claimants

(b)   Effect of advertisement.

Replace n.135 with:

28-032   [135] *Re Aldhous* [1955] 1 W.L.R. 459 at 462. In *Womble Bond Dickinson (Trust Corporation) Ltd v Persons Unamed* [2022] EWHC 43 (Ch) at [68] the court held that a trustee could not avoid their obligation to consider the objects of a class of discretionary beneficiaries by issuing a s. 27 advertisement for potential beneficiaries.

7. MAINTENANCE AND ADVANCEMENT

3. Statutory Power of Advancement

(a)   The power.

Replace paragraph with:

28-047   Under the section any capital money subject to a trust may at any time or times be paid or applied by trustees or personal representatives[214] for "the advancement or benefit" of any person entitled to the capital of the trust property or of any share thereof. Although the section refers to "capital money", assets can be conveyed in specie to avoid the circuitous course of advancing money to the beneficiary and then selling the assets to him.[215] This is confirmed by recent amendments to the power.[216] Further, capital is "applied" even if the beneficiary is merely given a life interest in the income of the capital fund.[217] The power applies[218] whether the beneficiary is entitled absolutely or contingently on his attaining any specified age or on the occurrence of any other event, including a double contingency, such as attaining the age of 21 years and surviving a life tenant.[219] It also applies where his interest is subject to a gift over on his death under any specified age or on the occurrence of any other event, and whether it is in possession or in remainder or reversion, and even if it is liable to be defeated by the exercise of a power of appointment or revocation, or to be diminished by the increase of the class to which he belongs.[220] The power also applies in respect of a beneficiary whose share of the trust fund is settled on a *Hancock v Watson*[221] type contingency.[221a] The power does not apply to capital money arising under the Settled Land Act 1925.[222]

[214] See TA 1925 s.68(17).

[215] *Re Collard's Will Trusts* [1961] Ch. 293 (see (1961) 77 L.Q.R. 161); *Pilkington v IRC* [1964] A.C. 612 at 639; and see para.5-029.

[216] The relevant provisions, Inheritance and Trustees' Powers Act 2014 s.9(1)–(2), (3)(a) and (4)–(5), were brought into force on 1 October 2014: see Inheritance and Trustees' Powers Act 2014 (Commencement) Order 2014 (SI 2014/2039) art.2. Once in force these provisions apply prospectively to any trusts, whenever created or arising: Inheritance and Trustees' Powers Act 2014 s.10(2).

[217] *Re Hastings-Bass* [1975] Ch. 25.

[218] TA 1925 s.32(1).

[219] *Re Garrett* [1934] Ch. 477.

[220] TA 1925 s.32(1).

[221] [1902] AC 14 [x-ref to section on resulting trusts where this case is discussed].

[221a] *Womble Bond Dickinson (Trust Corporation) Ltd v Glenn* [2021] EWHC 624, para 50.

[222] TA 1925 s.32(2). Settlements of land usually contain provisions for portions.

(b) Limitations on the power.

(3) Prior interests.

Replace paragraph with:

No advance can be made to the prejudice of a person entitled to a prior life or other interest, whether vested or contingent, unless he is in existence[231] and of full age and gives a written consent. "Prior" refers to the order in which the interests are enjoyed, for instance, that of a life tenant whose interest is enjoyed before that of a remainder beneficiary. The consent of beneficiaries with subsequent interests in capital, such as a contingent remainder beneficiary, are not required for the exercise of the power.[231a] The section does not require the consent of a person who is merely one of an indefinite number of objects of a discretionary trust,[232] even if the trust has come into operation[233]; but the court has no power to dispense with the consent of a person with whom it is impossible to communicate.[234]   **28-051**

[231] See *IRC v Bernstein* [1961] Ch. 399 at 411.

[231a] *Womble Bond Dickinson (Trust Corporation) Ltd v Glenn* [2021] EWHC 624, para.56.

[232] *Re Harris' Settlement* (1940) 162 L.T. 358.

[233] *Re Beckett's Settlement* [1940] Ch. 279.

[234] See *Re Forster's Settlement* [1942] Ch. 199 (express power of advancement).

(c)   The trustees' discretion.

Replace paragraph with:

28-052   The trustees may pay or apply the money for the "advancement or benefit" of the beneficiary "in such manner as they may, in their absolute discretion, think fit".[235] In construing the term "advancement or benefit" the courts are guided by the decisions on express powers.[236] "Benefit" is "the widest possible word one could have",[237] and so in a proper exercise of their discretion trustees may not only provide for the education of the beneficiary[238] but also make a payment directly to him[239] or make a settlement on him and his family, either for their immediate or their future benefit.[240] This is so even where the members of the family are not objects of the original trust; for it can be a benefit to a person that his family is provided for.[241] There is no particular formality required to exercise the statutory power, meaning that the power can be exercised orally or even by implication.[241a] In practice it is common for a will or trust instrument to require that the power be exercised by deed. In all cases it is essential that the trustees have formed an intention to exercise the power, and ignorance of its existence will prevent the power from being exercised, notwithstanding the advancement of capital to a beneficiary.[241b]

[235] TA 1925 s.32(1).

[236] *Pilkington v IRC* [1964] A.C. 612 at 634; see para.28-046. *Pilkington v IRC* was considered in *Re Pinto's Settlement* [2004] W.T.L.R. 879 (Jersey).

[237] *Re Moxon's Will Trusts* [1958] 1 W.L.R. 165 at 168, per Danckwerts J.

[238] Assumed in *Re Garrett* [1934] Ch. 477.

[239] *Re Moxon's Will Trusts* [1958] 1 W.L.R. 165. See generally *D.W.M. Waters* (1958) 22 Conv.(N.S.) 413.

[240] *Pilkington v IRC* [1964] A.C. 612.

[241] *Re Hastings-Bass* [1975] Ch. 25 at 39.

[241a] *Batt v Boswell* [2022] EWHC 649 (Ch) [128].

[241b] *Re Lawrence's Will Trusts* [1972] Ch 418, 430.

CHAPTER 29

THE DUTIES AND DISCRETIONS OF TRUSTEES

CONTENTS

THE CARES OF OFFICE

Replace n.1 with:

29-001   [1] *Knight v Earl of Plymouth* (1747) Dick. 120 at 126, per Lord Hardwicke LC.

DUTIES AT COMMON LAW AND UNDER THE TRUSTEE ACT 2000

Replace the fifth paragraph with:

29-003   Not all trustees are subject to the same rules. Thus the duties of a trustee in bankruptcy to the bankrupt are not those of an ordinary trustee towards a beneficiary, even though the bankrupt is entitled to any surplus assets; for a trustee in bankruptcy is primarily not a trustee for the bankrupt, but an assignee of his assets for the benefit of his creditors.[11] Whether the statutory duty care applies to bare trusts is not entirely clear. Trustees of bare trusts are often described as mere ciphers for the beneficiary,[11a] which would suggest that they simply hold the trust property as a nominee for the beneficiary. Yet it is clear that the beneficiary of a bare trust has no power to direct the trustee other than to compel them to convey the trust property.[11b] Conversely, it appears to be the case that bare trustees do have administrative powers, at least in some situations. Section 1(2) of the Trusts of Land and Appointment of Trustees Act 1996 expressly states that bare trusts fall within the definition of a 'trust of land', meaning that the general ownership powers conferred by s.6 of the Act apply to bare trustee of land. Elsewhere, the Trustee Act 1925 assumes that a bare trustee has a power to insure trust property.[11c] To the extent that trustees of bare trusts have powers to administer the trust fund, it is reasonable to assume that they fall within the statutory duty of care.

[11] See *Re A Debtor, Ex p. the Debtor v Dodwell* [1949] Ch. 236 at 240–243: *Re Leadbitter* (1878) 10 Ch. D. 388.

[11a] See *Kirby v Williams* [1929] 2 Ch 444 and *Christie v Ovington* (1875) 1 Ch D 279. In *Tomlinson v Glyn's Executor & Trustee Co* [1969] 2 W.L.R. 283 at 288 the court assumed that a beneficiary of a bare trust could give directions to a trustee. It is likely that this decision led to the statutory definition of a 'bare trust' found in Taxation of Chargeable Gains Act 1992 s.60, which refers to a beneficiary's ability "to direct how" trust property be dealt with.

[11b] *Re Brockbank* [1948] 1 Ch 206, *Ingram v HMRC* [1997] STC 1234 at 1259 and *McLaughlin v HMRC* [2012] UKFTT 174.

[11c] s.19 TA 1925, as modified by s.34 TA 2000.

1.   THE TRUST PROPERTY

1.   Reduction into Possession

After "to an executor.", add new n.13a:

29-004   [13a] Administration of Estates Act 1925, s.25(a).

4.   Investment and Pt II of the Trustee Act 2000

Replace first paragraph with:

29-007   The trustees' investment powers must be exercised in accordance with the purpose of the trust. Prima facie the purpose of the trust is best served by seeking the maximum return consistent with commercial prudence.[29a] In the case of a charity, the trustees have a discretion to exclude investments that potentially conflict with the purpose of the charity, although caution is necessary where the discretion is exercised for purely moral reasons.[29b] The duty of charitable trustees is to act honestly and reasonably in balancing the risks that particular investments would damage the reputation of the charity and alienate potential donors, against the potential financial effect of excluding such an investment.[29c]

[29a] *Cowan v Scargill* [1985] Ch. 270.

[29b] *Butler-Sloss v The Charity Commission* [2022] EWHC 974 (Ch), [76(6)-(7)]. The earlier case of *Harries v Church Commissioners* [1992] 1 W.L.R. 1241 at 124 suggested a stricter approach, whereby charitable trustees were not permitted to use the investment powers to as a means of making "moral statements". Whilst the court in *Butler-Sloss v The Charity Commission* did not disapprove of this statement, or otherwise suggest that *Harries* had been incorrectly decided, *Butler-Sloss* does confirm that charitable trustees have the discretion to exclude particular investments if they conflict with the charity's purpose.

[29c] *Butler-Sloss v The Charity Commission* [2022] EWHC 974 (Ch), [76(9)].

Create new second paragraph:
Originally the only proper investments were mortgages, Government Funds ("Consols") and any other investments authorised by the settlement. The range of authorised investments was substantially extended by a series of statutes, beginning with the Law of Property Amendment Act 1859,[32] and including the Trustee Act 1893,[33] and the Trustee Act 1925 s.1. These permitted trust funds to be invested in a substantial number of securities issued by the Government and various public bodies.

[32] See Law of Property Amendment Act 1859 s.32.

[33] See TA 1893 s.1.

Replace n.41 with:

[41] TA 2000 s.5. See *Brown v New Quadrant Trust Corporation Ltd* [2021] EWHC 1731 (Ch) at [29] for an example of a court approving of the trustees' decision not to obtain specialist advice on an investment decision.

3. Duty to Keep Accounts and Records and Disclosure of Trust Documents

1. The Duty

Replace paragraph with:
Another duty of a trustee[123] is to keep accounts and produce them to any **29-024** beneficiary when required.[124] The level of detail and formality required when providing an account will vary according to the size and nature of the trust, but the basic duty to account means that the trustee ought to be able to inform the beneficiary of what assets there were, what they have done with the assets, what the assets now are, and what distributions have taken place.[124a] Trustees must also when required give any beneficiary all reasonable information as to the manner in which the trust estate has been dealt with and as to the investments representing it.[125] When a beneficiary comes of age they must inform him of his interest under the trust.[126]

[123] For the position of judicial trustees as regards accounts, see para.27-020. For personal representatives, see AEA 1925 s.25, as substituted by AEA 1971 s.9.

[124] See *Pearse v Green* (1819) 1 Jac. & W. 135 at 140; *Armitage v Nurse* [1998] Ch. 241 at 255 (per Millett LJ); *James v Newington* [2004] W.T.L.R 1417 (Jersey).

[124a] *Ball v Ball* [2020] EWHC 1020, at [24].

[125] *Re Dartnall* [1895] 1 Ch. 474.

[126] *Hawkesley v May* [1956] 1 Q.B. 304. Contrast personal representatives: *Re Lewis* [1904] 2 Ch. 656; *Re Mackay* [1906] 1 Ch. 25 at 32.

2. Disclosure of Trust Documents

After "that the beneficiaries", replace "to" with:

29-025   do

After the second sub-section, add new sub-section:

2A. Requests for Personal Data

29-026A   Under the Data Protection Act 2018 an individual has various rights in respect of "personal data" that is processed by automated means, or which forms part of a "filing system",[148a] including a right of access to the personal data.[148b] "Personal data" means "any information relating to an identified or identifiable living individual",[148c] and a "data controller" is someone who processes personal data, by collecting it, recording it, organising and storing it."[148d] A trustee is a data controller, as they typically collect and store personal data on the beneficiaries of the trust. As such, a beneficiary may be entitled to make a "subject access" request to a trustee for personal information held in a filing system. Furthermore, the request may relate to personal information contained in documents that are usually not disclosable by other means, such as records of trustee deliberations or letters of wishes.[148e]

In *Dawson-Damer v Taylor Wessing LLP*[148e] the claimants, who were beneficiaries of a Bahamian discretionary trust, made a subject data request under the equivalent rules in the earlier legislation.[148f] The various decisions in the long-running dispute have established:

- The purpose of the beneficiary's request is not a relevant factor. The fact that the beneficiaries requested the personal information in order to further their claim was not a reason for refusing the request.[148g]
- Where the information is protected by legal professional privilege then the personal data is exempt.[148h] However, the exemption only applies where the information would be protected by legal professional privilege under English law.[148i]
- In respect of the requirement that the personal information be the subject of a "filing system", this requirement is met where the filing system is a structed set of data, accessible according to specific criteria related to individuals, which allows the data to be easily recovered.[148j]

The need for a relevant "filing system" limits the practical importance of the data protection legislation for beneficiaries. In *Dawson-Damer v Taylor Wessing LLP* the relevant paper files were labelled and structured according to the names of the settlement, not the individual beneficiaries, which meant that information relating to individual beneficiaries could not be easily recovered. As such, there was no relevant "filing system", and therefore no need to communicate the personal information to beneficiaries. The need for a relevant filing system is likely to be satisfied only where the trustees keep files labelled by reference to or structured around individual beneficiaries or classes of beneficiaries. If these requirements are met then beneficiaries will have a right of access to the information held upon them in the filing system. Two further points should be noted:

- The obligation under the Act is to communicate personal information to the individual, not disclose documents.[148k] As such, a beneficiary cannot use the legislation to request trust documents.
- Information relating to another party is exempt, unless it is reasonable to disclose the information without the consent of the other party.[148l] This means that one beneficiary cannot use the legislation to discover information about another beneficiary. It also creates difficulties where a beneficiary has requested access to information from a document that contains personal information both about themselves and another party.

[148a] DPA 2018, s.29(1).

[148b] DPA 2018, s.45(1).

[148c] DPA 2018, s.3(2).

[148d] DPA 2018, s.3(6).

[148e] In *Dawson-Damer v Taylor Wessing LLP* [2017] EWCA Civ 74 the request related to records of trustee deliberations.

[148e] [2017] EWCA Civ 74. Various issues were remitted to the High Court ([2019] EWHC 1258 (Ch); [2019] EWHC 1626), from which there was a further appeal to the Court of Appeal ([2020] Ch 746).

[148f] Data Protection Act 1998, s.7.

[148g] [2017] EWCA Civ 74.

[148h] DPA 2018, Sch.2, para.19.

[148i] [2020] Ch 746, [44]–[45], where the Court of Appeal held that privilege that applied under Bahamian law did not make the information exempt.

[148j] [2020] Ch 746 at [90]–[101].

[148k] DPA 1998, s.45(1).

[148l] DPA 1998, Sch.2, para.16(2).

4. CONTROL BY BENEFICIARIES

2. Rule in Saunders v Vautier

Replace the second paragraph with:

Again, where trustees are directed at their absolute discretion to pay or apply the **29-030** whole or any part of the income of a fund to or for the benefit of A, and are told to pay or apply to or for the benefit of B any part of the income not applied for A's benefit, A and B, if both sui juris, can together compel the trustees to pay the whole income as they direct, for they are the sole owners of each slice of income.[164] But the rule does not apply if other persons have possible interests in the income,[165] so that A and B alone could not control the trustees' application of the income. It is unclear whether the rule in *Saunders v Vautier* will apply in respect of a sole beneficiary where there is a power of addition of beneficiaries. In *Rusnano Capital AG (In Liquidation) v Molard International (PTC) Ltd* the Court of Appeal of Guernsey held that the sole beneficiary of a discretionary trust was entitled to call for the trust fund notwithstanding that the trustees had a power (which had not been exercised) of addition of beneficiaries.[165a] The decision concerned the construction of s.53 of the Trusts (Guernsey) Law 2007, which enacts a rule similar in terms to *Saunders v Vautier*. Although an important decision, its wider significance may be limited given that the issue in the case was the proper construction of a statutory provision which, the court noted, could not be assumed to have enacted every element of the rule in *Saunders v Vautier*.

[164] *Re Smith* [1928] Ch. 915; cf. *Re Nelson* (1918) [1928] Ch. 920n.

[165] *Berry v Geen* [1938] A.C. 575.

[165a] *Rusnano Capital AG (In Liquidation) v Molard International (PTC) Ltd* (2019) 23 I.T.E.L.R. 685. The case concerned the interpretation of Trusts (Guernsey) Law 2007 s.53(3), which enacts the *Saunders v Vautier* right.

4. Trusts of Land

Replace n.136 with:

29-032 [136] *Notting Hill Housing Trust v Brackley* [2001] 35 E.G. 106; *Pile v Pile* [2022] EWHC 2036.

5. CONTROL BY COURT

2. Supervision of Trustees

(a) The power.

Replace paragraph with:

29-034 It is not usual for trusts to be administered in court; for the court exercises a general controlling influence over all trustees, and has power to give directions and determine questions effecting the trustees and beneficiaries without making an order for administration.[182] The court's jurisdiction extends to persons potentially liable as constructive trustees.[183] In a proper case, the court may order an inquiry whether a particular investment ought to be continued, notwithstanding that the trustees claim to exercise their discretion without the interference of the court.[184] This general advisory jurisdiction is frequently invoked. Further, if a question of construction arises on the terms of a trust the Chancery Division may without hearing argument authorise the trustees to act in accordance with the opinion of a person who has had a right of audience in the High Court for 10 years.[185]

[182] For the procedure to be adopted when trustees or beneficiaries seek prospective costs in such proceedings see Civil Procedure Rules, Practice Direction 64A para 6. For an example of trustees successfully surrendering their discretion to the court, see *Womble Bond Dickinson (Trust Corporation) Ltd v Unamed Beneficiaries* [2022] EWHC 43 (Ch) at [65]. The trustees faced significant practical difficulties in identifying members of the class of beneficiaries and hence were at risk of liability for distributing in ignorance of the full class of beneficiaries. This was held to be a sufficiently good reason to surrender discretion to the court.

[183] *Bank of Scotland v A* [2002] 1 W.L.R. 751.

[184] *Re D'Epinoix's Settlement* [1914] 1 Ch. 890.

[185] Administration of Justice Act 1985 s.48 as amended by the Courts and Legal Services Act 1990 Sch.10 para.63; CPR Pt 50 r.50.1 and Sch.1, RSC, Ord. 93 r.21.

(b) Principles of interference.

Replace paragraph with:

29-035 Normally, however, if trustees have an absolute discretion as to the mode of executing the trust the court will not interfere with their discretion, provided they exercise it in good faith.[186] For instance, if a testator gives property to A, B and C to hold upon certain trusts, with power to sell it if they think fit, and A and B and some of the beneficiaries desire a sale but C, in the bona fide exercise of his discretion, refuses to sell, the court will not interfere, and the property cannot be sold.[187] The court will, however, interfere if the trustees refuse to exercise their discretion,[188] exercise it improperly[189] or threaten to commit a breach of fiduciary duty[189a]; and the trustees may, if they wish, surrender their discretion to the court and ask the court to exercise it for them in particular matters[190] though not indefinitely, e.g. under discretionary trusts.[191] In the case of *Lehitmaki v Cooper* the majority of the Supreme Court held (obiter) that in respect of charitable trusts the court has a power to intervene in exceptional cases and direct that a fiduciary exercise their discretion in a particular way even though there is no threatened or actual breach of duty.[191a] Where, instead of surrendering their discretion to the court the trustees seek the court's guidance and approval, the court's role is more limited and it will not without good reason substitute its views for the trustees' views.[192] The court will not compel trustees to take action, however advantageous to the beneficiaries, which will expose them to a breach of the currency regulations of a state whose law is the proper law of the trust.[193] These principles apply equally to express trusts and to statutory trusts for the sale of land.[194]

[186] *Gisborne v Gisborne* (1877) 2 App. Cas. 300; *Re Blake* (1885) 29 Ch. D. 913; *Re Charteris* [1917] 2 Ch. 379; *Re Steed's Will Trusts* [1960] Ch. 407; *Re Hayes's Will Trusts* [1971] 1 W.L.R. 758; and see above Ch.10.

[187] See *Tempest v Lord Camoys* (1882) 21 Ch. D. 571; and see *Re 90 Thornhill Road, Tolworth, Surrey* [1970] Ch. 261.

[188] *Prendergast v Prendergast* (1850) 3 H.L.C. 195; *Klug v Klug* [1918] 2 Ch. 67.

[189] *Tempest v Lord Camoys* (1882) 21 Ch. D. 571 at 578.

[189a] *Lehtimaki v Cooper* [2020] UKSC 33 at [217].

[190] See, e.g. *Re Ezekiel's Settlement Trusts* [1942] Ch. 230; *Marley v Mutual Security Merchant Bank and Trust Co Ltd* [1991] 3 All E.R. 198.

[191] *Re Allen-Meyrick's Will Trusts* [1966] 1 W.L.R. 499; contrast a discretionary trust, discussed at para.22-004.

[191a] *Lehtimaki v Cooper* [2020] UKSC 33. This was the basis of Lady Arden's decision at [119]; Lord Briggs, with whom the majority agreed, accepted this analysis but held that it was unnecessary as the trustee was threatening to breach his fiduciary duty (at [217]).

[192] *Royal Society for the Prevention of Cruelty to Animals v Attorney General* [2001] 3 All E.R. 530; *The Public Trustee v Cooper* [2001] W.T.L.R. 901.

[193] *Re Lord Cable* [1977] 1 W.L.R. 7.

[194] *Re Mayo* [1943] Ch. 302.

(c) Mode of interference.

Replace n.196 with:

[196] As in *Longmore v Broom* (1802) 7 Ves. 124; in *Womble Bond Dickinson (Trust Corporation) Ltd v Unamed Beneficiaries* [2022] EWHC 43 (Ch) at [72] equal division between the identified members of a large class of beneficiaries was considered to be the fairest approach where trustees had faced significant practical difficulties in exercising their discretion. **29-036**

(d) Statutory provision.

Replace n.199 with:

[199] TLATA 1996 s.15(1); and see *Oke v Rideout* [1998] 10 C.L. 559; and *W v W* [2003] EWCA Civ 924; [2004] 2 F.L.R. 321. In the latter case it was held that where there was a potential application under both the 1996 Act and the Children Act 1989 ordinarily an application should be brought under both Acts. See also *Re Kingley (Deceased)* [2020] 1 WLR 1909, where the court held that although an order under **29-037**

s.14 of the Act may engage Article 1 of the First Protocol (A1P1) to the ECHR (see *National Westminster Bank plc v Rushmer* [2010] 2 FLR 362) compliance with s.15 of the Act would satisfy A1P1.

3. Departure from the Terms of the Trust

(a) Management and administration.

(2) After 1925.

Replace paragraph with:

29-042   Since 1925 the court has been empowered by the Trustee Act 1925 s.57, to exercise a jurisdiction of this kind even though no emergency exists.[225] The section provides that "where in the management or administration of any property vested in trustees"[226] (other than Settled Land Act trustees[227]) any transaction is ·expedient[228] for the trust as a whole[229] but the trustees have no power to effect it,[230] the court may confer the necessary power upon the trustees[231]:

> "The object of s.57 was to secure that trust property should be managed as advantageously as possible in the interests of the beneficiaries and, with that object in view, to authorize specific dealings with the property which the court might have felt itself unable to sanction under the inherent jurisdiction, either because no actual 'emergency' had arisen or because of inability to show that the position which called for intervention was one which the creator of the trust could not reasonably have foreseen; but it was no part of the legislative aim to disturb the rule that the court will not rewrite a trust."[232]

The powers granted to trustees under s.57 must either enable the trustees to implement or undertake transactions with trust property, or be a necessary ancillary provision thereto.[232a] The section accordingly gives no power to vary the beneficial interests under a trust and is intended for the protection and benefit of persons who have claims under the relevant trust, not those who have claims against it.[233]

[225] For previous "benevolent" orders, see *Re Morrison* [1901] 1 Ch. 701 at 704.

[226] See *Re Downshire* [1953] Ch. 218 at 247 and *In the Matter of Instant Cash Loans Ltd* [2021] EWHC 1164 at [18].

[227] TA 1925 s.57(4).

[228] See *Riddle v Riddle* (1952) 85 C.L.R. 202.

[229] *Re Craven's Estate (No.2)* [1937] Ch. 431; and see *Re Earl of Strafford* [1980] Ch. 28 at 32, 33.

[230] See *Re Pratt's Will Trusts* [1943] Ch. 326; *Municipal and General Securities Co Ltd v Lloyds Bank Ltd* [1950] Ch. 212.

[231] And see Settled Land and Trustee Acts (Court's General Powers) Act 1943 s.1, for an extension of these powers in the case of trusts of land. (The original limit of time for the exercise of the extended powers was removed by the Emergency Laws (Miscellaneous Provisions) Act 1953 s.9 (repealed by Statute Law (Repeals) Act 1974 Sch. Pt X and again by Statute Law (Repeals) Act 1976 Sch.1 Pt XX)).

[232] *Re Downshire SE* [1953] Ch. 218 at 248, per Evershed MR and Romer LJ.

[232a] *Cotterell v Allendale* [2020] EWHC 2234 (Ch), [50].

[233] *Rennie & Rennie v Proma Ltd & Byng* (1990) 22 H.L.R.129 at 142.

(3) Operation of section.

Replace paragraph with:

29-043   This is an overriding section, the provisions of which are to be read into every settlement.[234] An application under s.57 is appropriate notwithstanding that the application could arguably be made under the Variation of Trusts Act 1958.[235] The statutory power has been used to authorise the sale of chattels settled on trusts which prevent sale,[236] the sale of land where a consent requisite to sale has been refused,[237] the sale of a reversionary interest,[238] the purchase of a residence for the tenant for life,[239] the partitioning of land where there was no power to partition it,[240] the blending of two charitable funds into one,[241] enlarging the trustees' power to appoint a non-professional co-trustee[241a] and the enlarging of the range of permissible investments.[242] But where a fund is settled on A for life on protective trusts, the statutory power cannot be used to enable the trustees to release the fund from the discretionary trusts which would arise if A surrendered his life interest.[243]

[234] *Re Mair* [1935] Ch. 562. For Canadian alarm, see (1943) 59 L.Q.R. 111.

[235] *Anker-Petersen v Anker-Petersen* [2000] W.T.L.R. 581. An application to enlarge administrative powers under the Variation of Trusts Act 1958 will be appropriate where it is part of a wider claim to alter beneficial interest. See *Duke of Somerset v Fitzgerald* [2019] EWHC 726 at [31].

[236] *Re Hope's Will Trusts* [1929] 2 Ch. 136; para.28-006.

[237] *Re Beale's Settlement Trusts* [1932] 2 Ch. 15.

[238] *Re Cockerell's Settlement Trusts* [1956] Ch. 372. Contrast *Re Heyworth's Contingent Reversionary Interest* [1956] Ch. 364.

[239] *Re Power* [1947] Ch. 572.

[240] *Re Thomas, Thomas v Thompson* [1930] 1 Ch. 194.

[241] *Re Harvey, Westminster Bank Ltd v Askwith* [1941] 3 All E.R. 284; *Re Shipwrecked Fishermen and Mariners' Royal Benevolent Society* [1959] Ch. 220; not following dicta in *Re Royal Society's Charitable Trusts* [1956] Ch. 87 at 91.

[241a] *Baker v BDS* [2021] EWHC 3755.

[242] *Re Shipwrecked Fishermen and Mariners' Royal Benevolent Society* [1959] Ch. 220; *Re Brassey's Settlement* [1955] 1 W.L.R. 192 at 196; *Mason v Farbrother* [1983] 2 All E.R. 1078 at 1086, 1087; and *Anker-Petersen v Anker-Petersen* [2000] W.T.L.R. 581 (but see *British Museum (Trustees of the) v Attorney General* [1984] 1 W.L.R. 418 at 425, 426).

[243] *Re Blackwell's Settlement Trusts* [1953] Ch. 218. And see *Re Basden's Settlement Trusts* [1943] 2 All E.R. 11; *Municipal and General Securities Co Ltd v Lloyds Bank Ltd* [1950] Ch. 212.

(e) Variation of Trusts Act 1958.

(2) Persons within the jurisdiction.

Replace list item "(i)" with:

(i) Incapacity: "any person having, directly or indirectly", a vested or contingent interest "who by reason of infancy or other incapacity is incapable of assenting".[274a]   **29-049**

[274a] See *MN v OP* [2019] EWCA Civ 679 for the correct approach to anonymity orders for minor beneficiaries in variation proceedings.

(3) Benefit.

Replace second paragraph with:

"Benefit" is not confined to financial benefit,[287] e.g. where the beneficiary is an irresponsible minor.[288] However, the court must exercise caution when asked to approve of an arrangement for non-financial reasons. It is not the function of the court to redistribute the trust fund according to some wise scheme; rather, the court is being asked to supply its consent on behalf of a beneficiary who is unable to do so, and in undertaking this function it is helpful to pose the question: **29-050**

"would a prudent adult, motivated by intelligent self-interest, and after sustained consideration of the proposed trusts and powers and the circumstances in which they may fall to be implemented, be likely to accept the proposal?"[288a]

Thus a provision forfeiting benefits on "practising Roman Catholicism" has been removed.[289] It may also be a benefit to a mentally incapable person to give away his property where the gift is one which he would have made if of sound mind.[290] But it is not for A's benefit to take from him property mistakenly given to him and give it to B, even if B is a member of the same family.[291]

[287] *Re Weston's Settlements* [1969] 1 Ch. 223 at 245; *Re Holt's Settlement* [1969] 1 Ch. 100 at 121.

[288] See *Re T's Settlement Trusts* [1964] Ch. 158.

[288a] *Wright v Gater* [2012] 1 WLR 802, [11].

[289] *Re Remnant's Settlement Trusts* [1970] Ch. 560.

[290] *Re CL* [1969] 1 Ch. 587.

[291] *Re Tinker's Settlement* [1960] 1 W.L.R. 1011.

CHAPTER 30

BREACH OF TRUST

2. ESTABLISHING A BREACH OF TRUST

1. Liability of Trustee for his Own Defaults

(a) Liability personal and not vicarious.

Replace second paragraph with:

30-005   The old case of *Townley v Sherborne*[7] illustrates the rule. A trustee who had joined with his co-trustees in signing receipts was liable, though he had received nothing, because the liability of the non-receiving trustee arose, not from his mere signing of the receipts, but from his subsequently leaving in the hands of his co-trustees the money that had been received. This was said to be an "evil-dealing" or, as we would now say, a breach of trust.

[7] *Townley v Sherborne* (1634) Bridg. J. 35 at 37, 38; and see *Brice v Stokes* (1805) 11 Ves. 319.

(b) Independent liability for act of co-trustee.

Replace n.13 with:

30-006   [13] *Lord Shipbrook v Lord Hinchinbrook* (1810) 16 Ves. 477; *Wynne v Tempest* (1897) 13 T.L.R. 360; contrast *Shepherd v Harris* [1905] 2 Ch. 310.

(c) Breaches by former trustees.

Replace n.18 with:

30-007   [18] *Hobday v Peters* (1860) 28 Beav. 603.

(e) Executors.

Replace n.23 with:

30-009   [23] *Clough v Bond* (1838) 3 My. & Cr. 490 at 496; *Joy v Campbell* (1804) 1 Sch. & Lef. 328 at 341; affirmed 2 Sch. & Lef. 740; *Re Gasquoine* [1894] 1 Ch. 470.

3. PERSONAL REMEDIES AGAINST THE TRUSTEE IN BREACH

2. Personal Remedies after Breach

(g) Interest and liability for lost income.

Replace first paragraph with:

30-020   The trustee may be liable to pay interest to compensate the trust for losses resulting from his breach.[79] Where the trustee applies the trust money for his own use, he may also have to account for his unauthorised profit made with the trust money. In principle, the rules for awarding interest should compensate the beneficiary fully for his lost investment returns or make the trustee disgorge his full profit.[80] Where trust money has been misapplied, the court should aim, as far as the evidence reliably allows, to award interest which reflects the cost to the trust beneficiaries of being kept out of their money.[81] The exercise of calculating the actual loss to the trust or gain to the trustee may be difficult: it may involve speculative inquiries into the possible income returns on the original capital sum, or the degree to which the trustee's profit was attributable to his use of the trust money. Where however the court has precise and reputable information about the expected returns on the trust investment, then interest should be awarded as a proxy for them.[81a]

[79] e.g. *Stafford v Fiddon* (1857) 23 Beav. 386; *Re Jones* (1883) 49 L.T. 91; *Re Waterman's WT* [1952] 2 All E.R. 1054 (trustee liable for interest representing lost income owing to undue delay in investing trust funds).

[80] S.B. Elliott [2001] Conv. 313 at 319–321.

[81] The principles are summarised in *Challinor v Juliet Bellis & Co* [2013] EWHC 620 (Ch); reversed on other grounds in [2015] EWCA Civ 59; [2016] W.T.L.R. 431; and *Watson v Kea Investments* [2019] EWCA Civ 1759, [2019] 4 W.L.R. 145.

[81a] *Watson v Kea Investments* [2019] EWCA Civ 1759, [2019] 4 W.L.R. 145 at paras [65], [71]-[74.]

Replace third paragraph with:

The special cases where the higher rate may be awarded in a private trust claim are:

(i)   Where the trustee is guilty of fraud or serious misconduct. The higher rate would also be compounded[87] with yearly[88] or even half-yearly rests.[89]

(ii)   Where the trustee has traded with the trust money for his own use. Here he is presumed to have earned more than the standard rate. Interest at the higher commercial rate is available where the beneficiary cannot prove and recover the profits actually made by the trustee with the trust money.[90] Normally compound interest is awarded[91] unless the trading has been for the benefit or partly for the benefit of the beneficiary.[92] Likewise, simple interest would be awarded if the money, while employed in a business or profession, was not used in the normal course of trading.[93]

Alternatively, the court may order an inquiry into the actual loss by the beneficiary owing to the trustee's breach, or the actual rate of return in fact made by the trustee with the trust money (this may include the total return of any investment, including any capital gain)[93a]:

(i)   thus where the trust claimant can establish what proportion of the trustee's profits was made by trading with the trust money, he must account for that profit rather than pay interest on trust money[94];

(ii)   where a trustee who applied trust money for his own benefit invested it at a rate above the standard trustee rate, he must account for the interest he actually received.[95]

In periods when there is a wide difference between commercial borrowing rates and investment rates, the court may vary from the usual higher rate of one per cent above bank base rate. It may take into account the purpose for which the claimant placed the money on trust with the defendant, and the standard rates of borrowing or investment return that a hypothetical person in the position of the claimant might have expected to pay or receive.[96]

[87] See *Westdeutsche Bank v Islington LBC* [1996] A.C. 669.

[88] See *Re Barclay* [1899] 1 Ch. 674.

[89] *Re Emmet's Estate* (1881) 17 Ch. D. 142. Half-yearly rests are rarely directed: *Burdick v Garrick* (1870) 5 Ch. App. 233.

[90] *Vyse v Foster* (1872) 8 Ch.App. 309 at 329 (affirmed L.R. 7 H.L. 318); *Re Davis, Davis v Davis* [1902] 2 Ch. 314; *Gordon v Gonda* [1955] 1 W.L.R. 885. The beneficiary may not claim the profits of a trader to whom the money has been improperly lent, even though the borrower knew that the money belonged to the trust: *Stroud v Gwyer* (1860) 28 Beav. 130.

[91] *Jones v Foxall* (1852) 15 Beav. 388; *Williams v Powell* (1852) 15 Beav. 461; *Wallersteiner v Moir (No.2)* [1975] Q.B. 373; and see *Westdeutsche Bank v Islington LBC* [1996] A.C. 669.

[92] *O'Sullivan v Management Agency and Music Ltd* [1985] Q.B. 428.

[93] *Burdick v Garrick* (1870) 5 Ch. App. 233.

[93a] *Watson v Kea Investments* [2019] EWCA Civ 1759, [2019] 4 W.L.R. 145.

[94] *Docker v Somes* (1834) 2 My. & K. 655.

[95] *Re Emmet's Estate* (1881) 17 Ch. D. 142.

[96] *Challinor v Juliet Bellis & Co* [2013] EWHC 620 (Ch); reversed on other grounds in [2015] EWCA Civ 59; [2016] W.T.L.R. 43.

4. DEFENCES AND ADJUSTMENTS TO TRUSTEE'S LIABILITY

1. Exemption Clauses and Express Modification of Duty

(b) Limits on permitted exclusion.

Replace n.116 with:

30-026 [116] *Walker v Stones* [2000] 4 All E.R. 412; following *Royal Brunei Airlines Sdn Bhd v Tan* [1995] A.C. 378. See para.30-079 below. An intentional breach of trust that was justifiably committed in the interests of the beneficiaries would not necessarily be dishonest in this sense. "The main duty of a trustee is to commit *judicious* breaches of trust": *Perrins v Bellamy* [1889] 1 Ch. 797, 798 in arg. A trustee who believes her acts are morally justified, or that her actions have not fallen below acceptable standards, may nonetheless be held to have acted dishonestly if an ordinary, honest trustee would not have acted as she did: *Wong v Burt* [2004] NZCA 174; [2005] W.T.L.R. 29; *Barnes v Tomlinson* [2006] EWHC 3115; [2007] W.T.L.R. 377. For the pleading a dishonest breach of trust where the trustee relies on an exoneration clause, see *Sofer v Swiss Independent Trustees SA* [2020] EWCA Civ 699.

5. PROPRIETARY REMEDIES AGAINST PROCEEDS OF BREACH OF TRUST

2. Title to Follow or Trace in Equity

(a) Fiduciary relationship or distinct equitable title.

Replace n.341 with:

30-054 [341] *El Ajou v DLH Plc* [1993] 3 All E.R. 717 at 734, per Millett J; *Twinsectra Ltd v Yardley* [1999] Lloyd's Rep. Bank. 438; reversed on other grounds [2002] 2 A.C. 164; [2002] UKHL 12. Similarly, an equity founding a claim in proprietary estoppel may confer a sufficient title to trace: *Re Sangha* [2021] EWHC 1599 (Ch). See further para.2-007 above.

3. Identification and Mixed Funds

(c) Other contributor innocent.

(2) Different rules for allocation.

Replace paragraph with:

30-060   Recent cases have recognised reasons to displace the rule in *Clayton's Case*. Although it remains the default rule, it may be displaced with relative ease in favour of a solution that produces a fairer result.[261] It would not apply where it was contrary to the actual presumed intentions of the contributors,[262] or was unjust or impractical in its operation.[263] The court may instead treat the mixed fund as subject to a "rolling charge" in favour of each innocent contributor.[264] Debits from the account are borne proportionately by each contributor according to the amount of their money in the account immediately before each withdrawal.[264a] But this approach may become unnecessarily complex or expensive to apply where the mixed fund derives from the deposits of many different contributors made over a long period.[264b]

The simpler solution is to treat all withdrawals from the account as borne rateably by all the contributors but to make no adjustment for sequence of deposits and withdrawals from the account.[265] The effect may be to allow a contributor to trace into a withdrawal from the account even though the withdrawal was made before his money had been deposited in the account.

[261] *Charity Commission for England and Wales v Framjee* [2014] EWHC 2507 (Ch); (2014) 17 I.T.E.L.R. 271 at [49].

[262] *Barlow Clowes International Ltd (In Liquidation) v Vaughan* [1992] 4 All E.R. 22; *Russell-Cooke Trust Co v Prentis* [2002] EWHC 2227 (Ch); [2003] All E.R. 478.

[263] *Commerzbank AG v IMB Morgan Plc* [2004] EWHC 2771 (Ch); [2005] 2 All E.R. (Comm) 564.

[264] See *Ontario Securities Commission and Greymac Credit Corp* (1985) 55 O.R. (2d) 673; discussed in *Barlow Clowes International Ltd (In Liquidation) v Vaughan* [1992] 4 All E.R. 22 at 27, 44.

[264a] This applies combines a version of the "lowest intermediate balance" rule in *Roscoe v Winder* [1915] 1 Ch. 62 with the "rolling charge" form of analysis: *Caron v Jahani* [2020] NSWCA 117. See para.30-057 above.

[264b] The authorities and reasons are gathered in *Caron v Jahani* [2020] NSWCA 117 at [106]-[122].

[265] *Barlow Clowes International Ltd (In Liquidation) v Vaughan* [1992] 4 All E.R. 22.

Change title of paragraph: **30-061**

(d)   Payment systems and backward tracing.

Replace paragraph with:
    Special difficulties arise where the trustee misapplies the claimant's money and passes it through a series of bank accounts, or where the trustee manipulates the timing of debits and credits in a network of accounts under his control. It may not be straightforward to identify the funds debited from the claimant's account with funds credited in the defendant's account. When the funds pass through a series of bank account, the claimant may succeed even without exact proof of each transactional link between himself and the defendant. There reason is that where defendant is a wrongdoer, he cannot defeat the possibility of tracing against him by creating an evidential "black hole" designed to frustrate the claimant's action against him.[265a] This is consistent with the punitive evidential presumption against a party who is at fault.[265b] It is not even strictly necessary for each relevant credit to come after each relevant debit. To a limited extent, the claimant may be allowed to trace "backward" into earlier credits. Thus a credit to the defendant's account may be treated as linked to the debit to the claimant's account when the rules of a payment system post the credit before the defendant's bank is reimbursed with funds attributable to the claimant.[265c] A traceable link might also be proved where the trustee has manipulated the timing of debits and credits in the accounts to effect a single transaction or as part of a coordinated scheme to launder the claimant's money.[266] Similarly, the claimant may be allowed to trace into a certain asset acquired on credit before his money was misapplied if the defendant acquired the asset in anticipation paying for it with the misapplied trust money.[267] Without some deliberate coordination of this kind, however, there is no general rule allowing the claimant to trace backward into an asset acquired before the trustee misapplied the claimant's money.[268]

[265a] *Sinclair Investments (UK) Ltd v Versailles Trade Finance Ltd* [2011] EWCA Civ 347; [2012] Ch. 453 at [135]–[139].

[265b] See para.30-057 above.

[265c] *Agip (Africa) Ltd v Jackson* [1990] Ch. 265; *Relfo Ltd (In Liquidation) v Varsani* [2014] EWCA

Civ 360; [2015] 1 B.C.L.C. 14; *Serious Fraud Office v Hotel Portfolio II UK Ltd (in liq)* [2021] EWHC 1273 (Comm) at [22]–[48].

[266] *El-Ajou v Dollar Land Holdings Plc* [1993] 3 All E.R. 717 at 733; reversed on other grounds [1994] 2 All E.R. 685; *Federal Republic of Brazil v Durant International Ltd* [2015] UKPC 35; [2016] A.C. 297 at [34], [38]; *Relfo Ltd (In Liquidation) v Varsani* [2014] EWCA Civ 360; [2015] 1 B.C.L.C. 14.

[267] *Serious Fraud Office v Hotel Portfolio II UK Ltd (in liq)* [2021] EWHC 1273 (Comm).

[268] *Relfo Ltd (In Liquidation) v Varsani* [2014] EWCA Civ 360; [2015] 1 B.C.L.C. 14; *Federal Republic of Brazil v Durant International Ltd* [2015] UKPC 35; [2015] 3 W.L.R. 599 at [40]–[41]; *Serious Fraud Office v Hotel Portfolio II UK Ltd (in liq)* [2021] EWHC 1273 (Comm) at [22]-[48]

6. PERSONAL LIABILITY OF THIRD PARTIES INVOLVED IN BREACH OF TRUST

2.   Knowing Receipt

(a)   Beneficial receipt.

Replace first paragraph with:

30-071   Where the defendant receives the property beneficially he may be liable to give restitution of its value in an action for knowing receipt. The basis of the defendant's liability is that he received property in which the claimant had a subsisting equitable interest, and was under a custodial duty to restore it immediately to the claimant.[297] It follows that the claim would not arise if the defendant received it as a bona fide purchaser for value or in a foreign jurisdiction that does not recognize the separate existence of an equitable interest.[298] The claimant may need to prove by the formal rules of following or tracing that the money received by the defendant was specifically attributable to him.[299] It would not be enough for him to prove in a more general way that the sum received by the defendant was the same as the sum misapplied from the trust.

[297] C. Harpum (1986) above at 267–269; *Byers v Saudi National Bank* [2022] EWCA Civ 43; [2022] 4 W.L.R. 22 at [69]-[79], developing the view of C Mitchell and S Watterson, ch 4 in C Mitchell (ed), *Constructive and Resulting Trusts* (2010).

[298] *Byers v Saudi National Bank* [2022] EWCA Civ 43; [2022] 4 W.L.R. 22.

[299] See para.30-051 above.

(b)   Fault.

Replace n. with:

30-072   [302] See generally D. Fox, *Property Rights in Money* (2008) paras 8.55–8.72. In modern-day banking transactions, the court may need consider the soundness of the defendant's automated processes for the detecting fraudulent payments as well as the conduct and state of mind of its employees: cf *Tecnimont Arabia Ltd v National Westminster Bank plc* [2022] EWHC 1171 (Comm).

4.   Dishonest Assistance

(c)   Dishonesty.

Replace n.391 with:

30-079   [391] *Royal Brunei Airlines Sdn Bhd v Tan* [1995] 2 A.C. 378, as explained in *Group Seven Ltd v Nasir* [2019] EWCA 614, [2020] Ch 129.

Replace second paragraph with:

When the test of dishonesty is applied, the defendant is not free to be judged according to his own standards. He is judged according the standards of an ordinary honest person, who would have the same knowledge of the circumstances as he does, and sharing some of his personal characteristics, such as his age and experience.[334] His conduct need not be dishonest by the standards of all people, since not all people may appreciate the kinds of specialised wrongdoing involved in certain kinds of commercial transaction.[335] In the past the authorities were uncertain whether the trustee also needed to realise that his conduct would be regarded as dishonest by the standard of an ordinary honest person. The better view, which is now accepted in England, is that the defendant need not also take a view on the propriety of his own conduct.[336] A finding that the defendant was dishonest only involves an assessment of his participation in the impugned transaction, judged in the light of his motives and his knowledge of the facts. Reckless participation in the impugned transaction is not the same as dishonesty unless the defendant's motive for acting was itself dishonest.[337]

[334] *Royal Brunei Airlines Sdn Bhd v Tan* [1995] 2 A.C. 378.

[335] *Starglade Properties Ltd v Nash* [2010] EWCA Civ 314.

[336] Compare the former view in *Twinsectra Ltd v Yardley* [2002] UKHL 165; [2002] 2 A.C. 164 at [32]–[35]; with *Barlow Clowes v Eurotrust International Ltd* [2005] UKPC 37; [2006] 1 All E.R. 333 at [15]–[16]. It is now beyond doubt that the later decision in *Barlow Clowes* case represents the correct view of English law: *Abou-Rahmah v Abacha* [2006] EWCA Civ 1492; [2007] W.T.L.R. 1; *Starglade Properties Ltd v Nash* [2010] EWCA Civ 314; *Group Seven Ltd v Nasir* [2019] EWCA 614, [2020] Ch 129, following *Ivey v Genting Casinos (UK) Ltd (trading as Crockfords Club)* [2017] UKSC 67, [2018] A.C. 391 (restating the corresponding rule in criminal law).

[337] *Clydesdale Bank v Workman* [2016] EWCA Civ 73; [2016] P.N.L.R. 18 at [51].

Replace n.338 with:

[338] *Attorney General of Zambia v Meer Care & Desai (a firm)* [2008] EWCA Civ 1007 at [21]; *Group Seven Ltd v Nasir* [2019] EWCA 614, [2020] Ch 129, at paras [59]-[60].

Replace n.341 with:

[341] *Barlow Clowes v Eurotrust International Ltd* [2005] UKPC 37; [2006] 1 All E.R. 333 at [28], per Lord Hoffmann; *Group Seven Ltd v Nasir* [2019] EWCA 614, [2020] Ch 129, at para [101]-[104].

CHAPTER 31

COLLECTION AND REALISATION OF ASSETS

1. GENERAL INTRODUCTION

1. Administration

Replace paragraph with:

When a person dies, whether testate or intestate, the property vested in him which **31-001** is available to meet his debts and other liabilities is called his "assets".[1] These assets must be collected and realised; the debts must be paid; and any surplus must be distributed to the persons beneficially entitled under the will or intestacy. These three tasks, known as the "administration of assets", are the duty of his personal representatives, i.e. the executors if he has appointed any, and otherwise his administrators.[2] Despite the name "personal representatives" an executor (and doubtless an administrator also) "does not act for a dead man or in his name, but

[265]

for the estate of the dead man".[3] The administration of the deceased's estate is normally conducted by the personal representatives out of court; but difficult or complex administrations may take place in court.[4]

[1] "Assets", from the French "assez" (enough) and Latin "ad satis" (to sufficiency).

[2] For the appointment of executors and administrators see *Williams, Mortimer and Sunnucks on Executors, Administrators and Probate*, 21st edn (London: Sweet & Maxwell, 2018); for wills, see *Williams on Wills*, 11th edn (London: Sweet & Maxwell, 2021); *Theobald on Wills*, 19th edn (London: Sweet & Maxwell, 2021); *Hawkins on the Construction of Wills*, 5th edn (London: Butterworths, 2000).

[3] *Stanhope v Stanhope* (1886) 11 P.D. 103 at 110, per Bowen LJ.

[4] See below para.34-002.

2. THE DEFINITION OF ASSETS

2. Realty

(c) Marshalling.

Replace n.13 with:

31-009 [13] *Aldrich v Cooper* (1803) 8 Ves. 382.

5. POWERS OF PERSONAL REPRESENTATIVES

1. Introduction

Replace n.50 with:

31-018 [50] *Re Crowhurst Park* [1974] 1 W.L.R. 583. See also *Rowles v 00182221 Ltd* [2021] EWHC 1170 (QB) (attempt by executrix to prove title to sue other than by grant of probate, and thereby obtain judgment, denied).

2. Powers of Disposition

Replace n.53 with:

31-019 [53] See, e.g. *Nugent v Gifford* (1738) 1 Atk. 463; *Corser v Cartwright* (1875) L.R. 7 H.L. 731 at 736.

CHAPTER 32

PAYMENT OF DEBTS

2. ORDER OF PAYMENT

2. Types of Administration

Replace n.12 with:

[12] See Administration of Insolvent Estates of Deceased Persons Order 1986 (SI 1986/1999) art.5(1). For **32-003** commentary on the Order, see I. Fletcher, *The Law of Insolvency*, 5th edn (London, Sweet & Maxwell, 2017) paras 12-002–12-008.

3. PAYMENT OF STATUTE-BARRED DEBTS

1. Right to Pay

Replace n.82 with:

[82] It seems the situation may be otherwise if the estate is insolvent: see SI 1986/1999 art.4(1); and **32-025** Fletcher, *Law of Insolvency*, 5th edn (2017) paras 9-007, 23-004.

CHAPTER 34

REMEDIES

1. ADMINISTRATION BY THE COURT

3. The Claim

Replace the second paragraph with:

If the claim is commenced before 22 April 2014 it may be brought in the county **34-004**
court only if the total value of the estate does not exceed £30,000.[25] For claims
brought on or after that date, the county court equity jurisdiction, which applies in
such circumstances, is £350,000.[26] If the claim is brought in the High Court, it must
be brought in the Chancery Division.[27] The claim should be issued in the Property,
Trusts and Probate List.[27a]

[25] County Courts Act 1984 ss.23(a), 147(1); County Courts Jurisdiction Order 1981 (SI 1981/1123).

[26] County Court Jurisdiction Order 2014 (SI 2014/503) art.3.

[27] See para.1-038; SCA 1981 s.61 and Sch.1 para.1(d); CPR r.64.1(3).

[27a] *Chancery Guide*, Ch.31, para.3(9).

3. GUIDANCE BY THE COURT

Replace paragraph with:

Administration by the court is complex and expensive, involving the taking of **34-016**
accounts and inquiries and the direction by the court at every stage of the

winding-up of the estate. In many cases, however, the personal representatives can manage the administration generally without the court's assistance, but merely require its guidance on some specific point, e.g. the meaning of a clause in the will[71] or the validity of a particular creditor's claim. Accordingly, the personal representatives may bring an action for the determination of any question arising in the administration of the estate, without seeking an order for administration by the court.[72] Provisions as to the procedure are set out in CPR Pt 64.[73] In particular, the claimant may make parties to the claim any persons with an interest in or claim against the estate whom it is appropriate to make parties having regard to the nature of the order sought.[74] Where directions are being sought whether to proceed against a beneficiary,[75] that beneficiary will usually not be entitled to see the evidence or take part in the proceedings for directions, even if he is a party.[76] Yet in the subsequent action the beneficiary can rely on the evidence as to fact given in such proceedings.[77]

[71] As to which see also Administration of Justice Act 1985 s.48, as amended by the Courts and Legal Services Act 1990 Sch.10 para.63; see para.29-034. The section provides that where any question of construction has arisen out of the terms of a will, the personal representatives may, after obtaining the written opinion of a person holding a 10-year High Court qualification (within the meaning of the Courts and Legal Services Act 1990 s.71) apply to the High Court for an order authorising them to act in reliance upon the opinion. Provisions as to the procedure are set out in CPR Pt 64; see also *Chancery Guide*, paras 29.29–29.35.

[72] CPR r.64.2(a)(i); and see CPR Pt 64 PD 64A para.1(1) for examples of claims that may be brought under the Rule. For the personal representatives' duty to lay full information before the court, see *Re Herwin* [1953] Ch. 701 at 708, 709, 714, 715. The personal representatives should not normally appeal against the court's guidance: *Re Londonderry* [1965] Ch. 918 at 930, 934.

[73] See also *Chancery Guide*, paras 29.29–29.35. As to costs, see *Re Buckton* [1907] 2 Ch. 406; *D'Abo v Paget (No.2)* [2000] W.T.L.R. 863; *Pennington v Wayne* [2003] W.T.L.R. 1011; CPR Pt 64 PD 64A para.6.

[74] CPR r.64.4(1)(c). The court may order that further parties be joined: see CPR Pt 19.

[75] A *Beddoe* application: see para.7-031.

[76] See *Re Moritz* [1960] Ch. 251; *Re Eaton* [1964] 1 W.L.R. 1269; *Three Professional Trustees v Infant Prospective Beneficiary* [2007] EWHC 1922 (Ch); [2007] W.T.L.R. 1631 (possibility of redacting material).

[77] *Midland Bank Trust Co Ltd v Green* [1980] Ch. 590 at 604–610 (Oliver J). In the appellate courts, this issue was not raised: [1980] Ch. 590 CA; [1981] A.C. 513 HL; see paras 4-018 et seq.

CHAPTER 35

LEGACIES

2. ADEMPTION AND ABATEMENT

2. No Ademption of General Legacies

Replace the first paragraph with:

Unlike a specific legacy, a general legacy is not within the principle of ademption. **35-007** Under this principle, a specific legacy fails if the chattel or fund given has ceased to exist as part of the testator's property in his lifetime; and the legatee is not entitled to any compensation out of the general assets, because nothing but the specific thing was given to him.[17] A legacy is also adeemed if the property is changed into something different, even if the thing into which it is changed is in the testator's possession at his death.[18] It is immaterial whether the change is effected by the testator himself or by external authority, for ademption is not dependent upon the intention of the testator.[19] It follows that the testator's ignorance of the change (e.g., on account of incapacity) is also irrelevant.[19a] However, an unauthorised change will work no ademption.[20] And a legacy may be adeemed pro tanto, as where the testator sells part of the property specifically bequeathed.[21]

[17] *Ashburner v Macguire* (1786) 2 Bro. C.C. 108.

[18] The existence of rights of pre-emption over the subject-matter of a gift, not created by the deceased and untriggered at the date of death, do not adeem the gift: *Pennington v Wayne* [2003] W.T.L.R. 1011.

[19] *Frewen v Frewen* (1875) 10 Ch. App. 610; *Harrison v Jackson* (1877) 7 Ch. D. 339; *Re Slater* [1907] 1 Ch. 665. Contrast *Re Jameson* [1908] 2 Ch. 111, where the change took place before the date of the will, so that there was a mere misdescription. But see also *Re Viertel* [1997] 1 Qd R 110 (Supreme Court of Queensland): specific legacy not adeemed when its subject-matter was sold by persons acting under a power of attorney, and the executrix had no knowledge of the sale. The correctness of *Re Viertel* was doubted (albeit in obiter dicta) by the NSW Court of Appeal in *RL v NSW Trustee and Guardian* (2012) 84 NSWLR 263 at [148]–[187].

[19a] *Rokkan v Rokkan* [2021] EWHC 481 (Ch) at [88].

[20] *Jenkins v Jones* (1866) L.R. 2 Eq. 323.

[21] *Humphreys v Humphreys* (1789) 2 Cox Eq. 184.

CHAPTER 37

CREATION AND SETTING ASIDE OF MORTGAGES

37-005 *Change title of section:*

2. MORTGAGES OF LAND

Add new paragraph:

Change footnote on title of section: The creation of mortgages of land is dealt with in outline only. For a detailed discussion of the creation, form and registration of such mortgages see, e.g. Megarry & Wade, *Law of Real Property*, 9th edn (London: Sweet & Maxwell, 2019); and see *Fisher & Lightwood's Law of Mortgage*, 15th edn (LexisNexis, 2019).

4. EQUITABLE MORTGAGES

3. Informal Mortgages

Replace fourth paragraph with:

37-021 Some decisions suggest that the courts might be willing to give effect to security agreements, notwithstanding a failure to comply with s.2 of the Law of Property (Miscellaneous Provisions) Act 1989, in reliance upon the doctrine of proprietary estoppel.[43] In *Cobbe v Yeoman's Row Management Ltd*, Lord Scott expressed his view that proprietary estoppel could not be used as a means of circumventing s.2, on the basis that equity ought not to contradict a statute by rendering enforceable an agreement that statute has declared to be void where the statute does not contain an express exemption for proprietary estoppel.[44] However, he made clear that this was an obiter comment,[45] and whereas Lord Mance agreed with Lord Scott's speech,[46] Lord Walker expressly considered it unnecessary and inappropriate to consider the issue relating to s.2.[47] Lord Scott's view is analogous to that which obtains where a surety denies the enforceability of a guarantee which does not comply with s.4 of the Statute of Frauds 1677.[48] Consistently with what the House of Lords has held in the surety context,[49] an informal agreement to create a mortgage which does not comply with s.2 ought not, by the mere fact of its existence, to generate a proprietary estoppel in favour of the mortgagee unless there is something further (beyond the mere fact of the mortgagor having agreed orally to create a mortgage) to found that estoppel. But s.2 should not rule out all possibility of an estoppel, if the facts genuinely support it.[50] Facts which might found an estoppel, notwithstanding s.2, could include an express representation that the mortgagor would not rely on the failure to comply with s.2 coupled with detrimental reliance on that representation, or "conscious encouragement"[51] by the mortgagor of the mortgagee's belief that there is a valid contract.[51a] The context within which such representations are made will also be important. *Cobbe v Yeoman's Row* involved commercial parties, who can legitimately be expected to protect themselves by complying with relevant formality requirements,[51b] which may not be the case in other contexts, such as familial relationships.[52] Commercial parties who have expressly negotiated "subject to contract" will not be able to avoid the consequences of taking that approach.[53] Section 2 should also not prevent a valid *Pallant v*

Morgan equity[54] from arising, which could generate a constructive trust over property notwithstanding a lack of writing signed by both parties.[55]

[43] *Cobbe v Yeoman's Row Management Ltd* [2005] EWHC 266 (Ch); *Kinane v Mackie-Conteh* [2005] EWCA Civ 45.

[44] *Cobbe v Yeoman's Row Management Ltd* [2008] UKHL 55 at [29]; [2008] 1 W.L.R. 1752.

[45] *Cobbe v Yeoman's Row Management Ltd* [2008] UKHL 55; [2008] 1 W.L.R. 1752.

[46] *Cobbe v Yeoman's Row Management Ltd* [2008] UKHL 55; [2008] 1 W.L.R. 1752 at [96].

[47] *Cobbe v Yeoman's Row Management Ltd* [2008] UKHL 55; [2008] 1 W.L.R. 1752 at [93]. Lord Hoffmann and Lord Brown agreed with the reasons of Lord Scott for allowing the appeal without indicating any view on the s.2 point: at [1] and [94].

[48] See below para.45-009.

[49] See *Actionstrength Ltd v International Glass Engineering IN GL EN SpA* [2003] UKHL 17; [2003] 2 A.C. 541.

[50] *Dowding v Matchmove Ltd* [2016] EWCA Civ 1233; [2017] 1 W.L.R. 749; *Whittaker v Kinnear* [2011] EWHC 1479 (QB) at [30]. See also *Herbert v Doyle* [2010] EWCA Civ 1095, esp. at [57]; *Ely v Robson* [2016] EWCA Civ 774; *Muhammad v ARY Properties Ltd* [2016] EWHC 1698 (Ch); and see the discussion in para.12–046 above; Neuberger, "The Stuffing of Minerva's Owl? Taxomony and Taxidermy in Equity" [2009] C.L.J. 537 at 546; Etherton, "Constructive Trusts and Proprietary Estoppel: The Search for Clarity and Principle" [2009] Conv. 104 at 120. *Kensington Mortgage Co Ltd v Mallon* [2019] EWHC 2512 (Ch) at [149].

[51] Neuberger [2009] C.L.J. 537 at 546.

[51a] For general discussion of the circumstances in which a proprietary estoppel might arise, see ch.12 above, esp. from para.12-032.

[51b] Although the mere fact that an arrangement is a commercial one does not necessarily preclude an estoppel arising: *Kensington Mortgage Co Ltd v Mallon* [2019] EWHC 2512 (Ch) at [144].

[52] See, e.g. *Thorner v Major* [2009] UKHL 18; [2009] 1 W.L.R. 776.

[53] See, e.g. *Generator Developments Ltd v Lidl UK GmbH* [2018] EWCA Civ 396. See also *Farrar v Miller* [2018] EWCA Civ 172 at [46].

[54] *Pallant v Morgan* [1953] Ch. 43.

[55] See s.2(5) of the Law of Property (Miscellaneous Provisions) Act 1989; *Farrar v Miller* [2018] EWCA Civ 172.

5.   SETTING ASIDE MORTGAGES FOR UNDUE INFLUENCE OR AS UNCONSCIONABLE BARGAINS

1.   The Three Party Situation

Delete n.58.   **37-023**

7.   STATUTORY PROVISIONS AFFECTING THE ENFORCEABILITY OF MORTGAGES

3.   Financial Services and Markets Act 2000

Replace n.122 with:

[122] See Financial Services and Markets Act 2000 (Regulated Activities) Order 2001 (SI 2001/544) art.61;   **37-036** and Financial Services and Markets Act 2000 s.22. In broad terms, the definition encompasses contracts where a lender provides credit to an individual or trustees, the obligation to repay is secured by a first legal mortgage over land in the EEA and at least 40 per cent of that land is to be used as a dwelling.

Replace second paragraph with:

Where the lender is authorised by the FCA to enter into a regulated mortgage contract, the FCA's Handbook contains a detailed code, the relevant part of which is called Mortgages: Conduct of Business ("MCOB"), that regulates the conduct of the lender's mortgage business. If the lender has acted in breach of the standards of conduct laid down in MCOB, the mortgagor may make a complaint to the Ombudsman[125] which has power to make a monetary award.[126] Such awards can be for financial loss (including consequential or prospective loss) or for pain and suffering or damage to reputation or distress and inconvenience, irrespective of whether a court would award compensation.[126a]

[125] Defined in the FCA Handbook as a person appointed by Financial Ombudsman Service Ltd.

[126] Such awards can now be up to £350,000.

[126a] See the FCA's Handbook on Dispute Resolution: Complaints ("DISP") esp at DISP 3.7.

4. Other Statutory Provisions

Replace n.128 with:

37-037 [128] See generally Megarry & Wade, *The Law of Real Property*, 9th edn (2019).

8. FORGERIES

Replace n.134 with:

37-038 [134] See Land Registration Act 2002 Sch.4. Rectification is not always possible: see paras 3(2) and 6(2) of Sch.4. On forgery and alteration of the register, see generally Fox, "Forgery and alteration of the Register under the Land Registration Act 2002" in Cooke (ed), *Modern Studies in Property Law* Vol.3 (Hart Publishing, 2005) Ch.2; and *NRAM Ltd v Evans* [2017] EWCA Civ 1013 at [48]-[59], [2018] 1 W.L.R. 639.

CHAPTER 40.

FLOATING CHARGES

Replace para.40-001 with:

This chapter addresses the nature of the floating charge and the general principles **40-001**
consequently applicable to it.[1] It discusses how case law and commercial practice
shaped the floating charge into a practically important security interest that enables
the debtor to raise finance against all or any part of its assets, including those that
form part of the going concern of the business while providing the creditor (the
chargee) with rights and powers that reduce the risk that the debt secured by the
floating charge will not be paid. This chapter also looks at protection of third parties who might be affected by the floating charge, both through general principles
and growing statutory regulation.

[1] For detailed treatment of the now vast amount of case law and statute law on the subject, see H Beale, M Bridge, L Gullifer and E Lomnicka, *The Law of Security and Title-based Financing* 3rd edn, (OUP, 2018).

Replace the first section with:

1. HISTORY

40-002   The story of the floating charge is generally thought to have started before the development of modern company law, when statutory companies began to grant mortgages over their undertakings.[2] The mortgage over an undertaking differed in many respects from the modern floating charge. Its role in the development of the floating charge is unclear but at the very least it gave currency to the idea of a security right over a company's undertaking,[3] and probably influenced the drafters of security documents for registered companies.

1. Mortgage over an undertaking granted by statutory companies

40-003   In the first half of the nineteenth century, before the emergence of recognisably modern companies legislation, incorporation of commercial enterprises was most commonly achieved by special Act of Parliament. The special Act which created a particular company often gave the company power to grant security over its "undertaking". A power to "mortgage the undertaking"[4] was included in the Companies Clauses Consolidation Act 1845. This Act applied (and continues to apply[5]) to companies constituted under specific Acts if the specific Act incorporated the 1845 Act. Courts understood the term "mortgage over an undertaking" to mean not a mortgage over the assets of the company but that the secured loan was to be paid from the earnings and returns on the completed work.[6] This was because a charge over the "undertaking" of a statutory company would be inconsistent with the company's statutory purpose if the land on which the undertaking was conducted could be seized and sold, so putting an end to the very undertaking authorised by Parliament.[7] This had certain consequences for the powers that the mortgagee was held to have: the mortgagee could not interfere with the going concern,[8] for example, by selling the company on a break-up basis.[9] However, the mortgagee had a power to apply to court to appoint a receiver[10] to collect the income (tolls) and profits, and to obtain an injunction to restrain judgment creditors from enforcing against tolls or from taking possession of the land or chattels where doing so would interfere with the mortgagee's right to the undertaking and tolls.[11]

40-004   A mortgage over a company's undertaking, created pursuant to a statutory power such as s.38 of the Companies Clauses Consolidation Act 1845, looks to modern eyes functionally similar to a floating charge in a sense that it allowed the mortgagor to continue its business free of the mortgagee's interest until default under the mortgage. However, by comparison to the modern chargee, the mortgagee did not have any interest in the company's assets, and had very limited enforcement powers.

2. Charge over an undertaking granted by registered companies

40-005   Registered companies formed under the Companies Acts continued the practice of granting security over their respective "undertakings".[12] Language familiar from one context was clearly used in another. There was much litigation about the meaning of a charge over a company's undertaking but the courts over time became willing to infer the existence of a charge over all the assets of a company, present and future, even where the language of the documentation was less than wholly felicitous.[13] Another issue concerned the rights that such a security interest created. If the charge were treated as a fixed charge, to use modern terminology, it would arguably be a breach of duty for directors to grant a fixed charge over the "undertaking" of a company, because such a charge would paralyse the very business of the company it was their duty to run. Such an argument was put to the court without success. In *Re Marine Mansions Co*, Page-Wood VC held that the charge was valid over all the debtor's assets, although he did not explain why the business was not paralysed.[14] The explanation was provided not long after in *Re Panama, New Zealand and Australian Royal Mail Co*, in which Sir GM Giffard LJ held that the continuation of the business until default was implied from describing the subject matter of the charge as 'undertaking' in the debenture.[15]

Drafters of legal documentation were well aware of these issues. In order to meet **40-006** the objection that a charge over the undertaking of a company would paralyse it, they explicitly reserved to the company powers to continue to use and dispose of assets in the course of its business.[16] This shows a charge on a company's undertaking—a floating charge, in today's terms—for what it is: an equitable charge coupled with chargor's authority to deal with charged assets free of the charge in certain circumstances.

A modern floating charge, unlike its mid-nineteenth century forebears, relies on **40-007** implication to establish the very existence of the chargor's freedom (authority) to deal free of the charge, rather than express terms; but such a charge often also contains express stipulations which modify and govern its extent and duration.[17] A modern floating charge can therefore be properly regarded as a set of default entitlements for chargor and chargee, evolved from previously express terms. Floating charges show, therefore, many common characteristics, which make it possible for courts to categorise a particular charge as floating (or fixed),[18] as they must now often do for the purposes of statute law.[19]

[2] R Pennington, "The Genesis of the Floating Charge" (1960) 23 M.L.R. 630 at 638.

[3] *Re Brumark Ltd* [2001] UKPC 28; [2001] 2 A.C. 710 at para.5 per Lord Millett.

[4] Companies Clauses Consolidation Act 1845, s. 38. The term "undertaking" was defined in s.2 of that Act as "the undertaking or works, of whatever nature, which shall by the special Act be authorized to be executed".

[5] While the legislation continues to be in force, the rarity of mortgages over an undertaking granted by statutory companies warrants treating the discussion here as of mainly historical interest, and justifies the use of the past tense.

[6] *Gardner v London, Chatham and Dover Railway* (1866) 2 Ch. App. 201 at 217 per Cairns LJ; *Re Parker, sub nom Wignall v Park* [1891] 1 Ch. 682 at 689-690.

[7] *Doe d Myatt v St Helen's & Runcorn Gap Railway Co* (1841) 2 Q.B. 364.

[8] *Furness v The Caterham Railway Co* (1859) 27 Beav 358 at 361 per Sir John Romilly MR; *Gardner v London, Chatham and Dover Railway* (1866) 2 Ch. App. 201 at 217 per Cairns LJ.

[9] *Walker v Milne* (1849) 11 Beav 507 at 518 per Lord Langdale MR.

[10] Such a power was typically set out under the special Acts of Parliament that incorporated statutory companies: see *Fripp v The Chard Railway Company* 68 ER 1264; *Gardner v London, Chatham and Dover Railway* (1866) 2 Ch App 201. See, too, Companies Clauses Consolidation Act 1845 s. 54.

[11] *Furness v The Caterham Railway Co* (1859) 27 Beav 358 at 362 per Sir John Romilly MR; *Legg v Mathieson* (1860) 2 Giff 71 at 80 per Sir John Stuart V-C.

[12] See, e.g. *Re Marine Mansions Co* (1867) L.R. 4 Eq. 605, which seems to be the first case concerning a charge on the company's "undertaking and property, and receipts and revenues". See also *Re New*

Clydach Sheet and Bar Iron Co (1868) L.R. 6 Eq. 514, concerning assignments of "the undertaking, and all the real and personal estate" of the company by way of mortgage to secure the repayment of a debt.

[13] See the trend shown by, e.g. *Gardner v London, Chatham, and Dover Railway Co* (1867) L.R. 2 Ch. App. 201; *Re New Clydach Sheet and Bar Iron Co* (1868) L.R. 6 Eq. 514; *Re Panama, New Zealand, and Australian Royal Mail Co* (1870) L.R. 5 Ch. App. 318; and *Re Florence Land and Public Works Co* (1878) 10 Ch. D. 530 CA.

[14] *Re Marine Mansions Co* (1867) L.R. 4 Eq. 605.

[15] *Re Panama, New Zealand, and Australian Royal Mail* (1869-70) LR 5 Ch App 318 at 322. See, too, *In re Florence Land and Public Works Co, ex p Moor* (1878) 10 Ch D 530 at 541 per Sir George Jessel MR; *Biggerstaff v Rowatt's Wharf Ltd* [1896] 2 Ch 93 at 101 per Lindley LJ, and at 103 per Lopes LJ.

[16] Sir Francis Beaufort Palmer, *Company Precedents*, 1st edn (1877) at 408.

[17] See para.40-032 below.

[18] See, e.g. *Re Yorkshire Woolcombers Association Ltd* [1903] 2 Ch. 284 at 294–295 per Romer LJ.

[19] See paras. 40-017 – 40-023 below.

Replace second section with:

2. THE NATURE OF THE FLOATING CHARGE

40-008   The floating charge poses some conceptual difficulties. It has features of both personal and property rights. If it is a personal right, it is hard to see why in certain circumstances it is capable of binding third parties, and how it can transform into a property right upon crystallisation, without a fresh act, enabling the creditor at a critical moment to gain a significant advantage over unsecured creditors on insolvency, where the general approach is that creditors share pari passu. If it is a property right in the subject matter immediately from the moment the charge is created, the challenge is to explain the susceptibility of this right to disposals of the charged assets by the chargor without chargee's consent, and why the susceptibility ceases on, for example, crystallisation.

1. Attempts at Definition

40-009   The floating charge defies easy definition[20], and its juridical nature is a source of considerable controversy.[21] One view is that until crystallisation the floating charge creates only personal rights between the chargor and the chargee, based on contract.[22] A clear illustration of this view can be found in the dicta of Lord Scott in *Re Spectrum Plus Ltd*:

> "Or suppose a case in which the charge were expressed to come into existence on the future occurrence of some event and then to be a fixed charge over whatever assets of a specified description the chargor might own at that time. The contractual rights thereby granted would, in my opinion, be properly categorised as a floating security. There can, in my opinion, be no difference in categorisation between the grant of a fixed charge expressed to come into existence on a future event in relation to a specified class of assets owned by the chargor at that time and the grant of a floating charge over the specified class of assets with crystallisation taking place on the occurrence of that event."[23]

This view is at odds with history and authority. It has been convincingly suggested that this dictum must have been intended to deal with the conceptual limitations of a fixed charge, and should not be read as meaning that a floating charge is a security which only comes into existence on the occurrence of a future event (crystallisation).[24] Contractual rights alone cannot constitute a security interest, fixed or floating, though they can be the source of either. Furthermore, in the very same case, Lord Walker said:

"Under a floating charge, by contrast, the chargee does not have the same power to control the security for its own benefit. The chargee has a proprietary interest, but its interest is in a *fund* of circulating capital, and unless and until the chargee intervenes (on crystallisation of the charge) it is for the trader, and not the bank, to decide how to run its business."[25]

The preferred view is that prior to crystallisation the floating charge is a charge over a fund of assets in the sense that the chargee has an immediate proprietary interest in identified assets owned by the chargor but the chargor is able to defeat this interest, or to subordinate it to other interests, by exercising its power to dispose of the charged assets. The chargee can logically be said to have consented to, or to have authorised, the defeasance of the charge in the charged assets or its subordination to other interests when the chargor exercises its power to dispose of the charged assets in the circumstances set out in the terms of the charge.[26] When upon disposition the charge ceases to encumber the assets, it typically captures the proceeds of the disposition because the charge agreement generally provides that this is so. In this sense, it is submitted, it is appropriate to refer to the floating charge prior to its crystallisation as an interest in a fund of circulating capital. However, whether the floating charge extends to proceeds of every authorised disposition depends on the terms on which the charge was created, namely whether the assets that form the proceeds are expressed to be the subject matter of the charge in the charge agreement.[27]

40-010

2.   Power to Deal Distinguished from Authority to Defeat the Charge

Where a company has granted a floating charge over its assets, it owns the charged assets (usually at law) but has granted to the chargee certain limited but nevertheless present equitable rights in those assets by way of security. While the chargee obtains a present proprietary interest in the charged assets, it also consents to (authorises) the charge being defeated or subordinated in the charged assets in a range of circumstances. Those circumstances are generally expressed in broad terms, either because the debenture provides that the chargor is free to deal with (dispose of) the charged assets in the ordinary course of business as if the charge did not exist, or because the chargor's freedom to do so is implied, probably in law, from the description of the subject matter of the charge as "the undertaking" or even from the description of the charge as "floating security".[28]

40-011

What constitutes a "disposition" that falls "in the ordinary course of business" depends on the terms of the charge, but the terms have generally been understood broadly by the courts. "Disposition" generally means any transaction that grants a third party a property right (a proprietary interest) in the charged assets, which could be by way of sale, lease, creation of other security interests, or even an execution levied against these assets (where the power to dispose is exercised irrespective of the chargor's will but clearly in a way that binds it). Such a dealing is typically thought to be "in the ordinary course of business" if, following it, the company's business continues.[29] Whether the disposition defeats or subordinates the floating charge depends on whether it is an outright disposition of the charged assets or the creation of an interest in them.

Notwithstanding the wide range of dispositions through which the chargor can defeat or subordinate the floating charge, the chargor's freedom to do so is not unlimited: some dispositions might fall outside the terms of the charge. One example is where a dealing is outside the ordinary course of business.[30] Another is where the terms of the charge restrict the chargor's (otherwise broad) freedom to defeat or subordinate the floating charge.

Where a disposition is outside the terms of the charge, the chargee does not consent to the floating charge being defeated or subordinated in the charged assets. It follows that such a disposition results in the disponee taking the assets subject to the floating charge. However, it is also possible for the disponee to defeat the floating charge in the charged assets or to subordinate it to the interest created by the disposition in those assets by raising a defence under the general law, for example that the disponee is a bona fide purchaser for value without notice that the disposition was outside the terms of the charge.[31]

This discussion shows that, as a matter of logic, there is a difference between the chargor's power to dispose of the charged assets and the chargor's freedom (sometimes also referred to in cases and debentures as a power[32] or liberty[33]) to dispose of the charged assets free of the floating charge. The chargor has a power to deal with the charged assets by virtue of owning them[34], and not by virtue of the grant of the charge. By contrast, the "power" to deal with the charged assets free of the floating charge until crystallisation *is* based on the grant of the charge, and the scope of this "power" is determined by the terms of the charge. Such terminology can be confusing and risks collapsing this important distinction. Therefore, it is useful to refer to the "power" to dispose free of the charge as an *authority to defeat or to subordinate the floating charge* in the assets that are being disposed of. Doing so makes it clearer to see that the exercise of the power to dispose of the charged assets can be either authorised or unauthorised under the terms of the floating charge, with different consequences following from each. In other words, the effects of the exercise of the power to dispose of charged assets are controlled by the limits on the authority to defeat or subordinate the charge in the charged assets.

3. Explaining the Operation of Floating Charges

40-012   This understanding of the floating charge explains many of its characteristics. For example, it explains why a third party who purchases property falling within the scope of the charge in the ordinary course of business takes it free of the floating charge; why an execution creditor who completes execution prior to crystallisation takes the assets free of the charge[35]; and why a third party taking a fixed charge over such property, takes priority over the floating charge.[36] It also provides the framework to explain the role and effect of negative pledge clauses,[37] and the events which will cause crystallisation—even automatic crystallisation—of the charge.[38]

This understanding also explains why dispositions that are not authorised (which generally means not in the ordinary course of the company's business) do not normally defeat or subordinate the floating charge in the assets disposed of, and why a party with actual or constructive notice that the disposition is not authorised by the terms of the charge will take subject to the charge: there is a subsisting charge which can bind a third party in accordance with the applicable rules of priority.[39] It also explains why the chargee can obtain an injunction to restrain the company from dealing with the assets other than in the ordinary course of business even whilst the charge remains uncrystallised,[40] and can equally seek the appointment of a receiver by the court when the security is in jeopardy[41]: again, there is a subsisting charge which can form the basis for these remedies.

The same understanding further explains that the proceeds of authorised dispositions do not automatically fall within the scope of the charge unless the terms of the charge so determine, and why the proceeds of unauthorised dispositions of charged assets similarly do not automatically fall within the scope of the charge, although the chargee might be able to assert a proprietary interest in them on some other basis.[42]

[20] For various judicial descriptions, see e.g. *Governments Stock and Other Securities Investment Co Ltd v Manila Railway Co* [1897] A.C. 81 at 86 per Lord Macnaghten; *Illingworth v Houldsworth* [1904] A.C. 355 at 358 per Lord Macnaghten; *Re Cimex Tissues Ltd* [1995] 1 B.C.L.C. 409 at 420–421; *Re Cosslett (Contractors) Ltd* [1998] Ch. 495 at [510c], per Millett LJ; *Re Spectrum Plus Ltd* [2005] UKHL 41; [2005] 2 A.C. 680 at [111] per Lord Scott, at [138]–[139], per Lord Walker.

[21] For the academic debate, see e.g. W Gough, *Company Charges* 2nd edn (1996) ch 13 (floating charge as an unattached and non-immediate interest); R Pennington, 'The Genesis of the Floating Charge' (1960) 23 MLR 630 at 644-646 (mortgage of future assets theory); B McFarlane, *Structure of Property Law* (2007) at 599-601 (power to acquire a persistent right theory); R Stevens, 'Contractual Aspects of Debt Financing' in: D Prentice and A Reisberg (eds), *Corporate Finance Law in the UK and EU* (2010) 213 at 221-222 (power in rem theory); R Goode, originally in *Legal Problems of Credit and Security* (1982), now L Gullifer (ed), *Goode and Gullifer on Legal Problems of Credit and Security* 6th edn (2018) at [4-04] (interest in a fund); J Farrar, "The Crystallisation of a Floating Charge" (1976) 40 Conv 397 at 397-398, and "World Economic Stagnation Puts the Floating Charge on Trial" (1980) 1 *The Company Lawyer* 83 at 83-87 (defeasible proprietary interest); S Worthington, "Floating Charges: An Alternative Theory" (1994) CLJ 81 and S Worthington, "Floating Charges: Use and Abuse of Doctrinal Analysis" in J Getzler and J Payne (eds), *Company Charges: Spectrum and Beyond* (2006) 25 at 39-44 (proprietary interest with a defeasible licence); R Nolan, "Property in a Fund" (2004) 120 LQR 108 at 129-130 (overreachable proprietary interest).

[22] W Gough, *Company Charges* 2nd edn (1996) ch.13, especially at 332-333, 343-344, 346-348, 359-360.

[23] *Re Spectrum Plus Ltd* [2005] UKHL 41; [2005] 2 A.C. 680 at [107].

[24] G Lightman, G Moss, I Fletcher, R Snowden and H Anderson (eds), *Lightman & Moss on The Law of Administrators and Receivers of Companies*, 6th edn (2017) at [3-029].

[25] *Re Spectrum Plus Ltd* [2005] UKHL 41; [2005] 2 A.C. 680 at [139].

[26] See para. 40-011 below, and for details, see M Raczynska, *The Law of Tracing in Commercial Transactions* (OUP, 2018) at [1.54]-[1.63], on which the discussion in this section and the section that follows is based. Of all academic and practitioner commentary, the discussion here is closest to, but not identical with, R Nolan, "Property in a Fund" (2004) 120 LQR 108. See also G Lightman, G Moss, I Fletcher, R Snowden and H Anderson (eds), *Lightman & Moss on The Law of Administrators and Receivers of Companies*, 6th edn (2017) at [3-031]-[3-033] and H Beale, M Bridge, L Gullifer and E Lomnicka, *The Law of Security and Title-based Financing*, 3rd edn (2018) at [6.72]-[6.75].

[27] Cf. R Nolan, "Property in a Fund" (2004) 120 LQR 108, who refers to the doctrine of overreaching to explain why the chargee's interest is capable of surviving in the proceeds of dispositions by the chargor so long as the disposition generates proceeds. For critique of this view, including the discussion of authorities on which this view is based, see M Raczynska, *The Law of Tracing in Commercial Transactions* (2018) at [4.38]-[4.48].

[28] See e.g. *Driver v Broad* [1893] 1 Q.B. 744 at 748.

[29] That the term "ordinary course of business" is given a broad meaning is discussed below at 40-030.

[30] *Hubbuck v Helms* (1887) 56 L.J. Ch. 536 at 538.

[31] See, for example, the discussion below concerning floating charge with negative pledge clauses, at 40-032.

[32] See e.g. *Biggerstaff v Rowatt's Wharf Ltd* [1896] 2 Ch. 93 at 100; *Re Bartlett Estates Pty Ltd (in liquidation)* (1988) 14 A.C.L.R. 512 at 516.

33 See e.g. *Driver v Broad* [1893] 1 Q.B. 744 at 748; *Biggerstaff v Rowatt's Wharf Ltd* [1896] 2 Ch. 93 at 94 and 105; *Re Benjamin Cope & Sons Ltd* [1914] 1 Ch. 800 at 806; *Stein v Saywell* (1969) 121 C.L.R. 529 at 556.

34 On and from 1 October 2009, a company, whenever incorporated, has unlimited objects, and hence capacity, unless its constitution provides otherwise: Companies Act 2006 s. 31.

35 See *Re Standard Manufacturing Co* [1891] 1 Ch. 627 at 641; *Evans v Rival Granite Quarries Ltd* [1910] 2 K.B. 979 at 995-996 per Fletcher Moulton LJ.

36 See paras. 40-030 – 40-031 below for the discussion of dispositions that fall in the ordinary course of business.

37 See para. 40-032 below.

38 See para. 40-037.

39 See section 7 below.

40 See, e.g. *Hubbuck v Helms* (1887) 56 L.T. 232; *Re Woodroffes (Musical Instruments) Ltd* [1986] Ch. 366 at 378A, per Nourse J; *Atkins v Mercantile Credit Ltd* (1985) 10 A.C.L.R. 153; *Wily v St George Partnership Banking Ltd* (1999) 30 ACSR 204 (Fed Crt of Aus) at 213 per Finkelstein J.

41 See, e.g. *Hubbuck v Helms* (1887) 56 LJ Ch 536; *McMahon v North Kent Ironworks Co* [1891] 2 Ch 148 at 150 per Kekewich J; *Edwards v Standard Rolling Stock Syndicate* [1893] 1 Ch 574 at 577 per North J; *Re Victoria Steamboats Ltd* [1897] 1 Ch. 158; *Re London Pressed Hinge Co Ltd* [1905] 1 Ch. 576 at 583 per Buckley J.

42 For details, see M Raczynska, *The Law of Tracing in Commercial Transactions* (2018) ch. 6.

Replace third section with:

3.   Conceptual Limits on Floating Charges

40-013   There are some limits on the extent to which parties can reserve rights to the chargor while still creating a charge: ultimately, the rights reserved to the purported chargor or to third parties may be so great that a court must hold that there is no charge, whether fixed or floating.[43] For example, there is no charge if the entitlement of the purported chargee to look to the asset for the discharge of the debt can be revoked by the purported chargor or a third party in the sense that the existence of this entitlement is within the control of the purported chargor or a third party. For there to be a charge, there must be an obligation to repay the loan out of an asset in favour of the creditor.[44] It cannot be revocable by the debtor or a third party. Correlated with this obligation is the chargee's right to enforce the charge.

40-014   Although the validity of the charge turns on the question whether the chargee has a right to enforce, a charge will not be invalid only because the chargee is in practice unable to assert this right. A floating charge granted over assets that are already subject to another security interest is consistent with the concept of the floating charge, even if it means that there are no free assets to which the chargee can have recourse at the time of enforcement.[45] There may, however, be a limit on the validity of the floating charge in situations where the parties' intention is that the purported charge is never to capture any assets of the company.[46] Such a "phantom" charge, it is submitted, is not a valid charge because the right to enforce the charge cannot exist without there being at least a possibility that it could be asserted against some assets, and without a right to enforce the creditor obtains no charge.[47]

40-015   The limits on the extent to which parties can reserve rights to the chargor while still creating a floating charge are widely drawn in English law. In England, a chargor's power to deal with charged assets free of a charge whilst remaining free to use the proceeds of the disposition for own benefit is seen as perfectly consistent with the existence of the charge. The contrary conclusion was reached in the

United States: attempts to create a floating security at common law were unsuccessful there.[48] This was because the chargor's power to dispose of charged assets without an obligation to account to the chargee for the proceeds of the disposition (by applying them to the payment of the secured debt or to the purchase of a substitute that would become subject to the charge) was seen as inconsistent with an effective creation of a charge.[49] Any such "argument of inconsistency" is an argument about some inconsistency between the terms of a particular transaction that purport to shape the content of an interest, and what the laws of a jurisdiction have established as the irreducible minimum content of the relevant interest. If such an inconsistency exists, the court may treat the purported interest at best as a nullity, at worst as a fraud. The position in the United States has since been reversed under Article 9 of the Uniform Commercial Code.[50]

[43] If it is established that there is a charge, the extent to which the rights are reserved to the chargor bears on the question of the characterization the charge, on which see section 6 below.

[44] See *Rodick v Gandell* (1852) 1 De G.M. & G. 763 at 777-778 per Lord Truro; *Palmer v Carey* [1926] A.C. 703 (P.C.) at 706-707 per Lord Wrenbury; *Kent & Sussex Sawmills* [1947] Ch. 177 at 180-181; *Swiss Bank Corporation v Lloyds Bank Ltd* [1982] A.C. 584 at 595-596 per Buckley LJ, affirmed by the House of Lords [1982] A.C. 584 at 613 per Lord Wilberforce; *Flightline Ltd v Edwards* [2003] EWCA Civ 63; [2003] W.L.R. 1200 at [45] per Jonathan Parker LJ; *Withers LLP v Langbar* [2011] EWCA Civ 1419 at [42]-[47] (Sir Robin Jacob).

[45] *Re Croftbell Ltd* [1990] B.C.C. 781 at 784 per Vinelott J; *SAW (SW) 2010 Ltd v Wilson* [2017] EWCA Civ 1001; [2018] Ch. 213 at [24], [28], [33] per Briggs LJ and [48], [51] per Arden LJ.

[46] This question was left open in *SAW (SW) 2010 Ltd v Wilson* [2017] EWCA Civ 1001; [2018] Ch. 213 at [49] per Arden LJ.

[47] Some support for this can be derived from *Re Spectrum Plus Ltd* [2005] UKHL 41; [2005] 2 A.C. 680 at [110] per Lord Scott.

[48] *Benedict v Ratner* 268 US 353 (1925) (Sup Crt of the United States). The decision was based on the law of New York but it was generally accepted in most other states: see G Gilmore, *Security Interests in Property*. Vol I (1965, reprinted 2011) at 270-271.

[49] *Benedict v Ratner* 268 US 353 (1925) esp. at 363–365 per Brandeis J. Note that a mere delivery of a report with an account to the chargee following the disposition (as opposed to an obligation to do so) was insufficient.

[50] Uniform Commercial Code, §9-205, and Official Comment 2.

Replace fourth section with:

4. PRACTICAL LIMITS ON FLOATING CHARGES

Floating charges are, in practice, only created by companies and some other **40-016** corporate bodies.[51] One exception is the floating charge created by farmers.[52] There are two main reasons why unincorporated persons do not grant floating charges, neither of which lies in principles of equity but in statute law. First, any security interest created in writing by an individual over goods would require compliance with the requirements set out in the Bills of Sale Acts 1878–1891.[53] The document must describe each asset within its scope, and each asset must be owned by the grantor at the time of creation, otherwise the document (and so, the security) is void.[54] It is practically impossible to comply with these requirements where the assets in question are used in trade as a circulating fund. Secondly, even if an individual wished to create a floating charge over assets that do not fall within the Bills of Sale Acts, such a security would be unattractive to lenders for lack of a statutory framework instituting publicity (registration) of such security. Without registration that would provide actual and constructive notice of the charge to others, in particular prospective lenders, it would be easy to defeat the chargee's interest. However, companies, for example, are outside the scope of the bills of sale legislation. A floating charge created by a company is registrable under Pt 25 of the Companies Act 2006[55], and that requirement can be met without any significant difficulty.

[51] The power of registered companies to create a floating charge is based on case law. In relation to other corporate bodies, the power to create a floating charge is based on statute law, which typically also stipulates how such a charge is to be registered, see e.g. Limited Liability Partnerships (Application of Companies Act 2006) Regulations 2009 SI 2009/1804, reg.32; Co-operative and Community Benefit Societies Act 2014 s.59 (for registered societies), Financial Services (Banking Reform) Act 2013 Sch.9, para. 4 (building societies), European Economic Interest Groupings Regulations1989 SI 1989/638 reg.18.

[52] Agricultural Credits Act 1928 s.5.

[53] The main acts are the Bills of Sale Act 1878 and the Bills of Sale Act 1878 (Amendment) Act 1882. The scope of the assets falling within those Acts is defined in s.4 of the 1878 Act.

[54] Bills of Sale Act 1878 (Amendment) Act 1882 ss.4, 5 and note s. 6, which makes an exception in relation to certain assets not owned by the grantor, namely growing crops and replacement plant, trade machinery, fixtures in substitution for those specifically described:

[55] Companies Act s.859A, and see s.895H for the consequences of lack of registration.

Replace fifth section with:

5.   THE UTILITY OF FLOATING CHARGES: BENEFITS AND COSTS

40-017   The floating charge is a very convenient way to align the interests of the chargor and chargee. The chargor retains the flexibility to deal with assets in the course of its business, free of the charge, and yet to offer them to a lender by way of security. The lender can take security over any type of asset, even a fluctuating class of assets, and thus benefit from priority over unsecured creditors. The lender is free to agree with the grantor to take a floating charge over all of grantor's property but it is far more common for lenders to take fixed security interests (such as mortgage, fixed charge, pledge) over non-fluctuating assets and a floating charge sweeping the remaining assets. Added to the convenience for the parties is the practice of taking different security interests in one document, a debenture.

40-018   Another advantage enjoyed by the chargee is the power to appoint an administrator out of court, if it holds a qualifying floating charge, as defined in the Insolvency Act 1986 and discussed below.[56] This is a useful method of enforcement, which is now based on statute but derives from the judicial recognition of a power to appoint a receiver in the debenture.

40-019   There is a cost, however, to creating a floating charge, as is the case with other security interests, and that cost falls on the unsecured creditors of the chargor. On the insolvency of the chargor, assets subject to security interests are applied to meet secured debts in full before any can be made available to meet the claims of unsecured creditors. While the parties to the security agreement may not object to this situation—indeed, they usually desire it—it is obviously unjust to those unsecured creditors who are unable to improve their position by private bargain with the debtor, either because they lack the opportunity to do so (for example, involuntary creditors such as tort claimants) or because they lack the economic power to strike such a bargain. The point is sometimes put more broadly that all unsecured creditors, including ordinary trade creditors who supply goods to a company, are at an unfair disadvantage.[57] This injustice has been attributed to the floating charge (rather than all security interests) partly due to the type of assets subject to it, and partly due to its very wide scope.[58]

As a result, statute law has intervened. The first such intervention came not long after the development of the floating charge: the Preferential Payments in Bankruptcy Amendment Act 1897.[59] At that time, floating charges were typically taken over raw materials and wholly or partially manufactured goods. Employees added value to such assets through their work, so it was thought that their wages should be paid out of assets subject to a floating charge before the chargee itself may be paid.[60] The class of preferential debts also included certain local and national taxes. It is possible to state the policy underpinning this intervention in broader terms, as a way of addressing the injustice of the floating chargee being able to "withdraw all or most of the assets of an insolvent company from the scope of a liquidation and leave the liquidator with little more than an empty shell and unable to pay preferential creditors".[61] The list of preferential claims is now contained in the Insolvency Act 1986.[62] When the 1986 Act was introduced, it comprised certain taxes, social security contributions, occupational pension scheme contributions, and employees' remuneration.[63] The first two of these were removed by the Enterprise Act 2002, which instead inserted s.176A into the Insolvency Act 1986, providing (subject to some exceptions) that a prescribed part of the assets subject to a floating charge created on or after 15 September 2003 shall be set aside for unsecured creditors.[64] The main unsecured creditor is typically the Crown in respect of taxes owed, so in practice the prescribed part replaced the preferential status of HMRC. Since the introduction of the 1986 Act, there have been a few additions to the list of preferential creditors[65] but the most significant modern statutory intervention in the rights of the floating chargee came with the Finance Act 2020. It re-introduced the Crown preference from 1st December 2020 in respect of certain taxes[66], without any cap or removal of the prescribed part, while the value of the prescribed part increased.[67]

The potentially wide scope of the floating charge has generated a concern that **40-020** the charge could be created in the twilight period before the onset of insolvency to the prejudice of unsecured creditors. Of all unsecured creditors, trade creditors are sometimes thought to be particularly at risk because a creditor taking a floating charge allows the debtor to trade and to buy assets on credit, which assets enlarge the scope of security at the expense of unpaid sellers.[68] No such prejudice exists if the debtor creates the charge in return for new value. Statutory interventions invalidating any late floating charge taken for past value have a long history. The first was introduced in the Companies Act 1907[69], and the current provision is found in s. 245 of the Insolvency Act 1986. It states that a floating charge created at a relevant time[70] is invalid except to the extent that new value is provided in consideration for the charge.[71]

Further costs to creating a floating charge arise for reasons other than protec- **40-021** tion of unsecured creditors. Some of them arise on administration, and appear to be attributable to the fact that an administrator is focused on maintaining liquidity of the company, which involves dealing with the sort of assets that are subject to a floating charge (as opposed to fixed security rights), meaning assets that the company generally deals with to operate its business.[72] First, on administration, the administrator has the power to dispose of the charged assets for the purposes of administration.[73] In relation to assets subject to the floating charge, by contrast to those secured by a fixed charge, the administrator can exercise this power freely, without the court's permission and without the obligation to pay the proceeds of the disposition to the chargee.[74] The only statutory safeguard is that the priority of the floating chargee is preserved with respect to the proceeds acquired by the administrator directly or indirectly.[75]

40-022 Secondly, the expenses of administration are payable out of floating charge assets.[76] These include the remuneration of the administrator and the debts arising out of contracts that the administrator entered into. They can be substantial, particularly if the administrator borrows money to continue trading. Expenses of liquidation, following the reform under the Companies Act 2006, are also payable out of floating charge assets.[77]

40-023 Some costs borne by the holders of the floating charge do not appear to be based on a clearly identifiable policy rationale. Where the company obtains a moratorium introduced by the Corporate Insolvency and Governance Act 2020[78] and enters winding up proceedings within twelve weeks from the day the moratorium ends, creditors who are owed certain pre-moratorium debts and those owed moratorium debts, including any new financing, are payable out of the company's assets in priority to all other claims.[79] Since the company's estate on winding up comprises assets subject to a floating charge, but not those subject to fixed security interests[80], it follows that rights of the floating chargee are affected. The standalone moratorium was introduced as part of a package of measures aimed at mitigating the impact of Covid-19 pandemic on business, and at improving the corporate rescue regime. It is not entirely clear why this limitation affects the holders of the floating chargee, rather than all secured creditors.

[56] See below, para. 40-039.

[57] See, e.g. *Re General South American Co* (1876) 2 Ch. D. 337 at 341 per Malins V-C; *Salomon v Salomon & Co Ltd* [1897] A.C. 22 at 53 per Lord MacNaghten; *Re London Pressed Hinge Co Ltd* [1905] 1 Ch. 576 at 583 per Buckley J.

[58] L Gullifer and J Payne, "The Characterization of Fixed and Floating Charges" in: J Getzler and J Payne (eds.) *Company Charges: Spectrum and Beyond* (2006) 51 at 78-81.

[59] Preferential Payments in Bankruptcy Amendment Act 1897, s. 2.

[60] Parliamentary debates U.K. H.C. Deb. 10 at cols. 72-73 (February 1897).

[61] *Agnew v Commissioner of Inland Revenue (Re Brumark Ltd)* [2001] UKPC 28; [2001] 2 A.C. 710 at [9] per Lord Millett.

[62] Insolvency Act 1986, ss. 175, 386, Sch. 6 and, in administration, Sch. B1, para. 65(2).

[63] This included and includes those who might be subrogated to employees' claims, which means the Secretary of State when employees' claims are paid from the National Insurance Fund: see Employment Rights Act 1996, s. 182, which replaces Employment Protection (Consolidation) Act 1978, s. 122(1), Insolvency Act 1985, s. 218(2) and Employment Act 1990, Sch. 2 para. 1(4).

[64] The calculation of the prescribed part is set out in the Insolvency Act 1986 (Prescribed Part) Order 2003 (SI 2003/2097), art. 3. Its value is capped, and the cap was raised from £600,000 to £800,000 by the Insolvency Act 1986 (Prescribed Part) (Amendment) Order 2020/211.

[65] These are: levies on coal and steel production, certain debts owed to the Financial Services Compensation Scheme (FSCS), deposits covered by the FSCS and certain other deposits: see Insolvency Act 1986, Sch. 6, paras. 15A, 15AA, 15B, 15BA and 15BB, with the debts in paras. 15BA and 15BB as secondary preferential debts.

[66] Insolvency Act 1986, Sch. 6, para. 15D and Insolvency Act 1986 (HMRC Debts: Priority on Insolvency) Regulations 2020 (SI 2020/983). They include value added tax, PAYE (pay as you earn tax), and national insurance contributions. All rank as secondary preferential debts, after the other ordinary preferential debts have been paid: Insolvency Act 1986, ss. 175(1B), 386(1B).

[67] See fn 72 above.

[68] *Report of the Review Committee, Insolvency Law and Practice* (1982, Cmnd. 8558), para. 1553. For criticism, see H. Bennett, "Late Floating Charges" in: J. Armour and H. Bennett (eds.) *Vulnerable Transactions in Corporate Insolvency* (2003) at [5.9]-[5.10].

[69] Companies Act 1907, s. 13.

[70] Relevant time means either one or two years ending with the onset of insolvency, depending on whether the chargee is a person connected with the company: Insolvency Act 1986, s. 245(3)-(5).

[71] For detailed discussion, see, e.g., H. Bennett, "Late Floating Charges" in: J. Armour and H. Bennett (eds.) *Vulnerable Transactions in Corporate Insolvency* (2003) at [5.39] – [5.94]; K van Zwieten (ed.) *Goode on Principles of Corporate Insolvency Law* 5th edn (2018) at [13-105] – [13.116].

[72] K van Zwieten (ed.) *Goode on Principles of Corporate Insolvency Law* 5th edn (2018) at [10-009].

[73] The purposes of administration are outlined in para 40-039 below.

[74] Insolvency Act 1986, Sch. B1, para. 70(1).

[75] Insolvency Act 1986, Sch. B1, para. 70(2) and (3).

[76] Insolvency Act 1986, Sch. B1, para. 99(3) and (4); Insolvency (England and Wales) Rules 2016/1026, rr. 3.50 and 3.51.

[77] Insolvency Act 1986, s. 176ZA, reversing the result in *Buchler v Talbot* [2004] UKHL 9; [2004] 2 A.C. 298. For the list of expenses and their order of priority, see Insolvency (England and Wales) Rules 2016/1026, rr. 6.42 and 7.108.

[78] Insolvency Act 1986, part A1, inserted by Corporate Insolvency and Governance Act 2020, s.1(1).

[79] Insolvency Act 1986, s 174A(4), inserted by the Corporate Insolvency and Governance Act 2020, s.2(1), Sch.3 paras 1, 13.

[80] See, e.g., *Re LB Holdings Intermediate 2 Ltd (In Administration)* [2020] EWHC 1681 (Ch.) at [87] per Marcus Smith J (obiter), reversed [2021] EWCA Civ 1523 but not on this point; K van Zwieten (ed.) *Goode on Principles of Corporate Insolvency Law* 5th edn (2018) at [8-04] and [8-17].

Replace sixth section with:

6. CHARACTERIZING A CHARGE: FIXED OR FLOATING?

1. The Nature of the Problem

The issue which has figured most prominently in case law has been how to determine whether a charge is fixed or floating. Since the early days of the floating charge, much has turned on that distinction, and statutory reforms over the last 120 years have deepened the significance of this distinction, as discussed above.[81] It is hardly surprising, therefore, that borrowers and lenders have tried to create a charge that would be categorised as fixed while giving the parties the same flexibility as a floating charge. It is equally unsurprising, given what is at stake for unsecured creditors, that the courts have resisted such attempts. It is therefore important to ascertain and understand the principles by which charges are categorised as fixed or floating.[82]

40-024

The problem is that statute law, for many purposes, draws a sharp distinction between a fixed charge and a floating charge, whereas in equity, a whole range of powers can be reserved to a chargor, to create a range of charges from those which give very little freedom to the chargor to deal with the charged assets (and their proceeds) free of the charge, to wide ranging powers which will obviously result in the creation of a floating charge. To put the point another way, the words "floating charge" are used as a defining (but itself undefined) phrase in statute, which must have clear boundaries, but only as a description in equity, without sharp boundaries, of a range of possible charges. So, the question is, from what point, on that spectrum of possibilities in equity, will a charge be properly characterized as "floating" for the many purposes of statute law.

2. The process of characterization

40-025   Assuming that the documentation creating the charge is not a sham,[83] characterization of the charge requires construction of the terms of the charge against the commercial background in order to categorise the charge correctly as a matter of law. The courts have made it clear that they are not bound by the label chosen by the parties to the transaction, but will instead look to its commercial substance. In the *Brumark* case, Lord Millett described the process of characterization as follows:

> "The question is not merely one of construction. In deciding whether a charge is a fixed charge or a floating charge, the court is engaged in a two-stage process. At the first stage it must construe the instrument of charge and seek to gather the intentions of the parties from the language they have used. But the object at this stage of the process is not to discover whether the parties intended to create a fixed or a floating charge. It is to ascertain the nature of the rights and obligations which the parties intended to grant each other in respect of the charged assets. Once these have been ascertained, the court can then embark on the second stage of the process, which is one of categorisation. This is a matter of law. It does not depend on the intention of the parties. If their intention, properly gathered from the language of the instrument, is to grant the company rights in respect of the charged assets which are inconsistent with the nature of a fixed charge, then the charge cannot be a fixed charge however they may have chosen to describe it. A similar process is involved in construing a document to see whether it creates a licence or tenancy. The court must construe the grant to ascertain the intention of the parties: but the only intention which is relevant is the intention to grant exclusive possession: see *Street v Mountford* [1985] A.C. 809, 826, per Lord Templeman. So here: in construing a debenture to see whether it creates a fixed or a floating charge, the only intention which is relevant is the intention that the company should be free to deal with the charged assets and withdraw them from the security without the consent of the holder of the charge; or, to put the question another way, whether the charged assets were intended to be under the control of the company or of the charge holder."[84]

The last sentence identifies the criterion for distinguishing between fixed and floating charges, which – as Lord Millett makes clear in the passage above – is needed in order to categorise the charge as a matter of law, and so to complete the process of characterization. In re Spectrum, the leading English authority, Lord Scott endorsed Lord Millett's view[85], and himself provided a description of the criterion in very similar terms, as did Lord Walker.[86]

3. Control over the Charged Assets

40-026   Both the *Brumark*[87] case and the *Spectrum*[88] case involved attempts to take fixed charges over the book debts of a company.[89] In each, the charge was held to be a floating charge. On the state of those authorities, it seems that for a charge to be fixed, there must be a total restriction on any disposal of the charged assets, book debts and proceeds, by the chargor without the consent of the chargee.[90] To ensure the charge is fixed the chargor could, for example, be prevented from collecting proceeds, or be required to pay the collected proceeds to the chargee in discharge of the charged debt.[91] If the parties prefer, as is likely, for the proceeds to be collected by the chargor and paid into a bank account (whether held with the chargee or a third party bank), that account must be under the control of the chargee for the charge to be fixed. The chargee has such control when the account is blocked.[92] Payments out of the account can be consistent with the charge being fixed, but these need to be under the control of the chargee. For example, payments out of a blocked account made at the chargee's absolute discretion and solely by way of individual instructions issued directly to the bank by the signatories of the chargee have been held to be consistent with a fixed charge over book debts and proceeds.[93] The chargee's blanket permission to release money from the account upon satisfaction of some conditions is unlikely to satisfy the requirement of control.

Lord Millet in *Brumark* stated that merely providing in the charge agreement that the account is blocked would not be enough "if it is not operated as one in fact".[94] It is not entirely clear what these words mean. One possibility is that they might be read to mean that practical (as opposed to agreed (legal)) control is required for the charge to be fixed. Assuming the test for distinguishing charges set out in *Brumark* and *Spectrum* applies generally to all charges (and there is no suggestion it does not), this interpretation is problematic. In relation to charges over tangibles, practical control would very likely mean possession, which would defeat the point of taking a charge as a *non-possessory* security interest. Such an interpretation should, therefore, be rejected. Another option is that a court might have some regard to the conduct of the parties *after* the execution of the charge. This is also problematic. The ordinary canon of construction is that the nature of a transaction (here, a charge) is to be ascertained at the moment of its inception.[95] It would be a radical change to such established principles of construction if behaviour after that point in time were to influence how the transaction is categorised. If no such radical change is intended, then behaviour subsequent to formation of the charge can be relevant in three possible ways, either as evidence of a sham, or as evidence of a variation of rights, or as facts on which to found some waiver or estoppel.[96] But all of these three possibilities might give rise to problems applying the Insolvency Act 1986, which defines a floating charge (unless the context otherwise requires) as a charge which, *as created*, was floating.[97] The difficulty raised by the wording of the statute could be overcome by considering the purpose of the relevant provisions: the idea was to preclude a floating chargee from circumventing the protections given on insolvency to unsecured creditors by arguing that by the time of insolvency the charge became fixed. There is no concern of this kind should a fixed charge become floating on or before insolvency, so it should not matter that a charge which is floating on insolvency was not created as floating.

Another area of difficulty concerns charges which allow the chargor limited **40-027** power to substitute one asset for another within the scope of the charge, rather than simply to deal with assets free of the charge whether or not the chargor must substitute a different asset (or equivalent value) for any asset it disposes to a third party free of the charge. Prior to *Brumark* and *Spectrum*, the courts indicated that some such limited power might not be inconsistent with categorisation of the charge as a fixed charge.[98] However, such views are difficult to reconcile both with older authority,[99] that regarded the power to substitute assets as indicative of a floating charge, and with *Brumark* and *Spectrum*, because the chargor's power to substitute is inconsistent with chargee's control in the sense of a total restriction on dispositions by the chargor. That said, it might be possible to construe a charge agreement with a power to substitute a new asset for another old asset as creating two charges: a charge over the old asset (which probably must now be a floating charge, for reasons just explained) and another charge over the new asset. The charge over the new asset can be fixed so long as the chargor does not have a power to replace the new asset, too (otherwise, the charge over that asset would likely also be floating).[100] The new asset would become subject to the charge as soon as it is acquired, and with effect from the charge agreement, assuming the intention of the parties to create this charge was immediate and unconditional.[101]

4. Charges over income-generating assets

40-028   When characterizing a charge over book debts, it matters what rights the chargee has with respect to proceeds of those debts: a charge over book debts cannot be fixed unless the chargee is also granted a fixed charge over the proceeds of those debts. This is because debts and their proceeds are very closely linked assets: a right to enforce the charge against a debt is worthless without a right to enforce against the proceeds.[102] This is clearly not the case for all assets. For example, characterization of a charge as fixed over a piece of machinery does not depend on the chargee being granted a fixed charge over, say, sale proceeds of the machinery. The question arises whether characterization of charges over any assets other than book debts depends on the rights the chargee has over their proceeds.

The *Brumark* and *Spectrum* cases do not address this but it is possible to look for an answer to this question by considering whether analogies can be drawn between, on one hand, book debts and their proceeds and, on the other, other assets and their proceeds. It is sometimes considered whether such an analogy can be drawn between certain income-generating assets and the income derived from them.[103] For example, such a parallel can be drawn between book debts and a right to be paid rent under lease agreements.[104] First, rent, like debt proceeds, arises not through the exercise of the chargor's power of disposition of the lease but through the realisation of the right to be paid held by the chargor by an act of a third party. Secondly, from the chargee's perspective, the right to enforce the charge against the lease without the right to rent is likely to be worthless in the following sense. Leases are not usually extinguished with a single payment (book debts usually are) but what the market is willing to pay for a lease decreases with every payment of rent until the last rent payment, which is very likely to make the lease worthless. Where the payment of income extinguishes the asset or has the potential to extinguish it over time, the existence of the chargee's right to enforce the charge against the asset is uncertain. This, it is submitted, is sufficient to draw a parallel with book debts, so that the fixed character of the charge over the asset (lease) depends on the chargee's control over the proceeds (rent).

[81] See paras. 40-017 – 40-023 above.

[82] This law is addressed in detail in H Beale, M Bridge, L Gullifer and E Lomnicka, *The Law of Security and Title-based Financing*, 3rd edn (2018) at [6.97]-[6.141], and see also L Gullifer and J Payne, "The Characterization of Fixed and Floating Charges" in: J Getzler and J Payne (eds.) *Company Charges: Spectrum and Beyond* (2006) 51.

[83] See *Snook v London and West Riding Investments Ltd* [1967] 2 Q.B. 786 at 802 per Diplock LJ. As to shams generally, see M. Conaglen, "Sham Trusts" [2008] C.L.J. 176; and para.22-067 above.

[84] *Re Brumark Ltd* [2001] UKPC 28; [2001] 2 A.C. 710 at [32].

[85] *Re Spectrum Plus Ltd* [2005] UKHL 41; [2005] 2 A.C. 680 at [111].

[86] *Re Spectrum Plus Ltd* [2005] UKHL 41; [2005] 2 A.C. 680 at [111] per Lord Scott, at [138]–[139], per Lord Walker.

[87] [2001] UKPC 28; [2001] 2 A.C. 710.

[88] [2005] UKHL 41; [2005] 2 A.C. 680.

[89] There were other cases involving the same issue: see, in particular, *Siebe Gorman & Co Ltd v Barclays Bank Ltd* [1979] 2 Lloyd's Rep 142, and *Re New Bullas Trading Ltd* [1994] 1 B.C.L.C. 485.

[90] See S Worthington, "Floating Charges: The Use and Abuse of Doctrinal Analysis" in: J Getzler and J Payne (eds.) *Company Charges: Spectrum and Beyond* (2006) 25 at 28; H Beale, M Bridge, L Gullifer and E Lomnicka, *The Law of Security and Title-based Financing*, 3rd edn (2018) at [6.110].

[91] See *Re Spectrum Plus Ltd* [2005] UKHL 41; [2005] 2 A.C. 680 at [54] per Lord Hope citing S Worthington, "An 'Unsatisfactory Area of the Law'—Fixed and Floating Charges Yet Again" (2004) 1 *International Corporate Rescue* 175 at 182.

[92] See *Re Brumark Ltd* [2001] UKPC 28; [2001] 2 A.C. 710 at [22], [48] per Lord Millett; *Re Spectrum Plus Ltd* [2005] UKHL 41; [2005] 2 A.C. 680 at [54] per Lord Hope, at [117], [119] per Lord Scott, at [140], [160] per Lord Walker. See also *Re Keenan Brothers Ltd* [1986] B.C.L.C. 242 (Irish Sup Crt).

[93] *Re Harmony Care Homes Ltd* [2009] EWHC 1961 (Ch) at [25]-[26].

[94] *Re Brumark Ltd* [2001] UKPC 28; [2001] 2 A.C. 710 at [48], endorsed cautiously in *Re Spectrum Plus Ltd* [2005] UKHL 41; [2005] 2 A.C. 680 at [160] per Lord Walker.

[95] Post-contractual conduct is not taken into account when interpreting a contract, see *Whitworth Street Estates (Manchester) Ltd v James Miller* [1970] A.C. 583 at 603 per Lord Reid, at 606 per Lord Hodson, at 611 per Viscount Dilhorne, at 615 per Lord Wilerforce; *L Schuler AG v Wickman Machine Tool Sales Ltd* [1974] A.C. 235, at 252 per Lord Reid, at 260 per Lord Morris, at 261 per Lord Wilberforce, at 265-268 per Lord Simon, at 272-273 per Lord Kilbrandon; *Dunlop Tyres Ltd v Blows* [2001] EWCA Civ 1032 at [21]-[22] per Lord Woolf. This is also the position in Australia (see *Agricultural and Rural Finance v Gardiner* (2008) 238 C.L.R. 570 at [35]) but not in New Zealand (*Gibbons Holdings v Wholesale Distributors* [2008] 1 N.Z.L.R. 277, *Bathurst Resources Ltd v L&M Coal Holdings Ltd* [2021] NZSC 85 at [84]-[90] (obiter), and at [149]-[151]).

[96] See H Beale, M Bridge, L Gullifer and E Lomnicka, *The Law of Security and Title-based Financing* 3rd edn, (2018) at [6.118]-[6.121].

[97] Insolvency Act 1986 ss. 40, 251 and Sch.B1 para. 111(1). Note, too, *Re Harmony Care Homes* [2009] EWHC 1961 (Ch) at [18].

[98] *Re TXU Europe Group Plc* [2004] 1 B.C.L.C. 519; and *Queens Moat Houses Ltd v Capita IRG Trustees Ltd* [2005] 2 B.C.L.C. 199.

[99] *Re Yorkshire Woolcombers Ltd* [1903] 2 Ch. 284 at [295] per Vaughan-Williams LJ.

[100] Given the very limited power to substitute discussed here, this analysis is unlikely to work in relation to a charge that includes a list of assets within a single charge with an power to dispose, for which see H Beale, M Bridge, L Gullifer and E Lomnicka, *The Law of Security and Title-based Financing* 3rd edn, (2018) at [6.106].

[101] *Holroyd v Marshall* (1862) 10 HL Cas. 191; *Tailby v Official Receiver* (1888) LR 13 App. Cas. 523, and see generally M Raczynska, *The Law of Tracing in Commercial Transactions* (2018) at [5.30]-[5.37].

[102] *Re Brumark Ltd* [2001] UKPC 28; [2001] 2 A.C. 710 at [46] per Lord Millett; *Re Spectrum Plus Ltd* [2005] UKHL 41; [2005] 2 A.C. 680 at [110] per Lord Scott.

[103] See M Raczynska, *The Law of Tracing in Commercial Transactions* (2018) at [5.47]-[5.66] for more detailed discussion, and for the discussion of characterization in relation to charges over other income-generating assets: insurance policies, intellectual property rights, shares, land, and long-term contracts.

[104] If the analysis correct, it is doubted whether *Re Atlantic Computer Systems Plc* [1992] Ch. 505 and *Re Atlantic Medical Ltd* [1992] B.C.C. 653 are good authorities following *Spectrum* and *Brumark*.

Replace seventh section with:

[293]

7. PRIORITIES

1. Introduction

40-029   The priority of floating charges is also explained by their structure.[105] It is a feature of a floating charge that the chargor has power to deal with the charged assets, and the exercise of this power is subject to the terms of the charge. The terms determine when the chargor is authorised to exercise the power free of the charge, thus defeating the charge in the disposed asset, or in a way that subordinates the interest of the chargee to that of another. So if the grant of a later charge is regarded as a transaction within the chargor's authority, the second charge will take priority over an earlier floating charge, even if the subsequent chargee has notice of the earlier charge.

The authority to defeat or subordinate the floating charge could in theory be set out by detailing authorised transactions, but it is far more common to describe the scope of authority with reference to the ordinary scope of business. If no such reference is made, the company's freedom to dispose of charged assets in the ordinary course of business is inferred from the term "floating" when describing the charge.[106] As discussed below, courts give a broad meaning to "ordinary course of business", so the chargor's authority is generally broad.[107] It is unsurprising that it became the practice of the parties to agree some limits through negative pledge clauses[108] and crystallisation clauses.[109] The chargor's authority to defeat or subordinate the floating charge is also terminated upon the occurrence of certain events identified by law.[110]

2. Authority to Defeat or Subordinate the Charge: Ordinary Course of Business

40-030   To determine whether a transaction is within the ordinary course of a company's business courts apply ordinary principles of interpretation to the charge document.[111] They first look at whether an objective observer, with knowledge of the company, would consider the transaction to be in the ordinary course of business, and secondly, whether there is anything in the document to manifest that the parties nevertheless did not intend for the transaction to be in the ordinary course of business.

While much depends on the document, it is clear that a wide range of transactions involving assets subject to a floating charge have been held to be within a company's ordinary course of business. Within the ordinary course of business have been, for example, the following: disposals of the charged assets in the course of trade[112], even if it is a quick sale to raise finance[113] or a substantial portion of charged assets is disposed[114]; disposals of the charged assets to meet expenses of the business[115]; sale and lease-back of charged assets[116]; grant of a fixed security interest (mortgage or fixed charge) over the charged assets; grant of a floating charge over part the charged assets[117]; assertion of rights of set-off, whether arising as legal or equitable set-off.[118] The courts were even willing to find that a completed execution is a disposition in the ordinary course of business.[119] They took the view that the floating charge is meant to be a security which leaves the secured assets free for use in connection with a company's business, so long as the company still has a business to run.[120] Not many transactions have been said to fall outside the company's ordinary course of business, but one example is a transaction intended to bring to an end, or have the effect of bringing to an end, the company's business.[121] Grant of another floating charge over the same charged assets is another.[122]

Where a transaction involving charged assets is in the ordinary course of busi-   **40-031**
ness, the third party takes free from the charge, which means that the third party is immune from the floating charge. Thus, an outright disposition of charged assets defeats the floating charge; disposition by way of creation of an interest or right in the charged assets subordinates the charge to the interest or right created, although in practice it might, like an outright disposition, have the consequence of defeat-ing the floating charge in those assets. For example, a grant of a mortgage or a fixed charge in the ordinary course of the company's business will take priority over an earlier floating charge, even if the subsequent chargee has notice of the earlier charge.[123]

By contrast, a disposition outside the ordinary course of business is outside the authority to defeat (or subordinate) the floating charge, so in principle the third party disponee is not immune from the floating charge. For example, a fixed charge granted outside the ordinary course of the company's business will be postponed to the floating charge according to normal priority rules, that is, the second (fixed) chargee will take subject to the first (floating) charge. However, a third party disponee may still take the assets free of the floating charge if they have some reason to displace ordinary time priority, such as bona fide purchase for value without notice.

3.   Limits on the Authority to Defeat or Subordinate the Charge

(a)   Negative pledge clauses   A negative pledge clause in a floating charge   **40-032**
agreement[124] generally means a clause restricting the chargor's authority to dispose of the charged assets in a way that would prejudice the rights of the floating chargee.[125] One of the most common is a restriction on the chargor's authority to create in favour of anyone else security interests that would rank pari passu or in priority to the floating charge. While such agreements are undoubtedly binding in contract as between chargor and chargee, so that breach would expose the chargor to a (probably worthless) claim in damages, such provisions can also have effect on third parties. Though the agreement creates only a "mere equity" or "personal equity",[126] if a third party has *actual* notice of the negative pledge clause, and does not obtain the consent of the floating chargee to the disposition, he will be bound by it and not be able to claim priority over the floating charge in respect of an inter-est granted to him in breach of the agreement.[127]

A question arises whether a third party could have *constructive* notice of the negative pledge. Prior to the 2013 reform of the Companies Act 2006[128] there was no basis on which a third party could have constructive notice of a negative pledge.[129] This was because constructive notice could only have been of charge details that were required to be registered with Companies House under the Companies Act 2006. The existence of a negative pledge clause was not among them: it was not a matter that a company was under a legal duty to register (i.e. there was no criminal sanction for the lack of registration unlike in relation to other matters). So, even if such a clause was registered voluntarily, it was only notice to those who actually searched the register, and not to those who did not, even though they might have been expected to search.[130]

Following the 2013 reform, the position on constructive notice of negative pledges is less clear.[131] The statue does not clarify this, and the courts have not had a chance to do so either. An argument against a third party having constructive notice of negative pledges is as follows. Under the new registration regime there is no duty to register any charge details: non-registration is no longer met with a criminal sanction, but merely that of invalidity of the charge on insolvency.[132] There is no breach of a duty if the charge remains unregistered. If the pre-2013 logic applies here, a third party might be thought not to have constructive notice of anything on the register, including any negative pledge clause. The outcome of this reasoning would be unfortunate as it would disincentivise any searches of the register, and so likely undermine the purpose of registration as a way of providing publicity of charges. On the other hand, in favour of constructive notice of negative pledges, it could be said that once a commercial decision to register a charge has been made, the law then stipulates which documents are to be delivered to the registrar and, in that sense, they are required to be registered. This includes a statement of charge particulars revealing whether the charge document contains a negative pledge or not.[133] On that basis, a third party expected to search the register (for example, a prospective chargee) has constructive notice of a negative pledge clause where the existence of the clause is indicated in the registered statement of particulars.[134] It is submitted that this is a preferable view as it is commercially more realistic.

40-033   **(b)   Crystallisation**   Crystallisation is the name given to the moment when a floating charge ceases to float and so becomes fixed on the assets within its scope.[135] The term "fixed" in this context is not particularly fortunate to the extent it might suggest that the comparative disadvantages of the floating charge on insolvency are avoided: they are not because under the insolvency legislation a charge is floating when it was created as one.[136] Crystallisation means that the chargor's authority to defeat or subordinate the floating charge is prospectively terminated. A floating charge may specifically provide that the chargor's authority to defeat or subordinate the charge may be terminated in respect of some assets rather than others, that is, that the charge should be crystallised over those assets but not others.[137] In the absence of such a stipulation, all the chargor's authority to do so is terminated on crystallisation,[138] and any attempt to terminate those powers in respect of some assets only will be ineffective.[139] Crystallisation can occur in various ways, which are discussed below.

40-034   *(1)   Crystallisation on cessation of business*   The reason the chargor has authority to defeat or subordinate the floating charge in charged assets is to enable it to operate its business. When the business ceases, the rationale behind the chargor's authority falls away, and so the floating charge crystalises. Cessation of business, and so crystallisation of the floating charge, takes place when the company is wound up[140] but it can take place for some other reason.[141] Charge agreement may expressly provide for crystallisation upon winding up of the company or cessation of business but if it does not, such a term is implied in law.[142]

40-035   *(2)   Crystallisation by intervention*   Crystallisation may also occur by the chargee's intervention[143] with the intention to crystallise the charge.[144] The intervention could be, for example, by the appointment of a receiver[145] or an administrator.[146] The grounds for intervening depend on the terms of the charge, but such grounds commonly include default in repayment, winding up, appointment of another receiver or administrator, execution on the property of the chargor, and unauthorised disposals of charged assets.[147] Crystallisation by appointment of a receiver was originally expressly stated in charge documentation to terminate the authority of the chargor to deal with assets free of the charge[148] but termination of authority and so crystallisation is now implied from the fact of appointment.[149] The same does not appear to be true in relation to an appointment of an administrator because an administrator has the power to carry on the business of the company, and does not owe the duties only to the chargee.[150] If the charge is to crystallise upon the appointment of an administrator an express provision to that effect is to be required.[151] Unless the parties agree otherwise, the mere fact that the grounds for intervention have arisen is insufficient to crystallise the charge.

(3) Crystallisation by notice   Crystallisation may also occur by service of notice **40-036** if the charge so provides.[152] Such clauses are referred to as semi-automatic clauses. The terms of the charge will determine whether notice may be served at will by the chargee, or on the occurrence of a specified event.[153] held that the approach in the *Brumark* case to whether a fixed charge has been created did not apply to interpretation of a clause providing for crystallisation by notice.

(4) Automatic crystallisation clauses   It is also possible to provide by the terms **40-037** of a floating charge that it shall crystallise automatically on the occurrence of certain stated events,[154] though provision for retrospective crystallisation (providing for crystallisation to have happened before certain events) is not possible.[155] There was once some doubt about whether automatic crystallisation was possible[156], but it is entirely in accordance with history and principle.[157] It is for the terms of the charge, not mandatory rules of law, to prescribe when the chargor's authority to defeat or subordinate the charge shall determine.[158]

There is naturally concern about the effect of automatic crystallisation on third parties; but those concerns are at the very least mitigated by a combination of general equitable doctrine and statute law. As a matter of general equitable doctrine, a third party will only be affected by a floating charge that has crystallised if she cannot raise a defence under the general equitable rules of priority[159] or use estoppel (apparent authority) reasoning.[160] Thus, the third party will not be bound if she takes legal title to charged property for value without notice that the charge has crystallised. She is not likely to have notice of crystallisation that takes place automatically upon a specified event: for example, this is not a matter registrable at Companies House.[161] Notice of the charge alone would not be sufficient because it is notice of the charge does not constitute notice of its contents.[162] Even if the third party cannot raise a bona fide purchaser defence, she might be able to argue that the chargee is estopped from asserting that the floating charge has crystallised where the chargor has apparent authority to dispose of assets free of the charge.

(5) De-crystallisation of charge   Finally, there is, as yet unresolved, a question **40-038** as to whether a floating charge, once crystallised, can be de-crystallised, or "refloated". This question often arises in the context of automatic crystallisation clauses, when crystallisation has occurred automatically (i.e. an event has been triggered) but is desired by neither the chargor nor the chargee. As a matter of general equitable principle, there appears to be no reason why not.[163] Re-floatation might occur by agreement of the chargor and chargee to restore the chargor's authority to defeat or subordinate the floating charge where the original charge documentation does not make provision for re-floatation. However, in those circumstances, it

is very likely that the parties' actions could be construed as the replacement of the original (now fixed) charge with a new (floating) charge. Were that the case, it could have severely disadvantageous consequences for the parties. The new charge would require fresh registration, though that might well be overlooked, with catastrophic consequences, if it were wrongly thought to be a continuation of the original, and duly registered, charge. There could also be grave consequences for any enforcement action taken pursuant to the original charge. Re-floatation might also occur where the original charge provided for it. As a matter of principle, it is hard to see why the charge, which after all, provides expressly or implicitly for the chargor's authority to dispose free the floating charge, could not do so in this more subtle way. This would, therefore, more likely be accepted as restoration of the chargor's authority, rather than replacement of an old charge with a new: the equitable security interest continues, though the authority to defeat it or to subordinate it are terminated and revived.

In addition, statute law further complicates the picture: it is hard to see how a charge can be "re-floated" where a receiver or an administrator has already been appointed. These office-holders have statutory duties and are subject to statutory regulation, irrespective of the wishes or intentions of the parties to the charge in question. Re-floatation might also have unforeseen and undesired effects under contracts to which chargor or chargee are party, or under guarantees for the secured indebtedness. Until these various doubts and issues are resolved, attempts to re-float a charge, or to provide for its re-floatation, are highly risky and best avoided.

[105] For priority of interests generally, see Ch.4.

[106] *Driver v Broad* [1893] 1 Q.B. 744 at 747.

[107] See paras. 40-030 – 40-031.

[108] See para. 40-032.

[109] See paras. 40-036 – 40-037.

[110] See paras. 40-034 – 40-035.

[111] For a useful summary of principles that emerge from cases, see *Ashborder BV v Green Gas Power Ltd* [2004] EWHC 1517 (Ch), [2005] B.C.C. 634 at [227].

[112] *In re Florence Land and Public Works Co, ex p Moor* (1878) 10 Ch. D. 530.

[113] *Hamer v London, City & Midland Bank Ltd* (1918) 87 L.J.K.B. 973.

[114] *Re HH Vivian & Co* [1900] 2 Ch. 654; *Bulbinder Singh Sandhu (t/a Isher Fashions UK) v Jet Star Retail Ltd (in administration)* [2011] EWCA Civ 459 at [10].

[115] *Re Panama, New Zealand, and Australian Royal Mail* (1869-70) L.R. 5 Ch. App. 318.

[116] *Reynolds Bros (Motors) Pty Ltd v Esanda Ltd* [1977] 1 W.L.R. 578.

[117] *Re Automatic Bottle Makers* [1926] Ch. 412.

[118] *Biggerstaff v Rowatt's Wharf Ltd* [1896] 2 Ch. 93 at 101 per Lindley LJ; *Edward Nelson & Co Ltd v Faber & Co* [1903] 2 K.B. 367. See also *Rother Iron Works Ltd v Canterbury Precision Engineers Ltd* [1974] Q.B. 1.

[119] *Robson v Smith* [1895] 2 Ch. 118 at 124-125 per Romer J; *Evans v Rival Granite Quarries Ltd* [1910] 2 K.B. 979. However, if the floating charge crystallises prior to the completion of the execution by sale of the seized assets, the sheriff (enforcement officer) is accountable to floating chargee: *Re Opera* [1891] 3 Ch. 260. For a useful discussion of cases, see *Wily v St George Partnership Banking Ltd* [1999] B.I.P.R 1030.

[120] See *Evans v Rival Granite Quarries Ltd* [1910] 2 K.B. 979, at 995 per Fletcher Moulton LJ.

[121] Courts are reluctant to formulate any test for determining whether a transaction falls within the ordinary course of business but a useful summary of principles that emerge from cases can be found in

Ashborder BV v Green Gas Power Ltd [2004] EWHC 1517 (Ch), [2005] B.C.C. 634 at [227] per Etherton J.

[122] *Re Benjamin Cope & Sons* [1914] 1 Ch. 800. It appears that this point was overlooked by Morritt J in *Griffiths v Yorkshire Bank Plc* [1994] 1 W.L.R. 1427, where a second floating charge, which crystallised by notice before the earlier floating charge over the same property, was held to have priority. For a cogent critique of the *Griffiths* case see Walters, "Priority of the Floating Charge in Corporate Insolvency" (1995) 16 *Company Lawyer* 291.

[123] *Re Hamilton's Windsor Ironworks* (1879) 12 Ch.D. 707; *Re Colonial Trusts Corp* (1879) 15 Ch.D. 465 at 472; *Wheatley v Silkstone & Haigh Moor Coal Co* (1885) 29 Ch.D. 715 at 724.

[124] When a floating charge is created, a negative pledge could be included in documents relating to the financing transaction other than the charge agreement, see L Gullifer and M Raczynska, "The English Law of Personal Property Security: Under-reformed?" in L Gullifer and O Akseli (eds), *Secured Transactions Law Reform. Principles, Policies and Practice* (2016) 271 at 281.

[125] Contrast negative pledge clauses used in international unsecured lending practice, where the clauses prohibit the debtor to grant a security interest or a title-based financing interest (such as where the financier retains title). For discussion, see H Beale, M Bridge, L Gullifer and E Lomnicka, *The Law of Security and Title-based Financing* 3rd edn, (2018) at [8-78]-[8.87]. Contrast, too, negative pledge clauses in documents intended to create a fixed charge, in which they are used in order to demonstrate that the chargor is not free to deal with the charged assets, and that the charge is not a floating charge: see L Gullifer and M Raczynska, "Secured Transactions" in S Paterson and R Zakrzewski (eds) *McKnight, Paterson, and Zakrzewski on The Law of International Finance* 2nd edn (2017) at [14.1.10.1.1].

[126] *Fire Nymph Products Ltd v The Heating Centre Pty Ltd* (1992) 7 A.C.S.R. 365 (New South Wales CA) at 377-378. For the distinction between equitable interests and mere equities, see generally Ch.2 above.

[127] *Re Valletort Sanitary Steam Laundry Co Ltd* [1903] 2 Ch. 654, 659-661 per Swinfen Eady J; *Cox v Dublin City Distillery Co* [1906] I.R. 446; *Wilson v Kelland* [1910] 2 Ch. 306 at 313 per Eve J; *Fire Nymph Products Ltd v The Heating Centre Pty Ltd* (1992) 7 A.C.S.R. 365 at 377. In *Griffiths v Yorkshire Bank Plc* [1994] 1 W.L.R. 1427, Morritt J doubted that third parties could be affected by a restrictive clause or negative pledge (at 1435F). These remarks are obiter and are not consistent with prior authority. See also Walters, "Priority of the Floating Charge in Corporate Insolvency" (1995) 16 *Company Lawyer* 291.

[128] Companies Act 2006 (Amendment of Part 25) Regulations 2013, SI 2013/600, reg. 2 and Sch. 1.

[129] The analysis in this paragraph continues to be relevant to charges created prior to 6th April 2013 to which pre-2013 reform law applies.

[130] *English & Scottish Mercantile Investment Co v Brunton* [1892] 2 Q.B. 700; *Standard Rotary Machine Co Ltd* (1906) 95 L.T. 829; *Wilson v Kelland* [1910] 2 Ch. 306; *Siebe Gorman & Co Ltd v Barclays Bank* [1979] 2 Lloyd's Rep. 142, 160; *Welch v Bowmaker Bowmaker (Ireland) Ltd* [1980] I.R. 251; *Re Salthill Properties Ltd* (2004) I.E.H.C. 145.

[131] For more detailed discussion of this and other matters relating to the 2013 reform, see L Gullifer and M Raczynska, "The English Law of Personal Property Security: Under-reformed?" in L Gullifer and O Akseli (eds), *Secured Transactions Law Reform. Principles, Policies and Practice* (2016) 271.

[132] Companies Act 2006, s. 859H.

[133] Companies Act 2006, s. 859D. Note that it is not possible to indicate the existence of a negative pledge if it is contained in a document other than the charge agreement (e.g. a loan agreement).

[134] It is doubtful that constructive notice is of the entire charge document, so if a negative pledge clause is not indicated in the statement of particulars, but is contained in the registered charge document, it is unlikely that a third party has constructive notice of the clause.

[135] See, e.g. *Evans v Rival Granite Quarries Ltd* [1910] 2 K.B. 979 at 999 per Buckley LJ; *NW Robbie& Co Ltd v Witney Warehouse Co Ltd* [1963] 1 W.L.R. 1324 at 1334 per Donovan LJ.

[136] See para 40-026 (fn 105).

[137] *Re Griffin Hotel Ltd* [1941] Ch. 129.

[138] *Evans v Rival Granite Quarries Ltd* [1910] 2 K.B. 979.

[139] *Evans v Rival Granite Quarries Ltd* [1910] 2 K.B. 979; *R. v Consolidated Churchill Copper Corp* (1978) 5 W.W.R. 652; (1978) 90 D.L.R. (3d) 357.

[140] *Re Panama, New Zealand, and Australian Royal Mail Co* (1870) L.R. 5 Ch. App. 318 at 322-323 per Sir G M Giffard LJ.

[141] See e.g. *Davey & Co v Williamson and Sons Ltd* [1898] 2 Q.B. 194 at 200-201; *Re Woodroffes Ltd* [1986] Ch. 366; *Re The Real Meat Co Ltd* [1996] B.C.C. 254.

[142] *Re Brightlife Ltd* [1987] Ch. 200 at 212 per Hoffmann J; *Re The Real Meat Co Ltd* [1996] B.C.C. 254 at 261 per Chadwick J.

[143] *Government Stocks and Other Securities Investment Co v Manila Railway Co* [1897] A.C. 81 at 86 per Lord Macnaghten.

[144] *Evans v Rival Granite Quarries Ltd* [1910] 2 K.B. 979 at 997 per Fletcher Moulton LJ.

[145] *Evans v Rival Granite Quarries Ltd* [1910] 2 K.B. 979 at 986-987 per Vaughan Williams LJ and at 1000 per Buckley LJ.

[146] This can also be an appointment of an administrative receiver where such appointment is possible. See para. 40-039.

[147] Note that following the introduction of a standalone moratorium under Corporate Insolvency and Governance Act 2020 (on which, see para. 40-023 above), stipulation for crystallisation of the floating charge upon the company's entry into such a moratorium is ineffective: Insolvency Act 1986, s. A22(3).

[148] See, e.g. Palmer, *Company Precedents*, 1st edn (London, Stevens & Sons, 1877) at 435-436.

[149] *Edward Nelson & Co Ltd v Faber & Co* [1903] 2 K.B. 367 at 376-377.

[150] See para. 40-039 below.

[151] See G Lightman, G Moss, I Fletcher, R Snowden & H Anderson,, *Lightman & Moss on The Law of Administrators and Receivers of Companies*, 6th edn (2017) at [3-081]; L Gullifer (ed), *Goode and Gullifer on Legal Problems of Credit and Security*, 6th edn (2018) at [4-45]; K van Zwieten (ed.) *Goode on Principles of Corporate Insolvency Law* 5th edn (2018) at [11-31].

[152] *Re Brightlife Ltd* [1987] Ch. 200. Statute law makes such clauses temporarily ineffective and in some very limited circumstances: see Insolvency Act 1986, s. A22(2) and see fn.147 above.

[153] On the relationship between crystallization by notice and the requirement of control by the chargee for creation of a fixed charge, see L Gullifer (ed), *Goode and Gullifer on Legal Problems of Credit and Security*, 6th edn (2018) at [4.59] discussing *Re JD Brian Ltd (In Liquidation)* [2011] I.E.H.C. 283, in which the Irish Supreme Court held that the approach in the Brumark case to whether a fixed charge has been created did not apply to interpretation of a clause providing for crystallisation by notice.

[154] *Re Brightlife Ltd* [1987] Ch. 200 at 212, per Hoffmann J; *Fire Nymph Products Ltd v The Heating Centre Pty Ltd* (1992) 7 A.C.S.R. 365 at 371, per Gleeson CJ. Statute law makes such clauses temporarily ineffective in very limited circumstances: see Insolvency Act 1986, s. A22(2) and see fn.147 above.

[155] *Fire Nymph Products* [1992] 7 A.C.S.R. 365.

[156] See e.g. *R v Consolidated Churchill Copper Corporation* [1978] 5 W.W.R 652.

[157] See G Lightman, G Moss, I Fletcher, R Snowden & H Anderson, *Lightman & Moss on The Law of Administrators and Receivers of Companies*, 6th edn (2017) at [3-083]. See also CH Tan, "Automatic Crystallisation, De-Crystallisation and Convertibility of Charges" [1998] *Company, Financial & Insolvency Law Review*. 41; A Boyle, "The Validity of Automatic Crystallization Clauses" [1979] *Journal of Business Law* 231.

[158] There are good reasons to be cautious about drafting automatic crystallization clauses with a wide range of crystallization events, see L Gullifer (ed), *Goode and Gullifer on Legal Problems of Credit and Security*, 6th edn (2018) at [4.56]-[4.57].

[159] *Fire Nymph Products* (1992) 7 A.C.S.R. 365 at 373 per Gleeson CJ. For priority, see Ch.4 above.

[160] Various commentators are in favour of the possibility of de-crystallisation: see, e.g., G Lightman, G Moss, I Fletcher, R Snowden & H Anderson, *Lightman & Moss on The Law of Administrators and Receivers of Companies*, 6th edn (2017) at [3-095]-[3-099] and H Beale, M Bridge, L Gullifer and E Lomnicka, *The Law of Security and Title-based Financing* 3rd edn, (2018) at [6.86]; T N Parsons, *Lingard's Bank Security Documents* 7th edn (2019) at [9.31].

[161] Contrast this with crystallisation that occurs on the appointment of a receiver, and which might occur on the appointment of an administrator when the appointments must be registered at Companies House: Companies Act 2006, s. 895K.

[162] See e.g. *Wilson v Kelland* [1910] 2 Ch. 306.

[163] See, generally, R Grantham, "Refloating a Floating Charge" [1997] *Company, Financial & Insolvency Law Review* 53; and CH Tan "Automatic Crystallisation, De-crystallisation and Convertibility of Charges" [1998] *Company, Financial & Insolvency Law Review* 41.

Replace eighth section with:

8.   ENFORCEMENT MECHANISMS

As noted earlier, enforcement of a floating charge is achieved by the appoint-   **40-039**
ment of a receiver or administrator.[164] Historically, the appointment of a receiver
was the means through which a mortgage or a charge was enforced as the receiver
would collect income from the property and pay it to the secured creditor. With the
development of the floating charge as a security interest over assets of an operat-
ing business, it became common to appoint a receiver not merely to collect the
income but to sell the business as a going concern, and in order for the receiver to
be able to sell it as such, to manage it in the meantime. Debentures creating fixed
and floating charges over all or substantially all assets of the company typically gave
the chargee the power to appoint a receiver (who came to be known as the
administrative receiver) and vested in him very broad powers to carry on the business of the company and to sell it as a going concern. This practice was
acknowledged by the Insolvency Act 1986, which provided for similarly wide
implied powers in administrative receivers.[165] However, policy makers came to the
view that administrative receivers, who acted in the interests of their respective ap-
pointors, did not sufficiently protect the interests of unsecured creditors of the
chargor. Consequently, the Enterprise Act 2002 abolished administrative receivership[166], with some very limited exceptions[167], and replaced it with the new statutory regime of administration.[168]

Following the 2002 Act, an administrator can be appointed, among other ways[169],
out of court by a creditor holding a "qualifying floating charge".[170] Administration
has three statutory purposes, which the administrator should seek to achieve in the
following order of priority[171]: (i) to rescue the company; (ii) to strive for a better
outcome for the creditors of the company as a whole than would be likely on
liquidation; (iii) to make distributions to one or more secured or preferential
creditors. In practice, an administrator appointed by a holder of a qualifying floating charge is likely to be alive to the needs of the appointor, and aim to achieve the
third purpose. In practice, therefore, the chargee can enforce its security through
administration in broadly the same circumstances in which it could previously use
administrative receivership although the procedure of doing so is now based on
statute, not the debenture. In addition, it remains common to confer on chargees
express powers to appoint a receiver and manager, and to include provisions regarding the receiver's powers in debentures.

[164] See, generally, G Lightman, G Moss, I Fletcher, R Snowden & H Anderson, *Lightman & Moss on The Law of Administrators and Receivers of Companies*, 6th edn (Sweet & Maxwell, 2017).

[165] By virtue of Insolvency Act 1986 s.29(2), an administrative receiver is, for the purposes of Pt III, Ch.1 of the Act, (a) a receiver or manager of the whole (or substantially the whole) of a company's property appointed by or on behalf of the holders of any debentures of the company secured by a charge which, as created, was a floating charge, or by such a charge and one or more other securities; or (b) a

person who would be such a receiver or manager but for the appointment of some other person as the receiver of part of the company's property. Powers of administrative receiver are set out in Insolvency Act 1986 Sch. 1.

[166] Insolvency Act 1986 s.72A(1). It continues to be possible for the chargee to appoint a receiver over one or more of the company's assets which are not subject to a "security over the whole, or substantially the whole, of the company's property" but such receivers can be removed by administrators: Insolvency Act 1986 Sch.B1, para.41.

[167] Insolvency Act 1986 ss.72B–72H, and Sch. 2A.

[168] For the appointment of administrators, see Insolvency Act 1986 s.8 and Sch.B1.

[169] An administrator can also be appointed by court: Insolvency Act 1986 Sch.B1, para. 10, and out of court by the company itself or its directors: Insolvency Act 1986 Sch.B1, para.22.

[170] Insolvency Act 1986 Sch.B1, para.14(1), and see paras 14(2) and (3), which sets out that the holder of a "qualifying floating charge" is one who (i) holds security over the whole, or substantially the whole, of the company's property; (ii) that security includes a floating charge; and (iii) the floating charge contains a power to appoint an administrative receiver or an administrator. The procedure of appointment is set out in Insolvency Act 1986 Sch.B1, para.18.

[171] Insolvency Act 1986 Sch.B1, para.3.

CHAPTER 44

LIENS

4. SOLICITORS' LIENS

2. Common Law Lien on Property Received Qua Solicitor

(b) Extent of lien.

Replace paragraph with:
   The lien extends to money paid into a joint account in the names of solicitors for   **44-018**

the parties to an action to abide the event of the action.[82] But it is confined to property which has come into the solicitor's hands in his character of solicitor and not otherwise[83]; it does not extend to property which was received by the solicitor in circumstances where the reason for receipt is inconsistent with the existence of a lien[83a] and it is confined to the solicitor's costs, i.e. to items properly included in his bill of costs,[84] and does not include debts.[85] But the lien is a general lien which extends to all costs due from the client, and is not restricted merely to the costs incurred in connection with the property over which the lien is claimed.

[82] *Halvanon Insurance Co Ltd v Central Reinsurance Corp* [1988] 1 W.L.R. 1122.

[83] *Ex p. Fuller* (1881) 16 Ch. D. 617.

[83a] *Withers LLP v Rybak* [2011] EWCA Civ 1419 at [19]-[22], [33] and [51]-[52]; [2012] 1 W.L.R. 1748.

[84] *Re Taylor, Stileman & Underwood* [1891] 1 Ch. 590 at 599.

[85] *Re Galland* (1885) 31 Ch. D. 296.

4. Loss of Lien

(c) Waiver.

Replace paragraph with:

44-022   The lien may be discharged by waiver, which will be inferred where the solicitor takes a security for costs which is inconsistent with the solicitor's lien, unless he expressly reserves his lien.[101] The enforcement of a judgment for costs[102] or the taking of security after the solicitor has ceased to act for the client[103] does not lead to the inference that the lien is waived, but a waiver can be inferred from the taking of additional security over the property which would otherwise be covered by the lien, or an acceptance that another creditor's claim to the property will have priority over the solicitor's claim.[103a] The fact that the solicitor has no positive intention to waive the lien does not prevent a waiver from being inferred where the new security arrangement is inconsistent with the lien.[104] The solicitor's duty to explain the combined effect of the new security arrangement and the lien to his or her client means it is easier to infer a waiver of the lien than in other cases, and merely arranging for the client to take independent advice about the terms of the new security arrangement does not enable the solicitor to avoid that duty.[104a]

[101] *Re John Morris* [1908] 1 K.B. 473; *Candey Ltd v Crumpler* [2020] EWCA Civ 26.

[102] *A v B* [1984] 1 All E.R. 265.

[103] *Twigg Farnell v Wildblood* [1998] P.N.L.R. 211.

[103a] *Candey Ltd v Crumpler* [2020] EWCA Civ 26.

[104] *Clifford Harris & Co v Solland International Ltd* [2005] EWHC 141 (Ch) at [40]; [2005] 2 All E.R. 334.

[104a] *Candey Ltd v Crumpler* [2020] EWCA Civ 26 at [56]-[57].

5. Equitable Lien on Property Recovered or Preserved

Replace paragraph with:

44-023   A solicitor has an equitable lien on a fund recovered by his exertions,[105] including any costs recovered.[106] This fund need not be cash,[107] but this lien does not extend to real property.[108] That limitation on the breadth of the lien led to the creation of a statutory jurisdiction to apply to court for a charge over property recovered or preserved,[109] which is of wider application (the statutory jurisdiction is discussed in the next section). The equitable lien is justified as promoting access to justice. Older authority held that the lien could only attach to property that was recovered, (or was due to be recovered[110]) by the solicitor's exertions in litigation (including under an agreement to settle the claim[111]) or arbitration.[112] But, recognising the nature of modern dispute resolution,[113] the equitable lien is now to attach where a solicitor provides services (within the scope of the retainer with the client) in relation to the making of a claim by the client (in the sense of asserting the client's legal entitlement, whether or not legal proceedings are formally initiated) which contribute significantly to the successful recovery of a fund by the client; that fund is subject to the lien.[114] The lien does not attach where the solicitor's work is transactional.[114a] The lien is also only available to secure payment of fees for which the solicitor's client is liable.[115]

[105] *Re Born* [1900] 2 Ch. 433; *Haymes v Cooper* (1864) 33 Beav. 431; *Re Meter Cabs Ltd* [1911] 2 Ch. 557.

[106] *Campbell v Campbell* [1941] 1 All E.R. 274.

[107] *West London Law Ltd v Sandhu* [2019] EWHC 828 (Ch) at [29].

[108] *Shaw v Neale* (1858) 6 H.L.C. 581. The reasoning in this decision is not completely satisfactory, apparently confusing the solicitor's equitable lien with the common law retaining lien, but the decision settled the law on the point: *Jackson v Richards* [2005] NSWSC 630 at [33], (2005) 12 B.P.R. 23,091.

[109] *Meguerditchian v Lightbound* [1917] 2 K.B. 298 at 307.

[110] *Khans Solicitors v Chifuntwe* [2014] 1 W.L.R. 1185 at [33]; *Gavin Edmondson Solicitors Ltd v Haven Insurance Co Ltd* [2018] UKSC 21; [2018] 1 W.L.R. 2052.

[111] *Gavin Edmondson Solicitors Ltd v Haven Insurance Co Ltd* [2018] UKSC 21 at [3]; [2018] 1 W.L.R. 2052.

[112] *Meguerditchian v Lightbound* [1917] 2 K.B. 298. For an indication of the extent to which the solicitor's exertions must have contributed to recovery of the fund, see *Gavin Edmondson Solicitors Ltd v Haven Insurance Co Ltd* [2018] UKSC 21 at [46] and [59]–[63]; [2018] 1 W.L.R. 2052.

[113] *Bott & Co Solicitors Ltd v Ryanair DAC* [2022] UKSC 8; [2022] 2 W.L.R. 634 at [145].

[114] *Bott & Co Solicitors Ltd v Ryanair DAC* [2022] UKSC 8; [2022] 2 W.L.R. 634 at [86].

[114a] *Bott & Co Solicitors Ltd v Ryanair DAC* [2022] UKSC 8; [2022] 2 W.L.R. 634 at [126], [154] & [175].

[115] It has thus been held that it does not apply to fees owing for legal aid work: *West London Law Ltd v Sandhu* [2019] EWHC 828 (Ch) at [25], [29].

Replace n.118 with:

[118] See *Loescher v Dean* [1950] Ch. 491; *Euro Commercial Leasing v Cartwright & Lewis* [1995] 2 B.C.L.C. 618; *Bott & Co Solicitors Ltd v Ryanair DAC* [2022] UKSC 8; [2022] 2 W.L.R. 634 at [20].

After "the fund itself.", add:

The lien may be waived, and waiver can be inferred from the taking of an inconsistent security right.[125a]

[125a] *Candey Ltd v Crumpler* [2020] EWCA Civ 26. See also para.44-022.

6.   Statutory Lien on Property Recovered or Preserved

(a)   Statutory lien.

Replace n.126 with:

[126] Solicitors Act 1974 s.73 (replacing earlier provisions: Solicitors Acts 1860 s.28; 1932 s.69; 1957 s.72).   **44-024**

Replace paragraph with:

This applies to every type of property, including realty.[127] An executor[128] or assignee[129] of the solicitor may also be declared entitled to this charge. Even where the solicitor has been discharged by the client, they may be given the charge, although this will be subject to a like charge in the new solicitor, whose charge will always have precedence.[130] The solicitor may also waive the right to apply for a statutory charge, where the solicitor takes an inconsistent security right.[130a]

[127] *Foxon v Gascoigne* (1874) 9 Ch. App. 654 at 660.

[128] *Baile v Baile* (1872) L.R. 13 Eq. 497.

[129] *Briscoe v Briscoe* [1892] 3 Ch. 543.

[130] *Rhodes v Sugden* (1886) 34 Ch. D. 155; *Knight v Gardner* [1892] 2 Ch. 368; *Hyde v White* [1933] P. 105.

[130a] *Clifford Harris & Co v Solland International Ltd* [2004] EWHC 2488 (Ch) at [15]. See also para.44-022.

5.   LIEN FOR SUMS SPENT ON PROPERTY OF ANOTHER

3.   Joint Owners

Replace n.186 with:

44-036   [186] See para.20-078 and *Cheung v Cheung* [2021] HKCFA 19.

CHAPTER 45

SURETYSHIP

6. REMEDIES OF SURETY: AFTER PAYMENT

3. Contribution between Co-sureties

(b) Modification of right by agreement.

Replace n.88 with:

45-025 [88] *Global Consulting Services Pty Ltd v Gresham Property Investments Ltd* [2018] NSWCA 255 at [65]–[66] and [102]–[103], (2018) 365 A.L.R. 143 (applying *Coulls v Bagot's Executor and Trustee Co Ltd* (1967) 119 C.L.R. 460, 480, 488; see also *Dunbar v Dunbar* [1909] 2 Ch. 639, 646); *Official Trustee in Bankruptcy v Citibank Savings Ltd* (1995) 38 N.S.W.L.R. 116, 118–119. This is based on the objectively ascertained common intention of the parties, rather than a judicial discretion to do justice between them: *Global Consulting Services Pty Ltd v Gresham Property Investments Ltd* [2018] NSWCA 255 at [77], (2018) 365 A.L.R. 143; *Hampton v Minns* [2002] 1 W.L.R. 1 at [66]; cf. *Trotter v Franklin* [1991] 2 N.Z.L.R. 92, 98.

INDEX